Teacher Preparation Classroom

TEACHER PREP

MERRILL
PRENTICE HALL

See a demo at
www.prenhall.com/teacherprep/demo

Your Class. Their Careers. Our Future. Will your students be prepared?

We invite you to explore our new, innovative and engaging website and all that it has to offer you, your course, and tomorrow's educators! Preview this site today at www.prenhall.com/teacherprep/demo. Just click on "go" on the login page to begin your exploration.

Organized around the major courses pre-service teachers take, the Teacher Preparation site provides media, student/teacher artifacts, strategies, research articles, and other resources to equip your students with the quality tools needed to excel in their courses and prepare them for their first classroom.

This ultimate online education resource will provide you and your students access to:

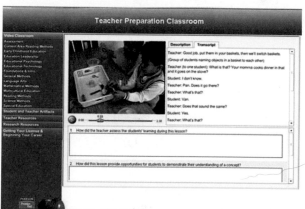

Online Video Library. More than 250 video clips—each tied to a course topic and framed by learning goals and Praxis-type questions—capture real teachers and students working in real classrooms.

Student and Teacher Artifacts. More than 200 student and teacher classroom artifacts—each tied to a course topic and framed by learning goals and application questions—provide a wealth of materials and experiences to help your students observe children's developmental learning.

Lesson Plan Builder. Step-by-step guidelines and lesson plan examples to support students as they learn to build high-quality lesson plans.

Articles and Readings. Over 500 articles from ASCD's renowned journal *Educational Leadership* are available. The site also includes *Research Navigator,* a searchable database of additional educational journals.

Strategies and Lessons. Over 500 research-supported instructional strategies appropriate for a wide range of grade levels and content areas.

Licensure and Career Tools. Resources devoted to helping your students pass their licensure exam; learn standards, law, and public policies; plan a teaching portfolio; and succeed in their first year of teaching.

Access Code previously been used?

Students:
- To purchase or renew an access code, go to **www.prenhall.com/teacherprep** and click on the "Register for Teacher Prep" button.

Instructors:
- Email **Merrill.marketing@pearsoned.com** and provide the following information:
  - Name and Affiliation
  - Author/Title/Edition of Merrill text

Upon ordering *Teacher Prep* for their students, instructors will be given a lifetime *Teacher Prep* Access Code.

Fundamentals of Early Childhood Education

fifth edition

GEORGE S. MORRISON

University of North Texas

PEARSON

Merrill
Prentice Hall

Upper Saddle River, New Jersey
Columbus, Ohio

Library of Congress Cataloging-in-Publication Data

Morrison, George S.
  Fundamentals of early childhood education / George S. Morrison.— 5th ed.
    p. cm.
  Includes bibliographical references and index.
  ISBN-13: 978-0-13-233129-6 (pbk.)
  ISBN-10: 0-13-233129-2 (pbk.)
  1. Early childhood education—United States.   I. Title.
  LB1139.25.M67 2008
  372.210973—dc22

                                                              2007013257

Vice President and Executive Publisher: Jeffery W. Johnston
Publisher: Kevin M. Davis
Acquisitions Editor: Julie Peters
Development Editor: Ben Sullivan Prout
Editorial Assistant: Tiffany Bitzel
Senior Production Editor: Linda Hillis Bayma
Production Coordination: Thistle Hill Publishing Services, LLC
Design Coordinator: Diane C. Lorenzo
Photo Coordinator: Lori Whitley
Cover and Text Designer: Candace Rowley
Front Cover Image: Geovanna Garzon, Little People Productions, Inc.
Production Manager: Laura Messerly
Director of Marketing: David Gesell
Marketing Manager: Amy Judd
Marketing Coordinator: Brian Mounts

This book was set in Garamond by Integra Software Services. It was printed and bound by C. J. Krehbiel. The cover was printed by Coral Graphic Services, Inc.

Photo Credits for Chapter Openers: Photo credits appear on page 398.

Pearson Prentice Hall™ is a trademark of Pearson Education, Inc.
Pearson® is a registered trademark of Pearson plc
Prentice Hall® is a registered trademark of Pearson Education, Inc.
Merrill® is a registered trademark of Pearson Education, Inc.

Pearson Education Ltd.
Pearson Education Singapore Pte. Ltd.
Pearson Education Canada, Ltd.
Pearson Education–Japan

Pearson Education Australia Pty. Limited
Pearson Education North Asia Ltd.
Pearson Educación de Mexico, S.A. de C.V.
Pearson Education Malaysia Pte. Ltd.

10 9 8 7 6 5 4 3
ISBN-13: 978-0-13-233129-6
ISBN-10:   0-13-233129-2

For Betty Jane—as always

about the author

George S. Morrison is a professor of early childhood education at the University of North Texas, where he teaches early childhood courses to undergraduate and graduate students. Professor Morrison's accomplishments include a Distinguished Academic Service Award from the Pennsylvania Department of Education and an Outstanding Service and Teaching Award from Florida International University. His books include *Early Childhood Education Today,* Tenth Edition; *Teaching in America,* Fourth Edition; *Education and Development of Infants, Toddlers, and Preschoolers; The World of Child Development; The Contemporary Curriculum;* and *Parent Involvement in the Home, School, and Community.*

Dr. Morrison is a popular author, speaker, and presenter. He is Senior Contributing Editor for the *Public School Montessorian* and contributes his opinions and ideas to a wide range of publications. His speaking engagements and presentations focus on the future of early childhood education, the changing roles of early childhood teachers, and the influence of contemporary educational reforms, research, and legislation on teaching and learning.

Dr. Morrison's professional and research interests include integrating best practices into faith-based programs; developing programs for young children and their families with an emphasis on readiness for learning; and the influences of families on children's development. He is also actively involved in providing technical assistance about graduate and undergraduate teacher education programs and early childhood practices to government agencies, university faculty, and private and public agencies in Thailand, Taiwan, and China.

Professor George S. Morrison with preschool children at the Child Development Laboratory on the campus of the University of North Texas, discussing their favorite books.

preface

When I ask early childhood educators how I can help them be better professionals, they repeatedly express their desire for an early childhood textbook that is user-friendly and applies theory to practice. *Fundamentals of Early Childhood Education,* Fifth Edition, meets this need for a textbook that is practical, is based on current research and thinking about how young children learn, and provides concrete examples for how best to teach them.

Fundamentals captures the important changes occurring in early childhood education today and shows how they apply to teaching young children and to collaborating with their parents and families. These changes include:

- New knowledge and ideas about how children grow and develop, and the conditions that support optimal learning.
- New views about how best to teach young children.
- Changing roles and responsibilities of early childhood professionals.
- Increasing demands from the public and politicians for accountability in ensuring that all children will learn to their fullest capacity.

As you, other early childhood professionals, scientists, and the public respond to the changing field of early childhood education, more opportunities arise for new programs, curricula, and appropriate practices to meet the ever-changing needs of children and families.

This textbook was designed to develop competent and confident early childhood education professionals. The following new features serve to support you in your course:

- The **TeacherPrep Website** contents are integrated into this edition, providing instant access to Classroom Videos, Children's Artifacts, Articles and Readings, and many other resources (an access code is included in your book).
- **Competency Builder** features teach you, step by step, how to do key early childhood teacher tasks.
- **Ethical Dilemmas** get you thinking and talking about common decision making in working with children and families and other professionals, based on the NAEYC Code of Ethical Conduct.
- **Coverage of environments and curriculum** for young children has been increased.
- Updated and new features emphasize how to meet the many and varied needs of today's **diverse learners**.

Understanding by Seeing and Experiencing Through the TeacherPrep Website

The TeacherPrep Website at www.prenhall.com/teacherprep includes videos of teachers and children in classrooms, children's artifacts to look at and analyze, articles to read, strategies to discover, career information, Praxis practice, a lesson plan building module, and many other resources. Integrated in the margins of your textbook are notes, such as the one to your left, that point out a resource the author suggests you review. These margin notes are extensions of the textbook content. Take the time to watch the recommended videos, learn a new teaching strategy from another experienced early childhood educator, or see what research has to say about child guidance, teaching math, or how to create a portfolio. To gain access to this site, an access code card is included with your textbook. Note how many of these resources include open-ended questions. These are written in a style similar to Praxis exam items. By answering these questions, you are essentially practicing for the Praxis exam and applying what you have learned based on your textbook reading and from the TeacherPrep Website.

Observe early childhood classrooms that demonstrate the **Montessori philosophy** at Video Classroom, Early Childhood Education, Module 4: Curriculum Planning and Programs, Video 2: Montessori.

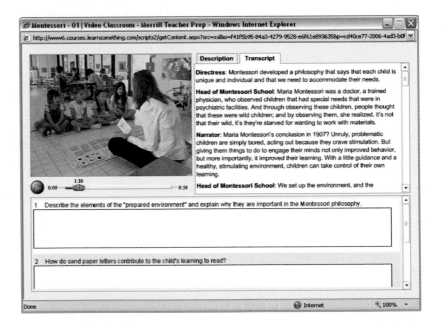

Building Competence

Other devices in the text that support your knowledge and growing expertise are the thirteen **Competency Builders**. These are highly practical step-by-step guides for how to specifically break down key tasks and teach them. How do you observe children? How do you develop curriculum for a two-year-old? How do you meaningfully incorporate state math standards for preschoolers into an integrated, engaging lesson plan? By reviewing the Competency Builders over and over, trying them out in field-based experiences, and returning to them later to refine your skills, you will learn and develop the professional competencies that all respected, competent early childhood professionals know how to do.

program in action

COMPETENCY BUILDER

How to Observe Children: Observing Will

Welcome to Ms. Liz's classroom! You will be observing Will, the energetic four-year-old in overalls and a yellow shirt. He is a bright, only child who is in his first year of school and has a mind of his own. You will also observe Ms. Liz, the classroom environment, and the ways children interact with Will, Ms. Liz, and each other. And by observing, you will try to determine whether Ms. Liz and the classroom environment support active learning. *Active learning* is an important part of early childhood practice. It is a challenge and a goal for all early childhood teachers to promote caring and learning in a child-centered classroom that supports active learning.

Look at the photos of Will, and implement the four steps for effective observation (see Figure 6.5).

STEP 1 PLAN FOR OBSERVATION
- Decide *who* you will observe, *how* you will observe (e.g., classroom visit, photos, or video), *what* you will observe, and *where* the observation will take place.
- Write your goal(s) for observation. Our goals for observing Will are to:
  - Determine if Ms. Liz's classroom supports active learning.
  - Make recommendations about what features of an active learning environment should be included in a classroom.

- Select your observational tool. For observing Will, an anecdotal record will achieve our goals and will provide the data necessary to make conclusions and recommendations. An anecdotal record is a short description of behavior over a period of time; it tells about the child's interaction with the physical and social environments. It should be as factual as possible. You might use an index card or some other form like the example shown below.

STEP 2 CONDUCT THE OBSERVATION
- Observe Will and try to answer the questions accompanying each photograph.
- Record your observations on index cards or forms you devise.

Ms. Liz is reading one of the children's favorite books. Will asked Ms. Liz if she would please read the book. Before she read it, Ms. Liz asked the children who their favorite characters were and why they wanted to hear the story again. Will said, "I like the way the boy helps the dog." P-1

Anecdotal Record

Child's name: Will   Date: September 8, 2008

Context: Ms. Liz's classroom

Picture 2: Will took the book from Ms. Liz. He pushed her arm away as she held on to it. Ms. Liz let Will take the book.

Picture 3: Will and his friend Greg built a tower. They worked well together and engaged in animated conversation. They were very excited and gleeful when their tower fell down on Larry.

Ethical Dilemmas are features that provide practice opportunities. They appear at the end of each chapter. The Ethical Dilemmas can be discussed in small groups, large groups, or in blogs and chatrooms. They address real situations experienced by teachers, parents, other professionals, and children. By studying these, and thinking about what you might do to address these sticky situations and ethically troubling issues, you will better prepare yourself for your current and future work.

The NAEYC Code of Ethical Conduct is reprinted in the Appendix and provides the basis for making ethical decisions and teaching in an ethical and professional manner.

Ethical Dilemma

"Test or Leave?"

Christina Lopez teaches in a preschool for three- to four-year-olds that is funded with federal dollars. Her administrator has sent out a memo announcing a testing program designed to measure children's preschool achievement and the effectiveness of programs funded with federal dollars. All four-year-olds will be tested on their knowledge, skills, and readiness for kindergarten with a federally developed paper-and-pencil achievement test. Christina believes it is developmentally inappropriate to "test" preschool children using the prescribed federal test.

What should Christina do? Should she share her concerns with the school administrator and risk the administrator's disapproval, or should she administer a test she believes is developmentally inappropriate?

More on Environments and Curriculum

Information about high-quality environments and curricula that support playing and learning has been expanded. Chapters 7 through 10 now show floor plans for each age group, describe content coverage appropriate for these ages, and identify key standards. I stress the use of developmentally appropriate practice (DAP) in environmental and curricular design. Implementation of DAP is a hallmark of this textbook and is emphasized throughout.

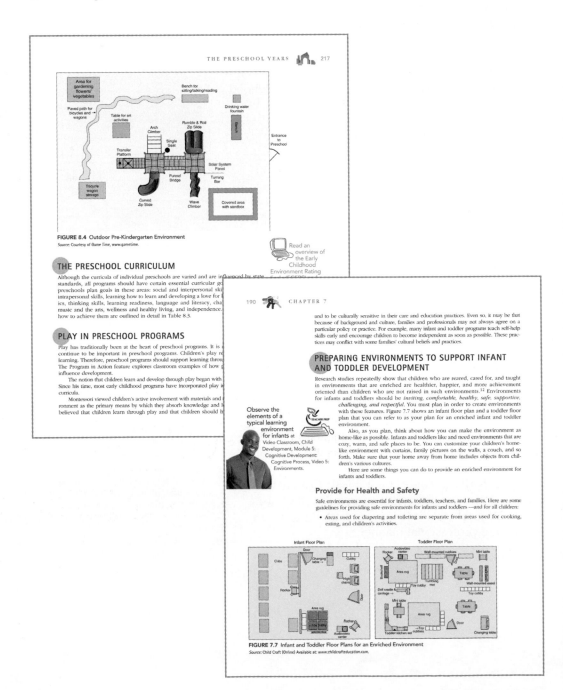

Understanding and Supporting Diversity

In the field of early childhood education, you will hear terms and phrases such as *finding strengths, cultural competence,* and *celebrating diversity.* These terms collectively reflect what I portray in *Fundamentals:* that early childhood professionals need to understand the vast array of people with whom they work—children, families, extended families, and a vast array of professionals. High-quality professionals look for the postive aspects in their work with children and families. *Fundamentals* discusses many types of diversity you find in society and early childhood settings: cultural, ethnic, socioeconomic, linguistic (language), gender, religious, and family structure. Diversity is woven through the textbook in Competency Builders, in the prose, and in the Diversity Tie-In features.

professionalism in practice

How to Help English Language Learners Succeed

COMPETENCY BUILDER

My attempts to learn Spanish have given me a lot of empathy for English language learners. Perhaps you have had the same experience of frustration with comprehension, pronunciation, and understandable communication. English language learners face these same problems and others. Many come from low socioeconomic backgrounds. Others come to this country lacking many of the early literacy and learning opportunities we take for granted.

INCREASING NUMBERS

Many school districts across the country have seen their numbers of English language learners skyrocket. For example, in the Winston-Salem/Forsyth County School District in North Carolina, more than 8 percent of the 49,797 student population are English language learners, representing seventy-seven different native languages.

The chances are great that you will have English language learners in your classroom wherever you choose to teach. There are a number of approaches you can use to ensure that your children will learn English and that they will be academically successful.

TIPS FOR SUCCESS

Judith Lessow-Hurley, a bilingual expert, says, "It's important to create contexts in which kids exchange meaningful messages. Kids like to talk to other kids, and that's useful."† Lessow-Hurley also supports sheltered immersion. She says, "A lot of what we call 'sheltering' is simply good instruction—all kids benefit from experiential learning, demonstrations, visuals, and routines. A lot of sheltering is also common sense—stay away from idioms, speak slowly and clearly, [and] find ways to repeat yourself."†

STRATEGY 1 **DEVELOP CONTENT AROUND A THEME**
The repetition of vocabulary and concepts reinforces language and ideas and gives English language learners better access to content.

STRATEGY 2 **USE VISUAL AIDS AND HANDS-ON ACTIVITIES TO DELIVER CONTENT**
Information is better retained when a variety of senses are used.

- Rely on visual cues as frequently as possible.
- Have students create flash cards for key vocabulary words. Be sure to build in time for students to use them.
- Encourage students to use computer programs and books with cassette tapes.

STRATEGY 3 **USE ROUTINES TO REINFORCE LANGUAGE**
This practice increases the comfort level of second-language learners; they then know what to expect and associate the routine with the language.

- One helpful routine is daily reading.

Picture yourself in this classroom. Which of the activites suggested here

---

DIVERSITY AND EARLY CHILDHOOD EDUCATION

Anti-Bias Curriculum. Conducting a developmentally and culturally appropriate program also means that you will include in your curriculum activities and materials that help challenge and change all biases of any kind that seek to diminish and portray as inferior all children based on their gender, race, culture, disability, language, or socioeconomic status. You can accomplish this goal by implementing an **anti-bias curriculum**.

The **Diversity Tie-In** feature is designed to help you be sensitive and responsive to issues of diversity in your classroom and program. Diversity is present in the entire fabric of contemporary life, and children bring their diverse backgrounds into the classroom. Specifically, each Diversity Tie-In feature:

- Encourages you to embrace the learning potential of all children and to develop multiple approaches to support children's learning.

- Presents you with issues relating to diversity and provides practical information and strategies to meet the needs of children from diverse backgrounds

- Enables you to understand the contexts and circumstances of diversity and how they influence your teaching and children's learning.

diversity tie-in

High-Stakes Tests Leave Minority Students Behind

Today, students from preschool to high school are subjected to an almost endless array of tests. These tests are designed to measure everything from achievement, abilities, interests, and reading level to friendship preferences. When these tests are used to make critical decisions about students that have serious school and life consequences, they are called *high-stakes tests.* For example, standardized achievement tests are used to make decisions about whether Maria or Mario should be promoted to the next grade or whether or not Jennifer or Johnny has to attend summer school. But grade promotion and summer school attendance are not the only high-stakes decisions about young children that are based on tests.

Take the case of Amir Diego Howard, a bright third grader at Sierra Vista Elementary School in Washo County, Nevada. Amir's teacher thought he was a perfect candidate for the school district's gifted and talented (GT) program, so she referred him. Amir did well in the first two steps of the district's three-step process for admission into GT. First, Amir had his teacher's recommendation. Second, he scored at the 96th percentile on a national standardized achievement test. The third step was the problem. Amir failed to score an IQ of 133 on the Kaufman-Brief Intelligence Test. "Sometimes they gave me these huge words that you don't even know," said Amir about the IQ test. "Like 'autobiography.' I don't know what that means. I'm only in the third grade."Unfortunately, across the country many language minority children like Amir fail to get into GT programs. Tests used to

establish admission criteria discriminate against English language learners (ELLs) and minority students. As Joe Garret, Washo County GT Curriculum Coordinator, points out, "The kids that are English language learners, if they don't have the language and they don't have the background experiences, they are not going to do well on standardized tests we use to identify kids."

The good news is that increasing numbers of school districts are doing something about the inequities of high-stakes testing and how criteria for GT and other programs discriminate against English language learners. For example, districts are broadening and/or changing their criteria by:

- Placing more emphasis on nonverbal criteria such as learning styles and creative behavior
- Eliminating passing scores on high-stakes tests as a condition of program admission
- Placing more emphasis on teacher recommendation
- Changing admission criteria to assure that more minority and ELL students are in GT programs
- Using language-free tests that don't discriminate against English language learners and minority children

Reflect on high-stakes assessment in light of NAEYC's position statement on assessment at http://www.prenhall.com/morrison, Chapter 5—Journal: Diversity Tie-In.

THEMES AND GOALS

The following core themes serve as an organizing framework for *Fundamentals:*

professionalism in practice

How to Scaffold Children's Learning

Vygotsky believed that cognitive development occurs through children's interactions with more competent others—teachers, peers, parents—who act as guides, facilitators, and coaches to provide the support children need to grow intellectually. Much of that support is provided through conversation, examples, and encouragement. When children learn a new skill, they need that competent other to provide a scaffold, or framework, to help them—to show them the overall task, break it into doable parts, and support and reinforce their efforts.

THE SCAFFOLDING PROCESS

Here are the basic steps involved in effective scaffolding. Study them carefully and then look for them in the three examples that follow:

STEP 1 OBSERVE AND LISTEN
You can learn a great deal about what kind of assistance is needed.

STEP 2 APPROACH THE CHILD
Ask what he or she wants to do, and ask for permission to help.

STEP 3 TALK ABOUT THE TASK
Describe each step in detail—what is being used, what is being done, what is seen or touched. Ask the child questions about the activity.

STEP 4 REMAIN ENGAGED IN THE ACTIVITY
Adjust your support, allowing the child to take over and do the talking.

STEP 5 GRADUALLY WITHDRAW SUPPORT
See how the child is able to perform with less help.

STEP 6 OBSERVE THE CHILD PERFORMING INDEPENDENTLY
After you have withdrawn all support, check to be sure the child continues to perform the task successfully.

STEP 7 INTRODUCE A NEW TASK
Present the child with a slightly more challenging task, and repeat the entire sequence.

EXAMPLE—WORKING A PUZZLE

Celeste has chosen a puzzle to work and dumps the pieces out. She randomly picks up a piece and moves it around inside the frame. She tries another. Look at her face: Is she smiling or showing signs of stress? Is she talking to herself?

Perhaps Celeste needs a puzzle with fewer pieces. If so, you can offer her one. But from prior observation, you may know she just needs a little assistance. Try sitting with Celeste and suggesting that you will help. Start by turning all the pieces right side up. As you do this, talk about the pieces you see: This one is red with a little green, this one has a straight edge, this one is curved. Move your finger along the edge.

• **Professionalism**—Being a professional is the foundation of high-quality programs for young children. Professionalism is the compass that guides and directs you throughout your work with children and families. In Chapter 1, you will complete a Professional Development Checklist that consists of sixteen core professional outcomes consistent with NAEYC and CDA professional guidelines. The checklist and its core outcomes create a professional profile that guides your professional thinking, reflection, and development throughout your career. Each chapter of this text begins with one or more of these sixteen professional outcomes that serve as an advance organizer for chapter content and Professionalism in Practice and Program in Action features, which provide authentic illustrations of effective practitioners and high-quality programs. Each chapter concludes with Activities for Professional Development, which are designed to help you achieve the professional development goals emphasized in the chapter. In this way, professionalism is integrated throughout each chapter and the entire book.

• **Theory to Practice**—This text helps you understand how teachers and programs translate theories of learning and educating young children into practice. The Program in Action and Professionalism in Practice features provide real-life insights into how teachers in programs across the United States endeavor to apply early childhood theories to their everyday practices. These features personalize the practice of early childhood education by adding faces, names, and authentic voices of practicing professionals and high-quality programs to chapter content. You will read firsthand about professional colleagues who make theories come alive in concrete ways that truly help children succeed in school and life.

• **Diversity**—The United States is a nation of diverse people, and this diversity is reflected in every early childhood classroom and program. You and your colleagues must have the knowledge and sensitivity to teach *all* students well, and you must understand how culture and language influence teaching and learning. Chapter 11, Educating Children with Diverse Backgrounds and Special Needs: Ensuring All Children Can Learn, helps you understand how all children are unique individuals with special strengths and challenges and emphasizes how all children, regardless of their multicultural, physical, mental, and emotional needs, can be included and fully taught in all early childhood classrooms. In addition, every chapter of this edition emphasizes the theme of diversity through narrative examples and program descriptions. (See page xi for a description of the Diversity Tie-In feature.)

program in action

How to Teach in a Child-Centered Program

The City & Country School, founded by Caroline Pratt in 1914, is located in the Greenwich Village district of New York City. It has a current enrollment of 250 students between the ages of two and thirteen and is an example of a progressive school that continues to educate children using the curriculum structure that was set forth over eighty years ago: "giving children experiences and materials that will fit their stage of development and have inherent in them unlimited opportunities for learning." Pratt, a teacher, sought to provide a school environment that suited the way children learn best—by doing.

BASIC VALUES OF A CHILD-CENTERED APPROACH

The essence of City & Country's philosophy is faith in children and their

• What are the children interested in?
• What is going on in their environment that interests them and is relevant to their lives?

OPEN-ENDED MATERIALS AND METHODS

It is City & Country School's belief that an early childhood curriculum based on open-ended materials and methods fosters independence, motivation, and interest, all essential components of learning. The younger groups (ages two through seven) use basic, open-ended materials to reconstruct what they are learning about the world and to organize their information and thinking in meaningful ways. Materials such as blocks, clay, water, paint, and wood are chosen because of their simplicity, flexibility, and the challenging possibilities that they offer. Children are encouraged to work out problems among themselves, with help from the teacher only when absolutely necessary.

Children move naturally into the more academic tasks as they need to find out more about what they're already doing. The three Rs are viewed as useful tools to further a child's education, not as ends in themselves; but in no way did Pratt, nor do we, undervalue their importance. In fact, every possible method is used to empower all children with the crucial skill of reading. It can be a natural process for many, but others require extra directed instruction.

- **Family-Centered, Community-Based Practice**—To effectively meet children's needs, you and other early childhood professionals must collaborate with families and communities. Today, successful partnerships at all levels are essential for effective teaching and learning. Chapter 13, Parents, Families, and the Community: Building Partnerships for Student Success, emphasizes the importance of family-centered practice, while every other chapter provides examples of successful partnerships and their influences on teaching and learning.

- **Timeliness**—This is a book for the twenty-first century. The information it contains is timely and reflects the very latest in trends and research. Every chapter has been thoroughly revised for this edition to reflect the changes in the field.

- **Developmentally Appropriate Practice**—The theme of developmentally appropriate practice is integrated and emphasized throughout this text. Developmentally appropriate practice is the foundation for all early childhood professional practice. It is important, therefore, that you, as an early childhood education professional, understand developmentally appropriate practice and become familiar

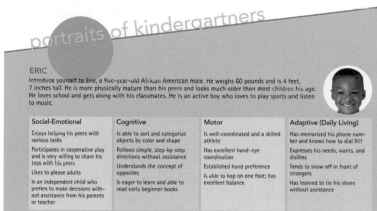

portraits of kindergartners

ERIC

Introduce yourself to Eric, a five-year-old African American male. He weighs 60 pounds and is 4 feet, 7 inches tall. He is more physically mature than his peers and looks much older than most children his age. He loves school and gets along with his classmates. He is an active boy who loves to play sports and listen to music.

Social-Emotional	Cognitive	Motor	Adaptive (Daily Living)
Enjoys helping his peers with various tasks	Is able to sort and categorize objects by color and shape	Is well-coordinated and a skilled athlete	Has memorized his phone number and knows how to dial 911
Participates in cooperative play and is very willing to share his toys with his peers	Follows simple, step-by-step directions without assistance	Has excellent hand–eye coordination	Expresses his needs, wants, and dislikes
Likes to please adults	Understands the concept of opposites	Established hand preference	Tends to show off in front of strangers
Is an independent child who prefers to make decisions without assistance from his parents or teacher	Is eager to learn and able to read early beginner books	Is able to hop on one foot; has excellent balance	Has learned to tie his shoes without assistance

with how to implement it in your teaching. Every chapter provides examples and illustrations to demonstrate how to apply developmentally appropriate practice to the teaching of young children. Portraits of Children features provide students with an overview of what children from infancy through age eight are like developmentally across the domains. These snapshots give you an authentic view of children at different ages, an understanding of universality and diversity, and insight into the interplay of nature and nurture.

- **Technology Applied to Teaching and Learning**—Technological and information literacy is essential for successful living and working in contemporary society. This edition provides you with the information and skills you need to integrate technology effectively into the curriculum and use new teaching approaches by integrating technology in your classroom practice. Each chapter has a Technology Tie-In feature that is designed to enable you to become more technologically proficient. Teachers and all professionals in education are expected to use technology in a number of ways and for multiple purposes; today's professional cannot plead technological ignorance.

- **Literacy Development**—Currently, there is a great deal of emphasis on promoting children's early literacy development and helping children learn how to read. This emphasis will continue well into the future. Therefore, it is imperative for you and every early childhood professional to know how to support and promote children's literacy development. For this reason, Chapters 7 through 10 place special emphasis on literacy development. Knowledge, information, and activities about literacy development are integrated throughout the text.

© Banana Stock Ltd.

OTHER SPECIAL FEATURE DESCRIPTIONS

- **Programs in Action**—The Program in Action features in every chapter enable you to experience actual programs designed for children in real-life classrooms and early childhood programs throughout the United States. These real examples of schools, programs, classrooms, and teachers enable you to explore the best practices of early childhood education and see "up close and personal" what teaching is really like. They also offer special opportunities to spotlight current topics such as standards-based education, helping children resolve conflicts, high-quality infant care and education, educating children with diverse backgrounds, applying brain research to early childhood practice, bilingual education, gifted education, inclusion, multicultural education, early literacy, and improving children's mental and physical health. This approach enables you to make the transition from thinking about being a teacher to becoming a competent professional.

- **Professionalism in Practice**—I believe it is important for the teacher's voice to be heard in and throughout this fifth edition of *Fundamentals of Early Childhood Education*. The Professionalism in Practice feature provides experienced teachers with the opportunity to explain their philosophies, beliefs, and program practices. These teachers actually mentor you as they tell how they practice early childhood education. Many of the Professionalism in Practice features have been contributed by national, *USA Today,* and state Teachers of the Year. Combined, these words of wisdom from award-winning teachers provide you with outstanding role models and mentors to guide your professional practice.

- **Margin and Text Notes**—Notes such as the one to the left direct you to related information on the Companion Website for this textbook, located at www.prenhall.com/morrison. In this way, you are supported in using the Internet and new technologies as sources of professional growth and development.

- **Technology Tie-Ins**—These features, included in each chapter, are designed to help you be technologically literate and incorporate technology of all kinds into your teaching. Each provides you with specific examples related to chapter content. They bridge theory and classroom practice and enable you to be a connected teacher. Collectively, the Technology Tie-In features help you to:

  - Apply technology to your teaching of young children. Every day you will want to explore the opportunities the curriculum provides for using technology to help young children learn.

  - Understand the full range of technology options: computer hardware and software, digital cameras, overhead projectors, tape recorders, handheld electronic devices, and assistive technology.

  - Empower young children with appropriate technology skills that will promote, enhance, and enrich learning.

  - Enhance collaboration with families. E-mail and word-processed newsletters are good ways to stay in touch with families and keep them informed. You can also help parents use the technology they have in their homes to help them assist their children and themselves in learning.

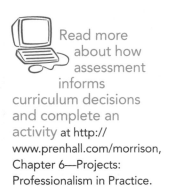
Read more about how assessment informs curriculum decisions and complete an activity at http://www.prenhall.com/morrison, Chapter 6—Projects: Professionalism in Practice.

SUPPLEMENTS TO THE TEXT

Instructor's Manual. Available both online and in print, the *Instructor's Manual* provides professors with a variety of useful resources, including learning outcomes, chapter outlines, teaching strategies, reflective prompts, classroom activities, and connections to the TeacherPrep Website content featured in this edition.

Online Test Bank. The test bank provides instructors electronic access to a number of high-quality multiple-choice, discussion, and essay questions for each chapter of the text.

TestGen—Test Management Software. The TestGen software can help professors manage their exams and gain insights into their students' progress. This software is available in a dual Macintosh and PC/Windows version, and can be downloaded from the Instructor's Resource Center at prenhall.com or ordered from a Prentice Hall sales representative.

Online PowerPoint Slides PowerPoint slides are also available for instructor use on the Instructor's Resource Center at www.prenhall.com, and are reproduced in lecture note format for the student on the Companion Website.

Companion Website. Located at www.prenhall.com/morrison, the Companion Website includes a wealth of resources for both students and professors. The following modules appear in each chapter of the CW content:

- ***Objectives: Focus Questions.*** Outline key concepts from the text.
- ***Multiple-Choice Questions.*** Complete with hints and automatic grading that provide immediate feedback for students.
- ***Essay Questions.*** Encourage students to analyze, synthesize, and apply chapter content. Each essay question also features hints and feedback.
- ***Web Links.*** Links to websites mentioned in the text and additional links for additional research on chapter topics and key issues.

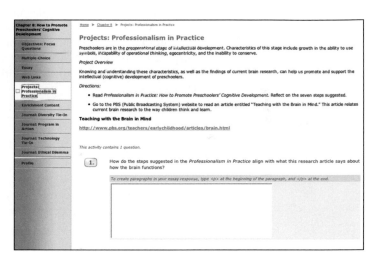

- ***Projects: Professionalism in Practice.*** Readings and research activities tied to individual Professionalism in Practice features throughout the text to enhance students' professional development.
- ***Enrichment Content.*** PowerPoint lecture notes, reproduced from the *Instructor's Manual,* are provided for each chapter along with glossary terms to familiarize students with key vocabulary.
- ***Journal: Diversity Tie-in.*** Additional readings and activities built around specific Diversity Tie-in features in the text.
- ***Journal: Program in Action.*** Additional readings and activities built around specific Program in Action features in the text.
- ***Journal: Technology Tie-in.*** Additional readings and activities built around specific Technology Tie-in features in the text.
- ***Journal: Ethical Dilemma.*** Students can complete this new feature and submit their responses to instructors.

WebCT and Blackboard Course Cartridges. The test items are available in formats compatible with existing WebCT and Blackboard courses. Cartridges may be downloaded from the Instructor's Resource Center.

ACKNOWLEDGMENTS

In the course of my teaching, service, and consulting, I meet and talk with many professionals who are deeply dedicated to doing their best for young children and their families. I am always touched, heartened, and encouraged by the openness, honesty, and unselfish sharing of ideas that characterize these professional colleagues. I thank all the individuals who contributed to the Professionalism in Practice, Program in Action, and other program descriptions. They are all credited for sharing their personal accounts of their lives, their children's lives, and their programs.

I value and respect the feedback and sound advice that the following reviewers provided: Diane Cerreto, Eastern Connecticut State University; Susan Gomez, California State University, Sacramento; Sherrill W. Hayes, Guilford Technical Community College; Richelle M. Johnson, Central Carolina Community College; Julie Williams, Pulaski Technical College; Cheryl Wright, University of Utah; and Nillofur Zobairi, Southern Illinois University at Carbondale.

In addition, I acknowledge the outstanding help and support of my research assistant Whitney Dwyer who is dependable, bright, dedicated and always gets the job done!

I am blessed to work with my colleagues at Merrill/Prentice Hall. Ann Davis, director of marketing, was the inspiration for this book. In fact, when she was the editor, *Fundamentals* was initially Ann's idea. I have always felt privileged to turn Ann's ideas into a new and different early childhood textbook. My editor, Julie Peters, is always positive, upbeat, and a constant source of bright and exciting ideas. I can always count on Julie for wise counsel about how to make *Fundamentals* more engaging and relevant for students and professors. Production editor Linda Bayma and Project Manager Angela Urquhart (Thistle Hill Publishing Services) are very attentive to detail and to making sure that things are done right. Many thanks to copy editor Lorretta Palagi who helped clarify by raising questions about content and style. Because of their persistence and insistence, *Fundamentals* is a much better book than it would have been without their devotion to excellence.

brief contents

CHAPTER 1 • • • **You and Early Childhood Education:**
Becoming a Professional   2

CHAPTER 2 • • • **Early Childhood Education Today:**
Understanding Current Issues   28

CHAPTER 3 • • • **History and Theories:**
Foundations for Teaching and Learning   52

CHAPTER 4 • • • **Implementing Early Childhood Programs:**
Applying Theories to Practice   86

CHAPTER 5 • • • **Standards and You:**
Teaching Children to Learn   120

CHAPTER 6 • • • **Observing and Assessing Young Children:**
Guiding, Teaching, and Learning   146

CHAPTER 7 • • • **Infants and Toddlers:**
Critical Years for Learning   170

CHAPTER 8 • • • **The Preschool Years:**
Getting Ready for School and Life   202

CHAPTER 9 • • • **Kindergarten Today:**
Meeting Academic and Developmental Needs   234

CHAPTER 10 • • • **The Early Elementary Grades: 1–3:**
Preparation for Life   264

CHAPTER 11 • • • **Educating Children with Diverse Backgrounds and Special Needs:**
Ensuring All Children Learn   294

CHAPTER 12 • • • **Guiding Children's Behavior:**
Helping Children Act Their Best   320

CHAPTER 13 • • • **Parents, Families, and the Community:**
Building Partnerships for Student Success   344

Appendix
NAEYC Code of Ethical Conduct and Statement of Commitment   367

Endnotes   375

Glossary   383

Index   387

contents

CHAPTER 1

You and Early Childhood Education:
Becoming a Professional 2

Who Is an Early Childhood Professional? 3
Professional Development Goals 3
    Goal 1: Content Knowledge 4
    Goal 2: Pedagogical Knowledge 5
    Why Diversity Tie-Ins? 8
    Goal 3: Professional Knowledge 9
    Goal 4: Professional Dispositions 13
Pathways to Professional Development 16
Why Technology Tie-Ins? 23
Using the Professional Development
    Checklist 23
Activities for Professional Development 23
    Ethical Dilemma 23
    Application Activities 24

CHAPTER 2

Early Childhood Education Today:
Understanding Current Issues 28

Issues Influencing the Practice of Early Childhood
    Education 29
    Changing Families 29
    Families and Early Childhood 30
    Wellness and Healthy Living 34
    Be a Role Model 35
    Socioeconomic Status and Children's
        Development 37
    Brain Research 39
    Violence 43
    Bullying 43
Politics and Early Childhood Education 45
Federal and State Involvement in Early Childhood
    Programs 46
    Expanded Federal Support for Early Childhood
        Education 46
    Public Schools and Early Education 46
    Growth and Preschools 47
New Directions in Early Childhood
    Education 48
Activities for Professional Development 50
    Ethical Dilemma 50
    Application Activities 50

CHAPTER 3

History and Theories:
Foundations for Teaching and Learning 52

Why Is the History of Early Childhood Education
    Important? 53
    Rebirth of Great Ideas 53
    Build the Dream—Again 53
    Implement Current Practice 54
Why Are Theories of Learning Important? 55
    Communicate 55
    Evaluate Learning 55
    Provide Guidance 56
Famous People and Their Influence on Early
    Childhood Education 57
    Martin Luther 57
    John Amos Comenius 57
    John Locke 57
    Jean-Jacques Rousseau 58
    Johann Heinrich Pestalozzi 59
    Robert Owen 60
    Friedrich Wilhelm Froebel 60
    Maria Montessori and the Montessori Theory 62
    John Dewey and Progressive Education Theory 62
    Jean Piaget and Constructivist Learning Theory 63
    Lev Vygotsky and Sociocultural Theory 71
    Abraham Maslow and Self-Actualization Theory 72
    Erik Erikson and Psychosocial Theory 75
    Urie Bronfenbrenner and Ecological Theory 76
    Howard Gardner and Multiple Intelligence
        Theory 79
From Luther to Today: Basic Concepts Essential to
    Good Educational Practices 81
    As They Relate to Children 81
    As They Relate to Teachers 81
    As They Relate to Parents 81
Activities for Professional Development 84
    Ethical Dilemma 84
    Application Activities 84

CHAPTER 4

Implementing Early Childhood Programs:
Applying Theories to Practice 86

What Are Early Childhood Education Programs? 87
    The Growing Demand for Quality Early Childhood
        Programs 87

Child Care: Serving Children and Families 88
  The Importance of Child Care 89
  Types of Child Care Programs 91
  What Constitutes Quality Education and Care? 92
  The Effects of Care and Education on Children 92
High/Scope: A Constructivist Model 93
  Basic Principles and Goals of the High/Scope Model 94
  The Five Elements of the High/Scope Model 97
  A Daily Routine That Supports Active Learning 100
  Advantages 102
The Montessori Method 102
  The Role of the Montessori Teacher 102
  The Montessori Method in Action 103
  Montessori and Contemporary Practices 106
Reggio Emilia 106
  Beliefs About Children and How They Learn 107
Waldorf Education: Head, Hands, and Heart 110
  Basic Principles 110
  Waldorf in Context 111
Federal Programs for Young Children 112
  Head Start 113
  Early Head Start 117
Early Childhood Programs and You 118
Activities for Professional Development 118
  Ethical Dilemma 118
  Application Activities 118

CHAPTER 5

Standards and You:
Teaching Children to Learn 120

What Are Standards 121
Why Standards? 121
  National Reports 122
  NCLB Discussion 124
  NAEYC Early Childhood Standards 125
  Appropriate Assessment 127
  Why Are Standards Important? 128
How Are Standards Changing Teaching and Learning? 130
  Standards and Teaching 134
  National Standards 136
Issues Surrounding Standards 139
Activities for Professional Development 145
  Ethical Dilemma 145
  Application Activities 145

CHAPTER 6

Observing and Assessing Young Children:
Guiding, Teaching, and Learning 146

What Is Assessment? 147
  Why Is Assessment Important? 147
  What Is Authentic Assessment? 149
  Formal Assessment 150
  Informal Assessment 151
Using Observation to Assess 153
  Purposes of Observation 153
  Steps for Conducting Observations 154
  Checklists 158
Using Portfolios to Assess 161
Screening Procedures 164
  Screening Instruments 164
Reporting to and Communicating with Parents and Families 164
Assessment in Context 165
What Are the Issues in the Assessment of Young Children? 165
  Assessment and Accountability 165
  Head Start National Reporting System 166
  High-Stakes Testing 167
Activities for Professional Development 168
  Ethical Dilemma 168
  Application Activities 169

CHAPTER 7

Infants and Toddlers:
Critical Years for Learning 170

What Are Infants and Toddlers Like? 171
Young Brains: A Primer 172
Nature, Nurture, and Development 174
Psychosocial and Emotional Development 175
  Social Behaviors 177
  Attachment and Relationships 177
  Temperament and Personality Development 178
Motor Development 180
Intellectual Development 181
  Stages of Sensorimotor Intelligence 181
Language Development 183
  Heredity and Language Development 183
  Theories of Language Development 183
  The Sequence of Language Development 184

Developmentally Appropriate Infant and Toddler
Programs 187

Multiculturally Appropriate Practice 189

Preparing Environments to Support Infant and Toddler
Development 190

Provide for Health and Safety 190

Support Developmental Needs 191

Provide Challenging Environments 191

**Promote Respectful Social Development
and Interactions 192**

Encourage Active Involvement 192

Curricula for Infants and Toddlers 192

Encourage Language Development 192

Provide Daily Routines 193

Infant Mental Health 193

What Is Infant Mental Health? 193

Portraits of Children 198

Activities for Professional Development 198

Ethical Dilemma 198

Application Activities 198

CHAPTER 8

The Preschool Years:
Getting Ready for School and Life 202

What Is Preschool? 203

**The Growing Popularity
of Preschools 203**

What Are Preschoolers Like? 205

Physical and Motor Development 205

Social and Emotional Development 206

Self-Regulation 206

Cognitive Development 207

Language Development 207

Ready to Learn: Ready for School 207

Readiness Skills 209

Readiness and Culture 214

Preschools and State Standards 214

The Preschool Environment 215

The Preschool Curriculum 217

Play in Preschool Programs 217

Kinds of Play 219

**Early Childhood Professionals
and Play 221**

The Preschool Daily Schedule 224

Successful Transitions to Kindergarten 229

Portraits of Children 230

Activities for Professional Development 230

Ethical Dilemma 230

Application Activities 233

CHAPTER 9

Kindergarten Today:
**Meeting Academic and Developmental
Needs 234**

The History of Kindergarten Education 236

Friedrich Froebel 236

Margarethe Schurz 236

Elizabeth Peabody 236

Susan Blow 236

Patty Smith Hill 236

What Are Kindergarten Children Like? 237

Physical Development 237

Social and Emotional Development 237

Cognitive and Language Development 238

Who Attends Kindergarten? 239

Universal Kindergarten 239

Kindergarten Today 240

The Changing Kindergarten 240

Environments for Kindergartners 241

The Physical Environment 241

The Social Environment 242

Curriculum in Kindergarten 243

Literacy and Reading in Kindergarten 243

Math in Kindergarten 249

Science in Kindergarten 250

Social Studies in Kindergarten 251

Arts in Kindergarten 255

Supporting Children's Approaches
to Learning 256

Kindergarten Issues 257

Redshirting 257

High-Stakes Kindergarten Testing 258

Kindergarten Entrance Age 259

Portraits of Children 261

Activities for Professional Development 261

Ethical Dilemma 261

Application Activities 261

CHAPTER 10

The Early Elementary Grades: 1–3:
Preparation for Life 264

Children in Primary Grades: Growth and
Development 267

Physical Development 267

Social Development 268

Emotional Development 269

Cognitive Development 271

Moral Development 272

The Contemporary Elementary School 273
  Pro-Social and Conflict Resolution Education 276
  Character Education 277
  Teaching Thinking 277
Environments That Support Learning 278
  The Physical Environment 280
  The Social Environment 282
Curriculum in the Primary Grades 283
  Literacy and Reading in the Primary Grades 283
  Math in the Primary Grades 284
  Science in the Primary Grades 286
  Social Studies in the Primary Grades 287
  Arts in the Primary Grades 289
Portraits of Children 289
Activities for Professional Development 289
  Ethical Dilemma 289
  Application Activities 293

CHAPTER 11

Educating Children with Diverse Backgrounds and Special Needs:
  Ensuring All Children Learn 294
  Children with Disabilities 295
    The Individuals with Disabilities Education Act (IDEA) 295
    Children with Autism 305
    Children with Attention Deficit Hyperactivity Disorder (ADHD) 307
    Strategies for Teaching Children with Disabilities 308
  Gifted and Talented Children 308
    Educating Gifted and Talented Children 310
  Education for Children with Diverse Backgrounds 312
    Multicultural Awareness 312
    Multicultural Infusion 313
  Activities for Professional Development 318
    Ethical Dilemma 318
    Application Activities 318

CHAPTER 12

Guiding Children's Behavior:
  Helping Children Act Their Best 320
  Why Guide Children's Behavior? 321
    What Is Guiding Behavior? 321
  A Social Constructivist Approach to Guiding Behavior 322
    Step 1: Use the Social Constructivist Approach to Guide Behavior 322

  Step 2: Clarify Your Beliefs About Guiding Behavior 325
  Step 3: Know and Use Developmentally Appropriate Practice 325
  Step 4: Meet Children's Needs 326
  Step 5: Help Children Build New Behaviors 327
  Step 6: Empower Children 329
  Step 7: Establish Appropriate Expectations 332
  Step 8: Arrange and Modify the Environment 332
  Step 9: Model Appropriate Behavior 334
  Step 10: Avoid Problems 335
  Step 11: Develop a Partnership with Parents, Families, and Others 337
  Step 12: Recognize and Value Basic Rights 337
  Step 13: Teach Cooperative Living and Learning 337
  Step 14: Use and Teach Conflict Management 339
Looking to the Future 342
Activities for Professional Development 343
  Ethical Dilemma 343
  Application Activities 343

CHAPTER 13

Parents, Families, and the Community:
  Building Partnerships for Student Success 344
  New Views of Parent/Family and Community Involvement 345
  Changing Parents and Families: Changing Involvement 346
    Grandparents as Parents 347
  Parent/Family Involvement: What Is It? 349
    Education as a Family Affair 352
    Family-Centered Teaching 352
    Two-Generation and Intergenerational Family Programs 353
    The Federal Government and Parent Involvement 354
    Activities for Involving Families 354
    Conducting Home Visits 357
    Conducting Parent–Teacher Conferences 358
    Making Contact by Telephone 359
    Communicating with Parents over the Internet 359
    Involving Single-Parent Families 360
    Involving Language-Minority Parents and Families 361

Community Involvement 362

School–Business Involvement 364

National Organizations 364

Website Connections 364

The Challenge 364

Activities for Professional Development 365

Ethical Dilemma 365

Application Activities 365

Appendix: NAEYC Code of Ethical Conduct and Statement of Commitment 367

Endnotes 375

Glossary 383

Index 387

Note: Every effort has been made to provide accurate and current Internet information in this book. However, the Internet and information posted on it are constantly changing so it is inevitable that some of the Internet addresses listed in this textbook will change.

special features

NEW! competency builders

program in action

How to Support Diversity in a Multicultural Child Care Setting

COMPETENCY BUILDER

Hampton Place Baptist Church is in the low-income region of Oak Cliff, an urban area of Dallas, Texas, that is composed of many minorities. The church provides child care services to primarily Hispanic, Spanish-speaking families. However, we also house a Laotian mission. Our preschool department includes approximately fifteen infants, ten toddlers, and fifteen preschoolers and serves both the Hispanic and the Laotian congregations. Here are some of the considerations and adjustments we make to accomodate these different cultures:

STRATEGY 1 GREET FAMILIES IN A CULTURALLY SENSITIVE MANNER
With Hispanic families, the father is greeted first, then the mother, and the children last

STRATEGY 2 PROVIDE INCLUSIVE ARTWORK
Murals include children with different skin and hair colors

STRATEGY 3 USE LINGUISTICALLY APPROPRIATE MATERIALS

infants are calmed through soft, smooth talking, cradling, and gentle rocking.

STRATEGY 5 MEET INDIVIDUAL AS WELL AS CULTURAL NEEDS
Some infants interact primarily person-to-others person; interact through toys.

STRATEGY 6 RESPECT DIFFERENT SOCIAL PREFERENCES
Hispanic toddlers tend to interact with peers, but Laotian toddlers tend to keep to themselves and sometimes want to be left alone. A Laotian child may need to be provided with a special place of his or her own.

STRATEGY 7 APPLY LIMITS TO CULTURAL ACCOMMODATION WHEN NECESSARY
Discuss compromises with parents. For example, some cultures allow infants to eat items they could choke on. In this case we explain the danger the food presents to the infants and ask parents to bring alternative snacks.

Multiculturalism and Professionalism: You Can't Have One Without the Other 10

How to Help English Language Learners Succeed 40

How to Scaffold Children's Learning 74

How to Teach in a Child-Centered Program 88

How to Plan Lessons That Meet Standards 136

How to Observe Children: Observing Will 160

How to Plan a Curriculum for Infants and Toddlers: Day to Day the Relationship Way 194

How to Promote Preschoolers' Cognitive Development 208

How to Integrate Science and Literacy in Kindergarten 252

How to Use Data-Driven Instruction 274

How to Support Diversity in a Multicultural Child Care Setting 314

How to Guide Hard-to-Manage Children to Help Ensure Their Success 340

Home and School: An Unbeatable Team! 348

diversity tie-ins

diversity tie-in

Getting Hispanic Parents Involved in Schools

Because parents play such a powerful role in their children's educational development, early childhood programs must make every effort to involve the parents and families of all children. Unfortunately, many minority parents are not included at all or not to the extent to which they should be. The urgency of involving minority parents becomes more evident when we look at the population growth of minorities. For example, the Bureau of the Census estimates that by 2025, 25 percent of all school-age children in the United States will be Hispanic.

"Historically, we know that Hispanics don't feel welcome in schools, and that's been a barrier to recruiting Hispanic parents," said Mark Townsend, Colorado PTA president and a board

- Always greet parents whenever they come to school for any reason.
- *Nonjudgmental communication*—Avoid making Hispanic parents feel that they are to blame for or are doing something wrong. Support parents for their strengths rather than judging them for perceived failings.
  - Be an active listener—pay close attention to what parents are saying and how they are saying it.
  - Be willing to compromise.
- *Bilingual support*—Communicate with Hispanic parents in both Spanish and English.
  - Send all notes and flyers home in Spanish.

Multiculturalism and Professionalism: You Can't Have One Without the Other 10

Achievement by Socioeconomic Status 38

Native American Education: Then and Now 58

Unique Characteristics of Native American Head Start Programs 114

Teaching, Standards, and You 129

High-Stakes Tests Leave Minority Students Behind 168

Infant Mental Health in a Cultural Context 197

Young English Language Learners 210

A Pre-K–First-Grade Program in Appalachia 262

The Rich Get Richer 266

Maternal Education and Student Achievement 315

Fathers, Socioeconomic Status, and Children's Behaviors 336

Making Sure All Parents Are Involved 357

Getting Hispanic Parents Involved in Schools 363

professionalism in practice

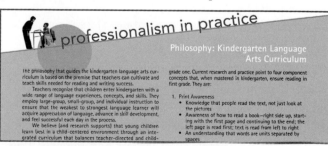

professionalism in practice

Philosophy: Kindergarten Language Arts Curriculum

The philosophy that guides the kindergarten language arts curriculum is based on the premise that teachers can cultivate and teach skills needed for reading and writing success.

Teachers recognize that children enter kindergarten with a wide range of language experiences, concepts, and skills. They employ large-group, small-group, and individual instruction to ensure that the weakest to strongest language learner will acquire appreciation of language, advance in skill development, and feel successful each day in the process.

We believe (and research supports) that young children learn best in a child-centered environment through an integrated curriculum that balances teacher-directed and child-

grade one. Current research and practice point to four component concepts that, when mastered in kindergarten, ensure reading in first grade. They are:

1. Print Awareness
   - Knowledge that people read the text, not just look at the pictures
   - Awareness of how to read a book—right side up, starting with the first page and continuing to the end; the left page is read first; text is read from left to right
   - An understanding that words are units separated by spaces

Caring and Kindness Are Keys to the Profession 14

Perspective on Early Childhood Education 22

How to Help English Language Learners Succeed 40

How to Scaffold Children's Learning 74

An "Educational History" Lesson 80

Making Homeless Children Feel at Home 92

The What and Why of Early Learning Standards 132

Teachers' Views About How Standards Have Changed
Their Teaching 138

Making a Difference 154

Power Tools for Teachers and Caregivers: The Three Rs 176

How to Promote Preschoolers' Cognitive Development 208

You Can't Fly by the Seat of Your Pants 222

Philosophy: Kindergarten Language Arts Curriculum 258

Igniting a Variety of Sparks Through Brain-Compatible
Learning 280

ESL Programs—"One of My Greatest Accomplishments" 318

Helping Gifted Children Through Challenging Curriculum 328

Home and School: An Unbeatable Team! 348

programs in action

The CDA 20

Head Start Children by "Heart Starting" Dads 32

Going to School in 1876 54

How to Teach in a Child-Centered Program 88

Magnia Child Care 94

A Reggio Parent-Teacher Cooperative 112

Inclusion and Collaboration 117

How to Plan Lessons That Meet Standards 136

How to Observe Children: Observing Will 160

Charlie and Emma's Very, Very Good Day at the Bright
Horizons Family Center 188

How to Plan a Curriculum for Infants and Toddlers: Day
to Day the Relationship Way 194

How Play Supports Literacy Development 220

How to Integrate Science and Literacy in Kindergarten 252

How to Use Data-Driven Instruction 274

Dual Languages for English Language Learners 276

Inclusion . . . Yours, Mine, Ours 307

How to Support Diversity in a Multicultural Child Care
Setting 314

Positive Guidance: Responsible, Motivated, Self-Directed
Learners 338

How to Guide Hard-to-Manage Children to Help Ensure
Their Success 340

Six Types of Parent/Family Involvement 350

technology tie-ins

How's Your Technology IQ? 24

Is the Use of Technology in Early Childhood Programs
"Bad" for Young Children? 48

From Mozart to Montessori: Teaching the Fine Arts to
Children 82

Promote Children's Social Development with Technology 107

Technology Across the Curriculum 135

Handheld Computers: Assessment Tools for a New
Generation 163

Using Technology to Record Infant and Toddler
Development 175

How to Use Technology as a Scaffolding Tool in the
Preschool Classroom 213

Five Effective Ways for Using Technology 247

The Technological Divides 288

Using Assistive Technology (AT) to Help Children with
Disabilities Learn 310

Helping Kids Help Themselves—Electronically 330

Homework Helpers 355

Fundamentals of Early Childhood Education

1

YOU AND EARLY CHILDHOOD EDUCATION
Becoming a Professional

professional development goal

Content Knowledge

A. I know the subject matter that I plan to teach and can explain important principles and concepts delineated in professional, state, and institutional standards.[1]

Pedagogical Knowledge

B. I reflect a thorough understanding of pedagogical content knowledge delineated in professional, state, and institutional standards. I have in-depth understanding of the subject matter that I plan to teach, allowing me to provide multiple explanations and instructional strategies so that all students learn. I present the content to students in challenging, clear, and compelling ways and integrate technology appropriately.[2]

Professional Knowledge

C. I demonstrate a complete comprehension of professional and pedagogical knowledge and skills delineated in professional, state, and institutional standards. I develop meaningful learning experiences to facilitate learning for all students. I reflect on their practice and make necessary adjustments to enhance student learning. I know how students learn and how to make ideas accessible to them. I consider school, family, and community contexts in connecting concepts to students' prior experience and applying the ideas to real-world problems.[3]

Professional Dispositions

D. I work with students, families, and communities in ways that reflect the dispositions expected of professional educators as delineated in professional, state, and institutional standards. I recognize when my own dispositions may need to be adjusted and are able to develop plans to do so.[4]

focus questions

1. Who is an early childhood professional?

2. What can you do to demonstrate the content knowledge necessary to be a highly qualified early childhood professional?

3. What can you do to demonstrate the pedagogical knowledge necessary to be a highly qualified early childhood professional?

4. What can you do to demonstrate the professional knowledge necessary to be a highly qualified early childhood professional?

5. What can you do to demonstrate the professional dispositions necessary to be a highly qualified early childhood professional?

Maria Cardenas is excited about her new assignment as a pre-kindergarten teacher. After years of study and serving as an assistant teacher, Maria now has her own classroom of three- and four-year-olds. "I can't believe this day has finally come! I've worked so hard, and now my dream has come true! I can't wait to get started! I want my children to learn and be all they can be!"

Maria did not become a teacher overnight. She spent two years at a local community college and three at the university, learning the content, pedagogical, and professional knowledge and dispositions necessary to be a highly qualified early childhood teacher. There was never any doubt in her mind or mine that she would achieve her goals! I first met Maria as her faculty advisor when she entered a university teacher education program. From the beginning, Maria was enthusiastic about her career choice and determined that she would be a high-quality professional. In addition to all of her coursework, Maria volunteered in many community and school-based programs to get the experiences she needed to help her prepare for the day when she would have her "own" classroom. After five years of going to school part time, Maria is ready to make a difference in the lives of "her" children. I hope you are as excited as Maria about your opportunity to teach young children.

Today, more than ever, the public and politicians are creating a lot of excitement by seeking ways to improve the quality of early childhood education and teaching.[5] As a result, you have a wonderful opportunity to work with young children and their families, develop new and better programs, and advocate for better practices and high-quality programs. Like Maria, you can be a leader in helping the early childhood profession make high-quality education a reality for all children.

WHO IS AN EARLY CHILDHOOD PROFESSIONAL?

You are preparing to be an **early childhood professional**, a person who works with, cares for, and teaches children between birth and age eight. You will work with parents, grandparents, other family members, and the community to bring high-quality education and services to all children. You are touching the future through the lives of the children you teach. What does it mean to be an early childhood professional?

Early childhood professionals have the content, pedagogical, and professional knowledge and dispositions necessary to teach and conduct programs so that all children learn. Professionals promote high standards for themselves, their colleagues, and their students. They are continually improving and expanding their skills and knowledge. They are multidimensional people who use their many talents to enrich the lives of children and families.

PROFESSIONAL DEVELOPMENT GOALS

Four professional development goals form the foundation of early childhood education: *content knowledge, pedagogical knowledge, professional knowledge,* and *professional dispositions.* These four goals are depicted in Figure 1.1, which shows how these goals surround and act as a compass to guide your professional practice.

Throughout this book, margin notes like the one on the following page direct you to a variety of multimedia items, including videos, children's artifacts, articles, and teaching

FIGURE 1.1 The Four Professional Development Goals

Photo: David Mager / Pearson Learning Photo Studio

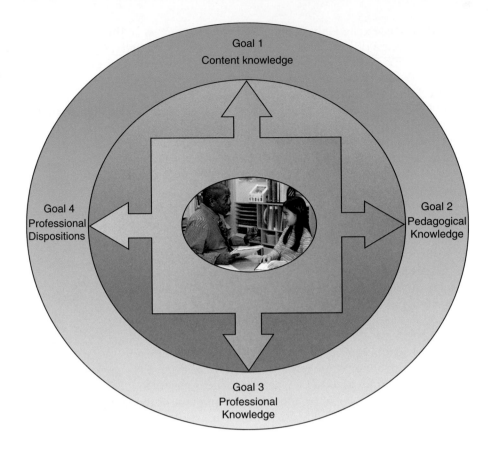

Observe two different teachers as they demonstrate examples of the four types of knowledge needed by teachers at Video Classroom, Foundations & Introduction to Teaching, Module 9: Developing As a Professional, Video 1: Types of Professional Knowledge.

strategies relating to and illustrating chapter topics. Log on to the Teacher Prep Website at http://www.prenhall.com/teacherprep/demo now to view two teachers exhibiting these four types of professional knowledge. An access code card, provided with this text, contains a password enabling you to access the site.

Goal 1: Content Knowledge

As an early childhood professional you will need to know the **content knowledge** you will be teaching young children. Content knowledge covers a wide range of disciplines and topics. This content knowledge includes child development and the academic disciplines. It is drawn from a number of sources including the Child Development Associate standards, the accreditation standards of the National Association for the Education of Young Children (NAEYC), the National Association of Early Childhood Specialists in State Departments of Education (NAECS/SDE), and state and national standards for teacher licensure and certification.

Child Development.   Knowledge of child development is fundamental for all early childhood educators regardless of their roles or the ages of the children they teach. It enables you to confidently implement developmentally appropriate practices with all children. All early childhood professionals ". . . use their understanding of young children's characteristics and needs, and of multiple interacting influences on children's development and learning, to create environments that are healthy, respectful, supportive, and challenging."[6]

Content Areas. Content areas are important to children's learning. Content areas form the basis for children's learning to read, write, do mathematics and science, and be creative. Consequently, early childhood professionals understand the importance of each content area in children's development and learning; demonstrate the essential knowledge and skills needed to provide appropriate environments that support learning in each content area; and demonstrate basic knowledge of the research base underlying each content area.[7] The content areas in early childhood are as follows:

- Language and literacy
- The arts: music, creative movement, dance, drama, and art
- Mathematics
- Physical activity and physical education
- Geography
- History
- Economics
- Social relations/civics.[8]

Throughout this book, you will learn what is included in each of the content areas and competencies that can help you teach each area.

Goal 2: Pedagogical Knowledge

Pedagogical knowledge and skills include concepts, theories, research, and approaches to effective teaching that enable you to develop and implement meaningful learning experiences that promote learning for all children. Say, for example, you were a beginning teacher with a group of English language learners (ELLs) in your class. You would want to know how ELLs learn best and how to teach them so they learn at high levels.

Effective pedagogical approaches include the following:

- Using developmentally appropriate practices,
- Selecting and using bias-free and culturally appropriate learning materials,
- Promoting children's oral language and communication,
- Supporting child-initiated learning,
- Scaffolding learning,
- Guiding children's learning and behavior,
- Promoting responsive relationships,
- Creating and maintaining learning environments both indoors and outdoors,
- Establishing and using learning centers,
- Using play as a foundation for children's learning, and
- Using technology as a teaching and learning tool.

Throughout this text, you are provided with the knowledge, concepts, and competencies necessary to become a confident teacher of all of these pedagogical approaches.

Developmentally Appropriate Approaches. Child development provides the foundation for conducting developmentally appropriate practices, which are essential curricula and instructional approaches on which all early childhood professionals must ground their work with young children.

Knowing Children. It is essential for you to have and demonstrate an understanding of child development. Child development knowledge enables you to understand how children grow and develop across all developmental levels—cognitive, linguistic, social, emotional, and physical. Knowledge of individual children, combined with knowledge of child growth and development, enables you to provide care and education that is developmentally appropriate for each child. **Developmentally appropriate practice (DAP)** means basing your teaching on how children grow and develop, and DAP is the recommended teaching practice of the profession. Ideas for how to conduct DAP are found throughout this book. These guidelines will serve as your road map of teaching. As you review the guidelines, consider how you can begin to apply them in your professional practice.

Review NAEYC's Position Statement on developmentally appropriate practice at http://www.prenhall.com/ morrison, Chapter 1—Web Links.

Developmentally and Culturally Appropriate Practice **(DCAP).**   Appropriate professional practice includes being sensitive to and responding to children's cultural and ethnic backgrounds and needs. The United States is a nation of diverse people and this diversity will continue. Children in every early childhood program represent this diversity. When children enter schools and programs, they do not leave their uniqueness, gender, culture, socioeconomic status, and race at the door. Children bring themselves and their backgrounds to early childhood programs. As part of your professional practice you will embrace, value, and incorporate **multiculturalism** into your teaching. Learning how to teach children of all cultures is an important part of your professional role. Figure 1.2 lists some popular and informative books that can help you achieve this goal. As you read these books, make a list of key ideas and how you can incorporate them into your teaching. In addition the anti-bias curriculum information that follows offers guidelines that will help you teach children from diverse backgrounds.

Anti-Bias Curriculum.   Conducting a developmentally and culturally appropriate program also means that you will include in your curriculum activities and materials that help challenge and change all biases of any kind that seek to diminish and portray as inferior all children based on their gender, race, culture, disability, language, or socioeconomic status. You can accomplish this goal by implementing an **anti-bias curriculum**. The book *Anti-Bias Curriculum: Tools for Empowering Young Children*[9] is the profession's primary resource for understanding and implementing an anti-bias curriculum. If you have not read this book, you should put it at the top of your list of professional books to read. An anti-bias curriculum:

> embraces an educational philosophy as well as specific techniques and content. It is value based: Differences are good; oppressive ideas and behaviors are not. It sets up a creative tension between respecting differences and not accepting unfair beliefs and acts. It asks teachers and children to confront troublesome issues rather than covering them up. An anti-bias perspective is integral to all aspects of daily classroom life.[10]

An anti-bias curriculum incorporates the positive intent of a multicultural curriculum and uses some similar activities, while seeking to avoid the dangers of a "tourist" approach, such as one that emphasizes differences by focusing primarily on holidays and foods. At the same time, anti-bias curriculum provides a more inclusive education: (1) it addresses more than cultural diversity by including gender and differences in physical abilities; (2) it is based on children's developmental tasks as they construct identity and attitudes; and (3) it directly addresses the impact of stereotyping, bias, and discriminatory behavior in young children's development and interactions.[11] Critical developmental identity tasks of early childhood include developing an *individual identity* and a *cultural identity*. Individual identity involves learning about the self— "Who am I?" Cultural identity involves learning about the culture of which the child is a part and how she relates to and functions in that culture. This is why you have to provide activities and an environmental context in which children can learn about their cultures, identify with them, and feel comfortable about being a part of their culture.

FIGURE 1.2

Books to Broaden Your Understanding of Multiculturalism in Schools and Other Programs

Delpit, L. (1996). *Other People's Children: Conflict in the Classroom.* New York: New Press.	In an interesting analysis of what is going on in American classrooms today, Lisa Delpit suggests that many of the academic problems attributed to children of color are actually the result of miscommunication as schools and "other people's children" struggle with the imbalance of power and the dynamics of inequality plaguing our system.
Derman-Sparks, L., & Ramsey, P. (2006). *What If All the Kids Are White? Anti-Bias Multicultural Education with Young Children and Families.* New York: Teachers College Press.	How do educators teach about racial and cultural diversity if all their students are white? The authors propose seven learning themes to help young white children resist messages of racism and build identity and skills for thriving in a multicultural country and world.
Jacobson, T. (2003). *Confronting Our Discomfort: Clearing the Way for Anti-Bias in Early Education.* Portsmouth, NH: Heinemann.	How do our attitudes get in the way of anti-bias in the classroom? Tamar Jacobson provides a framework for early childhood teachers to confront the issue head on. She guides the reader toward an anti-bias curriculum— showing how to see our own shortcomings, stop the perpetuation of negatives, and clear the way for children to gain a greater understanding of the world.
Jones, T. G., & Fuller, M. L. (2003). *Teaching Hispanic Children.* Boston: Allyn & Bacon.	This book presents information about the role of national origins and cultural backgrounds in teaching and learning and why it is important for teachers to know about culture in general and about Hispanic groups in particular.
Ladson-Billings, G. (1997). *The Dreamkeepers.* San Francisco: Jossey-Bass.	Ladson-Billings' portraits of teachers, interwoven with personal reflections, challenge readers to envision intellectually rigorous and culturally relevant classrooms that have the power to improve the lives of not just African American students but all children.

Here are a few anti-bias strategies you should follow in your classroom:

- *Evaluate your classroom environment and instructional materials to determine if they are appropriate for an anti-bias curriculum.* Get rid of materials that are obstacles to your anti-bias goals, such as books that include children of only one race. In my visits to early childhood classrooms, I observe many that are "cluttered," meaning they contain too many materials that do not contribute much to a multicultural learning environment. Include photos and representations from all cultures in your classroom and community.

- *Develop a plan for redesigning your classroom.* For example, you may decide to add a literacy center that encourages children to "read" and "write" about multicultural themes. Remember that children need the time, opportunity, and materials required to read and write about a wide range of anti-bias topics. In addition, since most classrooms don't have enough books on topics relating to gender, or cultural and ethnic themes, make sure you provide them.

View how a teacher teaches her students about race and ethnicity through children's literature at Video Classroom, Multicultural Education, Module 3: Ethnicity and Race, Video 1: Sensitive Illustrations.

- *Evaluate your current curriculum and approaches to diversity.* This will help you understand how your curriculum is or is not supporting anti-bias approaches. Learning experiences should be relevant to your students, their community, and their family's cultures.
- *Observe children's play and social interactions to determine what you have to do to make sure that all children are accepted and valued.* For example, some children of different cultural backgrounds may not be included in particular play groups. This information allows you to develop plans for ensuring that children of all cultures and genders are included in play groups and activities.
- *Evaluate how you interact with children.* You can reflect on your teaching, videotape your teaching, and/or have a colleague observe your teaching. In this way you will gain invaluable insight into how you interact with all children and make appropriate changes. I'm sure you have heard the saying "You can't see the forest from the trees." This frequently applies to our teaching practices. For example, you may unknowingly give more attention to boys than to girls. Also, you may be overlooking some important environmental accommodations that can support the learning of children with disabilities.
- *Include anti-bias activities in your daily and weekly classroom plans.* Intentional planning helps ensure that you are including a full range of anti-bias activities in your program. Intentional anti-bias planning also helps you integrate anti-bias activities into your curriculum for meeting national, state, and local learning standards.
- *Work with parents to incorporate your anti-bias curriculum.* Remember, parents are valuable resources in helping you achieve your goals.[12]

Anti-Bias Curriculum: Tools for Empowering Young Children provides guidelines and help with implementing these strategies.

Implementing an anti-bias curriculum will not be easy and it will require a lot of hard work and effort on your part. However, this is what teaching and being a professional is all about. You owe it to yourself, your children, and the profession to conduct programs that enable all children to live and learn in **bias-free** programs.

Why Diversity Tie-Ins?

Each chapter of this book has a Diversity Tie-In feature designed to do the following:

- Help you become a better person and a teacher who has a broad understanding of the diverse backgrounds of the children you teach.
- Enable you to teach all students regardless of their cultural, ethnic, or socioeconomic backgrounds.
- Provide you with learning ideas that support all children's intellectual, social, personal, and cultural development, regardless of cultural background, socioeconomic status, and gender.
- Help you apply multicultural knowledge and information to your teaching, exploring the opportunities the curriculum provides every day.
- Enable you and your children to live happily and productively in a multicultural world.

The Diversity Tie-In in this chapter is a Competency Builder that shares some important suggestions to guide you in making sure your professional practice is multicultural. Competency Builders are features of this text designed to help you increase your teaching competence and performance in specific professional areas. By completing the Competency Builder activities, you will enhance your professional development and contribute to your qualifications as a high-quality teacher.

Goal 3: Professional Knowledge

Early childhood professionals conduct themselves as professionals and identify with their profession.[13] Your identification with and involvement in your profession enables you to proudly say that you are a teacher of young children. Being a professional means that you (1) know about and engage in ethical practice; (2) engage in continuous lifelong learning and professional development; (3) collaborate with colleagues, parents, families, and community partners; (4) engage in reflective practice; and (5) advocate on behalf of children, families, and the profession.[14] These competencies represent the heart and soul of professional practice. You should be committed to increasing your knowledge in these areas throughout your career.

Lori Whitley / Merrill

Early childhood educators are professionals who, in addition to teaching and caring for children, are ethical, engage in lifelong learning, collaborate with colleagues and families, are reflective practitioners, and advocate for children and families.

Engaging in Ethical Practice. Ethical conduct—the exercise of responsible behavior with children, families, colleagues, and community members—enables you to confidently engage in exemplary professional practice. The profession of early childhood education has a set of ethical standards to guide your thinking and behavior. NAEYC has developed a Code of Ethical Conduct (see the Appendix or review the code online) and a Statement of Commitment, which follows:

> As an individual who works with young children, I commit myself to furthering the values of early childhood education as they are reflected in the NAEYC Code of Ethical Conduct. To the best of my ability I will
>
> Never harm children
> Ensure that programs for young children are based on current knowledge of child development and early childhood education
> Respect and support families in their task of nurturing children
> Respect colleagues in early childhood education and support them in maintaining the NAEYC Code of Ethical Conduct
> Serve as an advocate for children, their families, and their teachers in community and society
> Stay informed of and maintain high standards of professional conduct
> Engage in an ongoing process of self-reflection, realizing that personal characteristics, biases, and beliefs have an impact on children
> Be open to new ideas and be willing to learn from the suggestions of others
> Continue to learn, grow, and contribute as a professional
> Honor the ideals and principles of the NAEYC Code of Ethical Conduct.[15]

You can begin now to incorporate professional ethical practices into your interactions with children and colleagues. To stimulate your thinking, the Activities for Professional Development at the end of each chapter include an ethical dilemma.

> An ethical dilemma is a situation an individual encounters in the workplace for which there is more than one possible solution, each carrying a strong moral justification. A dilemma requires a person to choose between two alternatives; each has some benefits but also some costs. Typically, one stakeholder's legitimate needs and interest will give way to those of another. . . .[16]

As you reflect on and respond to each dilemma, use the NAEYC Code of Ethical Conduct as a valuable guide and resource.

diversity tie-in

Multiculturalism and Professionalism: You Can't Have One Without the Other

Think for a moment about all of the classrooms of children across the United States. What do you think their cultural, ethnic, and linguistic makeup is like? More than likely, the demographics of these children are different from those of the children you went to school with in kindergarten or first grade. Consider these data about America's children:

- In 2004, 58 percent of U.S. children were white-alone, non-Hispanic; 20 percent were Hispanic; 15 percent were black-alone; 5 percent were Asian-alone; and 5 percent were all other races.
- The percentage of children who are Hispanic has increased faster than that of any other racial or ethnic group.*

The increase in racial, ethnic, and cultural diversity in America is reflected in early childhood classrooms, which are also receiving increased numbers of children with disabilities and developmental delays. Consider the current student population at Susan B. Anthony Elementary School in Sacramento, California: 64 percent are Hispanic, 18 percent are Asian, 8 percent are African American, and 8 percent are white. Moreover, 100 percent of the children receive free lunches, and 41 percent are English-language learners.†

MEETING THE CHALLENGE

This diverse composition of early childhood classrooms challenges you to make your classroom responsive to the various needs of all your children, which is part of your professional responsibility. Let's look at some of the things you can do to be a responsible professional who is multiculturally aware and who teaches with respect and equity:

STRATEGY 1

BE CONCERNED ABOUT YOUR OWN MULTICULTURAL DEVELOPMENT

- Honestly confront your attitudes and views as they relate to people of other cultures. You may be carrying baggage that you have to get rid of to authentically and honestly educate all of your children to their fullest capacity.
- Read widely about your multicultural role as a professional.
- Learn about the habits, customs, beliefs, and religious practices of the cultures represented by your children.
- Ask some of your parents to tutor you in their language so you can learn basic phrases for greeting and questioning, the meaning of non-verbal gestures, and the way to appropriately and respectfully address parents and children.

STRATEGY 2

MAKE EVERY CHILD WELCOME

- Make your classroom a place where diversity is encouraged and everyone is treated fairly. Create a classroom environment that is vibrant and alive with

The goal of the NAEYC Code of Ethical Conduct is to inform, not prescribe, answers in tough decisions that teachers and other early childhood professionals must make as they work with children and families. The strategy inherent in the Code is to promote the application of core values, ideals, and principles to guide decision making.[17]

Continuous and Lifelong Professional Development Opportunities. A professional is never a "finished" product; you will always be involved in a process of studying, learning, changing, and becoming more professional. Teachers of the Year and others who share with you their philosophies and beliefs are always in the process of becoming more professional.

Becoming a professional means you will participate in training and education beyond the minimum needed for your current position. You will also want to consider your career objectives and the qualifications you might need for positions of increasing responsibility.

Collaborating with Parents, Families, and Community Partners. Parents, families, and the community are essential partners in the process of schooling. Knowing how to effectively collaborate with these key partners will serve you well throughout your career. Chapter 13, "Parents, Families, and the Community: Building Partnerships for Student Success," will help you learn more about this important topic.

the cultures of your children. You can do this with pictures, artifacts, and objects loaned by parents.

- Support and use children's home language and culture. Create a safe environment in which children feel free to talk about and share their culture and language. Encourage children to discuss, draw, paint, and write about what their culture means to them.

STRATEGY 3 — MAKE EVERY PARENT WELCOME

- Invite parents and families to share their languages and cultures in your classroom. Music, stories, and customs provide a rich background for learning about and respecting other cultures.
- Communicate with parents in their home languages.
- Work with parents to help them (and you) bridge the differences between the way schools operate and the norms of their homes and cultures.

STRATEGY 4 — COLLABORATE WITH YOUR COLLEAGUES

- Ask colleagues to share with you ideas about how to respond to questions, requests, and concerns of children and parents.
- Volunteer to form a faculty study group to read, discuss, and learn how to meet the cultural and linguistic needs of all children.

STRATEGY 5 — BECOME ACTIVE IN YOUR COMMUNITY

- Learn as much as you can about your community and the cultural resources it can provide. Communities are very multicultural places!

- Collaborate with community and state organizations that work with culturally and linguistically diverse families and populations. Ask them for volunteers who can help you meet the diverse needs of your children. Children need to interact with and value role models from all cultures.
- Volunteer to act as a community outreach coordinator to provide families with services, such as family literacy and school readiness information.

You can't be a complete early childhood professional without a multicultural dimension. As you become more culturally aware, you will increase your capacity for caring and understanding—and you and your students will learn and grow together.

*ChildStats.gov, "America's Children: Key National Indicators of Well-Being 2006," http://childstats.ed.gov/americaschildren/pop3.asp.
†greatschools.net, http://www.greatschools.net/cgi-bin/ca/other4675.

 Reflect on your cultural awareness at http://www.prenhall.com/morrison, Chapter 1—Journal: Diversity Tie-In.

Family education and support are important responsibilities of the early childhood professional. Children's learning begins and continues within the context of the family unit, whatever that unit may be. Learning how to comfortably and confidently work with parents and families is as essential as teaching children.

Reflective Practice. **Reflective practice** helps you think about how children learn and enables you to make decisions about how to best support their development and learning. Thinking about learning and understanding how children learn makes it easier for you to improve your teaching effectiveness, student learning, and professional satisfaction. In addition, thinking about learning and thinking about teaching are part of your reflective practice. Reflective practice involves deliberate and careful consideration about the children you teach, the theories on which you base your teaching, how you teach, what children learn, and how you will teach in the future. Although solitary reflection is useful, the power of reflective practice is more fully realized when you engage in such practice with your mentor teacher and colleagues. In a word, the reflective teacher is a thoughtful teacher. Reflective practice involves the three steps shown in Figure 1.3.

Advocacy. **Advocacy** is the act of pleading the causes of children and families to the profession and the public and engaging in strategies designed to improve the

11

Before

- What will I teach?
- How will I teach?
- What resources will I need?
- What background knowledge do my students have?

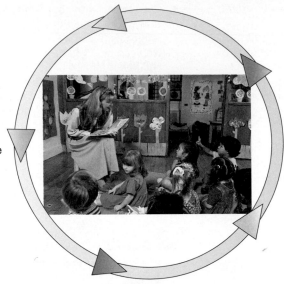

After

- Have I been self-reflective and thoughtful about my teaching?
- Did I assess the success of my students?
- How will I report students' achievements to parents?
- How will I provide feedback to my students?
- What will I do differently the next time I teach a similar lesson?

During

- Have I used students' prior knowledge to gain their interest and give them a focus?
- Am I presenting the lesson well?
- Am I constantly evaluating my students?
- Am I responding to the immediate needs of my students?
- Am I introducing new concepts and information?
- Am I motivating and challenging my students to pursue their own learning and investigation of the topic/subject/theme?

FIGURE 1.3 The Cycle of Reflective Practice: Thinking, Planning, and Deciding

Photo: Superstock Royalty Free

Read about how a teacher advocated for involving parents in their children's reading and writing at Strategies and Lessons, Early Childhood Education, Module 1: Advocacy, A Teacher's Experience in Involving Parents in Their Children's Reading and Writing

circumstances of those children and families. Advocates move beyond their day-to-day professional responsibilities and work collaboratively to help others. Children and families today need adults who understand their needs and who will work to improve the health, education, and well-being of all young children. You and other early childhood professionals are in a unique position to know and understand children and their needs and to make a difference in their lives.

There is no shortage of issues to advocate for in the lives of children and families. Some of the issues that are in need of strong advocates involve quality programs, abuse and neglect prevention, poverty, good housing, and health. To change policies and procedures that negatively affect children, you must become actively engaged. The following are some of the ways in which you can practice advocacy for children and families:

- *Join an early childhood professional organization,* such as NAEYC, the Association for Childhood Education International (ACEI), and the Southern Early Childhood Association (SECA). These organizations have local affiliates at colleges and universities and in many cities and towns and are very active in advocating for young children. You can serve on a committee or be involved in some other way.
- *Become familiar with organizations that advocate for children and families.*
  - Children's Defense Fund
  - Stand for Children
  - Voices for America's Children

- *Participate in community activities that support children and families.* Help others in your area who work to make a difference for children and families. For example, donate to an organization that supports children and families, volunteer your time at a local event that supports children, or participate in another way in a local organization that supports children and families.

- *Investigate the issues that face children and families today.* Read the news and become informed about relevant issues. For example, subscribe to an e-mail newsletter from a group that supports children and families; news updates are automatically sent on current issues. The share the news with colleagues, family, and friends.

- *Talk to others about the issues that face children and families.* Identify a specific concern you have for children and families, and talk to others about that issue. For example, if you are concerned about the number of children who do not have adequate health care, learn the facts about the issue in your community, and then talk to people you know about ways to solve that problem in your community. Begin with your own circle of influence: your colleagues, friends, family members, and other social groups in which you are a member.

- *Seek opportunities to share your knowledge of young children.* Inform others about the needs of young children by speaking with groups. For example, volunteer to meet with a group of parents at a local child care program to help them learn how to share storybooks with their young children, or meet with a local civic group that maintains the community park to discuss appropriate equipment for younger children.

- *Identify leaders in a position to make desired changes.* Learn who represents you in local, state, and national government. For example, identify the members of the local school board, and find out who represents you on the board. When issues arise, contact that person to express your concerns and offer solutions.

- *Enlist the support of others.* Contact others to help you disseminate information about an issue. For example, enlist the help of your local PTA in a letter-writing effort to inform town leaders about the need for safety improvements at the local playground.

- *Be persistent.* Identify an issue you are passionate about, and find a way to make a difference. There are many ways to advocate for children and families. Change takes time![18]

Begin exploring current issues in the field of Early Childhood Education at http://www.prenhall.com/morrison, Chapter 1—Web Links.

Within your own program or classroom, you will face many issues that should inspire you to advocate for your children and their families.

Goal 4: Professional Dispositions

I'm sure that you have a favorite teacher. I know I have many favorite teachers who taught me or with whom I work. One reason why they are my favorite teachers is because they act as professionals. They demonstrate the dispositions of highly qualified professionals.

Professional dispositions are the values, commitments, and professional ethics that influence behaviors toward students, families, colleagues, and communities and affect student learning, motivation, and development as well as the educator's own professional growth. Dispositions are guided by beliefs and attitudes related to values such as caring, fairness, honesty, and responsibility. For example, they might include a belief that all students can learn, a vision of high and challenging standards, or a commitment to a safe and supportive learning environment.[19] We have already discussed other dispositions such as ethical practice, collaborating with colleagues and families, and reflective practice. All programs that prepare professionals for the early childhood profession have a set of dispositions that are important for professional practice.

Caring and Kindness Are Keys to the Profession

Kindness is a simple eight-letter word that has the extraordinary power to make the world a better place. In our classroom we teach our students as we would want our own children to be taught. We practice what we teach by inspiring our students to share kindness with one another and to spread kindness wherever they go. To achieve that goal, we model kindness in these ways:

- Show enthusiasm for the subject matter and the children.
- Take time to know each child, both personally and academically (e.g., likes, dislikes, strengths, weaknesses, home environment).
- Be friendly and courteous, knowing that our attitudes can change children's attitudes.
- Be supportive and encouraging (e.g., saying "I am very proud of you," "Keep trying," "You're a great example for others").
- Avoid the use of criticism and ridicule.
- Don't choose favorites.
- Be sensitive to children's responses.
- Encourage mutual respect and trust.
- Create nurturing interactions with the children. (Our classroom motto, "Effort Creates Ability," makes students feel secure in trying new things.)

CLASSROOM PLEDGES

Each morning we begin the day by reciting three pledges. The first pledge is our Kindness Promise:

Every day, in every way,
I will show kindness to others.

When an unkind act occurs in our classroom, we ask the students involved to repeat the Kindness Promise and make an apology to the parties involved.

Our second pledge is our Helping Hands pledge. It is a quote from Helen Keller:

I am only one, but still I am one.
I cannot do everything, but still I can do something.
And because I cannot do everything, I will not refuse
to do the something that I can do.

This is our motto for community service projects in our classroom.

Our third pledge is our Learning Cheer:

L–Listen to others.
E–Expect to learn each day.
A–Act kindly toward others.
R–Remember the class rules.
N–Never give up on yourself.
1, 2, 3–First grade's cool!

All three pledges remind us that there is more to our classroom than the three Rs.

We show acts of kindness in our classroom through these special activities. We:

- Pause each morning for a moment of silence. We think kind-and-happy thoughts for our students who are absent, as well as for friends, family, pets, and situations that could benefit from our actions.
- Make a kindness critter, which is like a caterpillar. Each day our class thinks of one new way to show kindness. We write the idea on a new segment of the caterpillar. By the end of the school year, we have a very long critter with almost two hundred ways of showing kindness to others!
- Have regular class meetings to discuss situations in the classroom that relate to kindness (or its absence) and brainstorm solutions for those situations.

For the early childhood professional, *caring* is the most important of these dispositions. Professionals care about children; they accept and respect all children and their cultural and socioeconomic backgrounds. As a professional, you will work in classrooms, programs, and other settings where things do not always go smoothly—for example, children will not always learn ably and well, and they will not always be clean and free from illness and hunger. Children's and their parents' backgrounds and ways of life will not always be the same as yours. Caring means you will lose sleep trying to find a way to help a child learn to read and you will spend long hours planning and gathering materials. Caring also means you will not leave your intelligence, enthusiasm, and other talents at home but will bring them into the center, the classroom, administration offices, boards of directors' meetings, and wherever else you can make a difference in the lives of children and their families.

The theme of caring should run deep in your professional preparation and in your teaching. Listen to what Nel Noddings, a prominent teacher educator, has to say about caring:

- Insist that each student say please and thank you. We also remind our students to say "I'm sorry."
- Encourage students to compliment each other (e.g., "I like your picture" or "Congratulations, your team won the game").
- Display a rainbow fish in the classroom. Each time the teacher catches a child showing kindness, she can add a shiny scale to the rainbow fish.
- Form partnerships with organizations in the community. Our local chapter of Parent-Wise has developed a Bee Kind program, which comes to our school, sharing stories and creating hands-on activities that remind the students about the importance of kind acts, no matter how big or small.
- Host our "Have Lunch with Someone You Love" day! Each Friday in February, families are invited into our classroom to have lunch with their children. When parents cannot attend, grandparents, babysitters, or other family members fill in. Our intention is to provide kind and caring comments about their children. It is not a time for an academic or behavioral conference. It is just a time to let the parents know just how special their children are to us.
- Take pictures of our students, as they are involved in the classroom, and especially with our community service projects. At the end of the year, we give each student a "First-Grade Memory Book."
- Make our own "smiley face" classroom t-shirts. We wear them to special events in our school, and when we participate in community service projects outside of our school.

KINDNESS OUTSIDE THE CLASSROOM

There is no better way to promote and foster kindness and compassion in our world than by participating in community service projects. Here are ways we have taken caring and kindness outside our classroom:

- We made a lemonade stand and sold lemonade after each physical education class. We sent the proceeds of the sale to President Bush to be given to the children of Afghanistan.
- We traced the handprint of each of the students in our school onto red, white, or blue pieces of felt. We formed a six-by-eight-foot American flag from those hands and gave it to our state representative. It is now proudly displayed in our state capitol building.
- We raked leaves of veterans who live near our school on Veterans Day. We made patriotic wreaths for their doors and made no-bake cookies as a way of saying "thank you" to our veterans.
- We visited the pediatric floor of our local hospital. We used the bonus points from our Book Club to acquire age-appropriate books and prepared gift bags of hot chocolate, cups, and student-made bookmarks. Our theme was "Warm up with a good book; you'll feel so much better!" The books were given to each sick child as he or she was admitted to the hospital.
- We collected chewing and bubble gum and sent care packages to soldiers stationed in Iraq. Our theme "We Stick with Our Soldiers" was an inexpensive yet effective project that promoted kindness and caring attributes.
- We decorated lunch bags for our local "Meals-on-Wheels" program during our inside recess times. We were able to make 180 lunch bags per month for the elderly residents that live near our school and depend on Meals-on-Wheels for a nutritious meal. Meals-on-Wheels provided the bags and it cost us nothing but our recess time to make many elderly and, often, lonely people happy!
- We collected cans of soup and donated them to our local food bank for our own "Soup-er Bowl." As a culminating activity, we had a "tailgate party," complete with hot dogs, popcorn, and root beer!

Let your light shine! "All the darkness in the world cannot extinguish the light of a single candle."

Contributed by Christa Pehrson and Vicki Sheffler, 2002 USA Today First-Team Teachers, Amos K. Hutchinson Elementary School, Greensburg, Pennsylvania.

In an age when violence among school-children is at an unprecedented level, when children are bearing children with little knowledge of how to care for them, when the society and even the schools often concentrate on materialistic messages, it may be unnecessary to argue that we should care more genuinely for our children and teach them to care. However, many otherwise reasonable people seem to believe that our educational problems consist largely of low scores on achievement tests. My contention is, first, that we should want more from our educational efforts than adequate academic achievement and, second, that we will not achieve even that meager success unless our children believe that they themselves are cared for and learn to care for others.[20]

The Professionalism in Practice feature about caring and kindness illustrates this important point with many examples that you can use in your program or classroom.

PATHWAYS TO PROFESSIONAL DEVELOPMENT

The educational dimension of professionalism involves knowing about and demonstrating essential knowledge of the profession and professional practice. This knowledge includes the history and ethics of the profession, understanding how children develop and learn, and keeping up to date on public issues that influence early childhood and the profession.

Training and certification is a major challenge facing all areas of the early childhood profession and those who care for and teach young children. Training and certification requirements vary from state to state, and more states are tightening personnel standards for child care, preschool, kindergarten, and primary-grade professionals.

Many states have career ladders that specify the requirements for progressing from one level of professionalism to the next. Figure 1.4 outlines the early childhood practitioner's professional pathway for Oklahoma. What two things do you find most informative about this career pathway? How can you use the Oklahoma pathway to enhance your own professional development?

Review the Early Childhood Education course offerings of a community college at http://www. prenhall.com/ morrison, Chapter 1—Web Links.

Associate Degree Programs.   Many community colleges provide training in *early childhood education,* the services provided by early childhood professionals, that qualifies recipients to be **child care** aides, primary child care providers, and assistant teachers. For example, Southwest Florida College with campuses at Fort Myers and Tampa, Florida, offers a two-year early childhood education program curriculum leading to an associate's degree in the field. Coursework emphasizes emergent literacy, the exceptional child, documenting observations and using the data to plan lessons to meet the needs of children, the creation of developmentally appropriate curriculums, and assessment in classrooms. Students participating in the program are required to teach in an area school as the capstone course before graduating.

Baccalaureate Programs.   Four-year colleges provide programs that result in early childhood teacher certification. The ages and grades to which the certification applies vary from state to state. Some states have separate certification for **pre-kindergarten** programs and nursery schools; in other states, these certifications are "add-ons" to elementary (K–6, 1–6, 1–4) certification. At the University of South Florida, the age three through grade three teacher certification program includes coursework and extensive field experiences in early childhood settings to enable students to integrate theory with teaching practice.

Master's Degree Programs.   Depending on the state, individuals may gain initial early childhood certification at the master's level. Many colleges and universities offer master's programs for people who want to qualify as program directors or assistant directors or may want to pursue a career in teaching. Mary Ladd graduated with a bachelor's degree in business and worked for five years in a high-tech company. However she kept feeling a call to teach and satisfy her desire to work with young children. Mary earned a master's degree and teacher certification and now teaches first grade in an urban setting, where she enjoys helping young children read.

The CDA Program.   The **Child Development Associate (CDA)** National Credentialing Program is a competency-based assessment system that offers early childhood professionals the opportunity to develop and demonstrate competence in their work with children ages five and younger. Since its inception in 1975, the CDA program has provided a nationally recognized system that has stimulated early childhood training and education opportunities for teachers of young children in every state in the country and on military bases worldwide. The credential is recognized nationwide in state regulations for licensed centers as a qualification for teachers, directors, and/or family child care providers. The standards for performance that this program has established are used as a basis for professional development in the field.

Advanced degrees—MS, MA, PhD, EdD, JD, MD, RN

TRADITIONAL
- Occupational Child Care Instructor at technology centers
- Teacher Educator at a two-year college or four-year university
- Teacher/Administrator/Special Educator in a public or private elementary school–certification required
- Instructor/Curriculum Specialist in the armed services
- Child Development Specialist
- Child Guidance Specialist
- Researcher/Writer

RELATED
- Social worker
- Child Advocate/Lobbyist
- Librarian
- Pediatric Therapist–occupational and physical
- Human Resources Personnel in industry
- Child Life Specialist in a hospital
- Speech and Hearing Pathologist–Health Department, public/private school, private practice, university teaching
- Early Childhood Consultant
- Entertainer/Musician/Song Writer for children

- Author and Illustrator of children's books
- Physician/Pediatrician
- Pedodontist (works only with children)
- Dietitian
- Counselor
- Child Psychologist
- Psychiatrist
- Dietetic Assistant
- Recreation Supervisor
- Children's Policy Specialist
- Dental Hygienist
- Scouting Director

- Child Care Center or Playground/Recreation Center Designer
- Probation Officer
- 4-H Agent or County Extension Director
- Adoption Specialist
- Child Care Resource and Referral Director
- "Friend of the Court" Counselor
- Psychometrist
- Attorney with primary focus on children
- Religious Educator
- Certified Child and Parenting Specialist
- Family Mediator

Baccalaureate Level

TRADITIONAL
- Early Childhood Teacher in public school, Head Start, or child care settings
- Special Education Teacher
- Family Child Care Home Provider
- Nanny
- Administrator in Head Start program
- Child Care Center Director/Owner/Coordinator
- Child Care Center Director in the armed services

- Parents as Teacher's Facilitator
- Director of school-age (out-of-school time) program

RELATED
Some positions will require additional coursework at the baccalaureate level which will be in a field other than early childhood:
- Child Advocate/Lobbyist
- Recreation Director/Worker/Leader
- Web Master

- Journalist/Author/Publisher/Illustrator of children's books
- Children's Librarian
- Retail Manager of children's toy or book stores
- Licensing Worker
- Human Resource Personnel in industry
- Music Teacher, Musician/Entertainer for children
- Recreation Camp Director
- Camp Counselor/Scouts Camp Ranger

- Resource and Referral Trainer/Data Analyst/Referral Specialist/Child Care Food Program Consultant
- Childbirth Educator
- Gymnastic or Dance Teacher
- Pediatric Nurse Aide
- Child and Parenting Practitioner
- Producer of children's television shows and commercials
- Faith Community Coordinator and Educator

Associate Level

TRADITIONAL
- Head Start Teacher
- Child Care Teacher
- Family Child Care Home Provider
- Nanny
- Child Care Center Director

- School-Age Provider
- Early Intervention/Special Needs Program
- Para-Teacher/Aide

RELATED
In addition to those listed at the core level:

- Family and Human Services Worker
- LPN—specialized nurse training
- Entertainer for children at theme restaurants and parks
- Social Service Aide

- Playground Helper
- Physical Therapy Assistant
- Nursing Home Aide/Worker/Technician
- Faith Community Coordinators for families and children

Credential Level

- Head Start Teacher
- Child Care Teacher

- Family Child Care Home Provider
- Nanny

- Child Care Center Director
- Home Visitor

- Nursing Home Aide/Worker

Core Level
These positions require minimum education and training, depending on the position

TRADITIONAL
- Child Care Teaching Assistant
- Family Child Care Home Provider
- Head Start Teacher Assistant
- Nanny
- Foster Parent
- Church Nursery Attendant

- Related positions which involve working with children in settings other than a child care center, family child care home, Head Start or public school program

RELATED
Positions may require specialized pre-service training.

- Children's Storyteller, Art Instructor, or Puppeteer
- Recreation Center Assistant
- Salesperson in toy, clothing, or book store
- School Crossing Guard
- Children's Party Caterer
- Restaurant Helper for birthday parties
- Van or Transportation Driver
- Children's Art Museum Guide

- Receptionist in pediatrician's office
- Camp Counselor
- Special Needs Child Care Aide
- Live-in Caregiver
- Respite Caregiver
- Cook's Aide, Assistant Cook, Camp Cook, Head Start or Child Care Center Cook

FIGURE 1.4 Early Childhood Practitioner's Professional Pathway for Oklahoma

Source: The Center for Early Childhood Professional Development, College of Continuing Education, University of Oklahoma, 2000. Reprinted with permission.

The CDA program offers credentials to caregivers in four types of settings: (1) center-based programs for preschoolers, (2) center-based programs for infants/toddlers, (3) family child care homes, and (4) **home visitor programs.** Regardless of setting, all CDAs must demonstrate their ability to provide competent care and early educational practice in thirteen skill areas organized into six competency areas (which are outlined in Table 1.1). Evidence

TABLE 1.1 CDA Competency Goals and Functional Areas

CDA Competency Goals	Functional Areas
I. To establish and maintain a safe, healthy learning environment.	1. Safe: Candidate provides a safe environment to prevent and reduce injuries. 2. Healthy: Candidate promotes good health and nutrition and provides an environment that contributes to the prevention of illness. 3. Learning Environment: Candidate uses space, relationships, materials, and routines as resources for constructing an interesting, secure, and enjoyable environment that encourages play, exploration, and learning.
II. To advance physical and intellectual competence.	4. Physical: Candidate provides a variety of equipment, activities, and opportunities to promote the physical development of children. 5. Cognitive: Candidate provides activities and opportunities that encourage curiosity, exploration, and problem solving appropriate to the developmental levels and learning styles of children. 6. Communication: Candidate actively communicates with children and provides opportunities and support for children to understand, acquire, and use verbal and nonverbal means of communicating thoughts and feelings. 7. Creative: Candidate provides opportunities that stimulate children to play with sound, rhythm, language, materials, space, and ideas in individual ways and to express their creative abilities.
III. To support social and emotional development and to provide positive guidance.	8. Self: Candidate provides physical and emotional security for each child and helps each child to know, accept, and take pride in himself or herself and to develop a sense of independence. 9. Social: Candidate helps each child feel accepted in the group, helps children learn to communicate and get along with others, and encourages feelings of empathy and mutual respect among children and adults. 10. Guidance: Candidate provides a supportive environment in which children can begin to learn and practice appropriate and acceptable behaviors as individuals and as a group.
IV. To establish positive and productive relationships with families.	11. Families: Candidate maintains an open, friendly, and cooperative relationship with each child's family, encourages their involvement in the program, and suports the child's relationship with his or her family.
V. To ensure a well-run, purposeful program respective to participant needs.	12. Program Management: Candidate is a manager who uses all available resources to ensure an effective operation. The Candidate is a competent organizer, planner, record keeper, communicator, and a cooperative co-worker.
VI. To maintain a commitment to professionalism.	13. Professionalism: Candidate makes decisions based on knowledge of early childhood theories and practices. Candidate promotes quality in child care services. Candidate takes advantage of opportunities to improve competence, both for personal and professional growth and for the benefit of children and families.

Source: The Council for Professional Recognition, *Overview of the National CDA,* October 2002, http://www.nova.edu/msi/onlinecda/national_cda.html. Reprinted with permission.

of ability is collected from a variety of sources including firsthand observational evidence of the CDA candidate's performance with children and families. This evidence is weighed against national standards. The CDA national office sets the standards for competent performance and monitors this assessment process so that it is uniform throughout the country.

Since 1975, more than 160,000 individuals have received the CDA credential, with the vast majority (more than 80 percent) prepared to work in centers with three- and four-year-olds. Research studies have found that CDAs have a very high rate of retention in the field, move upward in terms of salaries and positions, and tend to continue their formal education toward college degrees.[21] Research studies have also shown that the CDA credential has a strong correlation with classroom quality and outcomes for young children.[22]

(CDA) *Participants.* Who becomes a CDA? Individuals working in all types of early education settings who want careers in early education—public schools, privately funded child care centers, church-based preschools, **Head Start** programs, and family child care homes. Anyone who is eighteen years old and holds a high school diploma is eligible. However, prior to application for assessment, individuals must acquire the required competencies by participating in some sort of professional preparation. Many two-year colleges, early childhood agencies and organizations, and some employers offer such CDA education and training programs. Scholarships to participate are also offered in many states, and since the CDA preparation often has a relationship with local colleges or universities to which community college students may transfer credits to gain additional education and/or a degree, general financial support for higher education is often available to CDA candidates. As it continues to grow in size and scope, the CDA program is playing a major role in enhancing the quality of education for young children.[23]

For more information, see the Program in Action feature. For more information on the CDA program, model curriculum materials for the preparation of CDAs, and other resources, visit the Council for Professional Recognition's website at http://www.cdacouncil.org.

Developing a Philosophy of Education. Professional practice entails teaching with and from a philosophy of education, which acts as a guidepost to help you base your teaching on what you believe about children.

A **philosophy of education** is a set of beliefs about how children develop and learn and what and how they should be taught. Your philosophy of education is based in part on your philosophy of life. What you believe about yourself, about others, and about life determines your philosophy of education. For example, we previously talked about optimism. If you are optimistic about life, chances are you will be optimistic for your children and we know that when teachers have high expectations for their children, they achieve at higher levels. Core beliefs and values about education and teaching include what you believe about children, what you think are the purposes of education, how you view the teacher's role, and what you think you should know and be able to do.

In summary, your philosophy of education guides and directs your daily teaching. Take a few minutes now and read Joann DesLauriers' perspective of education in the Professionalism in Practice feature, on page 22. As you read, reflect about what makes it special. What are some critical elements from her perspective that you can incorporate into yours? The following guidelines will help you develop your philosophy of education.

Read. Read widely in textbooks, journals, and other professional literature to get ideas and points of view. A word of caution: when people refer to philosophies of education, they often think of historical influences. This is only part of the information available for writing a philosophy. Make sure you explore contemporary ideas as well, for these will also have a strong influence on you as a professional. The Activities for Professional Development section at the end of the chapter will help you get started. In addition, Chapter 3, "History and Theories," provides helpful information for you to use in developing your philosophy.

At Green River Community College in Auburn, Washington, CDA training is offered over three quarters of the school year. An optional fourth quarter is available for students who would like to work further on their professional resource file and receive the Green River Community College CDA Preparation Certificate. CDA training covers specific topics relevant to early childhood education and helps the student prepare for the National CDA Assessment. Courses are designed to allow students to enter the program during any quarter while working in local child care centers, preschools, Montessori programs, or Head Start classrooms. In some cases, students can also take courses online via the Internet, linking theoretical knowledge to their work with young children and families. Students in the program come from various points in their life—the recent high school graduate, the mother who has assisted in her child's classroom, or the child care worker from Korea or the Ukraine. One of the outstanding elements of this training is that the credits earned while attending the CDA classes may apply toward students' early childhood degree.

ON-THE-JOB TRAINING

By demonstrating various areas of competency, the CDA candidates exemplify the concept of on-the-job training and prior learning. Through observing and recording children's behavior, students learn how to effectively plan a curriculum that meets the individual and cultural needs of the children they serve. The CDA instructor facilitates learning by providing direction and assigning relevant coursework. Assignments are designed to offer students real-life experiences. Some of these are (1) planning and implementing menus, (2) designing safe learning environments, and (3) presenting developmentally appropriate curricula, lessons, and activities to the children in their classrooms. Through a variety of learning experiences, including workshops and seminars, CDA candidates receive training in child development and early education. The strong connection between the families and the educator is supported as CDA students learn strategies and techniques that help them build these relationships in order to better meet the needs of the children.

PROFESSIONALISM IN ACTION

In the area of professionalism, students not only attend conferences, but they help plan them! Each year for the last twelve years, CDA candidates have made meaningful contributions to Green River Community College's annual Diversity Fair, a conference for educators, students, and primary caregivers. The Diversity Fair provides students opportunities to showcase what they've learned through displaying the curriculum they've created and by sharing their classroom experiences.

THE CDA IN ACTION

My passion for teaching the CDA program has its roots in my own success. I entered the field of early childhood education as a family child care provider. Over the years I attended work-

Reflect. As you read through and study this book, make notes and reflect about your philosophy of education. The following prompts will help you get started:

- I believe the purposes of education are. . . .
- I believe that children learn best when they are taught under certain conditions and in certain ways. Some of these are. . . .
- The curriculum—all of the activities and experiences—of my classroom should include certain "basics" that contribute to children's social, emotional, intellectual, and physical development. These basics include. . . .
- Children learn best in an environment that promotes learning. Features of a good learning environment are. . . .
- All children have certain needs that must be met if they are to grow and learn at their best. Some of these basic needs are. . . .
- I would meet these needs by. . . .
- A teacher should have certain qualities and behave in certain ways. Qualities I think important for teaching are. . . .

Discuss. Discuss with successful teachers and other educators their philosophies and practices. The personal accounts in the Professionalism in Practice boxes in each

shops and college classes to increase my knowledge of early childhood's best practices. Through the encouragement of my instructor and other professionals, I finally received my CDA. The CDA opened up a whole new vista of opportunities for me. Throughout my career I have been a family child care provider, owned and directed my own mini-center, directed a large for-profit child care center, and helped create a wonderful non-profit child care center that received NAEYC accreditation. All the while I continued to take one class at a time in order to complete my bachelor's degree. My current goal is to complete my master's degree in education.

CDA opened doors for me and gave me the confidence to continue my education and reach out into other areas of our field. Armed with practical experience and my CDA, I began training other child care providers for a local college. I helped facilitate a CDA support group that mentored students who were working toward their CDA credential. I also became involved in diversity work within my community.

As my enthusiasm for the CDA continued to grow, I took more CDA training from the college and became a CDA Representative for the Council for Professional Recognition. I have grown to understand and respect the incredible influence their work has on early childhood education. Shortly afterwards, I was offered a position at Green River to teach the CDA program. I have never wavered in my commitment to the early childhood community or in my efforts to help other providers see their potential and succeed in obtaining their CDA. Our program reaches out into our communities and offers individuals opportunities to learn more about obtaining a CDA. I am not shy in sharing with my students how powerful a CDA credential is to their future in early childhood. I am an example of just how wonderful the CDA experience can be.

Complete an activity on CDA credentials at http://www.prenhall.com/morrison, Chapter 1: Journal—Program in Action.

chapter of this text are evidence that a philosophy can help you be a successful, effective teacher. They also serve as an opportunity to "talk" with successful professionals and understand how they translate theory into practice.

Write. Once you have thought about your philosophy of education, write a draft and have other people read it. Writing and sharing helps you clarify your ideas and redefine your thoughts, because your philosophy should be understandable to others (although they do not necessarily have to agree with you).

Evaluate. Finally, evaluate your philosophy using this checklist:

- Does my philosophy accurately relate my beliefs about teaching? Have I been honest with myself?
- Is it understandable to me and others?
- Does it provide practical guidance for my teaching?
- Are my ideas consistent with one another?
- Does what I believe make good sense to me and others?

Now finalize your draft into a polished copy. A well-thought-out philosophy will be like a compass throughout your career. It may evolve but it will point you in the right direction and keep you focused on doing your best for children.

Joann DesLauriers
First-grade teacher
Hoover Elementary
Bartlesville, Oklahoma

After several decades as an educator, I still anticipate each August when I know it is time to meet a new class of first graders. I am acutely aware that I am one of the principal players in ensuring that the children who are placed under my care become readers and writers. This responsibility has led me to think constantly about my practice and to hold high standards for my own performance daily in the classroom. I have found that continued professional growth is the key to maintaining my love and passion for the teaching profession.

I continue to grow and learn because I keep current through professional reading. Teachers often feel so busy that they neglect maintaining professional reading. It is my strong belief and experience that developing a habit of staying current through educational journals and books is essential. Through membership in professional organizations such as the International Reading Association, I receive a monthly journal and information about recently published books. While reading these publications alone is necessary, this reading takes on a new dimension when teachers meet to discuss their readings. As new concepts and ideas are shared each of us begins to think about our classroom practice and its impact on student learning. The partnership of professional reading with professional conversation is powerful. The dialogue creates significant changes in practice and forms the basis for support from colleagues as we wrestle with how to incorporate what we have learned into our classrooms.

An abundance of knowledge is located within the walls of schools across the United States. Some of the best professional development I have had has been from fellow teachers. I make it a point to develop relationships with the most effective teachers on a staff. Teachers become like those with whom they associate. My advice to any new teacher is to locate the reflective teachers in their buildings and make them their model. Make opportunities to watch them in action. Invite them into your classroom to help you identify areas for improvement. Have conversations with them about what they do to help their students learn. I try to surround myself with strong, effective educators so that I, too, can become strong and effective.

Recently, the realization that many teachers have a deep understanding of how students learn has impacted the way professional development has been delivered. More and more schools are organizing professional learning communities. These are groups of teachers who meet regularly to evaluate teaching practices by looking at examples of student work or to design lessons and assessment techniques that meet specific standards. Teachers work together and combine their knowledge and ideas. Expectations for student learning and, therefore, for teacher performance are high. As teachers work collaboratively they share the work these high expectations bring. Participating in a collaborative team is "on-the-job" professional development. Specific strategies are developed around specific questions about the needs of a particular student or class, making them easier to implement and evaluate the impact. I have been involved with a professional learning community that brought videos of their teaching and examples of student work. The discussions that followed centered around student learning and how to improve it. These are the kinds of conversations teachers should be having as we work together to understand what students should know and be able to do. Being part of a collaborative team involves some risk as you make your practice "public." It requires being willing to share successes and failures. Only when we are willing to put our teaching practices "out there" for others to see can we really begin to grow. This sort of risk taking is what we ask our students to do each day. Teachers must be willing to take the same sort of risk to bring the best experiences and teaching practices to their students.

The primary motivation I have to continue to learn more about children and how they learn is the students. As teachers we must enter the doors of our classroom prepared to meet the needs of each one. This is our calling. They each deserve our best. Professional growth falls squarely on the teacher's shoulders; it is a choice we make. Choose to read professional literature. Choose to learn from the best teachers in your building. Choose to join professional learning communities. Your teaching will be richer and your students will reap the benefits.

 Begin working on your own Professional Development Notebook at http://www.prenhall.com/morrison, Chapter 1—Projects: Professionalism in Practice.

WHY TECHNOLOGY TIE-INS?

Each chapter of this book has a Technology Tie-In feature. Perhaps you are wondering "why?" I use these technology-focused features because they will:

- Enable you to become more technologically proficient. As the Technology Tie-In for this chapter illustrates, teachers and all educational professionals are expected to use technology in a number of ways and for multiple purposes. Today's professional cannot plead technological ignorance.
- Help you apply technology to your teaching of young children. Every day you will want to consider and explore the opportunities the curriculum provides for you to use technology to help young children learn. Technology includes more than computers. Technology also includes digital cameras, overhead projectors, tape recorders, and handheld electronic devices.
- Help you empower young children with appropriate technology skills that will promote, enhance, and enrich learning.
- Enhance collaboration with parents. E-mail is a good way to stay in touch with parents and keep them informed. You can also help parents use the technology they have in their homes to help them and their children learn.

 Observe a teacher's usage of a variety of types of technology **in the classroom** at Vedio Classroom, Foundations & Introduction to Teaching, Module 7: Technology, Video 1: Enhancing Learning Through Technology.

USING THE PROFESSIONAL DEVELOPMENT CHECKLIST

My purpose for writing this book is to support your professional development from the stage where you are—novice or midlevel to highly skilled expert. The professional development checklist (Figure 1.5) is a powerful tool you can begin to use now to achieve this goal. Each chapter emphasizes one or more professional outcomes from the checklist for you to consider and master. The Desired Professional Goals come from a number of sources: the initial certification standards for early childhood certification of the National Council for Accreditation of Teacher Education and National Teachers of the Year; award-winning teachers, National Board Certified teachers, and professors of early childhood education.

 To monitor your progress toward professionalism using the online version of the Professional Development Checklist, go to the Companion Website at *http://www.prenhall.com/morrison*, select Chapter 1, then choose the Professionalism in Practice module.

ACTIVITIES FOR PROFESSIONAL DEVELOPMENT

Ethical Dilemma

"Should I Report Her to. . . ?"

Elena is talking to Kim, her colleague at a preschool:

> Kim, you have been teaching here longer than I have, so maybe you can help me. I want to talk to you about the new preschool teacher they hired. I've talked with her a couple of times about how she implements the state pre-K standards, and she says she isn't too worried about them. I offered to help her with her lesson plans, but she told me she plans as she goes along. She said she knows what to do and developing a written plan gets in the way of her doing what comes naturally for her and the children. She also told me she thinks that the emphasis on early literacy is just a lot of hype—a passing fad. I'm concerned that her children won't be ready for kindergarten.

What should Elena do? Should she talk to her preschool supervisor and risk damaging her relationship with her fellow teacher and possibly hurt her career, or should she assume that another teacher's practices are not her business, even if they might be harmful to the children?

technology tie-in

Today, thousands of early childhood teachers use desktop and laptop computers with built-in modems, faxes, and CD-ROM drives; camcorders and digital cameras; optical scanners; and laser printers. They also use software for e-mail, word processing, desktop publishing, presentation graphics, spreadsheets, databases, and multimedia applications. You can begin now to prepare yourself to use technology to enhance your teaching and your students' learning. Colorado teachers are now required to demonstrate a broad usage of technology skills in the following twelve areas. In which of these areas are you competent? Quiz yourself on which of the competencies you possess. Access the entire set of competencies on the website provided. Based on your self-analysis, develop a plan for how you will develop the competencies you need to be technologically proficient.

Technology Competencies	Yes	No
1. Computer Operation **a.** Start and shut down computer systems and peripherals		
b. Identify and use icons, windows; menus		
2. Setup, Maintenance, and Troubleshooting **a.** Protect and care for storage media		
b. Make backup copies of documents and files		
3. Word Processing/Introductory Desktop Publishing **a.** Enter and edit text		
b. Cut, copy, and paste text		
4. Spreadsheet/Graphing **a.** Interpret and communicate information in an existing spreadsheet		
b. Enter data into an existing spreadsheet		
5. Databases **a.** Interpret and communicate information in an existing database		
b. Add and delete records		
6. Networking **a.** Use a file server (connect/log on, retrieve a program or document, save a document to a specified location)		
b. Share files with others on a network		

Application Activities

1. Recall the teachers who had a great influence on you. Which of their characteristics do you plan to incorporate into your philosophy of education?

2. Write your philosophy of education and share it with others. Ask them to critique it for comprehensiveness, clarity, and meaning. How do you feel about the changes they suggested?

3. Use a daily/monthly planner to develop a professional development plan for the next year. First list your career development goals and then on a monthly basis specify activities, events, and other ways that you will achieve these goals. For example, in addition to attending classes at a local community college, preschool teacher Rosa Vaquerio plans to read a book a month on a topic related to teaching.

4. Many local schools and school districts elect and honor their teachers of the year. Contact one of these teachers and have him or her share with you the core ideas and beliefs that enabled him or her to be selected as a teacher of the year. Ask the teacher to provide specific examples of how to apply ethical practice to teaching. How do you plan to integrate these qualities into your professional development plan?

5. To a great extent, your ongoing professional development is your responsibility. As a result, you should constantly be on the alert for ways to grow professionally. Interview

Technology Competencies	Yes	No
7. Telecommunications **a.** Connect to the Internet or an online service		
b. Use a web browser to access and use resources on the Internet and World Wide Web		
8. Media Communication and Integration **a.** Use imaging devices such as scanners, digital cameras, and/or video cameras with computer systems and software		
b. Connect video output devices and other presentation systems to computers and video sources for large screen display		
9. Curriculum **a.** Select and create learning experiences that are appropriate for curriculum and goals relevant to learners, and based on principles of effective teaching and learning; incorporate the use of media and technology for teaching where appropriate		
10. Design and Management of Learning Environments and Resources **a.** Develop performance tasks that require students to (1) locate and analyze information as well as draw conclusions and (2) use a variety of media to communicate results clearly		
11. Child Development, Learning, and Diversity **a.** Use media and technology to address differences in children's learning and performance		
b. Use media and technology to support learning for children with special needs		
12. Social, Legal, and Ethical Issues **a.** Follow school district policies and procedures, and federal law to ensure compliance with copyright law and fair-use guidelines		

Source: Colorado Technology Competency Guidelines for Teachers and Media Specialists, Essential Technology Skills, 2000.
http://www.aps.k12.co.us/rangeview/resources/Tech/CoTechComp/TechCompIndexa.html.

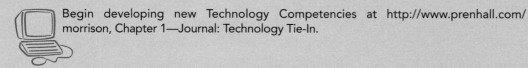 Begin developing new Technology Competencies at http://www.prenhall.com/morrison, Chapter 1—Journal: Technology Tie-In.

two pre-K to third-grade teachers. Ask them to identify specific things they do to promote their own professional development.

6. Dispositions as we have discussed are important for professional development. They are also a good way to think about yourself, your beliefs, and your teaching role. For example, some of the metaphors my students think are important include love of children, honesty, and respect for all children. Add to this list and then identify several dispositions that you plan to focus on during the coming year.

7. Developmentally appropriate practice will play an important role in your teaching. Each day you are with children, you will want to apply developmental information to your practice. For example, knowledge of child development influences how teachers help children develop oral language skills. Research this topic by accessing the website http://www.naeyc.org/about/positions.asp and then printing NAEYC's Developmentally Appropriate Practice in Early Childhood programs. Identify three other examples of how you would apply child development to your teaching to help children learn to communicate.

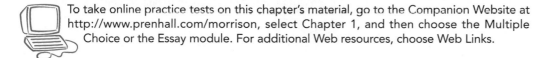 To take online practice tests on this chapter's material, go to the Companion Website at http://www.prenhall.com/morrison, select Chapter 1, and then choose the Multiple Choice or the Essay module. For additional Web resources, choose Web Links.

FIGURE 1.5

Sixteen Competencies to Becoming a Professional: A Development Checklist

Topic Number	Desired Professional Goals
1.	**Content Knowledge** I know the subject matter that I plan to teach and can explain important principles and concepts delineated in professional, state, and institutional standards.
2.	**Pedagogical Knowledge** I reflect a thorough understanding of pedagogical content knowledge delineated in professional, state, and institutional standards. I have in-depth understanding of the subject matter that I plan to teach, allowing me to provide multiple explanations and instructional strategies so that all students learn. I present the content to students in challenging, clear, and compelling ways and integrate technology appropriately.
3.	**Professional Knowledge** I demonstrate a complete comprehension of professional and pedagogical knowledge and skills delineated in professional, state, and institutional standards. I develop meaningful learning experiences to facilitate learning for all students. I reflect on their practice and make necessary adjustments to enhance student learning. I know how students learn and how to make ideas accessible to them. I consider school, family, and community contexts in connecting concepts to students' prior experience and applying the ideas to real-world problems.
4.	**Ongoing Professional Development** I have a professional career plan for the next year. I engage in study and training programs to improve my knowledge and competence, belong to a professional organization, and have worked or am working on a degree or credential (CDA, AA, BS OR B.A). I strive for positive, collaborative relationships with my colleagues and employer.
5.	**Professional Dispositions** I work with students, families, and communities in ways that reflect the dispositions expected of professional educators as delineated in professional, state, and institutional standards. I recognize when my own dispositions may need to be adjusted and am able to develop plans to do so.
6	**Philosophy of Teaching** I have thought about and written my philosophy of teaching and caring for young children. My actions are consistent with this philosophy.
7.	**Keeping Current in an Age of Change** I am familiar with the profession's contemporary development, and I understand current issues in society and trends in the field. I am willing to change my ideas, thinking, and practices based on study, new information, and the advice of colleagues and professionals.
8.	**Historical Knowledge** I am familiar with my profession's history, and I use my knowledge of the past to inform my practice.
9.	**Theories of Early Childhood Education** I understand the principles of each major theory of educating young children. The approach I use is consistent with my beliefs about how children learn.
10.	**Delivering Education and Child Care** I am familiar with a variety of models and approaches for delivering education and child care, and I use this knowledge to deliver education and child care in a safe, healthy learning environment.
11.	**Observation and Assessment** I pay attention to my students' actions and feelings. I evaluate students using appropriate and authentic measures. I use observation and assessment to guide my teaching.
12.	**Developmentally Appropriate Practice** I understand children's developmental stages and growth from birth through age eight, and use this knowledge to implement developmentally appropriate practice. I do all I can to advance the physical, intellectual, social, and emotional development of the children in my care to their full potential.
13.	**Educating All Students** I understand that all children are individuals with unique strengths and challenges. I embrace these differences, work to fulfill special needs, and promote tolerance and inclusion in my classroom. I value and respect the dignity of all children.
14.	**Guiding Behavior** I understand the principles and importance of behavior guidance. I guide children to be peaceful, cooperative, and in control of their behavior.
15.	**Collaborating with Parents and Community** I am an advocate on behalf of children and families. I treat parents with dignity and respect. I involve parents and community members in my program and help and encourage parents in their roles as children's primary caregivers and teachers (NCATE Standard 2).
16.	**Technology** I am technologically literate and integrate technology into my classroom to help all children learn.

Level of Accomplishment? (Circle One)	If High, Provide Evidence of Accomplishment	If Needs Improvement, Specify Action Plan for Accomplishment	Target Date for Completion of Accomplishment	See the following for more information on how to meet the Desired Professional Outcomes
High Needs Improvement				Chapter 1 All Chapters, "Professionalism in Practice" boxes, "Activities for Professional Development", and "Ethical Dilemmas"
High Needs Improvement				Chapter 1 All Chapters, "Professionalism in Practice" boxes, "Activities for Professional Development", and "Ethical Dilemmas"
High Needs Improvement				Chapter 1 All Chapters, "Professionalism in Practice" boxes, "Activities for Professional Development", and "Ethical Dilemmas"
High Needs Improvement				Chapter 1 All Chapters, "Professionalism in Practice" boxes, "Activities for Professional Development", and "Ethical Dilemmas"
High Needs Improvement				Chapters 1, 5 All Chapters, "Professionalism in Practice" boxes, "Activities for Professional Development", and "Ethical Dilemmas"
High Needs Improvement				Chapter 1 All Chapters, "Activities for Professional Development", and "Ethical Dilemmas"
High Needs Improvement				Chapters 2, 5 All Chapters, "Professionalism in Practice" boxes, and "Ethical Dilemmas"
High Needs Improvement				Chapter 3
High Needs Improvement				Chapter 4
High Needs Improvement				Chapter 4 All Chapters, "Program in Action" boxes, and "Ethical Dilemmas"
High Needs Improvement				Chapter 6 All Chapters, "Ethical Dilemmas"
High Needs Improvement				Chapters 1, 7, 8, 9, and 10 All Chapters, "Program in Action" boxes, and "Ethical Dilemmas"
High Needs Improvement				Chapter 11 All Chapters, "Diversity Tie-in" boxes, and "Ethical Dilemmas"
High Needs Improvement				Chapter 12 All Chapters, "Ethical Dilemmas"
High Needs Improvement				Chapter 13
High Needs Improvement				All Chapters, "Technology Tie-in" boxes

Note: These professional development outcomes are consistent with the core values of the NAEYC and the competencies of the CDA.

2

EARLY CHILDHOOD EDUCATION TODAY
Understanding Current Issues

professional development goal

Keeping Current in an Age of Change

A. I am familiar with the profession's contemporary development, and I understand current issues in society and trends in the field. I am willing to change my ideas, thinking, and practices based on study, new information, and the advice of colleagues and professionals.

B. I engage in continuous, collaborative learning to inform practice.[1]

C. I integrate knowledge, reflective practice, and critical perspectives on early childhood education.[2]

focus questions

1. What critical issues do children, families, and early childhood professionals face today?

2. How do contemporary issues influence curriculum, teaching, and the life outcomes of children and families?

3. How can early childhood professionals respond to contemporary social problems for the betterment of children and families?

4. What are some ways you can keep current in the rapidly changing field of early childhood education?

ISSUES INFLUENCING THE PRACTICE OF EARLY CHILDHOOD EDUCATION

Life is full of changes and so is early childhood education. These changes have and will continue to influence what and how you teach, as well as what your children learn.

Many contemporary social issues affect decisions families and early childhood professionals make about the education and care of young children. Child abuse; childhood diseases, such as asthma and lead poisoning; poverty; low-quality care and education; inequality of programs and services; and society's inability to meet the needs of all children are perennial sources of controversy and concern to which early childhood professionals seek solutions. New ideas and issues relating to the education and care of young children and the quest to provide educationally and developmentally appropriate programs keep the field of early childhood education in a state of continual change. In fact, change is one constant of the early childhood profession. You will be constantly challenged to determine what is best for young children and their families given the needs and political demands of society today.

The issues such as those shown in Figure 2.1 and those we discuss in this chapter have an influence on the profession and you. You cannot ignore these issues. You must be part of the solution to making it possible for all children to achieve their full potential. Education is political and those who ignore this reality do so at their own risk. Politicians and the public look to early childhood professionals to help develop educational solutions to social and political problems.

Agencies serving children and families, such as the Parent Teacher Association (PTA), offer "a voice for children" by expressing their views. For example, Anna Marie Weselak, president of the National PTA, says, "Every young mind needs a spark to light the way to a brighter future through learning. Teachers are that spark."[3] Part of your professional role as a children's advocate will be to help change the odds against children so they can succeed in school and life.

Let's examine some issues in early childhood and consider how you can respond to them.

Changing Families

Families are in a continual state of change as a result of social trends. Some of these include increased maternal employment, increased father absence, increased cultural diversity, and changing views about marriage. As a result, the definition of what a family is varies as society changes. Consider the following ways families are changing in the twenty-first century:

1. *Structure.* Many families now include arrangements other than the traditional nuclear family. Some of these contemporary families include single-parent families, headed by mothers or fathers; stepfamilies, including individuals related by either marriage or adoption; heterosexual, gay, or lesbian partners living together

FIGURE 2.1

Examples of Recent Newspaper Headlines Relating to Early Childhood Issues

Newspapers are full of articles relating to children and family news. These are just a few representative headlines that show the enormous range of topics. A good way to keep informed about such issues is to read daily newspapers. You will be well informed and you can talk knowledgeably with parents and colleagues.

- "In Kindergarten Playtime, a New Meaning for 'Play'," *The New York Times*
- "Push for Success Sends More Kids to pre-K Tutoring," *The Arizona Republic*
- "Disaster Planning at Day Care: Centers to Get New Guidelines for Emergencies," *The Wall Street Journal*
- "The Long Wait: Many Working Parents Need Assistance Paying for Good Child Care," *Winston-Salem Journal*
- "Preschool Space Is at a Premium," *The Washington Post*
- "Tutored at 2—Too Much, Too Soon?" *San Diego Tribune*
- "No Toy Is Better Than a Parent's Attention," *The Freelance Star*

Observe a child discussing his family at Video Classroom, Child Development, Module 3: Family, Culture, and Community, Video 3: Families.

as families; and extended families, which may include grandparents, uncles, aunts, other relatives, and individuals not related by kinship.[4] Grandparents as parents are growing in numbers and represent a fast-growing "new" family arrangement.[5] In Chapter 13, I discuss in more detail grandparents and their roles in children's lives.

2. *Roles.* As families change, so do the roles that parents and other family members perform. More parents work and have less time for their children and family affairs. Working parents must combine roles of both parents and employees. The number of hats parents wear increases as families change.

3. *Responsibilities.* As families change, many parents find it difficult to afford quality care for their children. Some parents find that buffering their young children from television and societal violence, child abusers, and crime is more than they can handle. Other parents are consumed by problems of their own and have little time or attention to give their children. Nonetheless, the responsibilities of parenthood remain and, increasingly, parents seek help from early childhood professionals to meet the demands and challenges of child rearing.

Families will continue to change. As they do, you must develop creative ways to provide services to children and families of all kinds.

Families and Early Childhood

Early childhood professionals agree that a good way to meet the needs of children is through their families, whatever the family units may be. Review Figure 2.2, which shows processes for educating both children and families. As families change, early childhood professionals have to develop new and different ways of meeting parents' and children's needs. Providing for children's needs through and within the family system makes sense for a number of reasons:

- The family system has the primary responsibility for meeting many children's needs. Parents are children's first teachers, and the experience and guidance they do or do not provide shapes their children for life. It is in the family that basic values, literacy skills, and approaches to learning are set and reinforced. This is why it is important to work with families and help them get a good start on parenting.

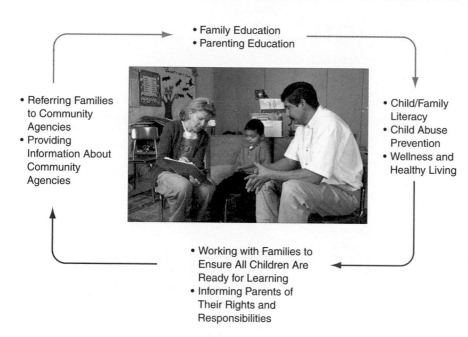

• Family Education
• Parenting Education

• Referring Families
to Community
Agencies
• Providing
Information About
Community
Agencies

• Child/Family
Literacy
• Child Abuse
Prevention
• Wellness and
Healthy Living

• Working with Families to
Ensure All Children Are
Ready for Learning
• Informing Parents of
Their Rights and
Responsibilities

FIGURE 2.2 Meeting
the Needs of Children
and Families

Photo: Michael Newman / PhotoEdit Inc.

• Teachers frequently need to address family problems and issues before they can help children effectively. For example, working with family services agencies to help parents access adequate, affordable health care means that the whole family, including children, will be healthier.

• Early childhood professionals can work with children and their families and benefit both. Family literacy is a good example. Helping children, their parents, and other family members learn to read and write helps the whole family. For example, the Texas Even Start Family Literacy Program provides literacy training for parents of families with newborns and children through age seven and assists families with parenting strategies in child growth and development.[6]

Families matter in the education and development of children. Working with parents becomes a win–win proposition for everyone. You are the key to making family-centered education work.

Working Parents. An increasing percentage of mothers with children are currently employed. In 2004, nearly 57 percent of mothers with children under age six and 73 percent of mothers with children ages six to seventeen were in the workforce.[7] This creates a greater demand for early childhood programs. Unfortunately, much of child care in the United States is of poor quality. One of your professional responsibilities is to partner with parents to raise the quality of child care and to make it affordable and accessible.

Fathers. Fathers are rediscovering the joys of parenting and interacting with young children. At the same time, early childhood educators have rediscovered fathers! Men are playing an active role in providing basic care, love, and nurturance to their children. Increasingly, men are more concerned about their roles as fathers and their participation in family events before, during, and after the birth of their children. Fathers want to be involved in the whole process of child rearing.

Children's development begins in the family system. The family system, with the help and support of early childhood programs, provides for children's basic needs. It makes sense for early childhood professionals to work with and through the family system to deliver their services.

Head Start Children by "Heart Starting" Dads

HEAD START A CHILD

At the National Center for Fathering, we seek to improve the well-being (health, education, and welfare) of all children by training and supporting men to be the fathers and father figures children need to lead them to success. This has been a real challenge in urban areas for the Urban Father-Child Partnership (UFP), where father absence and its impact on minority poor children is most severe. Many of these children have fallen behind.

Achievement Gap. According to the Education Department, only 20 percent of our minority kindergartners arrive with the skills needed to learn to read, compared with 50 percent of their classmates. There exists a wide achievement gap between rich and poor and white and minority students.

Parents as Primary Educator. How can these disadvantaged preschool and elementary school children be given a head start to compete in the economic race of life with their peers who do not face the same challenges? One strategy is to involve the parents of these children to help them develop as the primary educators and nurturers of their child. An involved father in education brings another important social asset to the aid of his child.

HEART START A DAD

Being a father is more of an art than science. It is an art that involves the heart. The heart of the father that is turned to his child paints a picture of success on the canvass of his child's life. The paint he uses goes well beyond the traditional societal paint of financial provider. The 2001 "Importance of Father Love" research reviewed over 100 studies and found that father love is as important for a child's happiness, well-being, and social and academic success as mother love. Research study after research study confirms the significant and lasting benefits of father involvement in children's education—fewer discipline problems, better academic performance, and a higher graduation rate.

Listen to Children. How important is father involvement? Listen to what children have to say. Rose, a second grader, says, "My Dad was my first date in the daddy daughter dance at school in our schools hall. My Dad took time off to be with me at this special event. My Dad is a very special person to me and no one can ruin that because I love him so much." Jarod, a first grader, says, "My dad is a hero to me. . . . I want to be like my dad when I grow up because then I'll be a hero, too."

MAKING A DIFFERENCE

Unfortunately, many fathers of today's children are repeating a generational cycle of uninvolvement. They did not have an involved father in education so they are not involved. How can you go another way unless you know another way? Furthermore, how can you know another way unless someone shows you another way? The Urban Father-Child Partnership is breaking

---

Because of the profession's increased understanding of the importance of fathers in children's development, there is now more research than ever before about fathers' roles in the lives of children. For example, research indicates that:

Read more about the importance of fathers' involvement to child development at http://www.prenhall.com/morrison, Chapter 2—Web Links.

- When fathers are involved with the children and interact with their children, do better in school.
- When fathers are involved with their children's cognitive development (reading to children, helping with school work, etc.), it helps counteract the negative effects of limited family and school resources. In other words, father involvement does, to some extent, make up for poor schools, poor neighborhoods, and low socioeconomic status.
- The positive effects of father involvement are not confined only to biological dads. When other adult males, such as adoptive fathers, grandfathers, and significant other males in the household, are involved, the same positive developmental outcomes and school-related benefits hold true.[8]

As you can see, helping fathers be involved with their children benefits children, families, schools, and society. The Program in Action feature illustrates how one father initiative encourages and supports father involvement with children.

Men are becoming single parents through adoption and surrogate childbearing. Also increasing in number are stay-at-home dads. Estimates of the number of fathers who stay

that cycle by showing another way through two breakthrough programs to reach out to urban fathers of preschool and elementary students.

Dads as Coaches. Our "Coach Dads" program is an innovative, noncompetitive preschool father involvement program that encourages dads to get involved in their child's development through play. The program is built around the "Coach Dads Play Book" that contains different "plays" dads lead that help develop the child physically, socially, cognitively, and representationally. The dads come to the site once a week to spend five to ten minutes at drop off or pick up to run a play from the book. Then they write a one-sentence entry about the experience in the journal section of the book.

Daily Reading. Our "R.E.A.D. to Kids" program (Reconnecting Education and Dads to Kids) involves the dad/father figure in his child's education by promoting the importance of practicing reading daily with his child, partnering with his child's teacher, and his presence at the school as an endorsement of school and practical fathering skills. The "R.E.A.D. to Kids" booklet contains five flexible sessions in the school library involving food, fun, and learning through projects for dad and his child.

Through programs like these we have seen how fathers can make a difference in their children's lives. Children, likewise, make a difference for fathers. Teachers, administrators, and mothers can help turn the hearts of these fathers to their children's education. Following are eight tips you can use to "heart start" dads:

1. See dads as part of the solution and an additional social asset for children's educational challenges.

2. Specifically target fathers and ask them to partner with you for their children's education.
3. Create a place at the school so that dads can share their interest and will feel competent.
4. Provide activities that strengthen the father–child relationship and use the fathering satisfaction of the relationship as the motivation for involvement.
5. Show dads the power of their influence on their children's development and teach them practical skills that will increase their fathering confidence.
6. Encourage fathers to form fathering support small groups to talk about issues related to their children that never get discussed anywhere else.
7. Allow for flexibility in fathers' schedules.
8. Take small attainable steps and celebrate the accomplishments of successful steps taken in the father-child relationship.

Fathers hold hope for giving children a head start in education and life. The "Coach Dads" and "R.E.A.D. to Kids" programs provide a boost for these children by engaging their fathers early in their children's education. We can all do our part in giving our children a head start in life by turning the hearts of fathers to their children.

Contributed by George R. Williams, MS, MFT, executive director of the Urban Father-Child Partnership for the National Center for Fathering.

 Reflect on additional ways early childhood professionals can involve fathers at http://www.prenhall.com/morrison, Chapter 2: Journal—Program in Action.

home with their children are just over one million.[9] Fathers are also receiving some of the employment benefits that have traditionally gone only to women, such as paternity leaves, flexible work schedules, and sick leave for family illness.

Single Parents. The number of one parent families, both male and female, continues to increase. Certain ethnic groups are disproportionately represented in single-parent families. These increases are due to several factors. First, pregnancy rates are higher among lower socioeconomic groups. Second, teenage pregnancy rates in poor white, Hispanic, and African American populations are sometimes higher because of lower education levels, economic constraints, and fewer life opportunities.[10] In 2004, 80 percent of single-parent families were headed by females and 20 percent were headed by males.[11]

The reality is that more women are having children without marrying. In fact, 35.7 percent of all births in 2004 were to unmarried women.[12]

Teenage Parents. Although teenage pregnancies have declined during the past several years, they still continue to be a societal problem. Each year, one out of ten, or 1.1 million, teenagers becomes pregnant. In addition: in 2004, there were 41 pregnancies for 1,000 teenagers, down from 75 pregnancies per 1,000 in 2002.

- As a group, Latino teenagers have the highest birthrate, with 82.6 births per 1,000, up from 82.3 per 1,000 in 2003.

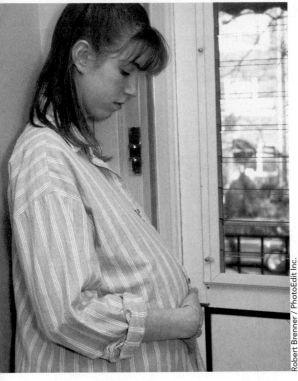

Robert Brenner / PhotoEdit Inc.

Teenage pregnancies continue to be a problem for a number of reasons. The financial costs of teenage childbearing are high, including costs to young mothers and their children. Teenage parents are less likely to complete their education and more likely to have limited career opportunities. How might early childhood programs help teenage parents meet their needs and the needs of their children?

Read about how children's nutrition and physical fitness trends have changed and the important role schools play in promoting physical health at Articles and Readings, Early Childhood Education, Module 2: Child Development, Article 1: Healthy and Ready to Learn.

TEACHER PREP

- Among states, New Mexico and Mississippi have the highest birthrates, with 61 and 62 births in 1,000, respectively, to mothers fifteen to nineteen years of age.[13]

Concerned legislators, public policy developers, and national leaders view teenage pregnancy as a loss of potential for young mothers and their children. From an early childhood point of view, teenage pregnancies create greater demand for infant and toddler child care and for programs to help teenagers learn how to be good parents.

Wellness and Healthy Living

As you know, when you feel good, life goes much better. The same is true for children and their families. One major goal of all early childhood programs is to provide for the safety and well-being of children. A second goal is to help parents and other family members provide for the well-being of themselves and their children. Poor health and unhealthy living conditions are major contributors to poor school achievement and life outcomes.[14] A number of health issues facing children today put their chances for learning and success at risk.

Illnesses. When you think of children's illnesses, you probably think of measles, rubella, and mumps. Actually, asthma, lead poisoning, and obesity are the three leading childhood diseases.

Asthma. **Asthma**, a chronic inflammatory disorder of the airways, is the most common chronic childhood illness in the United States. An estimated 6.2 million children under the age of eighteen suffer from asthma.[15] Asthma is caused in part by poor air quality, dust, mold, animal fur and dander, allergens from cockroaches and rodent feces, and strong fumes. Many of these causes are found in poor and low-quality housing. You will want to reduce asthma-causing conditions in your early childhood programs and work with parents to reduce the causes of asthma in their homes. Some things you can do to reduce the causes of asthma are: reduce or remove as many asthma and allergy triggers (such as smoke, mold, pet dander, cockroaches, and strong fumes or odors) as possible from homes and programs; use air filters and air conditioners—and properly maintain them; pay attention to the problem of dust mites, and keep in mind that vacuum cleaners with poor filtration and design characteristics release and stir up dust and allergens.[16]

Lead Poisoning. Lead poisoning is also a serious childhood disease. The Centers for Disease Control and Prevention (CDC) estimate that approximately 310,000 U.S. children between birth and age five have dangerous blood lead levels.[17] These children are at risk for low IQs, short attention spans, reading and learning disabilities, hyperactivity, and behavioral problems. The major source of lead poisoning is from old lead-based paint that still exists in many homes and apartments. Other sources of lead are from car batteries and dust and dirt from lead-polluted soil. Between 83–86 percent of homes built before 1978 have lead-based paint in them. Since then, lead has no longer been used in paint.[18] Lead enters the body through inhalation and ingestion. Young children are especially vulnerable since they put many things in their mouths, chew on windowsills, and crawl on floors. The Grace Hill Neighborhood Health Centers in St. Louis, Missouri, treat children for lead poisoning and send health coaches into homes of children with high levels of lead. These health workers cover peeling windowsills and provide vacuum cleaners with high-efficiency filters.

For more information about the Grace Hill Neighborhood Health Centers, visit http://www.gracehill.org.

Obesity. Today's generation of young children is often referred to as the "Supersize Generation." In fact, the Supersize Generation is getting younger! The 2006 statistical report of the American Heart Association reports that 10 percent of U.S. children, ages two to five, are now overweight![19]

Many contend that one of the reasons children are overweight is because of their tendency to supersize burgers, fries, and colas. The prevalence of **obesity** has quadrupled during the past 25 years among boys and girls.[20]

In addition, new waves of research report the relationship of obesity to other diseases and health problems, especially later in life. Excess weight in childhood and adolescence has been found to predict overweight in adults. Overweight children, ages ten to fourteen, with at least one overweight or obese parent, were reported to have a 79 percent likelihood of overweight persisting into adulthood.[21] Obesity can also cause heart problems. Another recent study revealed that children who are substantially overweight throughout much of their childhood and adolescence have a higher incidence of depression than those who aren't overweight. There were several significant findings related to this research involving one thousand children. First, a link was shown between obesity and psychiatric disorders. Second, researchers found that boys were at greater risk than girls for weight-related depression.[22]

The dramatic rise in obesity is due to a combination of factors, including less physical activity and more fat and calorie intake. More children spend more time in front of televisions and computer screens and fewer schools mandate physical education. Also, restaurant promotions to "supersize" meals encourage high-fat and high-calorie diets. Sarah Blumenschein at the University of Texas Southwestern Medical Center at Dallas says, "The number of overweight children has reached epidemic proportions, and fat children are likely to become fat adults."[23]

Visit sites dedicated to children's health at http://www.prenhall.com/morrison, Chapter 2—Web Links.

Be a Role Model

As the rate of obesity in American children continues to rise, it is especially important for you to keep yourself healthy and model healthy habits for the children you teach to ensure that they have a good role model as encouragement to develop healthy nutritional habits.

What can you do to help children and parents win the Obesity War?

- Provide parents with information about nutrition. What children eat—or don't eat—plays a major role in how they grow, develop, and learn. Diet also plays a powerful role in whether or not children engage in classroom activities with energy and enthusiasm. For example, send home copies of MyPyramid for kids (see Figure 2.3). Better yet, log onto http://www.mypyramid.gov, and individualize a food pyramid for each of your children. You can also send this information home to parents and share with them how to access and use the new MyPyramid.

- Counsel parents to pull the plug on the television. TV watching at mealtime is associated with obesity because children are more likely to eat fast foods such as pizza and salty snack foods. Also, children who watch a lot of television tend to be less physically active, and inactivity tends to promote weight gain.

- Cook with children and talk about foods and their nutritional values. Cooking activities are also a good way to eat and talk about new foods.

- Integrate literacy and nutritional activities. For example, reading and discussing labels is a good way to encourage children to be aware of and think about nutritional information. For example, calories provide energy; too much fat and sugar are not good for us, and protein is important, especially in the morning.[24]

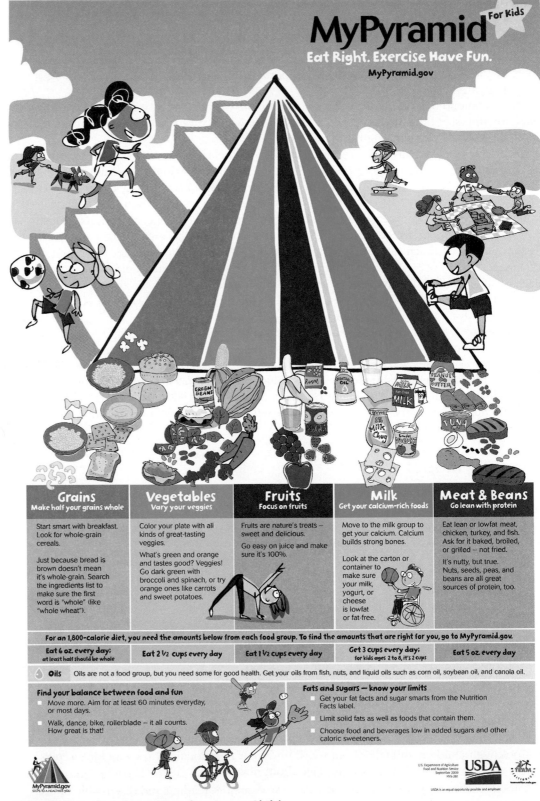

FIGURE 2.3 Good Nutrition for Young Children

Source: U.S. Department of Agriculture Food and Nutrition Service, retrieved February 27, 2007, from http://teamnutrition.usda.gov/Resources/mpk_poster2.pdf.

- Provide opportunities for physical exercise and physical activities everyday.
- If your school or program does not provide breakfast for children, be an advocate for starting it. School breakfasts can be both a nutritional and educational program.

For their part, schools are fighting the Obesity War by:

- Banning the sale of soda pop and candy bars in school vending machines during lunch hours;[25]
- Serving healthier foods in cafeterias—for example, in New York, school cafeterias are now serving whole-wheat pizza with low-fat cheese and Texas cafeterias are no longer serving deep-fat-fried foods;[26]
- Restoring recess and physical education to the elementary school curriculum; and
- Working with parents to help them get their children to be more active and to eat healthier foods at home.

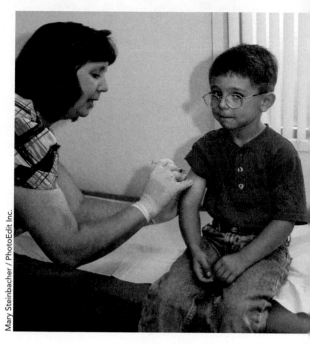

Mary Steinbacher / PhotoEdit Inc.

Socioeconomic Status and Children's Development

Throughout the course of their in-school and out-of-school lives, children's successes and achievement are greatly influenced by their family's socioeconomic status (SES).[27] This chapter's Diversity Tie-In feature discusses this topic further. SES consists of three broad but interrelated measures: parents' education level, parents' employment status, and family income. These three measures, acting individually as an integrated whole, influence:

- How children are reared,
- Family–child interactions,
- Home environments and the extent to which they do or do not support language development and learning,
- Kind and amount of discipline used, and
- Kind and extent of future plans involving children's education and employment.

Readiness is now viewed as promoting children's learning and development in all areas. Readiness includes general health such as being well rested, well fed, and properly immunized. UNICEF estimates that more than 30 million children around the world are unimmunized.

Poverty. **Poverty** has serious negative consequences for children and families. Over one-third of all children in the United States live in low-income families, meaning that their parents earn up to twice the federal poverty level, or $40,000 for a family of four. These families often face material hardships and financial pressures similar to those families who are officially counted as poor. More than 13.5 million children live in poor families, meaning their parents' income is $20,000 or less. These parents are typically unable to provide their families with basic necessities like stable housing and reliable child care.[28]

Poverty is a greater risk for children living in single-parent homes headed by females (approximately 35 percent) rather than males (approximately 17 percent).[29] Approximately 37 percent of African American children under the age of six live in poverty; this figure climbs to 53.8 percent in single-mother households. Poverty rates for Hispanic American children under the age of six are 29 percent overall and about 51.3 percent for those in single-mother homes.[30]

Living in poverty means children and their families don't have the income that allows them to purchase adequate health care, housing, food, clothing, and educational

You may have heard that children from low socioeconomic backgrounds do not achieve as well as they could or should in school. This is an overgeneralization, of course; many do succeed, although many do not. Although the following data shows a link between poverty and achievement in kindergarten children, it is not intended to convey a sense of determinism, nor lead to the conclusion that some children have no choice but to fail. Many examples exist that prove this is not the case. Such data should, instead, be used to encourage advocacy of policies that will help more poor children and their families find success in both school and life.

DATA RELATING TO SOCIOECONOMIC STATUS AND SCHOOL SUCCESS

- There are substantial differences by race and ethnicity in children's test scores as they begin kindergarten. Before even entering kindergarten, the average cognitive scores of children in the highest SES group are 60 percent above the scores of the lowest SES group. Moreover, average math achievement is 21 percent lower for blacks than for whites, and 19 percent lower for Hispanics.
- Race and ethnicity are associated with SES. For example, 34 percent of black children and 29 percent of Hispanic children are in the lowest quintile of SES compared with only 9 percent of white children. Cognitive skills are much less closely related to race/ethnicity after accounting for SES. Even after taking race differences into account, however, children from different SES groups achieve at different levels.
- Family structure and educational expectations have important associations with SES, race/ethnicity, and young children's test scores, though their impacts on cognitive skills are much smaller than either race or SES. Although 15 percent of white children live with only one parent, 54 percent of black and 27 percent of Hispanic children live in single-parent homes.
- Socioeconomic status is quite strongly related to cognitive skills. Of the many categories of factors considered—including race/ethnicity, family educational expectations, access to quality child care, home reading, computer use, and television habits—SES accounts for more of the unique variation in cognitive scores than any other factor by far.
- Low-SES children begin school at kindergarten in systematically lower quality elementary schools than their more advantaged counterparts.

One thing is certain, we do not need to accept the status quo. We can work to ensure that all children start school on an equal footing.

Professional development goal #12—Collaborating with parents and community—states, in part, "I am an advocate on behalf of children and families." Children and their socioeconomic status is a critical area in which you can develop and use your advocacy skills.

Some things you can advocate for and support in order to help all children and families include the following:

- Development of and access to high-quality preschool and kindergarten programs for all children, to ensure all children have equal opportunities to achieve. At the same time you would advocate that all children would enter preschool programs and kindergarten.
- Family literacy programs and other programs that will enable families to help their children learn before they come to school. Insofar as possible, we want to eliminate achievement gaps before children come to school.
- Public awareness of the importance of early learning and how early learning or the lack of it shapes children's futures. Part of your advocacy can include sharing the data about SES and school achievement. Also, you can share data that demonstrates the effectiveness of high-quality preschool programs. For example, the latest study by the High/Scope Education Research Foundation shows that adults who participated in a high-quality preschool program have higher earnings, are more likely to hold a job, and have committed fewer crimes. In addition, the study demonstrated a return to society of more than $17 for every tax dollar invested in the early care and education program. You can access this study at http://www.highscope.org/Research/Perry Project/Perry Age 40_sumweb.pdf.
- Equitable funding for all preschool and elementary programs and schools. All children deserve and need high-quality learning environments and teachers.
- Awareness of the importance that all children achieve the state standards specified for their grade level. All children must achieve the state standards, not just some. This means children from low-SES backgrounds will need more help and support from you, the schools, and the community.

Source: V. E. Lee and D. T. Burkham, Inequality at the Starting Gate: Social Background Differences in Achievement as Children Begin School, *Economic Policy Institute http://www.epinet.org/ content. cfm?id=617; and High Scope Education Research Foundation, "Long-Term Study of Adults Who Received High-Quality Early Childhood Care and Education Shows Economic and Social Gains, Less Crime," http://highscope.org/ Research/Perry Project/Perry Age 40_sumweb.pdf.*

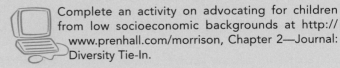

Complete an activity on advocating for children from low socioeconomic backgrounds at http://www.prenhall.com/morrison, Chapter 2—Journal: Diversity Tie-In.

services. The federal government annually revises its poverty guidelines, which are the basis for distribution of federal aid to schools and student eligibility for academic services such as Head Start, **Title I** (a federal program that provides low-achieving students additional help in math and reading), and free and reduced-price school breakfasts and lunches. The following are some examples of the effects of poverty:

- Living in a rural community and in a rural southern state increases the likelihood that families will live in poverty. Cities with the highest school-age poverty rate are in the South and East. In Arkansas, nearly one-third of all children are poor, well above the national average of 17.6 percent.[31]

- Living in urban cities increases the chances of being poor. With increases in rural and urban poverty come decreases in wealth and support for education. This in turn means that, as a whole, children living in poverty will attend schools that have few resources and poorly prepared teachers.

- Poverty is detrimental to students' achievement and life prospects. For example, children and youth from low-income families are often older than others in their grade level, move more slowly through the educational system, are more likely to drop out, and are less likely to find work. Poor children are more likely to be retained in school, and students who have repeated one or more grades are more likely to become school dropouts. Poverty affects students' health prospects as well. For example, more than one-half of all children who lack insured health care come from poor families.[32]

- Children in poverty are more likely to have emotional and behavioral problems and are less likely than others to be "highly engaged" in school.[33]

- Children living in poverty suffer twice as much tooth decay as their more affluent peers, and their disease is more likely to be untreated.[34]

So, improving the conditions that surround children of poverty is a major way teachers, politicians, and the public can collaborate to help children do better in all areas of life, including schooling.

Brain Research

Through brain research, the field of neuroscience continues to inform our practice of early childhood education. Brain research affirms what good early childhood educators have always known: Good parental care, warm and loving attachments, and positive age-appropriate stimulation from birth onward make a tremendous difference in children's cognitive development for a lifetime.[35]

New early childhood curricula apply brain research findings in a practical way. Finding practical ways to apply research is an important part of becoming a professional.

For example, **Zero to Three**, a national, nonprofit organization, focuses on the healthy development of infants, toddlers, and families by supporting and strengthening families, communities, and all who work on behalf of young children. Advocates of Zero to Three believe that a child's first three years are crucial for developing intellectual, emotional, and social skills. If these skills are not developed, the child's lifelong potential may be hampered. The organization supports professionals, parents, and policy makers and strives to increase public awareness, inspire leaders, and foster professional excellence through training, always emphasizing the first three years of a child's life.

Early childhood professionals hold the following beliefs about young children, based on brain research:

- *The most rapid period of intellectual growth occurs before age five.* The notion of promoting cognitive development implies that children benefit from enriched home

COMPETENCY BUILDER

My attempts to learn Spanish have given me a lot of empathy for English language learners. Perhaps you have had the same experience of frustration with comprehension, pronunciation, and understandable communication. English language learners face these same problems and others. Many come from low socioeconomic backgrounds. Others come to this country lacking many of the early literacy and learning opportunities we take for granted.

INCREASING NUMBERS

Many school districts across the country have seen their numbers of English language learners skyrocket. For example, in the Winston-Salem/Forsyth County School District in North Carolina, more than 8 percent of the 49,797 student population are English language learners, representing seventy-seven different native languages.

The chances are great that you will have English language learners in your classroom wherever you choose to teach. There are a number of approaches you can use to ensure that your children will learn English and that they will be academically successful.

TIPS FOR SUCCESS

Judith Lessow-Hurley, a bilingual expert, says, "It's important to create contexts in which kids exchange meaningful messages. Kids like to talk to other kids, and that's useful."* Lessow-Hurley also supports sheltered immersion. She says, "A lot of what we call 'sheltering' is simply good instruction—all kids benefit from experiential learning, demonstrations, visuals, and routines. A lot of sheltering is also common sense—stay away from idioms, speak slowly and clearly, [and] find ways to repeat yourself."†

Here are some other general tips Lessow-Hurley offers for assisting English language learners, along with some explicit classroom strategies:

STRATEGY 1

DEVELOP CONTENT AROUND A THEME

The repetition of vocabulary and concepts reinforces language and ideas and gives English language learners better access to content.

STRATEGY 2

USE VISUAL AIDS AND HANDS-ON ACTIVITIES TO DELIVER CONTENT

Information is better retained when a variety of senses are used.

- Rely on visual cues as frequently as possible.
- Have students create flash cards for key vocabulary words. Be sure to build in time for students to use them.
- Encourage students to use computer programs and books with cassette tapes.

STRATEGY 3

USE ROUTINES TO REINFORCE LANGUAGE

This practice increases the comfort level of second-language learners; they then know what to expect and associate the routine with the language.

- One helpful routine is daily reading.
- Use pictures, gestures, and a dramatic voice to help convey meaning.

Picture yourself in this classroom. Which of the activites suggested here would you select to help your student learn English?

environments that are conducive to learning and from early school-like experiences, especially for children in environments that place them at risk for learning problems.

- *Children are not born with fixed intelligences.* This outdated concept does not do justice to children's tremendous capacity for learning and change. The extent to which individual intelligence develops depends on many variables, such as experiences, child-rearing practices, economic factors, nutrition, and the quality of prenatal and postnatal environments. Inherited genetic characteristics set a broad framework within which intelligence develops. Heredity sets the limits, while environment determines the extent to which individuals achieve these limits.

- *Children reared in homes that are not intellectually stimulating might lag intellectually behind their counterparts reared in more advantaged environments.*[36] Implications concerning the home environment are obvious. Experience shows that children who lack an environment that promotes learning opportunities may be at risk throughout life. However, homes that offer intellectual stimulation and a print-rich environment tend to produce children who do well in school.

STRATEGY 4: ENGAGE ENGLISH LANGUAGE LEARNERS WITH ENGLISH SPEAKERS

Cooperative learning groups of mixed language abilities give students a meaningful content for using English.

Classroom activities such as those suggested here can help English language learners gain important skills.

- Pair English language learners with native speakers to explain and illustrate a specific word or phrase frequently heard in the classroom.
- Ask the students to make a picture dictionary of the words and phrases they are learning, using pictures they have cut out of magazines.
- Have small groups make vocabulary posters of categories of common words, again using pictures cut from magazines.

STRATEGY 5: ALLOW STUDENTS TO USE NONVERBAL RESPONSES

Permit students to demonstrate their knowledge and comprehension in alternative ways. For example, one teacher has early primary students hold up cardboard "lollipops" (green or red side forward) to indicate a yes or no answer to a question.

STRATEGY 6: DON'T CORRECT ALL NONSTANDARD RESPONSES.

It's better to get students talking, they acquire accepted forms through regular use and practice. A teacher can always paraphrase a student's answer to model Standard English.[†]

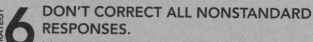

Photos by Hope Madden/Merrill.

["Acquiring English Schools Seek Ways to Strengthen Language Learning," Curriculum Update, Association for Supervision and Curriculum Development (Fall 2002). 6]

[† *Ibid.*]

[‡ *Ibid, 7.*]

Develop an activity for English Language Learners that integrates these strategies at http://www.prenhall.com/morrison, Chapter 2—Projects: Professionalism in Practice.

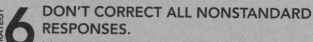

COMPETENCY BUILDER

For example, as Figure 2.4 illustrates, children reared in enriched language homes have a background of language experiences that far exceed the language experiences of their less advantaged peers. High-quality early language experiences count so much that it is very difficult for children who do not receive them to make up the deficit. The figure shows the estimated cumulative number of words of children's total language experience, assuming fourteen waking hours per day, or approximately one hundred hours per week of experience time. As you reflect on the implications of this data, consider what the researchers had to say. "When we examined the children's practice, we discovered that a child's talkativeness grew rapidly until it matched that of the child's parents and then stopped increasing. In each family the child's talkativeness came to be similar to the family."[37]

As a teacher of young children, you will more than likely teach children from different cultures and whose first language is not English. It is your responsibility to teach these children and to help them learn.[38] The accompanying Professionalism in

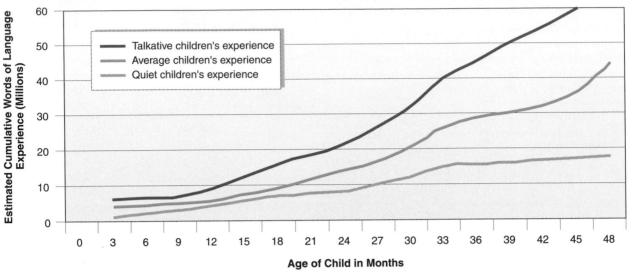

FIGURE 2.4 Children's Language Experiences and Language Development

Source: B. Hart and T. R. Risley, *The Social World of Children Learning to Talk* (Baltimore: Paul H. Bookes Publishing Co., 1999), p. 293. Reprinted by permission.

Practice box provides you with six strategies for becoming a successful teacher of linguistically and culturally diverse children.

- *Good parental care, warm and loving attachments, and positive, age-appropriate stimulation from birth onward make a difference in children's overall development for a lifetime.*[39] Even during the fetal stage, the kind of nourishment and care children receive affects neural development (i.e., the development of brain nerve cells). The majority of recent research shows that much of children's learning capacity is developed during the earliest years.

- *Positive interactions with caring adults stimulate children's brains in terms of establishing new synaptic connections and strengthening existing ones.*[40] For example, cuddling and singing to infants and toddlers stimulate brain connections and lay the foundation for learning throughout life. Those connections used over time become permanent, and those that are not used wither and become dormant. Increasingly, researchers are showing how early stimulation sets the stage for future cognitive processes.

In addition, positive emotional interactions and formations of secure attachments lay the foundation for healthy emotional development. As you know from your experiences, learning is emotional as well as cognitive. Your emotional state sets the tone for learning in your classroom and influences the emotional state of your children.

- *Early experiences during critical/sensitive periods and "windows of opportunity" are so powerful that they can completely change the way children develop.* The right input at the right time is crucial for children to fully develop cognitive potential. For example, the circuit for vision has a neuron growth spurt at two to four months of age, thus helping children begin to notice the shape of objects.[41] This neuron growth

As a result of new research, we are learning more about children than ever before. This new research accounts for the tremendous popularity of early childhood programs and curriculum. Practices in early childhood programs are now more "research based."

spurt peaks at eight months, suggesting the importance of providing appropriate visual stimuli early in life.

These six fundamental beliefs about children's brain development clearly demonstrate that the early years are important for brain development and the foundation for learning and life.

Violence

Violence seems to pervade American society. From television to video games to domestic violence, children are exposed to high doses of undesirable behavior.

Increasing acts of violence have led to proposals for how to provide violence-free homes and educational environments; how to teach children to get along nonviolently with others such as by using puppets who discuss feelings with younger children; or by role playing and discussing appropriate ways to behave on the playground with older children: and how to reduce violence on television, the movies, and in video games.[42] Reducing violence on television, for example, in turn leads to discussions and proposals for ways to limit children's television viewing. Such proposals include "pulling the plug" on television; using the V-chip, which enables parents to block out programs with violent content; boycotting companies whose advertisements support programs with violent content; and limiting violence shown during prime-time viewing hours for children. Figure 2.5 provides ideas for how to manage children's television viewing. Here are some other activities you can use to prevent/reduce violence in children's lives:

- Show children photographs and have children identify various emotions; discuss appropriate responses to these emotions.
- Have children role play how to respond appropriately to various emotions.
- Read children books about handling emotions and discuss how the story characters handled their emotions. Some good books to read are:
  - *Handling Your Ups and Downs: A Children's Book About Emotions* by Joy Wilt Berry and Ernie Hergenroeder,
  - *A to Z—Do You Ever Feel Like Me?* by Bonnie Hausman and Sandi Fellman, and
  - *The Oceans of Emotions* by Nicole K. Clark and John T. Clark.

Bullying

Programs to prevent and curb **bullying** are another example of how educators are combating the effects of violence on children. Although in the past bullying has been dismissed as "normal" or "kids' play," this is no longer the case, because bullying is related to personal and school violence. Bullying includes teasing, slapping, hitting, pushing, unwanted touching, taking personal belongings, name-calling, and making sexual comments and insults about looks, behavior, and culture. Many schools are starting to fight back against bullies and bullying through bully prevention programs.

Here are some things you can do to help prevent bullying in your classroom:

- Read books about bullying. You can read books about bullying during story time and group reading lessons, guided reading, and shared reading to and with your children. Some books you might want to read are:
  - *Arthur's April Fool* by Marc Brown. Arthur worries about remembering his magic tricks for the April Fool's Day assembly, and the bully Binky threatens to pulverize him.

TEACHER PREP

Read about how bullying and victimization are increasing at Articles and Readings, Special Education, Module 10: Emotional and Behavioral Disorders, Article 1: A Profile of Bullying at School.

FIGURE 2.5

Guiding Children's Television Viewing

Guiding children's television viewing is easier said than done. Television is a pervasive medium throughout American society. Here are some interesting facts about young children and television, and guidelines for monitoring its usage.

- A report, *Zero to Six: Electronic Media in the Lives of Infants, Toddlers, and Preschoolers,* revealed:
  - 36 percent of children have a TV in their bedroom.
  - Children with TVs in the bedroom watch an average of twenty-two more minutes of TV than children without them.
  - 43 percent of parents think that TV helps children learn.
  - 77 percent of children can operate a TV by themselves.
  - Children with parents who do not make rules about TV viewing watch an average of twenty-nine more minutes of TV per day than children whose parents have such rules.

So, how should we as early childhood professionals advise parents regarding their children's television viewing? Here are some tips:

- Set rules and guidelines early. Just like most habits, habits related to television viewing begin early. Therefore, it's better to develop good habits regarding television viewing early in life rather than have to try and break old habits later in childhood.
- Establish guidelines for children's television viewing. Some basic rules and limits include:
  - Limit the amount of time children spend watching television. A general public consensus is that most children spend more time than they should in front of the TV. The American Academy of Pediatrics recommends that children's television viewing be limited to no more than one or two hours a day.
  - Avoid watching television during meals. Television viewing during meals sets bad habits relating to family conversations and interactions. Children who eat while they watch television tend to eat more and therefore gain more weight.
  - Limit or eliminate children's snacks during television viewing. Children (and adults too) tend to consume sweet and salty snacks while watching television. After all, many television commercials, especially those aimed at kids, are for sweet and salty snacks. Therefore, the amount and kind of snacks children eat while watching television should be monitored and controlled.
- Monitor children's television viewing. Children should not be permitted to watch adult television, violent programs, or violent cartoons. This means that parents and other adults who are responsible for children have to screen and monitor what their children watch. When children are allowed to watch violent television, they not only learn violent and aggressive behavior, but they also become desensitized to violence.
- Keep televisions out of children's bedrooms. Generally speaking, children should not be permitted to have a television in their room; however, as our statistics show, 36 percent of children do have one in their room! When children have a television in their bedroom, their television viewing is not monitored and they can and do watch whatever they want.
- Don't use television as a babysitter. Television is not able to care for, protect, or nurture children. In other words, television cannot take the place of a parent. Likewise, television should not be used as a means of "keeping children busy."
- Participate with children. Parents should watch television with their children. This way parents can discuss program content with their children and can clarify actions and behaviors.
- Be a good role model. Parents can be good role models when they set good examples by the programs they watch. Parents should not view television with adult, sexual, or violent content when children are present.
- Help children learn from television. The majority of parents believe that children learn from television. So, encourage parents to watch educational shows with their children.

Source: V. J. Rideout, A. E. Vandewater, and E. A. Wartella, "Zero to Six: Electronic Media in the Lives of Infants, Toddlers and Preschoolers," The Henry J. Kaiser Family Foundation, http://www.kff.org/entmedia/upload/zero-to-six-electronic-media-in-the-lives-of-infants-toddlers-and-preschoolers-PDF.pdf.

- *Blubber* by Judy Blume. When overweight Linda gives an oral report on whales, the cruel and power-wielding class leader, Wendy, starts calling her "Blubber," and the name-calling escalates into more intense bullying and humiliation.
- *Dealing with Bullying* by Marianne Johnston. This text describes what is meant by bullying, and explains why bullies act as they do, how to deal with them, and how to stop being one.
- *Nobody Knew What to Do* by Becky R. McCain. When bullies pick on Ray, a boy at school, a classmate is afraid, but decides that he must do something.
- *Stop Picking on Me* by Pat Thomas. This picture book helps kids accept the normal fears and worries that accompany bullying, and suggests ways to resolve this upsetting experience.
- *The Berenstain Bears and the Bully* by Stan Berenstain. When she takes a beating from the class bully, Sister Bear learns a valuable lesson in self-defense—and forgiveness.

Additionally a good book for you to read to help you learn more about how to deal with bullying is *The Anti-Bullying and Teasing Book* by Barbara Sprung, Merle Froschl, and Blythe Hinitz. This text uses activities, the classroom environment, and family involvement to develop empathy in children and create a climate of mutual respect in the classroom.

- Talk to children individually and in groups when you see them engage in hurtful behavior. For instance, "Chad, how do you think Brad felt when you pushed him out of the way?"
- Intervene immediately when you see children starting to, or attempting to, bully others.
- Be constantly alert to any signs of bullying behavior in your classroom.
- Teach cooperative and helpful behavior, courtesy, and respect. Much of what children do, they model from others' behaviors. When you provide examples of courteous and respectful behavior in your classroom it sets a good example for children.
- Have children work together on a project. Then, have them talk about how they got along with and worked together.
- Make children and others in your classroom feel welcome and important.
- Talk to parents and help them understand your desire to stop bullying and have a bully-free classroom.
- Conduct a workshop for parents on anti-bullying behavior.
- Send books home on anti-bullying themes that your parents can read with their children.

POLITICS AND EARLY CHILDHOOD EDUCATION

The more early childhood is in the news, the more it generates public interest and attention; this is part of the political context of early childhood education. Whatever else can be said about education, it is this—it is political. Politicians and politics exert a powerful influence in determining what is taught, how it is taught, to whom it is taught, and by whom it is taught. Early childhood education is no exception.

FEDERAL AND STATE INVOLVEMENT IN EARLY CHILDHOOD PROGRAMS

Federal and state funding of early childhood programs has greatly increased during the past decade.[43] This trend will continue for these reasons. First, politicians and the public recognize that the early years are the foundation for future learning. Second, spending money on children in the early years is more cost effective than trying to solve problems in the teenage years.

As a result, all states are taking a lead in developing programs for young children, stimulated by these budgetary changes. As federal dollars shift to other programs, states are responding by initiating programs of their own, funded from both federal allocations and other sources, including lottery monies and increased taxes on commodities and consumer goods such as cigarettes.

The Florida Department of Education, for example, has an office dedicated to early intervention and school readiness. One of its programs is Florida First Start, a home–school partnership designed to give children at risk of future school failure the best possible start in life and to support parents in their role as their children's first teachers. Emphasis is on enabling families to enhance their children's intellectual, physical, language, and social development by involving parents in their children's education during the critical first three years of life. Through early parent education and support services, the program lays the foundation for later learning and future school successes, while fostering effective parent–school relationships. Further information is available on the Internet at http://title1.brevard.k12.fl.us/florida_1st_start.htm.

Expanded Federal Support for Early Childhood Education

At the same time states are exerting control over education, so is the federal government. One of the dramatic changes occurring in society is the expanded role of the federal government in the reform of public education. More federal dollars are allocated for specific early education initiatives than ever before.

The **No Child Left Behind Act** (Public Law 107–110) and other federal initiatives have focused national attention on developing educational and social programs to serve young children and families. Two areas in particular, reading and school readiness, are now major federal priorities in helping to ensure that all children succeed in school and life. The Early Reading First programs established by No Child Left Behind provide grants to school districts and preschool programs for the development of model programs to support school readiness of preschool programs and to promote children's understanding of letters, letter sounds, and the blending of sounds and words. For example, in 2006 the program granted the South San Antonio Independent School District $4.5 million to fund their project "Ready to Read, Preparing to Lead" (R2R-P2L).[44]

Public Schools and Early Education

Traditionally, the majority of preschool programs were operated by private agencies or agencies supported wholly or in part by federal funds to help the poor, the unemployed, working parents, and disadvantaged children. But times have changed how

Review additional information about the No Child Left Behind Act at http://www.prenhall.com/morrison, Chapter 2—Web Links.

preschool programs are conducted in the public schools. During the 2000–2001 school year, approximately 822,000 children were enrolled in 58,500 public elementary school pre-kindergarten classes nationwide. About 19,900 public elementary schools, roughly one-third of the public elementary schools in the country, offered these classes, and approximately 45,900 pre-kindergarten teachers taught them.[45] As preschool programs admit more three- and four-year-olds nationwide, employment opportunities for teachers of young children will grow.

Growth and Preschools

The public wants early childhood preschool programs for a number of reasons:

- Working parents believe the public schools hold the solution to child care needs so they advocate (rather strongly) for the public schools to provide preschool programs.

- Some parents cannot afford quality child care; they believe preschools, furnished at the public's expense, are a reasonable, cost-efficient way to meet their child care needs.

- The persistent belief that children are a nation's greatest wealth makes it seem sensible to provide services to avoid future school and learning problems.

- Many believe that early public schooling, especially for children from low-income families, is necessary if the United States is to promote equal opportunity for all. They argue that low-income children begin school already far behind their more fortunate middle-class counterparts and that the best way to keep them from falling hopelessly behind is for them to begin school earlier.

- Research supports the importance of preschool early literacy learning as a basis for successful reading.[46]

The alignment of the public schools with early childhood programs is becoming increasingly popular. Some think it makes sense to put the responsibility for educating and caring for the nation's children under the sponsorship of one agency—the public schools. For their part, public school teachers and the unions that represent them are anxious to bring early childhood programs within the structure of the public school system.

Despite the support of many parents for early childhood programs, the movement toward universal preschool remains controversial for these reasons:[47]

- For some parents, **universal preschool** means mandatory. These parents believe they should have the option to send their three- to five-year-olds to school. Generally the public supports universal and accessible, but not mandatory, preschool.[48]

- Money to support universal preschool is an issue. Universal preschools would involve a considerable expenditure of local, state, and federal funds. For example, voters in California recently voted down a universal preschool proposal.[49] Nonetheless, preschool is well on its way to becoming universal.

In summary, early childhood education and young children have captured the attention of the nation. This increased attention in turn creates many issues and controversies. Consequently, early childhood professionals must learn more about how to care for, educate, and rear children so they can advise parents, legislators, and others in determining what is best for the nation's children.

technology tie-in

Is the Use of Technology in Early Childhood Programs "Bad" for Young Children?

I want to be up-front with you. I am a strong advocate of using technology in the home and classroom—in appropriate ways. My answer to the title of this article is an unequivocal "No!" I support the use of technology with young children for a number of reasons.

First, today's children are the generation.com. They have a great deal of involvement with technology and have spent many years playing with and learning from technology. Children as young as nine months are using the computer, while nestled securely in their parents' laps. Programs such as Reader Rabbit and Jump-Start Baby are designed for the lapware set. These software programs and others like them constitute the fastest growing software on the market today. They are easy and fun to use, and children learn from them.

A second reason I support the use of technology with children is that the use of technology in early childhood programs can begin to level the educational playing field and close the digital divide that exists between the haves and have-nots of technology. Children from minority and low-income families have less access to computers and the Internet than do their more advantaged classmates.* Having access to and use of computers and other technology at school can help all children get the knowledge and skills they need to be successful in school and life.

I recommend that all early childhood classrooms have a technology center that includes a computer, access to the Internet, a printer, a digital camera, and appropriate learning software.

Here are some guidelines you can use to integrate various kinds of technology into your classroom and programs:

- Remember that technology does not replace the teacher. Computers and other technology are learning tools designed to help children learn and to extend and enrich their learning.
- Apply developmentally appropriate practices to your use of technology with young children. This means you should take into consideration the age, developmental levels, and the individual needs of your children when selecting technology and software for them.
- Collaborate with parents to help them work with their children so that they are not spending all of their time watching television or playing/working with computers.
- Advise parents about the American Academy of Pediatrics recommendation that children under two not be allowed to watch television or work on computers.[†]
- Monitor children's use of iPods and other forms of technology that use earphones. Research suggests that it's not how long children listen, but the volume at which they listen to the music.[‡]

*"Computers and Young Children,""Social Forces," 82, September 2003, 1.

† Nagourney, E., "Hazards: A Study Gauges the Risks for Ears with iPods," The New York Times, October 24, 2006.

‡ American Academy of Pediatrics, "Media Guidelines for Parents," retrieved February 27, 2007, from http://www.aap.org/healthtopics/mediause.cfm.

Read and respond to articles on the use of technology in Early Childhood Education programs at http://www.prenhall.com/morrison, Chapter 2—Journal: Technology Tie-In.

NEW DIRECTIONS IN EARLY CHILDHOOD EDUCATION

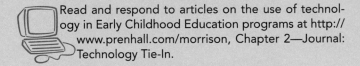

View teachers describing how different types of technology in their classrooms are improving their students' learning and their teaching experiences at Video Classroom, Educational Technology, Module 3: Computers, Video 1: Tablet Computers Facilitate Learning.

Changing needs of society and families and new research provide new directions in early childhood education. As a result, the field of early childhood education is constantly changing. These are some important changes occurring in early childhood education today that will influence how you and others practice the profession of early childhood education:

- *Full-day, full-year services.* Parents want full-day, full-year services for their children for a number of reasons.
- Such a schedule fits in with their work schedules and lifestyles. Working parents, in particular, find it difficult to patch together child care and other arrangements when their children are not in school.
- Parents believe that full-day, full-year services support and enhance their children's learning. Parents want their children to do well academically. As a result, we will see more full-day, full-year early childhood programs of all kinds.

- *Readiness for learning school readiness.* There is and will be an increase in programs designed to provide families, grandparents, and others with child development information, parenting skills, and learning activities that will help them get their children ready for school. Working with parents to help them get their children ready for learning and school is an important and growing part of early childhood services.

  For example, the *Child Care Executive Partnership Program* (CCEP) in Florida is designed to help employers meet the child care needs of their workforce. The Child Care Executive Partnership Act was established by the 1996 legislature, to expand child care subsidies for low-income working families by utilizing state and federal funds as incentives for matching local funds from local governments, employers, charitable foundations, and other sources.[50]

- *Wrap-around services.* Collaborative efforts in the form of wrap-around services (also referred to as an ecological approach) with professionals from other agencies and disciplines better use resources and avoid duplication of efforts. For example, many school districts work with social workers to help children and families meet their needs regarding nutrition, clothing, counseling services, and other means of support. Collaboration is all about working together to help make life better for children and families.

- *Support for whole child education.* Early childhood profesionals have always acknowledged that they must educate the whole child—physical, social, emotional, and cognitive aspects. However, another aspect, the spiritual aspect, has not received enough attention. A recent trend is a greater emphasis on supporting children's spiritual development through moral and character education.

- *Early literacy learning.* Brain research has created interest in the importance of early literacy development. There is a growing awareness of the critical role literacy plays in school and life success. Consequently, there are now more programs designed specifically to help young children get ready for learning to read. This emphasis on early literacy and learning to read will be evident in chapters throughout this book.

- *Increased use of technology.* More early childhood programs are seeking ways to enhance their effectiveness by helping children gain the cognitive and literacy skills they need to be successful in school and life. Many are turning to technology as a means of achieving these goals. The accompanying Technology Tie-In feature discusses technology's use in early childhood education programs.

- *Increased emphasis on subject matter.*

- *The politicalization of early childhood education.* There has been a dramatic increase in state and federal involvement in the education of young children. For example, the federal government is using Head Start as a means and model for reforming all of early childhood education. This federalization will likely continue and expand.

- *The increasing use of tests to measure achievement and school performance in the early years.* Increasing numbers of parents, professionals, and early childhood critics are advocating for less emphasis on *high-stakes testing* in the early years.

Changes in society constantly cause changes in the field of early childhood education. One of your major challenges as an early childhood professional is to keep current in terms of new changes and directions in your field. In this way you will be able to judge what is best for young children and implement the best practices that will enable young children to succeed in school and life.

This is a great time for early childhood education and a wonderful time to be a teacher of young children. Early childhood education has changed more in the last five years than in the previous fifty. These changes and the issues that accompany them provide many opportunities for you to become more professional, and they enable all children to learn the knowledge and skills necessary for success in school and life.

ACTIVITIES FOR PROFESSIONAL DEVELOPMENT

Ethical Dilemma

"My Child's Not Fat!"

The faculty and administration at Belvedere Elementary set up a pilot program to develop a curriculum for helping overweight children learn good nutrition skills and lose weight. Amanda Jones was asked to select three children from her kindergarten class to participate. She selected three children based on a comparison of the height and weight of her students with a height and weight chart of the National Academy of Pediatrics. One of the children's parents contacted Amanda and is angry that she selected her child. The parent believes that her child is not obese and should not be in a program for "fat kids." She believes Amanda is discriminating against her child and is threatening to contact the school board and the media.

What should Amanda do? Should she give in to the parent and remove her child from the program and risk that the child, who Amanda believes is very overweight, will suffer health-wise and from bullying and taunting? Or, should she risk alienating the parent and insist that her child would benefit from the program?

Application Activities

1. Reading daily newspapers is one way to keep up to date in a changing society and in a changing educational environment. For two weeks, scan online the following newspapers:

   New York Times
   Washington Post
   Los Angeles Times
   Chicago Tribune

   As you review, print one to two articles and discuss them in a small group.

2. Consult early childhood professionals and ask them what problems they face with the children in their programs as a result of divorce, abuse, and other types of stress in children's lives. Make a list of how they help children and families deal with these problems.

3. Interview early childhood professionals and ask them these questions:
   a. How have they kept up with changes in early childhood? What reading do they recommend?
   b. To what changes have they had the hardest time adjusting?
   c. What changes do they like the most? The least?
   d. What advice do they have for future educators about how to keep up with change?

4. Contact agencies that provide services to single parents, teenage parents, and families in need. How do these services influence early childhood education programs in your local community?

5. Over several weeks or a month, collect articles from journals, newspapers, and magazines relating to infants, toddlers, and preschoolers and categorize them by topic (child abuse, nutrition, child development, etc.). What topics were given the most coverage? Why? What topics or trends are emerging in early education, according to this media coverage?

6. Over the next three or four months, keep a journal about changes you notice in the field of early childhood. Include these topics:

a. What changes intrigue you the most?

b. Not all changes are for the better. Make a list of changes that you think have a negative effect on children (e.g., rising poverty).

c. Document the things you are doing personally and professionally to respond to changes in society and education.

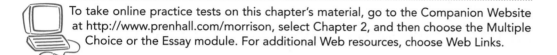

To take online practice tests on this chapter's material, go to the Companion Website at http://www.prenhall.com/morrison, select Chapter 2, and then choose the Multiple Choice or the Essay module. For additional Web resources, choose Web Links.

3

HISTORY AND THEORIES
Foundations for Teaching and Learning

· ·

professional development goal

History and Theories

A. I am familiar with my profession's history, and I use my knowledge of the past to inform my practice.

B. I understand the principles of each major theory of educating young children. The approach I use is consistent with my beliefs about how children learn.

C. I know, understand, and use effective approaches, strategies, and tools for early education.[1]

D. I know and understand the importance, central concepts, inquiry tools, and structures of content areas or academic disciplines.[2]

focus questions

1. Why is it important to know about the ideas, contributions, and learning theories of great educators?

2. What are the basic beliefs of the individuals who have had the greatest influence on early childhood education?

 3. How do the beliefs and practices of great educators influence early childhood education?

4. How do theories of learning influence the teaching and practice of early childhood education?

WHY IS THE HISTORY OF EARLY CHILDHOOD EDUCATION IMPORTANT?

There is a history of just about everything: a history of teaching, a history of schools, and a history of early childhood education. While we don't need to know the history of dolls in order to buy a doll, if you are a doll collector, knowing the history of dolls is essential. The same applies to you as an early childhood educator. You will be a much more informed and effective teacher if you know the roots of your profession. Knowing the history of your profession is essential to being a professional.

When we know the beliefs, ideas, and accomplishments of people who have devoted their lives to young children, we realize that many of today's early childhood programs are built on enduring beliefs about how children learn, grow, and develop. There are at least three reasons why it is important to know about ideas and theories that have and are influencing the field of early childhood education.

Rebirth of Great Ideas

Great ideas and practices persist over time and tend to be reintroduced in educational thought and practices in ten- to twenty-year cycles. For example, many practices popular in the past—such as the teaching of reading through phonics, multi-age grades or groups, and teacher-initiated instruction—are now popular once again in the first decade of the twenty-first century. I hope you will always be as amazed as I am about the way early childhood professionals recycle enduring ideas and practices and use them in their teaching.

Build the Dream—Again

Many ideas of famous educators are still dreams because of our inability to translate dreams into reality. Horace Mann, a nineteenth-century education reformer referred to as "the father of American public education," said this about the importance and necessity of educating all children:

> It is a free school system. It knows no distinction of rich and poor . . . it throws open its doors and spreads the table of its bounty for all the children of the state. . . . Education then, beyond all other devices of human origin, is the equalizer of the conditions of men, the great balance wheel of the social machinery.[3]

This goal of educating all children remains elusive, but nonetheless the goal remains. As Secretary of Education Margaret Spellings says, "It's our job to make sure every child has the knowledge and skills to succeed."[4]

The dream of educating all children to their full potential is a worthy one, and we can and should use it as a base to build meaningful teaching careers and lives for children

Perhaps you remember the grade school you went to. Think about how it is similar to and different from the schools of today. The following description of a schoolhouse from the 1800s lets you compare and contrast schools of yesterday with the schools you attended and the one you plan to teach in.

Rural schools were the traditional one-room schoolhouse; one teacher usually taught all grades, although schools in larger areas sometimes had more rooms and several teachers.

Restrooms were out back—one for boys and one for girls. The classroom had about five rows of double wooden desks with attached seats that were screwed into the floor. The teacher sat on a raised platform with a desk at one end of the room. There was a blackboard, and each school had one world globe, a map of the United States, and an unabridged dictionary.

The school was heated by an iron wood-burning stove that—like all other wood-burning stoves—nearly cooked the students sitting nearby while leaving those farther away out in the cold. For dark, cloudy days, there was an oil lamp hanging from the ceiling. A pail of water and a communal dipper to drink from was also available.

A standard school day began early. The teacher arrived first—probably by 7 a.m. to prepare for the day, which included starting a fire in the iron stove if it was cold weather. Students arrived at about 8 a.m. As they entered the classroom, each boy had to bow from the waist and each girl had to curtsey to the teacher.

The first lesson was reading, so everyone took out his or her McGuffey *Eclectic Readers.* Students read aloud and sometimes dramatized the McGuffey "pieces."

Arithmetic came next, including the popular exercise called "mental arithmetic." This was problem solving without using pen or paper. Problems from *The Common School Arithmetic* usually were practical, asking, for example: If a farmer erects 72 feet of fencing each day, how much fencing will he complete in a fortnight?

Recess was next. Children went outside to use the toilets and to play. Hide and go seek, marbles, kick the can, and pitching horseshoes were among the games played.

After recess, the students settled down for a writing lesson. They may have had pens and pencils or they may have still used slates, rectangular pieces of real slate in a wooden frame. Pupils wrote on slates with the point of a thin rod of compressed slate powder. Slates were really handy because anything could be wiped off the slate with a cloth or a shirt sleeve.

Children usually brought their lunch and ate in the classroom. Sometimes the teacher had a pot of soup simmering on the wood stove.

Afternoon lessons were in history and geography. A spelling bee would end the day, and the children left for home between 4 and 5 p.m., but not the teacher—he or she still had to clean up the classroom and sweep the floor. The teacher's contract included custodial work as well as teaching, all for a munificent sum ranging from $4 to $12 a month.

Contributed by Nita Thurman, Denton County (Texas) Historical Commission member and columnist, Denton Record-Chronicle.

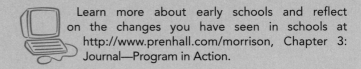

Learn more about early schools and reflect on the changes you have seen in schools at http://www.prenhall.com/morrison, Chapter 3: Journal—Program in Action.

and their families. We have an obligation to make the bright visions others have had for children our visions as well. After all, if we don't have bright visions for children, who will? The Program in Action feature spotlights how educational facilities have changed through the years.

Implement Current Practice

Beliefs of famous educators will help you better understand how to implement current teaching strategies, whatever they might be. For instance, Rousseau, Froebel, and Montessori all believed children should be taught with dignity and respect. Dignity and respect for all children are essential foundations of all good teaching and quality programs, and those traits apply today, just as they did hundreds of years ago. Here is what Theresa Stephens Stapler, Central Elementary School, Carrolton, Georgia, a *USA Today* all-USA Teacher, has to say about teaching with dignity and respect.

Students all over the world come to school with all types of baggage. Some are from loving homes; others are not. In my classroom I strive to do all I can do to help my students have a positive self-image and a good attitude. My main goal is to let the students know I love them and accept them for who they are. When students feel that level of belonging, they will do anything to succeed. At first the success is for me; then they start succeeding for themselves!

Students model the behavior demonstrated by the teacher. Treat students with love, respect and dignity, and they, in turn, will treat you the same. The Golden Rule should be the mantra of every teacher—"Do unto others as you would have them do unto you."

When I first meet my students, I always greet them with a smile and a handshake. I feel a handshake lets the students know that I am greeting them with an adult's way of showing respect. I am lucky because I have the pleasure to teach my students for three years. After being part of the student's life for three years, the handshake usually turns to hugs. I treat my students with respect and they in turn treat me with respect. My motto hanging in my class is "**I am the luckiest teacher because you are my student**."[5]

WHY ARE THEORIES OF LEARNING IMPORTANT?

When you try to explain plant growth to children or others you talk about soil, sun, water, and the need for fertilizer. Perhaps you even use the word *photosynthesis* as part of your theory of plant growth. Describing the processes of mental and physical growth of children, however, is not as straightforward. How do children develop? How do children learn? I'm sure you have ideas and explanations based on your experiences to help answer these questions. We also have the theories of others to help us explain these questions.

A **theory** is a statement of principles and ideas that attempts to explain events and how things happen; in our case, it is learning more about early childhood. We will learn about theories that attempt to explain how children grow, develop, and learn.

Learning is the process of acquiring knowledge, behaviors, skills, and attitudes. As a result of experiences, children change in their behavior, knowledge, skills, and attitude. So, we can also consider learning to be changes that occur in behavior over a period of time. Children who enter kindergarten in September are not the same children who exit kindergarten in May. Learning is a complex process, and many educators have developed theories to explain how and why learning occurs in children. We use child development to examine changes in children's lives. **Child development** is the study of how children change over time from birth to age eight. Theories about how children learn and develop are an important part of your professional practice for several reasons. Let's look at some of them.

Communicate

Theories enable you to explain to others, especially families, how the complex process of learning occurs and what you and they can expect of children. Communicating with clarity and understanding to parents and others about how children learn is one of the most important jobs for an early childhood professional. To do this, you need to know the theories that explain how children develop and learn.

Evaluate Learning

Theories also enable you to evaluate children's learning. Theories describe behaviors and identify what children are able to do at certain ages. You can use this information to evaluate learning and plan for teaching. Evaluation of children's learning is another important job for all teachers. We will discuss assessment of learning in Chapter 6.

TABLE 3.1 Contributions of Famous Individuals to Early Childhood Education

Individual and Dates	Major Contributions	Influences on Modern Theorists
Martin Luther (1483–1546)	• Translated the Bible from Latin to vernacular language, allowing people to be educated in their own language. • Advocated establishing schools to teach children how to read.	• Universal education. • Public support of education. • Teaching of reading to all children.
John Comenius (1592–1670)	• Wrote *Orbis Pictus,* the first picture book for children. • Thought early experiences formed what a child would be like. • Said education should occur through the senses.	• Early learning helps determine school and life success. • Sensory experiences support and promote learning.
John Locke (1632–1704)	• Said children are born as blank tablets. • Believed children's experiences determine who they are.	• Learning should begin early. • Children learn what they are taught—teachers literally make children. • It is possible to rear children to think and act as society wants them to.
Jean-Jacques Rousseau (1712–1778)	• Advocated natural approaches to child rearing. • Felt that children's natures unfold as a result of maturation according to an innate timetable.	• Natural approaches to education work best (e.g., family grouping, authentic testing, and environmental literacy).
Johann Pestalozzi (1746–1827)	• Advocated that education should follow the course of nature. • Believed all education is based on sensory impressions. • Promoted the idea that mother could best teach children.	• Family-centered approaches to early childhood education. • Home schooling. • Education through the senses.
Robert Owen (1771–1858)	• Held that environment determines children's beliefs, behaviors, and achievements. • Believed society can shape children's character. • Taught that education can help build a new society.	• Importance of infant programs. • Education can counteract children's poor environment. • Early childhood education can reform society.
Friedrich Froebel (1782–1852)	• Believed children develop through "unfolding." • Compared children to growing plants. • Founded the kindergarten "Garden of Children." • Developed gifts and occupation to help young children learn.	• Teacher's role is similar to a gardener. • Children should have specific materials to learn concepts and skills. • Learning occurs through play.

Provide Guidance

Theories help us understand how, why, where, and when learning occurs. As a result, they can guide you in developing programs for children that support and enhance their learning. For example, as we will see shortly, what Piaget believed about how children learn directly influences classroom arrangement and what is taught and how it is taught.

Developing programs and curriculum is an important part of your professional practice. Thus, the history of early childhood and theories about how children learn enable you to fulfill essential dimensions of your professional role. Table 3.1 summarizes the contributions of famous educators to the early childhood field. Those educators are profiled in the following section.

FAMOUS PEOPLE AND THEIR INFLUENCE ON EARLY CHILDHOOD EDUCATION

Throughout history many people have contributed to our understanding of what children are like and how to best teach them. The following accounts will help you understand the history of early childhood and theories about how to best teach children.

Martin Luther

Martin Luther (1483–1546) emphasized the necessity of establishing schools to teach children to read. Luther replaced the authority of the Catholic Church with the authority of the Bible. Luther believed that individuals were free to work out their own salvation through the Scriptures. This meant that people had to learn to read the Bible in their native tongue.

Luther translated the Bible into German, marking the real beginning of teaching and learning in people's native language. In these ways, the Protestant Reformation encouraged and supported popular universal education and the importance of learning to read.

Today, literacy for all is a national priority. As you can see by the following Diversity Tie-In box, ensuring that all children can read and be taught in their native language as Luther suggested are issues we are still dealing with today.

John Amos Comenius

John Amos Comenius (1592–1670) spent his life teaching school and writing textbooks. Two of his famous books are *The Great Didactic* and the *Orbis Pictus* ("The World in Pictures"), considered the first picture book for children.

Comenius believed education should begin in the early years because "a young plant can be planted, transplanted, pruned, and bent this way or that. When it has become a tree these processes are impossible.[6] Today, new brain research reminds us again that learning should begin early and that many "windows of opportunity" for learning occur early in life.

Comenius also thought that sensory education forms the basis for all learning and that insofar as possible, everything should be taught through the senses. This approach to education was endorsed by Montessori and forms the basis for much of early childhood practice to this day.

Learn more about the work of historical early childhood figures and theorists at http://www.prenhall.com/morrison, Chapter 3—Web Links.

John Locke

John Locke (1632–1704) is best known for his theory of the mind as a blank tablet, or "white paper." By this, Locke meant that environment and experience literally form the mind. According to Locke, development comes from the stimulation children receive from parents and caregivers and through experiences in their environment.

The implications of this belief are clearly reflected in modern educational practice. The notion of the importance of environmental influences is particularly evident in programs that encourage and promote early education as a means of helping children get a good foundation for learning early in life. These programs assume that differences in

Native American Education: Then and Now

Then: The Carlisle (Pennsylvania) Indian School, 1879

The Carlisle Indian School was founded in 1879 with the intention of assimilating American Indian children into the white, Protestant culture.

- A U.S. Army officer ran the school.
- Children were not allowed to speak in their native tongue.
- Children learned trades in the mornings and academics in the afternoon.
- Boys wore uniforms, and girls wore Victorian-style dresses; moccasins were not allowed.*

Now: Current BIA-Operated Schools

The education mission of the Bureau of Indian Affairs (BIA) is to "provide quality education for lifelong learning." Schools are empowered under a policy of indian self-determination.

- Tribes operate the majority of programs.
- Schools attempt to preserve the native language.
- Schools' curricula focus on literacy and math.
- Knowledge of native culture is encouraged.†

Irene Jones, a Native American Navajo, teaches seventeen Native American kindergarten students at Kenayta Primary School on the Navajo Nation in Kenayta, Arizona. Kenayta Primary serves 450 Native American children in kindergarten through second grade. Irene offers the following insights about what it is like to teach Native American children today.

My children are not as well prepared for school as I would like them to be. They are not prepared because they don't have the social skills to be with other children and to play with others. They don't have the boundaries they need. I have to teach them the social skills necessary to be in a school environment.

Half of my children come to school not knowing any alphabet or their numbers. This is generally true of the children who live in other towns who are bused in from thirty to forty miles away. The other half of my children know their alphabet and numbers. It is really like teaching two classes.

I make a lot of modifications in textbooks and materials so that my children understand what they are to do. My children are very visual learners—I can't just talk—I show them everything. For example, in teaching the letters of the alphabet and in writing, I use visuals and concrete materials. I show my children how to do things—I don't tell them.

Some of my children speak Navajo. At our school we encourage children to retain their language and culture. We have a Navajo culture class, which every child attends once a week.

Darlene Smith teaches in the Navajo Culture and Language Acquisition Program at Kenayta and has dedicated her teaching career to the preservation of Navajo culture and language.

learning, achievement, and behavior are attributable to environmental factors such as home and family conditions, socioeconomic background, and early education and experiences. The current move toward universal schooling for three- and four-year-olds is based on the premise that getting children's education right from the beginning can help overcome negative effects of poverty and neglect and can help erase differences in children's achievement due to difference in socioeconomic levels.

Jean-Jacques Rousseau

Jean-Jacques Rousseau (1712–1778) is best remembered for his book *Émile*, the opening lines of which set the tone for his education and political views: "God makes all things good; man meddles with them and they become evil."[7] Because of this belief, Rousseau advocated the "natural" education of young children, encouraging growth without undue interference or restrictions.

Rousseau also believed in the idea of *unfolding*, in which the nature of children—who and what they will be—unfolds as a result of development according to their innate

The Navajo tribe wants to have the young children learn their language and culture. I am Navajo, but I had lived off the reservation for a long time and lost a lot of my language skills. I had to get my Navajo language endorsement to teach bilingual, so I went back to school. It was tough for me to learn all of the native language sounds, but I did it. I have taught bilingual now for ten years. The emphasis now is to get more Navajo people to go into teaching. This wasn't always true. This emphasis on Native Americans teaching Native Americans began in the 1980s and 1990s, and I hope it continues. We need to preserve our culture and language, and this is one way to do it.

I teach students to read and write in Navajo, using a Navajo language curriculum that we developed here at Kenayta. The first thing we do is have the children learn their clans. Every child has a clan. There are four basic clans, and then there are clans within clans—they are all related. For example, Harry Yazzie, a kindergartner is a member of the Bitter Water Clan. According to our culture, Harry cannot marry into the Bitter Water Clan or a related clan—this is one reason for him to know his clan. Also, by knowing his clan, he knows his heritage and where he comes from. He also learns respect for the people who he is related to. Children today need to know this cultural information. Unfortunately, I have only thirty minutes for each class, and the children only come once a week, so I don't have a lot of time to teach all I want them to learn.

I think it is important for Navajo children to learn their language and culture. Our language is slowly dying, and if this generation doesn't learn it, I am afarid it will be lost. This is why I am so passionate about teaching our children our culture and language.

At San Felipe Pueblo Elementary School in San Felipe Pueblo, New Mexico, all 490 children are Native American.

Anna Beardsley, a native Navajo teacher, teaches twenty-two Native American children.

I teach the children in English. Keres, Tano, and Zuni are the three major language groups of the New Mexico pueblos. At San Felipe the dialect is Keres. The only time we use children's native language is when my aide translates or clarifies directions. If children use more Keres than English when they come to school, my aide uses the native dialect to clarify and help them understand. There is a difference here at San Felipe because some of our teachers are native language speakers, so we are helping our children retain their native language. In the village and school, we encourage the students to retain the language and the culture.

I have taught at several pueblos—there are eighteen pueblos in the state—and teaching varies from pueblo to pueblo. The biggest challenge at the beginning of the school year is to get children to listen and follow directions

We try our best to have all children achieve to their greatest potential. Our entire curriculum is aligned to the state standards, so we make sure our children are learning what the standards specify, If our children achieve at high levels, then they are more likely to be successful in the real world.

Contributed by Irene Jones, Darlene Smith, and Anna Beardsley through telephone interviews with the author.

*Landis, B. Carlise Indian Industrial School History [Online] Available at: http://home.epix.net/~landis/histry.html.
†Bureau of Indian Affairs, Office of Indian Education Programs [Online] Available at: http://www.oiep.bia.edu.

 Complete an activity on supporting the inclusion of other languages in the classroom at http://www.prenhall.com/morrison, Chapter 3—Journal: Diversity Tie-In.

timetables. Such an approach is at the heart of developmentally appropriate practice, in which childhood educators match their educational practices to children's developmental levels and abilities. Every day you will make decisions about how to make sure what you teach and how you teach it is appropriate for each child based on his/her developmental level.

Johann Heinrich Pestalozzi

Johann Heinrich Pestalozzi (1746–1827) was influenced by both Comenius and Rousseau. Pestalozzi believed all education is based on sensory impressions and that through the proper sensory experiences, children can achieve their natural potential. To achieve this goal, Pestalozzi developed "object lessons," manipulatives that encouraged activities such as counting, measuring, feeling, and touching. Pestalozzi also wrote two books—*How Gertrude Teaches Her Children* and *Book for Mothers*—to help parents teach their young children in the home. Today, enter any major bookstore (either online or in the shopping mall) and you will see shelves jammed with books on how to parent, how to teach young children, how to guide children's behavior, and many other topics. You will be able to help families by providing them with books and/or suggestions for books to read that will help them enhance their guidance skills.

Robert Owen

Robert Owen (1771–1858) believed children's environments contribute to their beliefs, behavior, and achievement just as we believe today. He maintained that individuals and society can use environments to shape children's character. Owen was also a utopian, believing that by controlling the circumstances and consequent outcomes of child rearing, it was possible to build a new and perhaps more perfect society. Such a view of child rearing makes environmental conditions the dominant force in directing and determining human behavior.

To implement his beliefs, Owen opened an infant school in 1816 in New Lanark, Scotland, designed to provide care for about a hundred children, ages eighteen months to ten years, while their parents worked in the cotton mills he owned. This emphasis on early education eventually led to the opening of the first infant school in London in 1818.

Several things about Owen's efforts and accomplishments are noteworthy. First, his infant school preceded Froebel's kindergarten by about a quarter century. Second, Owen's ideas and practices influenced educators concerning the importance of early education and the relationship between educational and societal improvements, an idea much in vogue in current educational practice. In addition, early childhood professionals also seek to use education as a means of reforming society and as a way of making a better world for everyone.

Observe the kindergarten classrooms of today and compare them to Froebel's kindergarten at Video Classroom, Early Childhood Education, Module 7: Professionalism, Video 1: Kindergarten Classroom.

Friedrich Wilhelm Froebel

Friedrich Wilhelm Froebel (1782–1852) is known as the "father of the kindergarten." Froebel's concept of children and learning is based in part on the idea of *unfolding*, also held by Comenius and Pestalozzi. According to this view, the teacher's role is to observe children's natural unfolding and provide activities that enable them to learn what they are ready to learn when they are ready to learn it.

Froebel compared the child to a seed that is planted, germinates, brings forth a new shoot, and grows from a young, tender plant to a mature, fruit-producing one. He likened the role of teacher to a gardener. Think for a moment how we still use the teacher as gardener metaphor to explain our role as teachers of young children. For example, I view myself as a planter of seeds in my work with young children. Froebel wanted his *kindergarten*, or "garden of children," to be a place where children unfolded like flowers. Froebel believed development occurred primarily through self-activity and play. Play will be discussed further in other chapters because the process of learning through play is as important today as it was in Froebel's time. The concepts of unfolding and learning through play are two of Froebel's greatest contributions to early childhood education.

To promote self-activity, Froebel developed a systematic, planned curriculum for the education of children based on "gifts," "occupations," songs, and educational games. Think of these as similar to the materials and toys we have today to promote children's learning. For example, we teach the alphabet and other concepts with songs, use blocks to teach size and shape, and use colored rods to teach concepts of length and seriation.

Gifts were objects for children to handle and use in accordance with teachers' instructions so they could learn shape, size, color, and concepts involved in counting, measuring,

	First Gift Six colored balls of soft yarn or wool
	Second Gift One 2-inch wooden sphere, one 2-inch cylinder, and two 2-inch tubes
	Third Gift Eight 1-inch cubes, presented together as a cube ($2 \times 2 \times 2 \times 2$)
	Fourth Gift Eight oblong blocks ($1/2 \times 1 \times 2$), presented as a 20-inch cube
	Fifth Gift Twenty-one 1-inch cubes, six half-cubes (triangular prisms), and twelve quarter cubes (triangular prisms), presented as a 3-inch cube
	Sixth Gift Eighteen oblong blocks; twelve flat, square blocks (caps) and six narrow columns
	Seventh Gift Parquetry tablets derived from the surfaces of the solid gifts including squares, equilateral triangles, right triangles, and an obtuse triangle, one circle, and one half-circle
	Eighth Gift Thirty-six straight sticks of wood, plastic, or metal in various lengths plus rings and half-rings of various diameters made from wood, plastic, or metal
	Ninth Gift Grid card and 576 wood dots, 64 of each of the following nine colors: red, orange, yellow, green, blue, violet, natural, white, black
	Tenth Gift Materials that utilize rods and connectors (similar to Tinkertoys)

FIGURE 3.1 Froebel's Gifts

Source: Used by permission of Scott Bultman, Froebel Foundation USA, http://www.froebelfoundation.org.

contrasting, and comparison. Figure 3.1 describes Froebel's gifts. Think of some specific examples of how they relate to educational toys and materials today.

Occupations were materials designed for developing various skills through activities such as sewing with a sewing board, drawing pictures by following the dots, modeling with clay, cutting, stringing beads, weaving, drawing, pasting, and folding paper. All of these activities are part of early childhood programs today.

Froebel devoted his life to developing both a program for young children and a system of training for kindergarten teachers. Many of his ideas and activities form the basis for activities in preschools and kindergartens today.

Pearson Learning Photo Studio

Froebel believed, as early childhood professionals believe today, that play is a process through which children learn. Learning flows from play. These children are engaged in play that supports their growth and development. Froebel urged early childhood educators to support the idea that play is the cornerstone of children's learning.

Maria Montessori and the Montessori Theory

Maria Montessori (1870–1952) developed a system for educating young children that has greatly influenced early childhood education. The first woman in Italy to earn a medical degree, she became interested in educational solutions for problems such as deafness, paralysis, and mental retardation.

At that time she said, "I differed from my colleagues in that I instinctively felt that mental deficiency was more of an educational than medical problem."[8]

While preparing herself for educating children, Montessori was invited to organize schools for young children of families who occupied tenement houses in Rome. In the first school, named the *Casa dei Bambini*, or Children's House, she tested her ideas and gained insights into children and teaching that led to the perfection of her system. Chapter 4 provides a full description of the Montessori method, which is currently used in over three thousand early childhood programs.

John Dewey and Progressive Education Theory

John Dewey (1859–1952) did more than any other person to redirect the course of education in the United States, and his influence is continuous.

Dewey's theory of schooling, usually called *progressivism*, emphasizes children and their interests rather than subject matter. From this child-centered emphasis comes the terms *child-centered curriculum* and *child-centered school*, two topics very much in the forefront of educational practice today. Dewey believed that education "is a process of living and not a preparation for future living" and that daily life should be a source of activities through which children learn about life and the skills necessary for living.[9]

Classroom work in Dewey's school was a carefully designed extension of the child's familiar life in the home. Rote exercises were minimized. Projects resembling those of a traditional household—crafts and cooking, for example—were used as ways to teach practical lessons of reading and arithmetic.[10]

Dewey's school was based on five basic principles, all of which are very contemporary and applicable to early childhood practice today:

- The child's early school experiences reflect the home life (cooking, sewing, construction); academic skills would be an outgrowth of these activities/occupations.[11]
- Children are part of a human community in school that focuses on cooperation.
- Learning is focused on problems that children solve (e.g., numbers would be learned through understanding relationships rather than memorizing multiplication tables).
- Motivation is internal to the experiences and the child.
- The teacher's role is to know the children and to choose stimulating problems for the children.

In a classroom based on Dewey's ideas, children are actively involved in activities, making and using things, solving problems, and learning through social interactions.

Dewey felt that an ideal way for children to express their interests was through daily life-skills activities such as cooking and through occupations such as carpentry.

Although Dewey believed the curriculum should be built on the interests of children, he also felt it was the teacher's responsibility to plan for and capitalize on opportunities to use these interests to teach traditional subject matter. This idea is the basis for the **integrated curriculum**, in which one subject area is used to teach another. For example, reading is taught in math and science, just as math and science are used to teach reading. Teachers who integrate subjects, use thematic units, and encourage problem-solving activities and critical thinking are philosophically indebted to Dewey.

John Dewey represents a dividing line between the educational past and the educational present and future. This would be a good time for you to review and reflect on Figure 3.2, a time line of the history of early childhood education.

Jean Piaget and Constructivist Learning Theory

Jean Piaget (1896–1980) was always interested in how humans learn and develop intellectually, beginning at birth and continuing across the life span. He devoted his life to conducting experiments, observing children (including his own), and developing and writing about his **cognitive theory** approach to learning.

Piaget's Cognitive Development Theory.   Piaget's theory explains how individuals think, understand, and learn. Piaget believed that intelligence is the cognitive, or mental, process by which children acquire knowledge. *Intelligence* is "to know" and involves the use of *mental operations* developed as a result of acting mentally and physically in and on the environment. Active involvement is basic to Piaget's theory that children develop intelligence through direct hands-on experiences with the physical world. These hands-on experiences provide the foundations for a "minds-on" ability to think and learn.

Observe young children demonstrating the theory of Piagetian schemes, object permanence, and conservation at Video Classroom, Child Development, Module 4: Cognitive Development: Piaget and Vygotsky, Video 1: Cognitive Development—Part 1.

Piaget also thought intelligence has a biological basis. All organisms, including humans, adapt to their environments. For example, in the process of physical adaptation, individuals react and adjust to their environments. Piaget applied the concept of adaptation to the mental level, using it to explain how children change their thinking and grow cognitively as a result of encounters with parents, teachers, siblings, peers, and the environment.

Constructivism in Play.   Play is one primary way for children to be actively involved in their environments and to think and learn. Play provides hands-on and "minds-on" opportunities so children can experience and learn through all kinds of materials—water, sand, clay, indoor and outdoor equipment, puzzles, blocks, real-life toys, housekeeping furniture, dolls, dress-up clothes, carpentry equipment, musical instruments, and so forth. The physical activity involved in play supports children's natural ways of learning by enabling them to touch, explore, feel, test, experiment, talk, and think. It is through these processes that children gain meaning of their world and learn how things work. As a result, children learn to make sense of the world.

Play with others also enables children to develop meaning of social relationships. When they play with others, children learn how to get along, learn about themselves, and come to understand that others have different points of view and values from their own. Through play with others, children learn how to solve problems and work cooperatively.

Active play also provides children opportunities to become confident about who they are, what they can accomplish, and enables them to become self-directed and self-regulated individuals.

Play then is a powerful means for providing children the physical and mental activity necessary to support cognitive development.

FIGURE 3.2

Time Line of the History of Early Childhood Education

1524   Martin Luther argued for public support of education for all children in his *Letter to the Mayors and Aldermen of All the Cities of Germany in Behalf of Christian Schools.*

1628   John Amos Comenius's *The Great Didactic* proclaimed the value of education for all children according to the laws of nature.

1762   Jean-Jacques Rousseau wrote *Émile*, explaining that education should take into account the child's natural growth and interests.

1801   Johann Pestalozzi wrote *How Gertrude Teaches Her Children*, emphasizing home education and learning by discovery.

1816   Robert Owen set up a nursery school in Great Britain at the New Lanark Cotton Mills, believing that early education could counteract bad influences of the home.

1817   Thomas Gallaudet founded the first residential school for the deaf in Hartford, Connecticut.

1836   William McGuffey began publishing the *Eclectic Reader* for elementary school children; his writing had a strong impact on moral and literary attitudes in the nineteenth century.

1837   Friedrich Froebel, known as the "father of the kindergarten," established the first kindergarten in Blankenburgh, Germany.

1837   Horace Mann began his job as secretary of the Massachusetts State Board of Education; he is often called the "father of the common schools" because of the role he played in helping set up the elementary school system in the United States.

1856   Mrs. Margaretha Schurz established the first kindergarten in the United States in Watertown, Wisconsin; the school was founded for children of German immigrants, and the program was conducted in German.

1860   Elizabeth Peabody opened a private kindergarten in Boston, Massachusetts, for English-speaking children.

1871   First teacher-training program for teachers of kindergarten began in Oshkosh Normal School, Oshkosh, Wisconsin.

1871   The first public kindergarten in North America was started in Ontario, Canada.

1873   Susan Blow opened the first public school kindergarten in the United States in St. Louis, Missouri, as a cooperative effort with superintendent of schools, William Harris.

1876   A model kindergarten was shown at the Philadelphia Centennial Exposition.

1884   The American Association of Elementary, Kindergarten, and Nursery School Educators was founded to serve in a consulting capacity for other educators.

1892   The International Kindergarten Union (IKU) was founded.

1896   John Dewey started the Laboratory School at the University of Chicago, basing his program on child-centered learning with an emphasis on life experiences.

1907   Maria Montessori started her first preschool in Rome called Children's House; her now-famous teaching method was based on the theory that children learn best by themselves in a properly prepared environment.

1911   Margaret and Rachel McMillan founded an open-air nursery school in Great Britain in which the class met outdoors; emphasis was on healthy living.

1915   Eva McLin started the first U.S. Montessori nursery school in New York City.

1918   The first public nursery schools were started in Great Britain.

1919   Harriet Johnson started the Nursery School of the Bureau of Educational Experiments, later to become the Bank Street College of Education.

1921   Patty Smith Hill started a progressive, laboratory nursery school at Columbia Teachers College.

1921   A. S. Neill founded Summerhill, an experimental school based on the ideas of Rousseau and Dewey.

1922   Abigail Eliot, influenced by the open-air school in Great Britain and basing her program on personal hygiene and proper behavior, started the Ruggles Street Nursery School in Boston.

1924   *Childhood Education,* the first professional journal in early childhood education, was published by the IKU.

1926   The National Committee on Nursery Schools was initiated by Patty Smith Hill at Columbia Teachers College; now called the National Association for the Education of Young Children, it provides guidance and consultant services for educators.

1926   The National Association of Nursery Education (NANE) was founded.

1930   The IKU changed its name to the Association for Childhood Education.

1935 First toy-lending library, Toy Loan, was founded in Los Angeles.

1943 Kaiser Child Care Centers opened in Portland, Oregon, to provide twenty-four-hour child care for children of mothers working in war-related industries.

1946 Dr. Benjamin Spock wrote the *Common Sense Book of Baby and Child Care.*

1950 Erik Erikson published his writings on the "eight ages or stages" of personality growth and development and identified "tasks" for each stage of development; the information, known as "Personality in the Making," formed the basis for the 1950 White House Conference on Children and Youth.

1952 Jean Piaget's *The Origins of Intelligence in Children* was published in English translation.

1957 The Soviet Union launched *Sputnik,* sparking renewed interest in other educational systems and marking the beginning of the "rediscovery" of early childhood education.

1960 Katherine Whiteside Taylor founded the American Council of Parent Cooperatives for those interested in exchanging ideas in preschool education; it later became the Parent Cooperative Preschools International.

1964 The Economic Opportunity Act of 1964 was passed, marking the beginning of the War on Poverty and the foundation for Head Start.

1965 The Head Start program began with federal money allocated for preschool education; the early programs were known as child development centers.

1967 The Follow Through program was initiated to extend Head Start into the primary grades.

1968 The federal government established the Handicapped Children's Early Education Program to fund model preschool programs for children with disabilities.

1971 The Stride Rite Corporation in Boston was the first to start a corporate-supported child care program.

1972 The National Home Start Program was initiated for the purpose of involving parents in their children's education.

1975 Public Law 94–142, the Education for All Handicapped Children Act, was passed, mandating a free and appropriate education for all children with disabilities and extending many rights to parents of such children.

1980 The first American lekotek (toy-lending library) opened its doors in Evanston, Illinois.

1982 The Mississippi legislature established mandatory statewide public kindergartens.

1984 The High/Scope Educational Foundation released a study that documented the value of high-quality preschool programs for poor children. This study will be cited repeatedly in coming years by those favoring expansion of Head Start and other early years programs.

1985 Head Start celebrated its twentieth anniversary with a Joint Resolution of the Senate and House "reaffirming congressional support."

1986 The U.S. Secretary of Education proclaimed the Year of the Elementary School, saying, "Let's do all we can this year to remind this nation that the time our children spend in elementary school is crucial to everything they will do for the rest of their lives."

1986 Public Law 99-457, the Education of the Handicapped Act Amendments, established a national policy on early intervention that recognizes its benefits, provides assistance to states for building systems of service delivery, and recognizes the unique roles of families in the development of their children with disabilities.

1988 Even Start was established by the U.S. Department of Education as a parent education/literacy program.

1989 The United Nations Convention on the Rights of the Child was adopted by the UN General Assembly.

1990 The United Nations Convention on the Rights of the Child went into effect following its signing by twenty nations.

1990 Head Start celebrated its twenty-fifth anniversary.

1991 Education Alternatives, Inc., a for-profit firm, opened South Pointe Elementary School in Miami, Florida, the first public school in the nation to be run by a private company.

1991 The Carnegie Foundation issued "Ready to Learn," a plan to ensure children's readiness for school.

1995 Head Start Reauthorization established a new program, Early Head Start, for low-income pregnant women and families with infants and toddlers.

1996 The Children's Defense Fund initiated the Stand for Children Campaign.

1997 White House Conference on Child Care was held.

1999 Florida became the first state in the nation to pass a statewide school voucher plan; the law gives children in academically failing public schools a chance to attend private, secular, and religious schools with public money.

(continued)

FIGURE 3.2   *continued*

2000	Head Start celebrated its thirty-fifth anniversary.	2005	Head Start celebrates forty years of success.
2000	Goals 2000 celebrated ten years.	2005	High/Scope's Perry Preschool Project marks the fortieth year of its study of participants and the effects of preschool education.
2001	NAEYC celebrated its seventy-fifth anniversary.		
2001	The No Child Left Behind Education Act provides funding for early literacy and learning to read.	2006	More than forty states enacted substantive child care and early education legislation under-scoring the popularity of programs for young children.
2003	Beginning of the Literacy Decade: All early childhood professionals are called to action by the United Nations to fight against illiteracy worldwide.		
2004	International Year of the Family (IYF) celebrates its ten-year anniversary.	2007	Montessorians around the world celebrate 100 years of Montessori education.

Constructivism and Cognitive Development.   Piaget's theory is a *constructivist* view of development. The **constructivist process** is defined in terms of the individual's organizing, structuring, and restructuring of experience—an ongoing, lifelong process—in accordance with existing schemes of thought. In turn, these very schemes become modified and enriched in the course of interaction with the physical and social world.[12]

Children, through activity and interaction with others, continuously organize, structure, and restructure experiences in relation to existing *schemes*, or mental images, of thought. As a result, children build their own intelligence.

Constructivist theory plays an important role in early childhood education. Review the following key concepts of constructivism and consider how you can apply these ideas to your teaching:

Read more about Piaget and the basic principles of constructivism at http://www.prenhall.com/morrison, Chapter 3—Web Links.

- Children construct their own knowledge through collaboration with others.
- Mental and physical activity is crucial for construction of knowledge. Knowledge is built step by step through active involvement—that is, through exploring objects in the environment and through problem solving and interacting with others.
- Children construct knowledge best through experiences that are of interest and meaningful to them.
- Cognitive development is a continuous process. It begins at birth and continues across the life span.
- Active learning is an important part of constructivism. Active learning means children are actively involved with a variety of manipulative materials in problem-solving activities.

Cognitive Development and Adaptation.   According to Piaget, the adaptive process at the intellectual level operates much the same as at the physical level. The newborn's intelligence is expressed through reflexive motor actions such as sucking, grasping, head turning, and swallowing. Early in life, reflexive actions enable children to adapt to the environment and their intelligence develops.

Through interaction with the environment, children organize sensations and experiences and grow mentally. Obviously, therefore, the quality of the environment and the nature of children's experiences play a major role in the development of intelligence. For example, José, with various and differing objects available to grasp and suck, and many opportunities for this behavior, will develop differentiated sucking organizations (and therefore an intelligence) quite different from those of Midori, who has nothing to suck but a pacifier. Consequently, one of your roles is to provide enriched environments for young children and work with parents to provide rich home learning environments.

Learning as the Adaptation of Mental Constructs.   *Assimilation.*   Piaget believed that adaptation is composed of two interrelated processes, assimilation and accommodation.

Assimilation is the taking in of sensory data through experiences and impressions and incorporating them into existing knowledge. Through assimilation, children use old methods or experiences to understand and make sense of new information and experiences. In other words, children use their experiences and what they have learned from them as a basis for learning more. This is why quality learning experiences are so important. All experiences are not equal. Out of all the possible learning experiences you could provide, make sure the ones you select have the highest potential to promote learning.

Accommodation. **Accommodation** is the process involved in changing old methods and adjusting to new situations. Robbie has several cats at home. When he sees a dog for the first time, he may call it a kitty. He has assimilated dog into his organization of kitty. However, Robbie must change (accommodate) his model of what constitutes "kittyness" to exclude dogs. He does this by starting to construct or build a scheme for dogs and thus what "dogness" represents.[13]

The processes of assimilation and accommodation, functioning together, constitute *adaptation*.

Equilibrium. If adaptation is the functioning together of assimilation and accommodation, then equilibrium is the balance between the two processes. According to Piaget's theory of intelligence, as assimilation and accommodation function with one another, there must be balance between the two in order to allow children to successfully understand new data.

Upon receiving new sensory and experiential data, children assimilate, or fit, these data into their already existing knowledge (scheme) of reality and the world. If the new data can be immediately assimilated, then equilibrium occurs. If unable to assimilate the data, children try to accommodate and change their way of thinking, acting, and perceiving to account for the new data and restore the equilibrium to the intellectual system. It may well be that Robbie can neither assimilate nor accommodate the new data; if so, he rejects the data entirely.

Anthony Magnacca / Merrill

Rejection of new information is common if experiences and ideas children are trying to assimilate and accommodate are too different from their past experiences and their level of knowledge and understanding. This partially accounts for Piaget's insistence that new experiences must have some connection or relationship to previous experiences. Child care and classroom experiences should build on previous life and school experiences.

Schemes. Piaget used the term *scheme* to refer to units of knowledge that children develop through adaptation. Piaget believed that in the process of developing new schemes, physical activity is very important. Physical activity leads to mental stimulus, which in turn leads to mental activity—our hands-on minds-on concept. Thus, it is not possible to draw a clear line between physical activity and mental activity in infancy and early childhood. Teachers and parents should provide classrooms and homes that support active learning by enabling all children to explore and interact with people and objects in meaningful ways.

Stages of Intellectual Development. Figure 3.3 summarizes Piaget's developmental stages and provides examples of stage-related characteristics. As you review these now, keep in mind that Piaget contended developmental stages are the same for all children and that all children progress through each stage in the same

Piaget believed that the opportunity to be physically and mentally involved in learning is necessary to mental development in the early years. What are some examples of how children's active involvement contributes to their learning?

CHAPTER 3

	Sensorimotor	Preoperational	Concrete Operational
When	Birth to two years	Two to seven years	Seven to twelve years
Basic Concept	Object permanence	Symbolic thinking	Reverse operations
Definition	The concept that people and objects have an independent existence beyond the child's perception of them.	Use symbols such as words or mental images to solve problems and think about things and people who are not present. Use system of symbols to communicate (language).	Both physical and mental processes can be reversed and canceled by others.
Implication	—Birth to one month: no response to an object's disappearance —One to four months: Gazes at place where object has disappeared —Four to eight months: Retrieves partially hidden objects —Eight to twelve months: Looks in familiar places for hidden objects; retrieves completely hidden objects —Twelve to eighteen months: Searches for hidden objects where last seen —Eighteen to twenty-four months: Achieved full object permanence	—Two to four years: language acquisition increasing rapidly– speech is egocentric —Four to seven years: egocentrism begins to decrease; capable of mental representations but cannot organize this thinking = intuitive thinking	—Logical thinking replaces intuitive thinking —Understand that change involving physical appearances doesn't necessarily mean change in quality or quantity —Can go back over and "undo" a mental action just accomplished

FIGURE 3.3 Piaget's Stages of Cognitive Development

Photos (from left to right): Krista Greco / Merrill; David Mager / Pearson Learning Photo Studio; Getty Images, Inc.–Photodisc

order. The ages identified with each stage are only approximate and are not fixed. The sequence of growth through the developmental stages does *not* vary; the ages at which progression occurs *do* vary.

Sensorimotor Stage.   The sensorimotor stage is the first of Piaget's stages of cognitive development. When children use their primarily reflexive actions to develop intellectually, they are in the *sensorimotor stage*. During this period from birth to about two years, children use their senses and motor reflexes to build knowledge of the world. They use their eyes to see, mouths to suck, and hands to grasp. These reflexive actions help children construct a mental scheme of what is suckable and what is not (what can fit into the mouth and what cannot) and what sensations (warm and cold) occur by sucking. Children also use the grasping reflex in much the same way to build schemes of what can and cannot be grasped. Through these innate sensory and reflexive actions, they continue to develop an increasingly complex, unique, and individualized hierarchy of schemes about their world. What children are to become physically and intellectually is related to these sensorimotor functions and interactions. This is why it is important for teachers and others to provide quality experiences and environments for young children.

Silver Burdett Ginn Needham

The following are characteristics of the sensorimotor period:

- Dependence on and use of innate reflexive actions, which are the basic building blocks of intelligence;
- Beginning development of object permanency, the understanding or awareness that objects exist even when they are not seen, heard, or touched;
- Egocentricity, the mental and emotional condition in which children see themselves as the center of the world and believe that they cause many events;
- Dependence on concrete representations (things) rather than symbols (words, pictures) for information; and
- By the end of the second year, less reliance on sensorimotor reflexive actions; beginning use of symbols for things that are not present.

Preoperational children's inability to perform operations makes it impossible for them to determine that the quantity of a group of objects does not change because some changes occur in how the objects look. Try the checker experiment discussed in the text with several children and see how they are thinking and making sense of their world based on how things look to them.

Preoperational Stage. The *preoperational stage*, the second stage of cognitive development, begins at age two and ends at approximately seven years. Preoperational children are cognitively different from sensorimotor children in these ways:

- Rapidly accelerating language development,
- Less dependence on sensorimotor actions, and
- Increased ability to internalize events and think by using symbols such as words to represent things.

Preoperational children continue to be egocentric in many ways, expressing ideas and basing perceptions mainly on how they perceive or see things. Children learn to use symbols such as words or mental images to solve problems and think about things and people who are not present. How things look to preoperational children is the foundation for several other stage-related characteristics. First, when children look at an object that has multiple characteristics, such as a long, round, yellow pencil, they will "see" whichever of those qualities first catches their eye. Preoperational children's knowledge is based mainly on what they are able to see, simply because they do not yet have operational intelligence or the ability to think using mental images.

Second, the inability to perform operations makes it impossible for preoperational children to *conserve,* or understand that the quantity of an object does not change simply because some transformation occurs in its physical appearance. For example, show preoperational children two identical rows of checkers. Ask whether each row has the same number of checkers. The children should answer affirmatively. Next, space out the checkers in one of the rows, and ask whether the two rows still have the same number of checkers. They may insist that more checkers are in one row "because it's longer."

Children base their judgment on what they can see—namely, the spatial extension of one row beyond the other row. This example also illustrates that preoperational children are not able to mentally reverse thoughts or actions, which in this case would require mentally putting the "longer" row back to its original length.

Preoperational children believe and act as though everything happens for a specific reason or purpose. This explains their constant and recurring questions about why things happen and how things work.

Preoperational children also believe everyone thinks as they think and acts as they do for the same reasons, and for this reason preoperational children have a hard time putting themselves in another's place. This helps explain why it is difficult for them to be sympathetic and empathetic.

Young children's egocentrism also helps explain why they tend to talk at each other rather than with each other. This dialogue between two children playing at a child care center illustrates one example of egocentrism:

Carmen: My mommy's going to take me shopping.
Mia: I'm going to dress this doll.
Carmen: If I'm good, I'm going to get an ice cream cone.
Mia: I'm going to put this dress on her.

The point is that egocentrism is a fact of cognitive development in the early childhood years. Developmentally appropriate practice means you will take this into account as you teach.

Preoperational Children and Make-Believe Play.   As we previously discussed, activity is a critical developmental force in children's physical, social, emotional, linguistic, and cognitive development. Activity in the form of play provides children opportunities to be active in early childhood classrooms.

During the preoperational stage, *make-believe play* (also called *dramatic* and *pretend play*) is one of children's favorite types of play. They engage in it with seriousness and purposefulness. For children, the world of make-believe play is their world.

Make-believe play helps children learn about their world; helps them deal with their feelings and emotions; enables them to try out roles (mommy, daddy, doctor, nurse, community helper, etc.); and helps them relate to others in ways they would not have the opportunity to do if they did not engage in make-believe play. Through make-believe play children learn:

- About themselves, their families, and the world around them;
- How to talk to others;
- How to get along with and work with others;
- How to plan and decide what to do;
- How to make plans for the things they need and for what they want to do;
- About their feelings;
- To be creative and solve problems;
- To develop physical skills by using large and small muscles;
- To understand the way others act, think, and feel; and
- To stick with a task until it's finished.[14]

Here are some things you can do to promote children's make-believe play:

- Provide the time and opportunity for children to engage in make-believe play.
- Provide props and materials (clothing and equipment) with which children can play.
- Provide a housekeeping area as a learning center in which children can play.
- Be supportive of children's make-believe play.

Concrete Operations Stage. **Concrete operations** is the third stage of operational or logical thought. Piaget defined an **operation** as an action that can be carried out in thought and in direct experiences and that is mentally and physically reversible. The concrete operations stage is often referred to as the "hands-on" period of cognitive development because the ability to reason is based on tangible objects and real experiences.

Children in the *concrete operations stage*, from about age seven to about age twelve, can reverse mental operations. For example, operational children know that the amount of water in a container does not change when it is poured into a different-shaped container. They can mentally reverse the operation.

You can encourage the development of mental processes during this stage through the use of concrete or real objects when talking about and explaining concepts. For example, instead of just giving the children a basket of beads to play with, ask them to sort the beads into a red group, a blue group, a yellow group, and a green group.

Concrete operational children begin to develop the ability to understand that change involving physical appearances does not necessarily change quality or quantity. They also begin to reverse thought processes, by going back over and "undoing" a mental action just accomplished.

The process of development from one cognitive stage to another is gradual and continual and occurs over a period of time as a result of maturation and experiences. No simple set of exercises will cause children to move up the developmental ladder. Rather, ongoing developmentally appropriate activities lead to conceptual understanding.

Formal Operations Stage. The fourth stage of cognitive development and the second part of operational intelligence is **formal operations**. The *formal operations stage* begins at about twelve years of age and extends to about fifteen years. During this stage, children become capable of dealing with increasingly complex verbal and hypothetical problems and are less dependent on concrete objects. Children also develop the ability to reason scientifically and more logically.

Lev Vygotsky and Sociocultural Theory

Read about preschools implementing Vygotsky's theories at Articles and Readings, Child Development, Module 5: Cognitive Development: Piaget and Vygotsky, Article 3: Uniquely Preschool.

Lev Vygotsky (1896–1934), a contemporary of Piaget, increasingly inspires the practices of early childhood professionals. Vygotsky's theory of development is particularly useful in describing children's mental, language, and social development. His theory also has many implications regarding how children's play promotes language and social development.

Vygotsky believed that children's mental, language, and social development is supported and enhanced by others through social interaction. This view is opposite from the Piagetian perspective, in which children are much more solitary developers of their own intelligence and language. For Vygotsky, development is supported by social interaction. "Learning awakens a variety of developmental processes that are able to operate only when the child is interacting with people in his environment and in collaboration with his peers. Once these processes are internalized, they become part of the child's independent developmental achievement."[15] Vygotsky further believed that children seek out adults for social interaction beginning at birth; development occurs through these interactions.

For early childhood professionals, one of Vygotsky's most important concepts is that of the **zone of proximal development (ZPD)**, which he defines as follows:

> The area of development into which a child can be led in the course of interaction with a more competent partner, either adult or peer. [It] is not some clear-cut space that exists independently of joint activity itself. Rather, it is the difference between what the child can accomplish independently and what he or she can achieve in conjunction with another, more competent person. The zone is thus created in the course of social interaction.[16]

Laima Druskis / PH College

To summarize, the ZPD represents the range of tasks that children cannot do independently but can do when helped by a more competent person—a teacher, adult, or another child. For tasks below the ZPD, children can learn independently. For tasks, concepts, ideas, and information above the ZPD, children are not yet able to learn, even with help.

In addition, Vygotsky believed that learning and development constitute a dynamic and interactive process.

Learning is not development; however, properly organized learning results in mental development and sets in motion a variety of developmental processes that would be impossible apart from learning. Thus, learning is a necessary part and universal aspect of the process of developing culturally organized, specifically human, psychological functions.[17]

The zone of proximal development is the mental and social state of concept development and learning in which children are about to "go beyond" and achieve at higher levels with the assistance of more competent "others." In this way, learning and development are very social processes.

In other words, learning drives development; the experiences children have influence their development. This is why it is important for teachers and primary caregivers to provide high-quality learning experiences for children.

Intersubjectivity is a second Vygotskian concept. Intersubjectivity is based on the idea that "individuals come to a task, problem, or conversation with their own subjective ways of making sense of it. If they then discuss their differing viewpoints, shared understanding may be attained. . . . In other words, in the course of communication participants may arrive at some mutually agreed-upon, or intersubjective, understanding.[18]

Vygotsky also believed communication or dialogue between teacher and child is very important and literally becomes a means for helping children *scaffold*, or develop new concepts and think their way to higher level concepts. **Scaffolding** is assistance of some kind that enables children to complete tasks they cannot complete independently. When adults "assist" toddlers in learning to walk, they are scaffolding from not being able to walk to being able to walk.

The idea of intersubjectivity is similar to Piaget's theory that disequilibrium sets the stage for assimilation and accommodation and, consequently, new schemes develop. Furthermore, Vygotsky believed that as a result of teacher–child collaboration, the child uses concepts learned in the collaborative process to solve problems when the teacher is not present. As Vygotsky said, the child "continues to act in collaboration even though the teacher is not standing near him. . . . This help—this aspect of collaboration—is invisibly present. It is continued in what looks from the outside like the child's independent solution of the problem."[19] According to Vygotsky, social interactions and collaboration are essential ingredients in the processes of learning and development.

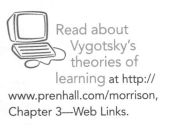

Read about Vygotsky's theories of learning at http://www.prenhall.com/morrison, Chapter 3—Web Links.

Many current practices such as cooperative learning, joint problem solving, coaching, collaboration, mentoring, and other forms of assisted learning are based on Vygotsky's theory of development and learning. Vygotsky believed that social and cultural features of the classroom play an important role in children's learning. By following the suggestions listed in Figure 3.4 you can apply Vygotsky's theories and help children learn to their fullest. Also, the accompanying Professionalism in Practice feature will help you learn how to put into practice this essential Vygotskian teaching skill.

Abraham Maslow and Self-Actualization Theory

Self-Actualization. Abraham Maslow (1908–1970) developed a theory of motivation called **self-actualization** based on the satisfaction of human needs. Maslow identified

Children are grouped by differing abilities.		Children are provided with the opportunity, time, and materials necessary to explore, experiment, and learn.
Ample opportunity for make-believe play with peers and adults.	Peer collaboration and cooperation on classroom projects.	Collaboration between adults, "expert" peers, and other more competent students (elementary, middle, and high school students, and other adults).
Activities, materials, and learning centers support independent discovery.		
Teachers guide child's learning in his/her "zone of proximal development." Vygotsky believed that challenging tasks promote maximum cognitive growth.		"Assisted discovery" is supported and encouraged as children help each other and as the teacher guides the children through scaffolding.
Diversity is valued, respected, and expected. Vygotsky believed children of different cultural backgrounds will develop somewhat different knowledge, skills, and ways of thinking.	Children are encouraged to help each other.	Teachers guide learning with explanations, verbal prompts, demonstrations, and modeling of behavior.
		Ample opportunity for child-care, child-children, teacher-child, and child-teacher conversations.

FIGURE 3.4 Features of a Vygotskian Classroom

Photo: Patrick White / Merrill

self-actualization, or self-fulfillment, as the highest human need but that children and adults don't achieve self-actualization until basic needs are satisfied.

Basic Needs.   Basic needs include life essentials such as food, safety, and security; belongingness and love; achievement and prestige; and aesthetic needs. Everyone has these basic needs regardless of sexual orientation, race, gender, socioeconomic status, or age. Satisfaction of basic needs is essential for children to function well and to achieve all they are capable of achieving.

Nutrition.   When children are hungry they perform poorly in school. Children who begin school without eating breakfast don't achieve as well as they should and experience difficulty concentrating on their school activities. This explains why many early childhood programs provide children with breakfast, lunch, and snacks throughout the day.

Safety and Security.   Safety and security needs play an important role in children's lives. When children think that their teachers do not like them or are fearful of what their teachers say and how they treat them, they are deprived of a basic need. As a consequence, they do not do well in school and become fearful in their relationships with others. Classrooms that have routines and predictableness provide children with a sense of safety and security.

Love and Belonging.   Children need to be loved and feel that they "belong" within their home and school in order to thrive and develop. All children have affectional needs that teachers can satisfy through smiles, hugs, eye contact, and nearness. For example, in my work with three- and four-year-old children, many want to sit close to me and want me to put my arms around them. They seek love and look to me and their teachers to satisfy this basic need.

Self-Esteem.   Recognition and approval are self-esteem needs that relate to success and accomplishment. Children who are independent and responsible, and who achieve well have high self-esteem. Today, many educators are concerned about how to enhance children's self-esteem.

COMPETENCY BUILDER

How to Scaffold Children's Learning

Vygotsky believed that cognitive development occurs through children's interactions with more competent others—teachers, peers, parents—who act as guides, facilitators, and coaches to provide the support children need to grow intellectually. Much of that support is provided through conversation, examples, and encouragement. When children learn a new skill, they need that competent other to provide a scaffold, or framework, to help them—to show them the overall task, break it into doable parts, and support and reinforce their efforts.

THE SCAFFOLDING PROCESS

Here are the basic steps involved in effective scaffolding. Study them carefully and then look for them in the three examples that follow:

STEP 1 OBSERVE AND LISTEN
You can learn a great deal about what kind of assistance is needed.

STEP 2 APPROACH THE CHILD
Ask what he or she wants to do, and ask for permission to help.

STEP 3 TALK ABOUT THE TASK
Describe each step in detail—what is being used, what is being done, what is seen or touched. Ask the child questions about the activity.

STEP 4 REMAIN ENGAGED IN THE ACTIVITY
Adjust your support, allowing the child to take over and do the talking.

STEP 5 GRADUALLY WITHDRAW SUPPORT
See how the child is able to perform with less help.

STEP 6 OBSERVE THE CHILD PERFORMING INDEPENDENTLY
After you have withdrawn all support, check to be sure the child continues to perform the task successfully.

STEP 7 INTRODUCE A NEW TASK
Present the child with a slightly more challenging task, and repeat the entire sequence.

EXAMPLE—WORKING A PUZZLE

Celeste has chosen a puzzle to work and dumps the pieces out. She randomly picks up a piece and moves it around inside the frame. She tries another. Look at her face: Is she smiling or showing signs of stress? Is she talking to herself?

Perhaps Celeste needs a puzzle with fewer pieces. If so, you can offer her one. But from prior observation, you may know she just needs a little assistance. Try sitting with Celeste and suggesting that you will help. Start by turning all the pieces right side up. As you do this, talk about the pieces you see: This one is red with a little green, this one has a straight edge, this one is curved. Move your finger along the edge.

Praise Children's Successes. Praising children's successes does wonders to boost children's abilities to do good work and keep on doing it. Give love and affection to every child everyday. Feeling loved and wanted is a cornerstone of self-esteem. Pay attention to children. Show children that you are interested in them. Build a foundation on which children can succeed. This foundation is built on this four-step process:

1. Tell children what you want them to do.
2. Show/model for children what to do.
3. Have children practice and demonstrate.
4. Have children work independently.

Teach children how to socialize and get along with others. Some children need help making friends. Friendship is a key to self-esteem. Teach cooperation and helpfulness. Instill new skills. Learning new skills forms the basis for achievement. Achievement is another cornerstone of high self-esteem. Have high and individually appropriate expectations for all of

Ask Celeste whether she can find a straight edge on the side of the puzzle and then whether she can find a piece with a straight edge that matches the color. Ask what hints the pieces give her. Repeat with several other pieces. Then pause to give Celeste the opportunity to try one on her own. As she does, describe what she is doing and the position, shape, and color of the piece. Demonstrate turning a piece in different directions while saying. "I'll try turning it another way." (If you just say, "Turn the piece," she will most likely turn it upside down.)

By listening to you verbalize and by repeating the verbalizing, Celeste is learning to self-talk, that is, to talk herself through a task. By practicing this private speech, children realize they can answer their own questions and regulate their own behavior. When the puzzle is complete, offer Celeste another of similar difficulty and encourage her to try it on her own while you stay nearby to offer assistance as needed, allowing her to take the lead.

EXAMPLE—BAKING

If you are teaching Isaac to bake, you can start by saying, "First we need to get everything out. Let's see what we need." Name the tools you will use as you lay them out.

- Draw pictures on cards to show each ingredient and the spoon(s) or cup(s) you will use to measure.
- Lay the cards out in the proper order, engaging Isaac by asking whether he recognizes each picture, can match it to the ingredient, and can tell you how many cups, teaspoons, etc., are needed.
  - Start with the first card.
  - Ask which cup or spoon should be used and how many times he will fill it.
  - Ask what the ingredient is.
- Encourage Isaac to start the measuring process.
- Observe Isaac. Can he fill the cup with flour? If not, guide his hand. Ask him whether he wants to try mixing, demonstrating if necessary.

The next time Isaac bakes, he will need less scaffolding and will be able to verbalize at least some of the steps for himself.

EXAMPLE—INTERACTING

Three girls are building a house in the block-building area. Joe watches and then asks, "Can I build with you?" In unison the girls respond, "No." When the girls start to move props into the house, Joe picks up a stop sign and places it at the end of the driveway. Arlene sharply reminds him, "We told you no." Joe responds, "But I just wanted to help" and walks away.

This is an opportunity for you to scaffold in a social situation. You must do more than say, "You need to find something else" or "The girls were here first," such as what the teacher in this photo is doing. Implement scaffolding by acknowledging that all the children want to build and helping them figure out how that might work.

Help the girls problem solve strategies for relating to Joe without completely shutting him out. Model appropriate responses. "When the house is finished, you'll be invited to a party" or "Joe, right now there are three of us and we think it will be too crowded" or "We're building the house. Would you like to plant some trees in the yard?" Have each child draw a picture of the incident that shows an ending in which everyone gains something.

Contributed by Catherine M. Kearn, EdD, early childhood professional and adjunct professor, Carroll College, Waukesha, Wisconsin. Also contributing were Elena Bodrova, senior researcher at Mid-Continent Research for Education and Learning, Denver, Colorado, and Deborah Leong, professor of psychology and director of the Center for Improving Early Learning, Metropolitan State College of Denver, Denver, Colorado. Photos by Krista Greco/Merrill (p. 74) and Anthony Magnacca/Merrill (above).

---

your children. Nothing diminishes self-esteem more than low or no expectations for a child. Acknowledge, accept, and celebrate children's cultures. Provide many opportunities for children to be recognized for their achievement.

When children have their basic needs met they become self-actualized. They have a sense of satisfaction, are enthusiastic, and are eager to learn. They want to engage in activities that will lead to higher levels of learning. Figure 3.5 outlines Maslow's hierarchy of needs. As you review these basic needs, think about how you can help children meet each of them.

Erik Erikson and Psychosocial Theory

Erik H. Erikson (1902–1994) developed his theory of **psychosocial development**, based on the premise that cognitive and social development occur hand in hand and cannot be separated. According to Erikson, children's personalities and social skills grow and develop within the context of society and in response to society's demands, expectations, values, and social institutions such as families, schools, and child care programs. Adults, especially parents and teachers, are key parts of these environments and therefore play a

FIGURE 3.5 Maslow's Hierarchy of Human Needs

Source: Diagram based on "The Hierarchy of Needs" from Maslow, Abraham H; Frager, Robert D. (Editor); Fadiman, James (Editor), *Motivation and Personality,* 3rd edition, 1987. Reprinted by permission of Pearson Education, Inc., Upper Saddle River, NJ.

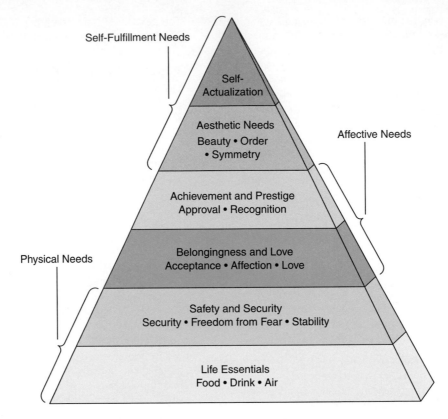

powerful role in helping or hindering children in their personality and cognitive development. For example, school-age children must deal with demands to learn new skills or risk a sense of incompetence, or a crisis of "industry"—the ability to do, be involved, be competent, and achieve—versus "inferiority"—marked by failure and feelings of incompetence. Many of the cases of school violence in the news today are caused in part by children who feel inferior and unappreciated and who lack the social skills for getting along with their classmates. Figure 3.6 outlines the stages of psychosocial development according to Erikson.

Urie Bronfenbrenner and Ecological Theory

Urie Bronfenbrenner's (1917–2005) ecological theory looks at children's development within the context of the systems of relationships that form their environment. There are five interrelating environmental systems: the microsystem, the mesosystem, the exosystem, the macrosystem, and the chronosystem. Figure 3.7 shows a model of these environmental systems and the ways each influences development. Each system influences and is influenced by the other.

The **microsystem** encompasses the environments of parents, family, peers, child care, schools, neighborhood, religious groups, parks, and so forth. The child acts on and influences each of these and is influenced by them. For example, four-year-old April might have a physical disability that her child care program accommodates by making the classroom more accessible. Five-year-old Mack's aggressive behavior might prompt his teacher to initiate a program of bibliotherapy.

The **mesosystem** includes linkages or interactions between microsystems. Interactions and influences there relate to all of the environmental influences in the microsystem. For example, the family's support of or lack of attention to literacy will influence the child's

FIGURE 3.6

Erikson's Stages of Psychosocial Development

Stage	Appropriate Age	Characteristics	Role of Early Childhood Educator
I. Basic trust versus mistrust: During this stage, children learn to trust or mistrust their environment and their caregivers. Trust develops when children's needs are met consistently, predictably, and lovingly. Children then view the world as safe and dependable.	Birth to 18 months  Krista Greco / Merrill	Infants learn to trust or mistrust that others will care for their basic needs, including nourishment, warmth, cleanliness, and physical contact.	• Meet children's needs with consistency and continuity. • Identify and take care of basic needs such as diapering and feeding. • Hold babies when feeding them—this promotes attachment and develops trust. • Socialize through smiling, talking and singing. • Be attentive—respond to infants' cues and signals. • Comfort infants when in distress.
II. Autonomy versus shame and doubt: This is the stage when children want to do things for themselves. Given adequate opportunities, they learn independence and competence. Inadequate opportunities and professional overprotection result in self-doubt and poor achievement; children come to feel ashamed of their abilities.	18 months to 3 years  Krista Greco / Merrill	Toddlers learn to be self-sufficient or to doubt their abilities in activities such as toileting, feeding, walking, and talking.	• Encourage children to do what they are capable of doing. • Do not shame children for any behavior. • Provide for safe exploration of classrooms and outdoor areas.
III. Initiative versus guilt: During the preschool years children need opportunities to respond with initiative to activities and tasks, which gives them a sense of purposefulness and accomplishment. Children can feel guilty if they are discouraged or prohibited from initiating activities and are overly restricted in attempts to do things on their own.	3 to 5 years  Teri Stratford / PH College	Children are learning and want to undertake many adult-like activities, sometimes overstepping the limits set by parents and feel guilty.	• Observe children and follow *their* interests. • Encourage children to engage in many activities. • Provide environments in which children can explore. • Promote language development. • Allow each child the opportunity to succeed.
IV. Industry versus inferiority: In this period, children display an industrious attitude and want to be productive. They want to build things, discover, manipulate objects, and find out how things work. They also want recognition for their productivity, and adult response to their efforts and accomplishments helps develop a sense of self-worth. Feelings of inferiority result when children are criticized or belittled or have few opportunities for productivity.	5 to 8 years  Krista Greco / Merrill	Children actively and busily learn to be competent or feel productive or feel inferior and unable to do things well.	• Help children win recognition by making things. • Help assure children are successful in literacy skills and learning to read. • Provide support for students who seem confused or discouraged. • Recognize children's achievement and success.

FIGURE 3.7 Ecological Influences on Development

Photo: Krista Greco / Merrill

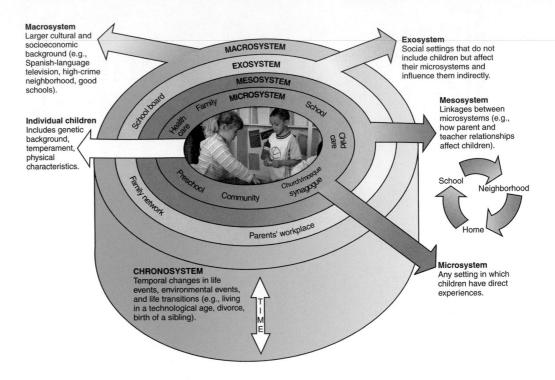

Macrosystem
Larger cultural and socioeconomic background (e.g., Spanish-language television, high-crime neighborhood, good schools).

Individual children
Includes genetic background, temperament, physical characteristics.

Exosystem
Social settings that do not include children but affect their microsystems and influence them indirectly.

Mesosystem
Linkages between microsystems (e.g., how parent and teacher relationships affect children).

Microsystem
Any setting in which children have direct experiences.

CHRONOSYSTEM
Temporal changes in life events, environmental events, and life transitions (e.g., living in a technological age, divorce, birth of a sibling).

TIME

Anthony Magnacca / Merrill

According to Gardner's theory of multiple intelligences, children demonstrate many types of intelligences. How would you apply his theory in the early childhood environment?

school performance. Likewise, school support for family literacy will influence the extent to which families value literacy.

The **exosystem** is the environmental system that encompasses those events with which children do not have direct interaction but which nonetheless influence them. For example, when school boards enact a policy that ends social promotion, this action can and will influence children's development. And when a parent's workplace mandates increased work time (e.g., a ten-hour workday), this may decrease parent–child involvement, which influences development.

The **macrosystem** includes the culture, customs, and values of society in general. For example, contemporary societal violence and media violence influence children's development. Many children are becoming more violent, and many children are fearful of and threatened by violence.

The **chronosystem** includes environmental influences over time and the ways they impact development and behavior. For example, today's children are technologically adept and are comfortable using technology for education and entertainment. In addition, we have already referred to how the large-scale entry of mothers into the workforce has changed family life.

Clearly, there are many influences on children's development. Currently there is a lot of interest in how these influences shape children's lives and what parents and educators can do to enhance positive influences and minimize or eliminate negative environmental influences as well as negative social interactions.

Howard Gardner and Multiple Intelligence Theory

Howard Gardner (b. 1943) has played an important role in helping educators rethink the concept of intelligence. Rather than relying on a single definition of intelligence, Gardner's philosophy of **multiple intelligences** suggests that people can be "smart" in many ways.

Gardner has identified nine intelligences: visual/spatial, verbal/linguistic, mathematical/logical, bodily/kinesthetic, musical/rhythmic, intrapersonal, interpersonal, naturalist, and existentialist. Gardner's view of intelligence and its multiple components has and will undoubtedly continue to influence educational thought and practice. Review Figure 3.8 to learn more about these nine intelligences and how to apply them to your teaching.

Read about designing learning experiences that combine children's multiple intelligences at Articles and Readings, Child Development, Module 7: Intelligence, Article 2: Orchestrating Multiple Intelligences.

Visual/Spatial	Children who learn best visually and who organize things spatially. They like to see what you are talking about in order to understand. They enjoy charts, graphs, maps, tables, illustrations, art, puzzles, costumes—anything eye catching.
Verbal/Linguistic	Children who demonstrate strength in the language arts: speaking, writing, reading, listening. These students have always been successful in traditional classrooms because their intelligence lends itself to traditional teaching.
Mathematical/Logical	Children who display an aptitude for numbers, reasoning, and problem solving. This is the other half of children who typically do well in traditional classrooms where teaching is logically sequenced and students are asked to conform.
Bodily/Kinesthetic	Children who experience learning best through activity: games, movement, hands-on tasks, building. These children were often labeled "overly active" in traditional classrooms where they were told to sit and be still!
Musical/Rhythmic	Children who learn well through songs, patterns, rhythms, instruments, and musical expression. It is easy to overlook children with this intelligence in traditional education.
Intrapersonal	Children who are especially in touch with their own feelings, values, and ideas. They may tend to be more reserved, but they are actually quite intuitive about what they learn and how it relates to themselves.
Interpersonal	Children who are noticeably people oriented and outgoing, and do their learning cooperatively in groups or with a partner. These children may have typically been identified as "talkative" or "too concerned about being social" in a traditional setting.
Naturalist	Children who love the outdoors, animals, and field trips. More than this, though, these students love to pick up on subtle differences in meaning. The traditional classroom has not been accommodating to these children.
Existentialist	Children who learn in the context of where humankind stands in the "big picture" of existence. They ask "Why are we here?" and "What is our role in the world?" This intelligence is seen in the discipline of philosophy.

FIGURE 3.8 Gardner's Nine Intelligences

Source: Reprinted with permission from Walter McKenzie, *Multiple Intelligences Overview.* [Online.] Available at http://www.surfaquarium.com.

An "Educational History" Lesson

Laura Bilbro-Berry
Second grade teacher
Director of Federal Programs Beaufort County Schools
Washington, North Carolina

When I think about the history of the teaching profession and how I have integrated it into my teaching, I remember an occasion when I shared with my students the delightful picture book, *My Great Aunt Arizona,* by Gloria Houston. The book's main character is a teacher who inspired children in the days of the one-room schoolhouse. The illustrations by Susan Condie Lamb that accompany the text clearly depict daily classroom life in the past.

While reading the story to my second-grade students, I turned the page to a description and illustration of an actual one-room class. When I read that the teacher taught children from multiple grade levels at the same time, my students were amazed. One child said, "You mean the teacher taught every grade all the time. Boy! I bet she was tired." I agreed that teacher, indeed, would have had a hard time teaching the younger and older children simultaneously.

Another child commented on the illustration of the classroom with its orderly rows of benches: "Where are the computers and shelves of math toys and books?" I explained that computers were not yet invented and that the manipulatives we use to learn were unheard of in those days. I also explained that books were very precious because they were so expensive and scarce. A classroom would not have anywhere near the books we have in our present-day classroom. The same child exclaimed, "Well, I sure am glad that I don't have to go to a school like that! How do they learn *anything* without computers?"

All of my students agreed that our classroom today was much better than that of the past. During this discussion, one child raised his hand and wanted to know what "that black box" in the middle of the room was. I explained to him that it was a wood stove that was used to heat the classroom, and that the teacher was responsible for making sure the stove had enough wood or coal to keep the room warm. I also shared that the teacher had to make sure the room was swept up and cleaned every day. The child who commented couldn't believe that the teacher had to be responsible for all those things. He asked, "Where was the custodian to do all that?" I had to explain that in a one-room schoolhouse there was only the teacher and the students—no computer, no math toys, and no custodian.

I was very pleased that the children were spontaneously asking the "right" questions. Not only were they listening and discussing an outstanding piece of literature, but also they were learning about the history of education. We were definitely enjoying a "teachable moment." I continued reading the story and sharing the illustrations. After a few pages, one student raised his hand and asked, "How come all the children are white?"

What great timing! Here was another chance for me to share about the history of schooling in the United States. I explained to my students that at the time when the story was to have taken place, African American children normally didn't go to school. If they did, they went to a separate school. My students were truly shocked. They wanted to know why the African American students couldn't go to the same school as white kids. As tactfully as I could, I explained that in the past some people felt that African Americans and white people should not be together anywhere.

One wonderfully outspoken student put her hands on her hips and said, "Well, that's just about the stupidest thing I've ever heard of!" The old adage "out of the mouths of babes..." immediately came to mind. I stopped at this point and shared with the children how much things have changed since the time in which this story was framed. I used this aspect of the story to encourage some Internet research about segregation and integration that afternoon. The group also created a Venn diagram comparing schools of the present day to schools of the past.

I certainly never imagined the direction this simple story session would take my class and me when I was preparing my lesson plan for that day. I can honestly say that this was one of the finest discussions I've ever experienced in all my years of teaching. The *knowledge* gained for both the class *and* the teacher were well worth the detour.

....
Laura Bilbro-Berry is a North Carolina Teacher of the Year.

 Complete an activity to place into your Professional Development Notebook at http://www.prenhall.com/morrison, Chapter 3—Projects: Professionalism in Practice.

Many people have influenced and changed the course of early childhood education. That process continues today. Part of your role as an early childhood professional is to stay up to date, be open to ideas and practices, and inspire children. And speaking of inspiring children, read the Professionalism in Practice about how one teacher used a history lesson from the past to inspire her children.

FROM LUTHER TO TODAY: BASIC CONCEPTS ESSENTIAL TO GOOD EDUCATIONAL PRACTICES

As They Relate to Children

- Everyone needs to learn how to read and write.
- Children learn best when they use all their senses.
- All children are capable of being educated.
- All children should be educated to the fullest extent of their abilities.
- Education should begin early in life. Today especially there is an increased emphasis on beginning education at birth.
- Children should be appropriately taught what they are ready to learn when they are ready to learn it and should be prepared for the next stage of learning.
- Learning activities should be interesting and meaningful.
- Social interactions with teachers and peers are a necessary part of development and learning.
- All children have many ways of knowing, learning, and relating to the world.

As They Relate to Teachers

- Teachers should love and respect all children, have high expectations for them, and teach them to their highest capacities.
- Teachers should be dedicated to the teaching profession.
- Good teaching is based on a theory, a philosophy, goals, and objectives.
- Children's learning is enhanced through the use of concrete materials.
- Teaching should move from the concrete to the abstract.
- Observation is a key way to determine children's needs.
- Teaching should be a planned, systematic process.
- Teaching should be centered on children rather than adults or subjects.
- Teaching should be based on children's interests.
- Teaching should collaborate with children as a means of promoting development.
- Teachers should plan so they incorporate all types of intelligence in their planning and activities.

As They Relate to Parents

- The family is the most important institution in children's education and development. The family lays the foundation for all future education and learning.
- Parents are their children's primary educators; they are their children's first teachers. However, parents need help, education, and support to achieve this goal.
- Parents must guide and direct young children's learning.
- Parents should be involved in every educational program their children are involved in.
- Everyone should have knowledge of and training for child rearing.
- Parents and other family members are collaborators in children's learning.
- Parents must encourage and support their children's many interests and their unique ways of learning (see the Technology Tie-In feature).

Since the beginning of the recorded history of early childhood education, music and the arts have had an important place in the education of young children. Educators have supported children's involvement in music and the arts in three ways: appreciation, performance, and creation. You and I may not agree on the kind of music and art we like, but one thing is certain: We all like music and the arts of some kind, and they all affect us in some way. The same is true for children. I have not met a child who does not like to sing, dance, paint, and create.

Aristotle believed that art and drama were good for people because through them they were able to work out their emotions vicariously and as a result be calmer and better persons. Maria Montessori believed that children should be involved in learning about art and artists. Art appreciation is part of the Montessori curriculum and many Montessori classrooms have paintings by famous artists on display. We have read in this chapter about the high value Abraham Maslow places on creativity and the importance of creating aesthetically pleasing classrooms for young children. Some early childhood programs provide keyboard lessons and experiences for all children based on the link some research shows between learning music and high academic achievement. You can involve your children in music and the arts in many ways as appreciators, performers, and creators. All early childhood programs should involve all children in the arts. Research studies have shown that students who listen to music have higher spatial scores on intelligence tests. Spatial intelligence is the ability to form mental images of physical objects and is a critical cognitive ability in young children.* The following software suggestions are just one avenue you can use to encourage and support your children's fine arts skills:

Curious George Paint & Print Studio (ages 4–9), Sunburst Technology
Draw & Paint Plus (ages 4–9), Forest Technologies
JumpStart Music (ages 5–8) Knowledge Adventure
Kid Works Deluxe (ages 4–9), Knowledge Adventure
Reader Rabbit Toddler (ages 2–4), The Learning Company
Create and Draw in Elmo's World (ages 4–9), Sesame Street

The following Web pages are for children to enhance and support their fine art skills:

http://www.kids-space.org/HPT/
http://datadragon.com/education/reading/
http://www.guitarlessonworld.com/exercises/index.html
http://webpages.marshall.edu/~ibanez2/disney.html
http://www.childrensmusic.org/
http://www.unclefred.com
http://sunsite.berkeley.edu/KidsClickl/topfine.html
http://www.creatingmusic.com

The following Web pages are resources for you to encourage and support your children's fine arts skills. On these pages, you will find several links to other helpful sites.

http://www.kn.pacbell.com/wired/fil
http://www.cln.org/lists/nuggets/art_mus.html

*Joyce Kelstorm, "Music's Effect on Academic Achievement," June 2006, http://www.agehr.org/overtone/otarticle050606.asp.

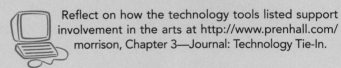

Reflect on how the technology tools listed support involvement in the arts at http://www.prenhall.com/morrison, Chapter 3—Journal: Technology Tie-In.

Throughout history all great educators have had a vision about what is best for young children and their families. Great educators are passionate about what they believe about children and how to best teach them what they need to know to be productive and involved citizens. The same is true today. Many educators, professional organizations, and politicians are passionately advocating for what they think are worthy goals and the best practices to achieve these goals. But how to do this is at the heart of many educational debates today. As a practicing professional you will be involved in these debates. You will be asked to identify ideas and theories that will help all children be successful in school and life. Knowing the history of your profession and the theories that guide approaches to education will help you in this critical part of your professional practice. See Table 3.2 for a summary of these theories.

TABLE 3.2 Learning Theories That Influence Early Childhood Education

Individual and Dates	Major Contributions	Influences on Modern Education
Maria Montessori (1870–1952)	• The Montessori Method for educating young children. • Learning materials to meet the needs of young children. • Sensory-based materials that are self-correcting. • Prepared environments are essential for learning. • Respect for children is the foundation of teaching.	• Large number of public and private Montessori schools that emphasize her approach, methods, and materials. • Renewed emphasis on preparing environment to support and promote children's learning. • Teacher training programs to train Montessori teachers.
John Dewey (1859–1952)	• Progressive education movement. • Children's interests form the basis of the curriculum. • Educate children for today—not tomorrow.	• Child-centered education. • Curriculum based on children's interests. • Discovery learning.
Jean Piaget (1896–1980)	• Theory of cognitive development based on ages and stages. • Children are "little scientists" and literally develop their own intelligence. • Mental and physical activities are important for cognitive development.	• Constructivist approaches to early childhood education. • Matching education to children's stages of cognitive development. • Active involvement of children in learning. activities. • Project approach to learning.
Lev Vygotsky (1896–1934)	• Sociocultural theory, which emphasizes importance of interpersonal relationships in social and cognitive development. • Concept of zone proximal development—children can learn more with the help of a more competent person. • Communication between teachers and children can act as a means of scaffolding to higher levels of learning.	• Use of scaffolding techniques to help children learn. • Use of cooperative learning and other forms of social learning.
Abraham Maslow (1908–1970)	• Theory of self-actualization based on needs motivation. • Human development is a process of meeting basic needs throughout life. • Humanistic psychology.	• Importance of meeting basic needs before cognitive learning can occur. • Teachers develop programs to meet children's basic needs. • Growth of the self-esteem movement. • Emphasis on providing safety, security, love, and affection for all children.
Erik Erikson (1902–1994)	• Theory of psychosocial development—cognitive development occurs in conjunction with social development. • Life is a series of eight stages with each stage representing a critical period in social development. • How parents and teachers interact with and care for children helps determine their emotional and cognitive development.	• Play supports children's social and cognitive development. • The emotional plays as great a role as the cognitive in development. • All children need predictable, consistent love, care, and education.

(continued)

TABLE 3.2 *continued*

Individual and Dates	Major Contributions	Influences on Modern Education
Urie Bronfenbrenner (1917–2005)	• Ecological systems theory views the child as developing within a system of relationships. • Five interrelating systems—microsystem, mesosystem, exosystem, macrosystem, and chronosystem—have a powerful impact on development. • Each system influences and is influenced by the other. • Development is influenced by children and their environments.	• Teachers are more aware of how different environments shape children's lives in different ways. • Parents and educators strive to provide positive influences in each system and minimize or eliminate negative influences. • Teachers and parents recognize that children's development depends on children's natures and their environments.
Howard Gardner (b. 1943)	• Theory of multiple intelligences. • Intelligence consists of nine abilities. • Intelligence is not a single broad ability, but rather a set of abilities.	• Teachers develop programs and curricula to match children's particular intelligences. • Teacher individualizes curricula and approaches to children's intelligences. • More awareness and attention to multiple ways in which children learn and think.

ACTIVITIES FOR PROFESSIONAL DEVELOPMENT

Ethical Dilemma

"Why Don't My Kids Get Their Fair Share?"

Latisha is a novice first-grade teacher in Rocky Springs School District. Her class of twenty-eight students includes fifteen Hispanic students, nine African American students, and four Vietnamese students. Latisha's room is sparsely furnished, many of the tables and chairs need repair, and the classroom library of thirty-seven books is old and worn. Last week at an orientation for pre-K–3 teachers held across town at the new elementary school, Latisha learned that the students there are 90 percent white and class size averages nineteen. A tour of the classrooms revealed the latest in furniture, learning materials, and technology with well-stocked classroom libraries. Latisha is concerned about the unequal distribution of resources in the school district, and she feels her children are not getting their fair share.

What should Latisha do? Should she just keep quiet and hope things get better; should she advocate for her children by getting a group of her colleagues together and sharing her concerns with them, or should she take some other course of action?

Application Activities

1. From John Dewey to the present, early childhood professionals have used children's interests as a basis for developing learning activities. In addition to being a good source of learning experiences, interests can also provide opportunities to develop skills and teach important information.

    a. Talk with some young children about what they like to do, their favorite activities, favorite television programs, and so on. Select several of these "interests" and plan three learning experiences you can use to teach skills related to literacy, math, and science.

b. Do you think it is possible to base your entire curriculum and teaching activities on children's interests? Why or why not?

2. Throughout the history of education, great educators have been concerned with what they believed was best for children; how best to teach them; and what it is worthwhile for children to know and be able to do.

   a. Based on the ideas and practices proposed by the educators discussed in this chapter, identify the teaching practices with which you most agree. State the learning outcomes you think are appropriate for all children.

   b. Review the curriculum goals and standards for the pre-K–3 grades in your local school district. Can you find examples to support that what educators identify as important knowledge and skills are substantiated by beliefs of great educators?

3. Think for a minute what would happen if you gave six-month-old Emily some blocks. What would she try to do with them? More than likely she would put them in her mouth. She wants to eat the blocks. However, if you gave blocks to Emily's three-year-old sister Madeline, she would try to stack them. Both Emily and Madeline want to be actively involved with things and people as active learners. This active involvement comes naturally for them. Observe children in a number of early childhood settings and identify five ways they learn through active learning.

4. You have just been assigned to write a brief historical summary of the major ideas of the educational pioneers you read about in this chapter. You are limited to fifty words for each person and are to write as though you were the person. For example:

Locke: "At birth the mind is a blank slate and experiences are important for making impressions on the mind. I believe learning occurs best through the senses. A proper education begins early in life and hands-on experiences are an important part of education."

To take online practice tests on this chapter's material, go to the Companion Website at http://www.prenhall.com/morrison, select Chapter 3, and then choose the Multiple Choice or the Essay module. For additional Web resources, choose Web Links.

4

IMPLEMENTING EARLY CHILDHOOD PROGRAMS

Applying Theories to Practice

professional development goal

Delivering Education and Child Care

A. I am familiar with a variety of programs and curricula for delivering education and child care. I use this knowledge to deliver education and child care in a safe, healthy learning environment.

B. I know, understand, and use a wide array of effective approaches, strategies, and tools to positively influence children's development and learning.

C. I use my knowledge and other resources to design, implement, and evaluate meaningful, challenging curriculum that promotes comprehensive developmental and learning outcomes for all young children.[1]

focus questions

1. Why are programs of early childhood education important?

2. What are the basic features of early childhood education programs, and how are they alike and different?

3. What decisions do you need to make to select challenging curricula and programs as a basis for your practice?

4. How can you apply developmentally appropriate practice to your practice of early childhood education?

WHAT ARE EARLY CHILDHOOD EDUCATION PROGRAMS?

When we talk about programs for young children, we mean the philosophy that guides our teaching and learning, the theories that underlie what we teach and how children learn, and the curricula that we select to guide the activities and experiences provided for children. Some teachers and administrators adopt a well-recognized program such as Montessori as the basis for their school or classroom. Others use an *eclectic* approach in which they integrate the best from a number of programs into their own unique approach to educating young children. High-quality early childhood teachers think seriously about what they want their children to learn and be able to do and how best to achieve these goals. They make decisions based on their knowledge and understanding of various programs and how the basic features agree with their philosophies of teaching and learning. As we discuss in Chapter 5, current state and local standards specify what pre-K–3 children will learn. Many programs incorporate these standards into their curriculum. Regardless of the approach you select to use as a basis for your program, the majority of early childhood professionals agree that the environment and teaching practices should be child centered. The accompanying Program in Action feature provides you with nine guidelines for ensuring that the environment and curricula of your program are child centered.

The Growing Demand for Quality Early Childhood Programs

Through 2004, the National Association for the Education of Young Children (NAEYC) accredited. 9,273 high-quality early childhood programs serving 800,000 children.[2] These programs are only a fraction of the total number of early childhood programs in the United States. Think for a minute about what goes on in these and other programs from day to day. For some children, teachers and staff have developed well-thought-out and articulated programs that provide for their growth and development across all the developmental domains—cognitive, linguistic, emotional, social, and physical. This should be the goal of programs. Today, the United States is once again discovering the importance of the early years. As a result, the public wants early childhood professionals to provide the following:

- Programs to ensure children's early school success and enable them to succeed in school and life. The public believes that too many children are being left out and left behind.[3]
- The inclusion of early literacy and reading readiness activities in programs and curricula that will enable children to read on grade level in grades one, two, and three.[4]

COMPETENCY BUILDER

The City & Country School, founded by Caroline Pratt in 1914, is located in the Greenwich Village district of New York City. It has a current enrollment of 250 students between the ages of two and thirteen and is an example of a progressive school that continues to educate children using the curriculum structure that was set forth over eighty years ago: "giving children experiences and materials that will fit their stage of development and have inherent in them unlimited opportunities for learning." Pratt, a teacher, sought to provide a school environment that suited the way children learn best—by doing.

BASIC VALUES OF A CHILD-CENTERED APPROACH

The essence of City & Country's philosophy is faith in children and their desire to learn. When we trust this truly child-centered ideal and set

about developing materials, experiences, and environments that foster and guide it, we remain true to Miss Pratt's work. Adults must constantly be open to learn from the children they teach and must be sensitive to their needs and experiences.

- What are the children interested in?
- What is going on in their environment that interests them and is relevant to their lives?

OPEN-ENDED MATERIALS AND METHODS

It is City & Country School's belief that an early childhood curriculum based on open-ended materials and methods fosters independence, motivation, and interest, all essential components of learning. The younger groups (ages two through seven) use basic, open-ended materials to reconstruct what they are learning about the world and to organize their information and thinking in meaningful ways. Materials such as blocks, clay, water, paint, and wood are chosen because of their simplicity, flexibility, and the challenging possibilities that they offer. Children are encouraged to work out problems among themselves, with help from the teacher only when absolutely necessary.

Children move naturally into the more academic tasks as they need to find out more about what they're already doing. The three Rs are viewed as useful tools to further a child's education, not as ends in themselves; but in no way did Pratt, nor do we, undervalue their importance. In fact, every possible method is used to empower all children with the crucial skill of reading. It can be a natural process for many, but others require extra directed instruction.

THE JOBS PROGRAM

The Lower School curriculum provides a firm foundation for the more formal academic skills that children must master in later years. The Jobs Program was developed to play this central role for students ages eight through thirteen. Each group of students has a specific job to perform that is related

- Programs that will help children develop the social and behavioral skills necessary to help them lead civilized and nonviolent lives. In the wake of September 11, 2001, and daily news headlines about shooting and assaults by younger and younger children, the public wants early childhood programs to assume an ever growing responsibility for helping get children off to a nonviolent start in life.[5]

As you read about and reflect on the programs in this chapter, think about the ways each tries to best meet the needs of children and families and the previously noted goals. Pause for a minute and review Table 4.1, which outlines the programs of early childhood education discussed in this chapter.

CHILD CARE: SERVING CHILDREN AND FAMILIES

Child care is assuming an increasingly prominent role in the American education system. It is part of the seamless system of providing for the nation's children and youth that begins at birth and continues through high school and beyond. For this important reason, it is included in this chapter.

to the school's functioning as an integrated community. These jobs provide both a natural impetus for perfecting skills in reading, writing, spelling, and mathematics and a relevant framework for the exploration of social studies and the arts.

Beyond their work with blocks and jobs, children at City & Country are given opportunities to experience art, music, dramatics, foreign languages, science, computers, and woodworking, often integrated with their classroom work.

GUIDELINES FOR A CHILD-CENTERED PROGRAM

Even though children learn naturally, teachers should arrange and manage the classroom environment to stimulate that learning. The following guidelines promote active, independent learning:

GUIDELINE 1 Arrange the classroom to support child-centered learning.

GUIDELINE 2 Provide easily accessible materials and supplies.

GUIDELINE 3 Provide opportunities for chilren to move around and engage in active learning.

GUIDELINE 4 Provide materials and space for hands-on activities.

GUIDELINE 5 Arrange learning centers and desks so that children can work and play together.

GUIDELINE 6 Support cooperative learning.

GUIDELINE 7 Provide for individual differences and individualized instruction.

GUIDELINE 8 Incorporate project-based activities.

GUIDELINE 9 Provide ample time for children to engage in projects and other cooperative activities.

City & Country School remains committed to its founding principles and will continue to promote and exemplify child-centered education.

....

Contributed by Kate Turley, Principal, City & Country School. Photos courtesy of City & Country School.

Complete an activity on implementing child-centered classroom strategies at http://www.prenhall.com/morrison, Chapter 4: Journal—Program in Action.

Child care is a comprehensive service to children and families that supplements the care and education children receive from their families. Comprehensive child care includes safety, nutrition, love and affection, and activities and experiences to support children's social, emotional, and academic development.

Child care is educational. It provides for the children's cognitive development and helps engage them in the process of learning that begins at birth. Quality child care does not ignore the educational needs of young children but incorporates learning activities as part of the curriculum. Futhermore, child care staff work with parents to help them learn how to support children's learning in the home. A comprehensive view of child care considers the child to be a whole person; therefore, the major purpose of child care is to facilitate optimum development of the whole child and support efforts to achieve this goal.

The Importance of Child Care   A

Child care is popular and important for a number of reasons. First, recent demographic changes have created a high demand for care outside the home. There are more dual-income families and more working single parents than ever before. For example, over

TABLE 4.1 Comparing Early Childhood Programs

Program	Main Features	Teacher's Role
Child Care	• Provides comprehensive health, social, and education services. • Program quality determined by each program. • Each program has its own curriculum.	• Provides care and education for the whole child. • Provides a safe and secure environment. • Collaborates with and involve families.
High/Scope	• Theory is based on Piaget, constructivism, Dewey, and Vygotsky. • Plan–do–review is the teaching–learning cycle. • Emergent curriculum is not planned in advance. • Children help determine curriculum. • Key experiences guide the curriculum in promoting children's active learning.	• Plans activities based on children's interests. • Facilitates learning through encouragement.* • Engages in positive adult–child interaction strategies.*
Montessori	• Theoretical basis is the philosophy and beliefs of Maria Montessori. • Prepared environment supports, invites, and enables learning. • Children educate themselves—self-directed learning. • Sensory materials invite and promote learning. • Has a set curriculum regarding what children should learn. Montessorians try to stay as close to Montessori's ideas as possible. • Children are grouped in multiage environments. • Children learn by manipulating materials and working with others. • Learning takes place through the senses.	• Follows the child's interests and needs. • Prepares an environment that is educationally interesting and safe.* • Directs unobtrusively as children individually or in small groups engage in self-directed activity.* • Observes, analyzes, and provides materials and activities appropriate for the child's sensitive periods of learning.* • Maintains regular communications with the parent.
Reggio Emilia	• Theory is based on Piaget, constructivism, Vygotsky, and Dewey. • Emergent curriculum is not planned in advance. • Curriculum is based on children's interests and experiences. • Curriculum is project oriented. • Hundred Languages of Children represents the symbolic representation of children's work and learning. • Learning is active. • Atelierista—a special teacher is trained in the arts. • Atelier—an art/design studio is used by children and teachers.	• Works collaboratively with other teachers. • Organizes environments rich in possibilities and provocations.* • Acts as recorder for the children, helping them trace and revisit their words and actions.*
Waldorf	• Theoretical basis is the philosophy and beliefs of Rudolf Steiner. • The whole child—head, heart, and hands—is educated. • The arts are integrated into all curriculum areas. • Study of myths, lores, and fairy tales promotes the imagination and multiculturalism. • Main-lesson teacher stays with the same class from childhood to adolescence. • Learning is by doing—making and doing.	• Acts as a role model exhibiting the values of the Waldorf school. • Provides an intimate classroom atmosphere full of themes about caring for the community and for the natural and living world.* • Encourages children's natural sense of wonder, belief in goodness, and love of beauty.* • Creates a love of learning in each child.

Program	Main Features	Teacher's Role
	• Learning is noncompetitive. • The developmental phases of each child are followed.	
Head Start	• Federally sponsored and funded early childhood program. • Programs must comply with federal performance standards and standards of learning. • Comprehensive approach to educating the whole child. • Comprehensive services approach including including health and nutrition. • Comprehensive program designed to strengthen familes. • Involves families and the community in delivery of program.	• Teach to and provide for all children's developmental areas—social, emotional, physical, and cognitive. • Provide programs for children that support their socioeconomic, cultural, and individual needs in developmentally appropriate ways. • Involve families and the community in all parts of the program.

*Information from C. Edwards, "Three Approaches from Europe: Waldorf, Montessori, and Reggio Emilia," *Early Childhood Research & Practice 4*, 1, 2002, http://ecrp.uiuc.edu/v4n1/edwards.html.

70 percent of mothers with children under age three are employed, and it is not uncommon for mothers to return to work as early as six weeks after giving birth.[6]

Second, child care is viewed as a critical early intervention program for both children and families. High-quality early child care promotes preacademic skills and readiness, enhanced language performance, and increased positive developmental outcomes. Thus, child care plays a vital role in the health, welfare, and general social and academic well-being of the nation's children.

As demand for child care increases, you and your colleagues must participate in advocating for and creating high-quality child care programs that meet the needs of children and families. In the Professionalism in Practice feature on page 92, Jackye Brown, executive director of Atlanta's Children's Shelter, discusses her commitment to helping homeless children and their families.

Krista Greco / Merrill

Types of Child Care Programs

Child care is offered in many places, by many persons and agencies that provide a variety of care and services. The options for child care are almost endless. However, regardless of the kinds of child care provided, the three issues of quality, affordability, and accessibility are always part of child care delivery of services. Table 4.2 outlines the types of child care, their purposes, and their functions. Review the eight kinds of child care and compare their similarities and differences. Reflect on why there are so many different kinds of programs. Do you think parents in the United States would be best served by only one kind of child care program?

The Program in Action feature, Magnia Child Care, on pages 94–95 will help you envision how good family child care is much more than babysitting. As you read, consider if you would want your child placed in this program.

For-profit child care is one of the fastest growing types of child care. As the name implies, for-profit child care is operated by individuals and companies to make a

Family child care is the preferred method of child care for many parents. Parents like a program for their children that approximates a home-like setting. What are some characteristics of a home-like setting you can incorporate into your classroom?

The Atlanta Children's Shelter, Inc. (ACS), is a nonprofit agency that provides a safe, caring, developmentally appropriate environment for homeless children during the day. My beliefs are grounded in my seventeen years of working with children and their families. My most basic belief is that all children can learn. This core belief guides all that I do. Believing in children's ability to learn is essential, especially when you provide services for homeless children.

The shelter is a model agency whose programs are oriented around (1) the care of children, (2) support of families, and (3) advocacy and networking. Our developmentally appropriate early childhood curriculum was originally published in 1992 and modified in 2005 to address the changing nature of the group of children served due to daily fluctuations in enrollment—and the variable and sometimes brief duration of the children's enrollment. It provides techniques for modifying classroom activities to an ever-changing group of children. A highlighted synopsis of the adaptations or accommodations for homelessness as it relates to our program is also included throughout the document.

The children we teach and care for are from unstable situations. They don't have a home to go to every day, so our program is their "home" while they are here. Our environment must foster the social, emotional, physical, cognitive, and language skills that are so vital for all children, but especially for homeless children. It is critical for us to help homeless children cope with their negative experiences so they can gain a positive outlook on life, have positive experiences, and develop to their fullest potential. We really care about our children, and this commitment to caring is important because of the trauma that our children and families have undergone. Teachers plan activities that are no longer a part of the child's life due to homelessness, including:

- Daily story reading,
- Cooking,
- Gardening,
- Shopping, and
- Field trips.

When people ask me why our program is so successful, I always respond that it is because we are uncompromising about certain basic core values, including quality, advocacy, and parent and community collaboration.

No program can or should sacrifice quality for young children. One way we address the quality issue is through NAEYC accreditation. Another is through seeing how we can better use our space so that we can provide enriched environments for young children. For example, it is important to provide some space in the classroom for preschoolers as their own personal space. There is often little sense of security or permanence in night shelters. The space provided in the classroom may be only an individual cubby for storage of their belongings, or the same spot each day for their cot at naptime, but it will make a child feel more secure and important. In the Infant Room, cribs are assigned and labeled so that babies sleep in the same place each day for health reasons and to help them develop a sense of security. Except for very young infants and sleeping babies, children should spend little time in cribs. They should be cuddled or free to interact with their caregivers and their

profit. The top ten for-profit child care centers in the United States are identified in Figure 4.1. They and others like them represent the booming entrepreneurial nature of child care. Indeed, you may spend some or all of your professional career in such programs.

What Constitutes Quality Education and Care?

Although there is much debate about the quality of child care and what it involves, we can nonetheless identify the main characteristics of quality programs. The dimensions and indicators of quality child care are outlined in Table 4.3. Of the ten components of quality listed, which do you think are the most important? Which of these do you think would be easiest or most difficult to advocate for?

The Effects of Care and Education on Children

Recent research reveals that high-quality early care and education have influences that last a lifetime. A valuable source of research about child care comes from the Study of Early Child Care and Youth Development (SECC) by the National Institute of Child Health and Human Development (NICHD). The SECC is a comprehensive longitudinal study

environment. Homeless children especially need this nurture and attention, and the opportunity to explore safely.

Our work with parents is as important as our work with children. Parents want to see their children do well in school and life. We serve a unique population. The parents are going through a traumatic time. They are homeless and many are battered women who are fleeing a violent situation. The role of the staff is to facilitate the parents' efforts to become independent, self-supporting, and effective in their parental roles. The goal of these efforts is to move from homelessness to self-sufficiency. Parents are provided comprehensive social services and are able to receive peer support from other families in crisis. Through our on-site services and community partnerships, parents receive individual, group, and family counseling; housing, financial, medical, legal, and credit counseling; and job readiness and employment assistance. Our Job Track Employment Program provides a centralized location where parents can achieve job readiness through skill assessment, job counseling, job search assistance, résumé development, and voice mailboxes to follow up on job leads. Our Aftercare Services Program guides formerly homeless families through their first year in their new homes, ensuring that no unexpected events hinder the family transition to post-homeless stabilization.

All early childhood programs, regardless of the clientele they serve, must have community partnerships to be successful. Part of our ongoing strategic plan is to develop ways that we can partner and collaborate with parents and the community. Recognizing that only through collaboration and partnerships with other service providers can we begin to address the depth of need our clients bring, ACS attempts to maintain and strengthen its collaborative relationships on an ongoing basis. This includes:

- Community advanced practice nurses—on-site medical care for children,
- Georgia Law Center for the Homeless—legal assistance for parents,
- Metro Atlanta Furniture Bank—household furniture for families,
- Atlanta Enterprise Center—job training and computer labs,
- Consumer Credit Counseling Service—credit checks, budget counseling, and
- Jefferson Place Transitional Program—resettlement rent assistance.

These partnerships help to improve the effectiveness and efficiency of services to our clients.

I make a special effort to work with and nurture our teachers. It is quite an adjustment for new teachers to acclimate to our population. We need teachers who can be consistent in their approach and who won't blame parents. They have to understand parents' situations. The parents are dealing with a whole lot of other things. To put it in terms of Maslow's hierarchy of needs, basic needs come first.

I am committed to seeing homeless children grow and develop. When I am having a down day, I go to the infant room and feed a baby or read a book to a toddler and I'm rejuvenated. Helping children and families is all the reward anyone needs in life.

Contributed by Dr. Jackye Brown, executive director, Atlanta Children's Shelter, Atlanta, Georgia.

 Explore issues in early childhood and your role as an advocate for young children at http://www.prenhall.com/morrison, Chapter 4—Projects: Professionalism in Practice.

initiated by NICHD in 1989 to answer the many questions about the relationship between child care experiences and characteristics and children's developmental outcomes. In 1991 the NICHD researchers enrolled 1,364 children from birth to age three in the study and conducted Phase I from 1991 to 1994. In Phase II, from 1995 to 2000, they followed the 1,226 children who continued to participate through their third year in school. Phase III of the study is currently being conducted to follow more than 1,100 of the children through their sixth year in school.[7] Figure 4.2 lists some of the study's findings on the use of child care and its effects on children and families. The study results make it clear that professionals must provide high-quality programs and must advocate for that high quality with the public and state legislators.

 Observe children engaging in the plan–do–review learning process, and identify the main aspects of the High/Scope curriculum at Video Classroom, Early Childhood Education, Module 4: Curriculum Planning and Programs, Video 4: High/Scope.

HIGH/SCOPE: A CONSTRUCTIVIST MODEL

The **High/Scope educational model** is based on Piaget's cognitive development theory. The curriculum is geared to the child's current stage of development and promotes the constructive processes of learning and broadens the child's emerging intellectual and social skills.[8]

I have been in the field of early care and education as a licensed family child care provider for sixteen years. My husband and I operate our program in our home. Magnia Child Care is accredited through the National Association for Family Child Care (NAFCC) and serves the needs of families with children from birth through age five. We are licensed for fourteen children and currently have eight enrolled. Because of the quality of our program, we are a training site for child development students from the local community college. As an Early Childhood Mentor Teacher—a program in California that pairs early childhood college students with experienced teachers in the field—I supervise these college students and offer first-hand experiences working with young children.

WHAT IS FAMILY CHILD CARE?

Family child care is the care of children in the provider's home. The provider must meet the necessary state and local licensing requirements, as well as health and safety standards. Family child care offers several benefits to parents that are not necessarily available in other early care settings:

- Smaller ratio of children to adults;
- Mixed-age groups of children, allowing siblings to be together;
- Consistent primary caregivers;
- Flexibility to meet the needs of families; and
- The nurturing environment of a home.

AN APPROPRIATE PROGRAM FOR ALL CHILDREN

At Magnia Child Care, we believe that our primary responsibilities include the following:

- Meeting the physical and emotional needs of children,
- Maintaining a safe and healthy environment,
- Supporting the parent-caregiver relationship,
- Performing administrative tasks, and
- Continuing our professional growth and education.

Because our program serves infants, toddlers, and preschool children, we offer a developmentally appropriate curriculum based on NAFCC guidelines. Along with planned activities for language and literacy, dramatic play, music and movement, and outdoor experiences, we also respect a child's ability to learn through self-discovery. Children in our program learn about science through their experiences with sand and water. They learn mathematics through the one-to-one ratio as they help pass out spoons or cups for lunchtime.

Counting freshly picked avocados with center owner Albert Magnia provides an authentic learning experience for young children.

Firm, smooth avocados are new to this child and worthy of the intense investigation that stimulates cognitive development.

High/Scope has three fundamental principles:

- Active participation of children in choosing, organizing, and evaluating learning activities, which are undertaken with careful teacher observation and guidance in a learning environment replete with a rich variety of materials located in various classroom learning centers;
- Regular daily planning by the teaching staff in accord with a developmentally based curriculum model and careful child observations; and
- Developmentally sequenced goals and materials for children based on the High/Scope "key developmental indicators."[9]

Basic Principles and Goals of the High/Scope Model

The High/Scope program strives to

develop in children a broad range of skills, including the problem solving, interpersonal, and communication skills that are essential for successful living in a rapidly changing

They learn about their community as we take walks in the neighborhood and speak with the postal carrier, a repairman, or a police officer and visit a grocery store.

Children at Magnia Child Care have opportunities to explore the outdoors on our tricycle path, in our sandbox, on the climbing structures and swings, and in the places we've provided for them to discover nature. Indoor activities allow children to play in groups or to investigate on their own. Our schedule also provides a quiet time for rest and napping.

RELATIONSHIPS WITH PARENTS

An important part of our work is the relationships we develop with parents. Together we form a partnership in caring for their children. We learn about the child from the parents, and in turn, the parents learn about their child's growth in our program. Over the years we have collected an assortment of articles on topics of interest to parents that relate to the typical skills of children, guidance suggestions, and dealing with difficult behaviors. Our Parent Files also include information on community resources that are available to children and their families. Coupled with our

Sharing the Parent File that is filled with articles on topics of interest to parents and information on community resources helps program owner/director Martha Magnia cement the teacher–parent relationship.

interactions with parents, this information serves to enhance the confidence of first-time parents as they inquire about their child's development.

AN EFFECTIVE FAMILY CHILD CARE PROVIDER

For an effective family child care provider, a strong background in child development is helpful. Understanding how children learn and how the environment affects their behavior, as well as learning about developmentally appropriate practices, influences the quality of child care. Taking part in professional organizations for early care and education is essential to our continued professional development.

A career in licensed family child care has many benefits. Being the director/owner of your own business is highly rewarding, as is incorporating your own program philosophy and developing your own policies, based on best practices. Your child care program can be flexible and accommodating to meet your needs and those of the families you serve.

Our greatest reward as licensed family child care providers is the pleasure we receive in working with young children and their families. It is gratifying to witness the growth and development of small infants into active, confident, ready-to-learn preschool children.

As with any profession, there are also challenges; unfortunately, some still assume that we are only babysitters. However, we continue to advocate and educate others about the valuable contribution that licensed family child care provides to children, to families, and to our communities.

Contributed by Martha Magnia, owner/director of Magnia Family Child Care and adjunct faculty at Fresno City College, where she teaches child development and family child care courses. Photos also courtesy of Martha Magnia.

society. The curriculum encourages student initiative by providing children with materials, equipment, and time to pursue activities they choose. At the same time, it provides teachers with a framework for guiding children's independent activities toward sequenced learning goals.

The teacher plays a key role in instructional activities by selecting appropriate, developmentally sequenced material and by encouraging children to adopt an active problem-solving approach to learning. . . . This teacher–student interaction—teachers helping students achieve developmentally sequenced goals while also encouraging them to set many of their own goals—uniquely distinguishes the High/Scope curriculum from direct-instruction and child-centered curricula.[10]

The High/Scope model influences the arrangement of the classroom, the manner in which teachers interact with children, and the methods employed to assess children. Review Figure 4.3 now to see how active learning forms the hub of the "wheel of learning" and is supported by the key elements of the curriculum.

TABLE 4.2 Types of Child Care Programs

Types of Child Care	Purpose and Function
Family and relative care	Children are cared for by grandparents, aunts, uncles, or other relatives. Child care by family members provides children with the continuity and stability parents desire for their children.
Family care/Family child care	Child care is provided in a child's own family, or in a family-like setting. An individual caregiver provides care and education for a small group of children in his or her home.
Intergenerational care	Intergenerational child care programs integrate children and the elderly into an early childhood and adult care facility. The programs blend the best of two worlds: children and the elderly both receive care and attention in a nurturing environment.
Center child care	Center child care is conducted in specially designed and constructed centers, churches, YMCAs and YWCAs, and other such facilities.
Employer-sponsored child care	The most rapidly growing segment of the workforce is married women with children under the age of one. To meet the needs of working parents, employers are providing affordable, accessible, and quality child care.
Proprietary child care	Some child care centers are being run by corporations, businesses, or individual proprietors for the purpose of making a profit. Many of these programs emphasize their educational component and appeal to middle-class families who can pay for the promised services. Providing care for the nation's children is big business.
Child care for children with medical needs	When children get sick, families must find someone who will take care of them or they must stay home. More and more programs are providing care for children with medical needs, such as care when they have illnesses (both contagious and noncontagious), broken bones, and other health problems that keep them from attending other regular child care programs.
Before- and after-school care	In many respects, public schools are logical places for before- and after-school care. They have the administrative organization, facilities, and staff to provide such care. Many taxpayers and professionals believe that schools should not sit empty in the afternoons, evenings, holidays, and summers.

These eight types of child care programs are all popular with parents. However, many families prefer family and relative care and like to have their children cared for in a home-like setting. For many parents, however, this type of care is not available.

FIGURE 4.1

The Ten Largest For-Profit Child Care Organizations in the United States

Organization	Headquarters	Centers	Capacity
Knowledge Learning Company	Portland, OR	2,454	256,000
La Petite Academy	Chicago, IL	650	84,000
Learning Care Group, Inc.	Novi, MI	417	—
Bright Horizons Family Solutions	Watertown, MA	620	67,000
Nobel Learning Communities	West Chester, PA	150	28,100
Child Care Network	Columbus, GA	135	18,299
The Sunshine House	Greenwood, SC	122	17,879
Mini-Skool	Scottsdale, AZ	89	16,000
New Horizon Child Care	Plymouth, MN	87	12,448
Minnieland Private Day School	Woodbridge, VA	93	10,884

Source: "The Exchange Top 40 North America's Largest For-Profit Child Care Organizations," *Child Care Exchange*, January/February 2006, p. 25, http://www.ccie.com/library/5016802.pdf.

TABLE 4.3 The Ten Components of High-Quality Child Care

Component	Indicator
Licensed programs following appropriate health and safety practices	Licensing ensures that a child care setting meets basic health and safety requirements.
Staff well trained in early childhood development	The strongest indicators for long-term success tied to early education and care are related to the caregivers' education and level of participation in ongoing training in the field of early childhood development and care.
Age-appropriate environments	Learning is an interactive process that involves continuous opportunities for exploration and interactions.
Small groups with optimal ratios	Group size and ratios determine the amount of time and attention that each caregiver can devote to each child.
Primary caregiver and continuity of care	Positive relationships between caregivers and children are crucial to quality child care.
Active and responsive caregiving to support children's development	The active and responsive caregiver takes cues from each child to know when to guide, teach, and intervene.
Emerging language and emerging literacy	The path to literacy begins with interaction between caregivers and young children.
Curricula, observation, and individualized programming	Learning involves activities, materials, and opportunities for exploration and interaction.
Family involvement and cultural continuity	High-quality programs incorporate practices reflecting the values and beliefs of the families and the cultures of their communities.
Comprehensive support services with multidisciplinary teams	High-quality child care serves as a protective environment for the child and a source of support for the child's family.

Source: FSU Center for Prevention & Early Intervention Policy, *10 Components of Quality Child Care.* http://www.cpeip.fsu.edu/ resource Files/resource File_1.pdf?CFID = 57777&CFTOKEN = 26715426. Reprinted by permission.

The Five Elements of the High/Scope Model

Professionals who use the High/Scope curriculum are fully committed to providing settings in which children actively learn and construct their own knowledge. Teachers create the context for learning by implementing and supporting five essential elements: active learning, classroom arrangement, the daily schedule, assessment, and the curriculum (content).

Active Learning.   Teachers support children's active learning by providing a variety of materials, making plans and reviewing activities with children, interacting with and carefully observing individual children, and leading small- and large-group active learning activities.

Classroom Arrangement.   The classroom contains five or more interest centers that encourage choice. The classroom organization of materials and equipment supports the daily routine. Children know where to find materials and what materials they can use. This encourages development of self-direction and independence.

The teacher selects the centers and activities to use in the classroom based on several considerations:

- Interests of the children (e.g., preschool children are interested in blocks, housekeeping, and art);
- Opportunities for facilitating active involvement in seriation (e.g., big, bigger, biggest), numbers (e.g., counting), time relations (e.g., before–after), classification (e.g., likenesses and differences), spatial relations (e.g., over–under), and language development; and
- Opportunities for reinforcing needed skills and concepts and functional (real-life) use of these skills and concepts.

Explore the materials and information available at High/Scope's homepage at http://www.prenhall.com/morrison, Chapter 4—Web Links.

FIGURE 4.2

Selected Results from the NICHD Study of Early Child Care and Youth Development

See what surprises you most as you review these study results. Then try to find other research data that confirm or contradict that finding.

Child care arrangements
- During the first year of life the majority of children in nonparental care experienced more than two different child care arrangements.
- More than one-third experienced three or more arrangements.

Hours in child care
- At their first entry into nonmaternal care, children averaged 29 hours of care per week.
- By twelve months, children care averaged 33.9 hours a week of care.

Kind of care
- The amount of time the children spent in care rose only slightly after the first year of life; children who were in care for thirty-six months averaged 34.4 hours per week.
- However, the type of care had changed considerably, with 44 percent in center care, 25 percent in child care home, 12 percent cared for by their father or their mother's partner, 10 percent cared for at home by nannies or babysitters, and 9 percent cared for by grandparents.

Child care and income
- Families with the lowest nonmaternal income were the most likely to place infants in care before the age of three months, probably because they were the most dependent on the mother's income.
- In contrast, infants from families with the highest maternal and nonmaternal incomes tended to start care between three and five months.
- The higher their mothers' earnings the more hours infants spent in nonmaternal care; however, the higher the *nonmaternal* earnings in the family the *fewer* hours they spent in care.

Maternal attitudes and child care
- Mothers who believed their children benefited from their employment tended to place their infants in care earlier and for more hours in nonauthoritarian, nonmaternal care.
- In contrast, mothers who believed maternal employment carried high risks for their children tended to put their infants in care for fewer hours and were especially likely to rely on the infant's father for child care.

Quality of nonmaternal care
- Observations at six months indicated that more-positive caregiving occurred when children were in smaller groups, child–adult ratios were lower, caregivers held less authoritarian beliefs about child rearing, and physical environments were safe, clean, and stimulating.
- Observed quality of care for poor children was generally lower than for nonpoor children when they were cared for by an unrelated caregiver.

Social, emotional, cognitive, and health-related child outcomes
- Observed quality of caregivers' behavior—particularly the amount of language stimulation provided—was positively related to children's performance on measures of cognitive and linguistic abilities at ages fifteen, twenty-four, and thirty-six months.
- Quality of care was also related to measures of social and emotional development. At twenty-four months, children who had experienced higher quality care were reported by both their mothers and their caregivers to have fewer behavior problems and were rated higher on social competence by their mothers. At thirty-six months, higher quality care was associated with greater compliance and less negative behavior during mother–child interactions and fewer caregiver-reported behavior problems.
- Over the first three years of life, higher quality child care among the families that used nonmaternal care was also associated with greater maternal sensitivity during mother–child interaction.
- Poor-quality child care was related to an increased incidence of insecure infant–mother attachment at fifteen months, but only when the mother was also relatively low in sensitivity and responsiveness.

Child outcomes
- The extent to which children's child care center classes met professional guidelines was related to developmental outcomes at twenty-four and thirty-six months.

- Children in classes that met the guidelines for child–staff ratio had fewer behavior problems and more positive social behaviors at both ages.
- Three-year-olds in classes that met the standards for caregiver training and higher education showed greater school readiness, better language comprehension, and fewer behavior problems.
- Quality of care continued to be associated with developmental outcomes throughout the preschool years.

Quantity of care

- The quantity of nonmaternal care was a statistically significant predictor of some child outcomes. When children spent more hours in child care, mothers were less sensitive in their interactions with their children (at six, fifteen, twenty-four, and thirty-six months) and children were less positively engaged with their mothers (at fifteen, twenty-four, and thirty-six months).
- Analyses of attachment at fifteen months showed that children who spent more hours in child care *and* had mothers who were relatively insensitive and unresponsive were at heightened risk for insecure infant–mother attachments.
- At twenty-four months, spending more hours in care was associated with mothers' reports of lower social competence and caregivers' reports of more problem behaviors.
- At the kindergarten assessment, quantity of care was associated with both teacher and mother ratings of problem behaviors.

Type of care

- Type of child care was clearly associated with rates of early communicable illnesses.
- Children attending child care centers and child care homes had more ear infections and upper respiratory illnesses than did children cared for at home, especially during the first two years of life.
- The number of other children in the child care setting was also positively related to frequency of upper respiratory illnesses and gastrointestinal illnesses through age three. However, these heightened rates of illness did not seem to have significant adverse developmental consequences over the first three years of life.

Family factors and child outcomes

- Analyses of the effects of child care experiences and family factors on child outcomes indicated that family characteristics were more consistent predictors of both social-emotional and cognitive child outcomes through age three than were child care factors.
- In the social-emotional domain, mothers' sensitivity, responsiveness, and overall psychological adjustment predicted infant–mother attachment security at fifteen months; but observed quality and amount of nonmaternal care, age at entry into care, and frequency of changes in care arrangements did not.
- Low-quality nonmaternal care, spending more than ten hours per week in care, and changes in care arrangements did increase the risk of insecure attachments when combined with low maternal sensitivity.
- Secure infant–mother attachment at fifteen months, in turn, predicted more positive infant–mother interaction at twenty-four months and fewer mother-reported behavior problems at thirty-six months.
- Maternal sensitivity during the first two years of life was a better predictor of self-control, compliance, and problem behaviors at twenty-four and thirty-six months than any aspect of children's early nonmaternal care experiences.
- In the cognitive domain, family factors accounted for a much larger share of the variance in cognitive and linguistic outcomes across the first three years of life than child care factors did.
- Maternal vocabulary and the quality of the home environment were significant predictors of cognitive and language development at fifteen, twenty-four, and thirty-six months.

Source: Reprinted by permission from Child Care and Child Development, *Results from the NICHD Study of Early Child Care and Youth Development* (New York: Guilford Press, 2005), 28–35.

Classroom arrangement is an essential part of professional practice in order to appropriately implement a program's philosophy. This is true for Montessori, for High/Scope, and for every other program with which you may be involved.

Daily Schedule. The schedule considers developmental levels of children, incorporates a sixty- to seventy-minute plan-do-review process, provides for content areas, is as consistent throughout the day as possible, and contains a minimum number of transitions.

Assessment. Teachers keep notes about significant behaviors, changes, statements, and things that help them better understand a child's way of thinking and learning. Teachers use

FIGURE 4.3 High/Scope
Curriculum Wheel

Source: Used with permission of
David P. Weikart, president,
High/Scope Educational Research
Foundation, 600 N. River
St., Ypsilanti, MI 48198–2898.

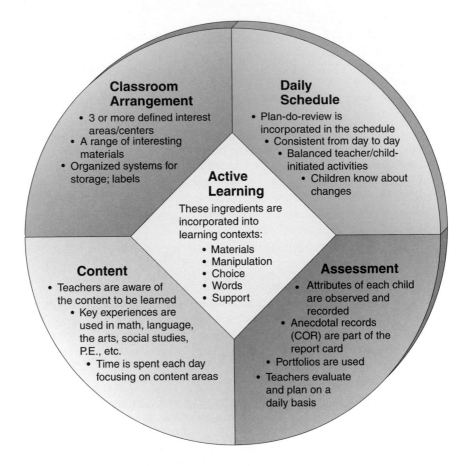

Classroom Arrangement
- 3 or more defined interest areas/centers
- A range of interesting materials
- Organized systems for storage; labels

Daily Schedule
- Plan-do-review is incorporated in the schedule
- Consistent from day to day
- Balanced teacher/child-initiated activities
- Children know about changes

Active Learning
These ingredients are incorporated into learning contexts:
- Materials
- Manipulation
- Choice
- Words
- Support

Content
- Teachers are aware of the content to be learned
- Key experiences are used in math, language, the arts, social studies, P.E., etc.
- Time is spent each day focusing on content areas

Assessment
- Attributes of each child are observed and recorded
- Anecdotal records (COR) are part of the report card
- Portfolios are used
- Teachers evaluate and plan on a daily basis

Children can learn mathematics skills through activities that involve the manipulation of concrete objects, like blocks. What other active learning experiences can you use to help children discover principles of mathematics?

two mechanisms to help them collect data: the key experiences note form and a portfolio. In addition, teachers use the Child Observation Record (COR) to identify and record children's progress in key behavioral and content areas.

Curriculum. The High/Scope curriculum comes from two sources: children's interests and the key experiences, which are lists of observable learning behaviors. Basing a curriculum in part on children's interests is very constructivist and implements the philosophies of Dewey and Piaget.

Figure 4.4 provides a partial list of key experiences in language and literacy. The key experiences listed are representative of the many that are available for teachers to choose from when identifying learning activities for children. In many ways, key experiences are similar to standards that state what children should know and do.

A Daily Routine That Supports Active Learning

The High/Scope curriculum's daily routine is made up of a plan–do–review sequence that gives children opportunities to express intentions about their activities while keeping the

---

FIGURE 4.4

Experiences in Language and Literacy for a High/Scope K–3 Curriculum

Speaking and Listening
Speaking their own language or dialect
Asking and answering questions
Stating facts and observations in their own words
Using language to solve problems
Participating in singing, storytelling, poetic, and dramatic activities
Recalling thoughts and observations in a purposeful context
Acquiring, strengthening, and extending speaking and listening skills
    Discussing to clarify observations or to better follow direction
    Discussing to expand speaking and listening vocabulary
    Discussing to strengthen critical thinking and problem-solving activities

Reading
Experiencing varied genres of children's literature
Reading own compositions
Reading and listening to others read in a purposeful context
Using audio or video recordings in reading experiences
Acquiring, strengthening, and extending specific reading skills
    Auditory discrimination
    Letter recognition
    Decoding—phonetic analysis (letter/sound associations, factors affecting sounds, syllabication), structural analysis (forms, prefixes, suffixes)
    Vocabulary development

Expanding comprehension and fluency skills
    Activating prior knowledge
    Determining purpose, considering context, making predictions
    Developing strategies for interpreting narrative and expository text
    Reading varied genres of children's literature

---

teacher intimately involved in the whole process. The following five processes support the daily routine and contribute to its successful functioning.

Planning Time. Planning time gives children a structured, consistent chance to express their ideas to adults and to see themselves as individuals who can act on decisions.

The teacher talks with children about the plans they have made before the children carry them out. This helps children clarify their ideas and think about how to proceed. Talking with children about their plans provides an opportunity for the teacher to encourage and respond to each child's ideas, to suggest ways to strengthen the plans so they will be successful, and to understand and gauge each child's level of development and thinking style. Children and teachers benefit from these conversations and reflections. Children feel reinforced and ready to start their work, while teachers have ideas of what opportunities for extension might arise, what difficulties children might have, and where problem solving may be needed.

Key Experiences. Teachers continually encourage and support children's interests and involvement in activities, which occur within an organized environment and a consistent routine. Teachers plan from key experiences that may broaden and strengthen children's emerging abilities. Children generate many of these experiences on their own; others require teacher guidance. Many key experiences are natural extensions of children's projects and interests. Refer again to Figure 4.4 to review a partial list of key experiences that support learning in the areas of language and literacy.

Work Time. This part of the plan–do–review sequence is generally the longest time period in the daily routine. The teacher's role during work time is to observe children to see how they gather information, interact with peers, and solve problems. When appropriate, teachers enter into the children's activities to encourage, extend, and set up problem-solving situations.

Cleanup Time. During cleanup time, children return materials and equipment to their labeled places and store their incomplete projects, restoring order to the classroom. All children's materials in the classroom are within reach and on open shelves. Clear labeling enables children to return all work materials to their appropriate places.

Recall Time. Recall time, the final phase of the plan–do–review sequence, is the time when children represent their work time experience in a variety of developmentally appropriate ways. They might recall the names of the children they involved in their plan, draw a picture of the building they made, or describe the problems they encountered. Recall strategies also include drawing pictures, making models, physically demonstrating how a plan was carried out, or verbally recalling the events of work time. The teacher supports children's linking of the actual work to their original plan.

This review permits children to reflect on what they did and how it was done. It brings closure to children's planning and work time activities. Putting their ideas and experiences into words also facilitates children's language development. Most important, it enables children to represent to others their mental schemes.

Advantages

Implementing the High/Scope approach produces several advantages. It offers you a method for implementing a constructivist-based program that has its roots in Piagetian cognitive theory. Second, it is widely popular and has been extensively researched and tested. Third, a rather extensive network of training and support is provided by the High/Scope Foundation. You can learn more about High/Scope through its website. Reviewing the website will help you decide if High/Scope is a program you would consider implementing in your classroom.

THE MONTESSORI METHOD

The **Montessori method** is attractive to parents and teachers for a number of reasons. First, Montessori education has always been identified as a quality program for young children. Second, parents who observe a good Montessori program like what they see: orderliness, independent children, self-directed learning, a calm environment, and children at the center of the learning process. Third, some public schools include Montessori in their magnet programs, giving parents choices in the kind of program their children will have at their school.

During the past decade, the implementation of Montessori education has increased tremendously in both private and public school early childhood programs. Maria Montessori would probably smilingly approve of the contemporary use of her method once again to help change the nature and character of early childhood education.

The Role of the Montessori Teacher

The Montessori teacher demonstrates certain behaviors to implement the principles of this child-centered approach. The teacher's six essential roles in a Montessori program are as follows:

- Respect children and their learning.
- Make children the center of learning.

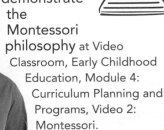

Observe early childhood classrooms that demonstrate the Montessori philosophy at Video Classroom, Early Childhood Education, Module 4: Curriculum Planning and Programs, Video 2: Montessori.

- Encourage children's learning.
- Observe children.
- Prepare learning environments.
- Introduce learning materials and demonstrate lessons.

Review these six roles and consider how you can apply them to your practice regardless of what kind of program you implement. Which of these six do you think is the most essential? Why?

Montessori contended, "It is necessary for the teacher to *guide* the child without letting him feel her presence too much, so that she may be always ready to supply the desired help, but may never be the obstacle between the child and his experience."[11] The teacher as a guide is a pillar of Montessori practice.

The Montessori Method in Action

In a prepared environment, certain materials and activities provide for three basic areas of child involvement: *practical life* or motor education, *sensory materials* for training the senses, and *academic materials* for teaching writing, reading, and mathematics. All of these activities are taught according to prescribed procedures.

Practical Life. The prepared environment emphasizes basic, everyday basic, everday motor activities, such as walking from place to place in an orderly manner, carrying objects such as trays and chairs, greeting a visitor, learning self-care skills, and doing other practical activities. For example, the "dressing frames" are designed to perfect the motor skills involved in buttoning, zipping, lacing, buckling, and tying. The philosophy for activities such as these is to make children independent of the adult and develop concentration. Water-based activities play a large role in Montessori methods, and children are taught to scrub, wash, and pour as a means of developing coordination. Practical life exercises also include polishing mirrors, shoes, and plant leaves; sweeping the floor; dusting furniture; and peeling vegetables.

Review articles on the impact of Montessori methods on learning at http://www.prenhall.com/morrison, Chapter 4—Web Links.

Montessorians believe that as children become absorbed in an activity, they gradually lengthen their span of concentration. As they follow a regular sequence of actions, they learn to pay attention to details. Montessori educators also believe that concentration and involvement through the senses enable learning to take place. Teacher verbal instructions are minimal; the emphasis in the instruction process is on *showing how*—modeling and practice.

Practical life activities are taught through four different types of exercises. *Care of the person* involves activities such as using the dressing frames, polishing shoes, and washing hands. *Care of the environment* includes dusting, polishing a table, and raking leaves. *Social relations* include lessons in grace and courtesy. The fourth type of exercise involves *analysis and control of movement* and includes locomotor activities such as walking and balancing.

Sensory Materials. For many early childhood educators the core of the Montessori program is the specialized set of learning materials that help children learn and that support Montessori's ideas about how to best facilitate children's learning. Many of these materials are designed to train and use the senses to support learning. Figure 4.5 shows basic Montessori sensory materials. Montessori sensory materials are popular, attractive, and they support children's cognitive development. Authentic Montessori materials are very well made and are durable.

As you review these materials, think about their purposes and how they act as facilitators of children's learning. Sensory materials include brightly colored rods and cubes and sandpaper letters. One purpose of these sensory materials is to train children's senses to focus on some obvious, particular quality. For example, with red rods, the quality of length; with pink tower cubes, size; and with bells, musical pitch. Montessori felt that

Material	Illustration	Descriptions and Learning Purposes
Pink tower		Ten wooden cubes of the same shape and texture, all pink, the largest of which is ten centimeters. Each succeeding block is one centimeter smaller. Children build a tower beginning with the largest block. (Visual discrimination of dimension)
Brown stairs		Ten wooden blocks, all brown, differing in height and width. Children arrange the blocks next to each other from thickest to thinnest so the blocks resemble a staircase. (Visual discrimination of width and height)
Red rods		Ten rod-shaped pieces of wood, all red, of identical thickness but differing in length from ten centimeters to one meter. The child arranges the rods next to each other from largest to smallest. (Visual discrimination of length)
Cylinder blocks		Four individual wooden blocks that have holes of various sizes and matching cylinders; one block deals with height, one with diameter, and two with the relationship of both variables. Children remove the cylinders in random order, then match each cylinder to the correct hole. (Visual discrimination of size)
Smelling jars		Two identical sets of white opaque glass jars with removable tops through which the child cannot see but through which odors can pass. The teacher places various substances, such as herbs, in the jars, and the child matches the jars according to the smells. (Olfactory discrimination)
Baric tablets		Sets of rectangular pieces of wood that vary according to weight. There are three sets—light, medium, and heavy—that children match according to the weight of the tablets. (Discrimination of weight)
Color tablets		Two identical sets of small rectangular pieces of wood used for matching color or shading. (Discrimination of color and education of the chromatic sense)
Cloth swatches		Two identical swatches of cloth. Children identify them according to touch, first without a blindfold but later using a blindfold. (Sense of touch)
Tonal bells		Two sets of eight bells, alike in shape and size but different in color; one set is white, the other brown. The child matches the bells by tone. (Sound and pitch)
Sound boxes		Two identical sets of cylinders filled with various materials, such as salt and rice. Children match the cylinders according to the sounds the fillings make. (Auditory discrimination)
Temperature jugs or thermic bottles		Small metal jugs filled with water of varying temperatures. Children match jugs of the same temperature. (Thermic sense and ability to distinguish between temperatures)

FIGURE 4.5 Montessori Sensory Materials

children need help discriminating among the many stimuli they receive. Accordingly, the sensory materials help make children more aware of the capacity of their bodies to receive, interpret, and make use of stimuli. In this sense, the Montessori sensory materials are labeled *didactic*, and are designed to instruct and help children learn.

Second, the sensory materials help sharpen children's powers of observation and visual discrimination. These skills serve as a basis for general beginning reading readiness. Readiness for learning is highly emphasized in early childhood programs.

Third, the sensory materials increase children's ability to think, a process that depends on the ability to distinguish, classify, and organize. Children constantly face decisions about sensory materials: which block comes next, which color matches the other, which shape goes where? These are not decisions the teacher makes, nor are they decisions children arrive at by guessing; rather, they are decisions made by the intellectual process of observation and selection based on knowledge gathered through the senses.

Finally, the sensory activities are not ends in themselves. Their purpose is to prepare children for the onset of the sensitive periods for writing and reading. In this sense, all activities are preliminary steps in the writing–reading process.

Materials for training and developing the senses have these characteristics:

- *Control of error.* Materials are designed so children, through observation, can see whether or not they have made a mistake while completing an activity. For example, if a child does not use the blocks of the pink tower in their proper order while building the tower, she does not achieve a tower effect.
- *Isolation of a single quality.* Materials are designed so that other variables are held constant except for the isolated quality or qualities. Therefore, all blocks of the pink tower are pink because size, not color, is the isolated quality.
- *Active involvement.* Materials encourage active involvement rather than the more passive process of looking. Montessori materials are " hands-on" in the truest sense of hands-on active learning.
- *Attractiveness.* Materials are attractive, with colors and proportions that appeal to children. In this sense, they help satisfy aesthetic needs for beauty and attractiveness.

Academic Materials for Writing, Reading, and Mathematics. The third type of Montessori materials is academic, designed specifically to promote writing, reading, and mathematics. Exercises using these materials are presented in a sequence that supports writing as a basis for learning to read. Reading, therefore, emerges from writing. Both processes, however, are introduced so gradually that children are never aware they are learning to write and read until one day they realize they are writing and reading. Describing this phenomenon, Montessori said that children "burst spontaneously" into writing and reading. She anticipated contemporary practices such as the contemporary whole-language approach in integrating writing and reading and in maintaining that through writing children learn to read.

Montessori believed many children were ready for writing at four years of age. Consequently, children who enter a Montessori program at age three have done most of the sensory exercises by the time they are four. It is not uncommon to see four- and five-year-olds in a Montessori classroom writing and reading. In fact, children's success with early academic skills and abilities serves as a magnet to attract public and parental attention.

Additional Features. Other features of the Montessori system are *mixed-age grouping* and *self-pacing*. A Montessori classroom always contains children of different ages, usually from two and a half to six years. This strategy is becoming more popular in many early childhood classrooms. Advantages of mixed-age groups are that children learn from one another and help each other, a wide range of materials is available for all ages of children, and older children become role models and collaborators for younger children. Contemporary instructional practices of student mentoring, scaffolding, and cooperative learning all have their roots in and are supported by multiage grouping.

In a Montessori classroom, children are free to learn at their own rates and levels of achievement. They decide which activities to participate in and work at their own pace. Through observation, the teacher determines when children have perfected one exercise and are ready to move to a higher level or different exercise. If a child is not able to correctly complete an activity, the teacher gives him or her additional help and instruction. Table 4.4 shows the instructional practices used in a Montessori program and how they

TABLE 4.4 Montessori Instructional Practices

Integrated curriculum	Montessori provides an integrated curriculum in which children are actively involved in manipulating concrete materials across the curriculum—writing, reading, science, math, geography, and the arts. The Montessori curriculum is integrated by age and developmental level.
Active learning	In Montessori classrooms, children are actively involved in their own learning. Manipulative materials provide for active and concrete learning.
Individualized instruction	Curriculum and activities should be individualized for children. Individualization occurs through children's interactions with the materials as they proceed at their own rates of mastery.
Independence	The Montessori environment emphasizes respect for children and promotes success, both of which encourage children to be independent.
Appropriate assessment	Observation is the primary means of assessing children's progress, achievement, and behavior in a Montessori classroom. Well-trained Montessori teachers are skilled observers of children and adept at translating their observation into appropriate ways for guiding, directing, facilitating, and channeling children's learning.
Developmentally appropriate practice	What is specified in developmentally appropriate practice is included in Montessori practice. It is more likely that quality Montessori practitioners understand, as Maria Montessori did, that children are much more capable than some early childhood practitioners think.

These instructional practices, combined with the roles of the Montessori teacher and the sensory materials (Figure 4.5), serve as the essential core of Montessori programs.

apply to teacher roles and the curriculum. Review these practices now and think how they are similar to or different from instructional practices you have observed in other early childhood programs.

Montessori and Contemporary Practices

The Montessori approach has had a tremendous influence on approaches to early education. Many instructional practices used in contemporary early childhood programs have their basis in Montessori materials and practices. The Montessori method has many features to recommend it as a high-quality early childhood program and this accounts for its ongoing popularity. As you observe in early childhood programs, search for examples of Montessori influences.

Furthermore, a growing body of research shows that the Montessori program works. For example, in one study children who completed Montessori primary education through age five outscored other children on tests of math and letter word recognition. Also, on tests of social abilities, Montessori children used reasoning to solve problems rather than socially unacceptable ways.[12] Technology can be used to promote children's social development. The accompanying Technology Tie-In provides you with ways you can use to promote such development.

REGGIO EMILIA

Reggio Emilia, a city in northern Italy, is widely known for its approach to educating young children. Founded by Loris Malaguzzi (1920–1994), Reggio Emilia sponsors programs for children from three months to six years of age. Certain essential beliefs and practices underlie the **Reggio Emilia approach**. These basic features are what defines

Perhaps you have heard the claim that computers and other technology interfere with children's social development. Let's look at this argument and consider some things you can do to ensure that your use of technology with young children supports and enhances their social development.

Social development involves interacting with and getting along with other children and teachers. Social development also includes the development of self-esteem, the feelings children have about themselves. During the early childhood years, true peer relationships begin to emerge. Children's interactions and relationships with others expand their views of the world and of themselves. Early childhood is also a time when children are learning self-control and self-reliance. Adults expect children to develop self-regulation, control aggression, and function without constant supervision. How children meet these expectations has tremendous implications for their social development.

You can use computers and other technology to help children develop positive peer relationships, grow in their abilities of self-regulation and self-control, and develop positive self-esteem. Here are some things you can do to accomplish these goals:

- Have children work on projects together in pairs or small groups. Several children can work on the computer and other projects at the same time.
- Make sure that each computer has several chairs to encourage children to work together. Learning through technology is not inherently a solitary activity. You can find many ways to make it a cooperative and social learning experience.
- Provide children opportunities to talk about their technology projects. Social development includes learning to talk confidently, explain, and share information with others.

- Encourage children to explore adult roles related to technology, such as newscaster, weather forecaster, and photographer. Invite adults from the community to share with children how they use technology in their careers. Invite a television crew to show children how they broadcast from community locations.
- Read stories about technology and encourage children to talk about technology in their lives and the lives of their families.
- Use the Internet and e-mail to connect children to other children. Have them exchange ideas and work on short reports. Remember that social development can occur electronically!
- Use technology to encourage a socially isolated child to develop social skills. "Sophia, let's use the video camera to interview Mrs. Little, the cafeteria manager, on good nutrition ideas for use at home."
- Create a learning center devoted to technology. The writing and publishing of a classroom newspaper is a great way to promote social interactions. Make sure *all* children have a job, for example, reporter, writer, or photographer.

As you use technology to promote children's social development, remember that all dimensions of children's development are integrated. The cognitive, linguistic, social, emotional, and physical support depend on each other, and technology can positively support all of these dimensions of development.

 Complete an activity on promoting children's social development with technology at http://www.prenhall.com/morrison, Chapter 4—Journal: Technology Tie-In.

the Reggio approach, makes it a constructivist program, and defines it as a model that attracts worldwide attention. The Reggio approach has been adapted and implemented in a number of U.S. early childhood programs.

Beliefs About Children and How They Learn

Relationships.   Education focuses on each child and is conducted in relation with the family, other children, the teachers, the environment of the school, the community, and the wider society. Each school is viewed as a system in which all of these interconnected relationships are essential for educating children. In other words, as Vygotsky believed, children learn through social interactions and, as Montessori maintained, the environment supports and is important for learning.

Observe children and teachers collaborating to develop emergent curriculum in a Reggio-inspired early childhood program at Video Classroom, Early Childhood Education, Module 4: Curriculum Planning and Programs, Video 3: Reggio Emilia.

TEACHER PREP

Teachers are always aware, however, that children learn a great deal in exchanges with their peers, especially when they interact in small groups. Such small groups of two, three, four, or five children provide possibilities for paying attention, hearing, and listening to each other, developing curiosity and interest, asking questions, and responding.

Time. Reggio Emilia teachers believe that time is not set by a clock and that learning continuity should not be interrupted by the calendar. Children's own sense of time and their personal rhythm are considered in planning and carrying out activities and projects. The full-day schedule provides sufficient time for being together among peers in an environment that is conducive to getting things done with satisfaction.

Teachers get to know the personal rhythms and learning styles of each child. This intensive getting to know children is possible in part because children stay with the same teachers and the same peer group for three-year cycles (infancy to three years and three years to six years).

Adults' Roles. Adults play a powerful role in children's lives. Children's well-being is connected with the well-being of parents and teachers. The well-being of all is supported by recognizing and supporting basic rights. Children have a right to high-quality care and education that supports the development of their potentials. This right is honored by adults and communities who provide these educational necessities. Parents have a right to be involved in the life of the school. As one parent remarked, "I'm not a visitor at school; this is my school!" Teachers have the right to grow professionally through collaboration with other teachers and parents.

The Teacher. Teachers observe and listen closely to children to know how to plan or proceed with their work. They ask questions and discover children's ideas, hypotheses, and theories. They collaboratively discuss what they have observed and recorded, and they make flexible plans and preparations. Teachers then enter into dialogues with the children and offer them opportunities for discovering, revisiting, and reflecting on experiences. In this sense, teachers support learning as an ongoing process. Teachers are partners and collaborators with children in a continual process of research and learning.

The Atelierista. An **atelierista** is a teacher trained in the visual arts, who works closely with other teachers and children in every preprimary school and makes visits to the infant–toddler centers. The atelierista helps children use materials to create projects that reflect their involvement in and efforts to solve problems.

Families. Families are an essential component of Reggio, and they are included in the advisory committee that runs each school. Family participation is expected and supported and takes many forms: day-to-day interaction, work in the schools, discussion of educational and psychological issues, special events, excursions, and celebrations.

The Environment. The infant–toddler centers and school programs are the most visible aspect of the work done by teachers and families in Reggio Emilia. They convey many messages, of which the most immediate is that they are environments where adults have thought about the quality and the instructive power of space.

The Physical Space. The layout of physical space, in addition to welcoming whoever enters, fosters encounters, communication, and relationships. The arrangement of structures, objects, and activities encourages children's choices, supports problem solving, and promotes discoveries in the process of learning.

Reggio centers and schools are beautiful. There is attention to detail everywhere: in the color of the walls, the shape of the furniture, the arrangement of objects on shelves and tables. Light from the windows and doors shines through transparent collages and weavings made by children. Healthy, green plants are everywhere.

The environment is highly personal and full of children's own work. Everywhere there are paintings, drawings, paper sculptures, wire constructions, transparent collages coloring the light, and mobiles moving gently overhead. Such things turn up even in unexpected spaces such as stairways and bathrooms.

The Atelier. The **atelier** is a special workshop or studio, set aside and used by all the children and teachers in the school. It contains a great variety of tools and resource materials, along with records of past projects and experiences.

In the view of Reggio educators, the children's use of many media is not art or a separate part of the curriculum but an inseparable, integral part of the whole cognitive/symbolic expression involved in the learning process.

Program Practices. Cooperation is the powerful mode of working that makes possible the achievement of the goals Reggio educators set for themselves. Teachers work in pairs in each classroom. They see themselves as researchers gathering information about their work with children by means of continual documentation. The strong collegial relationships that are maintained with teachers and staff enable them to engage in collaborative discussion and interpretation of both teachers' and children's work.

Documentation. Transcriptions of children's remarks and discussions, photographs of their activity, and representations of their thinking and learning using many media are carefully arranged by the *atelierista* and other teachers. These document children's work and the process of learning. This documentation has five functions:

1. To make parents aware of children's experiences and maintain their involvement.
2. To allow teachers to understand children and to evaluate their own work, thus promoting professional growth.
3. To facilitate communication and exchange of ideas among educators.
4. To make children aware that their effort is valued.
5. To create an archive that traces the history of the school and the pleasure of learning by children and their teachers.

Curriculum and Practices. The curriculum is not established in advance. In this sense, Reggio is a process approach, not a set curriculum to be implemented. Teachers express general goals and make hypotheses about what direction activities and projects might take. After observing children in action, teachers compare, discuss, and interpret together their observations and make choices that they share with the children about what to offer and how to sustain the children in their exploration and learning. In fact, the curriculum emerges in the process of each activity or project and is flexibly adjusted accordingly through this continuous dialogue among teachers and with children.

Read about how the Reggio approach is implemented in classrooms at http://www.prenhall.com/morrison, Chapter 4—Web Links.

Projects provide the backbone of the children's and teachers' learning experiences. These projects are based on the conviction that learning by doing is of great importance and that to discuss in groups and to revisit ideas and experiences is the premier way of gaining understanding and learning.

Ideas for projects originate in the experiences of children and teachers as they construct knowledge together. Projects can last from a few days to several months. They may start from a chance event, an idea or a problem posed by one or more children, or an experience initiated directly by teachers.

Considerations. Keep a number of things in mind as you consider the Reggio Emilia approach and how it might relate to your work as an early childhood educator. First, its theoretical base rests within constructivism and shares ideas compatible with those of Piaget, Vygotsky, Dewey, Gardner, and Diamond (reflect on Table 4.1 again) and the concept or process of learning by doing. Second, there is no set curriculum. Rather, the curriculum emerges or springs from children's interests and experiences. This approach is, for many, difficult to implement and does not ensure that children will learn basic academic skills valued by contemporary American society. Third, the Reggio Emilia approach is suited to a particular culture and society. How this approach works, flourishes, and meets the educational needs of children in an Italian village may not necessarily be appropriate for meeting the needs of contemporary American children. The Italian view of education is that it is the responsibility of the state, and the state provides high levels of financial support. While education is a state function in the United States, traditionally local community control of education is a powerful and sacrosanct part of American education. The Program in Action feature shows how the Reggio approach inspires professionals to adapt it to their programs.

WALDORF EDUCATION: HEADS, HANDS, AND HEART

Rudolf Steiner (1861–1925) was very interested in the spiritual dimension of education, and he developed many ideas for educating children and adults that incorporated it. Emil Molt, director of the Waldorf-Astoria cigarette factory in Stuttgart, Germany, was interested in Steiner's ideas and asked him to give a lecture to the workers regarding the education of their children. Molt was so impressed with Steiner's ideas that he asked him to establish a school for employees' children. Steiner accepted the offer, and on September 17, 1919, the Free Waldorf School opened its doors and the Waldorf movement began. Today, Waldorf education has developed into an international movement with close to nine hundred independent schools in fifty-five countries. There are more than 150 Waldorf schools in North America.

Waldorf schools emphasize the teaching of the whole child—head, hands, and heart. This dedication to teaching the whole child appeals to many teachers and parents.

Steiner believed that education should be holistic. In shaping the first Waldorf school, he said that from the start there was to be no classification of children into intellectual "streams," no class lists, no examinations, no holding back in a grade or promoting to a grade, no prizes, no honors boards, no reports, no compulsory homework, and no punishments of additional learning material. It was to be a school where teachers and children meet as human beings to share and experience the knowledge of human evolution and development in the world.[13]

Basic Principles

Waldorf education, like the other programs we have discussed, operates on a number of essential principles.

Anthroposophy. Anthroposophy, the name Steiner gave to "the study of the wisdom of man," is a basic principle of Waldorf education:

Anthroposophy, according to Steiner, is derived from the Greek: anthros "man" and sophia "wisdom." Anthroposophy, Steiner claimed, offered a step-by-step guide for spiritual research. Anthroposophical thinking, according to Steiner, could permit one to gain a "new" understanding of the human being—body and spirit.[14]

The development of the spiritual is embraced by Waldorf teachers; it is not tied to any particular religious tradition. The teacher, through devotion to truth and knowledge, awakens the student's reverence for beauty and truth. Steiner believed that each person is capable of tapping the spiritual dimension, which then provides opportunities for higher and more meaningful learning.

Respect for Development. Waldorf education is based squarely on respect for children's processes of development and their developmental stages. Individual children's development determines how and when Waldorf teachers introduce curriculum topics. Respecting children's development and the ways they learn is an essential foundation of all early childhood programs.

Music and Movement. The art of movement makes speech and music visible through action and gesture and enables children to develop a sense of harmony and balance. Thus, as they learn reading, they are also becoming the letters through physical gestures. According to Steiner, every sound—speech or music—can be interpreted through gesture and body movement; for example, in learning the letter *o*, children form the letter with their arms while saying the sound for *o*. In the main-lesson books that are the children's textbooks, crayoned pictures of mountains and trees metamorphose into letters *M* and *T*, and form drawings of circles and polygons that become the precursor to cursive writing. Mental imagery for geometrical designs supports the fine-motor skills of young children.[15]

Rhythm is an important component of all these activities. Rhythm (i.e., order or pattern in time) permeates the entire school day as well as the school year, which unfolds around celebrating festivals drawn from different religions and cultures.[16]

Nurturing Imagination. Folk and fairy tales, fables, and legends are integrated throughout the Waldorf curriculum. These enable children to explore the traditions of many cultures, thus supporting a multicultural approach to education. They also enrich the imaginative life of the young child and promote free thinking and creativity.

Providing for Diversity and Disability. Providing for and being sensitive to diversity is an important aspect of Waldorf education. From first grade the curriculum for all students includes the study of two foreign languages. In addition, the curriculum integrates the study of religions and cultures. As a result, children learn respect for people of all races and cultures.

Waldorf schools can also experience a certain level of success with children who have been diagnosed with disabilities such as dyslexia. Because Waldorf teaches to all of the senses, there is usually a modality that a child can use to successfully learn curriculum material.

Some Waldorf schools are devoted entirely to the education of children with special needs. For example, Somerset School in Colfax, California, offers a variety of programs designed to meet the special needs of students ages six to seventeen years who are unable to participate in regular classroom activities. Teachers, physicians, and therapists work closely with parents to create and implement individualized lesson plans.[17]

Waldorf in Context

Waldorf education has much that is appealing: its emphasis on providing education for the whole child, the integration of the arts into the curriculum, the unhurried approach to education and schooling, and the emphasis on learning by doing.

A Reggio Parent–Teacher Cooperative

Children First is a nonprofit NAEYC-accredited child care program that enrolls twelve children and is run by three staff members with the support and involvement of parents. The children range in ages from two to five, with two teachers available at all times of the day. The philosophy of the program views "children as strong, capable, infinitely valuable and profoundly unique individuals."

The curriculum has four main components: family centered, child centered, developmentally appropriate, and Reggio inspired. Essential features of Children First are:

- Teachers who provide children guidance without taking the initiative away from them;
- An environment that provides children a choice of various activities;
- Field trips that aid in connecting the children with nature and the larger community;
- Parents who are involved in all aspects of the program (parents serve on the board of directors and are encouraged to participate in the classroom);

- A genuine commitment to building a community among children, families, and teachers;
- A nontraditional approach to discipline (to create a "safe school," teachers use gentle, respectful techniques to guide behavior. Moreover, children have a strong voice in constructing the rules they live by as a community); and
- All children are competent and have a right to be both active in constructing the community and fulfilled by it.

"Perhaps the most important thing Reggio has taught us to do here," says Donna King, teacher and administrator at Children First, "is to build a program, from day to day and year to year, that is built around and belongs to the people—children, parents, and teachers—who inhabit it."

Donna King is a teacher, administrator, and one of the founders of Children First. Information based on the Children First Parent Handbook. Children First is a nonprofit organization based in a private residence.

On the other hand, Waldorf education, like the Montessori approach, seems better suited to private, tuition-based education and has not been widely adopted into the public schools.

Several reasons could account for this limited adoption. First, public schools, especially in the context of contemporary schooling, are much more focused on academic achievement and accountability. Second, Waldorf education may not be philosophically aligned with mainstream public education. Waldorf's emphasis on the spiritual aspect of each child may be a barrier to widespread public school adoption.

Third, critics object to a number of other features of Waldorf education. These include delaying learning to read, not using computers and other technology in the classroom until high school, and discouraging television viewing and the playing of video games.

Waldorf schools remain a popular choice for parents who want a less structured education for their children. The intimate learning atmosphere of small classes, the range of academic subjects, and the variety of activities can be very attractive.

FEDERAL PROGRAMS FOR YOUNG CHILDREN

The federal government exerts tremendous influence on early childhood education. Every dimension of almost every educational program—public, private, and faith based—is touched in some way by the federal government.

Head Start (children ages three to five) and Early Head Start (children from birth to age three) are comprehensive child development programs that serve children, families, and pregnant women. These programs provide comprehensive health, nutrition, educational, and social services in order to help children achieve their full potential and succeed in school and life. They are currently programs for poor children and families. In this regard, Head Start and Early Head Start are **entitlement programs**.

This means that children and families who qualify, in this case by low income, are entitled to the services. However, only about one-third of eligible children and families receive these services because of the lack of funding to support full implementation.

Observe different Head Start classrooms at Video Classroom, Early Childhood Education, Module 4: Curriculum Planning and Programs, Video 1: Head Start.

Head Start

Head Start, America's premiere preschool program, was implemented in 1965. The first programs were designed for children entering first grade who had not attended kindergarten. The purpose of Head Start was literally to give children from low-income families a "head start" on their first-grade experience and, hopefully, on life itself. As public schools have provided more kindergarten and preschool programs, Head Start has started to serve younger children. Head Start is administered by the Administration for Children and Families (ACF) in the department of Health and Human Services (HHS).

As of 2006, the national Head Start program has an annual budget of $6.8 billion and serves 907,000 low-income families. There are 1,604 Head Start programs nationwide, with a total of 19,800 centers and 49,235 classrooms. The average cost per child of the Head Start program is $7,287 annually. Head Start has a paid staff of 213,000 and 1,360,000 volunteers.[18]

Both Head Start and Early Head Start must comply with federal **performance standards**, designed to ensure that all children and families receive high-quality services (see Chapter 5). Head Start performance standards guide program development and implementation and cover child health and developmental services, education and early childhood development, child health and safety, child nutrition, child mental health, family and community partnerships, program management, and program governance. In addition, the performance standards stress that local programs emphasize the professional development of Head Start teachers, and include reading and math readiness skills in the curriculum. Although the Head Start Bureau provides guidance on meeting the performance standards, local agencies are responsible for designing programs to best meet the needs of their children and families. The Diversity Tie-In feature spotlights the need to customize programs. You can access the performance standards for Head Start and Early Start at http://www.head-start.lane.or.us/administration/regulations/45CFR130x.index.html.

Jo Hall / Merrill

Head Start Objectives. Five objectives for Head Start are defined in the program performance standards:

1. Enhance children's growth and development.
2. Strengthen families as the primary nurturers of their children.
3. Provide children with educational, health, and nutritional services.
4. Link children and their families to needed community services.
5. Ensure well-managed programs that involve parents in decision making.

Head Start programs implement standards of learning in early literacy, language, and numeracy skills. These nine standards of learning or indicators identify the following goals for children enrolled in Head Start:

- Develop phonemic, print, and numeracy awareness.
- Understand and use language to communicate for various purposes.

Federally funded programs such as Head Start are designed to provide for the full range of children's social, emotional, physical, and academic needs. Increasingly, however, federal- and state-supported early childhood programs are emphasizing literacy, math, and science skills. How can traditional play-based activities such as this one help children learn skills in these three areas?

GOVERNING BODY

The grantee and governing body for the Head Start program is the tribal council or a consortium of smaller tribes or villages. Standards of performance are established by the federal funding agency, as well as local tribally established standards. In some cases, state standards apply to tribal programs if state funds are used by the tribe.

Federally recognized tribes are considered sovereign nations, so many establish their own governing policies, procedures, and codes. An example of how that impacts tribal Head Start programs is in child abuse and neglect reporting. Head Start standards apply; tribal code specifies the reporting and investigative process; and state reporting requirements apply if the tribal center is state certified. The impact is that program policies and procedures must be written to maintain compliance with all the agency standards in order to continue funding, maintain certification, and ensure consistency in program service delivery.

The tribal government may have related programs available to indirectly support the Head Start program. Services may include facility repair and maintenance, transportation safety, emergency response, administrative services (payroll, purchasing, contracts, planning, etc.) and budget and grants management.

EARLY CHILDHOOD DEVELOPMENT

Head Start curriculum development addresses the culture and traditional practices of the tribal community. Native language may include more than one tribal language, because multiple tribes are often represented in the service area. It is necessary to determine the native languages spoken in the home and identify a native speaker in the program or request assistance from a tribal culture and heritage program employee or community member. Native language curriculum in Head Start programs includes words to describe body parts, colors, animals, family relatives (sister, brother, grandfather, aunt, etc.), as well as common phrases and greetings. The approach will vary depending on the cultural resources of the tribe. Some programs will provide pull-out instruction, immersion classrooms, or integrate native language throughout the normal school day.

Cultural activities in the program may include traditional mealtime practices; native food identification, gathering, preparation, and service; traditional social dancing; celebrations of significant tribal events; and storytelling and native arts and crafts.

HEALTH SERVICES

Head Start children who are members of federally recognized tribes or can prove Indian blood lineage and reside in the service area are eligible to receive health care from the Indian Health Service. Health care includes physical examinations, immunizations, medical and dental care, and follow-up after vision and hearing screenings. Referrals to specialists for special health or medical care are provided if unavailable in the outpatient clinic.

Consultation from the Indian Health Service is provided to Head Start program staff in the areas of nutrition, health policy development, and program planning. Assistance may include menu planning by a nutritionist, health and safety inspections from a sanitarian, routine classroom visits from a nurse, prevention information and training for parents, prenatal care for pregnant women, and well-baby clinics.

SERVICES FOR CHILDREN WITH DISABILITIES

Head Start children with identified or suspected disabilities receive services from local education service agencies or their subcontractors and the Indin Health Service. Services are delivered according to federal Institute of Occupational and Environmental Health legislation and state policies and procedures. Services include identification, placement, referral, treatment, transition, and case management.

Contributed by Julie Quaid, director of the Education Support Services Department, The Confederated Tribes of the Warm Springs Reservation of Oregon, P.O. Box C, Warm Springs, Oregon 97761.

Compare the Head Start programs described in this feature with other Head Start programs at http:// www.prenhall.com/morrison, Chapter 4—Journal: Diversity Tie-In.

- Understand and use increasingly complex and varied vocabulary.
- Develop and demonstrate an appreciation of books.
- In the case of non–English-background children, progress toward acquisition of the English language.
- Know that the letters of the alphabet are a special category of visual graphics that can be individually named.
- Recognize a word as a unit of print.

- Identify at least ten letters of the alphabet.
- Associate sounds with written words.

These nine standards of learning are being implemented by local programs. The federal government provides Head Start support by training Head Start teachers to use the best methods of early reading and language skills instruction in order to better teach these standards.[19] These standards and others, embedded in the Head Start performance standards, are having several influences on Head Start:

- The curriculum of Head Start is more academic.
- Literacy and reading are priorities.
- Teachers and programs are being held more accountable for children's learning.

You can also review how these nine indicators of learning are included in the Head Start Child Outcomes Framework shown in Figure 5.5 on pages 140–143. This outcome framework is important for several reasons:

- It specifies learning outcomes that are essential to children's success in school and life.
- It ensures that all Head Start children in all Head Start programs will have the same learning outcomes.
- It is and will continue to impact what children learn in all preschool programs, not just Head Start.

Head Start Program Options.   Head Start and Early Head Start programs have the freedom to tailor their programs to meet the needs of the children, families, and communities they serve. Every three years, local programs conduct a community survey to determine strengths and resources and then design the program option based on these data. There are four program options: center-based, home-based, combination, and local option.

1. The *center-based option* delivers services to children and families using the center as the base or core. Center-based programs operate either full day or half day for thirty-two to thirty-four weeks a year, the minimum required by the Head Start Performance Standards, while others operate full-year programs. Center staff make periodic visits to family homes.
2. The *home-based option* uses the family home as the center for providing services. Home visitors work with the parents and children. Twice a month, children and families come to gather for field trips and classroom experiences. The home-based option has these strengths:
   - Parent involvement is the very keystone of the program.
   - Geographically isolated families have an invaluable opportunity to be part of a comprehensive child and family program.
   - An individualized family plan is based on both a child and a family assessment.
   - The family plan is facilitated by a home visitor who is an adult educator with knowledge and training related to all Head Start components.
   - The program includes the entire family.
3. In the *combination option* or model, programs combine the center and home-based options.
4. The *local option*, as its name indicates, includes programs created specifically to meet unique community and family needs. For example, some Early Head Start programs provide services in family child care homes.

Ryan McVay / Getty Images, Inc.–Photodisc

Head Start provides medical, dental, mental health, and nutrition services to preschool children. How does providing health services help achieve Head Start's goal of overall social competence for all children?

Head Start has always prided itself on tailoring its local programs to the children and families in the local community. In fact, this goal of meeting the needs of families and children at the local level is one of the strengths, and one that makes it popular with parents.

Eligibility for Head Start Services.　To be eligible for Head Start Services, children must meet age and family income criteria. Head Start enrolls children ages three to five from low-income families. The income eligibility provision means that families establish eligibility on the basis of whether or not their incomes fall below the official poverty line set annually by the U.S. Department of Health and Human Services. Poverty guidelines for 2006 are $20,000 for a family of four.

Ninety percent of a Head Start's enrollment has to meet the income eligibility criteria. The other 10 percent of enrollment can consist of children from families that exceed the low-income guidelines. In addition, 10 percent of a program's enrollment must include children with disabilities.

Head Start always has been and remains a program for children of poverty. Increasing federal support for Head Start will likely increase the number of poor children served. However, keep in mind that the federal government is using Head Start to reform all of early childhood education. Federal officials believe the changes they make in the Head Start curriculum, what and how teachers teach, and how Head Start operates will serve as a model for other programs as well.

Parent Involvement/Family Partnerships.　From the outset, Head Start has been dedicated to the philosophy that to improve children's lives, corresponding changes must be made in parents' lives as well. Head Start provides a program that recognizes parents as (1) responsible guardians of their children's well-being, (2) prime educators of their children, and (3) contributors to the Head Start program and to their communities.

Health Services.　Head Start assumes an active role in children's health. Children's current health status is monitored and reported to parents, and corrective and preventive procedures are undertaken with their cooperation.

Head Start also seeks to direct children and parents to existing mental health delivery systems such as community health centers. It does not intend to duplicate existing services, but to help parents become aware of and use available services.

Nutrition.　Head Start programs teach children how to care for their health, including the importance of eating proper foods and maintaining good dental health.

A basic premise of Head Start is that children must be properly fed to have the strength and energy to learn. This philosophy calls for teaching children good nutrition habits that will carry over for the rest of their lives and be passed on to their children. In addition, parents are given basic nutrition education so they, in turn, can promote good nutrition in their families.

Head Start programs design and implement a nutrition program that meets the nutritional needs and feeding requirements of each child, including those with special dietary needs and children with disabilities. Also, the nutrition program serves a variety of foods that involve cultural and ethnic preferences and broaden the children's food experiences.[20]

The Head Start program of Upper Des Moines Opportunity, Inc., operates twenty-five fully inclusive preschool classrooms. We have three classrooms specific to toddlers, ages eighteen to thirty-six months. We also have twenty-two classrooms set up for children ages three to five. Our programs are designated for all children, regardless of race or disability.

Our Head Start programs take pride in the strength of our partnerships with local school districts and other local education agencies. Because of the strength of these relationships we are able to collaborate in program design and offer natural or least restriction environments to all children.

In Early Head Start, our staff have been trained in case management of children with special needs. They have taken the lead position in coordination of services to our children and their families. These services can be provided in the home, in the classroom, or in a child care setting. Support service staff trained in specific areas of early childhood development facilitate our toddler rooms. We use the Child Study model to continually update staff on individual progress, concerns, and needs of our children. We employ many interpreters of different languages as we serve a very diverse population.

Our Head Start classrooms for children ages three to five offer many opportunities for inclusion. In some centers we dually enroll children, allowing them the opportunity to spend half a day in Head Start and the other half in an early childhood special education (ECSE) classroom. We also have classrooms where Head Start teachers and ECSE teachers work side by side, allowing for full-day programming for all children in the least restrictive settings. We operate Head Start classrooms where the lead teacher has a degree in early childhood special education and associate(s) have backgrounds in early childhood, or, the lead teacher has a background in early childhood and associate(s) are qualified to work with children having special needs. Support service staff facilitate all of our classrooms for three- to five-year-olds, and they, too, use the Child Study team approach to communicate the progress needs, and concerns of all children.

Contributed by Mary Jo Madvig, Early Childhood Program director, Upper Des Moines Opportunity, Inc., Des Moines, Iowa.

Early Head Start

Early Head Start (EHS) is designed to promote healthy prenatal outcomes for pregnant women; enhance the development of very young children (birth through age three); and promote healthy family functioning. Early Head Start enrolls pregnant women. When the child is born, the mother is provided family services. As with Head Start, EHS is a program for low-income families who meet federal poverty guidelines. EHS serves about 62,000 infants and toddlers with a budget of $684 million. More than 650 grantees participate in the Early Head Start program.[21] Program services include:

- Quality early education both in and out of the home;
- Parenting education;
- Comprehensive health and mental health services, including services to women before, during, and after pregnancy;
- Nutrition education; and
- Family support services.

Head Start's entry into the field of infant and toddler care and education has achieved several things. It has given Head Start an opportunity to work with a long-neglected age and socioeconomic population. As the public schools have enrolled preschoolers at an accelerated rate, the infant and toddler field gives Head Start a new group to serve. It has enabled Early Head Start to be a leader in the field of infant and toddler education. Without a doubt, EHS has been a pioneer and catalyst in providing high-quality programs

Promoting good nutrition for children and their families is an important part of the Head Start curriculum and helps establish lifelong attitudes toward healthy living.

for infants and toddlers. The Program in Action feature describes a successful program in Des Moines, Iowa.

EARLY CHILDHOOD PROGRAMS AND YOU

As an early childhood professional, you will want to do several things now:

- Begin to identify which features of the programs you can and cannot support.
- Decide which of these programs and/or features of programs you can embrace and incorporate into your own practice.
- Decide what you believe is the best for children and families before you make decisions about what to teach.

ACTIVITIES FOR PROFESSIONAL DEVELOPMENT

Ethical Dilemma

"Why Can't We Serve Them All?"

For the past five years Kim has worked as a lead teacher at a large Head Start center in a major city. She is a supporter of Head Start and believes in its mission of helping low-income children and families. Last week the regional Head Start office released data showing that 1,253 children who are eligible for Head Start in Kim's city are not being served. Kim believes that all children should have the benefits of Head Start, and she is sick and tired of people saying that children are the nation's greatest resource but not putting money where their mouths are! In frustration, Kim meets with Marty, the center director, to tell her that she has talked with a community activist who suggests that she call a meeting of parents with Head Start–eligible children to discuss a plan of action to demand additional funding. However, Marty becomes angry and defensive. "Look Kim, I don't want you to rock the Head Start boat! We have to be satisfied with what we have. Head Start never has been and never will be fully funded."

What should Kim do? Does she ignore Marty and develop plans to organize the parents, perhaps risking her career and reputation, or does she reluctanly agree with Marty and resign herself to the fact that there is nothing she can do about a large governmental agency like Head Start, or does she pursue some other course of action to help the children?

Application Activities

1. As an early childhood professional, you will need to make decisions about what to teach and how to teach it. Choose one of the programs you read about in this chapter and explain how you would implement it in your classroom. In your plans include a daily schedule and activities for children.

2. Make a chart with these headings:

   "Program Features I Like" and "Program Features I Don't Like"

   Complete your chart for each of the programs we discussed in this chapter. Next, rank in order the programs according to your first choice, second, third, and so forth.

3. Review your philosophy of education again. Now write a paragraph about how your philosophy does or does not align with the theory and assumptions of each program we have discussed in this chapter.

4. Review the learning theories we discussed in Chapter 3. Explain, with specific examples, how these theories have influenced the programs discussed in this chapter.

5. The programs in this chapter reveal how fast the field of early childhood has changed and is changing. Which of these "changes" or new ideas surprised you?

To take online practice tests on this chapter's material, go to the Companion Website at http://www.prenhall.com/morrison, select Chapter 4, and then choose the Multiple Choice or the Essay module. For additional Web resources, choose Web Links.

5

STANDARDS AND YOU
Teaching Children to Learn

professional development goals

Providing High-Quality Curriculum and Instruction

A. I use curricula and learning materials that are appropriate and meaningful for my students and that are in alignment with national standards. I use a variety of instructional practices that will help my students achieve at their highest levels and which will enable them to meet national standards.

B. I understand the importance of each content area in young children's learning. I know the essential concepts, inquiry tools, and structure of content areas including academic subjects and can identify resources to deepen their understanding.[1]

C. I use my knowledge and other resources to design, implement, and evaluate meaningful, challenging curriculum that promotes comprehensive developmental and learning outcomes for all young children.[2]

focus questions

1. What are national standards?
2. Why are standards important?
3. What role will standards play in your teaching?
4. How can you teach effectively using standards?
5. How can you use standards to help children learn?

When I visit early childhood programs, I always ask teachers, "What are you teaching?" Some reply that they are teaching about "animals" or "holidays." Other teachers respond that they are teaching "themes." Some say they are teaching social skills, and some say they are teaching beginning reading. But what are these teachers really teaching their children? And more importantly, what are the children learning?

"What should I teach my children?" This is a question all teachers ask themselves. I am sure you have asked yourself this question as well. What is your answer? Perhaps you reply that you are going to teach your children reading, writing, and mathematics. Certainly, we want all children to know how to read, write, and compute. But let's look at your answer for a minute. What are the skills of reading that you are going to teach? Are you going to teach **phonics**? Word meaning? Vocabulary development? In what order will you teach these skills? To what achievement level will you teach these skills? These questions are not easily answered and not all teachers answer them in the same way. **Standards**, statements of what students should know and be able to do, help answer questions about what to teach children and about what they should achieve.

During the past decade, standards and the standards movement have influenced every facet of early childhood education and will continue to do so in the decades to come. You have probably heard a lot about standards. Perhaps you have thought about how standards will affect your teaching and your students' learning. The purpose of this chapter is to help you learn more about how you and the children you teach are influenced by standards.

WHAT ARE STANDARDS?

As noted earlier, standards are statements that specify what students should know and be able to do, they are expectations for student learning. Often, standards are specified by content area and grade (e.g., first-grade reading, second-grade science); these are known as *content standards*. Today, from preschool to high school, professionals are emphasizing **standards-based education (SBE)**, which focuses on basing the **curriculum** (all of the experiences children have while in school), teaching, and testing on local, state, and national standards. **Performance standards** indicate levels of performance students should attain and provide specific examples of what students should know and do to demonstrate (usually by a state or local test) that they have mastered the knowledge and skills stated in the content standards. Performance standards also specify a range of work to indicate that students can meet the standards in a variety of ways.

WHY STANDARDS?

The current popularity of standards and the controversies surrounding them did not just suddenly break forth upon the American educational landscape. In fact, the standards movement has been gaining steam for the last several decades. Politicians view standards as a way to make sure that the nation's children learn and are prepared to do well in school and the workplace.

Three federal initiatives have played a tremendous role in the creation of the SBE system we have today:

- *A Nation at Risk: The Imperative for Educational Reform, National Commission on Excellence in Education (1983):* The U.S. Department of Education created the National Commission on Excellence in Education to provide a report about the quality of education in America. The report stated that the poor quality of American education had helped put the nation gravely at risk.[3] Without major education reform, the commission said that America's leadership was in jeopardy.[4] The commission recommended, among other things, curriculum reform, higher expectations for the nation's students, and standards for learning.[5]

- *Goals 2000: Educate America Act (P.L. 103–227, 2000):* This act was designed to ensure that all students reached high levels of achievement. Goals 2000 established eight national education goals. Goal three specified that by the year 2000: "All students will leave grades 4, 8, and 12 having demonstrated competency over challenging subject matter including English, mathematics, science, foreign languages, civics and government, economics, the arts, history, and geography, and every school in America will ensure that all students learn to use their minds well, so they may be prepared for responsible citizenship, further learning, and productive employment in our nation's modern economy."[6]

Read about the benefits and criticisms of the No Child Left Behind Act at Articles and Readings, Early Childhood Education, Module 1: Advocacy, Article 3: What Does it Mean to Educate the Whole Child?

TEACHER PREP

Goals 2000 also created the National Education Standards and Improvement Council to encourage states and professional organizations to develop national standards to identify what all students should know and be able to do to live and work in the twenty-first century.[7] As a result, many professional organizations such as the National Council of Teachers of Mathematics (NCTM) wrote standards specifically for their discipline. The NCTM standards served as a model for other subject matter groups, state education agencies, and local districts to write their own standards specifying what students should know and be able to do. Today, all fifty state departments of education have standards documenting what students in each state should know and do. You can review excerpts from the NCTM standards in Figure 5.1.[8] Goals 2000 ceased to exist as of June 30, 2001, and its goals are no longer a part of official federal and state education policy. Nonetheless, they made professional and public education goal oriented and set in motion the SBE movement of today. Many professionals still use Goals 2000 to guide their thinking and program planning.

- *No Child Left Behind Act (2001):* The No Child Left Behind (NCLB) Act[9] required all states to implement statewide accountability systems covering all public schools and students. These systems are based on challenging state standards in reading and mathematics and annual testing for all students in grades three through eight.[10]

National Reports

Three widely read and influential reports by the National Research Council of the National Academy of Sciences have stimulated discussion and action regarding the importance of early learning: *Preventing Reading Difficulties in Young Children,*[11] *From Neurons to Neighborhoods: The Science of Early Childhood Development,*[12] and *Eager to Learn: Educating Our Preschoolers.*[13] These reports increased national interest in standards as a basis for making explicit and public what young children need to know and do to be successful in school and life.

FIGURE 5.1

National Council of Teachers of Mathematics Standards

Number and Operations
Instructional programs from prekindergarten through grade 12 should enable all students to:
- Understand numbers, ways of representing numbers, relationships among numbers, and number systems;
- Understand meanings of operations and how they relate to one another;
- Compute fluently and make reasonable estimates.

Algebra
Instructional programs from prekindergarten through grade 12 should enable all students to:
- Understand patterns, relations, and functions;
- Represent and analyze mathematical situations and structures using algebraic symbols;
- Use mathematical models to represent and understand quantitative relationships;
- Analyze change in various contexts.

Geometry
Instructional programs from prekindergarten through grade 12 should enable all students to:
- Analyze characteristics and properties of two- and three-dimensional geometric shapes and develop mathematical arguments about geometric relationships;
- Specify locations and describe spatial relationships using coordinate geometry and other representational systems;
- Apply transformers and use symmetry to analyze mathematical situations;
- Use visualization, spatial reasoning, and geometric modeling to solve problems.

Measurement
Instructional programs from prekindergarten through grade 12 should enable all students to:
- Understand measurable attributes of objects and the units, systems, and processes of measurement;
- Apply appropriate techniques, tools, and formulas to determine measurements.

Data Analysis and Probability
Instructional programs from prekindergarten through grade 12 should enable all students to:
- Formulate questions that can be addressed with data and collect, orgainze, and display relevant data to answer them;
- Select and use appropriate statistical methods to analyze data;
- Develop and evaluate inferences and predictions that are based on data;
- Understand and apply basic concepts of probability.

Problem Solving
Instructional programs from prekindergarten through grade 12 should enable all students to:
- Build new mathematical knowledge through problem solving;
- Solve problems that arise in mathematics and in other contexts;
- Apply and adapt a variety of appropriate strategies to solve problems;
- Monitor and reflect on the process of mathematical problem solving.

Reasoning and Proof
Instructional programs from prekindergarten through grade 12 should enable all students to:
- Recognize reasoning and proof as fundamental aspects of mathematics;
- Make and investigate mathematical conjectures;
- Develop and evaluate mathematical arguments and proofs;
- Select and use various types of reasoning and methods of proof.

Communication
Instructional programs from prekindergarten through grade 12 should enable all students to:
- Organize and consolidate their mathematical thinking through communication;
- Communicate their mathematical thinking coherently and clearly to peers, teachers, and others;
- Analyze and evaluate the mathematical thinking and strategies of others;
- Use the language of mathematics to express mathematical ideas precisely.

Connections
Instructional programs from prekindergarten through grade 12 should enable all students to:
- Recognize and use connections among mathematical ideas;
- Understand how mathematical ideas interconnect and build on one another to produce a coherent whole;
- Recognize and apply mathematics in contexts outside of mathematics.

Representation
Instructional programs from prekindergarten through grade 12 should enable all students to:
- Create and use representations to organize, record, and communicate mathematical ideas;
- Select, apply, and translate among mathematical representations to solve problems;
- Use representations to model and interpret physical, social, and mathematical phenomena.

NCLB Discussion

All states have responded to the No Child Left Behind Act of 2001 by writing learning standards for K–12. Many states have also written standards for preschool education. In addition, a federal early childhood initiative, *Good Start, Grow Smart,* encourages states to voluntarily develop early learning guidelines.[14] While the guidelines themselves are voluntary, they are a condition for receiving funding through the federal Child Care and Development Block Grant. This accounts for why most states have written or are writing preschool guidelines.

The No Child Left Behind Act of 2001 was intended to significantly reform K–12 education. Since its passage, it has radically and rapidly changed how America conducts its educational business. NCLB emphasizes state and district accountability, mandates state standards for what children should know and be able to do, puts in place a comprehensive program of testing in grades three to twelve, and encourages schools to use teaching methods that have demonstrated their ability to help children learn.

The NCLB Act targets six fundamental areas:

- Accountability,
- Literacy,
- Programs that work (based on scientific research),
- Professional development,
- Educational technology, and
- Parental involvement.

NCLB is a significant educational act that will continue to influence what and how you teach for many years to come. The act has influenced pre-kindergarten education because there is a major emphasis on getting children ready for school. Many federally funded programs now use guidelines and mandates in the No Child Left Behind Act to develop goals and objectives for their own programs. In other words, all facets of programs that serve young children have been and will continue to be influenced by the NCLB.

Evaluation Research. According to the federal government, NCLB is making a difference in the lives of children. For example, the most recent national test scores show that:

- In reading, nine-year-olds have made larger gains in the past five years than at any point in the previous twenty-eight years.
- In math, nine-year-olds and thirteen-year-olds earned the highest scores in the history of the test.
- In both reading and math, African American and Hispanic students are scoring higher, and are beginning to close the achievement gap with their Caucasian peers.[15]

Two NCLB programs that specifically influence the early childhood grades pre-K–3 are Reading First and Early Reading First.

Reading First
- Provides grants to states to help schools and school districts improve children's reading achievement through scientifically proven methods of instruction.
- Funds professional development, scientifically based instructional programs, materials, and strategies, valid and reliable screening, diagnostic and ongoing classroom assessments, and statewide accountability and leadership structures.
- Under the NCLB Act, funding for fiscal years 2002 through 2005 amounted to $3.96 billion for Reading First and $348 million for Early Reading First.[16]

Early Reading First

- Enhances children's language, cognitive, and early reading skills through professional development for teachers.
- Provides early language and reading development and instructional materials as developed from scientifically based reading research.
- Provides preschool-age children with cognitive learning opportunities in high-quality language and literature-rich environments.
- Uses screening assessments to effectively identify preschool children who may be at risk for reading failure.
- Improves existing early childhood programs by integrating scientifically based reading research into all aspects of the program (including instructional materials, teaching strategies, curricula, parent engagement, ande professional development).[17]

According to Amy Holcombe, Ph.D., principal of Falkener Elementary School in Greensboro, North Carolina, federally funded schools have benefited from the NCLB legislation in many ways:

- NCLB requires that all teachers working in Title I schools be highly qualified. Previously, lateral entry or uncertified teachers could work as teaching faculty at federally funded schools. Now that this is no longer allowed, teaching faculty at federally funded schools are 100 percent highly qualified.
- NCLB provides for federal funding for each student qualifying for a free or reduced-price lunch. With this funding, Title I schools are able to purchase many additional resources including teaching faculty, instructional supplies, professional development, student field trips, and parental involvement activities.
- NCLB has generated a more focused approach to teaching to the individual needs of students. Previously, if a school's overall percentage of on-grade-level students was high, they were considered to be performing well. Now that those data are disaggregated by subgroup, it has become apparent that some schools are not meeting the needs of all students equally. In an effort to meet the requirements of NCLB, schools are utilizing research-based strategies to ensure that students are receiving individualized instruction designed to meet their learning needs.

NAEYC Early Learning Standards

Since standards are part of the early childhood landscape, it is reasonable to expect that professional organizations should become more involved in providing guidance and suggestions regarding the use and influence of standards. The National Association for the Education of Young Children (NAEYC) and the National Association of Early Childhood Specialists in State Departments of Education (NAECS/SDE) have issued a joint position statement designed to guide the development and implementation of standards for young children. As you review the following guidelines for developing standards, reflect about how they can help you as you engage in standards-based teaching.

A developmentally effective system of early learning standards must include four essential features:[18]

1. *Effective early learning standards emphasize significant, developmentally appropriate content and outcomes.*
   - Effective early learning standards give emphasis to all domains of early development and learning.
   - The content and desired outcomes of effective early learning standards are meaningful and important to children's current well-being and later learning.

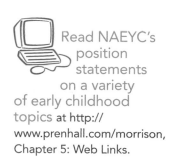

Read NAEYC's position statements on a variety of early childhood topics at http://www.prenhall.com/morrison, Chapter 5: Web Links.

- Rather than relying on simplifications of standards for older children, the content and desired outcomes of effective early learning standards are based on research about the processes, sequences, and long-term consequences of early learning and development.
- Effective early learning standards create appropriate expectations by linking content and desired outcomes to specific ages or developmental periods.
- The content of effective early learning standards, and expectations for children's mastery of the standards, must accommodate variations—community, cultural, linguistic, and individual—that best support positive outcomes. To do so, early learning standards must encompass the widest possible range of children's life situations and experiences, including disabilities.

Review an assortment of state and national early learning standards at http://www.prenhall.com/morrison, Chapter 5: Web Links.

2. *Effective early learning standards are developed and reviewed through informed, inclusive processes.*
- The process of developing and reviewing early learning standards relies on relevant, valid sources of expertise.
- The process of developing and reviewing early learning standards involves multiple stakeholders. Stakeholders may include community members, families, early childhood educators and special educators, and other professional groups. In all cases, those with specific expertise in early development and learning must be involved.
- Once early learning standards have been developed, standards developers and relevant professional associations ensure that standards are shared with all stakeholders, creating multiple opportunities for discussion and exchange.
- Early learning standards remain relevant and research based by using a systematic, interactive process for regular review and revision.

3. *Early learning standards gain their effectiveness through implementation and assessment practices that support all children's development in ethical, appropriate ways.*
- Effective early learning standards require equally effective curriculum, classroom practices, and teaching strategies that connect with young children's interests and abilities, and that promote positive development and learning.
- Tools to assess young children's progress must be clearly connected to important learning represented in the standards; must be technically, developmentally, and culturally valid; and must yield comprehensive, useful information.
- Information gained from assessments of young children's progress with respect to standards must be used to benefit children. Assessment and accountability systems should be used to improve practices and services and should not be used to rank, sort, or penalize young children.

4. *Effective early learning standards require a foundation of support for early childhood programs, professionals, and families.*
- Research-based standards for early childhood program quality, and adequate resources for high-quality programs, build environments where standards can be implemented effectively.
- Significant expansion of professional development is essential if all early childhood teachers and administrators are to gain the knowledge, skills, and dispositions needed to implement early learning standards.
- Early learning standards have the most positive effects if families—key partners in young children's learning—are provided with respectful communication and support.

Appropriate Assessment

The NAEYC and NAECS/SDE also take the position that policy makers, the early childhood profession, and other stakeholders in young children's lives have a shared responsibility to make ethical, appropriate, valid, and reliable assessment a central part of all early childhood programs.

To assess young children's strengths, progress, and needs, teachers need to use assessment methods that are:

- Developmentally appropriate,
- Culturally and linguistically responsive,
- Tied to children's daily activities,
- Supported by professional development,
- Inclusive of families, and
- Connected to specific beneficial purposes.

They also need to:

- Make sound decisions about teaching and learning.
- Indentify significant concerns that may require focused intervention for individual children.
- Help programs improve their educational and developmental interventions.[19]

Indicators of Effective Assessment.   The following are indicators of effective assessment that you can apply to your teaching.

- *Ethical principles guide assessment practices.* Ethical principles underlie all assessment practices. Young children are not denied opportunities or services, and decisions are not made about children on the basis of a single assessment.

- *Assessment instruments are used for their intended purposes.* Assessments are used in ways consistent with the purposes for which they were designed. If the assessments will be used for additional purposes, they are validated for those purposes.

- *Assessments are appropriate for ages and other characteristics of children being assessed.* Assessments are designed for and validated for use with children whose ages, cultures, home languages, socioeconomic status, abilities and disabilities, and other characteristics are similar to those of the children with whom the assessments will be used.

- *Assessment instruments are in compliance with professional criteria for quality.* Assessments are valid and reliable. Accepted professional standards of quality are the basis for selection, use, and interpretation of assessment instruments, including screening tools. NAEYC and NAECS/SDE support and adhere to the measurement standards set forth in 1999 by the American Educational Research Association, the American Psychological Association, and the National Center for Measurement in Education. When individual norm-referenced tests are used, they meet these guidelines.

- *What is assessed is developmentally and educationally significant.* The objects of assessment include a comprehensive, developmentally, and educationally important set of goals, rather than a narrow set of skills. Assessments are aligned with early learning standards, with program goals, and with specific emphases in the curriculum.

Read how to use assessment effectively in the classroom at Articles and Readings, Assessment, Module 2: Informal Classroom Assessment, Article 1: Classroom Assessment: Minute by Minute, Day by Day.

- *Assessment evidence is used to understand and improve learning.* Assessments lead to improved knowledge about children. This knowledge is translated into improved curriculum implementation and teaching practices. Assessment helps early childhood professionals understand the learning of a specific child or group of children; enhance overall knowledge of child development; improve educational programs for young children while supporting continuity across grades and settings; and access resources and supports for children with specific needs.

- *Assessment evidence is gathered from realistic settings and situations that reflect children's actual performance.* To influence teaching strategies or to identify children in need of further evaluation, the evidence used to assess young children's characteristics and progress is derived from real-world classroom or family contexts that are consistent with children's culture, language, and experiences.

- *Assessments use multiple sources of evidence gathered over time.* The assessment system emphasizes repeated, systematic observation, documentation, and other forms of criterion- or performance-oriented assessment using broad, varied, and complementary methods with accommodations for children with disabilities.

- *Screening is always linked to follow-up.* When a screening or other assessment identifies concerns, appropriate follow-up, referral, or other intervention is used. Diagnosis or labeling is never the result of a brief screening or one-time assessment.

- *Use of individually administered, norm-referenced tests is limited.* The use of formal standardized testing and norm-referenced assessments of young children is limited to situations in which such measures are appropriate and potentially beneficial, such as identifying potential disabilities. (See also the indicator concerning the use of individual norm-referenced tests as part of program evaluation and accountability.)

- *Staff and families are knowledgeable about assessment.* Staff are given resources that support their knowledge and skills about early childhood assessment and their ability to assess children in culturally and linguistically appropriate ways. Preservice and in-service training builds teachers' and administrators' "assessment literacy," creating a community that sees assessment as a tool to improve outcomes for children. Families are part of this community, with regular communication, partnership, and involvement.

Why Are Standards Important?

By now, you have gained a pretty good idea that standards are playing an important role in the lives of children, teachers, administrators, and family members. Let's examine some of the reasons for the prominent and important role standards have in education today.

Provide Clarity and Focus.   Standards enable you to know what a district expects of its children and teachers. In this regard, they bring clarity and focus to the program curriculum and teaching.

Integrate Concepts.   By knowing what your district expects, you will be able to integrate concepts, ideas, and skills into your teaching. For example, if you are a preschool teacher, knowing about kindergarten standards enables you to provide your preschoolers with the language, literacy, and other skills they must have for a successful transition to kindergarten. It is important for you and other professionals to know what is expected of children at each grade level, pre-K–3, so that you can ensure your children are well prepared for learning in the next grade.

Identify What Children Should Know.   Standards identify what every child in a particular state or district should know and be able to do. This is significant in that, with standards, the expectations are the same for all children, regardless of their socioeconomic

There's a lot of discussion today about the achievement gap. The achievement "gap is the difference between what certain groups of children know and are able to do as opposed to what other groups of children know and are able to do. The achievement gap is wide between white children and black and Latino children. Consider this example:

In reading, the achievement gaps between white and black and white and hispanic 4th-graders have fluctuated since 1992, but the gaps in 2005 were not measurably different from those in 1992. In 2005, at the 4th-grade level, Blacks scored, on average, 29 points lower than Whites (on a 0–500 scale), and Hispanics scored, on average, 26 points lower than Whites.*

The standards are often cited as one way that teachers and schools can help all children learn what they need to know, and as a result close the achievement gap. Certainly standards do play a role in helping close achievement gaps; however, standards by themselves cannot close achievement gaps. A number of other things are required, including the following:

- Providing programs for young children at an early age that will help them gain the knowledge skills and behaviors necessary to succeed in school,
- Providing every child with a high-quality teacher who is well prepared to teach all children regardless of diversity and socioeconomic background, and
- Providing programs designed to help parents gain knowledge and skills that will help them help their children get ready to learn before they come to school.

In addition, here are some things that you as a classroom teacher can do to make sure that you help all young children learn:

- Be familiar with your state and district standards. These standards are important because they outline what all children should know and be able to do, not just some children.
- Develop your lesson plans so that they incorporate state and district standards, and focus on the essential knowledge skills and behaviors that all children need to know.
- In your planning, focus on what your children will be tested on at the end of the year. You and other teachers should not "teach to the test"; however, you need to be aware of what your children will be tested on. (Chapter 6 discusses the consequences of high-stakes testing.)

- Differentiate your instruction so that you can provide for the diverse learning needs of your students. One approach does not fit all, and in today's educational environment increasing numbers of teachers are differentiating their instruction so that all students can learn.
- Make the best use of your classroom time for instructional purposes. When children are meaningfully engaged in learning activities, then there is a better chance for them to learn what they need to know and do. Remember that you have a limited amount of time with children, so you should strive to make the best use of it. At the same time, your teaching should be developmentally appropriate and children should be involved in activities they find interesting and worthwhile. Keep in mind also that children need opportunities to play and interact with each other.
- Integrate technology into your teaching and learning. Children enjoy technology, and technology adds interest while at the same time helping children learn what standards specify.
- Work with families and parents to help them understand what you are teaching their children and why. Seek family members' cooperation so that they can help support and encourage in the home what you are teaching in the classroom. Sending simple lessons home such as a packet of learning activities that children and family members can do in the home helps involve parents in the teaching–learning process and impresses on them and their children the importance of school achievement.

Closing the achievement gap between cultures, races, and socioeconomic groups is always an ongoing process, but it is a process to which you have to dedicate yourself. After all, helping all children succeed is why we teach and is what we dedicate our lives to.

*National Center for Education Statistics, "Trends in the Achievement Gaps in Reading and Mathematics," 2006, http://nces.ed.gov/programs/coe/2006/ section2/indicator14.asp.

Practice differentiating Pre-Kindergarten activities at http://www.prenhall.com/morrison, Chapter 5— Journal: Diversity Tie-In.

backgrounds, their culture, their race or ethnicity, or where they go to school. In this sense, standards level the educational playing field and help ensure that all students will learn the same content and will achieve at a high level. Implementing standards is one way to help close the achievement gap. Review the accompanying Diversity Tie-In for steps on what you can do to help close the achievement gap.

David Mager / Pearson Learning Photo Studio

Standards provide a number of challenges and opportunities for early childhood professionals. Determining developmentally effective ways to help children master the knowledge and skills in specified standards is a particular challenge. You can meet this challenge through involving children in active play with concrete materials that support their learning.

Provide Accountability. Standards serve as one means by which states and local programs can be accountable for teaching and learning. As we discussed in Chapter 2, not everyone agrees that using standards to hold teachers, schools, and programs accountable is beneficial to students. Critics of standards-based education argue that standards focus too much on academic achievement and that other areas of the curriculum such as social and emotional development get left behind. In addition, critics assert that standards promote a traditional back-to-basics approach to early childhood education at the expense of play-based and child-centered teaching and learning. Nonetheless, standards play a major role in the current accountability movement.

All four of these reasons point to the fact that standards are an essential part of early childhood today. Hardly a teacher or classroom in the country is not impacted in some way by standards. The Professionalism in Practice feature by Gaye Gronlund will help you make the best use of learning standards in your teaching.

HOW ARE STANDARDS CHANGING TEACHING AND LEARNING?

As indicators of what children should know and be able to do, standards are changing the ways teachers teach, how and what students learn, and the ways schools operate. Let's review some of the ways standards are shaping teaching and learning.

- *Standards serve as expectations of what teachers should teach.* When teachers ask the "What should I teach?" question, state and local standards help answer their question. However, good teachers teach more than the standards. They also teach an essential core that provides direction for the curriculum. Additionally, teachers teach individual children, plan for individual children's needs, and make decisions about what and how they should teach them; however, the standards serve as a baseline of expectations.

- *Standards are goals for student achievement.* Standards let the public, as well as parents or guardians, know what the state, district, or programs think their children should learn.

- *Standards are broad statements about what should be learned.* **Benchmarks** are more specific statements that clarify the standards. They specify the level at which students will learn and identify mastery levels. As a result, teachers and parents can use the benchmarks. For example, a reading standard which states that "students can comprehend what they read in a variety of literary and informational texts" may have a benchmark which states that "students can determine the meaning of new words from their context." In another example, a standard may specify that children should get memory from print. Benchmarks for this standard would propose that infants can pay attention to books as they are read to them; that toddlers can "retell" a simple story and that preschoolers can "read" picture books. The curriculum frameworks described academic standards students should achieve, but unlike a curriculum, did not include details about specific content, sequence, instructional materials, or pedagogical methods.

Figure 5.2 shows excerpts from the Illinois Early Learning Standards for Language Arts and Mathematics. This figure also gives you an example of what benchmarks are and how they are used.

FIGURE 5.2

A Portion of the Illinois Early Learning Standards for Language Arts and Mathematics

Language Arts

State Goal 1: Read with understanding and fluency.

Learning Standard A: Apply word analysis and vocabulary skills to comprehend selections.
- Understand that pictures and symbols have meaning and that print carries a message.
- Understand that reading progresses from left to right and top to bottom.
- Identify labels and signs in the enviroment.
- Identify some letters, including those in own name.
- Make some letter-sound matches.

Learning Standard B: Apply reading strategies to improve understanding and fluency.
- Predict what will happen next using pictures and content for guides.
- Begin to develop phonological awareness by participating in rhyming activities.
- Recognize separable and repeating sounds in spoken language.

Learning Standard C: Comprehend a broad range of reading materials.
- Retell information from a story.
- Respond to simple questions about reading material.
- Demonstrate understanding of literal meaning of stories by making comments.

Mathematics

State Goal 6: Demonstrate and apply a knowledge and sense of numbers, including numeration and operations (addition, subtraction, multiplication, division), patterns, ratios, and proportions.

Learning Standard A: Demonstrate knowledge and use of numbers and their representations in a broad range of theoretical and practical settings.
- Use concepts that include number recognition, counting, and one-to-one correspondence.
- Count with understanding and recognize "how many" in sets of objects.

Learning Standard B: Investigate, represent, and solve problems using number facts, operations (addition, subtraction, multiplication, division) and their properties, algorithms, and relationships.
- Solve simple mathematical problems.

Learning Standard C: Compute and estimate using mental mathematics, paper-and-pencil methods, calculators, and computers.
- Explore quantity and number.
- Connect numbers to quantities they represent using physical models and representations.

Learning Standard D: Solve problems using comparison of quantities, ratios, proportions, and percents.
- Make comparisons of quantities.

Source: Courtesy of the Illinois State Board of Education.

- *Standards serve as a basis for reform and accountability.* Standards help the public and politicians hold teachers and schools accountable for ensuring that children learn. As I pointed out in Chapter 2, using standards as a basis for accountability, teachers can no longer say, "I taught Maria reading." Now the question is, "Did Maria learn to read?" Even more important from an accountability point of view, "Did Maria achieve the benchmark of being able to read at or above her grade level?"

The What and Why of Early Learning Standards

Gaye Gronlund
Early childhood education consultant and author
Indianapolis, Indiana

As of 2007, early learning standards for preschool-age children had been developed by almost every state in the United States. Early childhood educators in each state worked hard to define reasonable expectations for three- and four-year-old children that reflect the values and uniqueness of their state, as well as comply with accepted developmental understanding of how young children learn and develop. There are many similarities across these standards, as well as unique features. The National Institute for Early Education Research has a State Standards Database at their website (http://www.nieer.org/standards/statelist.php) that enables comparison between the standards for each state. In addition, most states have provided easy Internet access to the early learning standards they developed. Early educators should become familiar with the standards in their state and incorporate them in their curriculum planning and assessment practices.

MAKING THE BEST USE OF STANDARDS

There are benefits to early learning standards. There are also potential problems if they are used inappropriately. The benefits include:

- Reinforcement of the incredible potential for learning and growth in young children;
- Help in establishing expectations for children at different ages and creating a commonality for communication among early educators;
- Creation of a framework for accountability—a way for early educators to show parents, the community at large, and themselves just what children are learning;

- Potential to be incorporated into curriculum that is developmentally appropriate for preschoolers—play and investigation, emergent curriculum and projects, small and large-group times, and daily routines such as snack time, toileting and hand washing, outdoor times, and transitions; and
- The capability to be assessed in ways that are authentic, based on teacher observation and documentation of children's progress through photographs and work samples that can be used to show children's progress on the early learning standards.

Caution should prevail when using early learning standards. Early educators committed to implementing them within a developmentally appropriate framework of curriculum and assessment must be careful to avoid the following:

- Teaching and curricular practices that overemphasize direct instruction and do not value child-initiated play and investigation with adult guidance and support; and
- Assessment practices that focus on testing or on-demand tasks that do not naturalistically reflect how the children demonstrate the early learning standards in everyday activities, play, investigation, and daily routines.

Learning the standards for your state takes time. Figuring out ways to incorporate them into activities and daily routines, as well as assessing children's progress in authentic and naturalistic ways, may require training, dialogue among colleagues, and even some trial and error as you get started and see what works and doesn't work in your setting. Early learning standards have changed the climate of early childhood education. The accountability associated with them may be frightening or seem oppositional to traditional early childhood practices. This is not the case! They can be implemented within the context of best practices for young children. Time and effort on the part of

- *Standards exert federal and state control over education.* Primarily, education is a state function. Historically, states have delegated the responsibility for education to local districts and programs. However, beginning in about 1995, states have increasingly taken more control for educating children, monitoring teaching, and holding schools accountable for student achievement. State standards are one example of this. Not everyone is happy about or satisfied with this state and federal control of education, for a number of reasons. First, they claim that federal control of education takes away from the ability of local programs to develop their own programs based upon what they think are best for their children. Essentially this is a local control of schools idea and is embedded in the belief that local communities know what is best for their children. Second, some early childhood educators believe that federal control is leading to the implementations of programs that are developmentally inappropriate for young children, especially preschool and kindergarten children. However, teachers and administrators will be required to do so in ways that are just right for preschoolers.

STANDARDS IN A PRESCHOOL CURRICULUM

There are two ways to think about standards in a preschool curriculum: naturalistically and intentionally.

Naturalistic Approaches. Naturalistically, standards are imbedded in all that goes on in a preschool classroom. You can look back over the day with children and think about what you saw children do and heard them say. Then, you can identify which standards they were demonstrating as they played in the dramatic play area, or created at the art table, or built with the blocks.

This requires conscientious attention to what children are doing and familiarity with your state's early learning standards. The more you reflect and think about this and the more you dialogue with colleagues, the more you will see the children's progress!

Intentional Approaches. Thinking intentionally about standards is a proactive approach. You can plan for activities and materials that will directly address specific early learning standards. Again, you do not need to think in terms of direct instruction only. Your plans for children's play, projects, group times, and field trips can incorporate early learning standards. You can:

- Put together specific materials or activities that address that standard;
- Write the goals on a lesson or activity plan; and
- Plan for how you will record what the children do in relation to that standard.

ASSESSING STANDARDS AUTHENTICALLY

As early educators work with children throughout each day, they are in a continual process of observing them and listening to them, as well as evaluating what they are seeing and hearing. Authentic assessment involves gathering information about a child as you work and play with him, watching him, listening to him, asking him open-ended questions to learn more about his thinking, and challenging him to try the next step. Then, you evaluate all of the information that you have learned about the child. This is where the standards come into play. They are the reference by which the child's accomplishments are measured. You ask yourself the following questions:

- Has the child accomplished a particular standard or not?
- If not, where is he on a spectrum of progress toward accomplishing the standard?
- If he has accomplished the standard, what is the next step in acquisition of skills and knowledge that he is ready for?
- What curricular plans will best meet this child where he is and help him to move on in his progress and accomplishments?

Authentic assessment through observation and reflection about each child's progress is time consuming. It is also the best and most appropriate way to get a true picture of how each child is developing in relation to the expectations in the standards. The time and effort put into documenting through observational notes, photographs, and work samples is worth it if the end result is a truer, more reliable evaluation of the child's capabilities.

CONCLUSION

Early learning standards have many benefits. They can be a wonderful guide to reasonable expectations and common goals for children in each state. They can be incorporated into developmentally appropriate preschool curriculum and authentic assessment practices. This takes commitment and hard work on the part of all involved to do what is right for young children!

Adapted with permission from Gaye Gronlund, Make Early Learning Standards Come Alive: Connecting Your Practice and Curriculum to State Guidelines *(St. Paul, MN: Redleaf Press, 2006); special edition published unchanged in 2007 by Merrill/Prentice Hall as part of the Merrill Education/Redleaf Press College Textbook Series.* © 2006 Gaye Gronlund.

standards are now a part of the political and educational landscape. They are not going to go away, for a number of reasons.

- *Standards address the educational needs of low-achieving students.* Most standards are considered to be the minimum necessary for grade-level achievement. In this way, they help assure that all children will be taught what they need to know to accomplish the skills appropriate for their grade level. There has always been a concern that low-socioeconomic status (SES) children are not being taught or challenged to achieve. Teaching to the standards addresses this issue and helps to prevent failure and school dropout.

- *Standards make the curriculum more academic.* In particular, standards have caused a greater emphasis on academics in pre-kindergarten and kindergarten. Almost all states have standards that describe what elementary school students should know and be able to do; however, only twenty-seven states lay out specific expectations for

FIGURE 5.3 Alignment
of Standards,
Curriculum, and Testing

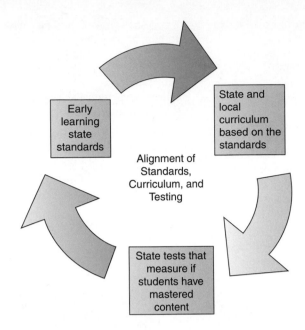

the kindergarten year.[20] Currently thirty-three states and the District of Columbia have specified standards for prekindergarten.[21] While there are standards for music and the arts, standards for reading, writing, math, and science receive the majority of the teaching attention.

- *Standards help bring teaching and the curriculum in alignment.* In **curriculum alignment**, the official curriculum of the school district and that taught by individual teachers is matched to the content standards. This alignment process, shown in Figure 5.3, also ensures that the tests used to assess student achievement really measure what the standards state. Alignment is the process of making sure that the curriculum and what teachers teach are what the standards specify. Standards encourage curriculum alignment and, as a result, teachers focus material and book selection and learning experiences on specific outcomes for children's learning. As federal pressure for accountability standards moves into the preschool arena, it is important for states to rapidly develop processes that align preschool standards with K–12 standards and evaluate how prepared children are to succeed in school. One method that districts and states can now use is integrating technology into the curriculum. Technology is a developmentally appropriate way to assess young children and measure their achievement. The Technology Tie-In feature helps you get a feeling for how one elementary school integrates technology across the curriculum to help children meet all state standards.

Standards and Teaching

I have said that standards have changed teaching and learning. But how have standards changed what teachers teach and how they teach it? Have standards changed more than teaching and learning? Have standards changed other dimensions of schooling as well, such as how schools are run and how teachers interact with their colleagues, parents, and families? One good way to answer our questions about standards is to ask teachers who are affected and influenced by them. Ask teachers to share with you their ideas about how standards have changed how they teach. The accompanying Program in Action and Professionalism in Practice features will help you get the most out of teaching with standards.

Technology Across the Curriculum

Preparing students to participate productively in a digital world is an important educational goal. Finding ways to achieve this goal is the challenge of all educators. Children, teachers, and schools all across the country are in different stages of using technology to facilitate and support teaching and learning. Many schools have progressed from simply teaching technology to integrating technology across the curriculum. As a result, teachers don't spend a lot of time teaching specific technology skills; rather, they spend their time helping children use technology to learn.

Carolina Beach Elementary School provides a good example of how teachers integrate technology in all curriculum areas. They use technology to teach skills and concepts related to the content areas (e.g., math, science, literacy), and knowledge and skills specified by North Carolina State Standards.

Vickie Holland, technology facilitator for Carolina Beach Elementary, believes that every lesson and topic can be taught using technology. Here are some examples of how students use technology:

Reading: Kindergarten

- *Science:* Classify Animals—Using Kid Pix software, students sort or stamp animals into groups. Examples: fur, scales, and feathers.
- *Language Arts:* Using Kid Pix software, students create pictures of words that start with an alphabet letter. Pictures are used in a classroom slideshow about the alphabet. Students use Island Adventure to learn the alphabet letters.
- *Math & Science:* Students use a software program called The Graph Club to make a graph of weather for a month.
- *Math:* Students use a software program called Whole Numbers in Math to sort different attributes.

First Grade

- *Social Studies:* Students create pictures of family members with a sentence about each family member. Pictures are used to create a family slide show.
- *Science:* In Kid Pix, students create a Venn diagram to teach, compare and contrast environments of animals. Label— Land, Water, and Both. Stamp animals in the correct area.
- *Language Arts:* Students use word processing to write a sentence or story. Import clip art to go with the lesson. Several software programs give students the individual help they need with blends, rhyming words, and beginning and ending sounds.
- *Math:* Students take digital pictures of math shapes and import them into a math slideshow.

Second Grade

- Use AlphaSmarts to create stories.
- *Science:* Students use a WebQuest on weather. Students create a picture with a sentence about each season during the year. At the end of the year they create a seasons slideshow.
- *Social Studies & Language Arts:* Students create a classroom book on community workers. Using a word-processing program, students write about their community workers and import a graphic on the subject for the book.
- Students search an Accelerated Reader database for books on their level.

Teachers at Carolina Beach are enthusiastic about their use of technology. For example, second-grade teacher Cathy Byrd says, "Technology allows me to differentiate learning in my classroom in a way we couldn't have imagined even ten years ago. It also allows me to expand the walls of my classroom so the children can virtually travel around the community and world."

Your use of technology to help you be a high-quality teacher depends on a number of factors:

- Your belief in the power of technology to help children learn,
- Your willingness to learn about and use technology in your teaching,
- The technology resources available to you and your school, and
- The support of administrators for using technology in the classroom.

Here are some things you can do to ensure that technology is an integrated part of your teaching:

- Collaborate with colleagues to develop ways to integrate technology in grade-level programs and across grades.
- Collaborate with and involve parents and the community. Many parents have technology skills and connections they can share with your students. Many community agencies, such as the police and health departments, use technology to solve problems. Community people make great classroom speakers and mentors.
- Create a classroom environment that encourages and enables students to help each other learn technology skills and applications. Children are very adept at helping their peers learn new skills.

Vickie Holland is technology facilitator and webmaster at Carolina Beach Elementary, Carolina Beach, North Carolina.

 Identify technology resources you would like to integrate into your classroom at http://www.prenhall.com/morrison, Chapter 5—Journal: Technology Tie-In.

When sitting down to create lesson plans, I always keep the following quotation in mind: "You cannot control the wind [i.e., state or district standrards] but you can adjust your sails [i.e., personal lesson plans]." As you review the following steps, remember that lesson plans are to *guide* instruction; they are not a blueprint that must control your every word. You should always follow a wonderful teachable moment, even if it is not written into your lesson plan. You will never regret where it leads you and your students.

STEP 1 BECOME FAMILIAR WITH BOTH STATE AND DISTRICT STANDARDS

The objectives in my district's teacher's guide are clearly stated and are usually cross-referenced with the broader Florida Sunshine State Standards. Realize that standards encompass broad categories and often do not change significantly from one grade level to another. For example, "Reads for meaning" and "Uses context clues" apply to many grade levels; what changes is the level of presentation.

STEP 2 INCORPORATE IN YOUR PLANS WHAT WILL BE ASSESSED ON HIGH-STAKES TESTS

I work into my lesson plans for all subjects the Florida Comprehensive Assessment Test task cards (e.g., compare/contrast, vocabulary, author's purpose, main idea, details, multiple representations of information, cause and effect) and the big five literacy components—phonological awareness, phonics, vocabulary, comprehension, and fluency.

STEP 3 PLAN A WEEK AHEAD

Planning ahead has several advantages:

* As you plan ahead, you think ahead. Just thinking about what you're going to teach enables you to see how standards and your instructional practices fit together.
* Planning ahead allows you to share ideas with your colleagues, get their advice, and make changes as appropriate.
* Planning ahead gives you time to gather all necessary materials and resources.

STEP 4 MEET WITH OTHER TEACHERS TO COORDINATE PLANS

As the chairperson for grade three, I hold a weekly planning meeting with the other third-grade teachers. We explore the information required to be presented the following week and plan together. Because my district uses the same authored curriculum across the county, we all teach from a particular reading series. This is extremely helpful with our somewhat transient population in Miami and allows for continuity as students move.

STEP 5 CREATE AND SAVE A FRAMEWORK FOR YOUR LESSON PLANS

Because parts of lessons are repeated week after week, using a consistent framework saves valuable time. On a computer I can cut and paste from week to week, adding or removing entries quickly. The table included on the next page shows a sample format, using Sunshine State Standards for literacy for third grade.

STEP 6 DIFFERENTIATE INSTRUCTION

Once the framework for lesson planning is understood you are ready to "adjust your sails"—that is, differentiate your instruction. As an inclusion teacher, one-third of my students have exceptional needs, so I differentiate my instruction. I must adjust my presentation rather than expecting my learners to modify themselves to my presentation. Because there are varied abilities and disabilities within any given

National Standards

National standards are, as the name implies, designed to be applicable to all children, regardless of individual state or local standards. Again, not everyone agrees that national standards from any source are good for the nation's children. Some argue that national standards, by their very nature, do not address the unique needs of children at the local level. They further argue that the needs of rural and urban children differ and that children's needs differ by geographic region. However, others argue that national standards help assure that all children in every state will learn a basic core of knowledge and skills. They further argue that this common curriculum does not preclude teachers in local districts and programs from teaching to the particular needs of children.

classroom, instructional practices and approaches should always be adapted to the students served within the classroom. In other words, instruction should meet the learners wherever they are and appeal to them on a multisensory level.

For instance, I plan vocabulary practice daily within every lesson plan (e.g., math vocabulary, science vocabulary, story vocabulary). Because not all students are at the same level in vocabulary development, I do the following:

- Present vocabulary on an overhead.
- Use colored markers on the overhead to separate and isolate vocabulary words.
- Use hearing and seeing sticks (i.e., rulers with an ear or an eye and a vocabulary word stapled on them). Students raise the stick when they hear or see the vocabulary word.
- Use a highlighter stick (i.e., a yardstick with an index card stapled to the end of it). When the vocabulary words are projected on the wall, I can hold the index card over a word and actually lift the word off the wall by lifting the card.

OTHER PLANNING AND INSTRUCTIONAL GUIDELINES

I recommend overplanning. Activities that you think will take a certain amount of time will often take much less or much more.

This is fine—you are working with children! Simply cut and paste a missed lesson into the next week's framework, or discontinue a lesson that is not working for you and move on to your next planned activity.

I also recommend moving your students often. Begin with a whole-group activity, and then transition to a partner activity. I place my students in groups of six rather than having them sit in rows. Within each grouping I place at least two children with special needs and have the group come up with a name and work as a small community. I also set up centers that allow for higher-order processing. Centers give me an opportunity to work with some students who may require more intensive instruction.

Lesson planning is a learned skill, and learned skills take time to master. Ask to see other teachers' lesson plans, ask them what works, and use any ideas that interest you.

....

Contributed by Lynn Carrier, third-grade teacher, Gulfstream Elementary, Miami, Florida, and 2007 Miami-Dade County Teacher of the Year.

Reflect on the guidelines for planning lessons suggested in this Competency Builder at http://www.prenhall.com/morrison, Chapter 5—Journal: Program in Action.

Reading/Language Arts (8:30–10:35 A.M.): Story Selection—*Across the Wide Dark Sea*

MONDAY	TUESDAY	WEDNESDAY	THURSDAY	FRIDAY
Standard 1: Reads text and determines the main idea	*Standard 2:* Identifies the author's purpose	*Standard 3:* Recognizes when a text is primarily intended to persuade	*Standard 4:* Identifies specific personal preferences relative to fiction and nonfiction reading	*Standard 5:* Reads and organizes information for a variety of purposes
Objective:	Objective:	Objective:	Objective:	Objective:
Activities:	Activities:	Activities:	Activities:	Activities:
ESOL strategies:	ESOL strategies:	ESOL strategies:	ESOL strategies:	ESOL strategies:
Vocabulary:	Vocabulary:	Vocabulary:	Vocabulary:	Vocabulary:
Home learning:	Home learning:	Home learning:	Home learning:	Home learning:
Assessment:	Assessment:	Assessment:	Assessment:	Assessment:

One set of national pre-kindergarten standards was developed by McGraw-Hill Publishing Company in consultation with early childhood experts from across the country. These standards provide a framework for what children between the ages of three and five should learn during their preschool years. These standards are organized around three domains and twelve guidelines, as shown in Figure 5.4.[22] These are useful in that they provide a set of national standards for prekindergarten children. In this regard, they provide much-needed direction for programs where states have developed standards for educating three to five year olds. However, critics argue that McGraw-Hill has a proprietary interest in selling products based on the standards. Nonetheless, these standards serve a number of very useful purposes. First, they represent a common core of standards that all pre-K programs can review and incorporate into their goals as appropriate. Second, the

Teachers' Views About How Standards Have Changed Their Teaching

Linda Housewright
Prekindergarten director/teacher
Dallas City, Illinois

1. **How have standards changed teaching and learning?** Standards have given classrooms a shared framework, based on developmentally appropriate practice, of what should be taught to children and how we know through their learning that they are growing socially, emotionally, physically, and academically. Standards have given education, especially early childhood education, credibility! Standards that are written in a friendly, usable format can also be used to help us explain to parents what their children are learning and achieving through play. They make the job of explaining the how's and why's of what we do easier.

2. **How do I teach with the standards?** I use the standards within my classroom as my curriculum. They guide the instruction and give meaning and credibility to what actually is happening in my room on a day-to-day basis. The standards give me long-range goals for each of my children. I also use the standards to create the environment in my classroom. Through this environment, I can do authentic ongoing assessment in a natural way.

3. **How do standards change my life?** I was one of the teachers chosen to field test the Illinois Early Learning Standards three years ago. Through this experience I became a more focused teacher. I acquired skills that helped me to really know where to look for learning within the environment I had created for the children in my classroom. I may have been a good teacher before I took ownership of the standards, but I became a better teacher because of my increased ability to focus. They also made me look at the "why" behind my instruction and to be more personally accountable for what was happening.

4. **How do standards affect the role of the teacher?** Standards are a teacher's road map. They are the guides used to create individual educational journeys. They tell what children should be able to do and what they should know. Standards are a child's "mile markers." Standards give teachers the tools necessary to meet the needs of all the children in the classroom in a way that allows each child to grow and to learn and not to be left behind.

5. **How do standards affect curriculum and instruction?** Standards tie curriculum and instruction together. They give us the "why" behind what we are doing in our classrooms. Curriculum, instruction, and assessment are all tied together and should be based around the standards. In past years, teachers created lessons that were "cute"... they did not look at the "why" behind what they were doing. Teachers do not have time to create "cute." The children we are seeing in our classrooms need an environment and a teacher who is being guided by a set of classroom standards that focus on where the child needs to go to become a critical thinker and a problem solver!

6. **Is addressing standards the only thing I do?** Standards are not something that I do, they are something I believe in and use to guide the direction I take my children. A focused teacher takes ownership of the standards and uses them as a "best friend."

7. **How do standards affect children?** If a teacher uses the standards to create the environment in the classroom the children will have a safe place to grow, learn, and discover themselves. The teacher will be able to sit back and make observations and to scaffold the learning in a way that is natural and authentic. When teachers "teach at" children, children do not always participate in a developmentally appropriate manner. We sometimes forget that play is the highest level of learning ... and that learning is not quiet!

 Conduct interviews with teachers about how standards have changed their teaching at http://www.prenhall.com/morrison, Chapter 5—Projects: Professionalism in Practice.

standards recognize that development and learning are integrated with each other. The recognition that development forms the basis for educating young children is the foundation to developmentally appropriate practice.

The Head Start Performance Standards (http://www.acf.hhs.gov/programs/hsb/performance/) and Outcomes Framework (http://www.kaplanco.com/ includes/content/classroom/UGCOF.pdf) are other examples of national standards. The Head Start Performance Standards guide programs in their operation. Major elements of the standards

FIGURE 5.4

McGraw-Hill Publishing Co. National Pre-Kindergarten Standards

Domain I: Children Will Be Equipped with Self-Knowledge, Social Skills, and Motivation to Learn

Guideline I: Children Will Develop Knowledge of Self

Guideline II: Children Will Develop Knowledge of Others and Social Skills

Guideline III: Children Will Gain Intrinsic Motivation for Learning

Domain II: Children Will Be Equipped with Their Culture's Basic Symbol Systems

Guideline IV: Children Will Gain Literacy and Language Learning

Guideline V: Children Will Possess Concepts of Mathematics

Guideline VI: Children Will Gain Initial Knowledge of World Languages

Domain III: Children Will Be Equipped with Knowledge of the World in Which They Live

Guideline VII: Children Will Gain Foundational Knowledge of Scientific Inquiry

Guideline VIII: Children Will Gain Foundational Knowledge of the Physical, Life, and Earth Sciences

Guideline IX: Children Will Gain Foundational Knowledge of Technologies

Guideline X: Children Will Gain Foundational Knowledge of the Social Sciences

Guideline XI: Children Will Gain Foundational Knowledge of Health and Physical Education

Guideline XII: Children Will Gain Foundational Knowledge of Visual Arts, Theater, and Music

Source: McGraw-Hill, *Pre-Kindergarten Standards,* 2003, http://www.ctb.com/media/articles/pdfs/resources/PreKstandards.pdf.

include early childhood development, health services, family and community partnerships, staffing, and program design and management. The Head Start Outcomes Framework acts as a national curriculum in that other preschool programs in addition to Head Start use them to guide what their children should know and do. The Outcomes Framework also helps ensure that all Head Start children, regardless of what state or program they are in, receive the same curriculum. Take a moment to review the Outcomes Framework shown in Figure 5.5 (see pages 140–143).

Read how to teach to meet standards and increase student **achievement** at Articles and Readings, Educational Leadership, Module 4: School Improvement Through Systematic Planning, Article 3: A Blueprint for Increasing Student Achievement.

ISSUES SURROUNDING STANDARDS

By now, through our discussion of standards, you are aware that a number of controversies and issues swirl around standards and their use. Let's examine some of these issues.

- Standards narrow the curriculum or force "teaching to the test." In some programs and classrooms, the standards may become the curriculum so that students pass

FIGURE 5.5

Head Start Child Outcomes Framework

Domain	Domain Element	Indicators
LANGUAGE DEVELOPMENT	Listening & Understanding	• Demonstrates increasing ability to attend to and understand conversations, stories, songs, and poems. • Shows progress in understanding and following simple and multiple-step directions. ☆ Understands an increasingly complex and varied vocabulary. ☆ For non–English-speaking children, progresses in listening to and understanding English.
	Speaking & Communicating	☆ Develops increasing abilities to understand and use language to communicate information, experiences, ideas, feelings, opinions, needs, questions and for other varied purposes. • Progresses in abilities to initiate and respond appropriately in conversation and discussions with peers and adults. ☆ Uses an increasingly complex and varied spoken vocabulary. • Progresses in clarity of pronunciation and towards speaking in sentences of increasing length and grammatical complexity. ☆ For non–English-speaking children, progresses in speaking English.
LITERACY	☆ Phonological Awareness	• Shows increasing ability to discriminate and identify sounds in spoken language. • Shows growing awareness of beginning and ending sounds of words. • Progresses in recognizing matching sounds and rhymes in familiar words, games, songs, stories, and poems. • Shows growing ability to hear and discriminate separate syllables in words. ☆ Associates sounds with written words, such as awareness that different words begin with the same sound.
	☆ Book Knowledge & Appreciation	• Shows growing interest and involvement in listening to and discussing a variety of fiction and non-fiction books and poetry. • Shows growing interest in reading-related activities, such as asking to have a favorite book read; choosing to look at books; drawing pictures based on stories; asking to take books home; going to the library; and engaging in pretend-reading with other children. • Demonstrates progress in abilities to retell and dictate stories from books and experiences; to act out stories in dramatic play; and to predict what will happen next in a story. • Progresses in learning how to handle and care for books; knowing to view one page at a time in sequence from front to back; and understanding that a book has a title, author and illustrator.
	☆ Print Awareness & Concepts	• Shows increasing awareness of print in classroom, home and community settings. • Develops growing understanding of the different functions of forms of print such as signs, letters, newspapers, lists, messages, and menus. • Demonstrates increasing awareness of concepts of print, such as that reading in English moves from top to bottom and from left to right, that speech can be written down, and that print conveys a message. • Shows progess in recognizing the association between spoken and written words by following print as it is read aloud. ☆ Recognizes a word as a unit of print, or awareness that letters are grouped to form words, and that words are separated by spaces.

Domain	Domain Element	Indicators
SOCIAL & EMOTIONAL DEVELOPMENT (cont.)	Social Relationships	• Demonstrates increasing comfort in talking with and accepting guidance and directions from a range of familiar adults. • Shows progress in developing friendships with peers. • Progresses in responding sympathetically to peers who are in need, upset, hurt, or angry; and in expressing empathy or caring for others.
	Knowledge of Families & Communities	• Develops ability to identify personal characteristics including gender, and family composition. • Progresses in understanding similarities and respecting differences among people, such as genders, race, special needs, culture, language, and family structures. • Develops growing awareness of jobs and what is required to perform them. • Begins to express and understand concepts and language of geography in the contexts of their classroom, home, and community.
APPROACHES TO LEARNING	Initiative & Curiosity	• Chooses to participate in an increasing variety of tasks and activities. • Develops increased ability to make independent choices. • Approaches tasks and activities with increased flexibility, imagination, and inventiveness. • Grows in eagerness to learn about and discuss a growing range of topics, ideas and tasks.
	Engagement & Persistence	• Grows in abilities to persist in and complete a variety of tasks, activities, projects and experiences. • Demonstrates increasing ability to set goals and develop and follow through on plans. • Shows growing capacity to maintain concentration over time on a task, question, set of directions or interactions, despite distractions and interruptions.
	Reasoning & Problem Solving	• Develops increasing ability to find more than one solution to a question, task or problem. • Grows in recognizing and solving problems through active exploration, including trial and error, and interactions and discussions with peers and adults. • Develops increasing abilities to classify, compare and contrast objects, events and experiences.
PHYSICAL HEALTH & DEVELOPMENT	Fine Motor Skills	• Develops growing strength, dexterity and control needed to use tools such as scissors, paper punch, stapler, and hammer. • Grows in hand-eye coordination in building with blocks, putting together puzzles, reproducing shapes and patterns, stringing beads and using scissors. • Progresses in abilities to use writing, drawing and art tools including pencils, markers, chalk, paint brushes, and various types of technology.
	Gross Motor Skills	• Shows increasing levels of proficiency, control and balance in walking, climbing, running, jumping, hopping, skipping, marching, and galloping. • Demonstrates increasing abilities to coordinate movements in throwing, catching, kicking, bouncing balls, and using the slide and swing.
	Health Status & Practices	• Progresses in physical growth, strength, stamina, and flexibility. • Participates actively in games, outdoor play and other forms of exercise that enchance physical fitness. • Shows growing independence in hygiene, nutrition and personal care when eating, dressing, washing hands, brushing teeth, and toileting. • Builds awareness and ability to follow basic health and safety rules such as fire safety, traffic and pedestrian safety, and responding appropriately to potentially harmful objects, substances and activities.

☆Indicates the four specific domain elements and nine indicators that are legislatively mandated.

Source: http://www.headstartinfo.org/pdf/im00_18a.pdf.

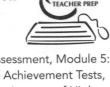

Read about high-stakes tests' effects on teaching and learning at Articles and Readings, Assessment, Module 5: Standardized Achievement Tests, Article 2: The Lessons of High-Stakes Testing.

state proficiency exams. While in a sense this issue may be true, it need not be so. There is no reason why standards should narrow the curriculum or what is taught. Effective teachers always have and always will teach a wide and rich range of knowledge and skills based on local community needs and the needs of young children.

- Standards impose too much structure on early childhood teachers who have a tradition of having the freedom to develop their own curriculum and classroom activities. As I previously indicated, effective teachers always teach what they think is important in the best way possible.

- Standards lead to an overemphasis on assessment and testing. This may well be true, but proponents of testing argue that it is necessary to help ensure that children learn. In reality, standards, instruction, and assessment, when well integrated, provide a process that helps ensure all children learn.

- Are the standards for all children? Not everyone agrees that they are. For example, do they apply to children with disabilities and special learning conditions? Many special educators believe that standards and tests designed for normally developing children are inappropriate for children with disabilities. This issue is far from resolved and we will hear more about it in the coming months and years.

Positive outcomes of the standards movement include:

David Mager / Pearson Learning Photo Studio

- Implementation and support of intentional teaching. Intentional teaching is the development of plans, and the selection of instructional strategies with the intended purpose of promoting learning.
- Increased and enhanced reporting and sharing of information with families and the community.
- Enhanced opportunities for professional training and education.

We can conclude our discussion of standards by asking ourselves, why is this important to us?

The standards movement has done a number of things for the early childhood profession as well as teachers and young children. Standards have helped the profession sharpen its focus about what young children should know and be able to do. As a result, many early childhood professionals have come to the conclusion that young children are more capable than they realized or gave them credit for. As the National Research Council Committee on Early Childhood Pedagogy points out,

> The accumulation of convincing evidence from research [is] that young children are more capable learners than current practices reflect and that good educational experiences in the preschool years can have a positive impact on school learning.[23]

As early childhood professionals have rediscovered the children they teach, they are in the process of rediscovering themselves. Teachers are engaged in more professional development than ever before and much of this professional development involves learning how to teach with standards. In this sense, standards have reenergized the teaching profession.

My hope for you is that you will embrace teaching with standards and that you will help all children learn to their highest levels.

Refer to Figure 5.4, page 139, Domain III, Guideline VII, of the McGraw-Hill National Standards states that "Children Will Gain Foundational Knowledge of Scientific Inquiry." What scientific foundational knowledge are children learning from this activity? Are they learning in a developmentally appropriate way? Identify two other activities that you could use to help kindergarten children learn scientific foundational knowledge.

ACTIVITIES FOR PROFESSIONAL DEVELOPMENT

Ethical Dilemma

"Test or Leave?"

Christina Lopez teaches in a preschool for three- to four-year-olds that is funded with federal dollars. Her administrator has sent out a memo announcing a testing program designed to measure children's preschool achievement and the effectiveness of programs funded with federal dollars. All four-year-olds will be tested on their knowledge, skills, and readiness for kindergarten with a federally developed paper-and-pencil achievement test. Christina believes it is developmentally inappropriate to "test" preschool children using the prescribed federal test.

What should Christina do? Should she share her concerns with the school adminis-trator and risk the administrator's disapproval, or should she administer a test she believes is developmentally inappropriate?

Application Activities

1. Do you think that standards are meeting their intended purpose of helping ensure that all children will achieve and learn? After you have reflected on the question, write a letter to your local school or a letter to the editor of your local newspaper expressing your opinions.

2. Review again your state standards for the grade you plan to teach. What insights do you have about your teaching and what children are learning after reviewing these standards? What will you have to do to prepare yourself to teach to the standards of your state?

3. What are your feelings about national standards? Interview teachers in preschool programs and ask them to explain how they do or do not use national standards to guide their program planning and teaching. Compare their thoughts with your thoughts. Make a list of five ways you could use the Illinois standards illustrated in Figure 5.2 to guide your teaching.

4. Select the grade in which you plan to teach (e.g., kindergarten) and compare the state standards for your grade with the standards from another state. What conclusions can you draw? Which state do you think has the better standards? Why?

5. Interview at least one teacher from all grades pre-K–3. Ask them how state standards are affecting their teaching. Ask them to share with you their feelings—pro and con—about standards.

6. Parents and community members have opinions about standards, too. Interview a parent, a politician, or a school board member about what roles they think standards should or should not play in early education.

 To take online practice tests on this chapter's material, go to the Companion Website at http://www.prenhall.com/morrison, select Chapter 5, and then choose the Multiple Choice or the Essay module. For additional Web resources, choose Web Links.

6

OBSERVING AND ASSESSING YOUNG CHILDREN
Guiding, Teaching, and Learning

professional development goal

Observation and Assessment

A. I evaluate students using developmentally appropriate and authentic measures. I use observation and assessment to guide my teaching.

B. I know about and understand the goals, benefits, and uses of assessment.[1]

C. I know about and use systematic observations, documentation, and other effective assessment strategies in a responsible way, in partnership with families and other professionals, to positively influence children's development and learning.[2]

focus questions

1. Why is it important for you to know how to assess?

2. What are the purposes and uses of observation and assessment?

3. What are some ways you can assess children's development, learning, and behavior?

4. How can you ensure that your assessment and observation is developmentally appropriate and adheres to the ethics of the profession?

Kindergarten teacher Tyron Jones wants to make sure Amanda knows the initial beginning sounds that he has taught the class during the last two weeks. First-grade teacher Mindy McArthur wants to see how many words on the class word wall César knows. Third-grade teacher José Gonzalez wants to know if his students can apply what they're learning to real-life situations. Decisions, decisions, decisions. All of these relate to how to assess learning and teaching.

Teachers' minutes, hours, and days are filled with assessment decisions. Questions abound: "What is Jeremy ready for now?" "What can I tell Maria's parents about her language development?" "The activity I used in the large-group time yesterday didn't seem to work well. What could I have done differently?" Appropriate assessment can help you find the answers to these and many other questions relating to how to teach and what is best for children in all areas of development.

WHAT IS ASSESSMENT?

Much of children's lives are subject to and influenced by your assessment and the assessment of others. As an early childhood professional, assessment will influence your professional life and will be a vital tool of your professional practice. Assessment well done is one of your most important responsibilities, and it can enhance your teaching and children's learning.

According to the National Association for the Education of Young Children, **assessment** is the process of observing, recording, and otherwise documenting what children do and how they do it as a basis for a variety of educational decisions that affect the child.

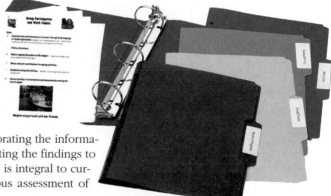

Assessment involves the multiple steps of collecting data on a child's development and learning, determining its significance in light of the program goals and objectives, incorporating the information into planning for individuals and programs, and communicating the findings to families and other involved people. Assessment of child progress is integral to curriculum and instruction. In early childhood programs, the various assessment of child progress procedures that are used serve several purposes:

(a) to plan instruction for individuals and groups
(b) to communicate with families
(c) to identify children who may be in need of specialized services or intervention
(d) to inform program development.[3]

Why Is Assessment Important?

Assessment is important because of all the decisions you will make about children when teaching and caring for them. The decisions facing our three teachers at the beginning of this chapter all involve how best to educate children. Like them, you will be called upon every day to make decisions before, during, and after your teaching. Whereas some of these decisions will seem small and inconsequential, others will be "high stakes," influencing the life course of children. All of your assessment decisions taken as a whole will direct and alter children's learning outcomes. Figure 6.1 outlines for you some purposes of assessment and how assessment can enhance your teaching and student learning. All of these purposes are important; if you use assessment procedures appropriately, you will help all children learn well.

The following general principles should guide both policies and practices for the assessment of young children:

- *Assessment should bring about benefits for children.* Gathering accurate information from young children is difficult and potentially stressful. Assessments must have a

Children

Families

Early Childhood Programs

Early Childhood Teachers

The Public

Children	Families	Early Childhood Programs	Early Childhood Teachers	The Public
• Identify what children know • Identify children's special needs • Determine appropriate placement • Select appropriate curricula to meet children's individual needs • Refer children and, as appropriate, their families for additional services to programs and agencies	• Communicate with parents to provide information about their children's progress and learning • Relate school activities to home activities and experiences	• Make policy decisions regarding what is and is not appropriate for children • Determine how well and to what extent programs and services children receive are beneficial and appropriate	• Identify children's skills, abilities, and needs • Make lesson and activity plans and set goals • Create new classroom arrangements • Select materials • Make decisions about how to implement learning activities • Report to parents and families about children's developmental status and achievement • Monitor and improve the teaching-learning process • Meet the individual needs of children • Group for instruction	• Inform the public regarding children's achievement • Provide information relating to student's school-wide achievements • Provide a basis for public policy (e.g., legislation, recommendations, and statements)

FIGURE 6.1 Purposes of Assessment

Photos (from left to right): Laura Bolesta / Merrill; Blair M. Seitz / Creative Eye/MIRA.com; Laura Bolesta / Merrill; Laura Bolesta / Merrill; Jeff Greenberg / PhotoEdit Inc.

clear benefit—either in direct services to the child or in improved quality of educational programs.

- *Assessment should be tailored to a specific purpose and should be reliable, valid, and fair for that purpose.* Assessments designed for one purpose are not necessarily valid if used for other purposes. In the past, many of the abuses of testing with young children have occurred because of misuse.

- *Assessment policies should be designed recognizing that reliability and validity of assessments increase with children's age.* The younger the child, the more difficult it is to obtain reliable and valid assessment data. It is particularly difficult to assess children's cognitive abilities accurately before age six. Because of problems with reliability and validity, some types of assessment should be postponed until children are older, while other types of assessment can be pursued, but only with necessary safeguards.

- *Assessment should be age appropriate in both content and the method of data collection.* Assessments of young children should address the full range of early learning and development, including physical well-being and motor development; social and emotional development; approaches toward learning; language development; and cognition and general knowledge. Methods of assessment should recognize that children need familiar contexts to be able to demonstrate their abilities. Abstract paper-and-pencil tasks may make it especially difficult for young children to show what they know.

- *Assessment should be linguistically appropriate, recognizing that to some extent all assessments are measures of language.* Regardless of whether an assessment is intended to measure early reading skills, knowledge of color names, or learning potential, assessment results are easily confounded by language proficiency, especially for children who come from home backgrounds with limited exposure to English, for whom the assessment would essentially be an assessment of their English proficiency. Each child's first- and second-language development should be taken into account when determining appropriate assessment methods and in interpreting the meaning of assessment results.

- *Parents should be a valued source of assessment information, as well as an audience for assessment.* Because of the fallibility of direct measures of young children, assessments should include multiple sources of evidence, especially reports from parents and teachers. Assessment results should be shared with parents as part of an ongoing process that involves parents in their child's education.[4]

Read how classroom assessments can improve learning at Articles and Readings, Content Area Reading Methods, Module 8: Content Area Assessment, Article 2: How Classroom Assessments Improve Learning.

What Is Authentic Assessment?

Authentic assessment is the evaluation of children's actual learning and the instructional activities in which they are involved. Figure 6.2 outlines characteristics of authentic assessment. As you examine these characteristics, think about how you will apply them to your professional practice. Following the authentic assessment strategies shown in Figure 6.2 will help ensure that the information you gather will be useful and appropriate for all children.

Authentic assessment is also referred to as *performance-based assessment.* Authentic assessment requires children to demonstrate what they know and are able to do. Meaningless facts and isolated information are considered inauthentic.

Here are some guidelines for authentic assessment:

- *Assess children based on their actual work.* Use work samples, exhibitions, performances, learning logs, journals, projects, presentations, experiments, and teacher observations.

Read more about authentic assessment at http://www.prenhall.com/morrison, Chapter 6: Web Links.

Employs a number of different ways to determine children's achievement and what they know and are able to do

Takes into account children's cultural, language, and other specific needs

Is ongoing over the entire school year

Is curriculum-embedded; children are assessed on what they are actually learning and doing

Assesses children and their actual work with work samples, portfolios, performances, projects, journals, experiments, and teacher observations

Is a cooperative process—involves children, teachers, parents, and other professionals; goal is to make assessment child-centered

Assesses the whole child rather than a narrow set of skills

Is part of the learning process

FIGURE 6.2 Characteristics of Authentic Assessment

Photo: Patrick White / Merrill

- *Assess children based on what they are actually doing in and through the curriculum.*
- *Assess what each individual child can do.* Evaluate what each child is learning, rather than comparing one child with another or one group of children with another.
- *Make assessment part of the learning process.* Encourage children to show what they know through presentations and participation.
- *Learn about the whole child.* Make the assessment process an opportunity to learn more than just a child's acquisition of a narrow set of skills.
- *Involve children and parents in a cooperative, collaborative assessment process.* Authentic assessment is child centered.
- *Provide ongoing assessment over the entire year.* Assess children continually throughout the year, not just at the end of a grading period or at the end of the year.

There are basically two kinds of assessment, formal and informal.

Formal Assessment

Formal assessment involves the use of standardized tests that have set procedures and instructions for administration and have been normed, meaning that it is possible to

TABLE 6.1 Formal Measures of Assessment Used in Early Childhood

Assessment Instrument	Age/Grade Level	Purpose
Battelle Developmental Inventory, 2nd edition *http://www.assess.nelson.com/test-ind/bdi.html*	Birth to age 8	Assesses key developmental skills in children up to age 8
Boehm Test of Basic Concepts–Revised *http://www.cps.nova.edu/~cpphelp/BTBC-R.html*	Kindergarten to grade 2	Assesses children's mastery of basic concepts that are fundamental to understanding verbal instruction and necessary for early school achievement
BRIGANCE® screens and inventories *http://www.curriculumassociates.com/products/ detail.asp?topic=TOA&sub=TOA2&title=BrigCIBS& Type=SCH&CustID=6590085734712131246053*	Prekindergarten to grade 9	Obtains a broad sampling of children's skills and behaviors to determine initial placement, plan appropriate instruction, and comply with mandated testing requirements
Developmental Indicators for the Assessment of Learning, 3rd edition (DIAL-3) *http://ags.pearsonassessments.com/Group.asp? nMarketInfoID=31&nCategoryInfoID2329& nGroupInfoID=a13700*	Ages 3 to 6	Identifies children who may have special educational needs
Peabody Picture Vocabulary Test–Revised (PPVT-R) *http://www.cps.nova.edu/~cpphelp/PPVT-R.html*	Ages 2.5 to 40	Tests hearing vocabulary; available in two forms

compare a child's score with the scores of a group of children who have already taken the same exam. In the following pages we discuss screening procedures, a formal type of assessment. Table 6.1 lists other types of formal assessment measures commonly used in early childhood teaching.

Note that screening procedures can also be informal. Informal screening is what you and other professionals do when you gather information to make decisions about small-group placements, instructional levels, and so forth.

Informal Assessment

Informal assessment is a procedure for obtaining information that can be used to make judgments about children's learning behavior and characteristics or programs using means other than standardized instruments. They are labeled as *informal* because they do not entail standard guidelines for administration and use. Authentic assessment relies heavily on informal procedures.

Observations, checklists, and portfolios are just some of the informal methods of assessment available to early childhood educators, as discussed in the following sections. Table 6.2 outlines methods for informal assessment, their purposes, and guidelines for using them. Study closely the ten kinds of informal assessments listed in the table—you will use all of them in your work with young children.

Also, visit http://www.naeyc.org to peruse a joint position statement on curriculum, assessment, and program evaluation. Pay particular attention to the section on indicators of effective assessment.

CC Studio / Photo Researchers, Inc.

Many school districts conduct a comprehensive screening for children entering kindergarten, which may include vision, hearing, and speech tests.

TABLE 6.2 Informal Methods of Assessment

Method	Purpose	Guidelines
OBSERVATION Kid watching—looking at children in a systematic way	Enables teachers to identify children's behaviors, document performance, and make decisions	Plan for observation and be clear about the purposes of the observation.
Anecdotal record Gives a brief written description of student behavior at one time	Provides insight into a particular behavior and a basis for planning a specific teaching strategy	Record only what is observed or heard; should deal with the facts and should include the setting (e.g., where the behavior occurs) and what was said and done.
Running record Focuses on a sequence of events that occurs over time	Helps obtain a more detailed insight into behavior over a period of time	Maintain objectivity and try to include as much detail as possible.
Event sampling Focuses on a particular behavior during a particular event (e.g., behavior at lunchtime, behavior on the playground, behavior in a reading group)	Helps identify behaviors during a particular event over time	Identify a target behavior to be observed during particular times (e.g., fighting during transition activities).
Time sampling Record particular events or behaviors at specific time intervals (e.g., five minutes, ten minutes)	Helps identify when a particular child demonstrates a particular behavior; helps answer the question, "Does the child do something all the time or just at certain times and events?"	Observe only during the time period specified.
Rating scale Contains a list of descriptors for a set of behaviors	Enables teachers to record data when they are observed	Make sure that key descriptors and the rating scale are appropriate for what is being observed.
Checklist A list of behaviors identifying children's skills and knowledge	Enables teachers to observe and easily check off what children know and are able to do	Make sure that the checklist includes behaviors that are important for the program and for learning (e.g., counts from 1 to 10, hops on one foot).
WORK SAMPLE Collection of children's work that demonstrates what they know and are able to do	Provides a concrete example of learning; can show growth and achievement over time	Make sure that the work sample demonstrates what children know and are able to do. Let children help select the items they want to use as examples of their learning.
PORTFOLIO Collection of children's work samples and other products	Provides documentation of a child's achievement in specific areas over time; can include test scores, writing work samples, videotapes, etc.	Make sure the portfolio is not a dumpster but a thoughtful collection of materials that documents learning over time.
INTERVIEW Engaging children in discussion through questions	Allows children to explain behavior, work samples, or particular answers	Ask questions at all levels of Bloom's taxonomy in order to gain insight into children's learning.

USING OBSERVATION TO ASSESS

Professionals recognize that children are more than what is measured by any particular standardized test. Observation is an "authentic" means of learning about children—what they know and are able to do, especially as it occurs in more naturalistic settings such as classrooms, child care centers, playgrounds, and homes, and it is one of the most widely used methods of assessment. **Observation** is the intentional, systematic act of looking at the behavior of a child or children in a particular setting, program, or situation. Observation is sometimes referred to as "kid-watching" and is an excellent way to find out about children's behaviors and learning.

Purposes of Observation

Observation is designed to gather information on which to base decisions, make recommendations, develop curriculum, plan activities and learning strategies, and assess children's growth, development, and learning. For example, when professionals and parents sometimes look at children, they do not really "see" or concern themselves with what the children are doing or why. However, the significance and importance of critical behaviors go undetected if observation is done casually and is limited to "unsystematic looking." In order for you to make your observation count, review the purposes of observation as outlined in Figure 6.3. Systematic observation each day will enable you to

FIGURE 6.3

Purposes of Observation

- *Determine the cognitive, linguistic, social, emotional, and physical development of children.* Using a developmental checklist is one way professionals can systematically observe and chart the development of children. (Figure 6.7 shows a checklist for inclusive classrooms.)

- *Identify children's interests and learning styles.* Today, teachers are very interested in developing learning activities, materials, and classroom centers based on children's interests, preferences, and learning styles.

- *Plan.* The professional practice of teaching requires planning on a daily, ongoing basis. Observation provides useful, authentic, and solid information that enables teachers to intentionally plan for activities rather than make decisions with little or no information.

- *Meet the needs of individual children.* Meeting the needs of individual children is an important part of teaching and learning. For example, a child may be advanced cognitively but overly aggressive and lacking the social skills necessary to play cooperatively and interact with others. Through observation, a teacher can gather information to develop a plan for helping him learn how to play with others.

- *Determine progress.* Systematic observation, over time, provides a rich, valuable, and informative source of information about how individuals and groups of children are progressing in their learning and behavior.

- *Provide information to parents.* Professionals report to and conference with parents on an ongoing basis. Observational information adds to other information they have, such as test results and child work samples, and provides a fuller and more complete picture of individual children.

- *Provide self-insight.* Observational information can help professionals learn more about themselves and what to do to help children.

Lu Ann Harger
Second-grade teacher
Hinkle Creek Elementary
Noblesville, Indiana

There are many ways to make a difference in a child's life. As a teacher, each year you are given the enormous honor of spending eight hours a day creating within a child a burning desire for learning. You have the opportunity to introduce your children to the wonders of numbers, letters, words, and to the history of their nation. You have the ability to create the "what if" and the "tell me more" in minds each day. But where to start this daunting task is difficult to say.

BEGINNING OF THE SCHOOL YEAR

All things have a beginning, and nothing equals a sound beginning. Each year as the school year is ready to begin, I call all my students to introduce myself and our classroom, Camp Can Do, and put their minds at ease. Fear of the unknown is a great deterrent to success, and this phone call goes a long way in calming that fear. I ask them to bring a thinking cap along to help on tough assignments and, of course, I keep mine handy all year too!

As they begin the first week of school, activities are planned to get to know each other and to evaluate levels of learning. Students play the M&M game by choosing a handful and speaking about themselves according to the colors. Each child gets a chance to say the alphabet, show me crayons to match color words, read a set of selected grade level word lists, and read a passage aloud to me. As a class we sit in community circle and use cards to stimulate discussions. That way I can check for verbal expression, use of vocabulary words, life experiences, and comfort levels. Students also fill out a reading inventory on their likes and dislikes, play math games to show computation skills, and copy some basic words to evaluate their fine-motor skills.

FAMILY PARTICIPATION

Now that I am on the right track evaluating my students, I work on my other team members, my family members. At the beginning of each school year at Parent Night, parents and guardians are asked to provide information about their child. Sure, I have permanent records to look over but the primary caregivers are the experts. They share fears and acts of bravery, favorites, past school experiences, and special traits of their children. With their help I will gain a better understanding of their child, and they will understand how much I value their input. During the meeting I explain how our classroom, or Camp Can Do, is run and what we do each day. I also explain the importance of their role as communicator, coach, and study partner. In the end, I read *Leo the Late Bloomer* and reiterate that my plan this year is for everyone to make it, just like Leo. Now I have the complete package: family input, student files, and my classroom evaluations. This is a sound beginning. Using this information, I can set up learning profiles for all my students that will be used throughout the year.

ASSESSMENT AND CURRICULUM

As the year's curriculum begins to unfold, I gather new information. In math, I pretest before each chapter to see what students know and do not know. Then throughout the lessons I group students according to their needs. Students work in many different groups by the year's end as their mastery of math skills is checked. Students are able to work on weak areas like time and money, but expand areas in which they are strong, like addition computation. In spelling, lists are modified according to learning levels. Everyone gets an opportunity to try the bonus words and earn a chance for spelling prizes. In reading and language arts, students work in small and large groups. They begin to take home simple readers or chapter books to become members of the Campfire Readers. Students work on partner reading books, enjoy the Scholastic Reader computer program books,

meet children's learning needs and be a more effective teacher. In the Professionalism in Practice feature, second-grade teacher Lu Ann Harger shares her perspective on assessment and evaluation.

Intentional observation is a useful, informative, and powerful means for informing and guiding teaching and for helping ensure that all children learn. The advantages of gathering data through observation are shown in Figure 6.4 on page 156. Review these six advantages now.

Steps for Conducting Observations

The four steps involved in the process of systematic, purposeful observation are listed in Figure 6.5 on page 157. Review them now in preparation for our discussion of each of them.

and add up pages read, and use trade books for readers during the year as well. Weekly reading conferences are held between students and myself to check on comprehension.

The use of various assessment tools provides me with a wide range of knowledge about each student. Some assessments can be as easy to use as a book discussion to determine my students' comprehension or a game to show knowledge gained. Assessments can also take the form of a Venn diagram for comparison or a poster giving facts about the animal students researched. Ongoing assessments, such as writing portfolios, can provide a big picture of skill growth by storing information in a time line fashion. Other assessments may be standardized, such as a math or reading test. No matter what type of assessment I might use, I think it is critical that my students be aware beforehand how they will be assessed and afterward take part in a discussion of the assessment tool. When I give a test of any kind, my students have a chance to talk over the items they missed. When using a less formal assessment such as a rubric, I give these out in advance. This gives students an idea of my expectations and a way to determine what they would like to accomplish.

No matter how you choose to assess your students, the most important thing to remember is that the assessment is only as good as the teacher using it. To keep the information meaningful, I look at the assessments I use with each unit I teach. Is there an area that I forgot to include? Are my students missing a question on a test in large numbers? Did this assessment give me the information I needed to know about my students' learning? What do the students think of the assessment? Is the information easy for me to understand? Is it easy to share with my students and my parents? Good assessments gather meaningful information that enhances children's learning. If my assessments are doing that, great! If not, I need to make a change so they are.

MAKING LEARNING MEANINGFUL

All of this information would mean nothing to the students or me if they were not engaged in their learning. Seven years ago, two colleagues and I investigated the idea of integrated instruction. Taking all our textbooks, we rebuilt our second-grade curriculum from the ground up using our social studies standards as the base.

The result was a full year of learning that was connected and meaningful. Students could learn about community workers and be reading a story for language arts on the same topic that week. The math lesson would also use community helpers as a base for the skill taught that week. The effort to make this possible was enormous and continues today as the plan is refined each year, but the results are worth it. Learning has become an "I get it" experience for my students. They see that our story for the week is about money and so are the math lessons. They understand that we are working on the skill of compound words because they are in our story for the week. Suddenly learning has an order and pattern that make their gathering of knowledge so much more genuine and long term. This connection of learning also brings strengths and weaknesses together that help improve both. This is real, lifelong learning!

Creating an environment where learning occurs is a huge key to successful students. We use these lifelong guidelines: Be truthful. Be trustworthy. Do your personal best. Appreciate others. Be an active listener. By expecting everyone in our classroom, including myself, to follow these guidelines, we create a place that is consistent, caring, and safe. Students know what to expect from day to day. By taking the time to listen to a story from home, provide a worry box to stuff concerns in, use mistakes as learning opportunities, or help ease a fear, I am modeling these expectations. I am creating a place where my students feel comfortable, can take risks, and will grow as learners. From my most able student to my least, I hear them saying: I can do this, I will try.

Can this make a difference? We sure think so in Room 12, or Camp Can Do as we like to call it. Never underestimate the potential of a child. If they shoot for the moon and miss, they will still wind up in the stars.

Lu Ann Harger is part of the *USA Today* ALL STAR Teacher Team.

Read more about how assessment informs curriculum decisions and complete an activity at http://www.prenhall.com/morrison, Chapter 6—Projects: Professionalism in Practice.

Step 1: Plan for Observation. Planning is an important part of the observation process. Everything you do regarding observation should be planned in advance of the observation. A good guide to follow in planning for observation is to ask the questions *who, what, where, when,* and *how.*

Setting goals for observation is a crucial part of the planning process. Goals allow you to reflect on why you want to observe and thus direct your efforts to what you will observe. Stating a goal focuses your attention on the purpose of your observation. For example, suppose you want to determine the effectiveness of your efforts in providing an inclusive classroom or program, and in fully including an exceptional child into the classroom. Your goals might read like this:

Goal 1: To determine what modifications might be necessary in the classroom to facilitate access to all parts of the classroom for Dana in her wheelchair.

FIGURE 6.4

Advantages of Gathering Data Through Observation

- Enables professionals to collect information about children that they might not otherwise gather through other sources. A great deal of the consequences, causes, and reactions to children's behavior can be assessed only through observation. Observation enables you to gather data that cannot be assessed by formal, standardized tests, questioning, and parent and child interviews.

- Is ideally suited to learning more about children in play settings. Observation affords you the opportunity to note a child's social behavior in a play group and discern how cooperatively he or she interacts with peers. Observing a child at play gives professionals a wealth of information about developmental levels, social skills, and what the child is or is not learning in play settings.

- Allows you to learn a lot about children's pro-social behavior and peer interactions. It can help you plan for appropriate and inclusive activities to promote the social growth of young children. Additionally, your observations can serve as the basis for developing multicultural activities to benefit all children.

- Provides a basis for the assessment of what children are developmentally able to do. Many learning skills are developed sequentially, such as the refinement of large-motor skills before fine-motor skills. Through observation, professionals can determine whether children's abilities are within a normal range of growth and development.

- Is useful to assess children's performance over time. Documentation of daily, weekly, and monthly observations of children's behaviors and learning provides a database for the cumulative evaluation of each child's achievement and development.

- Helps you provide concrete information for use in reporting to and conferencing with parents. Increasingly, reports to parents about children involve professionals' observations and children's work samples so parents and educators can collaborate to determine how to help children develop cognitively, socially, emotionally, and physically.

Krista Greco / Merrill

Observing is an excellent way to find out about a child's behavior and how well he is learning. What do you think you can learn about children from watching them complete puzzles and other fine-motor activities?

Goal 2: To assess the development of pro-social behavioral characteristics that other children display to Dana while interacting in the classroom.

Goal setting sharpens your observation and makes it more effective.

Step 2: Conduct the Observation. While conducting your observation, it is imperative that you be objective, specific, and as thorough as possible. For example, during your observation of Dana and her peers, you notice that there is not enough room for Dana to manipulate her wheelchair past the easel and shelf where the crayons are kept. None of her peers noticed that Dana could not reach the crayons and so did not help her get them. Dana had to ask one of the children to get the crayons for her. Now you have information that will enable you to take action.

Be sure to record your data as you observe. Here are four ways you can quickly and easily gather and manage observational data:

- Wear an apron (a carpenter's apron works very well) with pockets to carry pens, note cards, and Post-It notes.
- Use Post-It notes to record observations. These can be easily added to students' notebooks, folders, and so forth.

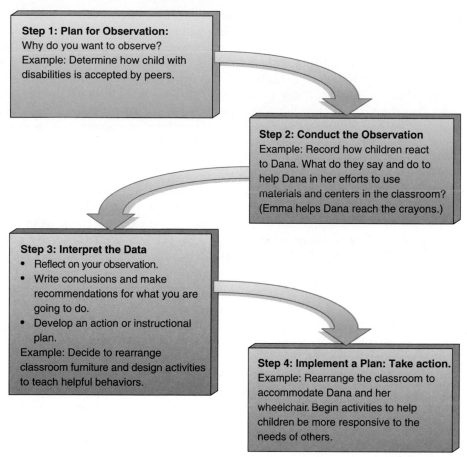

FIGURE 6.5 Four Steps for Effective Observation

- Use the observation checklist for inclusive classrooms shown later in Figure 6.7, checklists you make yourself, and checklists found in other books.
- Use tape recorders, videotapes, and digital cameras to gather information. A problem with using a tape recorder is you have to transcribe your notes. Video recorders are probably best reserved for group observations. However, digital cameras are an excellent means of gathering and storing data.

Step 3: Interpret the Data. All observations can and should result in some kind of **interpretation**. Interpretation serves several important functions. First, it puts your observations into perspective—that is, in relation to what you already know and do not know about events and the behaviors of your children. Second, interpretation helps you make sense of what you have observed and enables you to use your professional knowledge to interpret what you have seen. Third, interpretation has the potential to make you learn to anticipate representative behavior indicative of normal growth and development under given conditions, and to recognize what might not be representative of appropriate growth, development, and learning for each child. Fourth, interpretation forms the foundation for the implementation, necessary adaptations, or modifications in a program or curriculum. In your observation, you can note that Dana's only exceptionality is that she has a physical disability. Her growth in other areas is normal, and she displays excellent social skills in that she is accepted by others, knows when to ask for help, and is able to ask for help. When Dana asks for help, she receives it.

Step 4: Implement a plan. The implementation phase means that you commit to do something with the results or the "findings" of your observation. For example, although

Learn about using technology to observe and assess children at http://www.prenhall.com/morrison, Chapter 6: Web Links.

Dana's behavior in your observation was appropriate, many of the children can benefit from activities designed to help them recognize and respond to the needs of others. In addition, the physical environment of the classroom requires some modification in the rearrangement of movable furniture to make it more accessible for Dana. Implementation means you report to and conference with parents or others as necessary and appropriate. Implementation—that is, doing something with the results of your observations—is the most important part of the observation process. The following Program in Action feature is a Competency Builder that will help you learn how to observe in a classroom setting and use your observations as a basis for making decisions about how to teach young children. As you read this feature think about how you could apply observation and other assessment strategies to evaluate children's learning.

A sample observation form you can use is shown in Figure 6.6. This form can be a useful tool for gathering observational data and it will prove helpful when planning for teaching and conferencing with family members. You can also check other resources to develop more specific observation guides you could use as checklists to track developmental behaviors with individual children.

Checklists

Checklists are excellent and powerful tools for observing and gathering information about a wide range of student abilities in all settings. Checklists can be a regular part of your teaching and can be used on a wide variety of topics and subjects. Some checklists can be developmental; others can help you assess behaviors, traits, skills, and abilities. In addition, the same checklists used over a period of time enable you to evaluate progress and achievement. Figure 6.7 is a checklist for assessing children in inclusive classrooms

---

FIGURE 6.6

Sample Observation Form

Child's Name: _____

Date: _____

Time: _____

Location: _____

Classroom or Setting: _____

Purpose of Observation: _____

Prediction or Expectations of Findings: _____

Significant Events During Observation: _____

Reflective Analysis of Significant Event (this reflection should include what you have learned):

List at least three ways you can use or apply what you observed to your future teaching:

FIGURE 6.7

Observation Checklist for Inclusive Classrooms

Teacher: *Graciela Gonzalez*

School: *Mission Hill*

Date: *September 5, 2008*

Class: *Kindergarten*

Number of children in class: *16*

Number of children with disabilities in class: *1*

Types of disabilities: *Dana has moderate cerebral palsy (CP) and must use a wheelchair.*

Physical Features of the Classroom

1. Are all areas of the classroom accessible to children with disabilities?
   No, Dana cannot access the library/literacy center.
2. Are learning materials and equipment accessible for all children?
   There is not enough room for Dana to manipulate her wheelchair past the easel and the shelf with art materials.
3. Are work and play areas separated to minimize distractions?
   Yes, but pathways are too narrow for Dana's wheelchair.
4. Are special tables or chairs necessary to accommodate children's disabilities?
   Dana has a large work board/table that attaches to her wheelchair.

Academic Features of the Classroom

1. What special accommodations are necessary to help children with disabilities achieve state and local standards?
   I have to check on this.
2. Are principles of developmentally appropriate practice applied to all children, including those with disabilities?
   Yes
3. Is there a wide range of classroom literature on all kinds of disabilities?
   I have a few books—but not enough.

Classroom Interaction

1. Are children with disabilities included in cooperative work projects?
   I will work on this next week.
2. Do nondisabled children interact positively with children with disabilities?
   Dana is a very sociable child. Students interact well with her. Dana could not reach the crayons by herself, so she asked Emma for help. She and Emma seem to get along well.

Play Routines

1. Are children with disabilities able to participate in all classroom and grade-level play activities?
   I need to talk to the P.E. teacher. I also need to observe Dana during lunch and recess to see if she is involved in play and social activities during these times.

Conclusions

1. *I need to rearrange my classroom to make sure that Dana has access to all learning centers and materials.*
2. *The children are not as helpful to Dana as I want them to be.*
3. *The classroom library/literacy center needs books relating to children with disabilities.*
4. *There are a lot of questions I don't have the answers to at this time (e.g., meeting state standards).*
5. *I need to include more group work and cooperative activities in my planning.*

Recommendations

1. *I will ask a custodian to help me move a heavy bookshelf. I can move and rearrange the other things. I'll give the new arrangement a trial run and see how it works for all the children.*
2. *In our daily class meetings, I will talk about helpful behaviors and helping others.*
   a. *We can read books about helping.*
   b. *I plan to start a class buddy system; I can pair Dana and Emma.*
3. *In my lesson plans, I need to include activities for learning helpful behaviors.*
4. *I will search for books about children with disabilities.*
   a. *I'll consult with the school librarian.*
   b. *I'll talk to my grade-level leader and ask for money for books.*
5. *I will talk with the director of special education about meeting state standards. Dana is very smart, so I don't anticipate any problems.*
6. *I will develop a lesson involving group work and projects. I will include Dana and observe the children's interactions.*
7. *I will observe Dana at lunch and during recess.*

Welcome to Ms. Liz's classroom! You will be observing Will, the energetic four-year-old in overalls and a yellow shirt. He is a bright, only child who is in his first year of school and has a mind of his own. You will also observe Ms. Liz, the classroom environment, and the ways children interact with Will, Ms. Liz, and each other. And by observing, you will try to determine whether Ms. Liz and the classroom environment support active learning. *Active learning* is an important part of early childhood practice. It is a challenge and a goal for all early childhood teachers to promote caring and learning in a child-centered classroom that supports active learning.

Look at the photos of Will, and implement the four steps for effective observation (see Figure 6.5).

STEP 1 PLAN FOR OBSERVATION

- Decide *who* you will observe, *how* you will observe (e.g., classroom visit, photos, or video), *what* you will observe, and *where* the observation will take place.
- Write your goal(s) for observation. Our goals for observing Will are to:
  - Determine if Ms. Liz's classroom supports active learning.
  - Make recommendations about what features of an active learning environment should be included in a classroom.

- Select your observational tool. For observing Will, an anecdotal record will achieve our goals and will provide the data necessary to make conclusions and recommendations. An anecdotal record is a short description of behavior over a period of time; it tells about the child's interaction with the physical and social environments. It should be as factual as possible. You might use an index card or some other form like the example shown below.

STEP 2 CONDUCT THE OBSERVATION

- Observe Will and try to answer the questions accompanying each photograph.
- Record your observations on index cards or forms you devise.

Ms. Liz is reading one of the children's favorite books. Will asked Ms. Liz if she would please read the book. Before she read it, Ms. Liz asked the children who their favorite characters were and why they wanted to hear the story again. Will said, "I like the way the boy helps the dog."

P-1

Anecdotal Record

Child's name: Will   **Date:** September 8, 2008

Context: Ms. Liz's classroom

Picture 2:   Will took the book from Ms. Liz. He pushed her arm away as she held on to it. Ms. Liz let Will take the book.

Picture 3:   Will and his friend Greg built a tower. They worked well together and engaged in animated conversation. They were very excited and gleeful when their tower fell down on Larry.

---

and can be used as a template or model to make other checklists. Review Figure 6.7 now and think about how you could modify it to assess children's technology use and skills. Some things for you to keep in mind when making and using checklists are:

- Each checklist should contain the qualities, skills, behaviors, and other information you want to observe. In other words, tailor-make each checklist to a specific situation.
- Make sure you are observing and recording accurately.
- File all checklists in students' folders for future reference and use.
- Use checklists as a basis for conferencing with children and parents.
- Use the information from checklists to plan for small-group and individual instruction.

P-2

P-3

P-4

P-5

Note in P-2 how Ms. Liz supports Will's autonomy and the things he can do for himself. She allows Will to take the picture book from her. Would you have allowed this? Record what she does and how he appears, based on her actions and his ability to show the book to his peers. What can Ms. Liz do to involve the other children in Will's retelling of the story?

In P-3 you see Will and his friends building a tall tower. What can you tell about Will's willingness to engage in cooperative play with other children? What can you infer about the activity from Will's behavior and facial expression? Observe that the top of the red tower is falling on the child behind Will. Would you allow Will and his peers to build their tower as high as they are building it? Why or why not?

In P-4 observe how Will responds to the accident of the falling tower. What does Will's behavior tell you? What can you tell about Ms. Liz's behavior? What can you say about the behavior of Ryan, the child in the background behind Ms. Liz?

How would you categorize Will's and Megan's play behavior in P-5? Based on your observation, what are some things that Will and Megan are learning? Are the materials appropriate for them to use?

COMPETENCY BUILDER

STEP 3 INTERPRET THE DATA

- Review your goals for observing.
- Look at the observation data as a whole. Place your observation in the context of all that you know about young children and all that you know about Will.
- Reflect on your observation and look for patterns.
- Make decisions about what actions you want to pursue, based on your conclusions from the data.
- Your decision-making process can include consulting with other colleagues and professionals.

STEP 4 IMPLEMENT A PLAN

- Take action based on your interpretation of the data.
- Create a classroom arrangement that would support children's literacy development. Include several areas and use labels to identify materials for use in each area. Incorporate ideas from Ms. Liz's classroom, from your own professional ideas, and from information in this text.
- Share your classroom arrangement plan with teachers and colleagues. Ask them for helpful suggestions and comments.

Thanks to Director Vicki Yun, Ms. Liz, Will Sims, and the children of LaPetite Academy in Dublin, Ohio. Photos by Anthony Magnacca/Merrill.

*Janice Beaty, Observing the Development of the Young Child, 6th ed. (Upper Saddle River, NJ: Merrill/Prentice Hall, 2005).

Identify other plans you would implement based upon these observations at http://www.prenhall.com/morrison, Chapter 6—Journal: Program in Action.

USING PORTFOLIOS TO ASSESS

Today many teachers use **portfolios**—a purposeful compilation of children's artifacts (see Figure 6.8 on page 162), as well as teacher observations collected over time—as a basis for assessing children's efforts, progress, and achievement. Before compiling students' portfolios, you will need to make decisions about the criteria you will use to decide what to put in the portfolios. Remember, a portfolio is not a dump truck. You don't include everything in it. Some questions to ask yourself when deciding what to include in student portfolios are:

- How will students participate in decisions about what to include?
- Do the materials show student progress over time?

FIGURE 6.8 Electronic Artifact—Child's Letter to Parents

DeAr mom and dad,

Today I read the book "If you give a Pig a Pancake". It waS so fuNNy!

Love, KrystAL

Observe a teacher discussing her student's portfolio at Video Classroom, Educational Psychology, Module 13: Assessment, Video 1: Portfolios.

- Do the materials demonstrate student learning of program and district standards and goals?
- Can you use the materials and products to adequately and easily communicate with parents about children's learning?
- Do the materials include examples to positively support students' efforts and progress?

Student artifacts are children's products. They are pieces of evidence used to assess students' abilities and are often included to document a child's accomplishments and achievements. They can be electronic or nonelectronic and come in many different forms. The artifact in Figure 6.8 is an example of an electronic artifact that demonstrates a child's ability to read, write, and enjoy literature.

Examples of electronic and nonelectronic artifacts are:

- Artwork;
- Paper documents, such as written work samples;
- Electronic documents;
  - Electronic images;
  - DVDs;
  - Documents such as word processors, spreadsheets, and databases;
  - Photographs of projects;
  - Voice recording of oral skills—reading, speaking, singing;
  - Video recordings of performances—sports, musical, theatrical;
  - Scanned images of three-dimensional or large-scale art; and
  - Multimedia projects or Web pages exploring curriculum topics, current events, or social problems.

View an example of a student artifact at Student and Teacher Artifacts, Early Childhood Education, Module 2: Early Learning, Artifact 4: Flying Baseball.

Some teachers let children put their best work in their portfolios; others decide with children what will be included; still others decide for themselves what to include. Portfolios are very useful, especially during family-teacher conferences. Such a portfolio includes your notes about achievement, teacher- and child-made checklists, artwork samples, photographs, journals, and other documentation. The accompanying Technology Tie-In will give you an idea for using one type of technology, handheld computers, in the classroom.

A growing number of early childhood educators regard formative assessment, assessment conducted periodically during the school year, important in understanding students' learning needs and delivering instruction to meet these needs. Such assessment typically occurs three times each year to screen for students who are at risk and to monitor progress toward skill mastery. Many teachers find this scene familiar:

Kindergarten teacher Carrie Huggins has papers spread all over her dining room table. She tabulates scores on a calculator, writes notes about achievement levels for each student in her classroom, and adds comments to report cards to help parents understand assessment results. Carrie shifts papers into different piles, trying to organize small groups for children needing intervention on the same skills. Then she will create activities and lesson plans for the next week. Carrie finds all of this tedious and labor intensive.

However, the above scene is being replaced by this one more and more:

Rachel McBride uses a handheld computer to administer the assessment and record her students' responses. Later she connects her handheld device to a computer and uploads assessment results to a secure website where her students' data are recorded. Moments later, Rachel prints out a class summary, individual children summaries, small-group suggestions, and recommended instructional activities. The reports are easy to understand and include explanations of each skill assessed and student's level. Rachel then makes phone calls to parents to request conferences, as the reports show critical need areas that need to be addressed. Rachel gathers the materials needed for the small-group activities she will teach the following week. The teacher drops an extra copy of the reports into the principal's and the reading coach's mail boxes.

Cindy Lewis, a pre-K bilingual teacher and the 2006 Texas Elementary Teacher of the Year, has experienced both scenarios. She says, "The difference between teaching without, and then with, a handheld device is astounding. Hours of work were replaced by a simple click of a button that gave me more accurate, efficiently organized data, and support for planning my instruction. I found that in the school as a whole, the faculty talked about data regularly and collaborated in developing the right strategies for our students. The obvious impact of using this technology in my classroom was that I could do what I was trained for and do it even better—TEACH!"

Currently in the United States, more than 100,000 teachers use handheld computers to assess more than 2 million students. Many are in grades Pre-K–3, when formative assessment is usually observational—young children don't take bubble tests—and is often supported by federally mandated reading initiatives and funding. This number of teachers continues to grow as schools seek to impact all areas of teaching and learning through the more efficient collection and effective analysis of data. Benefits of using handheld computers for assessment include the following:

1. Teachers save time and can devote more instructional hours to the classroom.
2. Teachers can assess students more often for an understanding of what instruction they need.
3. All paperwork is eliminated.
4. Results are automatically delivered upon assessment completion.
5. The handheld promotes accurate administration and reliable results:

   - Prompts and instructions are displayed on the handheld, guiding the teacher and providing professional development in best practices.
   - Timing is integrated into the handheld—no need for a stopwatch.
   - Branching to the next assessment task is automated.
   - The handheld calculates all scores.

6. Immediate data aggregation and reporting support differentiated instruction:

   - Assessment information moves securely from the handheld to a secure website with a click of a button.
   - Reports allow educators to see student, class, school, and district progress toward key goals, growth over time, and all the key data needed to make critical instructional decisions.
   - Reports are individualized, allowing the teachers to select exactly which data they want to see.
   - Data are linked to instructional recommendations for individual students, groups, and classes.
   - Reports can be printed and shared, promoting conversations about data and learning among colleagues and with parents.

New educators have an advantage in using handheld devices because their generation has long been "plugged in." Veteran teachers might encounter a steeper learning curve, depending on their technology experience and willingness to try new approaches. But most educators quickly see that handheld technology makes assessment easier, more efficient, and more integral to their work in the classroom.

Contributed by Cindy Lewis, pre-K bilingual teacher, 2006 Texas Elementary Teacher of the Year.

 Complete an activity on the use of handheld computers in the early childhood classroom at http://www.prenhall.com/morrison, Chapter 6—Journal: Technology Tie-In.

SCREENING PROCEDURES

In your work with young children, have you ever wondered about the abilities of some children? Screening can help you, because it is the process of identifying the particular physical, social, linguistic, and cognitive needs of children in order to provide appropriate programs and services.

Screening procedures give you and others a broad picture of what children know and are able to do, as well as their physical and emotional status. As gross indicators of children's abilities, screening procedures provide much useful information for decisions about placement for initial instruction, referral to other agencies, and additional testing that may be necessary to pinpoint a learning or health problem. Many school districts conduct a comprehensive screening assessment program in the spring for children who will enter kindergarten in the fall. Screening can include the following:

- Gathering information from parents about their children's health, learning patterns, learning achievements, personal habits, and special problems.
- Conducting a health screening, including a physical examination, health history, and a blood sample for analysis. (Keep in mind in Chapter 2 we identified lead poisoning as a major childhood disease.)
- Conducting vision, hearing, and speech screening.
- Collecting and analyzing data from former programs and teachers, such as preschools and child care programs.
- Using commercial screening instruments to help make decisions regarding children's placement in programs and need for special services.

Schools and early childhood programs frequently conduct comprehensive screening programs for all children for one or two days. Data for each child is evaluated by a team of professionals who make instructional placement recommendations and, when appropriate, advise additional testing and make referrals to other agencies for assistance.

Screening Instruments

Several screening instruments provide information for grouping and planning instructional strategies. Most can be administered by people who do not have specialized training in test administration. Parent volunteers often help administer screening instruments, some of which can be administered in about thirty minutes.

Brigance® K and 1 Screen.   Brigance® K and 1 screen is an evaluation for use in kindergarten and grade one. Skills assessed include color recognition, vocabulary, counting, visual discrimination, large-motor skills, and the ability to follow directions.

Dial-3.   The Dial-3 (Developmental Indicators for the Assessment of Learning) is a norm-referenced instrument designed for screening large numbers of pre-kindergarten children. It requires approximately twenty-five to thirty minutes to administer and involves individual assessment in the following developmental areas: cognitive/basic concepts, language, motor, self-help, and social-emotional. The screening team consists of a coordinator, an operator for each of the skills areas screened, and aides or volunteers to register parents and children.

REPORTING TO AND COMMUNICATING WITH PARENTS AND FAMILIES

Part of your responsibility as a professional is to report to parents and other primary care-givers about the growth, development, and achievement of their children. Some of your colleagues may view reporting to family members as a bother and wish they didn't have to do it. Nonetheless, reporting to and communicating with families is one of your most important jobs. The following guidelines will help you meet this important responsibility of reporting your assessment information to the primary caregiver in your student's life:

- *Be honest and realistic with parents.* Too often, teachers do not want to hurt parents' feelings. They want to sugarcoat what they are reporting. However, parents and guardians need your honest assessments about what their children know, are able to do, and will be able to do. With this honest assessment you can solicit their help in helping their children.
- *Communicate with parents so they can understand.* What you communicate to parents must make sense to them. They must understand what you are saying. Reporting to parents often has to be a combination of written (in their language) and oral communication.
- *Provide parents with ideas and information that will help them help their children learn.* Remember that you and parents are partners in helping children be successful in school and life.

Read about the importance of encouraging communication with families at Articles and Readings, Early Childhood Education, Module 8: Families and Communities, Article 3: Listen First.

Systematic assessment of children represents a powerful way for you to learn about, guide, and direct children's learning and behavior. If you learn to use it well, you and your children will benefit.

ASSESSMENT IN CONTEXT

We have taken a look at individual processes of assessment—observation, screening, and individual tests—to gather data about children to help ensure achievement and learning. Now let's put all of this in context. Notice the four steps in Figure 6.9 and how they are all linked to each other. The four processes, taken as a whole, make assessment a meaningful and child-appropriate process. Notice also that assessment is an ongoing process throughout the program year. Finally, notice how the purpose—the end product—of assessment is to promote, support, extend, and enrich children's learning so that children are successful in school.

WHAT ARE THE ISSUES IN THE ASSESSMENT OF YOUNG CHILDREN?

As with almost everything that has been and will be discussed in this book, issues surround essential questions about what is good practice, what is inappropriate practice, and what is best for children and families. Assessment is no different. Let's examine some of the issues of assessment in early childhood.

Assessment and Accountability

There is a tremendous emphasis on the use of standardized tests to measure achievement for comparing children, programs, school districts, and countries. This emphasis will continue for a number of reasons. First, the public, including politicians and legislatures, sees assessment as a means of making schools and teachers accountable for teaching the nation's children. Second, assessment is seen as playing a critical role in the reform of education. As long as there is a public desire to improve teaching and achievement, we will continue to see an emphasis on assessment for accountability purposes.

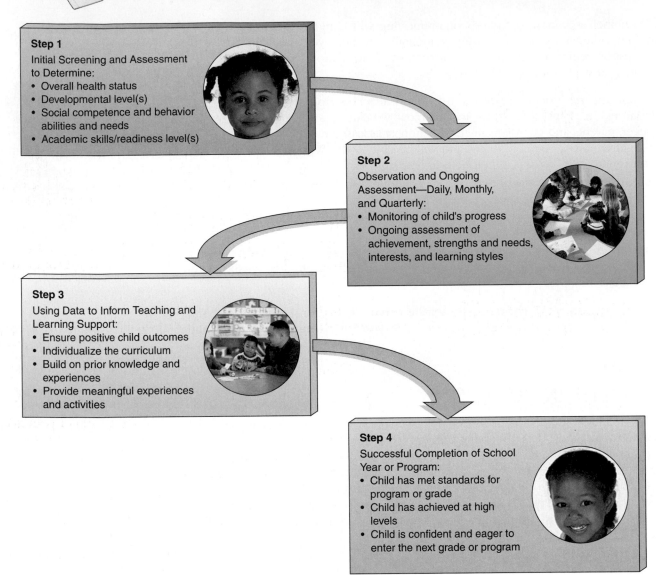

FIGURE 6.9 The Contexts of Observation, Assessment, and Evaluation

Photos: Step 1, © Dorling Kindersley; Step 2, David Buffington / Getty Images, Inc. –Photodisc;
Step 3, Karen Mancinelli / Pearson Learning Photo Studio; Step 4, David Mager / Pearson Learning Photo Studio

Head Start National Reporting System

The Head Start National Reporting System (HSNRS) is an example of how assessment and observation are used to gather data on Head Start children. It is also an example of how assessment and evaluation are affecting early childhood education and how they are in the center of political and educational controversy. The purpose of HSNRS is to create a database on the progress and accomplishments of four- and five-year-old Head Start children in the areas of literacy, math, and language skills. The Head Start program administers the HSNRS at the beginning and end of the program years. Results are sent to the National Head Start office electronically through the National Reporting System Computer-Based Reporting System.

The HSNRS is composed of four components:

- Comprehension of Spoken English,
- Vocabulary,

- Letter Naming, and
- Early Math.

The fifteen-minute assessment battery is composed of a short series of tasks that cover these four components. The tasks are feasible and interesting for preschoolers to carry out, and have been shown to be predictive of later school achievement or academic difficulties. There is an emphasis on tasks that relate to the acquisition of reading skills because reading is central to success in school and to later functioning in society. Children whose English-language proficiency is not sufficient for assessment in English and are from a Spanish-speaking household are given a Spanish version of the HSNRS.

Michael Newmar / PhotoEdit Inc.

Teacher ratings of children's social-emotional development are included as part of the HSNRS. Ratings are collected twice during the program year, once in the fall and again at the end of program year, in order to measure the children's growth in these areas.[5]

The HSNRS has drawn considerable amounts of criticism and has created much controversy. Issues surrounding HSNRS include:

- The argument that it is educationally and developmentally inappropriate to administer a standardized national test to three-, four-, and five-year-old children. Critics argue that young children are not good test takers and that the HSNRS does not adequately reflect Head Start children's abilities or program effectiveness.
- The belief that HSNRS as a national test threatens Head Start's local autonomy. Head Start leaders who value local program autonomy and control are wary of any program or national initiative that would dilute autonomy.
- The argument that the HSNRS is too "narrow" in that it focuses only on three areas (literacy, math, and language skills) and that Head Start's emphasis on the whole child is being undermined.
- The suspicion that HSNRS results may be used to shift Head Start resources from its traditional comprehensive mission to a narrow focus of early academics.

Over the coming years, the HSNRS will continue to be refined and used to assess children's achievement and program effectiveness. At the same time, politicians will seek to ensure that children learn and that programs are accountable for federal and state funds.

> Report your assessment findings accurately and honestly to the parents of your students. How might such communication build trust?

High-Stakes Testing

High-stakes testing occurs when standardized or other kinds of tests are used to make important, and often life-influencing, decisions about children. Standardized tests have specific and standardized content, administration, and scoring procedures and norms for interpreting scores. High-stakes outcomes include decisions about whether to admit children into gifted or other special programs, begin preschool or kindergarten, and whether to retain or promote children. Generally, the early childhood profession is opposed to high-stakes testing for young children because they are developing so rapidly in the early years. Also, high-stakes testing should be done by well-trained personnel. However, as part of the accountability movement, many politicians and school administrators view high-stakes testing as a means of ensuring that children learn and that promotions are based on achievement. Many school critics maintain that in the pre-K and primary grades

Explore some of the issues surrounding high-stakes testing at http://www.prenhall.com/morrison, Chapter 6: Web Links.

High-Stakes Tests Leave Minority Students Behind

Today, students from preschool to high school are subjected to an almost endless array of tests. These tests are designed to measure everything from achievement, abilities, interests, and reading level to friendship preferences. When these tests are used to make critical decisions about students that have serious school and life consequences, they are called *high-stakes tests*. For example, standardized achievement tests are used to make decisions about whether Maria or Mario should be promoted to the next grade or whether or not Jennifer or Johnny has to attend summer school. But grade promotion and summer school attendance are not the only high-stakes decisions about young children that are based on tests.

Take the case of Amir Diego Howard, a bright third grader at Sierra Vista Elementary School in Washo County, Nevada. Amir's teacher thought he was a perfect candidate for the school district's gifted and talented (GT) program, so she referred him. Amir did well in the first two steps of the district's three-step process for admission into GT. First, Amir had his teacher's recommendation. Second, he scored at the 96th percentile on a national standardized achievement test. The third step was the problem. Amir failed to score an IQ of 133 on the Kaufman-Brief Intelligence Test. "Sometimes they gave me these huge words that you don't even know," said Amir about the IQ test. "Like 'autobiography.' I don't know what that means. I'm only in the third grade."Unfortunately, across the country many language minority children like Amir fail to get into GT programs. Tests used to establish admission criteria discriminate against English language learners (ELLs) and minority students. As Joe Garret, Washo County GT Curriculum Coordinator, points out, "The kids that are English language learners, if they don't have the language and they don't have the background experiences, they are not going to do well on standardized tests we use to identify kids."

The good news is that increasing numbers of school districts are doing something about the inequities of high-stakes testing and how criteria for GT and other programs discriminate against English language learners. For example, districts are broadening and/or changing their criteria by:

- Placing more emphasis on nonverbal criteria such as learning styles and creative behavior
- Eliminating passing scores on high-stakes tests as a condition of program admission
- Placing more emphasis on teacher recommendation
- Changing admission criteria to assure that more minority and ELL students are in GT programs
- Using language-free tests that don't discriminate against English language learners and minority children

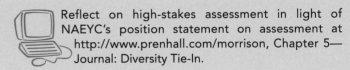 Reflect on high-stakes assessment in light of NAEYC's position statement on assessment at http://www.prenhall.com/morrison, Chapter 5—Journal: Diversity Tie-In.

there is too much social promotion—that is, passing children from grade to grade merely to enable students to keep pace with their age peers. The Diversity Tie-In feature tackles the issue of bias against minorities in high-stakes testing.

ACTIVITIES FOR PROFESSIONAL DEVELOPMENT

Ethical Dilemma

"He's No Guinea Pig!"

Stacy Hibauch teaches in an inclusive kindergarten classroom. One of her children, Shaun, has Down syndrome. Shaun's mother is very protective of him and tends to be, in Stacy's opinion, overprotective. A professor from the local university contacted Stacy and asked her permission to send students to observe in her classroom. In his request, he said "I want my students to see how you accommodate a child with Down syndrome." Stacy thought it would be a good idea to tell Shaun's mom about the classroom observation. Her response caught Stacy off guard, "I don't want any college kids observing my Shaun! He's no guinea pig!" Stacy thinks the college students would benefit from observing in her classroom.

What should Stacy do? Let the college class observe and not tell Shaun's mom? Or should she ask for a meeting with the school principal and Shaun's mom and try to work it out? Or should she just tell the college professor "No"?

Application Activities

1. Create an observation guide similar to Figure 6.7. Observe in an early childhood classroom and determine how effective you are at observing some aspect of children's development and learning.

2. Observe a particular child during play or another activity. Before your observation, make sure you follow the steps presented in this chapter. Use the information you gathered to plan a learning activity for the child. As you plan, determine what information you need that you didn't gather through observation. When you observe again, what will you do differently?

3. Interview several kindergarten and primary teachers and ask them to share with you their ideas and guidelines for assessing with portfolios. How can you apply this information to your teaching?

4. Review the contents of several children's portfolios. How are they similar and different? What do the contents tell you about the children? What would you include that wasn't included? What would you delete?

5. Frequently articles in newspapers and magazines address assessment and testing. Over a two-week period, review these sources and determine what assessment and evaluation issues are "in the news." Put these materials in your portfolio or teaching file.

6. Visit pre-K–3 programs in several different school districts. Make a list of the various ways they assess and of the instruments and procedures they use. Compare them with the ones identified in this chapter. How and for what purposes are the tests used? What conclusions can you draw from the information you gathered?

 To take online practice tests on this chapter's material, go to the Companion Website at http://www.prenhall.com/morrison, select Chapter 6, and then choose the Multiple Choice or the Essay module. For additional Web resources, choose Web Links.

7

INFANTS AND TODDLERS
Critical Years for Learning

Developmentally Appropriate Practice

A. I understand children's developmental stages and growth from birth through age eight, and use this knowledge to implement developmentally appropriate practice. I do all I can to advance the physical, intellectual, social, and emotional development of the children in my care to their fullest potential.

B. I use my understanding of young children's characteristics and needs, and of multiple interacting influences on children's development and learning to create environments that are healthy, respectful, supportive, and challenging for all children.[1]

1. How do infants and toddlers develop and how can I use this information to provide developmentally appropriate care and education?

2. What are the cognitive, language, and social milestones of infant and toddler development?

3. How is new knowledge about infants and toddlers influencing their care and education?

4. How can I provide high-quality environments, curricula, and programs for infants and toddlers?

Interest in infant and toddler care and education is at an all-time high; it will continue at this level well into the future.[2] The growing demand for quality infant and toddler programs stems primarily from the reasons discussed in Chapter 2. The popularity of early care and education is also attributable to a changing view of the very young and the discovery that infants are remarkably competent individuals.[3] Let's examine the ways that infants' and toddlers' early experiences shape their future development.

WHAT ARE INFANTS AND TODDLERS LIKE?

Think for a minute about your experiences with infants. What characteristics stand out most in your mind? I know that infants never cease to amaze me! Infants are capable of so many accomplishments. They are great imitators. Make a face at an infant and she will make a face back. Stick your tongue out at an infant and she will stick out her tongue at you. Talk to infants and they will "talk" back to you! One of the great delights and challenges of working with infants is that you will constantly discover the wonderful things infants can do.

Have you ever tried to keep up with a toddler? Everyone who tries ends up exhausted at the end of the day! A typical response is "They are into everything!" The infant and toddler years between birth and age three are full of developmental milestones and significant events. **Infancy**, life's first year, includes the first breath, the first smile, first thoughts, first words, and first steps. Significant developments continue during **toddlerhood**, the period between one and three years. Two of the most outstanding developmental milestones of these years are walking and rapid language development. Mobility and language are the cornerstones of autonomy that enable toddlers to become independent. These unique developmental events are significant for children as well as those who care for and teach them. How you and other early childhood professionals and primary caregivers respond to infants' first accomplishments and toddlers' quests for autonomy helps determine how they will develop and master life events.

As you work with infants, toddlers, and other children, constantly keep in mind that "normal" growth and development milestones are based on averages. "Average" is the middle ground of development. Table 7.1 gives average heights and weights for infants and toddlers. You must also consider the whole child and take into account cultural and family background, including nutritional and health history, to determine what is normal for individual children. Furthermore, when children are provided with good nutrition, health care, and a warm, loving emotional environment, development tends toward what is "normal" for each child.

TABLE 7.1 Average Height and Weight of Infants and Toddlers

Age (months)	Males		Females	
	Height (inches)	Weight (pounds)	Height (inches)	Weight (pounds)
Birth	19.75	7.75	19.5	7.5
3	24	13.25	23.25	12
6	26.5	17.5	25.75	15.75
9	28.25	20.5	27.5	18.75
12	29.75	22.75	29	21
18	32.25	25.75	31.75	24.25
24	34.25	28	33.75	26.5
30	36	29.75	35.75	28.5
36	37.75	31.5	37.25	30.5

Source: National Center for Health Statistics, "Clinical Growth Charts," 2001, http://www.cdc.gov/nchs/about/major/nhanes/growthcharts/clinical_charts.htm.

These descriptions of behaviors and abilities paint a picture of some commonly and frequently observed characteristics of infants. As you observe and care for infants, use this descriptive portrait to add other word descriptions. Keep in mind that all children are different and unique and that ages of development are approximate, especially in infancy.

YOUNG BRAINS: A PRIMER

We continue our look at young children with a discussion of the importance of the brain in ongoing growth and development. Brain and child development research has created a great deal of interest in the first three years of life. Let's review some interesting facts about infant and toddler brain development and consider the implications they have for how you practice as a professional. Also review Figure 7.1, which shows the regions of the brain and their functional processes.

The brain is a fascinating and complex organ. Anatomically, the young brain is like the adult brain, except it is smaller. The average adult brain weighs approximately 3 pounds. At birth, the infant's brain weighs 14 ounces; at six months, 1.31 pounds; and at three years, 2.4 pounds. So you can see that during the first two years of life the brain undergoes tremendous physical growth. The brain finishes developing at age ten, when it reaches its full adult size.

At birth, the brain has one hundred billion neurons, or nerve cells, which is the total amount it will ever have! It is important for parents and other caregivers to play with, respond to, interact with, and talk to young children because this is the way brain connections develop and learning takes place. As brain connections are used repeatedly, they become permanent. However, brain connections that are not used or used only a little may wither away. This withering away is known as **neural shearing** or **pruning**. This helps explain why children who are reared in language-rich environments do well in school, while children who are not reared in such environments may be at risk for academic failure.

Also by the time of birth, these billions of neurons have formed over 50 trillion connections, or synapses, through a process called **synaptogenesis**, the proliferation of neural connections; this process will continue to occur until the age of ten. The experiences

Read about classroom implications of recent brain research at Articles and Readings, Early Childhood Education, Module 2: Child Development, Article 3: What Do We Know from Brain Research?

TEACHER PREP

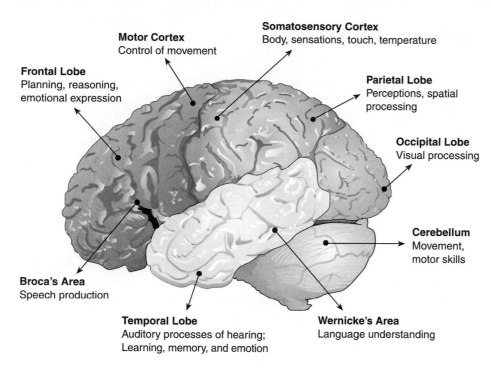

Motor Cortex
Control of movement

Somatosensory Cortex
Body, sensations, touch, temperature

Frontal Lobe
Planning, reasoning,
emotional expression

Parietal Lobe
Perceptions, spatial
processing

Occipital Lobe
Visual processing

Cerebellum
Movement,
motor skills

Broca's Area
Speech production

Temporal Lobe
Auditory processes of hearing;
Learning, memory, and emotion

Wernicke's Area
Language understanding

FIGURE 7.1 Brain
Regions

that children have help form these neural connections. Experiences count. If children don't have the experiences they need to form neural connections, they may be at risk for poor developmental and behavioral outcomes. In this regard, remember that while experiences count, not all experiences are equal! Children need high-quality experiences that contribute to their education and development.

In addition, children need the right experiences at the right times. For example, the critical period for language development is the first year of life. It is during this time that the auditory pathways for language learning are formed. Beginning at birth, an infant can distinguish the sounds of all the languages of the world. But at about six months, through the process of neuron shearing or pruning, infants lose the ability to distinguish the sounds of languages they have not heard. By twelve months, their auditory maps are pretty well in place.[4] It is literally a case of use it or lose it.

Having the right experiences at the right time also relates to critical periods, developmental "windows of opportunity" or sensitive periods (discussed in Chapter 3) during which it is easier to learn something than it is at another time. (See Table 7.2, which shows the progress of vocabulary development in the early years.) This is another example of how experiences influence development. An infant whose mother or other caregiver talks to her is more likely to have a larger vocabulary than an infant whose mother doesn't talk to her.

During the last decade, scientists and educators have spent considerable time and energy exploring the links between brain development and functions and classroom learning. Brain research provides many implications for how to develop enriched classrooms for children and for how to engage them in activities that will help them learn and develop to their optimal levels. Most important, brain research had made educators aware of the importance of providing young children stimulating activities early in life. We can draw some conclusions from our discussion about the brain:

Read about new discoveries in infant and toddler brain development at http://www.prenhall.com/morrison, Chapter 7: Web Links.

- Babies are born to learn. They are remarkable learning instruments. Their brains make them so.
- Children' brain development and their ability to learn throughout life rely on the interplay between nature (genetic inheritance, controlled by 80,000 genes) and nature (the experiences they have and the environments in which they are raised).

TABLE 7.2 Language Development in Infants and Toddlers

Months of Age	Language
Birth	Crying
1	Responds to sounds
2	Vocalizes sounds (cooing and gurgling)
3	Laughs
6	Turns toward sounds and voices
6	Imitates sounds
7	Imitates speech sounds (babbling)
8	Says "Dada and Mama" to both parents (not specific)
9	Makes word-like sounds
11	Says "Dada and Mama" to correct parent (specific)
11	One word
12	Jabbers word-like sounds
12	Two words
15	Vocabulary increases to up to five words
19	Strings words together in phrases
23	Can use up to fifty single words
24	Can create two-word sentences (i.e., "bye dada")

Note: This table shows the sequence of language development in infants and toddlers. Keep in mind that language development, like all other developmental processes, is individual for each child. Use the above language accomplishments to compare language development in infants and toddlers you know.

Source: Summarized from A. J. Capute and P. J. Accardo, "Linguistic and Auditory Milestones During the First Two Years of Life," *Clinical Pediatrics, 17(11),* November 1978, 848.

- What happens to children early in life has a long-lasting influence on how they develop and learn.
- Critical periods influence learning positively and negatively.
- The human brain is quite flexible. It has the ability to change in response to different kinds of experiences and environments.
- Prevention and early intervention are more beneficial than later remediation.
- The brain undergoes physiological changes in response to experiences.
- An enriched environment influences brain development.

NATURE, NURTURE, AND DEVELOPMENT

Does nature (genetics) or nurture (environment) play a larger role in development? This question is at the center of a never-ending debate. At this time there is no one right and true answer because the answer depends on many things. On the one hand, many traits are fully determined by heredity. For example, your eye color is a product of your heredity. Physical height is also largely influenced by heredity, as are temperament and shyness. Certainly height can be influenced by nutrition, growth hormones, and other environmental interventions, but by and large, an individual's height is genetically determined.

On the other hand nurturing and the environment in which children grow and develop also play an important role in development. For example, environmental factors that play a major role in early development include nutrition, quality of the environment, stimulation of the brain, affectionate and positive relationships, and opportunities to learn. Think for a moment about other kinds of environmental influences such as family, environment, school, and friends that affect development. The Professionalism in Practice feature will provide you with further insight into the powerful influences of caregiver relationships on infant and toddler development.

A decade or two ago, we believed that nature and nurture were competing entities and that one of these was dominant over the other. Today we understand that they are not competing entities; both are necessary for normal development, and it is the interaction between the two that makes us individuals.

SOCIAL AND EMOTIONAL DEVELOPMENT

We discussed Erik Erikson's theory of psychosocial development in Chapter 3. Review Figure 3.6 before reading this section. The first of Erikson's psychosocial stages, basic trust versus basic mistrust, begins at birth and lasts about one-and-a-half to two years. For Erikson basic trust means that "one has learned to rely on the sameness and continuity of the outer providers, but also that one may trust oneself and the capacity of one's organs to cope with urges,"[5] Whether children develop a pattern of trust or mistrust depends on the "sensitive care of the baby's individual needs and a firm sense of personal trustworthiness within the trusted framework of their culture's life-style."[6]

Basic trust develops when children are reared, cared for, and educated in an environment of love, warmth, and support. An environment of trust reduces the opportunity for conflict between child, parent, and caregiver.

Power Tools for Teachers and Caregivers: The Three Rs

Martha W. Pratt
Instructor
Early Childhood Education
College of Marin
Kentfield, California

Right now, every one of us is involved in a process of change. Whether you are preparing to become a teacher with your own classroom or have spent years in the profession, the process of change is ongoing.

We can choose to ignore the process or we can choose to value the process. I call what follows the three Rs for teachers. They are simple, but not easy. Making a commitment to use this process daily puts us each on the path of assuming a personal responsibility to the children we care for and teach. We become committed to improving our own caregiving/teaching practice.

The Three Rs for Teachers

- Reflect
- Reevaluate
- Renew

REFLECT

Imagine yourself watching a video of what you are doing as you are doing it. What do you feel inside at the moment? Is there frustration or anger toward the baby or perhaps resentment toward a colleague?

- Kate has been an infant care specialist for about six months. She is rocking eight-month-old Tim. She usually has no trouble quieting Tim for his nap, but today it is just not working. Kate does some reflecting. She can't see anything amiss as she mentally watches herself. She checks her feelings and realizes that she is still holding onto the sharp words she and Liz exchanged earlier in the day.

REEVALUATE

As you watch the video, try objectively comparing what you see to what you know would be the "best possible" practice.

- As Nancy sets the lunches on the table in the toddler room she does a mental reevaluation of what she is doing. "Watching" herself she sees the mechanical, routine way she is doing the task. She is not proud of herself. She knows that if she had instead interacted with each individual child she could have made this experience rich with good feeling.

RENEW

Your commitment to improving your personal professional practice.

- Both Nancy and Kate are highly competent infant/toddler teachers and their use of the three Rs helps them both catch themselves being less than competent from time to time. When this happens, they renew their commitment and improve their practice in the moment. How?
- Focus on the "you" of responding to infants and toddlers. Notice the inner thoughts you are having:

  - About yourself;
  - About the baby you hold;
  - About your beliefs concerning learning, teaching, and caregiving;
  - About your *feelings* while you are *doing;* and
  - About what would make this moment better for this child.

- Ask a colleague to observe and share what strengths they see in your interactions with babies and toddlers and what you could improve. There is always something that could be improved, but remember also that whatever changes we make must come strongly from our own nature if we are to connect effectively with others.

The change process continues. Your own willingness to *reflect, reevaluate,* and then *renew* your commitment to personal growth is what lets you to take advantage of this ongoing process and become a better teacher and caregiver.

Remember, infants and toddlers in particular learn how to see themselves by seeing their reflection through our eyes. We, their caregivers, have a responsibility to make that a crystal clear reflection of them, not of our own preoccupations.

Explore ways of incorporating "The Three Rs" into your daily routines in the classroom at http://www.prenhall.com/morrison, Chapter 7—Projects: Professionalism in Practice.

Social Behaviors

Social relationships begin at birth and are evident in the daily interactions between infants, parents, and teachers. Infants are social beings who possess many behaviors that they use to initiate and facilitate social interactions. Everyone uses *social behaviors* to begin and maintain a relationship with others. Consequently, healthy social development is essential for young children. Regardless of their temperament, all infants are capable of and benefit from social interactions.

Crying is a primary social behavior in infancy. It attracts parents or caregivers and promotes a social interaction of some type and duration, depending on the skill and awareness of the caregiver. Crying also has a survival value; it alerts caregivers to the presence and needs of the infant. However, merely meeting the basic needs of infants in a matter of fact manner is not sufficient to form a firm base for social development. You must react to infants with enthusiasm, attentiveness, and concern for them as unique persons.

Imitation is another social behavior of infants. They have the ability to mimic the facial expressions and gestures of adults. When a mother sticks out her tongue at a baby, after a few repetitions, the baby will also stick out his tongue! This imitative behavior is satisfying to the infant, and the mother is pleased by this interactive game. Since the imitative behavior is pleasant for both persons, they continue to interact for the sake of interaction, which in turn promotes more social interaction. Social relations develop from social interactions, but we must always remember that both occur in a social context, or culture.

Attachment and Relationships

Bonding and attachment play major roles in the development of social and emotional relationships. **Bonding** is the process by which parents or teachers become emotionally attached, or bonded, to infants. It is the development of a close, personal, affective relationship. It is a one-way process, which some maintain occurs in the first hours or days after birth. **Attachment** is the enduring emotional tie between the infant and the parents and other primary caregivers; it is a two-way relationship.

Attachment behaviors serve the purpose of getting and maintaining proximity; they form the basis for the enduring relationship of attachment. Parent and teacher attachment behaviors include kissing, caressing, holding, touching, embracing, making eye contact, and looking at the face. Infant attachment behaviors include crying, sucking, eye contact, babbling, and general body movements. Later, when infants are developmentally able, attachment behaviors include following, clinging, and calling.

Adult speech has a special fascination for infants. Interestingly enough, given the choice of listening to music or listening to the human voice, infants prefer the human voice. This preference plays a role in attachment by making the baby more responsive. Infants attend to language patterns they will later imitate in their process of language development; they move their bodies in rhythmic ways in response to the human voice. Babies' body movements and caregiver speech synchronize to each other: adult speech triggers behavioral responses in the infant, which in turn stimulate responses in the adult, resulting in a "waltz" of attention and attachment.

Multiple Attachments.   Increased use of child care programs inevitably raises questions about infant attachment. Parents are concerned that their children will not attach to them. Worse yet, they fear that their baby will develop an attachment bond with the caregiver rather than with them. However, children can and do attach to more than one person, and there can be more than one attachment at a time. Infants attach to parents as the primary teacher as well as to a surrogate, resulting in a hierarchy of attachments in which the latter attachments are not of equal value. Infants show a preference for the primary caregiver, usually the mother.

Parents should not only engage in attachment behaviors with their infants, but they should also select child care programs that employ caregivers who understand the importance of the caregiver's role and function in attachment. High-quality child care programs help mothers maintain their primary attachments to their infants in many ways. The staff keeps parents well informed about infants' accomplishments, but parents are allowed to "discover" and participate in infants' developmental milestones. A teacher, for example, might tell a mother that today her son showed signs of wanting to take his first step by himself. The teacher thereby allows the mother to be the first person to experience the joy of this accomplishment. The mother might then report to the center that her son took his first step at home the night before.

The Quality of Attachment.   The quality of infant–parent attachment varies according to the relationship that exists between them. A primary method of assessing the quality of parent–child attachment is the Strange Situation, an observational measure developed by Mary Ainsworth (1913–1999) to assess whether infants are securely attached to their caregivers. The testing episodes consist of observing and recording children's reactions to several events: a novel situation, separation from their mothers, reunion with their mothers, and reactions to a stranger. Based on their reactions and behaviors in these situations, children are described as being securely or insecurely attached, as detailed in Figure 7.2. The importance of knowing and recognizing different classifications of attachment is that you can inform parents and help them engage in the specific behaviors that will promote the growth of secure attachments.

Temperament and Personality Development

Children are born with individual behavioral characteristics, that, when considered as a collective whole, constitute **temperament**. This temperament, that is, what children are

FIGURE 7.2

Individual Differences in Attachment

Secure Attachment

Secure infants use parents as a secure base from which to explore their environments and play with toys. When separated from a parent, they may or may not cry; but when the parent returns, these infants actively seek the parent and engage in positive interaction. About 65 percent of infants are securely attached.

Avoidant Attachment

Avoidant infants are unresponsive/avoidant to parents and are not distressed when parents leave the room. Avoidant infants generally do not establish contact with a returning parent and may even avoid the parent. About 20 percent of infants demonstrate avoidant attachment.

Resistant Attachment

Resistant infants seek closeness to parents and may even cling to them, frequently failing to explore. When a parent leaves, these infants are distressed and on the parent's return may demonstrate clinginess, or they may show resistive behavior and anger, including hitting and pushing. These infants are not easily comforted by a parent. About 10 to 15 percent of infants demonstrate resistant attachment.

Disorganized Attachment

Disorganized infants demonstrate disorganized and disoriented behavior. Children look away from parents and approach them with little or no emotion. About 5 percent of children demonstrate disorganized attachment.

Source: Based on Mary Ainsworth, *Patterns of Attachment: A Psychological Study of the Strange Situation* (Hillsdale, NJ: Lawrence Erlbaum, 1978).

like, helps determine their personalities, which develop as a result of the interplay of the particular temperament characteristics and the environment.

The classic study to determine the relationship between temperament and personality development was conducted by Alexander Thomas, Stella Chess, and Herbert Birch.[7] They identified nine characteristics of temperament:

1. Level and extent of motor activity;
2. Rhythm and regularity of functions such as eating, sleeping, regulation, and wakefulness;
3. Degree of acceptance or rejection of a new person or experience;
4. Adaptability to changes in the environment;
5. Sensitivity to stimuli;
6. Intensity or energy level of responses;
7. General mood (e.g., pleasant or cranky, friendly or unfriendly);
8. Distractibility from an activity; and
9. Attention span and persistence in an activity.

Thomas and his colleagues developed three classes or general types of children according to how these nine temperament characteristics clustered together: the *easy child,* the *slow-to-warm-up child,* and the *difficult child* (see Figure 7.3).

It is important to develop a match between children's temperament and the caregiver's child-rearing style. The parenting process extends beyond the natural parents to include all those who care for and provide services to infants; therefore, it is reasonable to expect that all who are part of this parenting cluster will take infants' basic temperaments into account.

Observe how an infant's motor skills contribute to intellectual and skill development at Video Classroom, Child Development, Module 2: Physical Development, Video 5: Cognitive Development: Infancy.

FIGURE 7.3

Children's Temperaments

Reflect on each of these three classifications based on temperament, and provide examples of how each temperament could affect the outcome of children's development.

Easy Children
- Few problems in care and training
- Positive mood
- Regular body functions
- Low or moderate intensity of reaction
- Adaptability and positive approach to new situations

Slow-to-Warm-Up Children
- Low activity level
- Slow to adapt
- Withdrawing from new stimuli
- Negative mood
- Low intensity of response

Difficult Children
- Irregular body functions
- Tense reactions
- Withdrawing from new stimuli
- Slow to adapt to change
- Negative mood

Source: Based on A. Thomas, S. Chess, and H. Birch, "The Origin of Personality," *Scientific American,* 23, August 1970, 102–109.

EyeWire Collection / Getty Images–Photodisc

Motor development plays a major role in cognitive and social development. For example, learning to walk enables young children to explore their environment, which in turn contributes to cognitive development. Can you think of other examples?

MOTOR DEVELOPMENT

Think for a minute of all the life events and activities that depend on motor skills. Motor skills play an important part in all of life! Even more so, motor development is essential for infants and toddlers because it contributes to their intellectual and skill development. Table 7.3 below lists infant and toddler motor milestones. Here are some general principles that govern motor development:

- Motor development is sequential.
- Maturation of the motor system proceeds from gross (large) to fine (small) behaviors. For example, as part of learning to reach, Maria sweeps toward an object with her whole arm. Over the course of a month, however, as a result of development and experiences, Maria's gross reaching gives way to a specific reaching, and she grasps particular objects.
- Motor development is from cephalo to caudal — from head to foot (tail). This process is known as *cephalocaudal development*. At birth, Maria's head is the most developed part of her body; she holds her head erect before she sits, and her being able to sit precedes her walking.
- Motor development proceeds from the proximal (midline, or central part of the body) to the distal (extremities), known as *proximodistal development*. Maria is able to control her arm movements before she can control her finger movements.

Motor development also plays a major role in social and behavioral expectations. For example, toilet training is a milestone of the toddler period. Many parents want to accomplish toilet training as

TABLE 7.3 Infant and Toddler Motor Milestones

Behavior	Months of Age
Lifts head	1
Holds head steady	3
Can roll over	5
Reaches for objects	6
Sits without support	7
Begins to crawl	8
Stands alone for a few seconds	11
First step	9–12
Stands alone without support	12
Assisted walking	13
Walking without assistance	14–16

Note: When observing children's motor milestones, remember that children vary in the ages at which they achieve each milestone. What is important is that children achieve these milestones. When motor development is delayed, this may indicate a developmental problem.

Source: Summarized from William K. Frankenburg, Josiah Dodde, et al., *Denver II Training Manual,* 1992. Denver Developmental Materials, P. O. Box 6919, Denver, CO 80206–0919.

quickly and efficiently as possible, but frustrations arise when they start too early and expect too much of children. Toilet training is largely a matter of physical readiness, and most child-rearing experts recommend waiting until children are two years old before beginning the training process.

COGNITIVE DEVELOPMENT

Reflect on our discussion of cognitive development in Chapter 4, and think about how a child's first schemes are sensorimotor. Piaget said that infants construct (as opposed to absorb) schemes using reflexive sensorimotor actions.

Infants begin life with only reflexive motor actions that they use to satisfy biological needs. Consider sucking, for example, an innate sensorimotor scheme. Kathy turns her head to the source of nourishment, closes her lips around the nipple, sucks, and swallows. As a result of experiences and maturation, Kathy adapts or changes this basic sensorimotor scheme of sucking to include both anticipatory sucking movements and nonnutritive sucking, such as sucking a pacifier or blanket.

Children construct new schemes through the processes of assimilation and accommodation. Piaget believed that children are active constructors of intelligence through assimilation (taking in new experiences) and accommodation (changing existing schemes to fit new information), which results in equilibrium.

Read more about this critical period of intellectual, emotional, and social development at http://www.prenhall.com/morrison, Chapter 7: Web Links.

Stages of Sensorimotor Intelligence

Sensorimotor cognitive development consists of six stages (shown in Figure 7.4 and described in the following text). Let's follow Christina through her six stages of cognitive development.

Stage 1: Birth to One Month.   During this stage, Christina sucks and grasps everything. She is literally ruled by reflexive actions. Reflexive responses to objects are undifferentiated, and Christina responds the same way to everything. Sensorimotor schemes help her learn new ways of interacting with the world. New ways of interacting promote Christina's cognitive development.

Grasping is a primary infant sensorimotor scheme. At birth, Christina's grasping reflex consists of closing her fingers around an object placed in her hand. As Christina matures in response to experiences, her grasping scheme is combined with a delightful activity of grasping and releasing everything she can get her hands on!

Stage 2: One to Four Months.   Sensorimotor behaviors not previously present in Christina's repertoire of behavior begin to appear: habitual thumb sucking (indicates hand–mouth coordination), tracking moving objects with the eyes, and moving the head toward sounds (indicates the beginning of the recognition of causality). Christina starts to direct her own behavior rather than being totally dependent on reflexive actions.

Primary circular reactions begin. A **circular response** occurs when Christina's actions cause her to react or when another person prompts her to try to repeat the original action. The circular reaction is similar to a stimulus-response, cause-and-effect relationship.

Stage 3: Four to Eight Months.   Christina manipulates objects, demonstrating coordination between vision and tactile senses. She also reproduces events with the purpose of sustaining and repeating acts. The intellectual milestone of this stage is the beginning of **object permanence**, the concept that things that are out of sight continue to exist.

Secondary circular reactions begin during this stage. This process is characterized by Christina repeating an action with the purpose of getting the same response from an object or person. Christina will repeatedly shake a rattle to repeat the sound. Repetitiveness is characteristic of all circular reactions. Secondary here means that the reaction comes from

FIGURE 7.4

Stages of Sensorimotor Development During Infancy and Toddlerhood

Reflexive Action	Primary Circular Reaction	Secondary Circular Reaction	Coordination of Secondary Schemes	Experimentation (Tertiary Circular Reactions)	Representational Intelligence (Intention of Means)
Birth to 1 month	1 to 4 months	4 to 8 months	8 to 12 months	12 to 18 months	18 to 24 months
• Infant engages in the reflexive actions of sucking, grasping, crying, rooting, and swallowing • Reflexes are modified and become more efficient as a result of experiences; e.g., infant learns how much sucking is required to result in nourishment • Reflexive schemes become adaptive to the environment • Little or no tolerance for frustration or delayed gratification	• Acquired adaptations are formed • Reflexive actions are gradually replaced by voluntary actions • Beginning of understanding of causality; e.g., when infant tries to repeat action that prompted response from caregiver • Circular reactions result in modification of existing schemes	• Infants increase responses to people and objects • Intentional activities increase evidenced by infant's ability to initiate activities • Beginning of object permanency	• Increased deliberation and purposefulness in responding to people and objects • First clear signs of developing intelligence • Continued development of object permanency • Actively searches for hidden objects • Comprehends meanings of simple words	• Active experimentation begins, as evidenced through trial and error • Spends much time "experimenting" with objects to see what happens—insatiable curiosity • Differentiates self from objects • Realizes that "out of sight" is not "out of reach" • Can find hidden objects in first location hidden • Beginning of understanding of space, time, and causality of spatial and temporal relationships	• Mental combinations evidenced by thinking before doing • Representational intelligence begins—able to mentally represent objects • Engages in imitative behavior which is increasingly symbolic • Beginnings of sense of time • Aware of object permanence regardless of the number of invisible placements • Searches for an object in several places • Egocentric in thought and behavior

Source: Summarized from *Developmental Milestones Record*, http://www.nlm.nih.gov/medlineplus.

a source other than the infant. Christina interacts with people and objects to make interesting sights, sounds, and events happen and last. Given an object, Christina will use all available schemes, such as mouthing, hitting, and banging; if one of these schemes produces an interesting result, she continues to use the scheme to elicit the same response. Imitation becomes increasingly intentional as a means of prolonging interest.

Stage 4: Eight to Twelve Months.   During this stage, characterized by coordination of secondary schemes, Christina uses means to attain ends. She moves objects out of the way (means) to get another object (end). She begins to search for hidden objects, although not always in the places they were hidden, indicating a growing understanding of object permanence.

Stage 5: Twelve to Eighteen Months.   This stage, the climax of the sensorimotor period, marks the beginning of truly intelligent behavior. Stage 5 is the stage of experimentation.

Christina experiments with objects to solve problems, and her experimentation is characteristic of intelligence that involves tertiary circular reactions, in which she repeats actions and modifies behaviors over and over to see what will happen.

Christina and other toddlers are avid explorers, determined to touch, taste, and feel all they can. Novelty is interesting for its own sake, and Christina experiments in many different ways with a given object. For example, she will use any available item—a wood hammer, a block, a rhythm band instrument—to pound the pegs in a pound-a-peg toy.

Stage 6: Eighteen to Twenty-Four Months. This is the stage of symbolic representation, which occurs when Christina can visualize events internally and maintain mental images of objects not present. Representational thought enables Christina to solve problems in a sensorimotor way through experimentation and trial and error and predict cause-and-effect relationships more accurately. She also develops the ability to remember, which allows her to try out actions she sees others do. During this stage, Christina can "think" using mental images and memories, which enable her to engage in pretend activities. Christina's representational thought does not necessarily match the real world and its representations, which accounts for her ability to have other objects stand for almost anything: a wooden block is a car; a rag doll is a baby. This type of play, known as symbolic play, becomes more elaborate and complex in the preoperational period.

LANGUAGE DEVELOPMENT

Language development begins at birth. The first cry, the first coo, the first "da-da" and "ma-ma," the first words are auditory proof that children are participating in the process of language development. How does the infant go from the first cry to the first word a year later? How does the toddler develop from saying one word to several hundred words a year later? How does language development begin? What forces and processes prompt children to participate in this uniquely human endeavor? Let us examine some of the explanations.

Heredity and Language Development

Heredity plays a role in language development in a number of ways. First, humans have the respiratory system and vocal cords that make rapid and efficient vocal communication possible. Second, the human brain makes language possible. The left hemisphere is the center for speech and phonetic analysis and the brain's main language center. However, it does not have the exclusive responsibility for language. The right hemisphere plays a role in our understanding of speech intonations, which enables us to distinguish between declarative, imperative, and interrogative sentences. Without these processing systems, language as we know it would be impossible.

Observe an infant boy explore literacy activities at Video Classroom, Child Development, Module 7: Language Development, Video 1: Literacy: Infancy.

Theories of Language Development

The **maturationist theory** of language development holds that language acquisition is innate in all children regardless of country or culture.

This theory views speech production and related aspects of language acquisition as developing according to built-in biological schedules. They appear when the time is ripe and not until then, when a state of developmental "resonance" exists. Children become sensitive for language.

The idea of a sensitive period of language development makes a great deal of sense and held a particular fascination for Maria Montessori, who believed there were two such sensitive

Eddie Lawrence © Dorling Kindersley

Language development begins at birth. Infants and toddlers need to be surrounded by a rich linguistic environment that enables them to develop the literacy skills necessary for successful learning.

periods. The first begins at birth and lasts until about three years. During this time, children unconsciously absorb language from the environment. The second period begins at three years and lasts until about eight years. During this time, children are active participants in their language development and learn how to use their power of communication. Milestones of language development were listed in Table 7.2.

The Environmental Theory. This theory holds that while the ability to acquire language has a biological basis, the content of the language syntax, grammar, and vocabulary is acquired from the environment, which includes parents and other people as models for language. Development depends on talk between children and adults, as well as between children and children. Optimal language development ultimately depends on interactions with the best possible language models. The biological process may be the same for all children, but the content of their language will differ according to environmental factors.

The Sequence of Language Development

Children develop language in predictable sequences, and is an age–stage process, which are described next.

First Words. The first words of children are just that, first words. Children talk about people: dada, papa, mama, mommie, and baby (referring to themselves); animals: dog, cat, kitty; vehicles: car, truck, boat, train; toys: ball, block, book, doll; food: juice, milk, cookie, bread, drink; body parts: eye, nose, mouth, ear; clothing and household articles: hat, shoe, spoon, clock; greeting terms: hi, bye, night-night; and a few words for actions: up, no more, off.

Holophrasic Speech. Children are remarkable communicators without words. When children have attentive parents and teachers, they develop into skilled communicators, using gestures, facial expressions, sound intonations, pointing, and reaching to make their desires known and get what they want. Pointing at an object and saying, " uh-uh-uh" is the same as saying, "I want the rattle" or "Help me get the rattle." As a responsive caregiver you can respond by saying, "Do you want the rattle? I'll get it for you. Here it is!" One of the attributes of an attentive caregiver is the ability to read children's signs and signals, anticipating their desires even though no words are spoken.

The ability to communicate progresses from "sign language" and sounds to the use of single words. Toddlers are skilled at using single words to name objects, to let others know what they want, and to express emotions. One word, in essence, does the work of a whole sentence. These single-word sentences are called **holophrases**.

The one-word sentences children use are primarily referential (used primarily to label objects, such as "doll"), or expressive (communicating personal desires or levels of social interaction, such as "bye-bye" and "kiss"). The extent to which children use these two functions of language depends in large measure on the teacher and parent. For example, children's early language use reflects their mother's verbal style. This makes sense and the lesson is this: how parents speak to their children influences how their children speak.

Symbolic Representation. Two significant developmental events occur at about the age of two. First is the development of **symbolic representation**. Representation occurs when something else stands for a mental image. For example, a word is used to represent something else not present. A toy may stand for a tricycle, a baby doll may represent a real person. Words become signifiers of things, such as ball, block, and blanket.

The use of mental symbols also enables the child to participate in two processes that are characteristic of the early years: symbolic play and the beginning of the use of words and sentences to express meanings and make references.

Vocabulary Development.   The second significant achievement that occurs at about two is the development of a fifty-word vocabulary and the use of two-word sentences. This vocabulary development and the ability to combine words mark the beginning of rapid language development. Vocabulary development plays a very powerful and significant role in school achievement and success. Research repeatedly demonstrates that children who come to school with a broad use and knowledge of words achieve better than their peers who do not have an expanded vocabulary. Adults are the major source of children's vocabularies.

Telegraphic Speech.   You have undoubtedly heard a toddler say something like "Go out" in response to a suggestion such as "Let's go outside." Perhaps you've said, "Is your juice all gone?" and the toddler responded, "All gone." These two-word sentences are called **telegraphic speech**. They are the same kind of sentences you would use if you wrote a text message. The sentences are primarily made up of nouns and verbs. Generally, they do not have prepositions, articles, conjunctions, and auxiliary verbs.

Motherese or Parentese.   Many recent research studies have demonstrated that mothers and other caregivers talk to infants and toddlers differently than adults talk to each other. This distinctive way of adapting everyday speech to young children is called *motherese*,[8] or *parentese*. Characteristics of motherese are listed in Figure 7.5. Do all of the characteristics of motherese listed in this figure seem familiar to you? In working with parents of infants, what would you do to encourage them to use motherese with their children?

FIGURE 7.5

Characteristics of Motherese

- The sentences are short, averaging just over four words per sentence with babies. As children become older, the length of sentences mothers use also becomes longer. Mothers' conversations with their children are short and sweet.

- The sentences are highly intelligible. When talking to their children, mothers tend not to slur or mumble their words. This may be because mothers speak slower to their children than they do to adults in normal conversation.

- The sentences are "unswervingly well formed"; that is, they are grammatical sentences.

- The sentences are mainly imperatives and questions, such as "Give Mommie the ball" and "Do you want more juice?" Since mothers can't exchange a great deal of information with their children, their utterances are such that they direct their children's actions.

- Mothers use sentences in which referents ("here," "that," "there") are used to stand for objects or people: "Here's your bottle." "That's your baby doll." "There's your doggie."

- Mothers expand or provide an adult version of their children's communication. When a child points at a baby doll on a chair, the mother may respond by saying, "Yes, the baby doll is on the chair."

- Mothers' sentences involve repetitions. "The ball, bring Mommie the ball. Yes, go get the ball. The ball, go get the ball."

FIGURE 7.6

How to Promote Language Development in Infants and Toddlers

1. Treat children as partners in the communication process.	Engage in conversations, smile, sing nursery rhymes, and make eye contact. Infant behaviors, such as smiling, cooing, and vocalizing, serve to initiate conversation.
2. Conduct conversations.	Talk to children clearly and distinctly. Conversations are the building blocks of language development.
3. Talk to infants in a soothing, pleasant voice, with frequent eye contact, even though they do not "talk" to you.	Use *motherese*. Most mothers and teachers talk to their young children differently from the way they talk to adults. They adapt their speech so they can communicate in a distinctive way called *motherese* or *parentese*. Mothers' language interactions with their toddlers are much the same as with infants. When conversing with toddlers who are just learning language, simplify your verbalization—not by using "baby talk," such as "di-di" for diaper or "ba-ba" for bottle. Rather, speak in an easily understandable way. Instead of saying, "We are going to take a walk around the block so you must put your coat on," you would instead say, "Let's get coats on."
4. Use children's names when talking with them.	Use children's names while conversing with them. This personalizes the conversation and builds self-identity. The most important word to a child is his/her name. "My Sarah! You look beautiful!"
5. Use a variety of means to stimulate and promote language development.	Read stories, sing songs, and give children many opportunities to verbally interact with you and other children.
6. Converse and share information.	Encourage children to talk and share information with you, other children, and adults.
7. Converse in various settings.	Encourage children to learn to talk in various settings. Take them to different places so they can use their language with a variety of people. This approach also gives children ideas and events for using language.
8. Have children use language in different ways.	Teach children how to use language to ask questions and to explain feelings and emotions. Tell children what they have done and describe things. "Mario! Great job! You got the book all by yourself!"
9. Teach the language of directions and commands.	Give children experiences in how language is used for giving and following directions. Help children understand that language can be used as a means to an end—a way of attaining a desired goal. "Bruce, let's ask Christina to help us put the blocks back in the basket."
10. Converse with children about what they are doing and how they are doing it.	Help children learn language through feedback—asking and answering questions and commenting about activites—which shows children that you are paying attention to them and what they are doing. "Okay, let's read a story. Hillary, what book is your favorite?"
11. Use full range of adult language.	Talk to children in the full range of adult language, including past and future tenses. Talk about what happened yesterday, before a diaper change, and what will happen next. "Okay Cindy! We changed your diaper, now we are going to put on this pretty pink top."
12. Use new words and phrases.	Read stories and talk about the new words.

Negatives. If you took a vote on toddlers' favorite word, "no" would win hands down. When children begin to use negatives, they simply add "no" to the beginning of a word or sentence ("no milk"). As their "no" sentences become longer, they still put "no" first ("no put coat on"). Later, they place negatives appropriately between subject and verb ("I no want juice").

By the end of the preschool years, children have developed and mastered most language patterns. The basis for language development is the early years, and no amount of later remedial training can make up for development that should have occurred during this sensitive period for language learning.

Figure 7.6 provides concrete strategies to use to promote children's language development to make sure your children get off to the best language start possible. The accompanying Program in Action feature illustrates how one program is ensuring that all babies get off to a great start with language.

Baby Signing. Think of all the ways you use signs—gestures to communicate a need or emotion. You blow a kiss to convey affection and hold your thumb and little finger to the side of your head to signal talking on the telephone. I'm sure you can think of many other examples. Now apply this same principle to young children. Children have needs, wants, and emotional feelings long before they learn to talk. There is a growing movement of teaching children to use signs and gestures to communicate desires or signify objects and conditions. Beginning at about five months, babies can learn signals that stand for something else (e.g., a tap on the mouth for food, squeezing the hand for milk).

There is not universal agreement about whether to teach babies a common set of signs or to use ones that parents and children themselves make up. Linda Acredelo and Susan Goodwyn, popularizers of baby signing, identify these benefits: it reduces child and parent frustration, strengthens the parent–child bond, makes learning to talk easier, stimulates intellectual development, enhances self-esteem, and provides a window into the child's world.[9]

Krista Greco / Merrill

A major part of your role as an early childhood professional is to provide a developmentally appropriate environment and activities for young children. This means that you must know infant/child development and individual children. You must also know how to apply that knowledge to a curriculum that will enable children to learn what they need to know for successful learning and living.

DEVELOPMENTALLY APPROPRIATE INFANT AND TODDLER PROGRAMS

Most of the topics we discuss in this book have implications for infant and toddler education. First is the topic of developmental appropriateness. All early childhood professionals who provide care for infants and toddlers—indeed, for all children—must understand and recognize this important concept, which provides a solid foundation for any program. The NAEYC defines *developmentally appropriate* as having three dimensions:

- What is known about child development and learning knowledge of age-related human characteristics that permits general predictions within an age range about what activities, materials, interactions, or experiences will be safe, healthy, interesting, achievable, and also challenging for children.
- What is known about the strengths, interests, and needs of each individual child in the group to be able to adapt for and be responsive to inevitable individual variation.

Imagine a warm, sunny, homey room—one part living room, one part playroom/laboratory for messy little scientists—and an adjacent, quiet, comfortable area for cribs and nursing moms. Small cozy spaces, pillows, a couch, places to be together with friends, places to be alone, places to use all your new motor skills, lots of good books, and abundant conversation. There are always laps, hugs, and smiles.

CHARLIE'S DAY

Twenty-two-month-old Charlie burst through the door, his dad trailing behind with eleven-month-old Emma in his arms. "Bunnies," he said excitedly to his teacher Alicia as he dumped his jacket in his cubby and climbed up next to her on the couch. They talked about his bunny sighting and Alicia produced a book on bunnies, which Charlie pored over while she greeted others.

Charlie's friends trickled in, and he and almost-preschooler Jerrod built and crashed walls with the brick blocks while waiting for breakfast. After a brief group get-together to welcome each other, sing, and talk about bunnies, new clothes, feeding the fish and the parakeet, and other current events, Charlie's morning was spent experimenting with "chemistry and physics" with colored water and corks at the water table and a short visit to the infant room to spend time with Emma. He created a picture for Mom and moved around and over things, going in and out of the tent, "hiding" behind the couch, and spending forty-five minutes outdoors.

Lunch involved serious eating and silly discussions with Selena, who was teaching them some Spanish by speaking it to them, centering on, "Mi Madre takes me to." Charlie showed

Nicholas how he could pour his own milk from the tiny pitcher into his cup. Then it was time for the one story and two poems they always read before their nap, a successful trip to the potty, and a nap. A snack was ready for each child when he or she woke up, and then the group took a walk to find acorns and leaves for tomorrow's art. The rest of the afternoon was spent with Ashley and Nicholas playing with real pots, pans, and dishes. Best of all, Jerrod's ten-year-old brother read him a book on the couch after wrestling a bit with him. At 5:30 p.m. it was time to say good-bye and help Dad collect Emma.

EMMA'S DAY

What was the 352nd day of Emma's life like? After a weepy parting from Dad, she spent the day in "conversation"—great responsive language interactions. She explored the world with her mouth, nose, skin, and ears, and used her newfound skill of walking (actually, lurching about). She used the couch as a walking rail and a pull-me-up-space and had great delight using her whole body to explore the concepts of "over," "under," "around," "in," and "out" as she staggered and crawled around the room, over the footstool, under the table. She played peek-a-boo hiding in the big box. She splashed her fingers in the soapy tub of water with fourteen-month-old Keesha. She loved seeing her brother Charlie and survived his exuberant hug.

Between her three short naps, she ate lunch, lounged around with a bottle or two, and went for a buggy ride with Keesha, second favorite caregiver Tony, and two children from next door. Emma spent quite a bit of time being cared for by and endlessly "chatting" with her very special caregiver Kim,

---

- Knowledge of the social and cultural contexts in which children live to ensure that learning experiences are meaningful, relevant, and respectful for the participating children and their families.[10]

Based on these dimensions, you must provide different programs of activities for infants and toddlers. To do so, you must get parents and your professional colleagues to recognize that infants, as a group, are different from toddlers and need programs, curricula, and environments specifically designed for them. For example, we know that sudden infant death syndrome (SIDS) occurs in very young babies—a developmental, researched fact. We also use the practice recommended by the American Academy of Pediatrics: that infants under the age of one year be put down for a nap or for the night on their *backs*.[11] As another example, we know that mobile infants and toddlers developmentally need lots of physical activity and opportunities to explore, so quality programs accommodate this need. Designing programs and practices specifically for different age groups is at the heart of developmentally appropriate practice. The early childhood education profession is leading the way in raising

especially during the "prime times" of diapering and feeding. She was diapered three times with the requisite singing and tickle games and snuggled at least four or five times, reading picture books, rhyming, and having fascinating "conversations" as Kim talked about current events: the birds that they saw, the poop in her diaper, the water she drank, Charlie, and the zipper on her coat. She also watched closely as fourteen-month-old Nguyen and Tony did a finger play together.

The relaxed but full day of Charlie and Emma left them ready to go home with enough energy to handle the rush of reuniting with mom, sharing Charlie's picture, and spending some good time together before beginning it all over again the next day.

DECONSTRUCTING THE VERY, VERY GOOD DAY

Taking what we know about the development of children and the development of families, this was an extraordinarily good day for Charlie and Emma.

Responsive Interactions with Abundant Language.
Charlie and Emma's days are filled with conversations with adults and other children. They aren't just talked to or at, questioned, or responded to. These are real give-and-takes, often initiated by a vocalization by the children. Their days are laced with books, poems, and singing.

Undivided Attention.   There are a number of moments during the day when Charlie and Emma each have the undivided attention, the full human presence, of their primary caregiver—sometimes for chatting, sometimes for solace, and sometimes for helping them understand that group life has responsibilities. For that brief moment, the only thing in the world that matters is the interaction between the child and caregiver.

Exploration.   Days are full of exploration inside and out, not only with toys but materials from real life and nature.

Relationships.   Emma and Charlie spend the day in a community, not just a room with children just like themselves. They have relationships with older and younger children and adults throughout the center. When the beloved primary caregivers Vicki or Kim are out, it is still a secure place for them to be.

Expectations.   Charlie and Emma are respected as people and expected to behave appropriately. Charlie is learning social graces, and Emma is expected to fuss and cry as she navigates new waters.

Parent Partnership.   Charlie and Emma's mother and father are members of the family center community and are respected as the experts on their children. The care Emma and Charlie receive is based on a thorough mutual understanding between the family and the caregivers and on ongoing communication.

Why a Very, Very Good Day?   It was a very, very good day for Charlie and Emma because everything really important that they needed happened. Alicia, Kim, and all the staff work hard to try to make it great for each child and each family every day.

....

By Jim Greenman, senior vice president of Bright Horizons Family Solutions. This company operates more than 350 family centers in the United States, England, and Ireland.

Connect the routines at the Bright Horizons center with recent developments in brain research at http://www.prenhall.com/morrison, Chapter 7—Journal: Program in Action.

---

consciousness about the need to match what professionals do with children's development as individuals. We have a long way to go in this regard, but part of the resolution will come with ongoing training of professionals in child development and curriculum planning.

Finally, it is important to match teachers and child care providers with children of different ages. Not everyone is emotionally or professionally suited to provide care for infants and toddlers. Both groups need adults who can respond to their particular needs and developmental characteristics. Infants need especially nurturing professionals; toddlers, however need adults who are also nuturing and who can tolerate and allow for their emerging autonomy and independence.

MULTICULTURALLY APPROPRIATE PRACTICE

Children and families are not all the same. They do not all come from the same socioeconomic and cultural backgrounds, and they do not all rear their children the same way. Consequently, it is important for teachers and caregivers to get to know children and families and to be culturally sensitive in their care and education practices. Even so, it may be that because of background and culture, families and professionals may not always agree on a particular policy or practice. For example, many infant and toddler programs teach self-help skills early and encourage children to become independent as soon as possible. These practices may conflict with some families' cultural beliefs and practices.

PREPARING ENVIRONMENTS TO SUPPORT INFANT AND TODDLER DEVELOPMENT

Research studies repeatedly show that children who are reared, cared for, and taught in environments that are enriched are healthier, happier, and more achievement oriented than children who are not raised in such environments.[12] Environments for infants and toddlers should be *inviting, comfortable, healthy, safe, supportive, challenging, and respectful.* You must plan in order to create environments with these features. Figure 7.7 shows an infant floor plan and a toddler floor plan that you can refer to as your plan for an enriched infant and toddler environment.

Also, as you plan, think about how you can make the environment as home-like as possible. Infants and toddlers like and need environments that are cozy, warm, and safe places to be. You can customize your children's home-like environment with curtains, family pictures on the walls, a couch, and so forth. Make sure that your home away from home includes objects from children's various cultures.

Here are some things you can do to provide an enriched environment for infants and toddlers.

Observe the elements of a typical learning environment for infants at Video Classroom, Child Development, Module 5: Cognitive Development: Cognitive Process, Video 5: Environments.

Provide for Health and Safety

Safe environments are essential for infants, toddlers, teachers, and families. Here are some guidelines for providing safe environments for infants and toddlers —and for all children:

- Areas used for diapering and toileting are separate from areas used for cooking, eating, and children's activities.

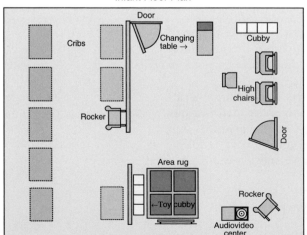

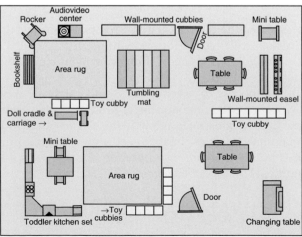

FIGURE 7.7 Infant and Toddler Floor Plans for an Enriched Environment

Source: Child Craft (Online) Available at: www.childcrafteducation.com.

- Mattresses used for infants are firm; avoid soft bedding, such as comforters, pillows, fluffy blankets, or stuffed toys.
- All infant and toddler toys are made of nontoxic materials and are sanitized regularly.
- All toys, classroom materials, and furniture are safe, durable, and in good condition.
- Garbage and trash are stored and disposed of in a safe, sanitary manner.
- All electrical outlets accessible to children are covered and maintained to prevent shock.
- All required policies and plans of action for health emergencies requiring rapid response (e.g., choking, asthma attacks) are posted.
- Locations and telephone numbers of emergency response systems, and posted and up-to-date family contact information and consent for emergency care are readily available.
- Playground equipment and surfaces are maintained to avoid injury to children.
- Teachers, staff, volunteers, and children wash their hands with soap and running water after diapering and toilet use, before and after food-related preparation or activity, after hands have become contaminated with blood or other body fluids, after handling pets or other animals, before and after giving medications, before and after bandaging a wound, and after assisting a child with toilet use.
- Staff and volunteers wear nonporous gloves when in contact with blood or other visibly bloody body fluids.
- Spilled body fluids are immediately cleaned up and disinfected according to professionally established guidelines. Tools and equipment used to clean spills are promptly disinfected, and blood-contaminated materials are disposed of in a plastic bag with a secure tie.[13]

Support Developmental Needs

Supportive environments enable infants to develop **basic trust** and toddlers to develop **autonomy** (see Chapter 3). Infant care should be loving and responsive to their needs. The trusting infant can depend on others to meet her needs. Toddlers want to do things for themselves and be independent.

- Meet infants' and toddlers' needs in warm, sensitive ways. Provide for their choices while taking into account their temperament, emotions, and individuatlity.
- Express love and be affectionate to your children. Tell them, "I love you!"
- Give infants and toddlers your undivided attention—respond to their actions.
- Treat each child as special and important.

Provide Challenging Environments

A challenging environment is one in which infants and toddlers can explore and interact with a wide variety of materials. It is important for you to provide all children with developmentally appropriate challenges. Challenging curriculum enables children to go from their present levels of development and learning to higher levels.

- Include a wide variety of multisensory, visual, auditory, and tactile materials and activities to support all areas of development—physical, social, emotional, and linguistic.
- Include materials for large and small muscles for reaching, grasping, kicking, pulling up, holding on, walking, and so forth.
- Provide materials for tactile and sensory stimulation.
- Hold, play with, and be responsive to infants and toddlers—you are the best toy a child has.

- Provide mirrors for infants and toddlers to look at themselves and others.
- Provide visually interesting things for children to look at such as mobiles, family pictures, and murals.
- Take infants and toddlers on walks so they can observe nature and people.

Promote Respectful Social Development and Interactions

- Play games and engage in activities that include small groups of children.
- Play with toys that involve more than one child. For example, use a wagon and let one child pull another.

Encourage Active Involvement

Review the Infant/Toddler Environment Rating Scale (ITERS) at http://www.prenhall.com/morrison, Chapter 7: Web Links.

- Provide toys and objects that children can manipulate, feel, suck, and grasp.
- Provide objects and containers that children can use to put things in and dump out.
- Provide responsive toys that make sounds, pop up, and change color as children manipulate or act on them.
- Provide safe floor space indoors and grassy areas outdoors so children can explore and move freely.
- Allow infants and toddlers to crawl, pull up, walk, move freely, and explore environments safely.
- Provide activities based on children's interests and abilities. This is a key to responsive and relational caregiving.
- Provide low, open shelves that allow children to see and select their own materials.
- Have a cubby for each child's personal belongings. Personalize these with a picture of each child.

CURRICULA FOR INFANTS AND TODDLERS

Curricula for infants and toddlers consist of all the activities and experiences they are involved with while in your care. The curriculum provides for the whole child—the physical, emotional, social, linguistic, and contitive aspects. Consequently, infant/toddler teachers plan for all activities and involvement: feeding, washing, diapering/toileting, playing, learning and having stimulating interactions, outings, being involved with others, and having conversations. You must plan the curriculum so it is developmentally appropriate.

Encourage Language Development

- Read, read, and read to infants and toddlers. Read aloud with enthusiasm, because this shows children how much you love to read.
- Read in all places and times—before naptime, when invited by children for special occasions, before and after outings, and so forth.
- Read from all kinds of books—stories, poems, and the alphabet.
- Provide books (washable, cloth, small board books, etc.) for children to "read," handle, manipulate, and mouth.
- Sing for and with children. Play a wide variety of music. Sing while changing diapers and doing other teacher–child activities.
- Read and sing nursery rhymes that provide children experiences with manipulating language.

All dimensions of the infant and toddler curricula are based on **responsive relation-ships**. This means that you are responsive to the *needs* and *interests* of each infant and toddler. For example:

We should watch and observe our babies much more closely. What are they doing? How are they playing? What are they trying to achieve? Ask them who they are, what they need, how they can be helped. Then listen and watch for the answer and let that guide what we choose to do with our babies. In this way the baby will truly direct his or her care. The baby will lead. This is hard work for caregivers. To truly attend to and "be there" emotionally for babies is not a skill, but a way of being. Engaging in loving, responsive relationships with each individual baby while at the same time fully supporting the family/child relationship is a tall order. It requires that caregivers have a depth and breadth of knowledge about infant and toddler development; a high degree of self-awareness; a wellspring of emotional resources; and intense dedication to the well-being of other people's children.[14]

The accompanying Program in Action Competency Builder will help you put the importance of *relationship care* into practice.

Provide Daily Routines

The infant and toddler curriculum is also built around routines of the daily organization and purposes of the programs. Routines include: (a) arrivals and departures; (b) diapering and toileting; (c) feeding, mealtimes, and snacks; and (d) naps and sleep time.

Organizing the curriculum around routines and including routines in the curriculum provides children with consistency, a sense of safety, security, an increase of trust, and a general sense of well-being.

INFANT MENTAL HEALTH

There is ongoing emphasis on how to support the social and emotional competence of young children. Early childhood teachers recognize that robust social and emotional development plays an essential role in children's overall growth development and well-being. Providing for the whole child includes ensuring that children have high-quality social and emotional experiences and support. At the same time, with national interest in school readiness at an all-time high, early childhood teachers also recognize the major roles emotional health and social competence play in children's cognitive development.

What Is Infant Mental Health?

Infant mental health is the "state of emotional and social competence of young children." It occurs in the context of the interplay between nature and nurture. The nurture context consists of many "nested" and interrelated processes and factors, including parents' mental health, educational background, and socioeconomic status; parents' parenting knowledge and competence; home conditions; child care; school and community quality and resources; and the values and practices of family cultures.

Infant mental health then can be viewed as a interrelated set of relationships between children, parents, early childhood programs, and community agencies. The essential question for you and other early childhood professionals is how to best provide for infants' mental health. The Diversity Tie-In feature highlights ways to ensure that your work with infants is culturally appropriate. Infant mental health is all about *relations—*

How to Plan a Curriculum for Infants and Toddlers: Day to Day the Relationship Way

Talitha (nine months old) leans against her teacher while laughing and giving her a quick hug.

Marcus (thirteen months old) figures out how to make music with a small drum.

Kareem (eighteen months old) climbs into a teacher's lap with a book in his hand.

Tanya (twenty-four months old) splashes water with her peers in a small water table.

All of these fortunate infants and toddlers have something in common. They attend programs in which teachers know how to plan a curriculum that is responsive and promotes relationships.

WHAT IS AN INFANT AND TODDLER CURRICULUM?

A curriculum for infants and toddlers includes everything that they experience (from their perspective) from the moment they enter the program until they leave to go home. Every experience makes an impression on how children view themselves, others, and the world. Caring teachers plan a curriculum that is (1) relationship based and (2) responsive to infants' and toddlers' needs, interests, and developmental levels as well as their families' goals for their children.

WHY ARE RELATIONSHIPS IMPORTANT IN CURRICULUM?

A relationship is a bond of caring between two people that develops over time. In a relationship-based program, teachers support all the relationships that are key to children's development—parent–child, teacher–child, teacher–family, and child–child relationships. Children need these sustaining, caring relationships to give them a sense of self-worth, trust in the positive intentions of others, and motivation to explore and learn. They need protection, affection, and opportunities to learn to thrive.

HOW CAN YOU PLAN AND IMPLEMENT A RESPONSIVE CURRICULUM?

In a responsive curriculum, teachers interact with children and plan day to day the relationship way. Teachers make daily and weekly changes in the environment and in their interactions in response to each child's needs, interests, goals, and exploration of concepts. How do you do this? First, you *respect,* then you *reflect,* and then you *relate.*

STEP 1 RESPECT

- **Respect infants and toddlers as competent, and honor their individual differences.** Recognize that infants and toddlers are active learners and thinkers who are using many different strategies to figure out how things work. In an emotionally supportive environment, they become problem solvers, make good choices, and care about others. Respect that children are unique human beings with different styles (e.g., some eat fast and others slow), different interests, and one-of-a-kind personalities. "Each child is valued as a child, not just for what adults want the child to become."*

- **Respect that children will have the motivation to learn if you provide a responsive environment.** It should engage them and appeal to a variety of ages, cultures, and individual needs. Provide opportunities for children to choose from such things as blocks, creative materials, sensory experiences, manipulatives, books, dramatic play, and active play opportunities.

- **Respect that play is the way that infants and toddlers learn.** When infants and toddlers aren't sleeping or eating, they are playing with toys, people, and objects (such as a string or a leaf). As they make choices, infants and toddlers focus on their important goals for learning and nurturing—opening and closing a door on a toy, filling a hole on the playground, playing with a friend, turning a page in a book, putting objects in containers, or climbing on a teacher's lap for a hug. As they play, they explore concepts such as how objects fit into various spaces, cause and effect, object permanence, how to comfort another child, or what they can do with different sizes of paper (e.g., crumple, stack, make into a ball, color on it, cover up toys). Children will pursue their goals in an emotionally supportive and physically interesting environment. For example, a child who feels secure might work on figuring out how to stack blocks for long periods of time. Anything that infants and toddlers decide to do in an interesting and relationship-based program supports their learning in all domains of development at the same time— emotional, social, cognitive, language, and motor. Nurturing and responsive adults stay close by, support children's play, and meet their emotional needs by using all of the strategies described in the next sections.

STEP 2 REFLECT

- **Reflect with families to learn about each child's unique interests, explorations, and culture.** If you are open and interested, families will share with you new words that their children are saying, their latest physical accomplishments, blossoming interests in bugs, how they celebrate holidays, or what they want for their children.
- **Reflect through observing children.** Each day observe children to know them well. Each teacher in the room should choose a few children to focus on each week and then take pictures or write notes to capture children's needs, interests, goals, and strategies. You can use an observation and planning guide such as the one shown here to capture your observations. Also, a developmental checklist such as the Ounce† allows you to capture the sequence and quality of a child's development over time and then use the information for responsive planning.
- **Reflect on your observations at least weekly with other teachers and often with families.**
  - What is the child trying to do, and how is the child trying to do it?
  - What is the child learning? (Not—what am I teaching?) What concepts (e.g., space, time, social interactions, expressing emotions, ways to open containers) is the child exploring?
  - What is the child telling you he or she needs? (More positive attention, more affection, new strategies to use when another child takes a toy, more room to learn to walk?)
  - What is new in the child's development? For example, is he or she learning to climb or jump, comfort peers, use two words together, or ask questions?

STEP 3 RELATE

- **Relate to children by providing the basics—moment-to-moment responsive adult interactions.** Infants and toddlers need to feel that you really care about them.
  - Comfort distressed children.
  - Respond to children's cues and signals—for example, a frown that indicates discomfort, a cry that

---

Individual Child Planning Guide

Child's Name: _____

Plans for Week of (Date): _____

Person(s) Completing the Guide: _____

Respect: Child's Emotions, Effort, Goals, Learning, and Relationships

Write an observation or use a photograph or other documentation here—date all notes:

Reflect	Relate
Date all notes: *What am I doing?*	What will you do to support my development and learning?
How am I feeling?	*Responsive Interactions and Building Relationships*
What am I learning?	
• Emotional: • Social with Peers: • Cognitive: • Language: • Motor:	*Environment, Toys, Materials, and Experiences*

Source: Adapted from Wittmer, D. S., & Petersen, S. H. (2006). *Infant and toddler development and responsive program planning,* p. 267. Upper Saddle River NJ: Merrill/Prentice Hall.

(continued)

(continued)

indicates distress, a plop in the lap with a book that means "Please read to me," sounds that indicate concentration and enjoyment, and words that communicate.

- Talk responsively with children, abundantly describe your own and the children's actions, provide reasons and explanations, and engage in cooing, babbling, and word conversations.
- Sing, read, play with children, and respond to children's need for sleep, food, and comfort.
- Guide children to learn how to be prosocial by noticing when they are kind, modeling helpfulness, and demonstrating how to care for others.
- Be open and receptive to what each child is learning in the moment, and follow each child's lead.
- Encourage the children to experiment and problem solve.
- When a child becomes frustrated, scaffold the child's learning and motivation by helping just enough to support the child's learning how to do the task.
- Remember that sometimes you facilitate children's concentration and peer play by sitting near and observing with engaged interest.

- **Relate during routines.** Consider routines such as diapering/toilet learning, feeding/group eating, and nurturing to sleep as central parts of the curriculum for infants and toddlers. Use these times to support children's emotional development and other learning. Talk to children to help them learn language, show affection to help them build a sense of self-worth, and respond to their cues of hunger and tiredness to help them learn to trust themselves and others.
- **Relate by using the observations and reflections to make changes**—day to day and week to week in your interactions, the environment, opportunities, and routines.
  - Plan new ways to support healthy relationships between teachers, children, peers, and families. For example, to help a child who has started to bite peers, plan for a teacher to stay near to help the child learn new behaviors to get needs met.
  - Choose a few new songs to sing, books, toys, changes in the environment, and new opportunities (e.g., art and sensory materials, puzzles, manipulatives, large-motor equipment) based on the children's interests and learning. However, keep most of the environment and materials the same for the children's sense of security and stability. Continue reading favorite books

and singing familiar songs while introducing a few new ones each week.

In the following two examples, teachers use the *respect–reflect–relate model* to plan a responsive, relationship-based curriculum. They trust that each child is expressing a need or conveying an interest. They communicate with families, observe the child, reflect on their observations, and then relate by planning changes in the environment, opportunities for the child, and moment-to-moment responsive interactions to build healthy relationships.

Tommy (twelve months old) was dumping toys out of containers. His teacher observed the dumping and asked, What is he trying to do? How is he trying to do it? What is he learning? What does he need? She asked Tommy's mother how Tommy was playing with his toys at home. Tommy's teacher decided that he was interested in how a container can be full one minute and then empty the next. She provided more containers full of safe objects that Tommy could dump. Soon he also began to fill the containers as he explored different strategies for how objects fit into different spaces.

Another teacher observed Latisha (fifteen months old). She seemed to need to stay near the teacher lately. Her teacher discussed this with Latisha's parents and the other teachers in the room. They decided together that Latisha seemed to need to be near her teacher for protection, affection, and encouragement. Her teacher decided to sit with Latisha more often, give her positive attention, and encourage other children to join them in play.

These teachers were being responsive to Tommy's and Latisha's relationship and learning needs, interests, and developmental changes. When teachers plan the curriculum in a responsive, relationship-based way, infants' and toddlers' motivation to learn and love gets stronger with each caring moment.

Contributed by Donna S. Wittmer and Sandra H. Petersen, *authors of* Infant and Toddler Development and Responsive Program Planning: A Relationship-Based Approach *(Upper Saddle River, NJ: Merrill/Prentice Hall, 2006). Donna is a professor of early childhood education at the University of Colorado at Denver and Health Sciences Center. Sandy works for Zero to Three with the National Infant Toddler Child Care Initiative and Early Head Start and is also an instructor for WestEd Laboratories with the Program for Infant and Toddler Caregivers (PITC).*

*R. N. Emde and J. K. Hewitt, Infancy to Early Childhood: Genetic and Environmental Influences on Developmental Change (Denver, CO: Oxford University Press, 2001), viii.

†TKW Consulting, Ounce Scale, http://www.tkwconsulting.com/ounce.htm.

relations between children, parents, child care programs, and other community agencies. Here are some relational guidelines suggested by the U.S. Department of Health and Human Services, Administration for Children and Families, of what relationships need to be:

The relational guidelines listed below identified cultural responsiveness as important for infant mental health.

Here are some things you can do to help ensure that your work with children and families is culturally appropriate and supports the positive development of infant mental health:

- Remember the important concept of individual differences. In any cultural group, there exist great differences between family practices, beliefs, and customs.
- Share stories about your own culture. Encourage others to share their culture and/or family's way of celebrating a particular holiday or milestone (e.g., birth of a child, wedding).
- Know and understand several basic phrases (e.g., hello, goodbye, thank you) in the language(s) represented by the families in your program.
- Explore your own cultural beliefs, practices, and assumptions.
- Provide training to staff in the role that culture plays in a child's development.

- Solicit songs and games from families from their home cultures—ask families and staff to provide bilingual labels for items found in the program.
- Ensure that all pertinent materials used by the program are available in the home languages of the families served.
- When food is served at a program-sponsored event, ensure that it is sensitive to the cultures of the families in the program.*

As you reflect on these eight key cultural approaches to supporting infant mental health, consider what you will have to do to implement them into your program.

---

*Adapted from Zero to Three—Center for Program Excellence, "Infant Mental Health and Cultural Competence," http://www.zerotothree.org/cpe/tip_2002_06.html.

Reflect on the importance of culturally responsive care and education of very young children at http://www.prenhall.com/morrison, Chapter 7—Journal: Diversity Tie-In.

- *Individualize attention.* Attention is given to the individual needs of the infant and the parents. Responsive caregiving of the infant acknowledges and addresses the infant's needs and behavioral temperament, and conveys the respect and security essential for early emotional development.
- *Emphasize strengths.* Early relationships must emphasize the strengths and resources of each participant. Everyone has strengths, even the newborn. Helping parents understand their infant's strengths, and the strengths that they bring to their caregiving, builds confidence within parents and supports their interactions with their infants.
- *Provide continuous and stable caregiving.* For the infant, continuous and stable caregiving builds confidence that their needs will be met. Especially in the earliest years, it is important for infants who are cared for out of the home to have a long-term relationship with a primary caregiver. For the parents, knowing that there are consistent people available to turn to—the child's caregiver, a home visitor, extended family, network of formal and informal support—is equally important.
- *Be accessible.* Relationships need to be accessible and responsive to when and how the infant and parent need attention and support. To achieve this for infants, adults need to understand the rhythm of the infants, being mindful of the cues infants send when seeking attention as well as those cues infants send when they are overstimulated. The parents and caregivers also need to be participants in supportive relationships. The extent to which the program staff and administration are available for parents helps to meet the individual needs of the adults, facilitating parents' responsive relationships with the infant.
- *Be culturally responsive.* You need to recognize the importance of understanding the values, beliefs, and practices of diverse cultures. Integrate diversity into your caregiving. In all interactions with children and their families honor, their home culture.[15]

PORTRAITS OF CHILDREN

I want you to understand what children are like. To help you achieve this goal, I have included a Portraits of Children feature. The portraits on pages 199–200 provide you with an "up-close" look at infants and toddlers. As you review each of these portraits, use them to consider how to apply what you have learned in this chapter. For example, for each child featured, what could you do to modify the environment to meet that child's particular needs?

ACTIVITIES FOR PROFESSIONAL DEVELOPMENT

Ethical Dilemma

"Should I Keep Quiet?"

Alexa is a toddler teacher at the Bent Tree Early Learning Center, a for-profit company. The state guidelines recommend a toddler ratio of 5:1. Generally, Alexa's room has ten children and two caregivers. However, the administration of Bent Tree overenrolls. One Bent Tree administrator justifies overenrollment in this way: "We can compensate for illnesses and other absences and always be fully enrolled. Full enrollment is important for our bottom line." As a result, on many days, Alexa has more children in her room than the recommended ratio. When the Bent Tree administration believes state licensing inspectors will visit the center, they shift children around from room to room so they are in compliance with the adult–child ratio. In addition, administrators often staff classrooms to comply with adult–child ratio guidelines.

What should Alexa do? Keep quiet and go along with the administrators' juggling of child–adult ratios, or should Alexa talk to the administrators about her concern that they are unethically manipulating the system to be in state compliance?

Application Activities

1. You are invited to speak to a group of infant and toddler caregivers about relationship-based caregiving. Develop your presentation and list five specific suggestions you will make about key relationship-based practices for infants and toddlers. Share your presentation with others or online in an early childhood discussion group.

2. Observe children between the ages of birth and eighteen months. Identify the six stages of sensorimotor intelligence by describing the behaviors you observed. Cite specific examples of secondary and tertiary reactions. For each of the six stages, develop two activities that would be cognitively and developmentally appropriate.

3. Visit two programs that provide care for infants and toddlers. Observe the curriculum to determine whether it is relationship based. Before you observe, develop an observational checklist based on guidelines provided in Chapter 6. What suggestions do you have for making the program more developmentally appropriate?

4. Relationship caregiving must also be culturally appropriate. Visit centers that care for young children of different cultures to determine the role culture plays in how we care for and educate children. List the specific activities and materials that supported children's cultures. How would you enhance the cultural appropriateness of the program?

 To take online practice tests on this chapter's material, go to the Companion Website at http://www.prenhall.com/morrison, select Chapter 7, and then choose the Multiple Choice or the Essay module. For additional Web resources, choose Web Links.

MARIELA

Introduce yourself to Mariela, a four-month-old Cuban female. Mariela weighs 15 pounds and is 2 feet tall. She frequently expresses her mood through facial expressions and vocal sounds. Mariela enjoys playing with here toys and has developed motor skills sucha as reaching, grasping, and kicking.

Social-Emotional	Cognitive	Motor	Adaptive (Daily Living)
Very vocal in expressing her needs and emotions	Attention is more efficient and focused	Holds up her head and chest	Is becoming more accepting of her primary caregiver
Is indiscriminate when smiling at people around her	Recognition of people, places, and objects has improved	Reaches and grasps for toys	Has developed a cycle of bowel movements
Social smile and laughter has emerged	Babbles and coos a lot	Sits up with support	Is beginning to eat formula with rice—eats every four hours
limitates father in face-to-face interaction	Attentive to surronding environment—looks at everything	Rolls from her back to one side	Reaches and cries for caregiver when hungry

CHARLES

Introduce yourself to Charles, a ten-month-old Caucasian male. Charles weighs 21 pounds and is 2 feet, 5 inches tall. He is inviting in nature and enjoys making eye contact with others. Charles is very trusting but gets visibly nervous when his mother leaves the room. He is full of personality and is a very happy baby.

Social-Emotional	Cognitive	Motor	Adaptive (Daily Living)
Pouts when frustrated or angry	Is learning to talk—says "mama" and "dada"	Grabs caregivers' fingers and walks with their assistance	Is beginning to eat solid foods
Has special attachments to familiar caregivers	Knocks things down and points and laughs	Sits upright without assistance	Points to bottle and whines when hungry—grasps cup and tries to feed himself
Exhibits stranger anxiety—distressed when faced with a stranger	Plays peek-a-boo with his mom	Pulls to stand—walks while holding on to furniture	Prefers pacifier at bedtime rather than bottle
Sleeps with favorite blanket	Fits shapes into shape sorter	Manipulates small objects and toys in play	Is taking swimming lessons with his mom

Questions About Developmentally Appropriate Practice:

- What are some of the common traits between Mariela and Charles?
- What differences are there?
- What roles do Mariela's and Charles' caregivers play in their cognitive development?
- What roles do Mariela's and Charles' caregivers play in their social and emotional development?
- Why is it important for Mariela's and Charles' caregivers to talk to them on a frequent basis?
- Why is it so important for caregivers to verbally and physically interact with their infants at this age?
- What role might culture play in what Mariela eats?
- Why is it important for you to be sensitive to cultural differences as you care for and teach young children?

portraits of toddlers

MARIAFE

Introduce yourself to Mariafe, an eighteen-month-old Peruvian Hispanic female. She weighs 24.5 pounds and is 1 foot, 6.25 inches tall. Mariafe is a very sociable girl and is talkative in Spanish. She loves to sing and is very independent; however, she looks for help from her caregiver when frustrated.

Social-Emotional	Cognitive	Motor	Adaptive (Daily Living)
Very sociable and talkative in Spanish	Loves to sing along with music	Walks up steps without help	Can feed self with spoon
Laughs when you call her name or make faces at her	Likes to pretend to be different animals. Cats are her favorite	Can build a tower with four cubes	Looks for help from caregiver when frustrated
Makes eye contact and smiles	Uses twenty-five to fifty words	Scribbles with crayons; loves to "write"; enjoys playing with play dough	Likes to do things by herself — very independent
Is warm and affectionate	Points to named body parts	Throws and catches a ball with both hands	Can undress herself

KENYA

Introduce yourself to Kenya, a twenty-four-month-old African American female. Kenya weighs 28 pounds and is 2 feet tall. She is a talkative child with an expansive vocabulary. Kenya is a highly creative child who enjoys drawing pictures as well as coloring in her coloring books.

Social-Emotional	Cognitive	Motor	Adaptive (Daily Living)
Self-conscious emotions such as pride, shame, embarrassment, and guilt are emerging	Knows the names of classmates—has vocabulary of more than 100 words	Mother began toilet training at twenty-one months—Kenya was responsive to the training and is now potty trained	Is beginning to use utensils when she eats
Shows signs of empathy—consoles her peers when they are upset	Knows names of colors and can count to ten	Is able to jump in place and walk on her tiptoes	Enjoys helping her mother with housekeeping activites
Does not share—very possessive	Interest in language has dramatically increased over the past two months	Walks up and down stairs without assistance	Gets upset when daily routine changes
Has favorite playmates	Can name familiar objects when caregiver points to them	Loves to draw—can draw both circular shapes and straight lines	Enjoys helping her mom choose her outfits for child care center

Questions About Developmentally Appropriate Practice:

- What role does Mariafe and Kenya's cultural background play in their socioemotional development?
- In what ways are Mariafe and Kenya alike and different?
- Given their temperaments, what types of supervision would best fit Mariafe and Kenya?

Photos: p. 198 (top), Eddie Lawrence © Dorling Kindersley; p. 198 (bottom), Getty Images, Inc.–Photodisc; p. 199 (top), Getty Images–Stockbyte; p. 199 (bottom), Eddie Lawrence © Dorling Kindersley

8

THE PRESCHOOL YEARS
Getting Ready for School and Life

professional development goal

Developmentally Appropriate Practice

A. I understand children's developmental stages and growth from birth through age eight, and I use this knowledge to implement developmentally appropriate practice. I do all I can to advance the physical, intellectual, social, and emotional development of the children in my care to their fullest potential.

B. I know, understand, and use a wide array of effective approaches, strategies, and tools to positively influence young children's development and learning.[1]

C. I understand the importance of each content area in young children's learning. They know the essential concepts, inquiry tools, and structure of content areas including academic subjects and can identify resources to deepen their understanding.[2]

focus questions

1. What are the essential physical and motor, socioemotional, cognitive, and language development characteristics of preschoolers?

2. How do the developmental characteristics of individual preschoolers influence how you will provide them with developmentally appropriate programs?

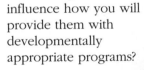

3. How are the changing purposes of preschools and state standards affecting how preschools operate?

4. What are characteristics of a high-quality preschool learning environment?

5. What is the role of play in children's learning?

T he road to success in school and life begins long before kindergarten or first grade. The preschool years are assuming a more important place in the process of schooling, and many view the preschool years as the cornerstone for learning.

WHAT IS PRESCHOOL?

Preschools are programs for three- to five-year-old children, before they enter kindergarten. Today it is common for many children to be in a school of some kind as early as age two or three. Forty-one states currently invest in preschool education, in the form of public preschools or support for Head Start. Some states such as Georgia and New York provide funds for educating every four-year-old whose parents want it. This is known as **universal preschool** and more states are moving in this direction. In 2003, the fifty states spent $3.2 billion on preschool care and education.

Figure 8.1 shows the educational and monetary benefits of investing in high-quality preschool programs. Often the public thinks that money invested in preschool programs does not have the impact that money invested in other programs has. That is wrong. Consider what the research about the three well-known early childhood interventions covered in Figure 8.1 reveals about spending taxpayer money in the early years. Preschool education continues to grow with greater numbers of four-year-olds entering preschools. Currently, about 900,000 children ages three to five are enrolled in public elementary school prekindergarten classes.[3]

The Growing Popularity of Preschools

A number of reasons help explain the current popularity of preschool programs. First, more parents are in the workforce than ever before.[4] With the changing attitudes toward work and careers, many parents believe it is possible to balance family and career. This in turn places a great demand on the early childhood profession to provide more programs and services, including programs for three- to five-year-olds. Many parents, however, are frustrated and dissatisfied with efforts to find quality and affordable care for their children. They believe the federal government, local communities, parents, policy makers, and scholars in the field should all work together to improve the quality of child care in the United States.[5]

Second, a more highly educated workforce will increase economic growth.[6] Business leaders see early education as one way of developing highly skilled and more productive workers.[7] Many preschool programs include work-related skills and behavior in their curriculum. For example, learning how to be responsible and trustworthy are skills that are learned early in life. Likewise, being literate begins in the early years. Research makes it clear that the foundation for learning is laid in the early years and that three-, four-, and five-year-old children are ready, willing, and able to learn.[8]

Third, parents, public policy planners, and researchers believe intervention programs designed to prevent social problems such as substance abuse and dropping out of school

FIGURE 8.1

What Research Says About Investing in Preschool

Program	Results and Benefits
Perry Preschool Project • Children are educated through child-planned activities. • Parents are involved through weekly home visits. • Teachers are trained, supervised, and assessed.	• For every dollar spent, $7.16 was saved in tax dollars. • 66 percent of the program group graduated from high school on time, compared to 45 percent of the control group. • The control group suffered twice as many arrests as the program group.
Chicago Child–Parent Center Program • Paents are required to participate in parent room or classroom activities at least twice a month. • Parent education on nutrition, literacy, development, and so forth is provided in the parent room. • Instructional approaches suit children's learning styles.	• For every dollar invested in the program, $7.10 was returned. • Participants had 51 percent reduction in child maltreatment. • Participants had a 41 percent reduction in special education placement.
Abecedarian Project • Primary medical care is provided on site. • Each child has individualized educational activities. • Activites promote cognitive, emotional, and social development, but focus on language.	• For every dollar invested, $4.00 was returned to taxpayers. • 35 percent attended a four-year college, compared to 13 percent of the control group. • 47 percent had skilled jobs, compared to 27 percent of the control group. • Participants had significantly higher reading and math skills.

Source: High/Scope Educational Research Foundation, *The Perry Preschool Project,* http://www.highscope.org/Research/PerryProject/perrymain.htm; The Child-Parent Center and Expansion Program, http://www.waisman.wisc.edu/cls/Program.htm; The Carolina Abecedarian Project, http://www.fpg.unc.edu/~abc/; and The Pew Charitable Trusts, http://www.pewtrusts.com/news/news_subpage.cfm?contentitem_id=1365&content_type_id=7&page=nr1.

Read about universal preschool at Articles and Readings, Early Childhood Education, Module 1: Advocacy, Article 1: A Call for Universal Preschool.

work best in the early years.[9] Research supports the effectiveness of this early intervention approach.[10] Quality early childhood programs help prevent and reduce behavioral and social problems.[11] Advocacy exists for publicly supported and financed preschools as a means of helping ensure that all children and their families, regardless of socioeconomic background, receive the benefits of attending high-quality preschool programs.

As preschool programs have grown in number and popularity, they have also undergone significant changes in purposes. In previous decades, the predominant purposes of preschools were to help socialize children, enhance their social-emotional development, and get them ready for kindergarten or first grade.[12] Today, there is a decided move away from socialization as the primary function for enrolling children in preschool. Preschools are now promoted as places to accomplish the following goals:

- Support and develop children's innate capacity for learning. The responsibility for "getting ready for school" has shifted from being primarily children's and families' responsibilities to being a cooperative venture between child, family, home, schools, and communities.[13] Review again the information on the importance of early learning for brain development discussed in Chapter 7. The same reasons for providing early education to infants and toddlers also apply to preschool children and their curriculum.

- Provide children the academic, social, and behavioral skills necessary for entry into kindergarten. Today a major focus is on developing preschool children's literacy and math skills.[14]

- Use the public schools to deliver a full range of health, social, economic, and academic services to children at an early age and their families. Family welfare is also a justification for operating preschools.

- Solve or find solutions for pressing social problems. The early years are viewed as a time when interventions are most likely to have long-term positive influences. Preschool programs are seen as ways of lowering the number of dropouts, improving children's health, and preventing serious social problems such as substance abuse and violence.[15]

These goals of the "new" preschool illustrate some of the dramatic changes that are transforming how preschool programs operate and how teachers teach. Given the changing nature of the preschool, it is little wonder that the preschool years are playing a larger role in early childhood education.

WHAT ARE PRESCHOOLERS LIKE?

Today's preschoolers are not like the children of previous decades. Many have already experienced one, two, or three years of child care. They have watched hundreds of hours of television. Many are technologically sophisticated. Many have experienced the trauma of family divorces or the psychological effects of abuse. Both collectively and individually, the experiential backgrounds of preschoolers are quite different from those of previous generations. These factors raise a number of imperatives for you and preschool teachers:

- Observe and assess children so that you know and understand what they know and are able to do.

- Conference and collaborate with families in order to discover their children's unique experiences, abilities, and needs.

- Develop programs to meet the needs of today's children, not yesterday's children. As children change, we must change our programs for them.

Physical and Motor Development

One noticeable difference between preschoolers and infants and toddlers is that preschoolers have lost most of their baby fat and taken on a leaner, lankier look. This "slimming down" and increasing motor coordination enables preschoolers to participate with more confidence in the locomotor activities so vitally necessary during this stage of growth and development. Both girls and boys continue to grow several inches per year throughout the preschool years. Table 8.1 shows the average height and weight for

TABLE 8.1 Average Height and Weight of Preschoolers

Age	Males		Females	
	Height (inches)	Weight (pounds)	Height (inches)	Weight (pounds)
3 years	37.5	31.75	37	30.75
4 years	40.5	36	39.75	35
5 years	43	40.75	42.5	39.75

Source: Based on data from the National Center for Health Statistics in collaboration with the National Center for Chronic Disease Prevention and Health Promotion, 2000, http://www.cdc.gov/growthcharts.

preschoolers. Compare these averages with the height and weight of preschoolers you know or work with.

Preschool children are learning to use and test their bodies. The preschool years are a time for learning what they can do individually and how they can do it. Locomotion plays a large role in motor and skill development and includes such activities as moving the body through space—walking, running, hopping, jumping, rolling, dancing, climbing, and leaping. Preschoolers use these activities to investigate and explore the relationships among themselves, space, and objects in space.

Preschoolers also like to participate in fine-motor activities such as drawing, coloring, painting, cutting, and pasting. Consequently, they need programs that provide action and play, supported by proper nutrition and healthy habits of plentiful rest and good hygiene. Good preschool programs provide for these unique physical needs of preschoolers and support their learning through active involvement.

Social and Emotional Development

A major responsibility of preschool teachers is to promote and support children's social and emotional development. Positive social and emotional development enables children to learn better and to succeed in all of school and life activities.

During the preschool years (ages three to five), children are in Erikson's psychosocial development stage of initiative versus guilt (see Chapter 3). During this stage, children are fully involved in locomotive activities and the enjoyment of doing things. They are very active and want to plan and be involved in activities. They want to move and be active.

You can help support children's initiative in these ways:

- Give children freedom to explore.
- Provide projects and activities that enable children to discover and experiment.
- Encourage and support children's attempts to plan, make things, and be involved.

Self-Regulation.   During the preschool years, children are learning **self-regulation**, the ability to control their emotions and behaviors, to delay gratification, and to build positive social relations with each other.

Teaching self-regulation (i.e., self-control) is a major teacher task during the preschool years. The following guidelines will help you teach self-regulation to preschool children:

- *Provide a variety of learning experiences.* Young children are very good at creating diversion when none is available. Often teachers think they cannot provide interesting learning experiences until the children are under control, when, in fact, the real problem is that the children are out of control because there is nothing interesting to do.
- *Arrange the environment to help children do their best.* Make sure block building activities are accorded enough space and are protected from traffic. Avoid arrangements that invite children to run or fight, such as long corridors or large open spaces.
- *Get to know each child.* Establish relationships with parents, and support children's strengths as well as their needs.
- *Set clear limits for unacceptable behavior.* Enforce them with rational explanations in a climate of mutual respect and caring.
- *Work with children to establish a few simple group rules.* Some appropriate rules are to take care of other people, take care of yourself, and take care of the classroom. Systematically teach and reinforce these rules throughout the school year.

- *Use the child's home language as often as possible.* Make every effort to show children you support their culture and respect their language.
- *Coach children to express their feelings verbally.* Help children use either their home language or English, and solve social problems with others using words. For many children, this will mean not only providing the words and offering some possible solutions, but being there to assist when situations arise.
- *Model self-control by using self-talk.* "Oh, I can't get this lid off the paint. I am feeling frustrated [take a deep breath]. Now I'll try again."[16]

Cognitive Development

Preschoolers are in the preoperational stage of intellectual development. As we discussed in Chapter 3, characteristics of the preoperational stage are (1) children grow in their ability to use symbols, including language; (2) children are not capable of operational thinking (an **operation** is a reversible mental action), which explains why Piaget named this stage preoperational; (3) children center on one thought or idea, often to the exclusion of other thoughts; (4) children are unable to conserve; and (5) children are egocentric.

Preoperational characteristics have particular implications for you and other early childhood professionals. You can promote children's learning during the preoperational stage of development by following the steps presented in the Professionalism in Practice feature. As you review these steps, start to plan for how you can apply them to your classroom.

Language Development

Children's language skills grow and develop rapidly during the preschool years. Vocabulary, the number of words children know, continues to grow. Sentence length also increases and children continue to master syntax and grammar.

During the preschool years, children's language development is diverse and comprehensive and constitutes a truly impressive range of learning. An even more impressive feature of this language acquisition is that children learn intuitively, without a great deal of instruction, the rules of language that apply to words and phrases they use. You can use many of the language practices recommended for infants and toddlers to support preschoolers' language development. The accompanying Diversity Tie-In feature provides you with specific examples of how you can support both home language and English language learning.

Getty Images-Stockbyte

Physical activities contribute to children's physical, social, emotional, linguistic, and cognitive development. It is essential that programs provide opportunities for children to engage in active play both in indoor and outdoor settings. What are some things that children can learn through participation in playground activities?

READY TO LEARN: READY FOR SCHOOL

School **readiness** is a major topic of debate in discussions of both preschool and kindergarten programs. The early childhood profession is reexamining "readiness," its many interpretations, and the various ways the concept is applied to educational practices.

For most parents, *readiness* means that their children have the knowledge and abilities necessary for success in preschool and for getting ready for kindergarten. Figure 8.2 shows important factors for kindergarten readiness. These are some of the things children should know and be able to do *before* coming to kindergarten. Thus they shape, influence, and inform the preschool curriculum and the activities of preschool teachers.

How to Promote Preschoolers' Cognitive Development

STEP 1 — FURNISH CONCRETE MATERIALS TO HELP CHILDREN SEE AND EXPERIENCE CONCEPTS AND PROCESSES

Children learn more from touching and experimenting with an actual object than they do from a picture, story, video, or a teacher's lecture. If children are learning about apples, bring in a collection of apples for children to touch, feel, smell, taste, discuss, classify, manipulate, and explore. Collections of things such as leaves, rocks, and bugs also offer children an ideal way to learn the names for things, classify, count, and describe.

STEP 2 — USE HANDS-ON ACTIVITIES THAT GIVE CHILDREN OPPORTUNITIES FOR ACTIVE INVOLVEMENT IN THEIR LEARNING

Encourage children to manipulate and interact with the world around them. In this way, construct concepts about relationships, attributes, and processes. Through exploration, preoperational children begin to collect and organize data about the objects they manipulate. For example, when children engage in water play with funnels and cups, they learn about concepts such as measurement, volume, sink/float, bubbles, prisms, evaporation, and saturation.

STEP 3 — GIVE CHILDREN MANY AND VARIED EXPERIENCES

Provide diverse activities and play environments that lend themselves to teaching different skills, concepts, and processes. Children should spend time daily in both indoor and outdoor activities. Give consideration to the types of activities that facilitate large- and fine-motor, social, emotional, and cognitive development. For example, outdoor play activities and games such as tag, hopscotch, and jump rope enhance large-motor development; fine-motor activities include using scissors, stringing beads, coloring, and using writing materials such as crayons, pencils, and markers.

STEP 4 — SCAFFOLD APPROPRIATE TASKS AND BEHAVIORS

The preoperational child learns to a great extent through modeling. Children should see adults reading and writing

FIGURE 8.2 The Basic Building Blocks of Kindergarten Readiness

Source: Applied Survey Research. (2005). "The Basic Building Blocks of Kindergarten Readiness" from *Assessment of Kindergarten Readiness in San Mateo and Santa Clara Counties Comprehensive Report,* p.12.

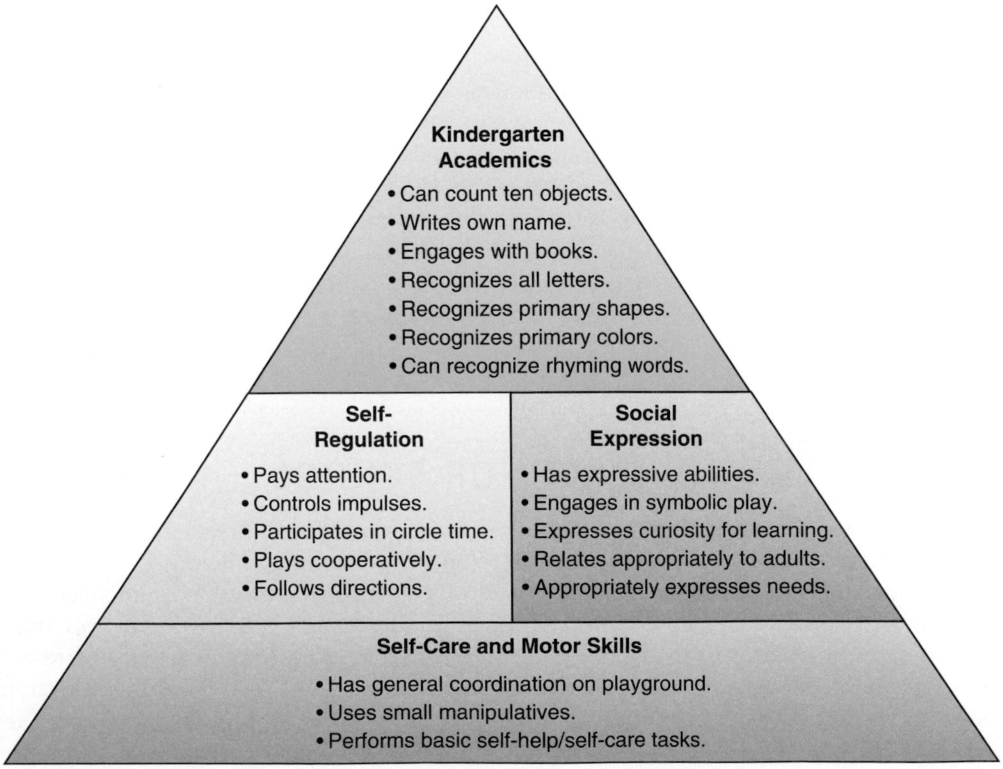

Kindergarten Academics
- Can count ten objects.
- Writes own name.
- Engages with books.
- Recognizes all letters.
- Recognizes primary shapes.
- Recognizes primary colors.
- Can recognize rhyming words.

Self-Regulation
- Pays attention.
- Controls impulses.
- Participates in circle time.
- Plays cooperatively.
- Follows directions.

Social Expression
- Has expressive abilities.
- Engages in symbolic play.
- Expresses curiosity for learning.
- Relates appropriately to adults.
- Appropriately expresses needs.

Self-Care and Motor Skills
- Has general coordination on playground.
- Uses small manipulatives.
- Performs basic self-help/self-care tasks.

daily. It is also helpful for children to view brief demonstrations by peers or teachers on possible ways to use materials. For example, after children have spent a lot of time in free exploration with math manipulatives, show children patterning techniques and strategies they may want to experiment with in their own play.

STEP 5 PROVIDE A PRINT-RICH ENVIRONMENT TO STIMULATE INTEREST AND DEVELOPMENT OF LANGUAGE AND LITERACY IN A MEANINGFUL CONTEXT

The physical environment should display room labeling, class stories and dictations, children's writing, and charts of familiar songs and finger plays. Provide a variety of literature for students to read, including books, magazines, and newspapers. Paper and writing utensils should be abundant to motivate children in all kinds of writing. Daily literacy activities should include opportunities for shared, guided, and independent reading and writing; singing songs and finger plays; and creative dramatics. Read to children every day.

STEP 6 ALLOW CHILDREN PERIODS OF UNINTERRUPTED TIME TO ENGAGE IN SELF-CHOSEN TASKS

Children benefit more from large blocks of time provided for in-depth exploration in meaningful play than they do from frequent, brief ones. It takes time for children to become deeply involved in play, especially imaginative and fantasy play. Morning and afternoon schedules should each contain at least two such blocks of time.

STEP 7 GUIDE CHILDREN IN PROBLEM-SOLVING SKILLS IN MATH AND SCIENCE

Apply and provide a variety of appropriate strategies to solve problems. Use graphic organizers in math. A graphic organizer such as a Venn diagram is a visual representation of material. The use of graphs is important. Children can graph many things—even their lunch requests! Many stories also offer a way to develop problem-solving skills. As you teach number concepts, use stories and visual representations. For example, there are five apples on the tree. Two apples fell on the ground. How many apples are on the tree? In science, ask questions such as "What do you think will happen if . . . ?"

Connect these strategies on promoting preschooler's cognitive development to current brain research at http://www.prenhall.com/morrison, Chapter 8—Projects: Professionalism in Practice.

Review these now and think about their implications for what you will teach preschoolers to know and do.

Discussions about readiness have changed the public's attitude about what it means. Responsibility for children's early learning and development is no longer placed solely on children and their parents but rather is seen as a shared responsibility among children, parents, families, early childhood professionals, communities, states, and the nation.

Readiness Skills

As you review Figure 8.2 note that important skills necessary for school success include language, independence, impulse control, interpersonal skills, experiential background, and physical and mental health. The following sections cover each of these topics. Use the information given and incorporate it into your planning and teaching.

Language. Language is the most important readiness skill. Children need language skills for success in school and life. Important language skills include:

- **Receptive language**, such as listening to the teacher and following directions;
- **Expressive language**, demonstrated in the ability to talk fluently and articulately with teacher and peers, the ability to express oneself in the language of the school, and the ability to communicate needs and ideas; and
- **Symbolic language**, knowing the names of people, places, and things, words for concepts, and adjectives and prepositions.

Young English Language Learners

Linda M. Espinosa, Ph.D.,
University of Missouri–Columbia
Columbia, Missouri

Increasingly, young children in the United States speak a language other than English in the home. The number of children enrolled in preschool and Head Start programs whose home language is not English (known as English-language learners or ELL) has been steadily increasing during the past two decades. During the 2004–2005 program year almost 30 percent of children enrolled in Head Start did not speak English as their home language. Of these, the vast majority are from Spanish-speaking homes with 139 other language groups also reported.

Recent research has consistently shown that most young children are not only capable of learning two languages, but also enjoy cognitive, cultural, and economic advantages as a result of being bilingual. Bilingualism has been associated with a greater awareness of and sensitivity to linguistic structure, an awareness that is transferred and generalized to certain early literacy and nonverbal skills. There are several important implications of this research for early childhood professionals:

- Children who have the opportunity to speak two languages should be encouraged to maintain both, so they can enjoy the benefits that may accompany bilingual status.
- Maintaining the home language is essential not just to the child's future academic and cognitive development, but also to the child's ability to establish a strong cultural identity, to develop and sustain strong ties with their immediate and extended families, and to thrive in a global, multilingual world.

- Becoming proficient in a language is a complex and demanding process that takes many years. As with any type of learning, children will vary enormously in the rate at which they learn a first and a second language.

TEACHING STRATEGIES THAT SUPPORT HOME LANGUAGE MAINTENANCE

Many specific teaching practices are available that support primary language development. Here are some things you can do:

- Provide instructional support including paraprofessionals (instructional assistants, parent volunteers, and older and more competent students) whenever possible.
- Incorporate children's home language into the daily classroom activities through song, poetry, dances, rhymes, and counting.
- Create materials in the children's home language to represent familiar stories, songs, or poems that will improve early primary language literacy.
- Provide simple print material in the children's home language in learning centers, labeled objects, and writing utensils. This further supports early literacy abilities for non-English speakers. Each language can be printed on different colored paper to help children distinguish between them.
- Encourage parents and other family members to continue to use the home language during family activities while also encouraging early literacy development in the primary language.
- Provide age-appropriate books and stories in the child's home language, loaning them to parents, with

Read about effective reading instruction for English language learners at Articles and Readings, Child Development, Module 8: Language Development, Article 3: Teaching Reading to Early Language Learners.

In addition, children need language skills related to reading readiness. Two of the most important reading readiness skills are the ability to recognize and name the letters of the alphabet and to make the sounds of the letters. More preschool programs are including these important skills in their curricula.

Teaching English Language Learners. A reality of teaching in the preschool today is that some students will come to your classroom not speaking any English. Others will be in stages of English acquisition ranging from speaking very little English to speaking it very well. Approximately ten million children speak a language other than English in the home.[17] Other than English, in the United States, Spanish is the most often spoken home language.[18] Other common home languages are Chinese and Vietnamese.[19] Furthermore, your chances of having to teach children English increases dramatically in high-minority population states such as California, Florida, Illinois, Arizona, New Jersey, New York, and Texas.[20]

Children whose home language is not English are called English language learners (ELLs). They are learning English as their second language. Preschool ELLs are like other

encouragement to engage in playful, interactive reading times. This will contribute to the child's motivation to read.

- Learn and use even just a few words of the students' home languages to communicate respect for the home language and culture. However, if you do attempt to speak the child's home language, it is important to pronounce the words correctly.
- Include family members and other community representatives in the classroom to provide language models in the home language. They can tell or read stories, help with translation if they are bilingual, and teach the rest of the class new words.

ENGLISH LANGUAGE FLUENCY

Many classroom instructional approaches are effective for English language learners. The following are specific suggestions to support English acquisition for young children who are not native English speakers. These strategies are based on research and can also promote children's bilingual development if combined with home language support:

- Embed all instruction in context cues that connect words to objects, visuals, and body movements. This is what Tabors calls "doubling the message."* By connecting words with concrete objects and physical movements, you are increasing the probability that children will understand their meaning.
- Provide a consistent and predictable routine that frequently uses cooperative learning groups, small-group interactions. These regular opportunities for ELLs to converse informally with English speakers support second-language learning.
- Use small peer groups that give children opportunities to learn English in nonthreatening, secure environments. This can also promote friendships among children who speak different languages.

- Allow children to practice following and giving instructions for basic literacy tasks such as turning pages during reading, using pictures to tell a story, telling a story in sequence, and noting the names of main characters in a story.
- Allow for chidren's voluntary participation instead of strictly enforced turn-taking or teacher-led lessons.
- Help young English learners become a part of the social fabric of the classroom by systematically including a mix of first- and second-language children in organized small-group activities.
- Teach English-speaking children in the classroom to act as language resources for second-language learners, which could "act as a catalyst to language development."
- Have students dictate stories about special personal events.
- Repeat words and directions frequently and explicitly throughout the day, calling attention to their sounds and meanings.
- Modify language use so that it is comprehensible for young second-language learners. Make it as simple, direct, and concrete as possible while systematically introducing new words that are unfamiliar.
- Speak at a standard speed with some pausing between phrases, use simple short sentences with clear referents, and use more gestures, movements, and facial expressions to help convey meaning.

*Tabors, P. (1997). One child two languages: A guide for preschool educators of children learning English as a second language. Baltimore, MD: Brookes Publishing Company.

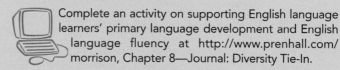

Complete an activity on supporting English language learners' primary language development and English language fluency at http://www.prenhall.com/morrison, Chapter 8—Journal: Diversity Tie-In.

preschoolers. Everything we have said about children's cognitive, physical, linguistic, and social-emotional development applies to them. They are bright, active, and they want to learn!

The following guidelines will provide you with teaching strategies you can apply to your teaching of ELLs:

- *Keep ELLs active and involved.* Provide motor and kinesthetic activities such as playing games involving basic English words, acting out stories, and helping with classroom chores.
- *Create a buddy system.* Pair ELLs with another child who is a native English speaker or who knows English well.
- *Teach daily living and vocabulary words and phrases.* Teach vocabulary and phrases that enable ELLs to greet others and identify objects in the classroom and home. Teach words they need to get along in everyday life such as days of the week. Have children make their own dictionaries of pictures labeled with words. They can have a picture dictionary for school and one for home. Help children learn oral language skills first. Then emphasize writing skills, followed by learning-to-read skills.

- *Incorporate children's culture into classroom activities*. Classroom activities and themes that focus on the children such as "all about me" enable you to support and celebrate children's unique cultural identities.
- *Integrate technology into children's English learning*. Use language learning software to help your students learn English such as the Zip Zoom English software by Scholastic that aids in developing critical language and reading skills for ELLs in grades K–3. The following Technology Tie-In feature explores ways in which technology can assist in *any* child's literacy development.

Independence.   **Independence** means the ability to work alone on a task, take care of oneself, and initiate projects without always being told what to do. Independence also includes mastery of self-help skills, including dressing skills, health skills (toileting, hand washing, and brushing teeth), and eating skills (using utensils and napkins, serving oneself, and cleaning up). Independence is a highly regarded American ability. However, it is not a capacity that is valued by all cultures. This means you will have to work with children and their parents in culturally sensitive ways as you support children's growing independence. Review again the guidelines for culturally appropriate practice in Chapter 7.

Impulse Control.   **Impulse control** includes working cooperatively with others; not hitting others or interfering with their work; developing an attention span that permits involvement in learning activities for a reasonable length of time; and being able to stay seated for a while. Children who are not able to control their impulses are frequently (and erroneously) labeled hyperactive (ADHD) or learning disabled (LD). These are also children who are *most* likely to *not* receive the individual attention they need and are therefore at risk for failure.

Interpersonal Skills.   **Interpersonal skills** include getting along and working with both peers and adults. Parents frequently say the primary reason they want their children to attend preschool is "to learn how to get along with others." All preschool programs are experiences in group living, and children should have the opportunity to interact with others to become successful in a group setting. Interpersonal skills include cooperating with others, learning and using basic manners, and, most important, learning how to learn from and with others. Recall that Lev Vygotsky believed that learning is a social activity. Constructivist practice is based on the important premise of social learning, that is, that people help people learn.

Experiential Background.   Experiential background is important to readiness because experiences are the building blocks of knowledge, the raw materials of cognitive development. Children must go places—the grocery store, library, zoo—and they must be involved in activities—creating things, painting, coloring, experimenting, discovering. Children can build only on the background of information they bring to new experiences. Varied experiences, for example, are the context in which children learn words, and the number and kinds of words children know is a major predictor of the ability to learn to read and of their school success.

Physical and Mental Health.   Children must have good nutritional, mental, and physical health habits that will enable them to participate fully in and profit from any program. They must also have positive, nurturing environments and caring professionals to help them develop a self-image for achievement. Today, more attention than ever is paid to children's health and nutrition.

technology tie-in

How to Use Technology as a Scaffolding Tool in the Preschool Classroom

Technology can be an exciting tool to help children acquire early literacy skills. Using cameras, printers, scanners, and software provides endless possibilities for personalizing literacy activities.

SELECT THE EQUIPMENT

You need several pieces of equipment to create literacy materials and activities.

Digital camera

An inexpensive camera may work just as well as a special model designed for children. There are a number of features to consider:

- Resolution—the sharpness of the pictures expressed in pixels (the higher the resolution, the better the picture)
- Optical zoom—magnifies the images using a multifocal-length lens
- Image capacity—memory capability for images shot at high resolution
- Expansion slot for memory card
- LCD display for children to review pictures

Digital video camera

- Use to document events in the classroom.
- Use a tripod to ease use and avoid accidents.

Printer and scanner

- A color printer is essential for book making and literacy material creation.
- Scanners can transfer children's writing samples and artwork into a digital format.

PDA (personal digital assistant)

- These handheld devices usually include a date book, address book, task list, memo pad, clock, and calculator software. Some models have Internet access, color screens, and audio capabilities, enabling them to show multimedia content.
- This important documentation tool can record a child's progress.
- Children's work can be captured in photo form.
- Software application is key to use with children's portfolio items.

LEARN TO USE THE EQUIPMENT

Most equipment is fairly user-friendly, requiring very little, if any, instruction to operate.

- Become familiar with all options and test them.
- Make sure equipment is easy for children to use.

The manufacturer may have tutorials that are downloadable from its website. Online training sites may also offer tips and training on using technology.

CHOOSE THE SOFTWARE

Before you choose software, decide on the literacy activity:

- For creating simple books or class slide shows, use a photo-management type of program—such as *iPhoto*, *Kodak EasyShare*, or *Photo Kit Junior*.
- For interactive books, authoring software is best—such as *IntelliPics Studio*, *HyperStudio*, or even *Microsoft Word*.

CREATE LITERACY ACTIVITIES FOR THE CHILDREN

When they create their own electronic books, children learn many print concepts, including reading text left to right and top to bottom, separating words with a space, and learning that words have meaning.

Electronic book templates

- Each child can create a book about him- or herself or can base it on a field trip, class project, or favorite book.
- Children can add their own pictures, voices, and text.
- Page-turning buttons in the bottom corners of each page allow children to navigate forward and backward through the book.

Child-created books

Children in preschool classes can learn to use digital cameras, download pictures to the computer, and use software to create books.

- Explain how to plug the camera into the computer and download the pictures.
- Show children how to use the photo management application.
- Teach children how to enter text and sounds into the program.
- Encourage children to work in small groups to benefit from cooperative play.

DOCUMENT THE LEARNING

- *Daily documentation.* Take digital photos in the classroom on an ongoing basis. Pictures of children's construction, artwork, or play activities can be shared immediately with them. The teacher may also want to share the images with the class as a review of the week's activities and projects.
- *Wall displays.* Displaying digital pictures in a hallway or on a classroom wall gives children documentation of events and an opportunity to review and revisit. Children's language skills are sparked as they review the pictures. They may also dictate a narrative about the pictures and events.
- *Portfolios.* Have digital photos, scanned photos, writing samples, and artwork in children's individual electronic portfolio files. At the end of the year, copy the images to a CD or DVD for families, or create an electronic book or movie about each child. Families might also create their own books during a workshop at the end of the year. With simple instructions and a template, you can choose the images to place in children's books.

Technology is a scaffolding tool for literacy when educators and families know how to use equipment and apply it to young children's needs. Children gain print concepts and other early literacy skills, and the technology serves as a valuable documentation tool.

Source: Contributed by Linda Robinson, assistant director, Center for Best Practices in Early Childhood, Western Illinois University, Macomb, Illinois.

*L. Robinson, "Technology as a Scaffold for Emergent Literacy: Interactive Storybooks for Toddlers," Young Children 58, no. 6 (2003): 42–48.

Identify ways in which NAEYC supports the use of computers in early childhood programs at http://www.prenhall.com/morrison, Chapter 8—Journal: Technology Tie-In.

Readiness and Culture

All children are always ready for some kind of learning. Children always need experiences that will promote learning and get them ready for the next step. As early childhood educators, we should constantly ask such questions as: What does this child know? What can I do to help this child move to the next level of understanding?

Many factors influence children's readiness for school. Reflect on the influence of parents, siblings, home, and schools on how children learn. Readiness is also a function of **culture**. Culture is a group's way of life, including basic values, beliefs, religion, language, clothing, food, and various practices. Professionals have to be sensitive to the fact that different cultures have different values regarding the purpose of school, the process of schooling, children's roles in the schooling process, and the family's and culture's roles in promoting readiness. You must learn about other cultures, talk with families, and try to find a match between the process and activities of schooling and families' cultures. Providing culturally sensitive, supportive, and responsive education is the responsibility of all early childhood professionals.

> . . . cultural variables influence how children present themselves, understand the world, and interpret experiences. Culture also affects the experiences through which children's earliest literacy and number knowledge are acquired. Some of these experiences may be explicitly focused on . . . learning, such as reading books to children or instructing them to count. More common are activities that provide implicit . . . support for various types of learning in the context of shared everyday activities, such as measuring ingredients when baking cookies or counting change at the grocery store. Significant, as well, are the adult activities that children witness and interpret as enjoyable or useful *because* their parents and relatives engage in them, such as reading for enjoyment or telling stories.
>
> Efforts to create effective classroom environments for young children from diverse cultural and linguistic backgrounds should be based, in part, on knowledge about the role that culture plays in shaping children's learning opportunities and experiences at home. From teachers' standpoints, it is critical to identify those aspects of children's cultural backgrounds that have the greatest relevance for children's adjustment, motivation, and learning at school. Cultural dimensions that influence children's school readiness include: (1) parents' attitudes and beliefs about early learning, (2) the nature and extent of parent–child interactions and other experiences that support the kinds of learning that schools tend to expect from children, and (3) social conventions that affect the ways in which knowledge and skills pertinent to early learning are communicated among and used by family members. The primary language used at home is . . . also a profoundly important factor that affects children's adjustment to school.[21]

PRESCHOOLS AND STATE STANDARDS

The purposes of preschool are changing dramatically. More and more, preschools are seen as places that get children ready for kindergarten. What was traditionally taught in kindergarten is now taught in the preschool. The preschool curriculum is now stressing academic skills related to reading, writing, and math as well as social skills. Increasingly, the responsibility for setting the preschool curriculum is being taken over by state departments of education through early learning **standards**, statements of what preschoolers should know and be able to do. (Recall the discussion in Chapter 5.) Currently, thirty-six states have guidelines or standards for what young children should know and do before they enter kindergarten. These early learning standards include literacy, mathematics, science, social studies, fine arts, health and safety, personal and social development, physical development, and technology applications. Two important points are associated with state preschool standards. One is that preschool goals and learning standards are being set by state departments of education, and as a result, states are determining the preschool curriculum. Second, the preschool curriculum is becoming much more academics focused.

Observe examples of indoor and outdoor preschool environments at Video Classroom, Early Childhood Education, Module 3: Appropriate Early Environments, Video 1: Environments—Early Childhood.

THE PRESCHOOL ENVIRONMENT

When we think of the preschool environment, we think of the physical dimension—the furniture, the materials, and the space. These are part of the preschool environment, but the preschool environment also includes child–staff interactions and behaviors, children's cultural needs and how they are met, mealtime, activities and interactions, quality of the staff, and so forth. Looking at the environment of preschools there are a number of things that you need to take into consideration. The indicators of a high-quality preschool environment are outlined for you in Table 8.2. For each quality indicator there is a quality description. All of the quality

TABLE 8.2 Indicators of High-Quality Preschool Environments

Quality Indicator	Quality Description
Preschool environment and setting	What are the physical accommodations like? Is the facility pleasant, light, clean, and airy? Is it a physical setting where you would want to spend time? (If not, children will not want to either.) Are plenty of materials available for the children to use?
Highly qualified staff	Are the staff highly qualified? Do they have two- or four-year college degrees? Do they have specialized training? Research is clear that children's learning and development depends on the educational qualifications of teachers.
Children's emotional states	Do the children seem happy and involved? Or passive? Is television used as a substitute for a good curriculum and quality professionals?
Types of materials	What kinds of materials are available for play and learning? Is there variety and an abundance of materials? Are there materials (like puzzles) that help children learn concepts and think?
Balance of activities	Is there a balance of activity and quiet play and of individual, small-group, and large-group activities? Child-directed and professional-directed activities? Indoor and outdoor play?
Health and safety	Is the physical setting safe and healthy? Do teachers model healthy practices by going outside and being physically active and eating nutritious foods?
Philosophy and goals	Does the school have a written philosophy and goals? Does the program philosophy agree with the parents' personal philosophy of how children should be reared and educated? Are the philosophy and goals appropriate for the children being served?
Literacy development	Is there an emphasis on early literacy development? Do teachers read to children throughout the day? A general rule of thumb is that teachers should read to children at least twenty minutes a day. Are there books and other materials that support literacy development? Another rule of thumb is that preschool children should be familiar with 100 different, high-quality books by the time they enter kindergarten.
Written curriculum	Is there a written curriculum designed to help children learn skills for literacy, math, and science? Does the curriculum provide for skills in self-help; readiness for learning; and cognitive, language, physical, and social-emotional development?
Daily plans	Does the staff have written plans? Is there a smooth flow of activities, or do children wait for long periods "getting ready" for another activity? Lack of planning indicates lack of direction. Although a program whose staff does not plan is not necessarily a poor program, planning is one indicator of a good program.
Adult:child ratio	What is the adult:child ratio? How much time do teachers spend with children one to one or in small groups? Do teachers take time to give children individual attention? Do children have an opportunity to be independent and do things for themselves?
Staff interaction	How does the staff relate to children? Are the relationships loving and caring?
Guiding behavior	How do staff members handle typical discipline problems, such as disputes between children? Are positive guidance techniques used? Are indirect guidance techniques used (e.g., through room arrangement, scheduling, and appropriate activity planning)? Is there a written discipline philosophy that agrees with the parents' philosophy?
Gender and cultural needs	Are staff personnel sensitive to the gender and cultural needs and backgrounds of children and families? Are the cultures of all children respected and supported?

(continued)

TABLE 8.2 *continued*

Quality Indicator	Quality Description
Outdoor activities	Are there opportunities for outdoor activities? Are there a variety of activities?
Mealtime	How is lunchtime handled? Are children allowed to talk while eating? Do staff members eat with the children? Is lunchtime a happy and learning time?
Staff continuity	Is there a low turnover rate for teachers and staff? Programs that have high and constant turnovers of staff are not providing the continuity of care and education that children need.
Director qualifications	Is the director well educated? The director should have at least a bachelor's degree in childhood education or child development. Can the director explain the program? Describing a typical day can be helpful. Is she or he actively involved in the program?
Staff-adult relationships	How does the staff treat adults, including parents? Does the program address the needs of children's families? Staff should provide for the needs of families as well as children.
Cost and affordability	Is the program affordable? If a program is too expensive for the family budget, parents may be unhappy in the long run. Parents should inquire about scholarships, reduced fees, fees adjusted to income level, fees paid in monthly installments, and sibling discounts.
Parent satisfaction	Are parents of children enrolled in the program satisfied? One of the best ways to learn about a program is to talk to other parents.
Hours and services	Do the program's hours and services match parents' needs? Too often, parents have to patch together care and education to cover their work hours.
Emergency care	What are the provisions for emergency care and treatment?
Ill children	What procedures are there for taking care of ill children?

Share these quality program indicators with parents and your colleagues. Taken as a whole, they will enable you to provide a quality program and will enable parents to select quality programs for their children.

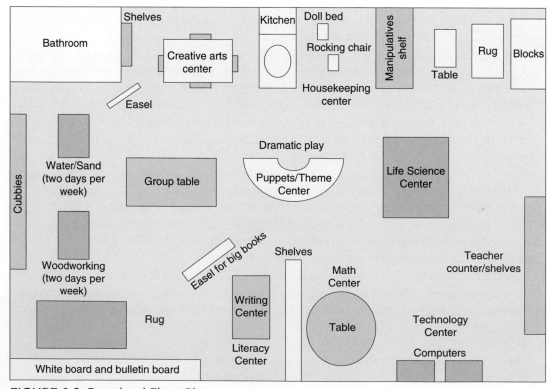

FIGURE 8.3 Preschool Floor Plan

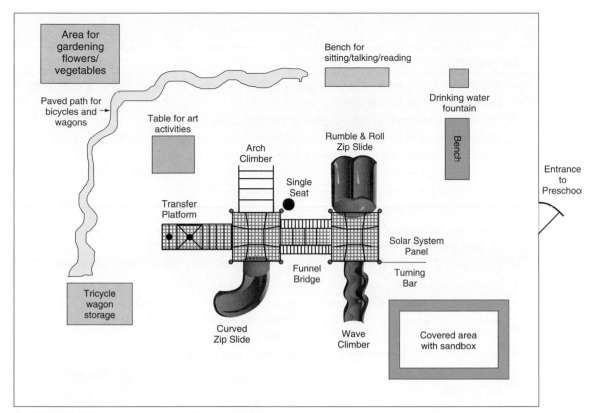

FIGURE 8.4 Outdoor Pre-Kindergarten Environment

Source: Courtesy of Game Time, www.gametime.

indicators taken as a whole make up the preschool environment. In addition, Figure 8.3, a sample preschool floor plan provides you with ideas for how to organize your own preschool classroom. Pay particular attention of how the arrangement supports different kinds of children's learning. Figure 8.4 provides a sample plan for children's outdoor environment.

THE PRESCHOOL CURRICULUM

Although the curricula of individual preschools are varied and are influenced by state standards, all programs should have certain essential curricular goals. Most quality preschools plan goals in these areas: social and interpersonal skills, self-help and intrapersonal skills, learning how to learn and developing a love for learning, academics, thinking skills, learning readiness, language and literacy, character education, music and the arts, wellness and healthy living, and independence. These goals and how to achieve them are outlined in detail in Table 8.3.

PLAY IN PRESCHOOL PROGRAMS

Play has traditionally been at the heart of preschool programs. It is and will continue to be important in preschool programs. Children's play results in learning. Therefore, preschool programs should support learning through play. The Program in Action feature explores classroom examples of how play can influence development.

The notion that children learn and develop through play began with Froebel. Since his time, most early childhood programs have incorporated play into their curricula.

Montessori viewed children's active involvement with materials and the prepared environment as the primary means by which they absorb knowledge and learn. John Dewey

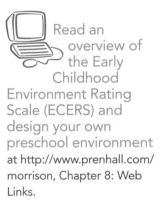

Read an overview of the Early Childhood Environment Rating Scale (ECERS) and design your own preschool environment at http://www.prenhall.com/ morrison, Chapter 8: Web Links.

Read about the importance of play at Articles and Readings, Early Childhood Education, Module 3: Early Learning, Article 3: The Importance of Being Playful.

TABLE 8.3 Preschool Goals

Goal	Dimensions
Social and interpersonal skills	• Helping children learn how to get along with other children and adults and how to develop good relationships with teachers • Helping children learn to help others and develop caring attitudes
Self-help and intrapersonal skills	• Modeling for children how to take care of their personal needs, such as dressing (tying, buttoning, zipping) and knowing what clothes to wear • Eating skills (using utensils, napkins, and a cup or glass; setting a table) • Health skills (how to wash and bathe, how to brush teeth) • Grooming skills (combing hair, cleaning nails)
Learning to learn and learning readiness	• Promoting self-help skills to help children develop good self-image and high self-esteem • Helping children learn about themselves, their family, and their culture • Developing a sense of self-worth by providing experiences for success and competence • Teaching persistence, cooperation, self-control, and motivation • Facilitating readiness skills related to school success, such as following directions, learning to work alone, listening to the teacher, developing an attention span, learning to stay with a task until it is completed, staying in one's seat, and controlling impulses
Academics	• Teaching children to learn their names, addresses, and phone numbers • Facilitating children's learning of colors, sizes, shapes, and positions such as under, over, and around • Facilitating children's learning of numbers and prewriting skills, shape identification, letter recognition, sounds, and rhyming • Providing for small-muscle development
Thinking skills	• Providing environments and activities that enable children to develop the skills essential to constructing schemes in a Piagetian sense—classification, seriation, numeration, and knowledge of space and time concepts—which form the basis for logical-mathematical thinking • Giving children opportunities to respond to questions and situations that require them to synthesize, analyze, and evaluate
Language and literacy	• Providing opportunities for interaction with adults and peers as a means of developing oral language skills • Helping children increase their vocabularies • Helping children learn to converse with other children and adults • Building proficiency in language • Developing literacy skills related to writing and reading • Learning the letters of the alphabet • Being familiar with a wide range of books
Character education	• Having a positive mental attitude • Being persistent • Having respect for others • Being cooperative • Being honest • Being trustworthy
Music and the arts	• Using a variety of materials (e.g., crayons, paint, clay, markers) to create original work • Using different colors, surface textures, and shapes to create form and meaning • Using art as a form of self-expression

Goal	Dimensions
	• Participating in music activities
	• Singing a variety of simple songs
	• Responding to music of various tempos through movement
Wellness and healthy living	• Providing experiences that enable children to learn the role of good nutritional practices and habits in their overall development
	• Providing food preparation experiences
	• Introducing children to new foods, a balanced menu, and essential nutrients
Independence	• Helping students become independent by encouraging them to do things for themselves
	• Giving children reasonably free access to equipment and materials
	• Having children be responsible for passing out, collecting, and organizing materials

These represent essential goals for all preschool programs that you will want to implement in your professional role of educator of young children.

believed that children learn through play and that children should have opportunities to engage in play associated with everyday activities (e.g., the house center, post office, grocery store, doctor's office).

Piaget believed play promotes cognitive knowledge and is a means by which children construct knowledge of their world. He thought that through active involvement, children learn.

Vygotsky viewed the social interactions that occur through play as essential to children's development. He believed that children, through social interactions with others, learn social skills such as cooperation and collaboration that promote and enhance their cognitive development.

Providing opportunities for children to choose among well-planned, varied learning activities enhances the probability that they will learn through play. Figure 8.5 shows some of the things children learn through play. In addition, the following Professionalism in Practice feature discusses how teachers can connect everything children do in their play to learning objectives.

Puppets and plays provide many opportunities for children to learn and interact with others. Indeed, the props that professionals provide for children to play with contribute to all of children's learning, but in particular their literacy development. What literacy skills are these children learning?

Kinds of Play

Children engage in many kinds of play. Mildren Parten (children's play researcher, now deceased) identified six stages and descriptions of children's social play:

- Unoccupied play is play in which the child does not play with anything or anyone; the child merely stands or sits, without doing anything observable.
- Solitary play is play where the child plays alone, seemingly unaware of other children.
- Onlooker play is play in which the child watches and observes the play of other children. The center of interest is others' play.
- Parallel play is play in which the child plays alone but in ways similar to other children and with toys or other materials similar to those of other children.
- In associative play, children interact with each other—perhaps by asking questions or sharing materials—but do not play together.
- In cooperative play, children actively play together, often as a result of organization by the teacher.[22]

Early childhood educators have long recognized the value of play for social, emotional, and physical development. Recently, however, play has attracted greater importance as a medium for literacy development. It is now recognized that literacy develops in meaningful, functional social settings rather than as a set of abstract skills taught in formal pencil-and-paper settings.

Literacy development involves a child's active engagement in cooperation and collaboration with peers; it builds on what the child already knows with the support and guidance of others. Play provides this setting. During observation of children at play, especially in free-choice, cooperative play periods, one can note the functional uses of literacy that children incorporate into their play themes. When the environment is appropriately prepared with literacy materials in play areas, children have been observed to engage in attempted and conceptual reading and writing in collaboration with other youngsters. In similar settings lacking literacy materials, the same literacy activities did not occur.

To demonstrate how play in an appropriate setting can nurture literacy development, consider the following classroom setting in which the teacher has designed a veterinarian's office to go along with a class study on animals focusing in particular on pets.

The dramatic play area is designed with a waiting room, including chairs; a table filled with magazines, books, and pamphlets about pet care; posters about pets; office hour notices; a "No Smoking" sign; and a sign advising visitors to "Check in with the nurse when arriving." On a nurse's desk are patient forms on clipboards, a telephone, an address and telephone book, appointment cards, and a calendar. The office contains patient folders, prescription pads, white coats, masks, gloves, a toy doctor's kit, and stuffed animals for patients.

Ms. Meyers, the teacher, guides students in using the various materials in the veterinarian's office during free-play time. For example, she reminds the children to read important information they find in the waiting area, to fill out forms about their pets' needs, to ask the nurse for appointment times, or to have the doctor write out appropriate treatments or prescriptions. In addition to giving directions, Ms. Meyers also models behaviors by participating in the play center with the children when first introducing materials.

This play setting provides a literacy-rich environment with books and writing materials; models reading and writing by the teacher that children can observe and emulate; provides the opportunity to practice literacy in a real-life situation that has meaning and function; and encourages children to interact socially by collaborating and performing meaningful reading and writing activities with peers. The following anecdotes relate the type of behavior Ms. Meyers observed in the play area.

Jessica was waiting to see the doctor. She told her stuffed animal dog, Sam, not to worry, that the doctor would not hurt him. She asked Jenny, who was waiting with her stuffed animal cat, Muffin, what the kitten's problem was. The girls agonized over the ailments of their pets. After a while they stopped talking and Jessica picked up the book *Are You My Mother?* and pretended to read to her dog. Jessica showed Sam the pictures as she read.

Preston examined Christopher's teddy bear and wrote a report in the patient's folder. He read his scribble writing out loud and said, "This teddy bear's blood pressure is twenty-nine points. He should take sixty-two pills an hour until he is better and keep warm and go to bed." At the same time he read, he showed Christopher what he had written so he could understand what to do.

When selecting settings to promote literacy in play, choose those that are familiar to children and relate them to themes currently being studied. Suggestions for literacy materials and settings to add to the dramatic play areas include the following:

- A fast-food restaurant, ice cream store, or bakery suggests menus, order pads, a cash register, specials for the day, recipes, and lists of flavors or products.
- A supermarket or local grocery store can include labeled shelves and sections, food containers, pricing labels, cash registers, telephones, shopping receipts, checkbooks, coupons, and promotional flyers.
- A post office to serve for mailing children's letters needs paper, envelopes, address books, pens, pencils, stamps, cash registers, and labeled mailboxes. A mail carrier hat and bag are important for children who deliver the mail and need to identify and read names and addresses.
- A gas station and car repair shop, designed in the block area, might have toy cars and trucks, receipts for sales, road maps for help with directions to different destinations, automotive tools and auto repair manuals for fixing cars and trucks, posters that advertise automobile equipment, and empty cans of different products typically found in service stations.

Source: L. M. Morrow, Literacy Development in the Early Years: Helping Children Read and Write, *5th ed. Needham Heights, MA: Allyn & Bacon, 2005.*

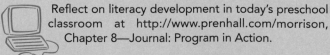 Reflect on literacy development in today's preschool classroom at http://www.prenhall.com/morrison, Chapter 8—Journal: Program in Action.

FIGURE 8.5

What Children Learn Through Play

- Learn concepts:
  - Physical concepts associated with the five senses—touching, tasting, smelling, seeing, and hearing
  - Logical-mathematical concepts associated with classification, seriation, numeration, space (over, under, etc.), and time (before, after, etc.)
- Develop social skills:
  - Sharing
  - Taking turns
  - Negotiating
  - Compromising
  - Leading
- Develop physical skills:
  - Using fine and large muscles
- Develop and practice language and literacy skills:
  - Phonological awareness—learning how sounds make up words and are used in words
  - Conversation skills (e.g., taking turns and responding appropriately)
- Enhance self-esteem:
  - Demonstrating accomplishments and abilities
  - Relating own accomplishments to those of peers
- Master life situations and prepare for adult life and roles:
  - Learning how to become independent
  - Thinking
  - Making decisions
  - Cooperating/collaborating with all others, including those who are different from the child culturally, racially, or in ability

Observing children's social play is a good way to sharpen your observation skills and to learn more about children's play and the learning that occurs through play.

Social play supports many important functions. First, it provides the means for children to interact with others and learn many social skills. Children learn how to compromise ("OK, I'll be the baby first and you can be the mommy"), be flexible ("We'll do it your way first and then my way"), resolve conflicts, and continue the process of learning who they are. Second, social play provides a vehicle for practicing and developing literacy skills. Children have others with whom to practice language and from whom to learn. Third, play helps children learn impulse control; they realize they cannot always do whatever they want. And fourth, in giving a child other children with whom to interact, social play negates isolation and helps children learn how to have the social interactions so vital to successful living.

In addition to social play, other types of play and their benefits and purposes are shown in Table 8.4. Carefully study these kinds of play and plan for how you will include them in your program.

Early Childhood Professionals and Play

You and your colleagues are the key to promoting meaningful play, which promotes a basis for learning. How you prepare the environment for play and the attitudes you have toward

You Can't Fly by the Seat of Your Pants

Deborah Austin
Retired principal, Early Childhood Learning Center
La Marque Independent School District
La Marque, Texas

As I look back on my years as a principal of an early childhood campus, I reflect on the beliefs we, as a faculty, had. The most important belief we had, as did John Dewey, was that children learn by doing and by getting involved with the learning process. Children need a concrete approach to learning and the opportunity to manipulate objects connected with that learning. We always have to remember that children require a hands-on approach and that they learn best by touching and making physical connections to words, concepts, and objects. We also tried to relate everything children do to the real world of people and things. This is what makes learning come alive in meaningful ways.

We also believed that children learn through play and that play should have an academic focus. Teachers must connect everything children do in their play to learning objectives. For example, are children using words and sentences appropriately in their conversations with their peers? You can incorporate math into children's play while they are in the home center. You can ask them how many are coming to dinner, how many forks, knives, and spoons they will need, and so forth. The writing connection can be made by providing paper and pencil in the home center and asking the children to make a list of the food they will need. Does it matter if they scribble? No, because this is the first step in making the reading/writing connection.

As a faculty we worked diligently on developing learning through real-life applications. For example, in the hallway, we had an attendance chart that showed the classrooms with perfect attendance each day. On the chart, for the month of December, a Christmas tree represented one day of perfect attendance, and a snowman represented five days of perfect attendance. Our preschoolers could tell which classroom had the most perfect attendance days, and who had the second most, and so on by reading the graph. Using symbols to represent multiple items is a first- and second-grade skill, but our preschoolers were able to understand the concept and interpret the data.

Not only is it important, but it is also imperative that teachers help students make real-world connections to learning. You can't just put a group of students in a block center and hope that they learn what they need to know. Pre-kindergarten guidelines specify what preschool children should be introduced to during their first year in school. Through practice in whole-group as well as small-group settings, students are given multiple opportunities to practice what has been introduced during the course of the year.

Although academics is greatly emphasized in early childhood settings, children also need opportunities to balance the academic with the social development. Play with a purpose allows for these opportunities to take place. Whether it is in the home center, the library center, the art area, the construction center, the math center, snack time, the outdoor play area, or any other time of the day, social skills are modeled, taught, and practiced. Language, manners, and respect are all part of the social development that took place at our school. When students leave our campus, we want them to be able to say that they learned and that they were loved.

Teachers are the keys to ensuring that children learn and are loved. A great deal of planning must take place in order for students to master the desired learning outcomes. Teaching is an organized profession, and it takes organized teachers to practice the art of teaching. You can't fly by the seat of your pants and hope to be a good teacher. You have to carefully plan for each day and for the individual needs of each child.

---

it determine the quality of the children's learning. Your responsibilities for supporting a quality play curriculum are shown in Figure 8.6. The suggestions given in the figure are just some of the ways you can create an environment that ensures children will have meaningful and joyful play experiences. After reviewing your responsibilities for play, think about what you need to do to prepare yourself to help ensure quality play experiences for all children.

Play and Emergent Curriculum. Today, with all of the discussions about standards and academics, sometimes play gets pushed out of the curriculum. This should not happen! Through play, you can help children meet state standards and achieve high academic levels.

When children play, they are involved in activities they are interested in. Through play, children learn by doing. Learning through interests and learning by doing are two hallmarks of developmentally appropriate practice. As children play, teachers follow

TABLE 8.4 Other Types of Play

Type of Play	Purpose/Benefit
Cognitive play	Froebel, Montessori, and Piaget recognized the value of cognitive play. They all saw children's active participation as a direct link to knowledge and development. From a Piagetian perspective, play is literally cognitive development.
Functional play	Functional play occurs during the sensorimotor period and in response to muscular activities and the need to be active. Functional play is characterized by repetitions, manipulations, and self-imitation. Functional play allows children to practice and learn physical capabilities while exploring their immediate environments. Very young children are especially fond of repeating movements for the pleasure of it. They engage in sensory impressions for the joy of experiencing the functioning of their bodies. Repetition of language is also a part of functional play.
Symbolic play	Piaget referred to symbolic play as "let's pretend" play. During this stage, children freely display their creative and physical abilities and social awareness in a number of ways—for example, by pretending to be something else, such as an animal. Symbolic play also occurs when children pretend that one object is another—that a building block is a car, for example—and may also entail pretending to be another person—a mommy, daddy, or firefighter.
Playing games with rules	This kind of play begins around age seven or eight and involves learning to play within rules and limits. Games with rules are common in middle childhood and adulthood as well.
Informal or free play	Informal play occurs when children play in an environment that contains materials and people with whom they can interact. Learning materials may be grouped in centers with similar equipment: a kitchen center, a dress-up center, a block center, a music and art center, a water or sand area, and a free-play center, usually with items such as tricycles, wagons, and wooden slides for promoting large-muscle development. The atmosphere of a free-play environment is informal, unstructured, and unpressured. Play and learning episodes are generally determined by the interests of the children. Outcomes of free play are socialization, emotional development, self-control, and concept development.
Sociodramatic (pretend) play	Dramatic play allows children to participate vicariously in a wide range of activities associated with family living, society, and their and others' cultural heritage. Dramatic play is generally of two kinds: *sociodramatic* and *fantasy*. Sociodramatic play usually involves everyday realistic activities and events, whereas fantasy play typically involves fairy tale and superhero play. In sociodramatic play, children have an opportunity to express themselves, assume different roles, and interact with their peers. Sociodramatic play acts as a nonsexist and multicultural arena in which all children are equal.
Outdoor play	Children's play outside is just as important as inside play. Outdoor environments and activities promote large- and small-muscle development and body coordination as well as language development, social interaction, and creativity. The outdoor area is a learning environment and, as such, the playground should be designed according to learning objectives. Indoor learning can also occur outdoors. Easels, play dough, and dramatic play props can further enhance learning opportunities.
Rough-and-tumble play	All children, to a greater or lesser degree, engage in rough-and-tumble play. One theory of play says children play because they are biologically programmed to do so; that is, it is part of children's (and adults') genetic heritage to engage in play activities. Rough-and-tumble play activities enable children to learn how to lead and follow, develop physical skills, interact with others in different ways, and grow in their abilities to give and take.

Play occurs in many types and forms. Your understanding of each of these will enable you to implement a meaningful program of learning through play.

Create environments that ensure children will learn through play. Create both indoor and outdoor environments that encourage play and support its role in learning.

Provide time for learning through play. Include play in the schedule as a legitimate activity in its own right.

Supervise play activities and participate in children's play. In these roles, help, show, and guide. Model when appropriate and intervene only when necessary.

Observe children's play. Teachers can learn how children play and the learning outcomes of play to use in planning classroom activities.

Educate assistants and families about how to promote learning through play.

Organize the classroom or center environment so that cooperative learning is possible and active learning occurs.

Provide materials and equipment that are appropriate to children's developmental levels and that support a nonsexist and multicultural curriculum.

Question children about their play. Discuss what children did during play, and "debrief" children about what they have learned through play.

Provide for safety in indoor and outdoor play.

Plan to implement the curriculum through play. Integrate specific learning activities with play to achieve learning outcomes. Play activities should match children's developmental needs and be free of gender and cultural stereotypes. Professionals have to be clear about curriculum concepts and ideas they want children to learn through play.

FIGURE 8.6 How Teachers Support Children's Play

Photo: Scott Cunningham / Merrill

Dramatic play promotes children's understanding of concepts and processes. These children are exploring their feelings and ideas about medical practitioners and medical settings.

Will & Deni McIntyre / Photo Researchers, Inc.

their lead and help them learn new concepts, knowledge, and skills. This is the essence of the emergent curriculum. For example, a state standard asks students to be able to count and engage in one-to-one correspondence. During play in the housekeeping center, the children are setting the table for lunch. The teacher asks children to count out the number of forks they will need for each place setting (counting) and then asks them to put a fork at each place setting (one-to-one correspondence).

On the other hand, children cannot learn all they need to know through play. There is a place in the curriculum for teacher-initiated instruction. For example, after her assessment of children's number knowledge, teacher Maria Gonzales decides that her children need more counting practice. She leads them in a lesson with counting bears in which the children count out five bears from the basket of bears on their table. Both child-initiated play and teacher-directed instruction are used in programs we discussed in Chapter 4.

The Preschool Daily Schedule

What should the preschool day schedule be like? Although a daily schedule depends on many things—your philosophy, the needs of children, families, beliefs, and state and local standards—the following descriptions illustrate what you can do on a typical preschool day.

This preschool schedule is for a whole-day program; many other program arrangements are possible. Some preschools operate half-day, morning-only programs five days a week; others operate both a morning and an afternoon session; others operate only two or three days a week. However, an important preschool trend is toward full-day, full-year programs.

Opening Activities. As children enter, the teacher greets each individually. Daily personal greetings make the children feel important, build a positive attitude toward school, and provide an opportunity to practice language skills. Daily greetings also give the teacher a chance to check each child's health and emotional status.

Children usually do not arrive all at one time, so the first arrivals need something to do while others are arriving. Offering a free selection of activities or letting children self-select from a limited range of quiet activities (such as puzzles, pegboards, or markers to color with) are appropriate.

Group Meeting/Planning. After all children arrive, they and the teacher plan together and talk about the day ahead. This is also the time for announcements, sharing, and group songs and for children to think about what they plan to learn during the day.

Learning Centers. After the group time, children are free to go to one of various learning centers, organized and designed to teach concepts. Table 8.5 lists types of learning centers and the concepts each is intended to teach. You should plan for the concepts and skills you want children to learn in each center. Also, every center should be a literacy center; that is, there should be materials for the development of writing and reading in every center.

Learning centers provide a number of useful functions. They enable you to meet the diverse learning needs and interests of your children and your community. In addition, learning centers:

SW Productions / Getty Images, Inc.–Photodisc

Although we want children to be involved in child-initiated and active learning, sometimes it is necessary to directly teach children certain concepts or skills. What concepts or skills is this teacher directly teaching these children?

- Encourage and promote collaboration, social interaction, and independent work.
- Provide you with a classroom organization that enables you to work with individual children and small groups while other children are meaningfully and actively involved.
- Provide for active and child-initiated learning.

When developing centers, keep these guidelines in mind:

- Teach children how to use each center. Provide appropriate rules for use, care of materials, and so on. Such guidelines can be covered with the whole group as well as in small groups or with individuals.
- Develop centers around your state's/district's pre-K guidelines or standards, children's interests, and your learning goals for the children. To get ideas for how to develop centers around state standards, review the Texas preschool guidelines in Chapter 5 and your own state pre-K standards. For example, a state standard or learning expectation for preschool might state that "children demonstrate emergent reading skills." To help meet this goal, you could develop a center that has a variety of age-appropriate printed materials such as books, magazines, catalogues, and so

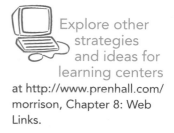

Explore other strategies and ideas for learning centers at http://www.prenhall.com/morrison, Chapter 8: Web Links.

TABLE 8.5 Types of Classroom Learning Centers

Theme-Based Centers	Concepts
Use theme centers as an extension of classroom themes: • Space • Dinosaurs • The Ocean • All About Me • My Family Generally a classroom theme lasts for one to two weeks and occasionally longer. Children can use theme centers for varying amounts of time from fifteen to thirty minutes and during their free time.	• Use language skills, participate in sociodramatic play, verbalize. • Identify role(s) as a family member. • Cooperate with others in joint activities. • Learn how to cooperate and practice good habits of daily living such as sharing, taking turns, and following rules.

Subject Centers	Concepts
• *Literacy/Language:* Be sure to change books frequently. Add ten new books every two to three weeks. The goal is to have preschoolers familiar with 100 books. Also include books from all genres: picture books, fiction, science, and so on.	• Verbalize; listen; understand directions, how to use books, colors, size, shapes, and names; print and book knowledge, vocabulary development, print awareness.
• *Writing:* Provide various and plentiful materials for writing: paper, blank books, folded paper, envelopes, markers, pencils, and so forth. Every center should have materials for writing.	• Learn word knowledge, alphabet, that words have meaning, that words make sentences, and so forth. • Learn that writing has many useful purposes, and that written words convey meaning.

• *Math:* Provide plastic number tiles, math cards, pegboards
  • Provide many concrete materials to promote hands-on experiences.
  • Provide picture books about math and read stories involving math.
	• Understand meanings of whole numbers.
	• Recognize the number of objects in small groups without counting and by counting.
	• Understand that number words refer to quantity.
	• Use one-to-one correspondence to solve problems by matching sets and comparing number amounts and in counting objects to ten and beyond.
	• Understand that the last word stated in counting tells "how many." They count to determine number amounts and compare quantities (using language such as "more than" and "less than").
	• Order sets by the number of objects in them.
	• Develop spatial reasoning by working from two perspectives on space as shapes of objects are examined and relative positions are inspected.
	• Find shapes in the environment and describe them.
	• Build pictures and designs by combining two- and three-dimensional shapes.
	• Solve such problems as deciding which piece will fit into a space in a puzzle.
	• Discuss the relative positions of objects with vocabulary such as "above," "below," and "next to."

Subject Centers	Concepts
	• Identify objects as "the same" or "different," and then "more" or "less," on the basis of attributes that can be measured.
	• Identify measurable attributes such as length, weight and solve problems by making direct comparisons of objects on the basis of those attributes.*
• *Science:* Provide books on science, materials for observing, for discovering relationships, and for learning about nature, plants, animals, and the environment.	• Develop skills in observation, size, shape, color, whole/part, figure/ground, spatial relations, classifying, graphing, problem-solving skills.
	• Learn how to observe, make comparisons, classify, and problem-solve.
	• Investigate and explore.
• *Life Science:* Provide various plants and animals, terrariums, and habitats.	• Understand plant and animal care and habitats.
• *Art/Music/Creative Expression:* Provide materials for painting, coloring, drawing, cutting, pasting.	• Listen to a wide range of musical styles.
	• Learn color relationships and combinations.
• Engage children in activities involving singing and movement.	• Engage in creative expression, aesthetic appreciation, satisfaction.
• Provide puppets and puppet theater to encourage dramatic and creative expression.	• Create representations of homes and places in the community.
	• Participate in group singing, finger plays, and rhythm.

Activity Centers	Concepts
• *Construction/Blocks:* Provide a variety of different kinds of blocks.	• Describe size, shape, length, seriation, spatial relationships.
	• Develop problem-solving skills.
• *Woodworking:* Use real tools and building materials. Be sure to provide for children's safety, i.e., goggles and so forth.	• Learning to follow directions; learn how to use real tools; planning, discovering whole/part relationships, process of construction.
• *Dramatic Play:* Provide various materials for home activities.	• Learn language skills, sociodramatic play, functions, processes, social skills.
• Provide many props such as clothing, costumes, hats, and shoes.	• Engage in pretend and imaginary play.
• Provide child-size stove, table, chairs, refrigerator, sink, etc.	• Learn roles and responsibilities of community workers.
• Provide outfits and props from many occupations: health, safety, etc.	
• Water/Sand Play	• Measures weights (what floats, capacity, etc.).
	• Learn social skills and responsibility, i.e., cleanup.

Technology Centers	Concepts
• *Computer/Technology:* Computers, printer, scanner, fax machine, digital camera, video camera. A computer center can have one or more workstations or can have one or more laptops or handheld devices.	• Learn socialization, keyboarding, how technology can solve problems.
	• Learn basic technology skills.
	• Write (using e-mail, word processing).
	• Use technology to learn basic math and language skills.
	• Use technology to play games.

Source: National Council of Teachers of Mathematics, "Curriculum Focal Points and Connections for Prekindergarten," 2006, http://www.nctm.org/focalpoints/bygrade_pk.asp.

forth. You would also provide opportunities in the center for children to "read" and participate in literacy-related activities.

- Use children's interests to develop learning centers. For example, on a nature walk around the center, the children were very interested in the dragonflies, grasshoppers, and crickets. You can develop a learning center in which children draw pictures of insects, tape record observations about insects, and sort pictures of insects by types.
- Develop ways for evaluating children's work processes and products while they are at the centers. Also develop ways for older children to self-evaluate. Chapter 6 provides many ideas for how to observe and assess children's products and achievement.

Bathroom/Hand Washing. Before any activity in which food is handled, prepared, or eaten, children should wash and dry their hands. Instructing children in proper hand-washing procedures can prevent the spread of illness and form lifelong habits.

Snacks. After center activities, a snack is usually served. It should be nutritionally sound and something the children can serve (and often prepare) themselves.

Outdoor Activity/Play/Walking. Outside play should be a time for learning new concepts and skills, not just a time to run around aimlessly. Children can practice climbing, jumping, swinging, throwing, and using body control. Teachers may incorporate walking trips and other events into outdoor play.

Bathroom/Toileting. Bathroom/toileting times offer opportunities to teach health, self-help, and intrapersonal skills. Children should also be allowed to use the bathroom whenever necessary.

Lunch. Lunch should be a relaxing time, and the meal should be served family style, with professionals and children eating together. Children should set their own tables and decorate them with place mats and flowers they can make in the art center or as a special project. Children should be involved in cleaning up after meals and snacks.

Relaxation. After lunch, children should have a chance to relax, perhaps to the accompaniment of teacher-read stories, records, and music. This is an ideal time to teach children breathing exercises and relaxation techniques.

Nap Time. Children who want or need to should have a chance to rest or sleep. Quiet activities should be available for those who do not need to or cannot sleep on a particular day. In any event, nap time should not be forced on any child.

Centers or Special Projects. Following nap time is a good time for center activities or special projects. Special projects can also be conducted in the morning, and some may be more appropriate then, such as cooking something for snack or lunch. Special projects might involve cooking, holiday activities, collecting things, work projects, art activities, and field trips.

Group Time. The day can end with a group meeting to review the day's activities. This meeting develops listening and attention skills, promotes oral communication, stresses that learning is important, and helps children evaluate their performance and behavior.

How you structure the day for your children will determine in part how and what they learn. You will want to develop your daily schedule with attention and care.

SUCCESSFUL TRANSITIONS TO KINDERGARTEN

A **transition** is a passage from one learning setting, grade, program, or experience to another. You can help ensure that the transitions preschool children make from home to preschool to kindergarten are happy and rewarding experiences.

You can help children and families make transitions easily and confidently in these ways:

- Educate and prepare children ahead of time for any new situation. Children can practice routines they will encounter when they enter kindergarten. For example, children practice putting their things away each day.
- Alert parents to new and different standards, dress, behavior, and parent–teacher interactions. Inform parents that attendance matters for children's achievement. Also make them aware of your state's requirements on attendance.
- Give children an opportunity to meet their new teachers. Invite a kindergarten teacher to your classroom to read to the children.
- Let parents know ahead of time what their children will need in the new program (e.g., lunch box, change of clothing).
- Provide parents of children with special needs and bilingual parents with additional help and support during the transition. Introduce them to new teachers and contact personnel.
- Offer parents and children an opportunity to visit programs. Children will better understand the physical, curricular, and affective climates of the new programs if they visit in advance.
- Cooperate with the staff of any program the children will attend to work out a transition plan.
- Exchange class visits between preschool and kindergarten programs. Class visits are an excellent way to have preschool children learn about the classrooms they will attend as kindergartners. Having kindergarten children visit the preschool and telling preschoolers about kindergarten provides for a sense of security and anticipation.
- Work with kindergarten teachers to make booklets about their program. These booklets can include photographs of children, letters from kindergarten children and preschoolers, and pictures of kindergarten activities. These books can be placed in the reading centers where preschool children can "read" about the programs they will attend.
- Hold a "kindergarten day" for preschoolers in which they attend kindergarten for a day. This program can include such things as riding the bus, having lunch, touring the school, and meeting teachers.

Remember that transitions can be traumatic experiences for children. When transitions are hurried, unplanned, and abrupt, they can cause social, emotional, and learning problems. Successful transitions can be good learning experiences for children.

PORTRAITS OF CHILDREN

Now that you have learned about transitions, this is a good time for you to think more about the children you will be helping to transition to kindergarten. Read, review, and reflect on the Portraits of Preschoolers on pages 231–232. As you answer the questions about developmentally appropriate practice, think how you would meet the needs of each of these children in your classroom. Also, you can refer to the Portraits of Kindergartners in Chapter 9 and review what kindergarten children are like.

ACTIVITIES FOR PROFESSIONAL DEVELOPMENT

Ethical Dilemma

"There's Only One Way"

Melissa teaches a class of 18 three- and four-year-old children from diverse cultures in a school district with a history of low achievement and test scores. The new superintendent has promised the board of education that he will turn the district around in three years. The superintendent has hired a new preschool coordinator because he believes that one of the best ways to close the district's achievement gap is to begin as early as possible. The new preschool coordinator has recommended the adoption of a skills-based curriculum that includes the use of direct instruction, other teacher-centered approaches, and a scripted curriculum. According to her, "There is only one way to teach children what they need to know, and that is to directly teach them. We can't fool around with all this child-centered stuff."

Direct instruction of basic skills and teacher-centered instructional practices are contrary to what Melissa learned in her teacher education classes at the university. In addition, these approaches do not fit with her view of child-centered and developmentally appropriate practice.

What should Melissa do? Should she inform the preschool coordinator that she will not use the materials when and if they are adopted, or should she convene a meeting of other teachers and ask their opinions about the materials, or should she keep her thoughts to herself and vow to use the new curriculum only when she has to? Or should she adopt another plan?

portraits of preschoolers

JESUS

Introduce yourself to Jesus, a three-year-old Cuban/Nicaraguan male. Jesus weighs 35 pounds and is 3 feet, 3 inches tall. Jonathan speaks Spanish and is slowly learning key words in English. Jesus comes from a large single-parent family—he is the youngest of seven children.

Social-Emotional	Cognitive	Motor	Adaptive (Daily Living)
Seeks attention and approval from caregivers	Enjoys repeating words and sounds that he hears	Likes to throw balls to other children	Is completely toilet trained
Has a strong sense of gender that could be attributed to cultural background	Enjoys hearing simple stories, rhymes, and songs—likes to participate in singing, rhyming, and so forth	Uses crayons and markers to draw	Puts legs into and pulls up pants without help
Recognizes feelings of others	Identifies colors and shapes	Likes to dance and jump on two feet	Drinks from a cup
Prefers to play with other boys	Is able to count from one to ten (in sequence)	Likes to build structures with toy blocks	Is able to zip and unzip his clothing

SOPHIE

Introduce yourself to Sophie, a three-year-old Caucasian female. Sophie weighs 34 pounds, is 3 feet, 2 inches tall and is a quiet child who exhibits a "slow to warm up" temperament. Once she becomes familiar with new people or new surroundings, she becomes much more talkative. She is an only child and receives a lot of attention from parents and extended family. Sophie loves to play "make-believe" and enjoys playing "dress-up."

Social-Emotional	Cognitive	Motor	Adaptive (Daily Living)
Very outgoing and sociable	Is very curious and frequently asks "Why?"	Is able to use hand–eye coordination when stringing beads	Dresses herself for school without assistance
Enjoys meeting new people	Is able to categorize items by colors and shapes	Enjoys painting and coloring	Is able to use the restroom without assistance
Enjoys talking with her caregivers	Puts puzzles together	Balances on one foot	Very self-confident and willing to try new things
Likes to play with selected friends	Has a very large vocabulary for a three-year-old	Is able to dress and undress herself when she is playing "dress-up"	Has no difficulty unwrapping food items independently
Exhibits parallel play; however, she does not try to influence others' play or behavior			

Questions About Developmentally Appropriate Practice:

- How do Jesus and Sophie differ in terms of their adaptive daily living skills?
- What might be some factors that have contributed to Sophie's language development?
- How might being from a large family affect Jesus' social-emotional development?

- Since Sophie is an only child and Jesus has three older brothers and three older sisters, how might these differing family dynamics play a role in their future development?

MONTREL

Introduce yourself to Montrel, a four-year-old African American male. Montrel weighs 33 pounds and is 3 feet, 3 inches tall. He is a very sociable child and enjoys participating in activities that involve other children. Montrel has been diagnosed with mild sensory integration dysfunction (SID), a neurological disability in which the brain is unable to appropriately process information from the senses. Montrel is particularly sensitive to loud noises and is easily distracted by most classroom background noises.

Social-Emotional	Cognitive	Motor	Adaptive (Daily Living)
Outgoing child who shows affection to others quite easily	Frequently imitates his brother's actions and words	Moves from one activity to another	Likes to comb his hair (by himself) before preschool
Acts out his frustrations by shouting and waving his arms	Has memorized the alphabet and is able to count to fifty	Likes to help his mother cook the family's meals	Is able to pour his own glass of milk
Covers his ears to shut out loud noises	Has trouble paying attention	Prints recognizable letters	Dresses himself for school
Is disruptive to others	Often tells elaborate, fictional stories	Is able to cut out shapes using scissors	Resists going to sleep—says he keeps hearing noises

KYM

Introduce yourself to Kym, a four-year-old Asian female. Kym weighs 34 pounds and is 3 feet, 3 inches tall. She is a very active and assertive preschooler. She enjoys coloring and playing in the home center at preschool. She is a natural leader and is very intelligent.

Social-Emotional	Cognitive	Motor	Adaptive (Daily Living)
Tends to be somewhat aggressive and bossy with other children	Is able to identify all the letters of the alphabet	Enjoys playing the piano	Washes her hands before eating and after using the restroom without prompting
Shows her frustration by raising her voice when she is upset	Is able to identify a variety of animals in picture books	Participates in a gymnastics class; able to do a forward roll and other movements	Brushes her teeth after meals without prompting from her caregivers
Enjoys spending time with friends and also being by herself	Expresses herself clearly—communication is easy for her	Rides a bike with training wheels	Is beginning to tie her own shoes
Is very interested in learning new skills such as reading and writing	Likes to "read" books—has several favorites	Demonstrates good balance and body control	Dresses herself each morning before school

Questions About Developmentally Appropriate Practice:

- What are two things you could do to adapt your classroom to help Montrel deal with being distracted by sounds?
- An occupational therapist provides Montrel sensory integration therapy three days a week. What would you need to do to prepare yourself to collaborate with special services teachers such as an occupational therapist?
- Knowing Kym's tendency to be bossy with her peers, how could you help her develop a more prosocial approach with her classmates?

- What developmental skills do Kym and Montrel need in preparation for attending kindergarten?

Application Activities

1. Visit preschool programs in your area. Determine their philosophies and find out what goes on in a typical day.

    a. How do their philosophies compare to your philosophy?

    b. Make a list of activities and practices you thought were developmentally appropriate. Make another list of developmentally inappropriate practices. How would you change the practices to make them appropriate?

2. Based on material presented in this chapter, develop a set of guidelines for ensuring that preschool programs would be developmentally appropriate. Develop guidelines for the environment, curriculum, and teaching practices.

3. Observe children's play, and give examples of how children learn through play and what they learn. Record the children's names, setting, day and time. Record some dialogue or the children's comments. Observe and record the materials used and your interpretations. Identify the type of play, based on Parten's stages of play.

4. Using the Internet, locate your state department of education's prekindergarten guidelines or standards. Compare these to the Illinois Early Learning Standards. Begin to decide how you can integrate your understanding of developmentally appropriate practice with what state standards are requiring that children should know and be able to do.

To take online practice tests on this chapter's material, go to the Companion Website at http://www.prenhall.com/morrison, select Chapter 8, and then choose the Multiple Choice or the Essay module. For additional Web resources, choose Web Links.

9

KINDERGARTEN TODAY
Meeting Academic and Developmental Needs

professional development goal

Developmentally Appropriate Practice

A. I understand children's developmental stages and growth from birth through age eight, and I use this knowledge to implement developmentally appropriate practice. I do all I can to advance the physical, intellectual, social, and emotional development of children to their fullest potential.

B. I use my understanding of young children's characteristics and needs, and of multiple interacting influences on children's development and learning, to create environments that are healthy, respectful, supportive, and challenging for all children.[1]

C. I use my knowledge and other resources to design, implement, and evaluate meaningful, challenging curriculum to promote positive outcomes.[2]

focus questions

1. How has the kindergarten changed from Froebel to the present?

2. What are appropriate goals, objectives, environments, and curriculum for kindergarten programs?

3. How can I use knowledge of developmentally appropriate practice to help me teach kindergarten children?

234

As we begin our discussion of kindergarten children and programs, perhaps you are thinking back to your kindergarten or **pre-first-grade** school experiences. I am sure that you have many pleasant memories and they include your teachers and classmates, what you learned, and how you learned it. It is good that you have fond memories of your kindergarten and/or other preschool experiences. However, we can't use just memories to build our understanding of what today's high-quality kindergartens are or should be like. If you have not visited a kindergarten program lately, now would be a good time to do so. You will discover that kindergarten education is undergoing a dramatic change. Compare the following changes that are transforming the kindergarten to your kindergarten observations:

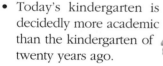

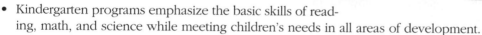

- Today's kindergarten is decidedly more academic than the kindergarten of twenty years ago.
- Kindergarten programs emphasize the basic skills of reading, math, and science while meeting children's needs in all areas of development.
- Kindergarten for all children, or **universal kindergarten**, is now a permanent part of the American education system.
- More states are providing more funding so districts can provide more kindergarten programs.[3]
- More kindergarten programs are full-day programs.[4]
- Kindergarten enrollment is exploding.
- Kindergarten programs are more challenging, and children are being asked to do and learn at higher levels.[5]

As a result of these and other changes we discuss in this chapter, the contemporary kindergarten is a place of high expectations and achievement for all children.

THE HISTORY OF KINDERGARTEN EDUCATION

Kindergarten has a long and interesting history that helps us to better understand the kindergartners of today.

Friedrich Froebel

Friedrich Froebel's educational concepts and kindergarten program were imported from Germany into the United States in the nineteenth century, virtually intact, by individuals who believed in his ideas and methods. His influence remained dominant for almost half a century. While Froebel's ideas still seem perfectly acceptable today, they were not acceptable to those in the mid-nineteenth century who subscribed to the notion of early education. Especially innovative and hard to accept was the idea that learning could be based on play and children's interests—in other words, that it could be child centered. Most European and American schools were subject oriented and emphasized teaching basic skills. In addition, Froebel was the first to advocate a communal education for young children outside the home. Froebel's ideas for educating children as a group in a special place outside the home were revolutionary.

Margarethe Schurz

Margarethe Schurz established the first kindergarten in the United States. After attending lectures on Froebelian principles in Germany, she returned to the United States and, in 1856, opened her kindergarten at Watertown, Wisconsin. Schurz's program was conducted in German, as were many of the new kindergarten programs of the time, since Froebel's ideas of education were especially appealing to bilingual parents. Schurz influenced Elizabeth Peabody, who was not only fascinated but converted to Froebel's ideas.

Elizabeth Peabody

Elizabeth Peabody opened her kindergarten in Boston in 1860. She and her sister, Mary Mann, also published a *Kindergarten Guide.* Peabody almost immediately realized that she lacked the necessary theoretical grounding to adequately implement Froebel's ideas. She visited kindergartens in Germany, then returned to the United States to popularize Froebel's methods. Peabody is generally credited as kindergarten's main promoter in the United States.

Susan Blow

The first public kindergarten was founded in St. Louis, Missouri, in 1873 by Susan E. Blow, with the cooperation of the St. Louis superintendent of schools, William T. Harris. Elizabeth Peabody had corresponded for several years with Harris, and the combination of her prodding and Blow's enthusiasm and knowledge convinced Harris to open a public kindergarten on an experimental basis. Endorsement of the kindergarten program by a public school system did much to increase its popularity and spread the Froebelian influence within early childhood education. In addition, Harris, who later became the U.S. Commissioner of Education, encouraged support for Froebel's ideas and methods.

Patty Smith Hill

The kindergarten movement, at first ahead of its time, became rigid and teacher centered rather than child centered. By the turn of the twentieth century, many kindergarten leaders thought that programs and training should be open to experimentation and innovation rather than rigidly following Froebel's ideas. Patty Smith Hill thought that, while the kindergarten should remain faithful to Froebel's ideas, it should nevertheless be open to innovation. She believed that the kindergarten movement, to survive, had to move into the twentieth century, and was able to convince many of her colleagues. More than anyone else, Hill is responsible for kindergarten as it was known prior to its twenty-first century transformation.

WHAT ARE KINDERGARTEN CHILDREN LIKE?

Kindergarten children are like other children in many ways. They have similar developmental, physical, and behavioral characteristics that characterize them as kindergartners—children ages five to six. Yet, at the same time, they have characteristics that make them unique individuals.

Physical Development

Kindergarten children are energetic. They have a lot of energy, and they want to use it in physical activities such as running, climbing, and jumping. Their desire to be involved in physical activity makes kindergarten an ideal time to involve children in projects of building—for example, making **learning centers** to resemble a store, post office, or veterinary office.

From ages five to seven, children's average weight and height approximate each other. For example, at six years, boys, on average, weigh 46 pounds and are 45 inches tall, while girls, on average, weigh about 44 pounds and are 45 inches tall. At age seven, boys weigh on average 50 pounds and are about 48 inches tall; girls weigh on average, 50 pounds and are about 48 inches tall (see Table 9.1).

Social and Emotional Development

Kindergarten children ages five to six are in Erikson's industry vs. inferiority stage of social and emotional development. During this stage kindergarten children are continuing to learn to regulate their emotions and social interactions.

Some things you can do to promote kindergartner's positive social and emotional development are:

- Provide opportunities for children to be physically and mentally involved in activities involving problem solving and social activities with others.
- Teach and role model how to make and keep friends.

TABLE 9.1 Average Height and Weight of Kindergartners

Age	Males		Females	
	Height (inches)	Weight (pounds)	Height (inches)	Weight (pounds)
5 years	43	40.5	42.25	40
6 years	45.25	45.5	45.25	44
7 years	48	50	47.75	50
8 years	50.5	56	50.25	56

Note: Remember that averages are just that—averages. Children are different because of their individual differences. Ongoing growth and development tend to accentuate these differences.

Source: 2000 CDC Growth Charts: United States, National Center for Health Statistics, http://www.cdc.gov/growthcharts.

Pearson Learning Photo Studio

- Model positive social and emotional responses. Read stories and discuss feelings such as anger, happiness, guilt, and pride.
- Give children opportunities to be leaders in projects and activities.
- State your expectations for appropriate behavior and discuss them with your children.

Most kindergarten children, especially those who have been to preschool, are very confident, are eager to be involved, and want to and can accept a great deal of responsibility. They like going places and doing things, such as working on projects, experimenting, and working with others. Socially, kindergarten children are at the same time solitary and independent workers and growing in their ability and desire to work cooperatively with others. They want to be industrious and successful. Their combination of a "can do" attitude and their cooperation and responsibility make them a delight to teach and work with.

Today, kindergarten is a universal part of schooling, enrolling children from different cultures and socioeconomic backgrounds and, subsequently, different life experiences. How can professionals help ensure that kindergarten experiences meet the unique needs of each child?

Cognitive and Language Development

Kindergarten children are in a period of rapid intellectual and language growth. They have a tremendous capacity to learn words and like the challenge of learning new words. This helps explain kindergarten children's love of big words and their ability to say and use them. This is nowhere more apparent than in their fondness for dinosaurs and words such as *brontosaur*. Kindergarten children like and need to be involved in many language activities.

Additionally, kindergartners like to talk. Their desire to be verbal should be encouraged and supported by allowing many opportunities to engage in various language activities such as singing, telling stories, being involved in drama, and reciting poetry.

What children know when they enter kindergarten helps determine their success in school and what and how they are taught. Figure 9.1 shows a national picture of the knowledge, health status, and behaviors of children entering kindergarten. Review it now to broaden your understanding of kindergarten children. As you read the information given in the figure, ask yourself these questions: Why can't greater percentages of children accomplish the identified academic skills? What implication does this information have for my work with parents? Keep in mind that kindergartners know more than what is described and many know a great deal less. For example, many immigrant children in border states, such as Texas and California, are illiterate in their native language.

Pearson Learning Photo Studio

Children are born to learn. Learning is not something children "get ready for," but is a continuous process. What factors do you think are critical to support children's readiness to learn?

WHO ATTENDS KINDERGARTEN?

Froebel's kindergarten was for children three to seven years of age. In the United States, kindergarten is for five- and six-year-old children before they enter first grade. Since the age at which children enter first grade varies, the ages at which they enter

FIGURE 9.1

What Do Kindergarten Children Know?

Academic Skill/Behavior	Percentage of Children
• Recognize lower-and uppercase letters by name	66%
• Know English print is read left to right—from the end of one line to the beginning of the next line; know where a story ends	61%
• Know beginning sounds of words	29%
• Know ending sounds of words	17%
• Count ten objects, identify numerals and shapes	94%
• Count twenty objects, judge relative length	58%
• Can read two-digit numerals, identify ordinal position (third flower in a row of four), and recognize the next number in a sequence	20%
Health Status	
• Excellent health	51%
• Very good health	83%
• Overweight	10%
Behavior Indicators	
• Consistently more active than peers	18%
• Difficulty paying attention	13%
• Difficulty articulating words	11%
• Exhibit positive approaches to learning—eager to learn, pay attention reasonably well, persist in completing tasks	75%

Source: U.S. Department of Education, National Center for Education Statistics, *Entering Kindergarten: A Portrait of American Children When They Begin School: Findings from the Condition of Education 2000,* Nicholas Zill and Jerry West, NCES 2001-035 (Washington, DC: U.S. Government Printing Office, 2001).

kindergarten also differ. Many parents and professionals support an older rather than a younger kindergarten entrance age because they think older children are more "ready" for kindergarten and will learn better. Whereas in the past children had to be five years of age prior to December 31 for kindergarten admission in many districts, today the trend is toward an older admission age.[6] Many school districts require that children be five years old by September 1 of the school year.

Universal Kindergarten

Just as support is growing for universal preschools, it should come as no surprise that there is wide public support for compulsory and tax-supported *universal public kindergarten*. Forty-two states mandate that school districts offer either whole- or half-day kindergarten. The national trend is for districts to offer full-day programs. However, only fourteen states require mandatory kindergarten attendance of age-eligible children.[7] Nonetheless, because of the widespread availability of kindergarten, 98 percent of American children attend at least a half-day of kindergarten before entering first

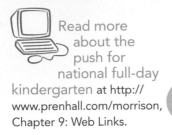

Read more about the push for national full-day kindergarten at http://www.prenhall.com/morrison, Chapter 9: Web Links.

grade.[8] As a result, public school kindergarten is now considered the first grade of school. It is important for you to know that kindergarten is considered a time for serious learning and accomplishment.

KINDERGARTEN TODAY

Kindergarten as it was known five years ago is not the same as kindergarten today. Kindergarten twenty years from now will be vastly different than it is today. Kindergarten is in a transitional stage from a program that focuses primarily on social and emotional development to one that emphasizes academics, especially early literacy, math and science, and activities that prepare children to think and problem solve. These changes represent a transformation of great magnitude and will have a lasting impact on kindergarten curriculum and teaching into the future.

Regardless of the grade or age group they teach, all early childhood teachers have to make decisions regarding what curriculum and activities they will provide for their children.

Observe teachers discussing the changes that have occurred in kindergarten classrooms at Video Classroom, Early Childhood Education, Module 7: Professionalism, Video 1: Kindergarten Classroom.

The Changing Kindergarten

Kindergarten education is literally changing before our eyes! These are some of the ways it is changing and the reasons why.

- *Longer school days and transition from half-day to full-day programs.* Reasons for longer school days and full-day programs include:
  - Changes in society,
  - An increase in the number of working parents,
  - Recognition that earlier is the best option, and
  - Research which shows that a longer school day helps children academically.[9]

- *Emphasis on academics including math, literacy and science.* Reasons for the emphasis on academics include:
  - Standards that specify what children should know and be able to do,
  - State standards that now include the kindergarten years, and
  - Political and public support for early education and skill learning because they reduce grade failure and school dropout.[10]

- *More testing.* Reasons for the increased testing include:
  - The accountability movement and
  - Recognition that district testing that begins in third grade and earlier puts more emphasis on what kindergarten children should learn.[11]

- *Enriched curriculum with emphasis on literacy designed to have children read by entry into first grade.* Reasons for literacy in the kindergarten include:
  - Recognition that literacy and reading are pathways to success in school and life, and
  - Recognition that learning to read is a basic right for all children.[12]

ENVIRONMENTS FOR KINDERGARTNERS

Both the physical environment and the social environment of the kindergarten classroom influence children's physical, cognitive, linguistic, and social-emotional development. In classrooms where the classroom environment supports children's learning, research shows that the occurrence of problem behaviors is reduced and the rate of children's social cooperation with their peers increases.[13]

The Physical Environment

Environments that support kindergarten children's learning are essential if we want all kindergarten children to be successful.

Classroom Arrangement and Organization. The classroom is organized to promote interaction and learning. Desks, tables, and workstations are clustered together; work areas have a variety of learning materials to encourage group projects, experiments, and creative activities. Figure 9.2 shows an example of a kindergarten floor plan. Note how stations, which we see in preschool classrooms, are still present in kindergarten classrooms. The sand/water table, computer station, play area, and reading area are organized for interactions, which Vygotsky theorized promotes cognitive and language development.

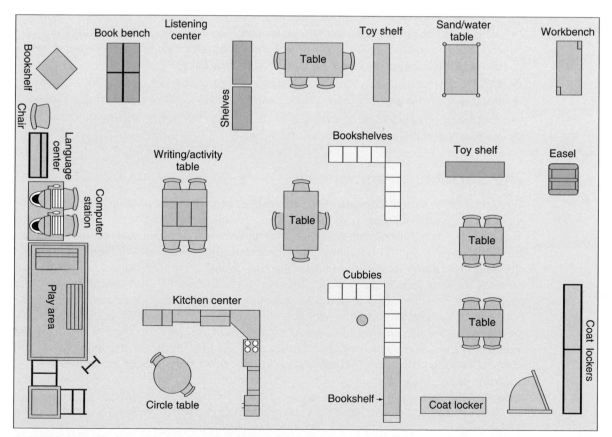

FIGURE 9.2 Kindergarten Floor Plan for an Enriched Environment

Source: Childcraft Education Corporation (Online). Available at: www.childcrafteducation.com.

Also, a high-quality kindergarten classroom is one in which children feel at home. Children's work is prominently displayed and they feel a sense of ownership. Here are some things you can do to provide high-quality kindergarten environments:

- Provide many materials that support children learning to read and write. Learning to read and write is a high priority of kindergarten, so be sure to offer a wide variety of all kinds of books and writing materials.
- Organize the children into groups of different sizes and ability levels. This provides for social interaction and cooperative learning and encourages children to help others (scaffolding).
- Use a variety of different instructional approaches such as:

  - Small group
  - Large group
  - Seat work
  - Center time
  - Free activity choice time
  - Individual teacher one-on-one work with children
  - Free play time.

- Develop your classroom arrangement so that it supports district and state learning standards. For example, to meet reading content standards, make books easily accessible to students. Also, make sure the classroom has a comfortable area for group and individual reading times.
- Adapt your classroom arrangement so it meets the learning and social needs of your children. For example, set aside time for students to work in groups, assign group projects, and assign projects dealing with different cultures.
- Collaborate with your children to "personalize" your classroom. Make your classroom home-like and cozy. Use plants, rugs, bean-bag chairs, pillows, and so on.
- Make supplies and learning materials accessible to children by storing them on open shelves with labels (using pictures and words).

Learn more about School-Age Care Environmental Rating Scale (SACERS) and view several kindergarten classrooms at http://www.prenhall.com/ morrison, Chapter 9: Web Links.

The Social Environment

The social environment consists of the immediate physical surroundings, social relationships, and cultural settings in which children function and interact. To help create a supportive social environment, all children of all cultures, genders, socioeconomic levels, and backgrounds should be valued and respected. Teachers treat children courteously, talk with them about in- and out-of-school activities and events, and show a genuine concern for them as individuals with specific needs. Unfortunately, not all children get the respect they need and want at home or at school. Some children, especially children with behavior and attention problems, can be subjected to verbal abuse by teachers and children.[14] Also, for shy children, the social environment can provide them with the social interaction they need, but they may have a difficult time initiating the interaction, and teachers need to help them find playmates. On the other hand, under the direction of an unaware or uncaring teacher, classroom activities and social interactions may encourage isolation and separation.

In developing positive teacher–child relationships, which is a key element of the social environment, it is important to remember to:

- Engage in one-to-one interactions with children.
- Get on the child's level for face-to-face interactions.

- Use a pleasant, calm voice and simple language.
- Provide warm, responsive physical contact.
- Follow the child's lead and interest during play.
- Help children understand classroom expectations.
- Redirect children when they engage in challenging behavior.
- Listen to children and encourage them to listen to others.
- Acknowledge children for their accomplishments and effort.[15]

CURRICULUM IN KINDERGARTEN

All kindergarten classrooms should be child centered and support developmentally appropriate practice in planning and implementing curriculum. Developmentally appropriate practice involves teaching and learning that is in accordance with children's physical, cognitive, social, linguistic, individual, and cultural development. Professionals help children learn and develop in ways that are compatible with how old they are and who they are as individuals (e.g., their background of experiences and culture). Early childhood professionals who embody the qualities of good kindergarten teachers are those who teach in developmentally appropriate ways.

Developmentally appropriate practice in kindergarten includes the following:

- Make learning meaningful to children and related to what they know. Children find things meaningful when they are interesting and they can relate to them.
- Individualize your curriculum as much as possible. All children do not learn the same way, nor are they interested in learning the same things as everyone else all the time.
- Make learning physically and mentally active. Actively involve children in learning that includes building, making, experimenting, investigating, and working collaboratively with their peers.
- Provide for hands-on activities with concrete objects and manipulatives. Emphasize real-life activities as opposed to workbook and worksheet activities.

Kindergarten curriculum includes not only activities that support children emotionally and socially in learning to be more competent people, but also more academic experiences, such as those in literacy and reading, math, science, social studies, and the arts. All experiences, however, should first be approached by considering five- and six-year-old's developmental capabilities and yearning to play as they learn.

Tom Watson / Merrill

Literacy and Reading in Kindergarten

Today, improving literacy is a major goal across all grade levels. All states and school districts have adopted an educational agenda with a strong literacy focus and have set the goal of having all children read on grade level by grade three.

What all of this means is that the reading goals for kindergarten learning are higher than they have ever been and they will continue to get higher.

The nation has set a goal of having all children read and write at or above level by grade three. What are some activities and practices you can implement to help ensure that all children achieve this national goal?

FIGURE 9.3

Michigan State Kindergarten English-Language Arts Content Standards

A. Reading
- Phonemic Awareness
  - Change the sounds of words by changing letters that can make new words. Example: "hat" becomes "_at, or <u>s</u>at, or <u>m</u>at."
  - Recognize that words are made of sounds blended together and that words have meaning.
  - Understand that sounds in words are represented by letters of the alphabet.

- Word Recognition
  - Follow the written text of familiar stories by pointing to known words.
  - Know the meaning of words heard and seen often.
  - Try to figure out the meaning of new words and phrases.

- Comprehension
  - Begin to connect and compare a story to their lives.
  - Predict what will happen next in a story, based on pictures or portions of the story.
  - Remember and use what has been read from other subject areas.

B. Writing
- Writing Genre
  - Write a brief personal story using pictures, words, and/or sentences.
  - Write a short informational piece using drawings, words, and/or sentences.
  - Help with a class research project by adding key information gathered from materials supplied by the teacher.

- Spelling
  - Correctly spell about eighteen words that are meaningful and seen often such as personal information (name), and some basic vocabulary words.
  - Use beginning and simple ending sounds, or word lists provided by the teacher, to figure out how to spell more words.

- Handwriting
  - Form upper- and lowercase letters.
  - Write from left to right and top to bottom leaving space between words.

Source: Michigan Department of Education, "A Parent's Guide to English Language Arts Grade Level Content Expectations," http://www.michigan.gov/documents/ELA_K_141486_7.pdf.

Literacy and Reading. Early childhood professionals place a high priority on children's literacy and reading success. **Literacy** means the ability to read, write, speak, and listen. Professionals view literacy as a process that begins at birth (perhaps before) and continues to develop across the life span, through the school years.

The process of becoming literate is also viewed as a natural process; reading and writing are processes that children participate in naturally, long before they come to school. No doubt you have participated with or know of toddlers and preschoolers who are literate in many ways. They "read" all kinds of environmental print such as signs (McDonald's), labels (Cheerios), and menus and other symbols in their environments.

Figure 9.3 lists Michigan's English-language arts content standards for kindergartners. *Language arts* refers to the subjects, including reading, spelling, and composition, aimed at developing reading and writing skills in early childhood education. Figure 9.4 defines common terms used when discussing literacy. These are terms you will want to know and use. They are an important part of being able to "talk the talk" of your profession. You will use these terms in your work with parents, colleagues, and the community.

FIGURE 9.4

Reading/Literacy Instructional Terminology

Alphabet knowledge The knowledge that letters have names and shapes and that letters can represent sounds in language. *Example:* Children recognize and name the letters of the alphabet.

Alphabetic principle Awareness that each speech sound or phoneme in a language has its own distinctive graphic representation and an understanding that letters go together in patterns to represent sounds. *Example:* Letters and letter patterns represent sounds of the language. Introduce just letters that are used a lot such as M, A, T, S, P, and H. Teach consonants first for sound–letter relationships.

Comprehension In reading, the basic understanding of the words and the content or meaning contained within printed material. *Example:* Keisha is able to retell the story. Mario is able to tell who the main character is.

Decoding Identifying words through context and *phonics. Example:* James can figure out how to read a word he does not know by using his knowledge of letters and sounds. Also, he uses context clues (information from pictures and the sentence before and the sentence after a word) to "decode" it. He looked at the picture with a "pile" of wood to figure out *pile*, a word he did not know.

Onset–rime The onset is any consonant(s) that precedes the vowel, and the rime is the vowel plus any succeeding consonants. *Example:* In pig, *p* is the onset and *ig* is the rime.

Orthographic awareness The ability to analyze visually the appearance and structure of words. *Example:* Ben knows the word *man* and uses that knowledge to read the word *fan*.

Phoneme The smallest unit of speech that makes a difference to meaning. *Example:* The word *pig* has three phonemes, /p/ /i/ /g/.

Phonemic awareness The ability to notice, think about, and work with the individual sounds in spoken words. *Example:* Alex can identify the words in a set that begin with the same sound: *boy, big, bike*.

Phonics The learning of alphabetic principles of language and knowledge of letter–sound relationships. *Example:* Children learn to associate letters with the phonemes (basic speech sounds) to help break the alphabetic code.

Phonological awareness The ability to manipulate language at the levels of syllables, rhymes, and individual speech sounds. *Example:* Maria can identify words that rhyme from those that don't rhyme. Whitney can match words that sound alike. Caroline can segment words into sounds. Angie can blend sounds into words.

Print awareness The recognition of conventions and characteristics of a written language. *Example:* Mario pretends to read a bedtime story to his teddy bear. Also, he recognizes the Kentucky Fried Chicken sign on his way to school.

Developing Literacy and Reading in Young Children.   Literacy and reading are certainly worthy national and educational goals, not only for young children but for everyone. However, how best to promote literacy has always been a controversial topic. What do children need to know to become good and skillful readers? Research identifies the following:[16]

- Knowledge of letter names,
- Speed at which children can name individual letters,
- Phonemic awareness (letter-sound awareness), and
- Experience with books and being read to.

Approaches to Literacy and Reading.   One of the ways you can give children experiences with books is by using technology effectively. The Technology Tie-In feature on page 247 provides you with ways to use technology in your program.

  Sight Words.   Basal approaches and materials used for literacy and reading development often emphasize one particular method. One of the most popular methods is the **sight word approach** (also called *whole-word* or *look-say*) in which children are presented whole words (*cat, bat, sat*) and develop a "sight vocabulary" that enables them to begin reading and writing. Many early childhood teachers label objects in their

Observe a teacher discussing a book with his students to develop literacy at Video Classroom, General Methods, Module 1: The Effective Teacher, Video 1: Using Student Ideas and Contributions.

classrooms (door, bookcase, etc.) as a means of teaching a sight vocabulary. Word walls are popular in kindergarten and primary classrooms. A word wall is a bulletin board or classroom display area on which high-frequency and new words are displayed. The words are arranged alphabetically.

Phonics.   A second popular approach is based on **phonics instruction**, which stresses teaching letter–sound correspondences. By learning these connections, children are able to combine sounds into words (C-A-T). The proponents of phonics instruction argue that letter–sound correspondences enable children to make automatic connections between words and sounds and, as a result, to sound out words and read them on their own. From the 1950s up until the present time there has been much debate about which of these two approaches to literacy development is best. Today, there is a decided re-emphasis on the use of phonics instruction. One reason for this emphasis is that the research evidence suggests that phonics instruction enables children to become proficient readers.[17]

Language Experience.   Another method of literacy and reading development, the **language experience approach (LEA)**, follows the philosophy and suggestions inherent in progressive education philosophy. This approach to reading instruction is child centered, links oral and written language, and maintains that literacy education should be meaningful to children and should grow out of experiences that are interesting to them. LEA is based on the premise that what is thought can be said, what is said can be written, and what is written can be read. Children's experiences are a key element in such child-centered approaches. Many teachers transcribe children's dictated "experience" stories and use them as a basis for writing and for reading instruction.

Whole Language.   Beginning about 1980, early childhood practitioners in the United States were influenced by literacy education approaches used in Australia and New Zealand. These influences gradually developed into what is known as the **whole-language approach** to literacy development. Since whole language is a philosophy rather than a method, its definition often depends on who is using the term. This approach nonetheless advocates using all aspects of language—reading, writing, listening, and speaking—as the basis for developing literacy. Children learn about reading and writing by speaking and listening; they learn to read by writing, and they learn to write by reading.

Shared Reading.   Because children love books and reading, shared reading is a good way for you to capitalize on their interest and help them learn to read. **Shared reading** is a means of introducing young beginners to reading, using favorite books, rhymes, and poems. Teachers model reading for the students by reading aloud a book or other text and ultimately inviting students to join in.

Shared reading builds on children's natural desire to read and reread favorite books. The repeated reading of texts over several days, weeks, or months deepens children's understanding of them because each time the reading should be for a different purpose: to extend, refine, or deepen a child's abilities to read and construct meaning.

The shared reading routine requires that you have on hand a big-book form of the book to be read, as well as multiple little-book copies for individual rereading later. You then follow these three steps:

1. *Introduce the book.* Gather the children where they can all see the big book.
   - Show and discuss the book cover: read the title, author, illustrator, and other appropriate book features.
   - Discuss some of the pages in the book, but don't give away the entire story.
   - Invite children to predict what they think will happen in the book. If they have difficulty, model thinking aloud to show them how you would predict. Record their predictions on a chart for later reference.

technology tie-in

Five Effective Ways for Using Technology

There are several ways to use technology to enhance the educational experience for young children:*

1. *Tell a story.* Reading and writing are more effective when taught together. To create illustrations use a simple paint program, draw and scan images into the computer or get them from an online source. Children can use the images to illustrate or create their own stories. Have the children record the story. They love hearing their stories played over and over again.

2. *Create a memory book.* Use a digital camera to record a special activity or field trip to make a memory book. Children can share their memories of the event by dictating or writing captions, drawing illustrations, and making recordings. Children can work together to create a slideshow that covers the event. The memory book can then be viewed online or printed as a book. Revisiting the photos reinforces the learning associated with the event. Transcribing recordings will allow children to see how spoken language can be translated into written words. Even as a group activity, the memory book allows the children to express themselves in individual ways.

3. *Document and display projects through photos.* Technology can be used to celebrate children's achievements. Take digital pictures of children doing everything from performing to working on various projects.[†] Display pictures around school, in newsletters, on a class Web site, and in a school yearbook. When children see their pictures, they take pride and ownership in who they are and in their accomplishments.

4. *Explore.* Use images from a digital camera or the Web. Zoom in to magnify features not immediately obvious to the children. Collect digital pictures of the community or famous places and encourage children to create their own virtual tour. Hands-on experiences build literacy through conversation and the opportunity to learn new vocabulary. When computers are available for children to use, you can guide them through several interesting, child-oriented Web sites using TrackStar (http://trackstar.4teachers.org). With this online tool, you can easily build your own track or use one of the thousands of tracks already developed by other teachers.

5. *Compare and contrast.* Collect and organize things that are of interest to children. Categorize them and arrange them in a physical graph format. This experience will help children to visualize and understand information in new ways. As an alternative, you can use magnets personalized with the children's names on the chalkboard or white board to illustrate how the children fall into different categories: primary color of clothes, pets vs. no pets, color of hair, and so forth. Then use a computer-based program to enter data and display a pictograph.

When considering the use of technology with young children, ask yourself these key question:[†]

- Is it developmentally appropriate?
- Will the activity benefit children, or will it replace some other, more meaningful learning activities?

Using technology for the sake of technology is not very useful. Kindergartners benefit most from technology in the classroom under these circumstances:[§]

- The lesson or project is directly connected to the classroom curriculum.
- The technology allows for active learning and discovery.
- The lesson or project is open ended, allowing learners to proceed at their own pace.
- Technology is applied to real situations for a real purpose.
- Computers are part of the classroom, rather than set apart in a separate room or lab.

Technology can be fun and engaging and, when used appropriately, can enhance a child's learning experience.

Web-based resources for teachers of young children include:

- *Early Connections: Technology in Early Childhood Education.* Web site developed by Northwest Educational Technology Consortium. It provides resources and information to educators on "connecting technology with the way young children learn." Available at http://www.netc.org/earlyconnections/.
- *4teachers.* Web site maintained by ALTEC at the University of Kansas. It provides online tools and resources designed to help teachers integrate technology into their classrooms. Tools include the popular RubiStar, TrackStar, and QuizStar software. A classroom architect tool is available to help teachers create a floor plan for their classroom. Available at http://www.4teachers.org.

Contributed by Linda Merillat, M.Ed., and Jennifer Holvoet, Ph.D.

*Northwest Educational Technology Consortium. (2002). Five effective ways for young children to use technology [Brochure]. Portland, OR: Author. Available at http://www.netc.org/earlyconnections/pub/brochure.pdf.

[†]Van Scoter, J., Ellis, D., & Railsback, J. (2001). Technology in early childhood education: Finding the balance [Brochure]. Portland, OR: Northwest Regional Educational Laboratory. Available at http://www.netc.org/earlyconnections/byrequest.pdf.

[†]Idid, p. 15.

[§]Northwest Educational Technology Consortium. (n.d.) Early Connections kindergarten: Technology and curriculum. Retrieved February 14, 2007, from http://www.netc.org/earlyconnections/kindergarten/curriculum.html.

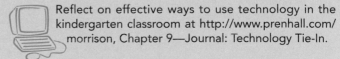

Reflect on effective ways to use technology in the kindergarten classroom at http://www.prenhall.com/morrison, Chapter 9—Journal: Technology Tie-In.

2. *Read and respond to the book.* Read the book aloud to the children, holding it so they can see each page. As you read, run your hand or a pointer under each line of print to help children develop a sense of left-to-right orientation, speech-to-print match, and other concepts of print. If some children wish to join in, encourage them to do so.

As you read, you may stop briefly to discuss the story or to respond to reactions, but you should progress through the entire book rather quickly to give children a complete sense of the story. At the conclusion of the reading, encourage children to respond, using questions such as these:

- Were your predictions right?
- What did you like in this story?
- What was your favorite part?
- What made you happy (or sad)?
- Who was your favorite character? Why?

Then return to the book, rereading the story and inviting children to read along. Many will feel comfortable doing this right away, but others may not join in until another day. After the second reading, many children will say, "Let's read it again"— especially for books, songs, or rhymes that are lots of fun. Under most circumstances, when children are excited and want to reread, you *should* reread.

After you have read the book again, have children respond, using activities such as these:

- Talk with a friend about a favorite part.
- Retell the story to a partner.
- Draw a picture about the story and write a word or a sentence about it.
- Draw and write about a favorite character.
- Write a list of favorite characters.

Help children become comfortable with making decisions by giving them only a couple of choices initially.

Katelyn Metzger / Merrill

Reading and written language acquisition is a continuum of development. Think of children as being on a continuous journey toward full literacy development! Regardless of what method you use to teach children how to read, the goal is that they should learn to read—and read on or above grade level— so they can do well in school and life.

3. *Extend the book.* You may want to wait until children have read a book several times before extending it, or you may wait unit they have read several books within a thematic unit and combine them for extension activities. Although each repeated reading may seem to be just for fun, each should have a particular focus. You might first invite children to recall what the title was and what the book was about, prompting and supporting them if necessary.

Then tell the children why they are rereading the book, using statements such as the following:

- "As we reread this book, let's think about who the important characters are" (comprehension).
- "In our story today, notice how the author repeats lines over and over" (exploring language).
- "Today, as we reread one of our favorite stories, look for places to use phonic skills we have been learning" (decoding).[18]

A Balanced Approach. As with most things, a **balanced approach** is the best, and many early childhood advocates are encouraging literacy approaches that provide a balance between whole-language methods and phonics instruction and that meet the specific needs of individual children. One thing is clear: systematic instruction that enables children to acquire skills they need to learn to read is very much in evidence in today's early childhood classrooms. It is likely that the debate over "the best approach" will continue. At the same time, efforts will increase to integrate the best of all approaches into a unified whole to make all children confident readers. The "Professionalism in Practice: Philosophy: Kindergarten Language Arts Curriculum" on pages 258–259 explores the language arts curriculum used in one kindergarten classroom.

Supporting Children's Learning to Read. A primary goal of kindergarten education is for children to learn how to read. Teachers must instruct, support, and guide children in helping them learn what is necessary for them to be successful in school and life. Here are some of the things you can do to motivate children's learning to read:

- Include a variety of different types of books, such as picture books without words, fairy tales, nursery rhymes, picture storybooks, realistic literature, decodable and pre-dictable books, information books, chapter books, biographies, big books, poetry, and joke and riddle books.
- Provide other types of print such as newspapers, magazines, and brochures.
- Introduce and discuss several books each week (may be theme related, same authors, illustrators, types of books, etc.).
- Have multiple copies of popular books.
- Provide a record-keeping system for keeping track of books read (may include a picture-coding system to rate or evaluate the book).
- Showcase many books by placing them so covers are visible, especially those that are new, shared in read-aloud sessions, or theme related.
- Organize books on shelves by category or type (may color code).
- Provide comfortable, inviting places to read (pillows, rugs, a sofa, large cardboard boxes, etc.).
- Encourage children to read to "friends" (include stuffed animals and dolls for "pretend" reading).
- Have an Author's Table with a variety of writing supplies to encourage children to write about books.
- Have a Listening Table for recorded stories and tapes.[19]

Also, stop for a minute and reflect on what we said in Chapter 3 about Vygotsky's theory of scaffolding children's learning.

Math in Kindergarten

Your teaching of mathematics in kindergarten should be in alignment with the National Council of Teachers of Mathematics (NCTM) Curriculum Focal Points. Curriculum focal points are important mathematical topics for each grade level, pre-K–8. In addition, your integration of your curriculum with the curriculum focal points should promote these processes:

- Problem solving,
- Reasoning,
- Communication,

FIGURE 9.5

Kindergarten Curriculum Focal Points

1. *Numbers and Operations:* Representing, comparing, and ordering whole numbers and joining and separating sets

Children use numbers, including written numerals, to represent quantities and to solve quantitative problems, such as counting objects in a set, creating a set with a given number of objects, comparing and ordering sets or numerals by using both cardinal and ordinal meanings, and modeling simple joining and separating situations with objects. They choose, combine, and apply effective strategies for answering quantitative questions, including quickly recognizing the number in a small set, counting and producing sets of given sizes, counting the number in combined sets, and counting backward.

For example, they might sort solids that roll easily from those that do not. Or they might collect data and use counting to answer such questions as "What is our favorite snack?" They re-sort objects by using new attributes (e.g., after sorting solids according to which ones roll, they might re-sort the solids according to which ones stack easily).

2. *Geometry:* Describing shapes and space

Children interpret the physical world with geometric ideas (e.g., shape, orientation, spatial relations) and describe it with corresponding vocabulary. They identify, name, and describe a variety of shapes, such as squares, triangles, circles, rectangles, (regular) hexagons, and (isosceles) trapezoids presented in a variety of ways (e.g., with different sizes or orientations), as well as such three-dimensional shapes as spheres, cubes, and cylinders. They use basic shapes and spatial reasoning to model objects in their environment and to construct more complex shapes.

For example, children integrate their understandings of geometry, measurement, and number. For example, they understand, discuss, and create simple navigational directions (e.g., "Walk forward ten steps, turn right, and walk forward five steps").

3. *Measurement:* Ordering objects by measurable attributes

Children use measurable attributes, such as length or weight, to solve problems by comparing and ordering objects. They compare the lengths of two objects both directly (by comparing them with each other) and indirectly (by comparing both with a third object), and they order several objects according to length.

For example, children identify, duplicate, and extend simple number patterns and sequential and growing patterns (e.g., patterns made with shapes) as preparation for creating rules that describe relationships.

Source: Reprinted with permission from "Curriculum Focal Points for Prekindergarten through Grade 8 Mathematics: A Quest for Coherence," National Council of Teachers of Mathematics (NCTM), 2006. p. 11.

- Making connections, and
- Designing and analyzing representations.[20]

Review now the NCTM kindergarten curriculum focal points in Figure 9.5.

Science in Kindergarten

Science plays an increasingly important part of the kindergarten curriculum. The following Program in Action feature provides you with important guidelines for how to make sure your children are becoming scientifically literate.

Scaffolding with Science.   We do not want to forget that in all of our teaching of young children we should be alert to how to apply the theories that we discussed in Chapter 3 to practice. For example, science offers many wonderful opportunities to apply Vygotsky's ideas, especially scaffolding. For example, in meeting the science

FIGURE 9.6

Sample Problem-Solving Chart

Identify Problem	Preview Solution	Assemble Resources
What kind of soil will a bean seed grow in: soil from outside our classroom, humus, sand, water, rocks, or clay?	We think that a bean seed will grow best in humus because it has nutrients in it.	We need soil from outside our classroom, humus, sand, water, rocks, clay, see-through cups, beans, and a well-lit place in our classroom.

Analyze Resources and Plans	Select Plan and Begin Doing It	Monitor the Process
We need to make sure each cup gets the same amount of light.	Each group of four students needs to plan the experiment and do it.	What is happening to the seeds?
We need to make sure we use the same amount of planting material.		After 4 days? After 8 days? Why is this happening?

Source: Williams, Kerry C., *Launching Learners in Science, PreK–5*, p. 122, Copyright 2007 by Corwin Press Inc. Reprinted by Permission of Corwin Press Inc.

content standard *science as inquiry* (see Chapter 10), a problem-solving chart like that shown in Figure 9.6 can help you not only teach science as inquiry but also help students learn the process of scientific inquiry in their study of plants and how they grow.

Social Studies in Kindergarten

In the kindergarten, the social sciences most often included are history, geography, economics, and civics.[21] For each of these disciplines you will want to include knowledge, concepts, and themes. Your teaching of the social studies should be content based and child centered, and you will want to make sure that you consult your state's content standards for social studies.

Historically, social studies in the kindergarten have focused on the **expanding horizons** or **expanding environments approach** for sequencing and selecting content. In this approach the child is at the center of the expanding horizons, and at each grade level is immersed in a widening environment. Refer to Figure 9.7 to see how children are immersed in a slowly widening environment through the expanding horizons approach in grades K–3. In kindergarten, teaching of the social studies is generally focused on topics such as "All About Me." In recent years, the expanding horizons approach has come under criticism. Critics of this approach maintain that it is simplistic, it lacks rigorous social science content, and it does not engage children in a serious study of the social studies.

Although the expanding horizon approach is much maligned, nonetheless, the teaching of the social studies generally begins with who the children are and where they are geographically. In addition, approaches to the study of the social studies in the kindergarten also try to be child centered and developmentally appropriate. A good example of these criteria is from the Georgia Department of Education.

Lightning is flashing and thunder is rolling in my bilingual kindergarten classroom. The children are trying to say how the storm is scaring them. But they don't know how to describe what's going on. They can only say that there's a lot of rain and wind. They've never heard the words for thunder or lightning—in either Spanish or English! Since many of these children are performing at high levels in other areas, this underdevelopment of oral language in science is amazing. No wonder we see such high failure rates in state science test scores.

If our children are to develop a love of science and the ability to think and express themselves scientifically, they need to learn about scientific concepts, methods, and attitudes while they are young. This gives them a foundation for future work in the sciences, math, language and the arts.

WHY IS TEACHING SCIENCE IN KINDERGARTEN IMPORTANT?

- Science is an ideal vehicle for developing children's questioning minds about the natural world.
- Implementing the National Science Education Standards can help our students take their place in a scientifically literate society.
- When children explore science they acquire oral and written language for scientific expression—and learn to read in new contexts.
- Science teaches children to appreciate the diversity of life and its interconnectedness.
- When children learn about nature they respect and care for our planet and its natural resources.
- Learning scientific methods teaches children to view themselves as scientists.
- Exciting lessons in science can foster a lifelong love for the subject.

KINDERGARTNERS CAN ACT LIKE SCIENTISTS

Teaching children what a scientist is and what scientists do is fundamental to science education. Scientists observe with their five senses (sight, touch, taste, smell, and hearing). They draw what they see, write about their observations, classify, ask questions, make predictions, create models, design experiments, count accurately, test their hypotheses, repeat their experiments, and keep on trying. Children learn

this scientific method and practice it from pre-kindergarten to grade twelve.

HOW TO INTEGRATE SCIENCE

ELEMENT 1 PLAN AN ACTIVITY AND ADDRESS STANDARDS

Always plan activities that provide opportunities to engage, explore, explain, elaborate, and evaluate—the 5-E model. Central to teaching science is developing scientific concepts and methodology rather than merely studying some favorite topic or, worse yet, displaying some dramatic effect, such as a foaming "volcano." State and district standards will have science learning objectives. Plan activities as you consider the standards.

Example: Use "Planting Pumpkin Seeds" (a small part of an ongoing unit) to teach the following objectives as stated in the *Texas Essential Knowledge & Skills* publication:

- Students will ask questions about organisms, objects, and events.
- Students will plan and conduct simple descriptive investigations and communicate their findings.
- Examples will follow.

ELEMENT 2 INCLUDE HANDS-ON EXPERIENCES

Because children come from diverse backgrounds, they may not all have experience with a particular topic. To "level the playing field," begin every science unit with an activity that engages the students with a shared, hands-on experience.

Example: Bring a real pumpkin to the classroom and let the children touch it. Ask them to describe it and encourage them to ask questions.

Teacher:	"What do you notice about the pumpkin?"
Jonathan:	"It's orange."
Sara:	"It's like a ball."
Carolina:	"It's has brown spots on it."
Anthony:	"It has lines on it."
Edward:	"It's big."
Teacher:	"What do you wonder about the pumpkin?"
Kevin:	"Is it real?"
Carolina:	"Are there seeds inside?"
Daniela:	"Will it get bigger?"
Pedro:	"Is it heavy?"

ELEMENT 3 · INCORPORATE WRITING AND DRAWING

- Model writing for the class by recording on a chart what children say about the pumpkin.
- Encourage interactive writing. With guidance from the teacher, children take turns with a marker on a large piece of paper writing their observations as a group and using invented spelling.
- Teach children to make direct observations by individually drawing only what they see—in their science journals or on recording sheets.
- Depending on the children's developmental levels, they will either write about their observations, or you will record their observations.

ELEMENT 4 · INCORPORATE LITERATURE

- Incorporate both nonfiction and fiction materials for read-alouds, free reading, and research. *Apples and Pumpkins* (Rockwell, Anne), *Calabazas/Pumpkins* (Berger, Melvin & Gilda), *From Seed to Plant* (Fowler, Allan), *From Seed to Pumpkin* (Pfeffer, Wendy), *Pumpkin Circle* (Levenson, George) (Spanish version: *El círculo de las calabazas*), *Pumpkin Jack* (Hubbell, Will), *Perfect Pumpkins* (Bauer, Jeff), *Pumpkin, Pumpkin* (Titherington, Jeanne), *Too Many Pumpkins* (White, Linda).
- Choose nonfiction books with photos (including children if possible). *Perfect Pumpkins* (Bauer, Jeff), *Pumpkin Circle* (Levenson, George) (Spanish version: *El círculo de las calabazas*).
- Use charts of songs and poems for shared reading to teach scientific vocabulary and concepts.
- Explain science text features such as table of contents, diagram labels, glossary, and index.

ELEMENT 5 · ASK QUESTIONS TO PROMOTE STUDENT-DESIGNED EXPERIMENTS

- Start children wondering. Model asking testable questions for the children:
  "What would happen if we watered these seeds?"
  "What would happen if we didn't water some others?"
  "What would happen if these seeds got a lot of light?"
  "What would happen if these seeds got a little light?"
- Ask: "Which of these would grow faster and how could we find out?"
- Now say:
  "Let's put three seeds in each cup with some soil."
  "We'll put one cup where it will get a *lot* of light and *water* the seeds.
  "We'll put one cup where it will get a *lot* of light and *not water* the seeds.
  "We'll put one cup where it will get a *little* bit of light and *water* the seeds.
  "We'll put one cup where it will get a *little* bit of light and *not water* the seeds."
- Prompt the class to make predictions and record their answers.

  Brandon: "I think the seeds will grow in three days."
  Samantha: "I think the seeds will grow in five days."

- The children will check the seeds every few days and record the results in their science journals.
- Use plastic connecting cubes or some other nonstandard unit of measure such as paper clips to determine which plants are growing faster.
- Discuss the results.

ADDITIONAL STRATEGIES

Go into depth with a few topics rather than scratching the surface of many. Place additional materials in the science center for the children to explore and extend their studies of seeds, plants, and life cycles. Some examples are a tray with paper, crayons and rubbing plates of leaves; field identification guides of leaves, trees, and other plants; seeds for sorting and sorting sheets; rubber stamps of the life cycle of a plant for the children to use to sequence the life cycle of a plant; and plant puzzles.

Contributed by Lori D. Cadwallader, bilingual kindergarten teacher, Rivera Elementary School, Denton, Texas, and staff development trainer for "SALSA" (Science and Literacy Saturday Academy) and "The Nature of Science," Denton ISD, Denton, Texas.

Complete an activity on the use of hands-on experiences in kindergarten at http://www.prenhall.com/morrison, Chapter 9—Journal: Program in Action.

FIGURE 9.7 Expanding Horizons Approach, Grades K–3

Photo: Katelyn Metzger/ Merrill

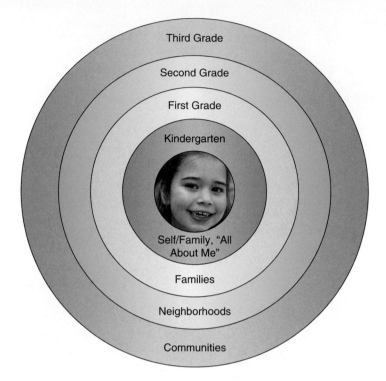

The teaching of social studies in kindergarten in Georgia, consists of six 30-day units. Here are the unit titles and lesson plan titles from the first 30-day unit for kindergarten:

1. *Unit Title:* "School Life"
   - *Lesson Plan Titles:* "Meet the Faculty," "Our Fearless Leader," "Teacher Feature," "Rules of the Room," "Let Me Tell You About My School"
2. *Unit Title:* "All About Me"
   - *Lesson Plan Titles:* "Getting to Know You Through Interview," "Name Games," "Call Me!" "There's No Place Like Home," "What's the Difference?" "The Old Me, The New Me," "I Like Myself Just the Way I Am," "A Few of My Favorite Things"
3. *Unit Title:* "All in the Family"
   - *Lesson Plan Titles:* "Different as Night and Day," "The Working Family," "Family Traditions: Part One," "Family Traditions: Part Two," "Sharing My Family"[22]

Today's teaching of the social studies is designed to provide children with content knowledge and skills from the four social sciences: history, geography, economics, and civics. So, in your teaching of the social studies you will want to make sure that children are provided with authentic content and are engaged in activities that help them learn knowledge, apply knowledge, and engage in critical thinking.

Ideas for Teaching Social Studies.   The following are some ideas that you can use to help you teach the social studies content standards of your state and school district:

- **Geography.** Ms. Thompson taught her kindergarten class about different cultures by placing one end of a ribbon on a map on the United States and the other end on the country they are learning about. Ms. Thompson discussed with the students about the different modes of transportation that could be used to travel to the country. Pictures

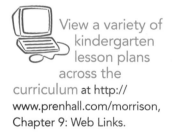

View a variety of kindergarten lesson plans across the curriculum at http://www.prenhall.com/morrison, Chapter 9: Web Links.

were then placed on the map above that country pertaining to the culture there. Students were then instructed to draw a picture, write a story, or create a poem to put on the map as well.

- **Economics.** Ms. Carter taught her children about assembly lines through the use of creative arts. She drew a picture of a stick figure person with each line drawn using a different color crayon. After displaying the drawing up on the wall she then separated her class into small groups and gave each group member a different color crayon and one piece of paper per group. The piece of paper was then passed down the line of students, and each students drew one line with their crayon matching Ms. Carter's drawing. The class then discussed the importance of assembly lines, why each member must do his part, and the different products that are made by assembly lines.

- **Civics.** Mr. Phillipes had his kindergarten children make a United States flag collage using large paper, magazines, crayons, scissors, and glue. He then discussed with the class that the flag is a national symbol, explained what the stars and stripes stand for, and discussed the role national symbols play in society. Students then told Mr. Phillipes where they've seen the American flag flown before, and he made a list of these places on the chalkboard. After the discussion, students individually drew pictures of other flags they had seen.

- **History.** Ms. Hubbard taught her kindergarten children about ancient cultures through photographs and online reproductions of wall paintings from ancient civilizations that illustrate aspects of life as it was lived in ancient times. She then asked the students to give her ideas about which animals lived at that time, which animals the people hunted, and what games the people played. Ms. Hubbard then had her students illustrate a picture of a day in their lives using markers, crayons, or paint. The pictures included scenes such as driving to school, reading in class, recess, lunch, and playing with pets or siblings at home. After their drawings were complete, Ms. Hubbard hung the students' pictures next to the pictures of the ancient civilization. The class then held a discussion about the similarities and differences in the ancient civilizations and their own.

Arts in Kindergarten

Teaching of the arts in kindergarten consists of knowledge, skills, and concepts from these four areas: music, art, dance, and theater. The standards were developed by the American Alliance for Theater and Education, Music Educators National Conference, the National Art Education Association, and the National Dance Association.

In your role as a kindergarten teacher, you will want to integrate the arts into everything that you do. Children love to participate in activities relating to the arts, so you should capitalize on their natural creative inclinations and provide them with these experiences. As with anything else, the integration of the arts depends on these factors: time, opportunity, and materials.

Time. By integrating the arts into your curriculum, you are solving the time issue by enabling children to participate in all of these activities while they are learning reading/literacy, math, science, and social studies. For example, here are some ideas for integrating the arts into each of these areas:

- *Reading/literacy.* Students can act out the stories of their favorite book; students can illustrate a story that they and/or the class have written.

- *Math.* Students can use art materials to make charts and graphs and design and make different kinds of shapes. Students can also develop rules to describe the relationships of one shape to another, for example, "You can put two identical triangles together to make a rectangle."

- *Science.* Children can use their artistic skills to draw and paint various examples of life cycles of organisms or write and produce a public service announcement on the importance of personal health in the kindergarten classroom.
- *Social studies.* Students can learn about and sing many of the songs popular in their state's history; students can learn the folk dances of various cultural groups in their state.

Opportunity.   There are many opportunities during the school year for children to engage in projects that involve the arts. For example, puppetry can be integrated into all of the content areas, and stories provide many opportunities for children to engage in theater and dramatic play. For example, in preparation for, and while reading the story *The Three Billy Goats Gruff*, children can make paper masks to depict the goats and could build a bridge out of blocks and/or other materials. Also, students could have a starring role playing the troll. Every thematic unit provides opportunities for all of the arts, and children should be encouraged to explore ways to express ideas from the thematic units in an artistic way.

Materials.   Materials are just as important as time and opportunity. Materials include all of the materials related to the visual arts—paints, crayons, markers, brushes, and so on— as well as materials necessary for music and dance. For example, you could provide materials such as DVDs of folk dances, popular songs, and sing-along tunes. To encourage theater expression, children need props—clothes, hats, puppets, and plenty of materials such as cardboard boxes, glue, and tape for making their own stage settings and backgrounds. Keep in mind that the *process* of exploring the creative arts is more important than the finished *product.* Children are learning to enjoy learning when the process is respected by teachers.

SUPPORTING CHILDREN'S APPROACHES TO LEARNING

The experiences children have before they come to kindergarten often influence the success of their kindergarten years. Three areas are particularly important in influencing children's success in kindergarten: children's skills and prior school-related experiences, children's home lives, and preschool and kindergarten classroom characteristics. Research demonstrates the following in relation to these three areas[23]:

- Children who are socially adjusted do better in school. For example, kindergarten children whose parents initiate social opportunities for them are better adjusted socially and therefore can do better.
- Rejected children have difficulty with school tasks.
- Children with more preschool experiences have fewer adjustments to make in kindergarten.
- Children whose parents expect them to do well in kindergarten do better than children whose parents have low expectations for them. Children who have teachers with high expectations also do better in school.
- Books, videos, computer-based learning materials, and other materials designed for children in the home improve the chances that children will be successful in school.
- Developmentally appropriate classrooms and practices promote easier and smoother transitions for children from home to school, from grade to grade, and from program to program.

The nature, extent, creativity, and effectiveness of transitional experiences for children, parents, and staff will be limited only by the commitment of all involved. If we are

```
┌─────────────────────────────────────────────────────────────────────────┐
│                    My Weekly Home Reading Journal                         │
│                                                                           │
│  Name: Daniel Sheffield                                                   │
│                                                                           │
│  Week of: December 12                                                     │
│                                                                           │
│  Day            Book Read                              Who I Read To      │
│  Monday:        The Biggest, Best Snowman              mother             │
│  Tuesday:       A Bed for the Winter                   sister             │
│  Wednesday:     The Penguin Who Wanted to Fly          father             │
│  Thursday:      Bad Kitty                              brother            │
│  Friday:        Bear Snores On                         baby brother       │
│  Saturday:      There Was an Old Lady Who Swallowed a Bell  my dog "Butch" │
│  Sunday:        Who Will Help Santa This Year?         mother             │
│                                                                           │
│  Parent's Signature: Marie Sheffield                                      │
└─────────────────────────────────────────────────────────────────────────┘
```

FIGURE 9.8 Reading Logs Encourage Children and Their Parents to "Read Together"

interested in providing good preschools, kindergartens, and primary schools, then we will include transitional experiences in the curricula of all these programs.

How successful children are in kindergarten depends on how well all who have a stake in children's education cooperate. More and more we realize that when early childhood teachers work with parents, children's achievement increases. For example, you can involve your students' parents in a family literacy project that supports children's learning to read. One way to do this is to encourage children and their parents to "read together." The use of a reading log such as the one shown in Figure 9.8 motivates children to read at home and involves the whole family.

KINDERGARTEN ISSUES

You would think that with all that is happening in the new kindergarten, we would have discussed all the issues! Not only is kindergarten education a fascinating topic, but coming as it does almost at the beginning of formal education, there are a number of issues that relate to beginnings.

Redshirting

You may have heard of the practice of redshirting college football players. This is the practice of holding a player out a year so he can grow and mature. The theory is that the extra year will result in better football players. The same practice applies to kindergarten children. The U.S. Department of Education estimates that about 9 percent of entering kindergarten children are *redshirted*—held out of school for a year.[24] Parents and administrators who practice redshirting think that the extra year will give children an opportunity to mature intellectually, socially, and physically. On the one hand, redshirting might have some benefit for children who are immature and whose birth dates fall close to the school entrance date cutoff. On the other hand, some affluent parents redshirt their children, their sons in particular, because they want them to be the oldest members of the kindergarten class. They reason that their children will be class leaders, will get more attention from the teachers, and will have another year under their belt, which will help them handle the increasing demands of the kindergarten curriculum.

Philosophy: Kindergarten Language Arts Curriculum

Phyllis Trachtenburg
Elementary reading specialist
Moorestown Public Schools
Moorestown Township, New Jersey

The philosophy that guides the kindergarten language arts curriculum is based on the premise that teachers can cultivate and teach skills needed for reading and writing success.

Teachers recognize that children enter kindergarten with a wide range of language experiences, concepts, and skills. They employ large-group, small-group, and individual instruction to ensure that the weakest to strongest language learner will acquire appreciation of language, advance in skill development, and feel successful each day in the process.

We believe (and research supports) that young children learn best in a child-centered environment through an integrated curriculum that balances teacher-directed and child-initiated activities.

Kindergarten children's language development is enhanced through:

- Exposure to quality literature (nursery rhymes, poetry, classic tales)
- Frequent demonstrations of proficient reading and writing by the teacher and other adults
- Formal and informal practice (workbook, journal writing, retellings, dramatizations, songs, artwork, creative play)

A key priority is to prepare children with the prereading foundation skills directly related to successful reading achievement in grade one. Current research and practice point to four component concepts that, when mastered in kindergarten, ensure reading in first grade. They are:

1. Print Awareness
   - Knowledge that people read the text, not just look at the pictures
   - Awareness of how to read a book—right side up, starting with the first page and continuing to the end; the left page is read first; text is read from left to right
   - An understanding that words are units separated by spaces
2. Knowledge of the Alphabet
   - Being able to recognize and name all the letters (in and out of order)
3. Phonemic Awareness
   - Knowing that letters represent speech sounds that can be manipulated (added, deleted, transposed)
4. Sight Vocabulary
   - Ability to recognize a number of words (fifteen to eighteen) instantly (at sight)

Read how high-stakes testing can affect teaching and learning at Articles and Readings, Assessment, Module 5: Standardized Achievement Tests, Article 2: The Lessons of High-Stakes Testing.

TEACHER PREP

High-Stakes Kindergarten Testing

Children at all grade levels are being subjected to more testing. For kindergarten children, this testing not only includes achievement testing but also developmental and readiness screening. **Developmental screening** is designed to assess current developmental status and identify children's language, cognitive, and social-emotional delays. Traditionally, this information is used to modify existing curriculum and/or provide specific learning activities and programs designed to help children learn. This is what developmental practice is all about. However, increasing numbers of kindergarten children and their parents are confronting **readiness screening**, designed to determine if children have the cognitive and behavioral skills necessary for kindergarten success. Unfortunately, many children may be " screened-out" of kindergarten rather than have a school experience that will help them succeed. Many of the children who are screened out of programs are the children who need a high-quality school program.

There are a number of other issues with readiness tests:

- Many lack validity; that is, they don't measure what they say they are measuring.
- Many readiness tests measure things that require teaching, such as colors, letters, and shapes. Consequently, children who would benefit most from a kindergarten program are judged not ready.

- Usually acquired through frequent story reading (with the child encouraged to follow along) and by attending to environmental print

For young children, the language arts (reading, writing, listening, and speaking) mutually reinforce one another. Growth in one leads to growth in the others—hence, the term *integrated language arts.*

GUIDING PRINCIPLES OF OUR INTEGRATED LANGUAGE ARTS CURRICULUM

1. Oral language proficiency is related to growth in reading and writing. Therefore, children need frequent opportunities for verbal expression.
2. Children learn from the language they hear. Therefore, the richer the language environment, the richer the language learning.
3. Children imitate the language they hear and read and use it as part of their own. Therefore, teachers select high-quality, award-winning children's literature to read to children daily.
4. Writing opportunities have been proven to facilitate word analysis and word recognition in young children. Therefore, teachers engage children in journal writing and functional writing (writing for real purposes and real audiences), although they may not yet be able to read.

RATIONALE

Encouraging kindergarten children to write (after they know approximately ten to fifteen consonant sound–symbol associations) heightens phonemic awareness. Strong phonemic awareness results in greater receptivity to phonics instruction (formally taught in first grade).

Children are encouraged to write words the way they sound. This practice is frequently called "inventive," "developmental," or "transitional" spelling. Because strong phonemic awareness leads to receptivity to phonics instruction, early writing has become a kindergarten priority and is widely practiced. This writing "experimentation" is temporary and is followed by a gradual and predictable transition to conventional spelling.

The kindergarten language arts curriculum integrates reading, writing, listening, and speaking with age-appropriate activities that support children of varying experiences and abilities. The curriculum balances teacher-directed and child-initiated activities using the finest children's literature and research-supported practices such as providing early writing opportunities for pregrade readers. Major emphasis is placed on the teaching of print awareness, knowledge of the alphabet, phonemic awareness, and sight word acquisition. It is paramount that parents know and understand our goals for their children. Therefore, we consider parent communication a priority. We also realize the critical role that parent participation plays in the literacy acquisition of young children. Hence, we provide many opportunities for parents to join in this important endeavor of producing children who can use language skillfully and effectively.

 Explore the balanced approach to reading and writing instruction at http://www.prenhall.com/morrison, Chapter 9—Projects: Professionalism in Practice.

- There is a mismatch between what readiness tests measure and what kindergarten teachers say is important for school success.

Kindergarten Entrance Age

Undoubtedly, there will be ongoing debates and discussions about the appropriate age for kindergarten entrance. Current legislative policies and initiatives support delaying kindergarten entrance ages. For example, Maryland recently raised the age at which children can be admitted to kindergarten. Now children must be five by September 1 rather than the previous date of December 31. The state's superintendent of schools said the change was necessary because of the increased academic focus in today's kindergartens.[25]

Rather than the constant juggling of entrance ages, what is needed are early childhood programs designed to meet and serve the needs of all children, regardless of the ages at which they enter school. At the heart of this issue of age and time is whether maturation or school is the more potent factor in children's achievement. Research studies comparing age and school effects suggest educational intervention contributes more to children's cognitive competence than does maturation.[26]

These and other issues will continue to fuel the educational debates and will make learning about and teaching in kindergarten even more fascinating as the years go by. Read now about the real-life practices at Belpre Elementary School described in the Diversity Tie-In feature.

Anne Monterosso
Former principal
Belpre Elementary School
Belpre, Ohio

Belpre, is a small community located on the edge of the Ohio River in the far southeastern corner of Ohio. Belpre is considered a part of the Appalachian region. Our student population is approximately 99 percent Caucasian. About 40 percent of our student body qualifies for free/reduced lunch. Many families are transient and move in and around our county, as well as across the state line into West Virginia. Our preschool serves special education students coupled with norming peers.

Supplemental services such as speech, physical therapy, and occupational therapy are provided by personnel who serve multiple schools. Special education enrollment figures are low at our level because an appropriate amount of instructional time has not been devoted to accurately identifying children with special needs. As a result, we share a special education teacher with another school.

COLOCATED FACILITY

Belpre Elementary is located on a high school campus. High school students are able to complete academic projects with our students. "High school students enjoy working with K–1 students and it is a great experience for both groups of children" according to first-grade teacher Mrs. C. Mrs. C. also believes that the high school students "make good role models for the young students, and the K–1 students really look forward to seeing them." The proximity, however, created logistical problems. Traffic patterns had to be modified to secure our students' safety from high school drivers. Also, sharing facilities such as our lunchroom, gym, and music room with the high school campus uses a substantial amount of time for travel and causes our students to walk outside in all types of weather at least once a day.

HIGH-QUALITY CURRICULUM

Our school implements a research-based, phonics-based reading program for ninety minutes daily. Students are placed in the reading groups based on data that is collected every nine weeks. Assessment information, teacher recommendation, and homework completion are considered for grouping.

Our math program is also intense; approximately one hour of math instruction is provided each day. Math lessons consist of a math meeting where students review basic math skills such as time, money, patterns, and calendar. Each teacher has an area in his or her classroom dedicated to the math meeting. This daily math practice "provides opportunity for frequent skill review instead of the traditional once a year review" says Mrs. K., first-grade teacher. A second, more traditional math session is usually scheduled later in the day. The structure of the lesson is consistent; each lesson begins with a daily facts review. Students are taught to master not only facts and basic procedures, but also strategies to use when solving various types of problems. Manipulatives such as fact wraps, clocks, money, rulers, counters, and food items are frequently used. Daily homework assignments are consistent and "encourage families to become involved with their child's school work" according to first-grade teacher Mrs. A.

Outside of our school day, students who are at risk might be involved in after-school language arts programs that focus on phonics-based reading instruction and writing skills.

IMPACT OF FEDERAL AND STATE MANDATES

Overall, our staff is a strong and dedicated group of educators. The grade-level teachers function as a team, yet there can be friction between the grade levels and also between the various schools in the district. With the increased accountability of state assessments that is being placed on all school districts, it seems that instruction in previous grade levels can be an easy target. This makes it particularly difficult at times for teachers in the lower grades. Early educators often wish those upper-grade-level teachers could come and spend the day and see what limited knowledge a child brings to school on day one of kindergarten! Suggestions for early childhood educators include the following:

- Implement ninety minutes of reading/language arts instruction daily.
- Incorporate thematic learning, science, social studies, spelling, and handwriting instruction into reading and language arts instruction.
- Read aloud from high-quality literature every day.
- Increase the length of the day for at-risk learners.
- Incorporate the use of manipulatives daily in math instruction. Find a balance between fact-based and inquiry learning.
- Develop a system for parent communication. Be consistent in your communication with parents and at the same time collect documentation of such dialogue.
- Keep homework assignments consistent. Eliminate confusion by having clear and consistent expectations.
- Use your personal strengths to increase the quality of the total school environment.
- Connect with the school community.
- Read educational research, attend professional conferences and understand the legal issues surrounding education.
- Find a mentor in your school, ask questions and listen.

Read more about rural early childhood programs and complete an activity at http://www. prenhall.com/ morrison, Chapter 9: Chapter 9—Journal: Diversity Tie-In.

PORTRAITS OF CHILDREN

Now that we have discussed what kindergarten is like, let's return our attention to kindergarten children. The Portraits of Kindergartners feature on the following pages helps you get an up-close, real-life insight into what the children you will teach are like. As you study the portraits, respond to the accompanying questions as though each child were in your classroom.

ACTIVITIES FOR PROFESSIONAL DEVELOPMENT

Ethical Dilemma

"No More Social Promotion"

Maria's school district has implemented a new policy that all kindergarten students must pass a first-grade readiness test before they can be promoted to first grade. Two of Maria's children did not have a passing score on the test. She believes the school district's policy is unfair because it bases promotion on the results of one test score. In addition, she thinks the children who did not pass the readiness test will do well in first grade.

What should Maria do? Should she keep quiet and say nothing, or should she talk with the school principal and present her case? Or should she organize the parents and ask them to help her change the school district's policy, or should she choose another ethically appropriate solution?

Application Activities

1. Do you think as a teacher you are oriented more toward a kindergarten program based on academics or social-emotional play? How would you explain your beliefs on this topic during an interview for a teaching job?

2. Do you support an earlier or later entrance age to kindergarten? Why? If your local legislator wanted specific reasons, what would you say? Ask two other teachers their opinion on this topic and compare their viewpoints to yours.

3. Give examples from your observations of kindergarten programs to support one of these opinions:
   a. Society is expecting too much of kindergarten children.
   b. Many kindergartens are not teaching children enough.
   c. Current changes occurring in the kindergarten are necessary and appropriate.

4. How to conduct developmentally appropriate practices in the ever-changing kindergarten is a major issue. Interview two kindergarten teachers and ask them for their "Top Five Developmentally Appropriate Practices."

To take online practice tests on this chapter's material, go to the Companion Website at http://www.prenhall.com/morrison, select Chapter 9, and then choose the Multiple Choice or the Essay module. For additional Web resources, choose Web Links.

ERIC

Introduce yourself to Eric, a five-year-old African American male. He weighs 60 pounds and is 4 feet, 7 inches tall. He is more physically mature than his peers and looks much older than most children his age. He loves school and gets along with his classmates. He is an active boy who loves to play sports and listen to music.

Social-Emotional	Cognitive	Motor	Adaptive (Daily Living)
Enjoys helping his peers with various tasks	Is able to sort and categorize objects by color and shape	Is well-coordinated and a skilled athlete	Has memorized his phone number and knows how to dial 911
Participates in cooperative play and is very willing to share his toys with his peers	Follows simple, step-by-step directions without assistance	Has excellent hand–eye coordination	Expresses his needs, wants, and dislikes
Likes to please adults	Understands the concept of opposites	Established hand preference	Tends to show off in front of strangers
Is an independent child who prefers to make decisions without assistance from his parents or teacher	Is eager to learn and able to read early beginner books	Is able to hop on one foot; has excellent balance	Has learned to tie his shoes without assistance

ELENA

Introduce yourself to Elena, a five-year-old Hispanic female. She weighs 39 pounds and is 3 feet, 11 inches tall. Elena's family immigrated to the United States when she was an infant; therefore, her parents are learning the English language along with Elena. She has been cared for by not only her parents, but also her maternal grandmother who has taught Elena many cultural songs from their Hispanic culture.

Social-Emotional	Cognitive	Motor	Adaptive (Daily Living)
Given her bilingual status, she tends to talk to her classmates In Spanish, not realizing that they do not understand that language	Is able to recite the alphabet in both English and Spanish	Helps her grandmother make homemade tortillas	Has memorized her address and phone number
Seeks approval from the adults in her life (parents, grandmother, and teacher)	Is able to sing songs her grandmother taught her	Is learning to tie her shoes by herself	Is able to recognize her mother's car when she arrives to pick her up from school
Shows guilt over misbehavior	Recognizes many letters and words	Shows increased skill with simple tools and writing utensils	Enjoys playing noisy rhythm instruments
Is a vibrant child who is very talkative in school and at home	Is able to identify the parts of a story (beginning, middle, and end)	Enjoys skipping and hopping	Is able to bathe herself while her mother supervises her

Questions About Developmentally Appropriate Practice:

- How could Elena's teacher incorporate Elena's cultural heritage into the classroom so that the other classmates could learn about new cultures?
- Name several social tasks you think are important for Elena and Eric to master before reaching the first grade.
- How can a child's individuality become an asset in the classroom?

- Why do you think Eric has mastered the skill of tying his shoes, whereas Elena has not?
- How can you support Elena's ongoing learning of her national language?

HARRY

Introduce yourself to Harry, a six-year-old Asian male. He weighs 54 pounds and is 4 feet tall. Harry is a quiet child who has an "easy" temperament. He prefers to play in small groups and enjoys reading picture books by himself. Harry is an attentive listener, but at times will remain focused on a task when being spoken to. He has tremendous concentration skills and tends to be a perfectionist when trying to write the letters in his name.

Social-Emotional	Cognitive	Motor	Adaptive (Daily Living)
Tends to keep to himself and exhibits shy behavior	Is reading above his grade level	Prefers less active activities such as reading, writing, and mathematics, rather than physical activities	Makes his bed every morning before going to school
Is more social in smaller groups	Loves to listen to stories being read to him	Has refined writing skills for his age; his printing is very legible	Is anxious to know how to do things so that he can do them by himself in the future
Tends to try to figure things out on his own rather than ask his teacher for help	Enjoys writing letters of the alphabet	Is able to stay in the lines while coloring	Is good about putting his dirty clothes into the dirty clothes hamper—does not like a "messy" environment

HANNAH

Introduce yourself to Hannah, a six-year-old Caucasian female. Hannah weighs 39 pounds and is 3 feet, 7 inches tall. She is an assertive kindergartner and loves to explore. She is involved in many extracurricular activities such as karate, choir, gymnastics, and Spanish lessons.

Social-Emotional	Cognitive	Motor	Adaptive (Daily Living)
Is adopted and very comfortable with the issue—her parents are very open about her adoption	Enjoys being read to and reciting the story back to an adult	Enjoys dancing and perfecting her gymnastic routines	Expresses strong wants and dislikes
Enjoys playing with her neighborhood friends	Knows all the letters of the alphabet and can count to one hundred	Is very good at activities involving fine-motor skills	Is not a very neat child—she must be reminded to pick up after herself
Is very sensitive to criticism	Enjoys dramatic play	Is able to maintain balance while standing on one foot with eyes closed	Is becoming a finicky eater
Cries easily and is a somewhat impulsive child	Enjoys learning new Spanish words in her Spanish class	Is beginning to ride her bike without training wheels	Enjoys new responsibilities such as feeding the dog and cat

Questions About Developmentally Appropriate Practice:

- What could be some of the reasons why Harry is a quiet child and Hannah is an assertive child?
- Knowing that Hannah is adopted, how could you as a teacher make sure she is socially and emotionally secure?
- How can children's individuality such as Hannah's and Harry's become assets in your classroom?
- Given that obesity is an epidemic in America, how could you encourage Harry to do more physical activities rather than less active ones?

Photos: p. 262 (top), Silver Burdett Ginn; p. 262 (bottom), Silver Burdett Ginn; p. 263 (top), John Paul Endress/Modern Curriculum Press/Pearson Learning; p. 263 (bottom), Katelyn Metzger/Merrill

10

THE EARLY ELEMENTARY GRADES: 1–3
Preparation for Life

Developmentally Appropriate Practice

A. I understand children's developmental stages and growth from birth through age eight, and I use this knowledge to implement developmentally appropriate practice. I do all I can to advance the physical, intellectual, linguistic, social, and emotional development of the children in my care to their fullest potential.

B. I use my understanding of young children's characteristics and needs and of multiple interacting influences on children's development and learning to create environments that are healthy, respectful, supportive, and challenging for all children.[1]

C. I understand the importance of each content area in young children's learning. I know the essential concepts, inquiry tools, and structure of content areas including academic subjects and can identify resources to deepen their understanding.[2]

1. What are the unique physical, cognitive, language, and psychosocial characteristics of children in grades 1–3?

2. What are the political, social, and educational forces changing grades 1–3?

3. How is the curriculum in grades 1–3 structured?

4. How can I apply developmentally appropriate practice to my teaching of children in grades? 1–3?

In Chapters 7, 8, and 9, we discussed how the education of infants, toddlers, preschoolers, and kindergartners is changing. Change is also sweeping across grades 1–3. Teaching children ages six through nine is different today than a decade ago because of educational reform, which comes about as a result of changes in society. Some of these societal changes include:

- *Violence.* Violence in real life and in the media is a constant influence in the lives of children. The kind and level of violence from cartoons to adult-themed programming affects how this generation of children views the world and interacts with others. For example, heavy doses of violent episodes on television encourage children to respond to others in violent, rather than peaceable and socially acceptable, ways. Children become desensitized to violence and see violence as a way of problem solving. As a result, teachers, parents, and society seek ways to buffer children from violence and incorporate peaceful living and anti-bullying strategies into school curricula.

  Another example of violence involves reactions to the terrorist attacks of September 11, 2001, and the effects they have had on children. Children, adults, and all of American society are much more concerned about safety and how to live safely. Many schools and child care centers have made keeping children safe at school a top priority. This context of how to live safe lives changes how children view the world. This, in turn, influences how society and adults care for, protect, and educate children.

- *Obesity.* Today's children are getting heavier—almost one-third (31 percent) of young children are overweight![3] Reasons for this epidemic of childhood obesity are as follows: Children eat too much; they watch too much television; play and exercise too little; are bombarded by fast food adds that encourage them to eat too much of the wrong kinds of foods; and are in charge of their own diets at earlier ages.[4] In addition, children and families consume more convenience foods, which contain high amounts of sodium and calories. Combine this with fewer opportunities for eating together as a family and you have a recipe for poor nutrition. As a result, you will be asked to teach good nutritional habits, see that children play and exercise more, and be an advocate for healthy practices at home and school.

- *Technological developments.* Children are different today than a decade ago because of new and different kinds of technology.[5] Today"s generation is the dot.com or Net Generation. Children have grown up surrounded by technology and are familiar and comfortable with it. Children are much more comfortable writing their friends text messages than handwritten notes. Children's involvement with computer games enables them to think abstractly and to make rapid-fire decisions. Many children live in homes with access to the Internet. This connectivity enables children to have almost immediate access to vast amounts of information that enrich their lives and learning. Also, consider how the use of cell phones and text messaging change how children communicate. Here is what two third graders shared with each other about a school project through text messaging:

Student 1: do u want 2B partners 4 the project y/n?

Student 2: y.msg me L8tr on im

As a result of today's children being immersed in technology from the beginning of life, you need to find many opportunities for children to learn with technology. You need to provide children activities that enable them to access the Internet, use digital cameras to gather information and document learning, make and transport reports on the Internet, and engage in electronic creativity discussions and sharing of ideas.

- *Political changes.* What politicians and lawmakers believe is best for children and how to teach them changes with each election. Changes in politics in turn change how we teach children and what we teach them. For the past decade, politicians have placed a major emphasis on standards and academic achievement. The No Child Left Behind Education Act of 2001 has focused teaching and learning on meeting state standards in reading and math.

What we expect of children, however, may not be possible with the quality of the schools and materials we provide for them. Take a look at our Diversity Tie-In feature. It addresses issues and consequences of children from low socioeconomic homes, neighborhoods, and schools having fewer educational materials to learn from than children from higher socioeconomic backgrounds.

As a result of the previously listed changes, you and your colleagues must look at teaching in grades 1–3 differently from how you approach kindergartners. You will want to consider new and appropriate approaches for your teaching in these three important grades. We begin now our journey of rediscovering grades 1–3 with a look at what children (typically ages six, seven, eight, and nine) are like in these grades.

Read how schools can help fight childhood obesity at Articles and Readings, Child Development, Module 3: Physical Development, Article 2: Healthy and Ready to Learn.

CHILDREN IN PRIMARY GRADES: GROWTH AND DEVELOPMENT

All children share common developmental characteristics, yet each child is a unique individual. Although the common characteristics of children guide our general practice of teaching, we still must always account for the individual needs of children.

Physical Development

Two words describe the physical growth of primary age children: *slow* and *steady*. Children at this age experience continual growth, develop increasing control over their bodies, and explore the things they are able to do.

From ages six to nine, children's average weight and height approximate each other, as shown in Table 10.1. The weight of boys and girls tends to be the same until about age nine, when girls pull ahead of boys in both height and weight. Wide variations appear in both individual rates of growth and development and among the sizes of individual children.

The Rich Get Richer

INEQUALITY OF EDUCATIONAL RESOURCES

The title of this Diversity Tie-In may seem perplexing to you. After all, when we think about the rich getting richer, we think of money and other things associated with the rich and the famous. However, the same applies to schools and schooling. Think for a moment about some of the things that contribute to rich learning experiences and environments, such as the children and the teacher. Although they are important, there are other dimensions to rich learning environments that contribute to student achievement. For example, in addition to a high-quality teacher, children also need high-quality classroom environments with materials that support learning. To learn to read and write well, children need books and other materials that support the reading and writing processes. Unfortunately, these materials are not evenly distributed across all classrooms in the country. In fact, they are generally distributed by the socioeconomic status (SES) of the children who attend these classrooms.

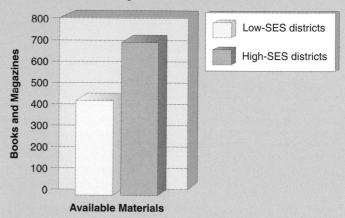

Books and Materials in the First-Grade Classroom Libraries of High- and Low-SES Children

Legend: Low-SES districts, High-SES districts. Y-axis: Books and Magazines (0–800). X-axis: Available Materials.

INEQUALITIES OF LEARNING MATERIALS

Let's look at the inequality of the distribution of classroom learning materials by SES status. We see that children from high-SES environments get more of the materials that support literacy than do their less-advantaged low-SES peers. So, in the very real world of learning to read and reading achievement, children who have adequate learning materials do indeed get richer in that they are able to learn to their fullest capacity. When researcher Nell Duke looked at classrooms of low-SES students, she found wide discrepancies between the classrooms of high-SES first graders and those of low-SES first graders. As our graph illustrates, children from high-SES schools had almost 50 percent more books and learning materials in their classroom libraries than did low-SES first graders. Additionally, Duke found that ". . . it was not simply that the high-SES classroom libraries contained and displayed more materials; there were more opportunities for students to use them."

MAKING CLASSROOMS MORE EQUAL

So, what does this mean for you as a classroom teacher? Here are four things you can do:

1. Make sure that you're using all of your classroom materials to their fullest. Using materials and allowing children to have access to them is an essential first step in making sure that children are getting a foundation for reading and literacy.
2. Read, read, and read to your children. Reading to children is one of the best ways to improve vocabulary, word knowledge, and meaning, and to promote interest in and enthusiasm for reading.
3. Work with families and the community to get the materials that you need. You can be an advocate for getting your children the materials that they need to learn how to read and write. Your advocacy will include conducting fund-raisers, seeking support from local businesses, and spreading the word that children need materials if they are to learn effectively and well.
4. Conduct family literacy programs for your parents. In these programs, you can help parents learn the importance of reading and literacy, and the vital role that books and other reading materials play in children's lives.

Source: Nell K. Duke, "For the Rich It's Richer," American Educational Research Journal, 37 (2), Summer 2000, 460.

Read and reflect on additional articles about low-SES classrooms at http://www.prenhall.com/morrison, Chapter 10—Journal: Diversity Tie-In.

These differences in physical appearance result from genetic and cultural factors, nutritional intake and habits, health care, and experiential background. Refer now to the "Portraits of Children" at the end of this chapter to compare and contrast the physical development of primary grade children.

TABLE 10.1 Average Height and Weight for Primary Age Children

Conduct your own survey of the height and weight of primary age children. Compare your findings with this table. What conclusions can you draw?

Age	Males		Females	
	Height (inches)	Weight (pounds)	Height (inches)	Weight (pounds)
6 years	45.25	45.5	45.25	44
7 years	48	50	47.75	50
8 years	50.5	56	50.25	56
9 years	52.25	62	52.5	64

Source: 2000 CDC growth charts: United States. *National Center for Health Statistics.* [Online.] Available at http://www.cdc.gov/growthcharts.

The primary years are also a time to use and test developing motor skills. Children's growing confidence and physical skills are reflected in games involving running, chasing, and kicking. A nearly universal characteristic of children in this period is their almost constant physical activity.

Differences between boys' and girls' motor skills during the primary years are minimal—their abilities are about equal. Teachers, therefore, should not use gender as a basis for limiting boys' or girls' involvement in activities. Children in the primary grades are also more proficient at school tasks that require fine-motor skills, such as writing, making artwork, and using computers. In addition, primary children want to and are able to engage in real-life activities. They want the "real thing." In many ways this makes teaching them easier and more fun, since many activities have real-life applications.

Katelyn Metzger / Merrill

Today there is a greater emphasis on children's cognitive development and activities that promote reading, math, and science. What are some things you can do to help children be successful in these areas?

Social Development

Children in grades 1–3 (ages six through nine) are in the Erikson's industry vs. inferiority stage of social-emotional development. This period, also known as **middle childhood**, is a time when children gain confidence in and ego satisfaction from completing demanding tasks. Children want to act responsibly and are quite capable of achieving demanding tasks and accomplishments. Children take a lot of pride in doing well. All of this reflects the industry side of social-emotional development.

Children during this stage are at varying levels of academic achievement. Those who are high in academic self-esteem credit their success to such **mastery-oriented attributions** as trying hard (industriousness), paying attention, determination, and stick-to-itiveness. If they have difficulty with a task, they belive that by trying harder they will succeed.

At the same time, children in this stage compare their abilities and accomplishments to their peers. When they perceive that they are not doing as well as they can or as well as their peers, they may lose confidence in their abilities and achievement. This is the inferiority side of this stage of social-emotional development. Some children attribute their failures to a lack of ability and develop **learned helplessness**. This is where you the teacher can be helpful and supportive of children, providing them with tasks they can accomplish and encouraging them to do their best.

Here are some things you can do to accomplish this goal:

- Provide activities children can reasonably accomplish so they can experience the satisfaction that comes from a job well done.
- Apply Gardner's theory of multiple intelligences to your teaching (see Chapter 3). Let children excel at things they are good at. All children develop skills and abilities in particular areas. Build a classroom environment that enables children to be competent in their particular intelligence.
- Be supportive and encouraging of children's efforts. For example, "Good job Carol! See what good work you can do when you really try!"

Emotional Development

Think for a moment about how important emotions are in your life and how emotions influence what and how you learn. When you are happy, life goes well! When you are sad, it is harder to get enthused about doing what you have to do. The children you teach are no different. Emotions are an important part of children's everyday lives. One of your responsibilities is to help them develop positive emotions and to express their emotions in healthy ways.

The following activities give you specific ideas for how to support the positive social-emotional development of children in the industry vs. inferiority stage of development:

1. *Use literature to discuss emotions.* Children in grades 1–3 like to talk about their emotions and the emotions of characters in literature. They are able to make emotional inferences about characters' emotional states and discuss how they are or are not appropriate to the story. They can then relate these emotional states to their own lives and to events at home and in the classroom. Some good books to use to discuss emotional states include these:
    - *How Are You Peeling? Foods with Moods* by Saxton Freymann and Joost Elffers offers brief text and photographs of carvings made from vegetables that introduce the world of emotions by presenting leading questions such as "Are you feeling angry?"
    - *Today I Feel Silly: And Other Moods That Make My Day* by Jamie Lee Curtis follows a little girl with curly red hair through thirteen different moods including silly, grumpy, mean, excited, and confused.
    - *When Sophie Gets Angry . . . Really, Really Angry* by Molly Bang conveys young Sophie's anger when her mother allows her younger sister to play with her stuffed gorilla, the eventual calm she feels after running outside and crying, and the calm and relaxed return home.
2. *Encourage children to express their emotions.* Beginning and ending the day with a classroom circle-time discussion is a good way to help children express their thoughts and feelings. This provides children a safe and secure outlet to say how they felt about their day.
3. *Write about feelings.* Give children opportunities to keep journals in which they can write about home, life, and classroom events and how they feel about them. One teacher has her children keep several journals, one that they share only with her and another journal that they share with their classmates if they choose.

    Figure 10.1 shows a journal entry seven-year-old Cindy wrote in reaction to her feelings about the main character in a book she read. Cindy will decide if she wants to share her thoughts about the book with her teacher and classmates. In this journal entry, pay

FIGURE 10.1 A Seven-Year-Old's Journal Entry

> I am just done with book. I really like this book that I chose and it was a good chose. She dose not go back to San Fransico and find her peo pals he stay io the Arctic. , I would be sared too and cold. Mya X has survied there. About done.

particular attention to several things. First, note Cindy's invented spelling, which enables her to be a writer and express her thoughts. She is well on her way to mastering the writing and reading processes. Second, note how sensitive she is to others. Cindy is developing the capacity for empathy—being able to identify with the feelings of others.

4. *Provide opportunities for play.* Play is a powerful outlet for releasing energy and expressing emotional states. Through fantasy and superhero play, children can express feelings and try out their growing range of emotions.

5. *Provide for cultural differences.* Be aware of how the various cultures represented by your children feel about emotional expression. Some cultures are very emotive, whereas others are not. Work with parents to learn how their cultures express certain emotions such as joy and sadness and what are not culturally acceptable ways to express emotions.

Play and Recess Support Children's Social and Emotional Development. Think for a minute how you feel when you have engaged in some kind of physical activity. Perhaps you feel good and in an upbeat mood. This physical activity has the same effects on children. It promotes their well-being, encourages a sense of contentment and happiness, and creates an atmosphere in which they are more inclined to engage in school and other activities.

Unfortunately, many of today's children do not have the opportunity to exercise as much as they need or sometimes want. Television viewing and passive activities such as computer games, which promote sedentary lifestyles, and a general de-emphasis of the value of physical activities all tend to undermine children's health. In response to increased demands for academics, school districts are decreasing the amount of time children have for physical activity and recess. The good news is that more schools that deleted recess from the school day are bringing it back. Currently 88 percent of elementary schools report offering recess once a day for their children. The average length of this recess time is 27.8 minutes per day. Also more schools are using more educational activities such as dance and nontraditional ones such as kickboxing to make physical education classes more enjoyable.[6] Some states such as Texas have mandated 30 minutes of physical activity a day.[7] Many parents whose school districts are not offering opportunities for physical activity are upset that their children don't have an opportunity to participate in recess and other physical activities. Some are taking proactive steps to restore recess to the school day. For example, parents at Rivers Edge Elementary in Richmond, Virginia, have banded together to launch a "rescuing recess" campaign. They are involving children in letter writing campaigns directed at school officials in which they explain the reasons for restoring recess.[8]

As an early childhood teacher, you will want to make sure that you provide time in your program for children to play indoors and outdoors, and to engage in group projects that enable children to be up out of their seats and active in the classroom.

Mental Health in Middle Childhood.   Just as we are concerned about the mental health of infants, toddlers, and preschoolers, so too are we very concerned about the mental health of children in the middle years. We are particularly concerned about **childhood depression**. As many as one in thirty-three children have depression.[9] Childhood depression manifests itself in the following ways:

- Persistent sadness;
- Withdrawal from family, friends, and activities that were once enjoyed;
- Increased irritability or agitation;
- Changes in eating and sleeping habits (e.g., significant weight loss, insomnia, excessive sleep);
- Frequent physical complaints, such as headaches and stomachaches;
- Lack of enthusiasm or motivation;
- Decreased energy level and chronic fatigue;
- Play that involves excessive aggression toward self or others or that involves persistently sad themes;
- Indecision, lack of concentration, or forgetfulness;
- Feelings of worthlessness or excessive guilt; and
- Recurring thoughts of death or suicide.[10]

Risk factors of childhood depression include:

- Chronic illness such as diabetes, anxiety disorders, or attention deficit hyperactivity disorder (ADHD);
- Parental depression or family history of depression;
- Neglect or abuse (physical, emotional, or sexual);
- General stressors including low socioeconomic status; and
- Loss of a loved one.[11]

Cognitive Development

Concrete operational thought is the cognitive milestone that enables children in the early elementary grades to think and act as they do. Logical operations, although more sophisticated than in preoperational children, still require concrete objects and referents in the here and now. Abstract reasoning comes later, in the formal operations stage during adolescence.

Children in the *concrete operations stage*, from about age seven to about age twelve, begin to use mental images and symbols during the thinking process and can reverse operations. For example, operations include many mathematical activities involving addition and subtraction, greater than and less than, multiplication, division, and equalities. A child is able to reverse operations when she can understand that when, for example, she adds two to three to get five, she can reverse this operation by subtracting two from five to get three. This is why it is a good idea for you to use concrete materials (e.g., rods, beads, buttons, blocks) to help children physically see operations as an aid for mental representation.

Concrete operational children begin to develop the ability to understand that change involving physical appearances does not necessarily change quality or quantity. They also begin to reverse thought processes by going back over and "undoing" a mental action just accomplished. Other mental operations children are capable of during this stage include:

- *One-to-one correspondence.* One-to-one correspondence is the basis for counting and matching objects. The concrete operations child has mastered the ability, for example, to give one cookie to each of her classmates and a pencil to each member of her work group.
- *Classification of objects, events, and time according to certain characteristics.* For example, a child in the concrete operations stage can classify events as occurring before or after lunch.
- *Classification involving multiple properties.* Multiple classification occurs when a child can classify objects on the basis of more than one property such as color and size, shape and size, shape and color, and so forth.
- *Class inclusion operations.* Class inclusion also involves classification. For example, if you showed a child who was in concrete operations five apples, five oranges, and five lemons, and asked him if there were more apples or fruit, he would be able to respond "fruit."

The concrete stage does not represent a period into which children suddenly emerge after having been preoperational. The process of development from stage to stage is gradual and continual and occurs over a period of time as a result of maturation and experiences. No simple sets of exercises will cause children to move up the developmental ladder. Rather, ongoing developmentally appropriate activities lead to conceptual understanding.

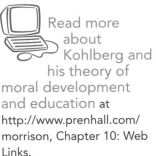 Read more about Kohlberg and his theory of moral development and education at http://www.prenhall.com/morrison, Chapter 10: Web Links.

Moral Development

Jean Piaget and Lawrence Kohlberg are the leading proponents of a developmental stage theory of children's moral growth. Table 10.2 outlines their stages of moral development during the primary years. Review these now and consider how you can apply the

TABLE 10.2 Moral Development in the Primary Years

Theorist	Moral Stage and Characteristics	Implications for Teachers
Jean Piaget	1. Relations of Constraint: Grades 1–2 Concepts of right and wrong determined by judgments of adults—morality is based on judgments of adults. 2. Relations of Cooperation: Grades 3–6 Exchange of viewpoints with others helps determine what is good/bad and right/wrong.	• Provide children with many opportunities to make moral decisions and judgments. • Look for opportunities every day in every classroom for moral decisions. Responsibility comes from opportunities to be responsible. • Provide many examples of moral values and decisions. This can occur through stories.
Lawrence Kohlberg	1. Preconventional Level: Ages 4–10 Morality is a matter of good or bad based on a system of punishment and rewards as administered by adults in authority positions. • Stage 1–Punishment and obedience: Children operate within and respond to physical consequences of behavior. • Stage 2–Instrumental-relativist orientation: Children's actions are motivated by satisfaction of needs (you scratch my back, I'll scratch yours).	• Use children's out-of-classroom experiences as a basis for discussion involving moral values. • Provide children many opportunities to interact with children of different ages and cultures.

implications to your teaching. Remember that children's moral and character development are important topics, especially after tragic events such as the terrorist attacks of September 11, 2001.

THE CONTEMPORARY ELEMENTARY SCHOOL

As we have discussed, reform is sweeping across the educational landscape. Schooling in the primary years has become a serious enterprise for political, social, and economic reasons. Educators, parents, and politicians realize it is better to prevent illiteracy, school dropout, and many social problems in the early childhood years than wait until middle and senior high school, when changing students is more difficult and expensive. Also, the public is not happy about continuing reports of declining educational achievement. So, demands for higher achievement and more rigorous teaching and learning begin in first grade and continue in grades two and three.

Here are some ways teaching and learning have changed in grades 1–3:

- **Diversity.** Schools and classrooms are more diverse than ever before. This diversity means you will be teaching children from many diverse cultures and backgrounds. It means you will have to take into account children's families' cultures in your planning and teaching. In addition to diversity of cultures, diversity is also reflected in socioeconomic status.

- **Achievement.** Achievement of all students is a high priority. Schools and teachers place a premium on closing the achievement gap that exists by race and socioeconomic status. High-quality teachers are dedicated to ensuring that all children learn.

- **Data-driven instruction.** Data-driven instruction is one instructional strategy teachers are using to ensure children achieve. The Program in Action feature introduces you to the topic and gives you six steps for how to implement it.

- **Testing.** Testing is a way of school life and is part of contemporary school culture. You will be involved in helping students learn appropriate grade-level content so that they can pass local, state, and national tests. In addition, test data is used as a basis for planning.

- **Standards.** The curriculum of the schools is aligned with local, state, and national standards. As a result, you will be teaching content designed to help students learn what the state standards specify. This may mean that you don't always get to teach exactly what you want to teach, when you want to teach it, or how you want to teach it. It is becoming more common for schools to develop and/or adapt curricula designed to help students learn to the state standards. However, good teachers always find ways to include in the curriculum what they believe is important and developmentally appropriate. They also teach it in their own relative ways. "Teaching to the standards" does not have to be dull and boring; you can make learning interesting and relevant to your students' lives.

- **Academics.** The contemporary grade 1–3 curriculum is heavy on reading, math, and science. In spite of this, there is also an emphasis on the arts, social studies, character education and developing health and wellness through physical education. Many of these curricular areas, however, are integrated with the basic curriculum.

- **Obesity prevention.** Physical education at all levels, pre-K–12, is undergoing a renaissance. A primary reason for the rejuvenation of PE, especially in the primary and elementary grades, is the concern about the national epidemic of childhood obesity and increases in childhood diabetes. Physical education classes and programs are viewed as a way of providing children with the knowledge and activities they need to get in shape and stay that way over their lifetimes. The American

How to Use Data-Driven Instruction

You don't have to go back to *Little House on the Prairie* to find a teaching style that is predicated on "getting through" the curriculum. Curriculum coverage is not the same as student learning. Recent accountability initiatives, including No Child Left Behind, have brought about a shift in focus from covering subject matter to meeting the needs of each student. There is only one way to determine whether or not the needs of the students are being met and that is through an ongoing analysis of data collected from assessing children.

BACKGROUND

Lead Mine Elementary School reflects the changing demographics taking place in America today. More than 43 per-

cent of our students are eligible for free or reduced lunches, and for many students, English is not their primary language. Yet despite these challenges, our test scores have shown steady growth over the years. Our teachers had to learn to teach smarter and to use technological resources as their ally.

WHAT IS DATA-DRIVEN INSTRUCTION?

Data-driven instruction is a system of teaching in which instructional decisions are based on the analysis of assessment data collected to determine how best to meet the needs of each individual student.

THE PROCESS OF IMPLEMENTING DATA-DRIVEN INSTRUCTION

STEP 1

START THE SCHOOL YEAR BY ANALYZING EXISTING DATA

Before your students arrive, examine their cumulative record files to get a general profile of each student. We conduct

a formal initial assessment process for incoming kindergartners before creating our kindergarten class lists.

STEP 2

ALIGN ASSESSMENTS TO OBJECTIVES

Plan collaboratively with your grade-level colleagues to determine when you will be teaching district and state standards and how you will assess each standard.

STEP 3

BEGIN THE DATA COLLECTION PROCESS

There are a number of ways to collect classroom data. You may use formal assessments such as written assignments, quizzes, and tests. You may use informal assessments such as observation and discussions. You may also use technology to help you collect data. A variety of instructional learning systems on the market now will allow you to track student progress with instructional software.

STEP 4

ANALYZE DATA

At the completion of the data collection process for a unit of study, you should sit down with your grade-level colleagues and look at the data for trends. Did the majority of the students reach the standard? Does the data reveal needs that have to be addressed?

STEP 5

USE DATA ANALYSIS TO DECIDE THE NEXT COURSE OF STUDY

After examining the data, use it to guide your next steps in the instructional process. Which students

Academy of Pediatrics recommends "Comprehensive, preferably daily, physical education for children in grades kindergarten through 12."[12]

Additionally, one of the Institute of Medicine's recommendations is that schools do all they can to "Ensure that all children and youth participate in a minimum of 30 minutes of moderate to vigorous physical activity during the school day, including expanded opportunities for physical activity through classes, sports programs, clubs, lessons, after-school and community use of school facilities, and walking and biking to-school program."[13]

are ready to move on? Which students need remediation? Which students need enrichment? In creating your plan to meet the needs of all students you may be involving resource teachers such as the academically gifted teacher, the ESL teacher, a special education teacher, the computer lab manager, or any other specialists in the school who could be employed to help meet the specific needs of each child. Students may also be assigned to appropriate software.

STEP 6

REPEAT THE PROCESS

Making data-based decisions to guide instruction is an ongoing process. Throughout the school year teachers are constantly assessing your students, analyzing their data, and readjusting the plans you have made to best meet their educational needs.

USING ASSESSMENTS PROPERLY

The two types of assessments used in the schools are *formative* and *summative*. Formative assessments are used to keep you apprised of students' progress. Running records, discussions, observations of the children at their centers, pretests, and journal entries are all ways to learn more about what and how the child is learning. Teachers use this information to diagnose the needs and strengths of the students before prescribing a plan of instruction for them.

Formative assessments are used to help you create flexible groups, alert you to the need for additional help, discover concepts that need to be retaught, or reveal students who need more enrichment. Formative assessments are there to support improvement in the teaching/learning process. They make up the meat of the discussions you will have about the effectiveness of the instruction.

Summative assessments assign a level or designation to a student. With the No Child Left Behind Act, every state now uses some sort of high-stakes, standardized test to show how students fared against a standard at the end of the year. These tests give some idea about how your students performed over an extended period of time as an indicator of the effectiveness of your instruction. Remember that these tests offer a view of how well your students performed over a couple of days on a select number of items that reflect a sampling of the curriculum standards. Your ongoing formative assessments will present a broader picture of the students' abilities.

HELP FROM TECHNOLOGY

Technology is used at Lead Mine to help with assessments. Software provides the teachers with data, instructional support, and an important means of differentiation. All of our kindergarten and first- and second-grade students come to the lab twice a week to take part in the program. After the initial placement, the children come to the lab to receive fifteen minutes of math and fifteen minutes of reading per session. Each child receives instruction at his or her own level, as determined by the computer placement assessment. This is a unique opportunity for students to receive completely individualized instruction. The lab manager prints out reports for the teachers, which become a part of the body of data used to make instructional decisions about students. The lessons on the computer are aligned with the North Carolina Standard Course of Study. The program also provides enrichment opportunities and lessons in Spanish.

Our district is dedicated to continuous improvement for all students. Making that happen requires that we follow a fairly simple formula for success: Pinpoint the needs of each child and then direct all of the resources available to meet those needs. It is virtually impossible to follow that plan without employing data-driven decision making.

....
Contributed by Gary W. Baird, principal, Lead Mine Elementary School, Raleigh, North Carolina. Photos by Gary W. Baird.

- ***Professional development.*** Teachers are involved in frequent and ongoing staff development designed to enhance skills, teach new methods, and ensure that teaching is aligned with standards. A large portion of your professional development will occur through staff development.
- ***Parent involvement.*** Parent and community involvement are highly valued and encouraged. As a result you will spend more time and effort promoting and supporting family/parent/community collaboration. We will discuss the specifics of parent/community involvement in Chapter 13.

Dr. Carlos J. Finlay Elementary is a dual-language professional development school that teaches prekindergarten through fifth grade and has an enrollment of over 650 students. It is located on the campus of Florida International University in Miami, Florida. "Transmitting Education Beyond Expectations" is the motto for every teacher. The strategic setting of our school allows for the Florida International University faculties and Finlay's faculty to collaborate together to facilitate high levels of learning, promote an exemplary school environment for preparing teachers, and stimulate academic, social, and emotional growth.

The bilingual design of the school offers every child enrolled the opportunity to simultaneously learn Spanish and English. Sixty percent of the day is taught in English and 40 percent taught in Spanish. The implementation of the dual program is an essential part of the adaptation process for many of the immigrant students enrolled in this school, in that it allows them to continue to succeed academically in their native language.

In addition, to assist our population with the assimilation process, we provide the parents with an outreach program called Families Learning at School and Home (FLASH). This program operates on the premises that linguistically and culturally diverse parents can be active partners in the educational process of their children when provided with training tailored to their specific needs. The program design consists of instruction to facilitate the acquisition of English language literacy skills, thus allowing a better understanding of the school system in the United States.

Dr. Carlos J. Finlay is a Title I school, based on the socioeconomic population that serves as our boundaries. More than 75 percent of our students receive free and reduced lunches.

Based on the relatively low-income bracket of the area surrounding the school, the students are in need of support to secure the basic resources that will enable them to actively be involved in their learning. These multi-family households are in need of financial assistance since many lack secure employment. Our parents are also faced with obstacles beyond the English language and employment, such as lack of literacy in their native language. To overcome these barriers, our teaching staff provides parents with workshops, FLASH, in-house tutoring for students, and an array of extracurricular activities. Many times the teachers offer workshops in order to reach some of the parents and establish a working relationship with the entire family. For example, many parents are not aware of how detrimental it is when students miss school days or are withdrawn from the school site early in the school day. The teachers stress with parents that they cannot provide all the help the children need unless they are in school. Many times, it takes several measures of intervention strategies (phone calls, home visits, and parent meetings) before any concrete results are noted. Luckily a large number of the teaching staff are second generation immigrants themselves, and have been educated in the United States. This allows them to be even more sensitive to the needs and concerns of the parents and students.

Contributed by Lourdes P. Gimenez, principal, Dr. Carlos J. Finlay Elementary, Miami, Florida.

Explore other dual-language early childhood programs at http://www.prenhall.com/morrison, Chapter 10—Journal: Program in Action.

- *Collaboration.* Teamwork and collaboration are hallmarks of the culture of many schools. Administrators and faculty understand it takes teamwork to accomplish educational goals. Children with special learning needs rely on a team of professionals to help them succeed such as a psychologist, physical therapist, speech therapist, and an occupational therapist. Also, to be an effective teacher, you should seek out more knowledgeable teachers to help you and vice versa.

By now you are learning that the modern elementary school of today is not the same as it was when you attended. The Program in Action box describes how the changing population demands changed elementary schools. As more children of diverse cultures and linguistic backgrounds come to school, schools and teachers have to develop programs that meet their needs: academically, socially, and behaviorally.

Pro-Social and Conflict Resolution Education

All early childhood professionals, parents, and politicians believe that efforts to reduce incidents of violence and uncivil behavior begin in preschool, kindergarten, and grades 1–3.

Consequently, they place emphasis on teaching children the fundamentals of peaceful living, kindness, helpfulness, and cooperation. You can follow these suggestions below to foster the development of pro-social skills in your classroom:

- Be a good role model for children. Demonstrate in your life and relationships with children and other adults the behaviors of cooperation and kindness that you want to encourage in children. Civil behavior begins with courtesy and manners. You can model these and help children do the same.

- Provide positive feedback and reinforcement when children perform pro-social behaviors. When rewarded for appropriate behavior, children tend to repeat the behavior. ("I like how you helped him. I'll bet that made him feel better.")

- Provide opportunities for children to help and show kindness to others. Cooperative programs between primary children and nursing and retirement homes are excellent opportunities to practice kind and helping behaviors.

- Conduct conflict-free classroom routines and activities. Provide opportunities for children to work together and practice skills for cooperative living. Design learning centers and activities for children to share and work cooperatively.

- Provide practice in conflict resolution skills. Skills include taking turns, talking through problems, compromising, and apologizing. A word of caution regarding apologies: too often, an apology is a perfunctory response on the part of teachers and children. Rather than just saying the often-empty words "I'm sorry," it is far more meaningful to help one child understand how another is feeling. Encouraging empathic behavior in children is a key to developing pro-social behavior.

- Infuse anti-bias principles into classroom activities. Respect diversity, be aware of tendencies in yourself and students to stereotype and be vocal about it and correct sexist behaviors.

- Read stories to children that exemplify pro-social behaviors and provide such literature for them to read.

- Counsel and work with parents to encourage them to limit or eliminate altogether their children watching violence on television, attending R-rated movies, playing video games with violent content, and buying CDs with objectionable lyrics.

- Catch them while they're "good." To help children feel good about themselves, build strong self-images, and be competent individuals, notice when they are behaving pro-socially and tell them that you are pleased with their actions. Children who are happy, confident, and competent feel good about themselves and are more likely to behave positively toward others.

Mary Kate Denny/PhotoEdit Inc.

Children not only have to learn how to count, but they need to know what counts. Helping children develop positive character traits is now a standard part of the curricula of many early childhood programs. What are some character traits that you believe should be taught to young children?

Character Education

Character education is closely aligned with pro-social and conflict resolution education. Character education is rapidly becoming a part of many early childhood programs. The three Rs have been expanded to six: reading, writing, arithmetic, reasoning, respect, and responsibility. Respect and responsibility are now part of the primary curriculum for a number of reasons. Although everyone believes children have to learn how to count, the public and educators also believe that schools have to teach children what counts. Character education is now a high priority for all early childhood educators. Character education activities designed to teach specific character traits are now commonplace in the curriculum of the primary grades.

Whereas educators may argue over what character traits to teach, there is no longer a debate over whether they should be taught. Some common characteristics being taught in the schools are:

Review online resources and standards for character education at http://www.prenhall.com/morrison, Chapter 10: Web Links.

- Responsibility
- Cooperation
- Respect for others
- Compassion
- Self-discipline

- Selflessness (friendship)
- Tolerance
- Courage
- Friendship
- Optimism

- Honesty
- Perseverance
- Future-mindedness
- Purposefulness.

Teaching Thinking

As stated previously, reasoning has been added as one of the six Rs of early childhood programs. Educators believe that if students can think, they can meaningfully engage in subject matter curriculum and the rigors and demands of the workplace and life. As a result, many teachers are including the teaching of thinking in their daily lesson plans.

Figure 10.2 shows examples of questions you can use to promote thinking. They are based on Benjamin Bloom's hierarchy of questioning levels. A major teaching objective is to ask students questions from top to bottom of the hierarchy. Your questions not only challenge children to think, they also promote linguistic, social, and behavioral skills. For example, recall of knowledge is the lowest level of thinking and evaluation is the highest. In addition, instead of asking children to recall information, teachers ask them to think critically about information, solve problems, and reflect. To promote thinking in your classroom follow these guidelines:

- Give children the freedom and security to be creative thinkers.
- Encourage children to search for other answers and alternative solutions rather than settling for one "right" answer. Ask open-ended questions ("why do you think that?") rather than questions that require a "yes" or "no" response.
- Create classroom cultures in which children have the time, opportunity, and materials with which to be creative.
- Integrate thinking into the total curriculum so that children learn to think during the entire school day.

In the accompanying Professionalism in Practice box, Millie Harris shares her experiences using cognitively appropriate teaching practices.

ENVIRONMENTS THAT SUPPORT LEARNING

As we have discussed, the environment plays a major role in children's learning and success and is also a major determinant of what and how well children learn. Figure 10.3 shows some of the critical features of an effective primary classroom designed to help children learn in today's demanding educational environment. Classrooms not only support children's learning, but they also help ensure that all children learn to their full capacities. Part of your role is to use these features to help you provide the best learning environment possible for all children. How might you do that in grades 1–3?

Six Levels in the Cognitive Domain   **Examples of Questions to Ask Children**

Evaluation

- Compare and discriminate between ideas
- Make judgments about
- Give arguments/reasons for an opinion
- Verify that evidence is/is not correct
- Judge which is better

- Which of these pictures is your favorite? Why?
- How would you deal with the situation?
- Mario, is there a better way to arrange your display?

Synthesis

- Invent a new way of doing something
- Generalize from given facts
- Relate knowledge from several areas
- Explain reasons for . . .

- What do you think will happen if we mix red and yellow together?
- Caleb, how would you solve the girl's problem we just read about in our story?
- What are three things you can do with a paper clip?

Analysis

- See patterns—compare and contrast
- Organize parts into a whole
- Investigate and find out why
- Identify components

- Why did the girl change her mind about what she was going to do?
- How are the two boys we read about similar and different?
- Jessica, can you explain what we have to do to make this better?

Application

- Classify information and apply to new situations
- Use methods concepts, theories in new situation
- Solve problems using required skills or knowledge

- How would you organize these pictures to show your parents which one you like best and which one you like least?
- Matthew, if you could change one thing in our classroom, what would it be?
- What questions will we ask the firefighter when she visits our classroom?

Comprehension

- Explanation of information
- Discuss events
- Translate knowledge into new context
- Interpret facts, compare contrast
- Describe events

- Maria, what do you think happens next in our story?
- Can you tell me what this word means?
- How is the main character in our story like the main character in the story we read yesterday?
- Whitney, can you write a description of what happened?

Knowledge

- Observe and recall information
- Recall dates, events, and places
- Explain events and processes
- Name facts

- How would you describe the color of the monkey in the story we just read?
- Can you name the three characters in our story?
- Hector, how many days have you been in school?
- Which of the following is true or false?

FIGURE 10.2 Applying Bloom's Taxonomy to Early Childhood Classrooms

Source: Based on the Counseling Services of University of Victoria website, http://www.coun.uvic.ca/learn/program/hndouts/bloom.html. From Bloom, B. S. (Ed.), 1956 *Taxonomy of Educational Objectives: The Classification of Education Goals, Handbook I. Cognitive Domain.* New York; Toronto: Longmans, Green.

Igniting a Variety of Sparks Through Brain-Compatible Learning

Millie Harris
*2001 Department of Defense Education Activity
Teacher of the Year
Stowers Elementary School
Fort Benning, Georgia*

During my twenty years of teaching the culturally diverse students of our nation's soldiers, I have found that children are more alike than they are different. Military schools are truly a colorless society, demonstrating that whether students are Hispanic, Asian, Native American, Caucasian, or African American, they are capable of outstanding achievement when expectations are high and instruction is effective. These students are poorer and more racially diverse than the nation's average. At least half qualify for free or reduced lunches. Two in five are either Hispanic or black, a full 10 percent above the national average. Forty percent finish the school year in a different school than where they started. Although standardized tests are not typically administered to these early childhood students, data that is available on fourth grade and above indicate that they achieve at rates far beyond those of the civilian world. Eighty percent of these students attend college, as compared to 67 percent nationwide.

The outstanding success the military has had in teaching poor, racially diverse, transient students can be attributed to several factors. Effective discipline is maintained through open communication with parents. Parents are actively involved. Technology is integrated into the curriculum. Teachers are provided ongoing training in research-based best teaching practices. Specialists and classroom teachers are also encouraged to engage in regular co-teaching and consultation, creating a community of teacher learners who work together studying, practicing, and refining best teaching practices, particularly brain-compatible learning.

As a specialist in talented and gifted education, one of the most valuable experiences I have had in sharing and learning is co-teaching with regular education teachers. I have extended the critical and creative thinking methods of gifted education into the general curriculum, while learning about effective practices from classroom teachers. Co-teaching is a powerful tool in alleviating the sense of isolation that many teachers feel. It also creates a "win–win" learning environment.

One of the most profound of these win-win experiences was one I had co-teaching with Barbara Culwell, who teaches first- and second-grade students at Stowers Elementary of the Fort Benning Schools. Mrs. Culwell is a strong proponent of brain-compatible learning, holding teacher training and leading study groups. She served as my mentor in my exploration of teaching children to learn effectively through the extensive neuro-research of the past ten years. I found that whatever children's cultural backgrounds may be, a universal truth is that their brains are wired in essentially the same way.

Classrooms like Mrs. Culwell's that incorporate brain-compatible learning are a far cry from many of the past, when the teacher served as the "drill and kill" dispenser of knowledge. She creates a safe learning environment in which risk taking and original ideas are valued. Her instruction technique includes skillful questioning that elicits higher order thinking. She incorporates varied learning styles and multiple intelligences into her instruction. Mrs. Culwell accommodates the physical needs of students, including water, snacks, and movement, to ensure that optimal learning occurs.

A VISIT TO THE CLASSROOM

I walk into Barbara Culwell's classroom first thing Monday. The children are working together in groups or in pairs. They seem to know what to do before the teacher gives directions. They are actively going about the business of learning.

Observe how to effectively create a supportive classroom environment at Video Classroom, Classroom Management, Module 1: Organizing Your Classroom and Supplies, Video 1: Arranging Furniture and Materials.

The Physical Environment

The following conditions support learning in the primary classroom:

- Materials are in abundant supply for reading, writing, language development, and content area development (e.g., books about math, science, social studies, and the arts).
- Learning centers reflect content areas.
- Children are seated in chairs at tables or in clusters of desks for roughly three to six children.
- Literature of all genres supports content area learning centers, and materials provide for and emulate real work experiences (i.e., the waiting room, the restaurant).

A variety of choices, crucial to brain-based learning, are available for all the students who are arriving at different times during the thirty-minute span before the school day officially begins at 8:30. Children are engrossed in different academic computer programs, including "How to Speak Chinese," since the class is involved in a study of the Chinese New Year. Others are busy reading their favorite books and playing thinking board games. Not a mind is idle.

A parent volunteer works at one computer rotating students, testing them on books they had read during the past week. The presence of family members is crucial to classroom management and makes a distinct neural connection, bridging the importance of school and home. It is no secret that parental involvement and school success are positively correlated.

Weekly homework folders are placed on each child's desk. Every day's assignments are neatly typed for students and parents. The few needed worksheets are enclosed in the pocket folder. The children take these home on Monday and return them on Friday. Expectations are clear to every child and parent. Students develop their intrapersonal intelligence, assessing their own academic growth.

After all the students arrive, Mrs. Culwell instructs them, "Fill up your water bottles." Dehydration is a problem that is connected to weak learning. Since the brain is made up of a higher percentage of water than any other organ, a lack of it causes a loss of attention and increased sluggishness.

The old adage "To teach it is to learn it" is alive and well in this classroom. Students volunteer to teach others vocabulary words integrating the technology of the InFocus, which projects a computer screen onto the chalkboard, with their spelling lesson. Mrs. Culwell teaches word processing skills through questioning, "How can we make our font really big? How can we change it?" First graders are becoming adept at technology and increasing their vocabularies simultaneously.

Children practice metacognitive skills through making their own rubrics for their writing assignment with the vocabulary words. They agree a smiling face at the end means that they understood what each word means; that they wrote at least three good sentences, using words correctly in these sentences; and that they started each sentence with a capital letter and ended it with a period. A straight face means that they think they did well, but not perfectly. A frowning face means that they did not try or did not do well.

Mrs. Culwell instructs, "Get your thoughts clear and think of the night sky." As the youngsters begin their writing activity, soft classical Chinese music (Chinese New Year theme) plays in the background. Victoria writes, "I went outside one night. A star blazed across the sky. It was lovely. So now I know how pretty stars can be. I like stars." Use of music is priming the neural pathways so that learning is occurring, as seen in this student's exemplary writing.

After a three-minute stand-up, move-about break and a snack, Mrs. Culwell transforms the spelling, vocabulary, writing lesson into a science lesson about tips for watching the night sky, growing further dendrites for neuron connections. These youngsters are skilled at identifying numerous constellations such as Orion, Taurus, and Leo.

Later, the children practice symmetry, measurement, and following directions by making Chinese lanterns. They use manipulatives to discover the solution to the math problem of the day, displaying their problems on their own PowerPoint slides, and writing journals as to how they arrived at their answers.

At lunchtime I reflect back on a morning well spent in meaningful learning. I witnessed man-made boundaries of race, culture, and economics being broken through nature's common medium—the human brain and a teacher who cares enough to shatter old myths.

....

Millie Harris is a specialist in talented and gifted education in Fort Benning, Georgia.

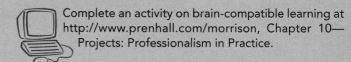

Complete an activity on brain-compatible learning at http://www.prenhall.com/morrison, Chapter 10—Projects: Professionalism in Practice.

- Materials and instruction provide for interdisciplinary integrated approaches.
- Program, learning, and environment are coordinated so that materials support and align with outcomes and standards.
- Teacher instruction (teacher-directed instruction and intentional teaching) and active student involvement are balanced.
- Centers support literacy. All centers have materials that support reading and writing.
- Children's products are displayed and valued.
- Schedules are posted where children can read them.
- Technology supports and enriches basic skill and concept learning. Children use technology to make presentations, projects, and reports.

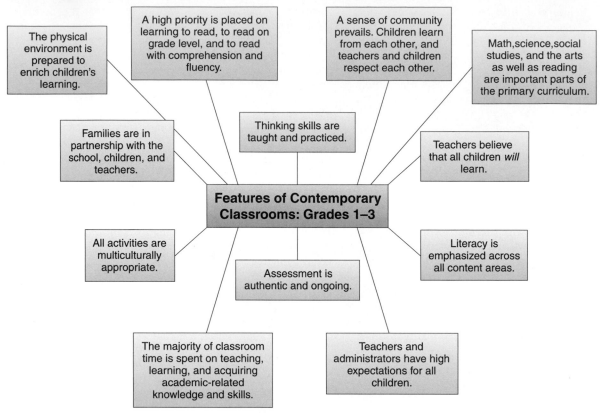

The physical environment is prepared to enrich children's learning.

A high priority is placed on learning to read, to read on grade level, and to read with comprehension and fluency.

A sense of community prevails. Children learn from each other, and teachers and children respect each other.

Math, science, social studies, and the arts as well as reading are important parts of the primary curriculum.

Families are in partnership with the school, children, and teachers.

Thinking skills are taught and practiced.

Features of Contemporary Classrooms: Grades 1–3

Teachers believe that all children *will* learn.

All activities are multiculturally appropriate.

Assessment is authentic and ongoing.

Literacy is emphasized across all content areas.

The majority of classroom time is spent on teaching, learning, and acquiring academic-related knowledge and skills.

Teachers and administrators have high expectations for all children.

FIGURE 10.3 Features of Contemporary Classrooms: Grades 1–3

Observe a teacher explaining how she executed a literacy lesson plan at Video Classroom, Classroom Management, Module 3: Planning and Conducting Instruction, Video 1: Celebrating Learning.

Review an example of a second-grade floor plan in Figure 10.4. As you examine the floor plan in Figure 10.4, here are some things to think about. Notice the tables and chairs for four children. This arrangement is designed to encourage and support group work and interaction. The desks can be combined to allow larger groups of children to work together and can be moved to different areas of the room to provide for quiet activities. The small-group learning center is designed to enable the teacher to work with a group of children or individually with a child to teach specific knowledge and skills. Notice also how the book cases are arranged in the reading center to provide a quiet and relaxing environment for pleasurable reading.

The Social Environment

The following conditions support an enriching emotional and social environment:

- Families, other adults, and the community are connected to classroom learning.
- Children are valued and respected. The classroom is a community of learners.
- Children live and learn in peace and harmony.
- High expectations for all are an essential part of the classroom culture.
- Assessment is continuous and appropriate and is designed to support teaching and learning.
- Thinking is considered a basic skill and is integrated through all areas of the curriculum.

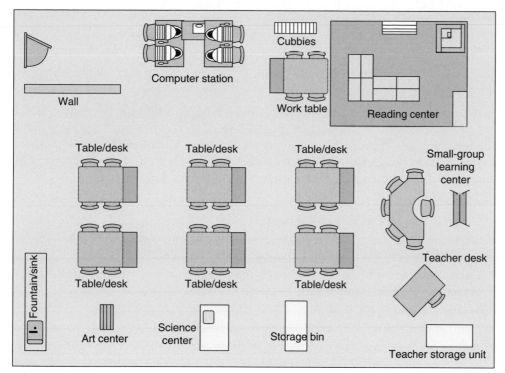

FIGURE 10.4 Second-Grade Floor Plan for an Enriched Environment

View photos of a third-grade classroom at http://www.prenhall.com/morrison, Chapter 10: Web Links.

CURRICULUM IN THE PRIMARY GRADES

Literacy and Reading in the Primary Grades

Just like preschool and kindergarten programs, today's primary grades emphasize literacy development and reading. In fact, this emphasis is apparent in all the elementary grades, from pre-K to six. Parents and society want children who can speak, write, and read well. As discussed in Chapter 9 and as a result of No Child Left Behind, more teachers are adopting a balanced approach. They integrate many different activities into a complete system of literacy development:

- Using the fundamentals of letter–sound correspondence, word study, and decoding, as well as, holistic experiences, in reading, writing, speaking, and listening;

- Incorporating many reading approaches, such as shared reading (see Chapter 9), guided reading (discussed next), independent reading, and modeled reading (reading out loud);

- Using many forms of writing, such as shared writing, guided writing, and independent writing;

- Integrating literacy across the curriculum; for example, having students write in journals or composition books about their experiences and investigations in math and science;

- Integrating literacy across cultures, that is, using literacy to communicate with and about people in other cultures;

- Using children's written documents as reading material, as well as literature books, vocabulary-controlled and sentence-controlled stories, and those containing predictable language patterns; choosing the best children's literature available to read to and with children;

- Organizing literacy instruction around themes or units of study relevant to students; and
- Having children create stories, write letters, keep personal journals, and share their written documents with others.

Connections with others, especially families, are important in making literacy meaningful for children.

Guided Reading. Guided reading is designed to help children develop and use strategies of independent reading. During guided reading, children read texts that are at their developmentally appropriate reading level and have a minimum of new things to learn. The children read in small groups (usually five to eight) with their teacher. The following guidelines should help you learn to use guided reading:

1. *Introduce the book.*
   - Give each student a copy of the book.
   - Show the book cover. Read the title and discuss information on the cover. Ask students to *predict* what is going to happen in the text. Record their predictions.
   - Conduct a picture walk. Turn through the pages, and note the pictures, illustrations, and graphics. Do not give away the ending.
2. *Read and respond to the book.*
   - Direct students to read the book silently to see whether their predictions are accurate.
   - At the very beginning stages of reading, students may read aloud softly to themselves.
   - As the children read, observe their behaviors. Are some having difficulty with certain words or types of words? Are some tracking with their fingers while others are not?
   - Are children applying the decoding skills they have been taught? You can check this when you provide opportunities for them to read sections orally.
   - Look for one or two things you might help the children with. For example, if several children seem to have trouble with the word *day,* print it on the board and help them sequentially decode or read through the word by identifying each sound in order if they have the skills.
   - After they have read the book, discuss what students predicted and what actually happened in the text.
   - Teach any decoding or comprehension skill or strategy needed.
3. *Extend the book.*
   - Have children reread the book alone or with a partner.
   - Children may also choose to act out or role-play the story with partners.[14]

Math in the Primary Grades

Mathematics is being reemphasized as an essential part of primary education. Just as reading is receiving a great deal of national attention, so too is mathematics.

The term *new math* is not new. It has been around since the 1960s. What differentiates the "old" math from the "new"? Memorization and drill characterize the old or traditional math. The new math, sometimes referred to as the "new-new math," emphasizes hands-on activities, problem solving, group work and teamwork, application and use of mathematical ideas and principles to real-life events, daily use of mathematics, and an understanding of and use of math understandings and competencies. The new math seeks to have students be creative users of math in life and workplace settings but also includes the ability to recall addition sums and multiplication products quickly.

The ten standards of the National Council of Teachers of Mathematics (NCTM) identify these understandings and competencies as number and operations, algebra, geometry, measurement, data analysis and probability, problem solving, reasoning and proof, communication, connection, and representation. The following sample standard from the NCTM will help you understand the standard of algebra and how it is applied to the primary grades:

In prekindergarten through grade 2 all students should:

- Sort, classify, and order objects by size, number, and other properties;
- Recognize, describe, and extend patterns such as sequences of sounds and shapes or simple numeric patterns and translate from one representation to another;
- Analyze how both repeating and growing patterns are generated.[15]

Your teaching of math in the primary grades will also most likely be in alignment with the NCTM's new Curriculum Focal Points, which outline important mathematical topics for each grade level. For example, the Curriculum Focal Points and children's connections to them for grade two are as follows:

1. *Numbers and Operations:* Developing an understanding of the base-ten numeration system and place-value concepts.
   - Children develop an understanding of the base-ten numeration system and place-value concepts (at least to 1000). Their understanding of base-ten numeration includes ideas of counting in units and multiples of hundreds, tens, and ones, as well as a grasp of number relationships, which they demonstrate in a variety of ways, including comparing and ordering numbers. They understand multi-digit numbers in terms of place value, recognizing that place-value notation is shorthand for the sums of multiples of powers of 10 (e.g., 853 as 8 hundreds + 5 tens + 3 ones).
   - Children use place value and properties of operations to create equivalent representations of given numbers (such as 35 represented by 35 ones, 3 tens and 5 ones, or 2 tens and 15 ones) and to write, compare, and order multi-digit numbers. They use these ideas to compose and decompose multi-digit numbers. Children add and subtract to solve a variety of problems, including applications involving measurement, geometry, and data, as well as non-routine problems. In preparation for grade 3, they solve problems involving multiplicative situations, developing initial understandings of multiplication as repeated addition.

2. *Number and Operations* and *Algebra:* Developing quick recall of addition facts and related subtraction facts and fluency with multi-digit addition and subtraction.
   - Children use their understanding of addition to develop quick recall of basic addition facts and related subtraction facts. They solve arithmetic problems by applying their understanding of models of addition and subtraction (such as combining or separating sets or using number lines), relationships and properties of number (such as place value), and properties of addition (commutativity and associativity). Children develop, discuss, and use efficient, accurate, and generalizable methods to add and subtract multi-digit whole numbers. They select and apply appropriate methods to estimate sums and differences or calculate them mentally, depending on the context and numbers involved. They develop fluency with efficient procedures, including standard algorithms, for adding and subtracting whole numbers, understand why the procedures work (on the basis of place value and properties of operations), and use them to solve problems.
   - Children use number patterns to extend their knowledge of properties of numbers and operations. For example, when skip counting, they build foundations for understanding multiples and factors.

3. *Measurement:* Developing an understanding of linear measurement and facility in measuring lengths.

- Children develop an understanding of the meaning and processes of measurement, including such underlying concepts as partitioning (the mental activity of slicing the length of an object into equal-sized units) and transitivity (e.g., if object A is longer than object B and object B is longer than object C, then object A is longer than object C). They understand linear measure as an iteration of units and use rulers and other measurement tools with that understanding. They understand the need for equal-length units, the use of standard units of measure (centimeter and inch), and the inverse relationship between the size of a unit and the number of units used in a particular measurement (i.e., children recognize that the smaller the unit, the more iterations they need to cover a given length).

- Children estimate, measure, and compute lengths as they solve problems involving data, space, and movement through space. By composing and decomposing two-dimensional shapes (intentionally substituting arrangements of smaller shapes for larger shapes or substituting larger shapes for many smaller shapes), they use geometric knowledge and spatial reasoning to develop foundations for understanding area, fractions, and proportions.[16]

Science in the Primary Grades

When teaching science in the primary grades, you must be aware of the National Science Content Standards put forth by the Center for Science, Mathematics, and Engineering, and take strides to follow these standards in your teaching of science in the primary grade classroom. Review these standards now in Figure 10.5.

FIGURE 10.5

Science Content Standards for Grades K–4

Unifying Concepts and Processes	Science As Inquiry	Physical Science	Life Science
• Systems, order, and organization • Evidence, models, and explanation • Change, constancy, and measurement • Evolution and equilibrium • Form and function	• Abilities necessary to do scientific inquiry • Understandings about scientific inquiry	• Properties of objects and materials • Position and motion of objects • Light, heat, electricity, and magnetism	• Characteristics of organisms • Life cycles of organisms • Organisms and environments
Earth and Space Science	**Science and Technology**	**Science in Personal and Social Perspectives**	**History and Nature of Science**
• Properties of earth materials • Objects in the sky • Changes in earth and sky	• Abilities of technological design • Understandings about science and technology • Abilities to distinguish between natural objects and objects made by humans	• Personal health • Characteristics and changes in populations • Types of resources • Changes in environments • Science and technology in local changes	• Science as a human endeavor

Source: National Science Education Standards (1996), Center for Science, Mathematics, and Engineering Education. Reprinted with permission from the National Academies Press. Copyright 2000 National Academy of Science.

FIGURE 10.6

Essential Features of an Inquiry-Based Classroom and Their Variations

Essential Feature	Variations			
1. Learner engages in scientifically oriented questions.	Learner poses a question.	Learner selects among questions, poses new questions.	Learner sharpens or clarifies question provided by teacher, materials, or other source.	Learner engages in question provided by teacher, materials, or other source.
2. Learner gives priority to **evidence** in responding to questions.	Learner determines what constitutes evidence and collects it.	Learner directed to collect certain data.	Learner given data and asked to analyze.	Learner given data and told how to analyze.
3. Learner formulates **explanations** from evidence.	Learner formulates explanation after summarizing evidence.	Learner guided in process of formulating explanations from evidence.	Learner given possible ways to use evidence to formulate explanation.	Learner provided with evidence and how to use evidence to formulate explanation.
4. Learner connects explanations to scientific knowledge.	Learner independently examines other resources and forms the links to explanations.	Learner directed toward areas and sources of scientific knowledge.	Learner given possible connections.	
5. Learner communicates and justifies explanations.	Learner forms reasonable and logical argument to communicate explanations.	Learner coached in development of communication.	Learner provided broad guidelines to use to sharpen communication.	Learner given steps and procedures for communication.

Source: National Academy Press, "Inquiry and the National Science Education Standards: A Guide for Teaching and Learning," p. 13, 2000, http://newton.nap.edu/html/inquiry_addendum/ch2.html.

Today's science teaching is *inquiry based;* that is, it is all about helping children solve problems. **Inquiry learning** is involvement of children in activities and processes that lead to learning. The process of inquiry involves:

- Posing questions,
- Observing,
- Reading and researching for a purpose,
- Proposing solutions and making predictions, and
- Gathering information and interpreting it.

What does an inquiry-based classroom look like? Figure 10.6 provides you with the essential features of an inquiry-based classroom. Such a classroom focuses on student constructed learning, and is important for science concept development. Use the features in this figure as ideas for implementing inquiry-based learning in your own classroom.

Social Studies in the Primary Grades

Social studies are the integrated study of the social sciences and humanities to promote civic competence. Within the school program, social studies provide coordinated, systematic study drawing on such disciplines as anthropology, archaeology, economics, geography, history, law, philosophy, political science, psychology, religion, and sociology, as

technology tie-in

Although the use of computers by children ages five to seventeen is widespread, there are many "divides" that separate children and their use of and access to technology. Review the data in the figure to the right.

Notice these "divides":

- Different races differ in technology use; for example, only 37 percent of Hispanics have access to the Internet.
- Having a disability means you are less likely to use a computer or have access to the Internet than someone who doesn't have a disability.
- As potential educational attainment increases, so too does children's computer use and Internet access.
- Children in single-parent households are less likely to use computers or have Internet access.
- As family income increases, so does computer use and Internet access.

Here are some things you can do to help close or eliminate these digital divides:

- Work with your school district to find ways for parents to use computers and the Internet at your school.
- Collaborate with the PTA and community agencies to secure funding or partial funding to provide families with computers. Also, investigate the opportunities for collaboration with local libraries.
- Provide your students with high-quality experiences with computers and the Internet. Schools and classrooms can compensate for the lack of home opportunities.
- Be a strong advocate for closing digital divides. You and your professional colleagues must tell the public that the digital divides are not acceptable. Equity of access to computers and the Internet for all families and children should be a goal for all early childhood professionals.

Characteristics	Percent Using Computers	Percent Using the Internet
Child Characteristics		
Age		
5–7	80.5	31.4
8–10	90.5	53.5
Sex		
Female	90.0	58.6
Male	89.1	58.3
Race/Ethnicity		
White	93.4	66.7
Black	85.0	45.3
Hispanic	78.7	37.2
Asian	89.7	64.6
American Indian	89.8	53.5
Disability Status		
Has a disability	80.0	48.9
Does not have a disability	89.8	59.4
Family and Household Characteristics		
Parent educational attainment		
Less than high school credential	75.6	31.6
High school credential	87.2	50.2
Some college	92.0	63.2
Bachelor's degree	94.2	69.3
Graduate education	96.4	74.4
Family/household type		
Two-parent household	91.3	62.2
Male householder	86.9	54.3
Female householder	85.5	48.8
Other arrangement	75.2	48.8
Family income		
Under $20,000	80.1	36.5
$20,000–$34,999	86.3	48.8
$35,000–$49,999	82.0	62.8
$50,000–$74,999	93.6	67.1
$75,000 or more	96.2	75.4

Source: K. M. Culp, M. Honey, and E. Mandinach, "A Retrospective on Twenty Years of Education Technology Policy," Education Development Center—Center for Children and Technology, 2003. [Online.] Available at http://www.ed.gov/rschstat/eval/tech/20years.pdf.

Reflect on the appropriate and equitable use of technology in the early childhood classroom at http://www.prenhall.com/morrison, Chapter 10—Journal: Technology Tie-In.

well as appropriate content from the humanities, mathematics, and natural sciences. The primary purpose of social studies is to help young people develop the ability to make informed and reasoned decisions for the public good as citizens of a culturally diverse, democratic society in an interdependent world.[17]

Arts in the Primary Grades

In the primary grades, the creative arts most often included in the curriculum are music, theater, dance, and art. For each of these disciplines you will want to include knowledge, concepts, and themes. Your teaching of the arts should be content based and child centered, and you will want to make sure that you consult your state's content standards for the arts.

Ideas for Teaching Creative Arts.   Today's teaching of the arts is designed to provide children with content knowledge and skills from the four disciplines listed in the preceding paragraph. So, in your teaching of the arts you will want to make sure that children are provided with authentic content and are engaged in activities that help them learn and apply knowledge of the arts. The following is an idea that you can use to help you teach your students about music and dance:

- **Dancing to Music.** Ms. Dwyer encourages her students to appreciate, and examine different styles of music as well as create dance presentations that are specifically related to the music. She plays music and asks her students to listen to it carefully, think about what it is about and how it makes them feel. She plays the music again and asks her students to move to the music. If the music is fast, she encourages them to move fast. At the same time, she asks her students to show her how the music makes them feel, happy, sad, and so forth.[18]

Making sure all students have access to technology is another important factor when planning curricula that promote learning and motivation. The technology tie-in feature shows the differences children face in their access to technology.

PORTRAITS OF CHILDREN

We have discussed a lot of information about the curriculum and environments of the primary grades, but what about the children? Classrooms and programs are for the children, and we must always remember that children are the reason we teach. On the following pages are some Portraits of Children for you to review and to think about how you would teach each one in your classroom.

ACTIVITIES FOR PROFESSIONAL DEVELOPMENT

Ethical Dilemma

Program Incentives

Amy and Allison teach first grade in a middle- to low-income school district where a lot of children have difficulty learning to read. Allison believes that the parents should do more to support their children's learning to read. She has joined the sales force of a national company that markets a beginner reading program targeted at struggling beginner readers. Allison has asked Amy for names, addresses, and phone numbers of families of children in her class who are experiencing reading difficulty. Allison feels she can help the children and make some extra money.

What should Amy do? Should she give Allison the list of names? Or should she refuse Allison's request and risk alienating her as a coworker? Or should Amy pursue another plan of action?

HECTOR

Meet Hector, a seven-year-old Spanish boy. Hector weighs 47 pounds and is 3 feet, 11 inches tall. He is a talkative first grader and loves learning anything that involves animals. Hector has a hard time paying attention in class and is easily distracted.

Social-Emotional	Cognitive	Motor	Adaptive (Daily Living)
Comes from a single-parent family and does not have a male role model	Easily memorizes odd facts about animals	Likes to climb and run during recess	Helps his mother with household chores
Spends a lot of time with his grandmother because his mother works full time	Is beginning to learn to add and subtract small numbers	Likes to play competitive sports and games	Makes his own breakfast in the morning
Shows off in new situations	Is confident with individual sounds	Is action oriented, rather than verbal	Is becoming more independent
Tries very hard to fit in with other boys	Likes to read by himself	Is somewhat aggressive and tends to get into fights	Folds and puts away his own clothes

CANDACE

Meet Candace, a seven-year-old African American female. Candace weighs 45 pounds and is 3 feet, 9 inches tall. She is a very boisterous child who is outgoing and loves to talk with her friends in class. Candace is highly intelligent and loves to read.

Social-Emotional	Cognitive	Motor	Adaptive (Daily Living)
Likes to tell riddles and jokes	Is able to count to 200 without difficulty	Enjoys participating in her cheerleading class and has great coordination	Is able to fix a snack by herself
Tends to get in "trouble" at school for talking too much in class	Enjoys learning about space and the solar system	Likes to create dance routines with her friends	Likes to do her own hair each morning
Shows a growing concern about popularity among her peers	Has concrete math concepts	Is able to ride a bicycle without training wheels	Knows how to cross a street safely
Is often "performing" songs for her parents	Is able to recognize denominations of currency	Likes to draw the planets of the solar system	Puts herself to bed

Questions About Developmentally Appropriate Practice:

- What are the major differences between Hector and Candace? How might their unique characteristics affect their approaches to learning?

- As a teacher, how could you help Hector grow socially and emotionally? Do you think having a male role model is important for Hector? How could you provide Hector with adult male influences?

- As Hector's teacher, what would you do to help him pay attention?

Photos: Silver Burdett Ginn (top); Getty Images, Inc.–Photodisc (bottom)

JULIO

Meet Julio, an eight-year-old Hispanic male. He weighs 68 pounds and is 4 feet, 3 inches tall. Julio is an active child who is impulsive and very social. He can become aggressive while playing and is often asked to "settle down" while on the playground. Julio has difficulty with reading and likes math.

Social-Emotional	Cognitive	Motor	Adaptive (Daily Living)
Is very loud and tends to yell out answers in class before raising his hand	Is a creative thinker who enjoys making up fictional stories	Has difficulty writting in paragraph form the fictional stories he likes to make up	Is able to make his own breakfast in the morning
Has difficulty controlling his emotions when he is upset	Prefers being read aloud to rather than reading quietly to himself	Is able to dribble and shoot a basketball and understands the basic rules of sports and games	Feeds his dog each morning and night
Is easily embarrassed	Resists adult guidance at times	Writes and draws with increasing skill	Is beginning to understand his role in household duties
Often intimidates his peers with his aggressive behavior and impulsive social skills	Is able to multiply double-digit numbers with little difficulty	Is learning to write in cursive	Is able to manage his small weekly allowance

TAMEKA

Meet Tameka, an eight-year-old African American female. Tameka weighs 58 pounds and is 4 feet, 4 inches tall. Tameka is very outspoken and likes to be the center of attention. Tameka enjoys extra attention from her teacher.

Social-Emotional	Cognitvie	Motor	Adaptive (Daily Living)
Lives full time with her grandmother	Is gradually learning concepts related to addition and subtraction	Is somewhat aggressive when playing with other children	Makes her bed every morning
Is extremely social and talkative—is a very happy child	Learns best in a tactile environment	Likes to play jump rope with other children on the playground	Has a strong, loving relationship with her grandmother—makes friends easily
Is beginning to become concerned about her height and weight	Is proud when she completes tasks	Has a lot of energy and stamina	Is very independent—likes to do things for herself
Is influenced by others, especially older females	Enjoys science but not math or reading	Likes to braid classmates' hair	Gets her own snacks without assistance from her grandmother

Questions About Developmentally Appropriate Practice:

- As a teacher, identify three activities that you could use to teach to Tameka's and Julio's strengths.
- What gender differences of Julio and Tameka influence their classroom behavior?
- How can you work with Tameka's grandmother to help her parent Tameka?
- How could you use math to help Julio with his reading?

Photos: Silver Burdett Ginn (top); Getty Images, Inc.–Photodisc (bottom)

TRAN

Meet Tran, a nine-year-old Asian boy. Tran weighs 70 pounds and is 4 feet, 7 inches tall. Tran is a very intelligent third grader who excels when he is challenged. He prefers individual activities to those that involve a group. He is somewhat reserved and shy. He enjoys the company of adults rather than children his own age.

Social-Emotional	Cognitive	Motor	Adaptive (Daily Living)
Is an intraverted child and keeps to himself	Reads two grades above the third-grade level	Is nonaggressive in physical play	Dresses and grooms himself before school
Is very sensitive	Enjoys reading chapter books	Writes very legibly in cursive	Is very attached to his parents—prefers to stay "close" to them
Tends to be critical of himself	Uses reference books and the Internet to write research papers	Has very good manual dexterity	Shows a strong desire to complete his tasks
Is "ahy" around children his age but is very interactive with adults	Excels in all subjects except physical education	Enjoys art activities and likes to paint and draw	Helps his mother with chores around the house such as sweeping and putting away dishes

ALEXIS

Meet Alexis, a nine-year-old Caucasian female who is in the third grade. Alexis weighs 69 pounds and is 4 feet, 5 inches tall. Alexis attends a private school and is in accelerated reading and math classes. She is a sensitive child who has a studious nature. Alexis spends most of her time reading or talking with her best friend. She is very outgoing, mannerly, and makes friends easily.

Social-Emotional	Cognitive	Motor	Adaptive (Daily Living)
Can have her feelings hurt rather easily but bounces back—has a positive attitude	Loves to read—has read all the books on the "Fun to Read" list	Has excellent balance and is able to twist on her tip toes without falling—enjoys her ballet classes	Very fashion conscious and likes to be well dressed
Has a large circle of friends to and outside of school	Can write lengthy paragraphs with little assistance and minimal spelling errors—enjoys using the computer to write stories	Is involved in many out-of school activities—has won a blue ribbon for her equestrian skills	Has her own cell phone and enjoys talking to her friends—also adopt at text messaging
Very independent and self-assured	Has developed personal standards of right and wrong	Draws with great detail—thinks she may be an artist when she growns up	Is very curious—wants to know about everything
Actively seeks praise and affirmation of her good accomplishments	Is above average in math skills	Likes to dance and is able to stand on one leg for long periods of time without falling	Is becoming "boy" conscious and can be "silly" in relationships with them

Questions About Developmentally Appropriate Practice:

- How could you as a teacher help Tran be more socially assertive?
- Would it be helpful to pair Tran and Alexis with children who are not so academically advanced?
- What would be your plan to further enhance Alexis' development and education?

- What are some possible reasons for Alexis' "advanced" education and development?

Photos: © Dorling Kindersley (top); Getty Images, Inc.–Photodisc (bottom)

Application Activities

1. One of the goals of the federal government and many states is that all children should be able to read on grade level by grade three.

   a. Why do you think this has become such an important goal?

   b. Why do you think this goal was set for grade three rather than another grade?

   c. What are some things you can do to help children achieve this goal in developmentally appropriate ways?

2. Early childhood professionals are able to articulate their reasons for wanting to teach a particular grade.

   a. Explain in detail why you would or would not want to teach one of the primary grades.

   b. Based on your reasons, make revisions in your philosophy of teaching.

3. What do you think are the most important subjects of the primary grades? Why? How would you agree or disagree with those who think any subjects other than reading, writing, and arithmetic are a waste of time?

4. Inquire whether any schools in your area offer character education programs.

   a. Compile a list of character traits you believe are most important for teaching young children.

   b. Ask parents and community members what they believe are the most important character traits.

 To take online practice tests on this chapter's material, go to the Companion Website at http://www.prenhall.com/morrison, select Chapter 10, and then choose the Multiple Choice or the Essay module. For additional Web resources, choose Web Links.

11

EDUCATING CHILDREN WITH DIVERSE BACKGROUNDS AND SPECIAL NEEDS
Ensuring All Children Learn

Educating All Students

A. I understand that all children are individuals with unique strengths and challenges. I embrace these differences, work to fulfill children's special needs, and promote tolerance and inclusion in my classroom. I value and respect the dignity of all children.

B. I use my understanding of young children's characteristics and needs, and of multiple interacting influences on children's development and learning, to create environments that are healthy, respectful, supportive, and challenging for all children.[1]

C. I integrate my understanding of and relationships with children and families; my understanding of developmentally effective approaches to teaching and learning; and my knowledge of academic disciplines to design, implement, and evaluate experiences that promote positive development and learning for all children.[2]

D. I use my own knowledge and other resources to design, implement, and evaluate meaningful, challenging curriculum that promotes comprehensive developmental and learning outcomes for all young children.[3]

1. How can you meet the special needs of all children in developmentally appropriate ways?

2. What is the basis for inclusion of children with disabilities in early childhood programs?

3. What is multicultural education and how can you infuse multicultural content in your programs and activities?

294

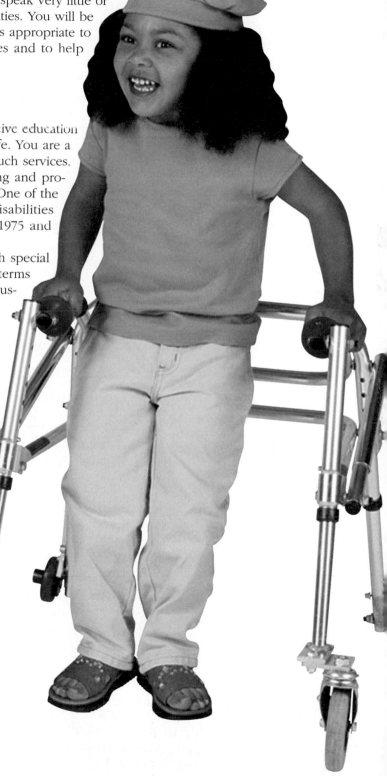

Children with diverse backgrounds and special needs are in every program, school, and classroom in the United States. You will teach students with a variety of special needs. They might come from low-income families and various racial and ethnic groups; they might speak very little or no English; they may have exceptional abilities or disabilities. You will be challenged to provide for all students an education that is appropriate to their physical, intellectual, social, and emotional abilities and to help them achieve their best.

CHILDREN WITH DISABILITIES

Children with special needs and their families should receive education and services that will help them succeed in school and life. You are a key player in the process of ensuring that they receive such services. The federal government has passed many laws protecting and promoting the rights and needs of children with disabilities. One of the most important federal laws is the Individuals with Disabilities Education Act (IDEA), which was originally enacted in 1975 and was reauthorized by Congress in 2004.

As with many special areas, the field of children with special needs has a unique vocabulary and terminology. The terms defined in Figure 11.1 will help you as we begin our discussion of IDEA and as you work with children and families.

The Individuals with Disabilities Education Act (IDEA)

The purpose of IDEA is to ensure that all children with disabilities have available to them a free appropriate public education that emphasizes special education and related services designed to meet their unique needs, to ensure that the rights of children with disabilities and their parents or guardians are protected, to assist states and localities to provide for the education of all children with disabilities, and to assess and ensure the effectiveness of efforts to educate children with disabilities.[4]

IDEA defines **children with disabilities** as those children with mental retardation, hearing impairments (including deafness), speech or language impairments (including blindness), serious emotional disturbance, orthopedic impairments, autism, traumatic brain injury, other health impairments, or specific learning disabilities; and who, by reason thereof, need special education and related services.[5] The number of persons from age six to age eleven served under IDEA in the 2001 school year included:

- All disabilities: 2,729,822
- Specific learning disabilities: 897,833
- Speech and language impairments: 981,716
- Mental retardation: 168,595

FIGURE 11.1

Glossary of Terms Related to Children with Special Needs

Adaptive education: Modifying programs, environments, curricula, and activities to provide learning experiences that help all students achieve desired education goals.

Children with disabilities: Replaces former terms such as *handicapped.* To avoid labeling children, do not use the reversal of these words (e.g., *disabled children*).

Co-teaching: The process by which a regular classroom professional and a special educator or a person trained in exceptional student education team teach, in the same classroom, a group of regular and mainstreamed children.

Disability: A physical or mental impairment that substantially limits one or more major life activities.

Early education and care settings: Promotes the idea that all children learn and that child care and other programs *should* be educating children birth to age eight.

Early Intervention: Providing services to children and families as early in the child's life as possible to prevent or help with a special need or needs.

English language learners (ELLs)*:* Students with a primary language other than English.

Exceptional student education: Replaces the term *special education;* refers to the education of children with special needs.

Full inclusion: The mainstreaming or Inclusion of all children with disabilities into natural environments such as playgrounds, child care centers, preschool, kindergarten, and primary grades.

Individualized education program (IEP)*:* A written plan for a child stating what will be done, how it will be done, and when it will be done.

Individualized family service plan (IFSP)*:* A written plan for providing early intervention services for a child and his family that is based on the child's strengths and needs. The plan lists outcomes for the child and family and describes the services and coordination that will get to those outcomes. Family members decide what is written on the plan, they can veto any input from professionals, and the plan can be amended at any time by the family.

Integration: The education of children with disabilities along with typically developing children. This education can occur in mainstream, reverse mainstream, and full-inclusion programs.

Least restrictive environment (LRE)*:* Children with, disabilities are educated with children who have no disabilities. Special classes, separate schooling, or other removal of children with disabilities from the regular educational environment occurs only when the nature or severity of the disability is such that education in regular classes with the use of supplementary aids and services cannot be achieved satisfactorily.

Limited English proficiency (LEP)*:* Describes children who have limited English skills.

Mainstreaming: The social and educational Integration of children with special needs into the general instructional process; usually a regular classroom program.

Merged classroom: A classroom that includes—merges—children with special needs and children without special needs and teaches them together in one classroom.

Natural environment: Any environment in which it is natural for any child to be, such as home, child care center, preschool, kindergarten, and primary grades.

Reverse mainstreaming: The process by which typically developing children are placed in programs for children with disabilities. In reverse mainstreaming, children with disabilities are in the majority.

Typically developing children: Children who are developing according to and within the boundaries of normal growth and development.

- Emotional disturbance: 131,254
- Multiple disabilities: 50,450
- Hearing impairments: 31,889
- Orthopedic impairments: 30,041
- Other health impairments: 229,344
- Visual impairments: 11,448
- Autism: 109,869
- Deaf-blindness: 592
- Traumatic brain injury: 7,876
- Development delay: 78,915.[6]

About 10 to 12 percent of the nation's children have disabilities. What this means for you is that in your classroom of twenty to twenty-five students you will have at least two to three children with some kind of disability.

IDEA's Seven Principles. IDEA establishes seven basic principles to follow as you provide educational and other services to children with special needs:

1. *Zero reject.* IDEA calls for educating all children and rejecting none from receiving an appropriate education. Whereas before IDEA many children were excluded from educational programs or were denied an education, this is not the case today.

2. *Nondiscriminatory evaluation and multidisciplinary assessment.* A fair evaluation is needed to determine whether a student has a disability, and, if so, what the student's education should consist of. IDEA specifies the use of nondiscretionary testing procedures in labeling and placement of students for special education services. These include:

   - Testing of students in their native or primary language, whenever possible, and
   - Use of evaluation procedures selected and administered in such a way as to prevent cultural or racial discrimination.

3. *Multidisciplinary assessment.* This is a team approach in which a group of people use various methods in a child's evaluation. Having a **multidisciplinary assessment (MDA)** helps ensure that a child's needs and program will not be determined by one test or one person.

Anthony Magnacca / Merrill

4. *Appropriate education.* Instruction and related services need to be individually designed to provide educational benefits to students in making progress toward meeting their unique needs. Basically, IDEA provides for a **free and appropriate education (FAPE)** for all students between the ages of three and twenty-one. *Appropriate* means that children must receive an education suited to their age, maturity level, condition of disability, past achievements, and parental expectations.

5. *Least restrictive placement/environment.* All students with disabilities have the right to learn in the **least restrictive environment (LRE)**—an environment consistent with their academic, social, and physical needs. Such a setting may or may not be the general classroom, but 96 percent of children with disabilities spend at least part of their school day in general classrooms.[7]

6. *Due process.* IDEA provides schools and parents with ways of resolving their differences by mediation and/or hearings before impartial hearing officers or judges.

All early childhood programs should address the individual needs of children with disabilities. How can you use the IEPs to ensure that those needs are being met?

7. *Parental and student participation.* IDEA specifies a process of shared decision making whereby educators, parents, and students collaborate in deciding a student's educational plan.[8]

Figure 11.2 lists the disabilities covered under IDEA. You can be reasonably assured that you will have children with some of these disabilities in your classroom. Make yourself familiar with each of these and consider how you might meet the needs of children with these disabilities.

Guaranteeing a Free and Appropriate Education.   As previously mentioned, IDEA mandates a free and appropriate education (FAPE) for all persons between the ages of three and twenty-one. In addition, IDEA provides federal money to state and local educational agencies to guarantee students a free appropriate public education.

State and local agencies, however, must agree to comply with the federal law or else they will not receive federal money. One of the facts of public education is that there is a lot of federal money for special services to children, such as the school lunch program, bilingual programs, and exceptional student education. Some of the exceptional education and related services specified by IDEA are listed in Figure 11.3. When providing services for children with disabilities, it is important for them to receive specific services that will help them learn. This is why IDEA identifies some, but not all, of the services that will help achieve this goal.

Observe professionals discussing a student's IEP with one of her parents at Video Classroom, Special Education, Module 2: Collaboration, Co-Teaching, and the IEP, Video 1: IEP Meeting.

Creating an Individualized Education Program.   Exceptional student education laws mandate the creation of an **individualized education program (IEP)**, which requires a plan for the individualization of each student's instruction. The IEP is one of the most important educational documents in the education of children with disabilities. It literally constitutes a contract between the school system, the children, and parents. Writing an IEP and the document itself are the most important parts of compliance with IDEA. When the IEP is prepared as intended by law:

- Students' needs have been carefully assessed.
- A team of professionals and the parents have worked together to design an education to best meet the student's needs.
- Goals and objectives are clearly stated so that progress in reaching them can be evaluated.[9]

An IEP requires creating learning objectives and basing students' learning plans on their specific needs, disabilities, and preferences, as well as on those of their parents. A collaborative team of regular and special educators creates these objectives. The IEP must specify what will be done for the child, how and when it will be done, and by whom, and this information must be in writing. In developing the IEP, a person trained in diagnosing disabling conditions, such as a school psychologist, must be part of the IEP team, which includes the parent and, when appropriate, the child. Figure 11.4 on page 301 identifies the members of the IEP team as mandated by federal law. Certain individuals must be involved in writing a child's Individualized Education Program. An IEP team member may fill more than one of the team positions if properly qualified and designated. For example, the school system representative may also be the person who can interpret the child's evaluation results.

Purposes of the IEP.   The IEP has several purposes, including these:

- Protecting children and parents by ensuring that planning will occur.
- Guaranteeing that children will have plans tailored to their individual strengths, weaknesses, and learning styles.

FIGURE 11.2

Disabilities Covered Under IDEA

As an early childhood educator, you will have children with special needs in your classroom. The following disabilities qualify children for special education services under IDEA:

1. *Autism:* A developmental disability significantly affecting verbal and nonverbal communication and social interaction, generally evident before age three, that adversely affects educational performance.

2. *Deafness:* A hearing impairment which is so severe that a child is impaired in processing linguistic information through hearing, with or without amplification, which adversely affects educational performance.

3. *Deaf-blindness:* Simultaneous hearing and visual impairment, the combination of which causes such severe communication and other developmental and educational problems that a child cannot be accommodated in special education programs solely for children with deafness or children with blindness.

4. *Emotional disturbance:* A condition exhibiting one or more of the following characteristics over a long period of time and to a marked degree, which adversely affects educational performance: (a) an inability to learn that cannot be explained by intellectual, sensory, or health factors; (b) an inability to build or maintain satisfactory interpersonal relationships with peers and teachers; (c) inappropriate types of behavior or feelings under normal circumstances; (d) a general pervasive mood of unhappiness or depression; or (e) a tendency to develop physical symptoms or fears associated with personal or school problems. The term includes children who have schizophrenia. The term does not include children who are socially maladjusted, unless it is determined that they have an emotional disturbance.

5. *Hearing impairment:* A hearing impairment, whether permanent or fluctuating, which adversely affects a child's educational performance but which is not included under the definition of "deafness."

6. *Mental retardation:* Significantly subaverage general intellectual functioning existing concurrently with deficits in adaptive behavior and manifested during the developmental period, which adversely affects a child's educational performance.

7. *Multiple disabilities:* Simultaneous impairments (such as mental retardation/blindness or mental retardation/orthopedic impairment), the combination of which causes such severe educational problems that the child cannot be accommodated in a special education program solely for one of the impairments.

8. *Orthopedic impairment:* A severe orthopedic impairment that adversely affects a child's educational performance. The term includes impairments caused by a congenital anomaly (e.g., clubfoot, absence of some member).

9. *Other health impairment:* Having limited strength, vitality, or alertness, due to chronic or acute health problems such as a heart condition, attention deficit disorder, rheumatic fever, nephritis, asthma, sickle cell anemia, hemophillia, epilepsy, lead poisoning, leukemia, or diabetes, which adversely affects a child's educational performance. According to the Office of Special Education and Rehabilitative Services' clarification statement of September 16, 1991, eligible children with AIDS may also be classified under "other health impairment."

10. *Specific learning disability:* A disorder in one or more of the basic psychological processes involved in understanding or in using language, spoken or written, which may manifest itself in an imperfect ability to listen, think, speak, read, write, spell, or do mathematical calculations. The term includes such conditions as perceptual disabilities, brain injury, minimum brain dysfunction, dyslexia, and developmental aphasia. The term does not include children who have learning problems which are primarily the result of visual, hearing, or motor disabilities, of mental retardation, of emotional disturbance, or of environmental, cultural, or economic disadvantage.

11. *Speech or language Impairment:* A communication disorder, such as stuttering, impaired articulation, a language impairment, or a voice impairment, which adversely affects a child's educational performance.

12. *Traumatic brain injury:* An injury to the brain caused by an external physical force, resulting in total or partial functional disability of psychosocial impairment, or both, which adversely affects educational performance. The term does not include brain injuries that are congenital or degenerative, or brain injuries induced by birth trauma.

13. *Visual impairment, including blindness:* A visual impairment that, even with correction, adversely affects a child's educational performance. The term includes both children with partial sight and those with blindness.

Source: Adapted with permission of the National Dissemination Center for Children with Disabilities (NICHCY), "General Information about Disabilities: Disabilities That Qualify Infants, Toddlers, Children, and Youth for Services Under the IDEA," http://www.nichcy.org/pubs/genresc/gr3.htm#categories.

FIGURE 11.3

Services Provided by IDEA

1. "Assistive technology and services" are any items, pieces of equipment, or product systems that directly assist a child with a disability and increase, maintain, or improve functional capabilities of that child.

2. "Audiology" includes identification of children with auditory impairment; determination of the range, nature, and degree of hearing loss; and the provision of services for prevention of hearing loss.

3. "Family training, counseling, and home visits" means services provided by social workers, psychologists, or other qualified personnel to assist the family in understanding the special needs of the child and enhancing the child's development.

4. "Health services" means services necessary to enable a child to benefit from other early intervention services during the time that the child is receiving the other early intervention services.

5. "Medical services" means services provided by a licensed physician to determine a child's developmental status and need for early intervention services.

6. "Nutrition services" include conducting individual assessments in nutritional history and dietary intake, feeding skills and feeding problems, and food habits and food preferences; and developing and monitoring appropriate plans to address nutritional needs.

7. "Occupational therapy" includes services that are designed to improve the child's functional ability to perform tasks in home, school, and community settings.

8. "Physical therapy" includes services to address the promotion of sensorimotor function, and provide services or treatment to prevent, alleviate, or compensate for movement dysfunction and related functional problems.

9. "Psychological services" include administering psychological and developmental tests and other assessment procedures; interpreting assessment results; obtaining, integrating, and interpreting information about child behavior and conditions relating to learning, mental health, and development; and planning and managing a program of psychological services, including psychological counseling for children and parents, family counseling, consultation on child development, parent training, and education programs.

10. "Respite care" includes temporary child care services that are short term and nonmedical in nature, provided either in or out of the home.

11. "Social work services" include making home visits to evaluate a child's living conditions and patterns of parent–child interaction; preparing a psychosocial developmental assessment of the child within the family context; providing individual and family-group counseling; working with those problems in a child's and family's living situation that affect the child's maximum utilization of early intervention services; and mobilizing community resources and services to enable the child and family to receive maximum benefit from early intervention services.

12. "Special instruction" includes the design of learning environments and activities that promote the child's acquisition of skills in a variety of developmental areas; curriculum planning that leads to achieving the outcomes in the child's IFSP; providing families with information, skills, and support related to enhancing the skill development of the child; and working with the child to enhance the child's development.

13. "Speech-language pathology" includes the identification, diagnosis, and appraisal of children with communicative or oropharyngeal disorders; referral for medical or other professional services; and provision of services for the habilitation, rehabilitation, or prevention of communicative or oropharyngeal disorders and delays in development of communication skills.

14. "Transportation and related costs" include the cost of travel and other costs that are necessary to enable children with disabilities and their families to receive early intervention services.

15. "Vision services" include the evaluation and assessment of visual functioning, including the diagnosis and appraisal of specific visual disorders, delays, and abilities.

16. "Services to infants and toddlers" include all services listed above to those infants and toddlers who have special needs to be met by special services.

Source: Office of Special Education and Rehabilitative Services, U.S. Department of Education, "IDEA Part C Data Fact Sheet." Accessed March 14, 2007, from http://www.ideadata.org/docs/efactsheetservices.doc.

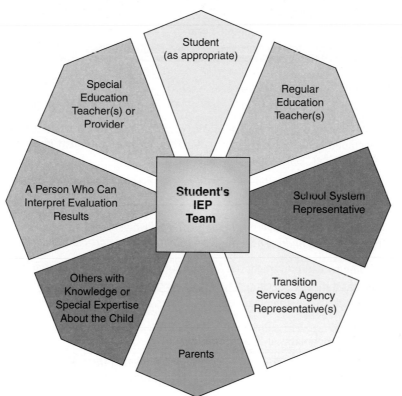

FIGURE 11.4 IEP Team Members

Source: Office of Special Education and Rehabilitative Services, *A Guide to the Individualized Education Program* (Washington, DC: U.S. Department of Education, 2000), http://www.ed.gov/parents/needs/speced/iepguide/iepguide.pdf.

- Helping professionals and other instructional and administrative personnel focus their teaching and resources on children's specific needs, promoting the best use of everyone's time, efforts, and talents.
- Ensuring that children with disabilities will receive a range of services from other agencies. The plan must not only include an educational component, but also specify how the child's total needs will be met.
- Helping to clarify and refine decisions as to what is best for children, where they should be placed, and how they should be taught and helped.
- Ensuring that children will not be categorized or labeled without discussion of their unique needs.
- Ensuring that reviews are conducted at least annually; encouraging professionals to consider how and what children have learned, determining whether what was prescribed is effective, and prescribing new or modified strategies.

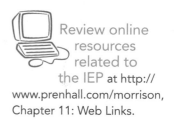

Review online resources related to the IEP at http://www.prenhall.com/morrison, Chapter 11: Web Links.

An example of a completed IEP for a preschooler is shown in Figure 11.5 on pages 302–304.

Individualized Family Service Plan. Infants, toddlers, and their families also have the right to an **individualized family service plan (IFSP)**, which specifies what services they will receive. The IFSP is designed to help families reach the goals they have for themselves and their children. The IFSP provides for:

- Multidisciplinary assessment developed by a multidisciplinary team and the parents. Planned services must meet developmental needs and can include special education, speech and language pathology and audiology, occupational therapy, physical therapy, psychological services, parent and family training and counseling services, transition services, medical diagnostic services, and health services. Meet with a special educator in your program or school district to determine specific examples of how these services are provided for young children.

Sample Form

Individualized Education Program (IEP)

Jeremy Carlson

September 26, 2007

_____ | _____
Student Name | Date of Meeting to Develop or Review IEP

Note: For each student with a disability beginning at age 14 (or younger, if appropriate), a statement of the student's transition service needs must be included under the applicable parts of the IEP. The statement must focus on the courses the student needs to take to reach his or her post-school goals.

[a general statement of the transition needs of the student; must be updated annually]

Present Levels of Educational Performance

[includes a description of how the disability affects involvement and progress or (for preschool children) how the the disability affects participation]

- When asked to write his name, Jeremy can print the letter "J," but does not print the remaining letters.
- Given a free-play setting, Jeremy has difficulty selecting play items, changing activities, and remaining engaged in activities.
- When given the opportunity, Jeremy can greet familiar adults and peers and make unprompted eye contact with them, but he does not do so consistently.

Measurable Annual Goals [Including Benchmarks or Short-Term Objectives]

[clearly stated goals that lay out the plan for meeting the child's needs for improvement as well as all other educational needs]

- By the end of the school year, Jeremy will demonstrate comprehension of a spoken story's main idea by selecting representative pictures from arrays of three with 90 percent accuracy.
- By the end of the school year, Jeremy will utter two- and three-word phrases as the result of natural environmental cues without prompting in eight out of every ten opportunities presented to him.
- By the end of the school year, Jeremy will greet three specific peers (Manny, Sarah, and Roland) at least once a day with unprompted eye contact and unprompted one- and two-word greetings such as "Hi, Manny," "Hey, Sarah," and "Roland!"

Jeremy's Benchmarks

- At the end of the first month of instruction, Jeremy will point as prompted with 100 percent accuracy to one pictorial representation (selected from an array consisting only of that picture) of a spoken story's main character or event.
- At the end of the third month of instruction, Jeremy will point as prompted with 60 percent accuracy to the correct pictorial representation (selected from an array consisting of two pictures) of a spoken story's main character or event.
- At the end of the fifth month of instruction, Jeremy will point as prompted with 90 percent accuracy to the correct pictorial representation (selected from an array consisting of two pictures) of a spoken story's main character or event.
- At the end of the seventh month of instruction, Jeremy will point as prompted with 70 percent accuracy to the correct pictorial representation (selected from an array consisting of three pictures) of a spoken story's main character or event.
- At the end of the ninth month of instruction, Jeremy will point, without prompting and with 90 percent accuracy, to the correct pictorial representation (selected from an array consisting of three pictures) of a spoken story's main character or event.

When Services, Modifications, and Accommodations Will Begin and Their Anticipated Frequency, Duration, and Location

- Services will begin as soon as parental agreement is obtained and will continue throughout the school year. Special education and related services will be delivered daily in the preschool.
- Upon receipt of parental agreement, speech/language therapy will occur in the preschool therapy room for thirty minutes each day for the first three months the IEP is in effect, and will be offered for thirty minutes, three times per week thereafter.
- The early childhood special education teacher and the Montessori teacher will develop a schedule of periodic visits (i.e., biweekly, then weekly) for Jeremy (with and without his parents) to the Montessori classroom during the last month of this year's preschool program.

FIGURE 11.5 An Example of a Preschool IEP

[listing of all services, aids, and special modifications needed along with specific details]

- The lead special education teacher and paraprofessionals, as necessary, will develop and use pictorial "social stories" (Gray, 2000) to describe and exemplify acceptable and successful ways of greeting peers. Three peers (one with and two without disabilities) will serve as peer supports for this instruction. Other personnel at the preschool will cooperate with modeling and prompting as necessary.
- The lead special education teacher and paraprofessionals, as necessary, will use "comic strip conversations" (Rogers and Myles, 2001) to establish nonverbal, unobtrusive ways to provide Jeremy with feedback and cues as he interacts with his peers.
- The speech-language therapist and the lead special education teacher will collaborate, plan, and deliver spoken-language training in comprehension and production on the basis of the training model developed by Ivar Lovaas (McKeachin, Smith, and Lovaas, 1993).

Explanation of Extent, if Any, to Which Child Will Not Participate in Regular Education Classroom

[description of child's lack of interaction with other children in regular class setting]

- Jeremy is in an integrated preschool and participates fully with nondisabled children.

ADMINISTRATION OF STATE AND DISTRICT-WIDE ASSESSMENTS OF STUDENT ACHIEVEMENT

Any Individual Modifications in Administration Needed for Child to Participate in State or District-Wide Assessment(s)

[a listing of any special requirements needed for child to participate in assessments]

- Jeremy will not take these tests as a preschool child. Typically, children are first assessed in the intermediate elementary grades.

If IEP Team Determines That Child Will Not Participate in a Particular State or District-Wide Assessment

- Why isn't the assessment appropriate for the child?
- Describe alternative assessment.

How Child's Progress Toward Annual Goals Will Be Measured

[clear statement of measurement procedures]

- In light of the intent to place Jeremy in a general kindergarten program next year, progress monitoring is essential. Jeremy's IEP team will review each goal's status on a monthly basis. His lead teacher will prepare a brief report of this review for Jeremy's parents. The teacher will offer to call meetings for clarification purposes as necessary.
- Jeremy's progress toward annual goals will be assessed monthly through a review of his relevant performance data by the IEP team. His parents will receive monthly written reports of these reviews.

How Child's Parents Will Be Regularly Informed of Child's Progress Toward Annual Goals and Extent to Which Child's Progress Is Sufficient to Meet Goals by End of Year

[description of plan for working with parents and informing them of child's progress]

- Developing and maintaining clear communication between Jeremy's parents and all the professionals involved with him will be important. Formal progress reports will be provided to Jeremy's parents each month. It would be a good idea, however, to establish weekly "check-ins," either by phone or by e-mail.

[Beginning at age 16 or younger if determined appropriate by IEP team] Statement of Needed Transition Services (Including, If Appropriate, Statement of Interagency Responsibilities or Any Needed Linkages)

[takes into account special considerations involved with older children, including student preferences and interests]

- Jeremy is too young for postsecondary transition services to be considered. However, he will make a critical transition next year to a Montessori kindergarten. Although it is not required, it would be wise for the IEP team to begin concerted planning for this transition early in the fourth quarter of the school year.
- As suggested in the preceding section, the team should arrange for Jeremy, with and without his parents, to make periodic visits to the Montessori classroom during the last month of this year's preschool program.

FIGURE 11.5 *continued*

- Although moving from an integrated preschool to kindergarten is not part of the explicit intent of the transition statement in the IEP, the IEP team should nonetheless acknowledge the importance of Jeremy's transition to the Montessori kindergarten program by providing a plan for coordinating this transition.

[In a state that transfers rights to the student at the age of majority, the following information must be included beginning at least one year before the student reaches the age of majority]

The student has been informed of the rights under Part 8 of IDEA, if any, that will transfer to the student on reaching the age of majority. Yes

[guarantees that student is fully informed of rights regarding services available under IDEA]

References:

Gray, C. 2000. *Writing social stories with Carol Gray.* Arlington, TX: Future Horizons.

Rogers, M.F., and B.S. Myles. 2001. Using social stories and comic strip conversations to interpret social situations for an adolescent with Asperger's syndrome. *Intervention in School and Clinic,* 36:310–3.

McKeachin, J. J., T. Smith, and O. Lovaas. 1993. Long-term outcome for children who received early behavioral treatment. *American Journal on Mental Retardation,* 97:359–72.

FIGURE 11.5 *continued*

Sources: IEP outline from Morrison, George S., *Teaching in America,* Fourth Edition. Published by Allyn & Bacon, Boston, MA. Copyright © 2006 by Pearson Education. Reprinted by permission of the publisher. Adapted from U.S. Office of Special Education Programs, "A Guide to the Individualized Education Program." (2000). (Online). Available at www.ed.gov/offices/OSERS/OSEP/Products/IEP_Guide/. Examples from Knowlton, Earle, *Developing Effective Individualized Education Programs: A Case Based Tutorial,* 2nd edition, © 2007. Electronically reproduced by permission of Pearson Education, Inc., Upper Saddle River, New Jersey.

- A statement of the child's present levels of development; a statement of the family's strengths and needs with regard to enhancing the child's development; a statement of major expected outcomes for the child and family; the criteria, procedures, and timeliness for determining progress; the specific early intervention services necessary to meet the unique needs of the child and family; the projected dates for initiation of services; the name of the case manager; and transition procedures from the early intervention program into a preschool program.

Helping parents of children with disabilities is an important role of all early childhood professionals. Administrators can help teachers and parents by:

- Establishing parent resource centers to help parents and teachers develop good working relationships.
- Providing basic training to help parents understand special education and the role of the family in cooperative planning as well as offering workshops on topics requested by parents.
- Making available up-to-date information and resources for parents and teachers.
- Encouraging creation of early childhood and preschool screening programs and other community services that can be centered in the schools.

Teachers can:

- Make it clear to parents that you accept them as advocates who have an intense desire to make life better for their children.
- Provide parents with information about support groups, special services in the school and the community, and family-to-family groups.
- Offer parents referrals to helpful groups.
- Encourage parents to organize support systems, pairing families who can share experiences with each other during school activities.
- Involve parents in specific projects centered on hobbies or special skills that parents can share with students in one or several classes.

- Discuss a child's special talents with parents and use that positive approach as a bridge to discuss other issues.[10]

Chapter 13 will provide you with a comprehensive program for involving and collaborating with parents and families.

The Program in Action feature on page 307 offers a profile of inclusion at a Florida elementary school and a look at an early intervention program for infants and toddlers with disabilities and their families.

A Continuum of Inclusive Services. A continuum of services means that a full range of services is available for children from the most restrictive to the least restrictive placements. This continuum implies a graduated range of services, with one level of services leading directly to the next. For example, a continuum of services for students with disabilities would define institutional placement as the most restrictive and a general education classroom as the least restrictive. There is considerable debate over whether providing such a continuum is an appropriate policy. Advocates of inclusion say that the approach works against developing truly inclusive programs in regular education classrooms. Figure 11.6 shows educational options for students with disabilities that range from the most physically integrated, in which the regular classroom teacher meets most of a child's needs with help and support, to the least integrated, a residential setting providing a therapeutic environment.

Inclusive classrooms offer many benefits for children. They demonstrate increased acceptance and appreciation of diversity, develop better communication and social skills, show greater development in moral and ethical principles, create warm and caring friendships, and demonstrate increased self-esteem.

Anthony Magnacca / Merrill

Inclusive classrooms educate students with disabilities in the least restrictive educational environment. What would you say to a parent of a child without a disability who questions the idea of an inclusive classroom?

Children with Autism

Autism is a complex developmental disability that typically appears during the first three years of life and is the result of a neurological disorder that affects the normal functioning of the brain, impacting development in the areas of social interaction and communication skills. Children with autism typically show difficulties in verbal and nonverbal communication, social interactions, and leisure or play activities. Autism affects each child differently and at varying degrees.[11] Autism is diagnosed four times more often in boys than girls. Its prevalence is not affected by race, region, or socioeconomic status. Since autism was first diagnosed in the United States, the occurrence has climbed to an alarming 1 in 150 people across the country.[12]

Autism is one of five disorders that falls under the umbrella of **pervasive developmental disorders (PDDs)**, a category of neurological disorders characterized by severe and pervasive impairment in several areas of development. The five disorders classified under PDD are:

Learn how to make inclusion successful at Articles and Readings, Special Education, Module 3: Inclusion, Article 1: Making Inclusive Education Work.

- Autistic disorder,
- Asperger's disorder,
- Childhood disintegrative disorder (CDD),
- Rett's disorder, and
- PDD—not otherwise specified (PDD–NOS).[13]

Level	Educational Delivery System	Professional Responsibility

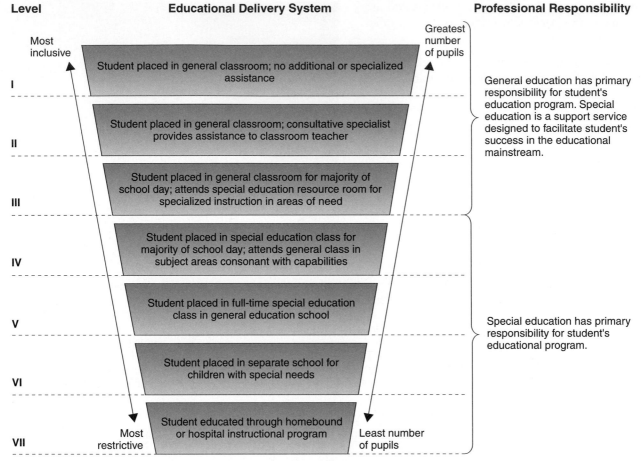

FIGURE 11.6 Educational Service Options for Students with Disabilities

Source: Extracted from Michael L. Hardman et al., *Human Exceptionality: School, Community, and Family,* 8e. Published by Allyn & Bacon, Boston, MA. Copyright © 2005 by Pearson Education. Reprinted by permission of the publisher.

Autism is the fastest growing serious developmental disability in the United States. More children will be diagnosed with autism this year than with AIDS, diabetes, and cancer combined. It costs the nation more than $90 billion per year, a figure expected to double in the next decade, but receives less than 5 percent of the research funding of many less prevalent childhood diseases.[14]

Children with autism typically demonstrate the following characteristics:

- Impaired social and communication skills,
- Repetitive behaviors,
- Limited interests, and
- May have trouble keeping up with conversations.[15]

The cause of autism remains unknown; however, evidence points to genetic factors playing a prominent role in causing the disorder. Twin and family studies have suggested an underlying genetic vulnerability to autism.[16]

An effective intervention method that you can apply to autistic children in your classroom is **applied behavior analysis (ABA)**. Applied behavior analysis is the theory that behavior rewarded is more likely to be repeated than behavior ignored. Other methods of effective intervention include a highly supportive teaching environment; predictability and routine; family involvement; and working with young children in small teacher-to-child ratios, often one to one in the early stages.[17]

Alimacani Elementary School is a National Model Blue Ribbon school located in Jacksonville, Florida. The faculty, staff, and community have consistently worked together to live up to their vision that "Alimacani is a place where education is a treasure and children are inspired to reach for their dreams."

The school serves pre-K–5 students. It originally included self-contained classes for kindergarten children with varying exceptionalities. After several years of serving the youngsters using a traditional self-contained model and mainstreaming individually as appropriate, frustration ran high. Although the children with disabilities were occasional visitors to the kindergarten classes, they were never a part of the general classroom learning and social community. As our team of kindergarten teachers looked at this model of serving children, we brainstormed ideas of how to better meet the needs of individual students. After many difficult conversations, we agreed to focus on a model that would best serve the needs of all of our children. We decided to take the entire population of children with special needs and include them in regular kindergarten classes, matching children with teacher strengths.

As our vision for inclusion was first formed, we were anxious and unsure. We would have to teach with other teachers and give up ownership of children and space. All of our roles would change. We had read about the benefits of collaboration with our colleagues, but we knew that the reality of so intimate a bond would require trust, respect, a great deal of faith, and a strong sense of humor!

Despite our reservations and uncertainty, we were full of enthusiasm! Our expectations changed daily. Even our assignments changed, as we enrolled and identified a record number of kindergarten children with special needs. In partnership with parents of the children with disabilities and with parents of typically developing children, we stretched, bent, and broadened our ideas. In most cases, visitors could not identify the children with disabilities in our classrooms from their typically developing peers. They

also could not always identify general education teachers from special educators. Eighteen children with a variety of special needs were included in three different kindergarten classes during that initial year, including children with Down syndrome, autism, mild physical and mental disabilities, attention deficit hyperactivity disorder, Asperger's syndrome, fetal alcohol syndrome, learning disabilities, and developmental delays.

To say that the first year was a success is an understatement. Without exception, we felt that we had done a better job of educating exceptional children than we had ever achieved in our self-contained model. We also learned that we did not have to sacrifice the many for the few. Our typically developing population of kindergartners thrived with the new responsibilities of helping their peers. As we came together to develop alternative methods of instruction for children with special needs, we found many of those same methods reaching our typically developing children. We were extremely proud of all of our kindergartners at the end of the year as they marched ahead into first grade.

Even with our own successes, we have come to believe that inclusion is not for everyone. We believe that there must continue to be an array of services to meet individual needs. We believe that we must learn to first look at the needs of our students, and then design programs and assign personnel to make learning successful.

Visit the inclusive classrooms of Dayle Timmons, Marie Rush, Kerry Rogers, and Lori Medlock on the Web.

Contributed by Dayle Timmons, Marie Rush, Kerry Rogers, and Lori Medlock of Alimacani Elementary School, Jacksonville, Florida.

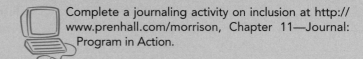

Complete a journaling activity on inclusion at http://www.prenhall.com/morrison, Chapter 11—Journal: Program in Action.

Children with Attention Deficit Hyperactivity Disorder (ADHD)

Students with **attention deficit hyperactivity disorder (ADHD)** generally display cognitive delays and have difficulties in three specific areas: attention, impulse control, and hyperactivity. To be classified as having ADHD, a student must display for a minimum of six months before age seven at least eight of the characteristics outlined here:

Inattention

- Often fails to give close attention to details or makes careless mistakes in schoolwork, work, or other activities.
- Has difficulty sustaining attention in tasks or play activities.

- Does not seem to listen when spoken to directly.
- Does not follow through on instructions and falls to finish schoolwork or chores.
- Has difficulty organizing tasks and activities.
- Avoids, dislikes, or is reluctant to engage in tasks that require sustained mental effort.
- Frequently loses things necessary for tasks or activities.
- Is often easily distracted by extraneous stimuli.

Impulsivity

- Blurts out answers before questions have been completed.
- Has difficulty awaiting turn.
- Interrupts or intrudes on others.

Hyperactivity

- Fidgets with hands or feet or squirms in seat.
- Frequently leaves seat in classroom or in other situations in which remaining seated is expected.
- Often runs about or climbs excessively in situations in which it is inappropriate.
- Has difficulty playing or engaging in leisure activities quietly.
- Often "on the go" or acts as if "driven by a motor."
- Talks excessively.[18]

ADHD is diagnosed about three times more often in boys than in girls and affects 4 to 12 percent of all students.[19] Frequently, the term *attention deficit disorder* (ADD) is used to refer to ADHD, but ADD is a form of learning disorder, whereas ADHD is a behavioral disorder. Teachers work with school psychologists and other professionals to help correctly identify children with ADHD. Remember, the primary purpose of identification is to provide appropriate services, instruction, and programs.

Strategies for Teaching Children with Disabilities

Sound teaching strategies work well for all students, including those with disabilities. You must plan how to create inclusive teaching environments. The ideas shown in Figure 11.7 will help you teach children with disabilities and create inclusive settings that enhance the education of all students. In addition, the accompanying Technology Tie-In feature will provide you with tips for ensuring all your students achieve and are successful. Good teaching is good teaching regardless of where you teach. However, you will want and need to make modifications in your program and curriculum to meet the unique needs of children with disabilities. Also, Figure 11.8 outlines a model for how you can teach effectively in your inclusive classroom. As the figure indicates, you will need special kinds of knowledge and skills about students, the curriculum, and working with others. Which knowledge and skills do you possess? Which will you have to make a special effort to acquire?

GIFTED AND TALENTED CHILDREN

In contrast to children with disabilities, children identified as gifted or talented are not covered under IDEA's provisions. Congress has passed other legislation specifically to provide for these children. The Jacob K. Javits Gifted and Talented Students Education Act defines **gifted and talented children** as those who "give evidence of high performance capabilities in areas such as intellectual, creative, artistic, or leadership capacity; or in specific academic fields, and who require services or activities not ordinarily provided by the school in order to fully develop such capabilities."[20] The definition distinguishes between giftedness,

FIGURE 11.7

Tips for Teaching Children with Disabilities

- Accentuate the positive. One of the most effective strategies is to emphasize what children can do rather than what they cannot do. Children with disabilities have talents and abilities similar to other children, and by exercising professional knowledge and skills you can help these and all children reach their full academic potential.

- Use appropriate assessment, including work samples, cumulative records, and appropriate assessment instruments. Discussions with parents and other professionals who have worked with the individual child are sources of valuable information and contribute to making accurate and appropriate plans for children.

- Use concrete examples and materials.

- Develop and use multisensory approaches to learning. For example, when conducting a lesson on counting have the children learn simple dance movements for each number and speak them aloud.

- Model what children are to do rather than just telling them what to do. Have a child who has mastered a certain task or behavior model it for others. Ask each child to perform a designated skill or task with supervision. Give corrective feedback.

- Let children practice or perform a certain behavior, involving them in their own assessment of that behavior.

- Make the learning enviroment a pleasant, rewarding place to be. For example, make the physical setting of the classroom accessible to all students; create clear classroom rules accompanied by pictures; be cautious of too many visual or audio distractions; vary instructional materials and teaching styles; and be sure to reward students for participation, good behavior, and so on.

- Create a dependable classroom schedule. Young children develop a sense of security when daily plans follow a consistent pattern. Allowing for flexibility also is important, however.

- Encourage parents to volunteer at school and to read to their children at home.

- Identify appropriate tasks children can accomplish on their own to create in them an opportunity to become more independent of you and others.

- Use cooperative learning. Cooperative learning enables all students to work together to achieve common goals. Cooperative learning has five components:

  - *Positive interdependence.* Group members establish mutual goals, divide the prerequisite tasks, share materials and resources, assume shared roles, and receive joint rewards.

  - *Face-to-face interaction.* Group members encourage and facilitate each other's efforts to complete tasks through direct communication.

  - *Individual accountability/personal responsibility.* Individual performance is assessed, and results are reported back to both the individual and the group. The group holds each member responsible for completing his or her fair share of responsibility.

  - *Interpersonal and small-group skills.* Students are responsible for getting to know and trust each other, communicating accurately and clearly, accepting and supporting each other, and resolving conflicts in a constructive manner.

  - *Group processing.* Group reflection includes describing which contributions of members are helpful or unhelpful in making decisions and which group actions should be continued or changed.

technology tie-in

Using Assistive Technology (AT) to Help Children with Disabilities Learn

IDEA defines assistive technology (AT) as "any item, piece of equipment, or product system, whether acquired commercially off the shelf, modified, or customized, that is used to increase, maintain, or improve functional capabilities of individuals with disabilities."*

Assistive technology covers a wide range of products and applications, from battery-operated toys to computer-assisted instruction. Assistive technology should be included as an important tool in your work with children with special needs.

One of your students with special needs may have trouble holding a pencil. Putting a pencil grip on her pencil makes it easier for her to hold it. The pencil grip is an example of low-tech assistive technology.

Dictionary skills are an important part of language and literacy. If a student has trouble holding and handling a dictionary, an assistive technology solution would be to use an electronic dictionary on the Internet, which also has voice pronunciation.

As this text has stressed, literacy development and learning to read are given a high priority in all grades, pre-K to 3. Children with special needs can learn to read with the help of assistive technology. Here are some programs that can help you achieve this goal.

PHONEMIC AWARENESS/EMERGENT LITERACY SKILLS

Earobics-Cognitive Concepts
Sesame Street Elmo's Reading: Preschool & Kindergarten, The Learning Company
First Phonics, SUNBURST
I Want to Read, DK Family Learning

PHONOLOGICAL DECODING

Curious George Learns Phonics, Houghton Mifflin Interactive
Let's Go Read: 1 & 2, Riverdeep & Edmark
Jumpstart Phonics, Knowledge Adventure
Sound It Out Land: A Musical Adventure in Phonics and Reading, Learning Upgrade LLC

READING COMPREHENSION

Reader Rabbit Learn to Read with Phonics, The Learning Company
Reading Blaster, Knowledge Adventure
Arthur's Reading Games, The Learning Company
Reading Readiness 1, School Zone

TALKING STORYBOOKS

Discis Books, Harmony Interactive
Disney's Animated Storybooks, Disney Interactive
Interactive Storybooks, Encore Software

*Lou Danielson, U.S. Office of Special Education, Research to Practice Division. [Online.] Available at: http://www.ed.gov/offices/OSERS/ Policy/IDEA/.

Sample a variety of software programs designed to assist young learners with literacy development at http://www.prenhall.com/morrison, Chapter 11—Journal: Technology Tie-In.

Observe a child using assistive technology at Video Classroom, Special Education, Module 11: Assistive Technology, Video 1: Headsprout Reading.

TEACHER PREP

characterized by above-average intellectual ability, and talented, referring to individuals who excel in such areas as drama, art, music, athletics, and leadership. Students can have these abilities separately or in combination. A talented five-year-old may be learning disabled, and a student with orthopedic disabilities may be gifted.

Although children may not display all these signs, the presence of several of them can alert parents and early childhood professionals to make appropriate instructional, environmental, and social adjustments.

Educating Gifted and Talented Children

Professionals tend to suggest special programs and sometimes schools for meeting the needs of the gifted and talented. Regular classroom teachers can provide for gifted children in their classrooms through enrichment and acceleration. Enrichment provides an opportunity for children to pursue topics in greater depth and in different ways than planned for in the curriculum. Acceleration permits children to progress academically at their own pace.

Many schools have resource rooms for gifted and talented students, in which children can spend a half-day or more every week working with a professional who is interested

KNOWLEDGE OF STUDENTS AND THEIR NEEDS

- Learn characteristics of students with special needs.
- Learn legislation regarding students with special needs.
- Develop a willingness to teach students with special needs.
- Foster social acceptance of students with special needs.
- Use assistive and educational technologies.

CLASSROOM LEADERSHIP AND CLASSROOM MANAGEMENT SKILLS

- Plan and manage the learning environment to accommodate students with special needs.
- Provide inclusion in varied student groupings and use peer tutoring.
- Manage the behavior of special needs students.
- Motivate all students.

KNOWLEDGE AND SKILLS IN CURRICULUM AND INSTRUCTION

- Develop and modify instruction for students with special needs.
- Use a variety of instructional styles and media and increase the range of learning behaviors.
- Provide instruction for students of all ability levels.
- Modify assessment techniques for students with special needs.
- Individualize instruction and integrate the curriculum.

PROFESSIONAL COLLABORATION SKILLS

- Work closely with special educators and other specialists.
- Work with and involve parents.
- Participate in planning and implementing IEPs.

FIGURE 11.8 Effective Teaching in Inclusive Classrooms

Photo: Scott Cunningham / Merrill

and trained in working with them. There are seven primary ways to provide for the needs of gifted and talented children:

1. *Enrichment classroom.* The classroom professional conducts a differentiated program of study without the help of outside personnel.
2. *Consultant professional.* A program of differentiated instruction is conducted in the regular classroom with the collaboration of a specially trained consultant.
3. *Resource room pullout.* Gifted students leave the classroom for a short period of time to receive instruction from a specially trained professional.
4. *Community mentor.* Gifted students interact with an adult from the community who has special knowledge in the area of interest.
5. Independent study. Students select projects and work on them under the supervision of a qualified professional.
6. *Special class.* Gifted students are grouped together during most of the class time and are instructed by a specially trained professional.
7. *Special schools.* Gifted students receive differentiated instruction at a special school with a specially trained staff.[21]

Of these seven methods, the resource room pullout is the most popular.

Read about instructional strategies for gifted learners at http://www.prenhall.com/morrison, Chapter 11: Web Links.

Scott Cunningham / Merrill

Early childhood educators must consider the diverse needs of students—including gender, ethnicity, race, and socioeconomic factors—when planning learning opportunities for their classes.

EDUCATION FOR CHILDREN WITH DIVERSE BACKGROUNDS

The population of the United States is changing and will continue to change. For example, projections are that by 2050, over one-fifth of the population will be Hispanic.[22]

The population of young children in the United States reflects the population at large and represents a number of different cultures and ethnicities. Thus, many cities and school districts have populations that express great ethnic diversity, including Asian Americans, Native Americans, African Americans, and Hispanic Americans. For example, the Dade County, Florida, school district has children from 172 countries, each with its own culture.[23] Table 11.1 shows the proportion of minority students in the nation's ten largest school districts. As a result of changing demographics, more students will require special education, bilingual education, and other special services. Issues of culture and diversity will shape instruction and curriculum. These demographics also have tremendous implications for how you teach and how your children learn.

Multicultural Awareness

Multicultural awareness is the appreciation for and understanding of people's cultures, socioeconomic status, and gender. It includes understanding one's own culture. Multicultural awareness programs and activities focus on other cultures while making children aware of the content, nature, and richness of their own. The terms and concepts for describing multicultural education and awareness are shown in Figure 11.9. Knowing the terminology of the profession is important. Review these terms, become familiar with them, and use them appropriately. Learning about other cultures concurrently with their own culture enables children to integrate commonalities and appreciate differences without inferring inferiority or superiority of one or the other.

TABLE 11.1 Proportion of Minority Students in the Ten Largest Public School Districts in the United States

Name of Reporting School District	State or Commonwealth	Percentage of Minority Students
New York City Public	NY	85.2
Los Angeles Unified	CA	90.9
City of Chicago	IL	90.9
Dade County	FL	89.6
Broward County	FL	63.7
Clark County	NV	56
Houston Independent	TX	90.9
Philadelphia City	PA	85.4
Hawaii Department of Education	HI	79.8
Hillsborough County	FL	51.3

Source: National Center for Education Statistics, "Characteristics of the 100 Largest Public Elementary and Secondary School Districts in the United States: 2003–04," http://nces.ed.gov/pubs 2006/2006 329.pdf.

Promoting multiculturalism in an early childhood program has implications far beyond your school, classroom, and program. Multiculturalism influences and affects work habits, interpersonal relations, and a child's general outlook on life. Early childhood professionals must take these multicultural influences into consideration when designing curriculum and instructional processes for the impressionable children they will teach. One way to accomplish the primary goal of multicultural education—to positively change the lives of children and their families—is to infuse multiculturalism into early childhood activities and practices, as evidenced by the accompanying Program in Action feature.

Being a multiculturally aware teacher means that you are sensitive to the socioeconomic backgrounds of children and families. For example, we know that low family socioeconomic status tends to dampen children's school achievement. The same is true with children's school achievement and maternal education as the Diversity Tie-In on page 315 illustrates. By learning about family background you can provide children from diverse backgrounds the extra help they may need to be successful in the school.

Read how to connect with Hispanic students at Articles and Readings, Multicultural Education, Module 7: Language, Article 2: Connecting with Latino Learners.

Multicultural Infusion

Multicultural infusion means that multicultural education permeates the curriculum to alter or affect the way young children and teachers think about diversity issues. In a larger perspective, infusion strategies are used to ensure that multiculturalism becomes a part of the entire center, school, and home. Infusion processes foster cultural awareness; use appropriate instructional materials, themes, and activities; teach to children's learning styles; and promote family and community involvement. Let's take a closer look at each of these practices.

FIGURE 11.9

Glossary of Multicultural Terms

The following terms will assist you as you provide bias-free and multiculturally appropriate education for your children and families.

Bias-free: Curriculum, programs, materials, language, attitudes, actions, and activities that are free from biased perceptions.

Bilingual education: Education in two languages. Generally, two languages are used for the purpose of academic instruction.

Cultural diversity: The diversity between and within ethnic groups. The extent of group identification by members of ethnic groups varies greatly and is influenced by many factors such as skin color, social class, and professional experience.

Cultural pluralism: The belief that cultural diversity is of positive value.

Culturally fair education: Education that respects and accounts for the cultural backgrounds of all learners.

Diversity: Refers to and describes the relationships among background, socioeconomic status, gender, language, and culture of students, parents, and communities.

English as a second language (ESL): Instruction in which students with limited English proficiency attend a special English class.

Infusion: The process of having multiculturalism become an explicit part of the curriculum throughout all the content areas.

Multicultural awareness: Ability to perceive and acknowledge cultural differences among people without making value judgments about these differences.

Multiculturalism: An approach to education based on the premise that all peoples in the United States should receive proportional attention in the curriculum.

program in action

How to Support Diversity in a Multicultural Child Care Setting

Hampton Place Baptist Church is in the low-income region of Oak Cliff, an urban area of Dallas, Texas, that is composed of many minorities. The church provides child care services to primarily Hispanic, Spanish-speaking families. However, we also house a Laotian mission. Our preschool department includes approximately fifteen infants, ten toddlers, and fifteen preschoolers and serves both the Hispanic and the Laotian congregations. Here are some of the considerations and adjustments we make to accommodate these different cultures:

STRATEGY 1 GREET FAMILIES IN A CULTURALLY SENSITIVE MANNER
With Hispanic families, the father is greeted first, then the mother, and the children last.

STRATEGY 2 PROVIDE INCLUSIVE ARTWORK
Murals include children with different skin and hair colors.

STRATEGY 3 USE LINGUISTICALLY APPROPRIATE MATERIALS
Books in English and Spanish should be provided.

STRATEGY 4 ADJUST TEACHER–INFANT INTERACTION STYLE ACCORDING TO CULTURE
Although most Hispanic infants are calmed with quick, repetitive, choppy phrases and back patting, Laotian infants are calmed through soft, smooth talking, cradling, and gentle rocking.

STRATEGY 5 MEET INDIVIDUAL AS WELL AS CULTURAL NEEDS
Some infants interact primarily person-to-person; others interact through toys.

STRATEGY 6 RESPECT DIFFERENT SOCIAL PREFERENCES
Hispanic toddlers tend to interact with peers, but Laotian toddlers tend to keep to themselves and sometimes want to be left alone. A Laotian child may need to be provided with a special place of his or her own.

STRATEGY 7 APPLY LIMITS TO CULTURAL ACCOMMODATION WHEN NECESSARY
Discuss compromises with parents. For example, some cultures allow infants to eat items they could choke on. In this case we explain the danger the food presents to the infants and ask parents to bring alternative snacks.

STRATEGY 8 RECOGNIZE THAT ALL FAMILIES HAVE INDIVIDUAL CULTURES
Be careful not to stereotype by ethnicity.

Contributed by Amy Turcotte, developmental specialist.

Foster Cultural Awareness. As an early childhood professional, keep in mind that you are the key to a multicultural classroom. The following guidelines will help you foster cultural awareness:

- *Recognize that all children are unique.* Children have special talents, abilities, and styles of learning and relating to others. Make your classroom a place in which children are comfortable being who they are. Always value uniqueness and diversity.
- *Get to know, appreciate, and respect the cultural backgrounds of your children.* Visit families and community neighborhoods to learn more about cultures and religion and the ways of life they engender.
- *Infuse children's culture (and other cultures as well) into your teaching.*
- *Use authentic situations to provide for cultural learning and understanding.* For example, a field trip to a culturally diverse neighborhood of your city or town provides children an opportunity for understanding firsthand many of the details about how people live. Such an experience provides wonderful opportunities for involving children in writing, cooking, reading, and dramatic play activities. What about setting up a market in the classroom?

Maternal Education and Student Achievement

Socioeconomic status (SES), the social and economic background of an individual or individuals, is a reflection of family income, maternal education level, and family occupation. You may be surprised by the inclusion of maternal education level in this list, but in fact it is a powerful predictor of how well students do in school. As a mother's education increases, so does student achievement (see figure below). This helps explain why, from a social and educational policy perspective, a U.S. priority is to prevent teenage mothers from dropping out of school.

Family income also correlates with how well students do in school, whether or not they drop out, the kind and type of schools they attend, and the quality of their teachers. Students' socioeconomic status is used to determine eligibility for many state and federal programs such as Head Start and Title I programs. One Head Start eligibility criteria, for example, is that the child's family meets federal poverty income criteria for enrollment, and many schools provide free or reduced school lunches based on family income.

....

Sources: K. Denton and E. Germino-Hausken, America's Kindergartners (NCES No. 200–070) (Washington, DC: National Center for Education Statistics, U.S. Department of Education, 2000); Mathematics and Science in the Eighth Grade: Findings from the Third International Mathematics and Science Study (NCES No. 2000–014), Washington, DC: National Center for Education Statistics, U.S. Department of Education, 2003).

Reflect on the classroom implications of poverty at http://www.prenhall.com/morrison, Chapter 11—Journal: Diversity Tie-In.

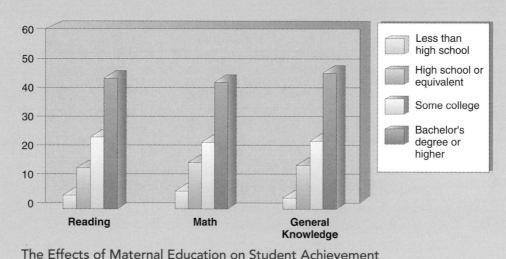

Legend:
- Less than high school
- High school or equivalent
- Some college
- Bachelor's degree or higher

The Effects of Maternal Education on Student Achievement

- *Use authentic assessment activities to assess fully children's learning and growth.* Portfolios (see Chapter 6) are ideal for assessing children's learning in nonbiased and culturally sensitive ways.

- *Infuse culture into your lesson planning, teaching, and caregiving.* Use all subject areas—math, science, language arts, literacy, music, art, and social studies—to relate culture to children's cultures.

- *Be a role model by accepting, appreciating, and respecting other languages and cultures.* In other words, infuse multiculturalism into your personal and professional lives.

- *Use children's experiences to form a basis for planning lessons and developing activities.* This approach makes students feel good about their backgrounds, cultures, families, and experiences.

- *Be knowledgeable about, proud of, and secure in your own culture.* Children will ask about you, and you should be prepared to share your cultural background with them.

Use Appropriate Instructional Materials. You need to carefully consider and select appropriate instructional materials to support the infusion of multicultural education. The following are some suggestions for achieving this goal.

Scott Cunningham / Merrill

All classrooms must be places where people of both genders and all cultures, races, socioeconomic backgrounds, and religions are welcomed and accepted. If students learn to embrace diversity within the classroom, they will also embrace diversity outside of it.

Review online resources for multicultural children's literature at http://www.prenhall.com/morrison, Chapter 11: Web Links.

Multicultural Literature. Choose literature that stresses similarities and differences regarding how children and families live their *whole lives*. Avoid books and stories that note differences or teach only about habits and customs.

Themes. Early childhood professionals may select and teach through thematic units that help strengthen children's understanding of themselves, their culture, and the cultures of others. Some appropriate theme topics are:

- Getting to Know Myself, Getting to Know Others
- What Is Special About You and Me?
- Growing Up in the City
- Growing Up in the Country
- Tell Me About Africa (South America, China, etc.)

All of these themes are appropriate for meeting various state standards and standards of the National Council for the Social Studies (NCSS).

Personal Accomplishments. Add to classroom activities, as appropriate, the accomplishments of people from different cultural groups, women of all cultures, and individuals with disabilities.

When selecting materials for use in a multicultural curriculum for early childhood programs, make sure:

- People of all cultures are represented fairly and accurately;
- To represent people of color, many cultural groups, and people with exceptionalities;
- Historical information is accurate and nondiscriminatory;
- Materials do not include stereotypical roles and language; and
- There is gender equity—that is, boys and girls are represented equally and in non-stereotypic roles.

Teach to Children's Learning Styles and Intelligences. Every child has a unique learning style. Although every person's learning style is different, we can cluster learning styles for instructional purposes.

Different Children, Different Learning Styles. It makes sense to consider students' various **learning styles** and account for them when organizing the environment and developing activities. "Learning style is the way that students of every age are affected by their (1) immediate environment, (2) own emotionality, (3) sociological needs, (4) physical characteristics, and (5) psychological inclinations when concentrating and trying to master and remember new or difficult information or skills."[24]

Learning styles consist of the following elements:

- Environmental—sound, light, temperature, and design;
- Emotional—motivation, persistence, responsibility, and the need for either structure or choice;
- Sociological—learning alone, with others, or in a variety of ways (perhaps including media);

- Physical—perceptual strengths, intake, time of day or night energy levels, and mobility; and

- Psychological—global/analytic, hemispheric preference, and impulsive/reflective.

Teaching to children's learning styles is a good way to infuse multiculturalism into your program. Also, review now our discussion of multiple intelligences in Chapter 3.

Howard Gardner maintains that all children possess all nine of the multiple intelligences, although some intelligences may be stronger than others. This accounts for why children have a preferred learning style; different interests, likes, and dislikes; different habits; preferred lifestyles; and preferred career choices.

The Professionalism in Practice feature on pages 318–319 describes how a 2004 National Teacher of the Year, Kathy Mellor, uses mainstreaming with her ESL students and what effect it has had on her teaching career.

Promote Family and Community Involvement. You will work with children and families of diverse cultural backgrounds. As such you will need to learn about the cultural background of children and families so that you can respond appropriately to their needs. For example, let's take a look at the Hispanic culture and its implications for parent and family involvement.

Throughout Hispanic culture is a widespread belief in the absolute authority of the school and teachers. In many Latin American countries it is considered rude for a parent to intrude into the life of the school. Parents believe that it is the school's job to educate and the parent's job to nurture and that the two jobs do not mix. A child who is well educated is one who has learned moral and ethical behavior.

Hispanics, as a whole, have strong family ties, believe in family loyalty, and have a collective orientation that supports community life. They have personalized styles of interaction, a relaxed sense of time, and a need for an informal atmosphere for communication. Given these preferences, a culture clash may result when Hispanic students and parents are confronted with the typical task-oriented style of most American teachers.

Whereas an understanding of the general cultural characteristics of Hispanics is helpful, it is important not to overgeneralize. Each family and child is unique, and care should be taken not to assume values and beliefs just because a family speaks Spanish and is from Latin America. It is important that you spend the time to discover the particular values, beliefs, and practices of the families in the community.

In addition to having Hispanic children in your classroom or program, chances are you will also have children from one of the many Asian American family subgroups. Asian Americans now represent one of the fastest growing minority populations in the United States.

It is always risky to generalize about peoples and their cultures. When we do make generalizations about ethnic groups that compromise the domain of Asian Americans, we run the risk of assuming that the generalization applies to all groups. It may not. In addition, we always have to consider individual children and families, regardless of their cultural background. With this in mind, some broad generalizations about Asian Americans and values that influence the rearing and education of children include the following: a group orientation as opposed to an individual orientation, the importance of family and family responsibilities, emphasis on self-control and personal discipline, educational achievement, respect for authority, and reverence for the elderly.[25]

Educating students with diverse backgrounds and special needs makes for a challenging and rewarding career. As society, families, and children change, as diversity increases, and as more students with special needs come to school, you will have to change how and what you teach. How to constantly improve your responses to students' special needs and improve learning environments and curricula will be one of your ongoing professional responsibilities. Your students with special needs are waiting for you to make a difference in their lives!

ESL Programs—"One of My Greatest Accomplishments"

Kathy Mellor
2004 National Teacher of the Year
Teaches English as a second language in
North Kingstown, Rhode Island.

When I was four years old, I entered a private kindergarten before it was required as part of the public school program. I loved the activities, the learning, and the way my teacher made everyone feel—smart and special. We played, we worked, and we learned a lot. I learned to read. I was impressed by my teacher. What a great job being a teacher must be! For the next five years in elementary school, I was blessed with teachers who had the same effect on me. Each of those classes was large—well over forty students. There was less play and a lot more work, but just as much excitement in learning.

In third, fourth, and sixth grades, I was assigned to split grades, where I learned a lot by osmosis, watching the teacher work with the other group or as she taught us together. I had the same teacher for third, fourth, and fifth grades. Early on, I experienced the benefits of multi-aged groupings and looping—moving up a level with a class and then returning to the lower grade to do the same with another class. With such wonderful experiences as a student, I knew that I would love being a teacher myself.

My parents valued education. Like many of their contemporaries, they had to leave school to go to work to help support their families. My parents spoke openly about how important school was. "A house without books is like a house without windows," proclaimed my father, who encouraged me on my first day of first grade to stay in school so my hands wouldn't look like his. It was a defining moment in my life.

ACTIVITIES FOR PROFESSIONAL DEVELOPMENT

Ethical Dilemma

"We Shouldn't Cater to Them!"

Beth has just been hired to teach first grade in River Bend School District, which has had an influx of minority students during the past few years. The minority students are almost the majority. Not everyone thinks that the rapid increase in the minority student population is beneficial to the school district or town. Some of Beth's colleagues think that the school district is bending over (too far) backward to meet minority students' needs. At Beth's first meeting with Harry Fortune, her new mentor teacher, he remarked, "Respecting minorities and catering to them are two different things. I'm going to stress with my parents that this is America and American culture comes first, and that includes speaking English!"

What should Beth do? Should she agree with her mentor teacher, adopting a policy of English first, or should she seek out the director of multiculturalism for her school district and discuss Harry's comments with her, or should she pursue another course of action?

Application Activities

1. Visit a classroom or program where children with special needs are included, and observe the children during play activities. You can develop an observational checklist based on guidelines provided in Chapter 6. Follow a particular child and note the materials available, the physical arrangement of the environment, and the number of other children involved. Try to determine whether the child is really engaged in the play activity. Hypothesize about why the child is or is not engaged. Discuss your observations with your colleagues.

2. Visit an early childhood special education classroom and a regular preschool classroom and compare how their methods for guiding children's behavior are similar and different.

Before I completed elementary school, I had decided that I would become a teacher.

Mainstream teachers and ESL/bilingual teachers must function as a team, fully sharing responsibility for the students they have in common. They need each other's expertise, and the students need them to work toward the same goals, reinforcing each other's efforts on behalf of the students. Today, ESL instruction in my district has evolved into a program set up to deal successfully with the many variables the students present. Children remain integrated in their home schools. They are a shared responsibility between the ESL and content-area teachers. As a result, the program is cognitively demanding, and the students are not isolated from their English-speaking peers, so a great deal of natural language acquisition takes place. The ESL component of the program is a developmental language program that provides each student with one to three periods of instruction per day according to the child's proficiency level in the areas of listening, speaking, reading, and writing.

I consider this ESL program to be one of my greatest accomplishments in education. Unlike many districts, the students are not segregated into separate classrooms or schools.

They are integrated into all programs within the district and are held to the same high standards. The program, the students, and their families are accepted and respected.

Academically, teaching is the challenge of maximizing student growth regardless of ability level or previous achievement. It requires teachers to be responsible for and responsive to every child in the classroom. I believe that my achievement as a teacher is directly related to the success and achievement of my students. Effective teaching establishes goals and expectations that are clear, consistent, and attainable.

I believe the teaching environment must be conducive to learning. It is our job as educators to see that it is. I strongly believe that teachers are responsible for every child enrolled in their classroom and must be each child's advocate. Isn't that what we would want for ourselves?

Conduct an observation of an ESL program at http://www.prenhall.com/morrison, Chapter 11— Projects: Professionalism in Practice.

3. Visit several public schools and ask to review either IEPs or IFSPs. How are these plans meeting the needs of children and families? What are some services that you think are unique about each plan?

4. How is curriculum and instruction in a class for gifted and talented students different from that in other classes? Get permission to visit and observe such a class. Then compare that class with others you have observed or experienced. On the basis of your observations, describe how you might teach a student who is gifted and talented within your inclusive classroom.

5. How does a teacher modify the classroom environment, classroom routines, learning activities, student groupings, teaching strategies, instructional materials, assessments, and homework assignments to meet all students' special needs? What human and material resources for successful inclusion are available to teachers and to students with special needs? How do students show social acceptance for their classmates with special needs? Visit an inclusive classroom and take notes on what you observe. Compare and discuss your observations with classmates who have visited different settings across all grade levels.

6. Effective educational programs provide children with opportunities to develop an understanding of other persons and cultures. List ways for how you would accomplish the following objectives in your classroom:

    a. Provide children with firsthand, positive experiences with different cultural groups.

    b. Help children reflect on and think about their own cultural group identity.

    c. Help children learn how to obtain accurate information about other cultural groups.

7. Select ten children's books that have multicultural content. Decide how you would use these materials to promote awareness and acceptance of diversity. Read these books to children and get their reactions.

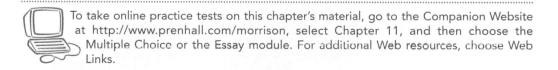

To take online practice tests on this chapter's material, go to the Companion Website at http://www.prenhall.com/morrison, select Chapter 11, and then choose the Multiple Choice or the Essay module. For additional Web resources, choose Web Links.

12

GUIDING CHILDREN'S BEHAVIOR
Helping Children Act Their Best

Guiding Behavior

A. I understand the principles and importance of behavior guidance. I guide children to be peaceful, respectful, cooperative, and in control of their behavior.

B. I know, understand, and use positive relationships and supportive interactions as the foundation for my work with young children.[1]

C. I know, understand, and use a wide array of effective approaches, strategies, and tools to positively influence children's development and learning.[2]

1. Why is it important to help children guide their own behavior?

2. What theories of guiding children's behavior can I apply to my teaching?

3. What are some basic strategies that I can successfully use to guide children's behavior?

4. What can I do now to develop the knowledge and skills to successfully help children guide their behavior?

WHY GUIDE CHILDREN'S BEHAVIOR?

As an early childhood professional, you will be assuming major responsibility for guiding children's behavior in up-close and personal ways. You will spend many hours with young children as a parent/family surrogate. As a result, you need to know how to best guide children's behavior and help them become responsible. There are a number of reasons for knowing how to best guide children's behavior:

- Helping children learn to guide and be responsible for their own behavior is as important as helping them learn to read and write. You may think that this notion is far-fetched, but think for a moment about how many times you have said or have heard others say, "If only the children would behave, I could teach them something!" Appropriate behavior and learning go together. One of your primary roles as an early childhood teacher is to help children learn the knowledge and skills that will help them act responsibly.

- Helping children learn to act responsibly and guide their behavior lays the foundation for lifelong responsible and productive living. As early childhood educators, we believe that the early years are the formative years. Consequently, what we teach children about responsible living, how we guide them, and the skills we help them learn will last a lifetime.

- The roots of delinquent and deviant behavior are in the early years. From research we know what behaviors lead to future behavior problems. For example, some characteristics of preschool children that are precursors of adolescent behavior problems and delinquency include disruptive behavior; overactivity, irritability, noncompliance, aggression toward peers, and poor regulation of impulses.[3]

- The public is increasingly concerned about the erosion of civility, and what it perceives as a general breakdown of personal responsibility for bad behavior. One reason the public funds the public educational system at all levels is to help keep society strong and healthy. Parents and the public look to early childhood professionals for assistance in helping children learn to live cooperatively and civilly in a democratic society. Getting along with others and guiding one's behavior is a culturally and socially meaningful accomplishment.

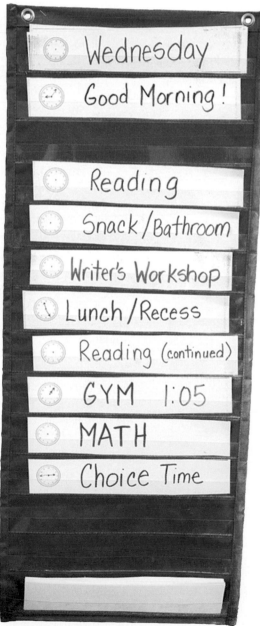

What Is Guiding Behavior?

Guiding children's behavior is a process of helping children build positive behaviors. Discipline is not about compliance and control but involves **behavior guidance**, a process by which all children learn to control and direct their behavior and become independent and self-reliant. In this view, behavior guidance is a process of helping children develop skills useful over a lifetime.

As you work with young children, one of your goals will be to help them become independent and have the ability to regulate or govern their own behavior. **Self-regulation** is the child's ability to plan, guide, and monitor his or her behavior according to changing life circumstances.

A SOCIAL CONSTRUCTIVIST APPROACH TO GUIDING BEHAVIOR

Step 1: Use the Social Constructivist Approach to Guide Behavior

In Chapter 3, "History and Theories: Foundations for Teaching and Learning," we discussed theories of learning and development and how you can use them in your teaching. Reacquaint yourself now with the theories of Piaget, Vygotsky, Maslow, and Erikson so their ideas will be fresh in your mind as we apply them to guiding children's behavior.

Read about the importance of teachers' actions and control in the classroom at Articles and Readings, Classroom Management, Module 2: Establishing Classroom, Norms and Expectations, Article 3: The Key to Classroom Management.

The Social Constructivist Approach: Piaget and Vygotsky.   Piaget's and Vygotsky's theories support a social constructivist approach to learning and behavior. Teachers who embrace a **social constructivist approach** believe that children construct or build their behavior as a result of learning from experience and from making decisions that lead to responsible behavior. Your primary role in the constructivist approach is to guide and help children construct or build their behavior and use it in socially appropriate and productive ways. This process begins in homes and classrooms.

In Chapter 3, we also discussed Vygotsky's theories of **scaffolding** and the **zone of proximal development (ZPD)**. We now apply these two theories to our approach for guiding children's behavior and add two additional essentials to Vygotskyian constructivist theory: **adult/child discourse** and child **self-discourse** (or **private speech**). Foundational to Vygotskyian and constructivist theory are the central beliefs that the development of a child's knowledge and behaviors occurs in the context of social relations with adults and peers. This means that learning and development are socially mediated as children interact with more competent peers and adults. As children gain the ability to master language and appropriate social relations, they are able to intentionally regulate their behavior.

Guiding Behavior in the Zone of Proximal Development.   The ZPD is the cognitive and developmental space that is created when the child is in social interaction with a more competent person (MCP) or a more knowledgeable other (MKO). As Vygotsky explains, the ZPD is the "actual development level as determined by independent problem solving and the level of potential development as determined through problem solving under adult guidance or in collaboration with more capable peers."[4] Problem solving is what guiding behavior is all about. Teachers take children from the behavioral and social skills they have in their ZPD and guide them to increasingly higher levels of responsible behavior and social interactions. Also, although we often think of guiding behavior as a one-on-one activity, this is not the case. Your role in guiding behavior includes large and small groups, as well as individual children. Figure 12.1 illustrates the ZPD and illustrates how to guide children's behavior within it. The ZPD is constantly moving and changing, depending on children's behavioral accomplishments and the assistance and scaffolding provided by others.

Guiding Behavior with Scaffolding.   Scaffolding is one of the ways teachers can guide children in the ZPD. Recall that scaffolding is the use of informal methods such as conversations, questions, modeling, guiding, and supporting to help children learn concepts, knowledge, and skills that they might not learn by themselves. When more competent others provide "help," children are able to accomplish what they would not have been able to do on their own. In the ZPD, children are capable of far more competent behavior and achievements as they receive guidance and support from teachers and parents.

Adult/Child Discourse.   The scaffolding script that follows is illustrative of adult/child discourse. Discourse also involves talking about how children might solve problems, guide their own behavior, interact and cooperate with others, understand norms of social conduct,

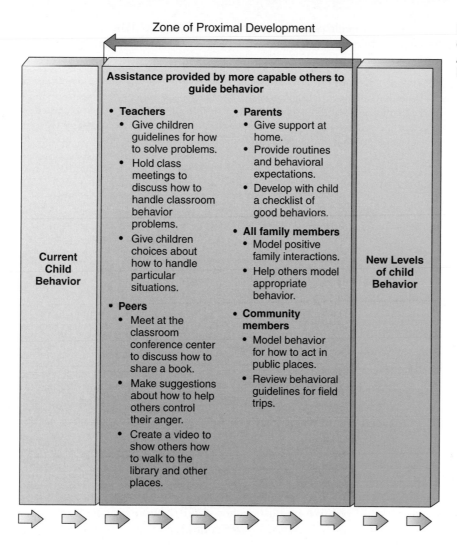

FIGURE 12.1 The Zone of Proximal Development Applied to Guiding Behavior

and learn values related to school and family living. Teachers must initiate and guide these discourses and help children learn new skills that will assist them in developing self-regulation. Here is an example of a "learning conversation" that invites student participation. This discourse centers on how student authors should act while they are sharing their stories.

Ms. Fletcher: Maybe we should now think about how to behave as the author during author's chair. What do authors do? Who can remember? Tina, would you like to start?

Tina: The author sits in the author's chair and speaks loud and clear.

Crystal: The author should not be shy and should be brave and confident.

Ms. Fletcher continues to invite students to participate providing ideas and suggestions, using this type of scaffolding. The children create a list of responsibilities to guide their behaviors while sharing stories.[5]

Private Speech and Self-Guided Behavior.   Jennifer, a four-year-old preschooler, is busily engrossed in putting a puzzle together. As she searches for a puzzle piece, she asks herself out loud, "Which piece comes next?" I'm sure you have heard children talk to themselves. More than likely, you have talked to yourself while working on a task! Such conversations are commonplace in the lives of young children and adults.

Private speech plays an important role in problem solving and self-regulation of behavior. Children learn to transfer problem-solving knowledge and responsibility from adults to themselves:

> When adults use questions and strategies to guide children and to help them discover solutions, they elevate language to the status of a primary problem-solving tool. This use of language by adults leads children to use speech to solve problems. Research reveals that the relation of private speech to children's behavior is consistent with the assumption that self-guiding utterances help bring action under the control of thought.[6]

Vygotsky Guidance Guidelines. Based on Vygotsky's theory, here are some strategies you can use to guide children's behavior:

- Guide problem solving:
  - "Tanya, what are some things you can do to help you remember to put the books away?"
  - "Keyshawn, you and Juana want to use the easel at the same time. What are some ideas for how you can both use it?"
- Ask questions that help children arrive at their own solutions:
  - "Jesse, you can't use both toys at the same time. Which one do you want to use first?"
  - "April, here is an idea that might help you get to the block corner. Ask Amy, 'Would you please move over a little so I can get to the blocks?'"
- Model appropriate skills:
  - Practice social skills and manners (e.g., say "please and thank you").
  - Listen attentively to children and encourage listening. For example, say, "Harry has something he wants to tell us. Let's listen to what he has to say."

Teacher Effectiveness Training. Thomas Gordon (1918–2002) developed a child guidance program based on teacher–student relationships. Gordon developed Parent Effectiveness Training (PET) for parents and Teacher Effectiveness Training (TET) for teachers. Both programs use communication as the primary means of helping parents and teachers build positive parent/teacher–child relationships that foster self-direction, self-responsibility, self-determination, self-control, and self-evaluation.[7]

Problem Ownership. The first cornerstone of the TET approach to guiding behavior is to identify who owns the behavior problem. When a problem arises, as problems inevitably do in human relationships, you, the teacher, have to determine if the child (or children) owns the problem or if you own the problem. For example, preschool teacher Maria Escobar observes that several of her children are noisy and disruptive and are not following the guidelines for using the woodworking center. As Maria thought about the children's lack of self-direction, she concluded that the children owned the problem. They didn't fully understand the center directions and how to follow them. In response to this conclusion, Maria gathered the children and explained the guidelines for using the woodworking center in a different way, using herself as an example and having the children repeat the steps aloud to promote class participation and interest in the center.

On another occasion, Maria was becoming increasingly irritated with always having to deal with Hector's interrupting behavior during circle time. As Maria thought about Hector's behavior, she realized that *she* owned the problem. She was allowing Hector's behavior to irritate her rather than working on specific ways to help Hector learn new ways of behaving and interacting.

> The difference between student-owned and teacher-owned problems is essentially one of tangible and concrete (*or real*) effect. Teachers can separate their own problems from those of their students by asking themselves: "Does this behavior have any *real*, tangible, or concrete effect on me? Am I feeling unaccepting because I am being interfered with,

damaged, hurt, or impaired in some way? Or am I feeling unaccepting merely because I'd like the student to act differently, not have a problem, and behave the way I think he should?" If the answer is "yes" to the latter, the problem belongs to the student. If it is "yes" to the former, the teacher certainly has a real stake in the problem.[8]

Active Listening.   **Active listening** is the second cornerstone of TET. Active listening will help you identify who has the problem, and it will help you communicate with children. Active listening involves interactions with a child to provide him with proof that you understand what he is talking about. This proof might come in the form of feedback. Determining who owns the problem is an essential part of being able to guide children's behavior well.

I Messages.   Letting children know about your problem is the third cornerstone of TET. If, upon reflection, you determine you own the problem, then you will want to deliver **"I" messages**. I messages are designed to let children know that you have a problem with their behavior and that you want them to do something to change the behavior. Let's join Maria and Hector again. Maria can send an I message by responding, "Hector, when I am constantly interrupted, I can't teach what I need to, and this makes me feel like I'm not a good teacher." Notice how Maria described the behavior (interrupting), the consequences of the behavior (I can't teach), and her feelings (I'm not a good teacher). These three components constitute a good I message.

Laura Bolesta / Merrill

Practice Makes Perfect.   I have briefly reviewed with you some of the major concepts associated with Vygotskyian, constructivist, and TET ideas and practices. Using these strategies effectively requires much determination and practice. They are worth the effort, and you will be rewarded with their beneficial results as you learn to guide children's behavior.

Guiding children's behavior consists of essential guidelines, including helping children build new, appropriate behaviors and helping them to be responsible for their behaviors. Why is it important for children to learn to guide their own behavior rather than having teachers and parents always telling them what to do?

Step 2: Clarify Your Beliefs About Guiding Behavior

A good way to clarify your beliefs is to develop a philosophy about what you believe concerning child rearing, guidance, and children. Review the information on how to develop your philosophy of education in Chapter 1 to help you do this. Knowing what you want for your children at home and school helps you decide what to do and how to do it. Knowing what you believe also makes it easier for you to share with parents, help them guide behavior, and counsel them about discipline. Take a few minutes now and write a paragraph titled "My Basic Beliefs About Guiding Children's Behavior." This will help you get started on clarifying your beliefs.

Step 3: Know and Use Developmentally Appropriate Practice

Knowing child development is the cornerstone of developmentally appropriate practice. Children cannot behave well when adults expect too much or too little of them based on their development or when parents expect them to behave in ways inappropriate for them as individuals. Thus, a key for guiding children's behavior is to *really know what they are like.* This is the real meaning of developmentally appropriate practice. You will want to study children's development and observe children's behavior to learn what is appropriate

Observe a teacher using developmentally appropriate practice to guide the behavior of his student at Video Classroom, Special Education, Module 7: Emotional and Behavioral Disorders, Video 1: Managing Behavior.

for all children and individual children based on their needs, gender, and culture. The portraits of children in Chapters 7, 8, 9, and 10 will help you learn and apply developmentally appropriate practice.

Step 4: Meet Children's Needs

A major reason for knowing children and child development is so that you will be able to meet their needs. Abraham Maslow felt that human growth and development were oriented toward self-actualization, the striving to realize one's potential. Review Maslow's hierarchy in Chapter 3 and consider how children's physical needs, safety and security needs, belonging and affection needs, and self-esteem needs culminate in self-actualization. An example of each of these needs will illustrate how to apply them to your guiding children's behavior.

Physical Needs. Children's abilities to guide their behaviors depend in part on how well their physical needs are met. Children do their best in school, for example, when they are well nourished. Families and schools should provide for children's nutritional needs by giving them breakfast. Recent brain research, discussed in Chapter 2, also informs us that the brain needs protein and water to function well. You should encourage children to drink water throughout the day and also provide frequent nutritional snacks.

Safety and Security. Just as you can't teach when you are fearful for your safety, children can't learn in fear. Children should feel comfortable and secure at home and at school. Consider also the dangers many children face in their neighborhoods, such as crime, drugs, and violence, and the dangers they face at home, such as abuse and neglect. Part of guiding children's behavior includes providing safe and secure communities, neighborhoods, homes, schools, and classrooms. For many children your classroom may be their only haven of safety and security. In addition, you may need to assume a major role of advocacy for safe communities.

© Ellen B. Senisi / Ellen Senisi

Helping children become more independent by warmly supporting their efforts is one of the most effective forms of guidance. Identify some ways you and other professionals can support children's efforts to do things for themselves.

Belonging and Affection. You need love and affection and children do too. Love and affection needs are satisfied when parents hold, hug, and kiss their children and tell them, "I love you." Teachers meet children's affectional needs when they smile, speak pleasantly, are kind and gentle, treat children with courtesy and respect, and genuinely value each child. Today, many children are starving for affection and recognition. For these children you may be their sole or main source of affectional needs.

Self-Esteem. Children who view themselves as worthy, responsible, and competent feel good about themselves and learn better. Children's views of themselves come from parents and early childhood professionals. Experiencing success gives children feelings of high self-esteem. It is the responsibility of parents and teachers to give all children opportunities for success. Success and achievement are the foundations for self-esteem.

Self-Actualization. Children want to do things for themselves and be independent. Teachers and parents can help children become independent by helping them learn to dress themselves, go to the restroom by themselves, and take care of their environments. They can also help children set achievement and behavior goals ("Tell me what you are going to build with your blocks") and encourage them to evaluate their behavior ("Let's talk about how you cleaned up your room"). Self-actualization is a process of becoming all you can be, and we want this goal for all children. The Professionalism in Practice feature on pages 328–329 discusses strategies teachers can use to set achievement and goals for gifted students within the regular classroom.

Step 5: Help Children Build New Behaviors

Helping children build new behaviors means that you help them learn that they are primarily responsible for their own behavior and that the pleasures and rewards for appropriate behavior are internal, coming from within them as opposed to always coming from outside (i.e., from the approval and praise of others). This concept is known as **locus of control**, the source or place of control. The preferred and recommended locus of control for young children is internal.

The process of developing an internal locus of control begins at birth, continues through the early childhood years, and is a never-ending process throughout life. We want children to control their own behavior. When their locus of control is external, children are controlled by others; they are always told what to do and how to behave. In addition, we want children to take responsibility for their behavior. What we want to avoid is having children blame their behavior on others ("Chandra took my pencil") or on circumstances ("I didn't have time"). Legitimate excuses are appropriate, but always blaming others or external events is not. Learning to do it right and trying again after a failure are other important positive behaviors.

Affirming and acknowledging children's appropriate behaviors is a good way to build new behaviors—everyone likes to be praised and affirmed for a job well done, good efforts, and their best work. Figure 12.2 provides examples on how to do this. Helping

Read about encouraging children to make positive choices at http://www.prenhall.com/morrison, Chapter 12: Web Links.

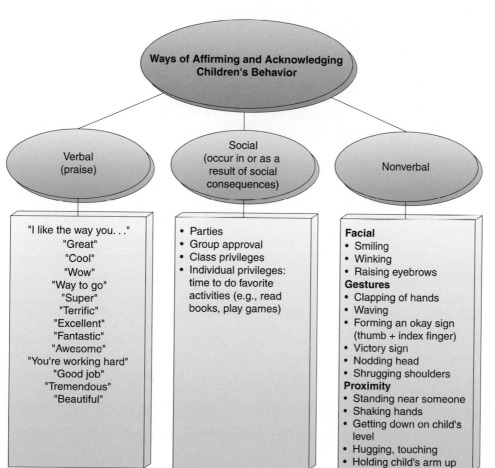

FIGURE 12.2 Example of Ways to Affirm and Acknowledge Young Children's Behavior

Helping Gifted Children Through Challenging Curriculum

Susan Winebrenner
Author and consultant

It may shock you to know that of all the students in mixed-abilities classrooms, those who are at greatest risk of learning the least during a regular school year are those at the top in academic ability. Although this condition has always been present in our schools, it is occurring more often due to the national attention to raising the achievement levels for students scoring below expected standards. Many teachers pay much less attention to students who can easily score well on state and standardized tests or who are getting high grades. If we define learning as one's forward progress during the present year's curriculum, we can appreciate the significant problems faced by gifted students at all grade levels.

When schools promise that "all kids can learn," gifted students should also be able to reap the benefits of that promise.

LESS PRESSURE ON PERFECTION: CONSISTENT OPPORTUNITIES FOR STRUGGLE AND CHALLENGE

Students who get high grades or praise with little or no effort conclude that smart means easy. The longer their effortless success continues, the more likely they are to resist challenge when it comes because they fear it will send a message that they are not really smart after all. They may conclude from their experience that teachers, parents, and peers expect them to be perfect at all times. Risk-taking behavior will be diminished.

Teachers and parents must help these students value hard work when learning. Encouragement to try things that do not come easily can help students reconnect with intrinsic motivation. Teachers' willingness to work with these students during their struggle, rather than expecting them to learn all things easily, can give courage to those who may have lost it.

WHAT IS CURRICULUM COMPACTING?

Compacting describes the process of reducing the amount of time gifted students need to spend on the regular curriculum by allowing them to demonstrate what they already know and providing them with alternate learning activities so they can move forward in their own learning. The student who experiences a compacted curriculum will probably be more motivated to be productive in school than students who find themselves wasting precious learning time working on content they have already mastered or that they could learn in a significantly shorter period of time than age peers. We can compact the content, and we can compact the pacing.

Gifted students may resist compacting opportunities if they perceive there will be more work for them to do, or that their grades will be lower than if they did the regular class work. Explain to the students how it will be "safe" for them to participate in the compacting.

Students who are experiencing compacting are expected to follow what I call the "Three Simple Rules" at all times. When working on something different than other students:

1. Don't bother anyone, including the teacher when she is with other students.
2. Don't call attention to yourself or the fact that you are doing something different than the regular work—it's no big deal.
3. Do the work you choose to do.

COMPACTING THE CONTENT

1. Identify the learning objectives or standards all students must learn in an upcoming chapter or unit.
2. Plan a menu of extension activities related to the content being studied that incorporates more depth and complexity.

---

children learn new behaviors and change or modify old behaviors is also an important part of guiding children's behavior.

Responsible choices and support are key ways to help children develop responsible behavior that internalizes their locus of control. Helping children with behavior and emotional problems learn to take control of and guide their own behavior can be a challenge. One source of help is KidTools Support System, which is the focus of this chapter's Technology Tie-In on pages 330–331. Review the program now to see how it works.

3. Ask all students to take a few minutes to examine the upcoming content to assess the degree to which they believe they already know it.
4. Offer a pretest to volunteers who believe they can demonstrate mastery of the upcoming curriculum.
5. Eliminate all review, drill, and practice for students who demonstrate mastery. This includes review work for state tests.
6. On days when you are teaching what students have mastered, allow them to work instead on extension activities they have chosen from the menu you prepared. Always allow room for their independent choices, with your approval.
7. On days when you are teaching what students have not mastered, they are expected to participate in the direct instruction lesson and activities.

COMPACTING STRATEGY: MOST DIFFICULT FIRST

Prepare a menu of extension activities related to the unit concepts but which requires more depth and complexity from the students.

1. Any time you have given a directed lesson and are assigning practice items, decide which five items are the most difficult in the entire set.
2. Tell all class members that any person who completes the most difficult items first (before the other items), and gets no more than one wrong, is done practicing for that day and does not need to continue the practice for homework. You may correct the work yourself or provide an answer key.
3. Students must maintain an average of 90 percent or higher in this particular subject area to continue to be eligible for most difficult first.

Remember: The grade that is recorded for the student is only what describes their ability with the grade-level work. If you grade the extension activities and that leads to lower grades, students will decide to end their participation in these compacting opportunities.

Careful records must be kept of which students experience compacting and on which extension activities they work. By the second half of second grade and up, teachers can show students how to do the record keeping themselves.

COMPACTING THE PACING

When the content cannot be pretested because it is new to students, we can compact the pacing by allowing them to move through the new content at a faster pace than their classmates. This allows them to spend a significant amount of time during the unit working on topics related to the regular content but which extend the curriculum into areas the teacher does not have time to include for all students. The areas in which this strategy works best are science, social studies, more sophisticated math concepts, and/or thematic integrated units in any subject area.

INDEPENDENT STUDY ON TOPICS OF PERSONAL INTEREST

Students who always complete their compacted work quickly may be interested in working on an independent study project on a topic in which they have a passionate interest. This topic does not necessarily have to be related to the regular school curriculum. Ask the student and his or her parents for topic suggestions.

CONCLUSION

In order for gifted students to be challenged in mixed-ability classes, it is imperative for them to spend considerable time working on tasks that provide challenge and interest for them. This vignette has described several strategies you can use to facilitate exciting learning for your gifted students.

Contributed by Susan Winebrenner, author-consultant and president of Education Consulting Service, Inc. More information is available at www.susanwinebrenner.com.

 Complete an activity on intrinsic motivation and guidance strategies at http://www.prenhall.com/morrison, Chapter 12—Projects: Professionalism in Practice.

Step 6: Empower Children

Helping children build new behaviors creates a sense of responsibility and self-confidence. As children are given responsibility, they develop greater self-direction, which means that you guide them at the next level in their zone of proximal development. Some professionals and parents hesitate to let children assume responsibilities, but without responsibilities, children are bored and frustrated and become discipline problems—the very opposite of

Every classroom and early childhood program has children with emotional and behavioral disabilities. To help these children, a new type of computer software, called electronic performance support tools, have been developed and tested at the University of Missouri–Columbia. Known as the *KidTools* Support System (KTSS), the computer programs help children take responsibility for their own learning and behavior by providing easy-to-use templates for students to personalize and use independently in school and home settings.

The *KidTools* programs assist children with problem-solving and use self-management skills. The early childhood version, *eKidTools*, provides tools for children to identify behaviors, develop strategies to change or control these behaviors, prepare self-talk cues, and create self-monitoring cards. The software

consists of fifteen tool templates that are kid friendly with colorful graphics, text-with-audio directions, and simple formats. Figure 1 displays the main menu screen for the program. Figure 2 provides an example of a completed self-monitoring card. In this example, the child has named three behaviors for monitoring, selected pictures from a graphics library, and prepared the card for printing. Once created, the child uses the card to manage his or her own behavior at school or home.

The *KidSkills* programs provide organizational and learning strategy tools for children to support independence and success. The early childhood version, *eKidSkills*, provides tools for children to get organized, learn new information, complete homework, and do projects. The software consists of eighteen tool templates that operate identical to those in *eKidTools*. Figure 3

FIGURE 1 Menu in *eKidTools*

FIGURE 2 Picture Point Card Tool

what is intended. Guidance is not a matter of adults getting children to please them by making remarks such as "Show me how perfect you can be," "Don't embarrass me by your behavior in front of others," "I want to see nice groups," or "I'm waiting for quiet."

To reiterate, guiding behavior is not about compliance and control. Rather, it is important to instill in children a sense of independence and responsibility for their own behavior. For example, you might say, "You have really worked a long time cutting out the flower you drew. You kept working on it until you were finished. Would you like some tape to hang it up with?"

Parents and early childhood professionals can do a number of things to help children develop new behaviors that result in empowerment:

- *Give children responsibilities.* All children, from an early age, should have responsibilities—that is, tasks that are their job to do and for which they are responsible. Being responsible for completing tasks and doing such things as putting toys and learning materials away promote a positive sense of self-worth and convey to children that in a community people have responsibilities for making the community work well.

- *Give children choices.* Life is full of choices—some require thought and decisions; others are automatic, based on previous behavior. But every time you

FIGURE 3 Menu in *eKidSkills*

FIGURE 4 Homework Planner Tool

displays the main menu screen for the program. Figure 4 provides an example of the homework planner tool. In this example, the child plans weekly activities and times for doing homework.

In both programs, graphic characters serve as "guides" to the different tools and provide audio directions in children's voices. The text and audio utilize the natural language of children. The audio directions supplement the simplified text instructions and can be turned off or on as desired.

Children and teachers who used the software in classroom research projects enthusiastically supported the programs. Children said *KidTools* is "cool" and it "helps you be better because you pay attention to how you act." Teachers reported children were intrigued by the software and became independent with it. Many described behavior change attributed in part to the tool approaches that help children think before they act.

Gail Fitzgerald, co-developer of the programs, believes the use of electronic computer tools provides a nonintrusive method of supporting children with behavioral disabilities by providing easy-to-use tools that are functional and motivating.

She states, "Often teachers attempt to control children's behavior without really involving them in that decision-making process or giving them the resources to be successful. The focus in this software is to help children make the shift from external to internal management."

The programs are available in both Windows and Mac versions and can be downloaded from the project website at http://kidtools.missouri.edu. This website also contains teacher orientation and practice materials.

Source: G. Fitzgerald and K. Koury, The KidTools Support System (KTSS) *(Columbia: The University of Missouri–Columbia). Funded in part by the United States Department of Education Project H327A000005.*

Explore ways technology can be used to help children manage their behavior at http://www.prenhall.com/morrison, Chapter 12—Journal: Technology Tie-In.

make a decision, you are being responsible and exercising your right to decide. Children like to have choices, and choices help them become independent, confident, and self-disciplined. Making choices is key for children developing responsible behavior and inner control. Learning to make choices early in life lays the foundation for decision making later. Guidelines for giving children choices are as follows:

- Give children choices when there are valid choices to make. When it comes time to clean up the classroom, do not let children choose whether they want to participate, but let them pick between collecting the scissors or the crayons.
- Help children make choices. Rather than say, "What would you like to do today?" say, "Sarah, you have a choice between working in the woodworking center or the computer center. Which would you like to do?"
- When you do not want children to make a decision, do not offer them a choice.

- *Support children.* As an early childhood professional, you must support children in their efforts to be successful. Arrange the environment and make opportunities available for children to be able to do things. Successful accomplishments are a major ingredient of positive behavior.

Step 7: Establish Appropriate Expectations

Expectations set the boundaries for desired behavior. They are the guideposts children use in learning to direct their own behavior. Like everyone, children need guideposts along life's way.

Teachers and parents need to set high and appropriate expectations for children. When children know what to expect, they can better achieve those expectations. Up to a point, the more we expect of children, the more and better they achieve. Generally, we expect too little of children and ourselves.

The following are some things you can do to promote appropriate expectations.

The classroom environment is one of the most important factors that enables children to develop and use appropriate behavior. The classroom should belong to children, and their ownership and pride in it makes it more likely that they will act responsibly.

Set Limits. Setting limits is closely associated with establishing expectations and relates to defining unacceptable behavior. Setting clear limits is important for three reasons:

1. Setting limits helps you clarify in your own mind what you believe is acceptable, based on your knowledge of child development, children, their families, and their culture.
2. Limits help children act with confidence because they know which behaviors are acceptable.
3. Limits provide children with security. Children want and need limits.

As children grow and mature, the limits change and are adjusted to developmental levels, programmatic considerations, and life situations. Knowing what they can and cannot do enables children to guide their own behavior.

Develop Classroom Rules. Plan classroom rules from the first day of class. As the year goes on, you can involve children in establishing classroom rules, but in the beginning, children want and need to know what they can and cannot do. For example, rules might relate to changing groups and bathroom routines. Whatever rules you establish, they should be fair, reasonable, and appropriate to the children's age and maturity. Keep rules to a minimum; the fewer the better. Figure 12.3 Shows some sample classroom rules.

Observe a teacher discussing classroom rules with his students at Video Classroom, Educational Psychology, Module 12: Classroom Management, Video 1: Classroom Rules.

Step 8: Arrange and Modify the Environment

Environment plays a key role in children's ability to guide their behavior. Arrange the environment so that it supports the purposes of the program and makes appropriate behavior possible. Appropriate room arrangements signal to children that they are expected to guide and be responsible for their own behavior and enable teachers to observe and provide for children's interests. Also, it is easier to live and work in an attractive and aesthetically pleasing classroom or center. We all want a nice environment—children should have one, too. The guidelines shown in Figure 12.4 can help you think about and arrange your classroom to support children as they guide their own behavior. Apart from the physical environment, other characteristics of classrooms that support children as they learn how to guide their own behavior include:

FIGURE 12.3

Examples of Classroom Rules, Pre-K–3

Pre-kindergarten	• Helping Hands
	• Listening Ears
	• Looking Eyes
	• Quiet Voices
	• Walking Feet

Kindergarten	• Be kind to everybody
	• Raise your hand when you want to speak
	• Use inside voices
	• Walk inside the room
	• Listen to the teachers
	• Follow the school rules

First grade	• Respect other people
	• Keep your hands and feet to yourself
	• Raise your hand for permission to speak in class
	• Walk quietly in the hallways
	• Move about quietly in the classroom

Second grade	• Be a good listener
	• Be a good friend
	• Be polite
	• Be a hard worker
	• Be the best you can be

Third grade	• Listen to and follow directions
	• Raise your hand
	• Work quietly
	• Keep hands and feet to yourself
	• Walk silently in the halls
	• Be kind to others

Note: Carrollton Elementary School, Carrollton, Texas (pre-kindergarten); Chapin Elementary School, Chapin, South Carolina (kindergarten); Garrison-Pilcher Elementary School, Thomasville, Georgia (first grade); Elwood Public School, Elwood, Nebraska (second grade); H. L. Horn Elementary, Vinton, Virginia (third grade).

Source: Vanessa Levin and Theresa Stapler

- An atmosphere of respect and caring.
- Consistent behavior from teachers and staff. They model appropriate behavior and expect it of children.
- Established and maintained routines.
- A belief shared by all staff that children can and will learn. The teachers also believe they are good teachers.
- A partnership between teachers and children.
- Community and a culture of caring.
- Open communication between
  - Children–children,
  - Teacher–children,
  - Children–teacher,
  - Teacher–parents, and
  - Parents–teacher.

Make the classroom a rewarding place to be. It should be comfortable, safe, and attractive.

Locate materials so that children can easily retrieve them. When children have to ask for materials, this promotes dependency and can lead to behavior problems.

Create center areas that are well defined and accessible to children and have appropriate and abundant materials. Provide children with guidelines for how to use centers and materials, and make center boundaries low enough so that you and others can see over them for proper supervision and observation.

Establish a system so that materials are easily stored, and so that children can easily put them away. A rule of thumb is that there should be a place for everything and everything should be in its place.

Have an open area in which you and your children can meet as a whole group. This area is essential for story time, general class meetings, and so on. Starting and ending the day with a class meeting provides an opportunity for children to discuss their behaviors and suggest ways they and others can do a better job.

Provide for all kinds of activities, both quiet and loud. Try to locate quiet areas together (reading area and puzzle area) and loud centers together (woodworking and blocks).

 Provide opportunities for children to display their work.

FIGURE 12.4 How to Arrange the Classroom to Support Positive Behavior

Photo: Katelyn Metzger / Merrill

- Clear expectations and high expectations.
- Sufficient materials to support learning activities.
- A balance between cooperation and independent learning.

The Diversity Tie-In on page 336 details how a child's environment influences how he or she behaves.

Step 9: Model Appropriate Behavior

Telling is not teaching. Actions speak louder than words. Children see and remember how other people act. Modeling plays a major role in helping children guide their behavior.

Teachers and parents lay the first—and most important—foundation for children's appropriate habits and behaviors. You must be the best role model you can for children and help parents be good role models too. Whether they want to or not or like it or not, teachers have to accept responsibility for helping raise responsible children who will become responsible adults.

Another good way both you and parents can become good role models for children is through books that encourage prosocial behaviors. The picture books listed in Figure 12.5 provide you many opportunities to model appropriate behavior through good books.

FIGURE 12.5

Children's Books That Encourage Prosocial Behaviors in Young Children

A Chair for My Mother by Vera Williams. New York: Scholastic, 1982 (Ages 5–6).

After losing all her possessions in a fire, a young girl learns compassion and perseverance as she and her mother and grandmother rebuild their lives.

Ira Sleeps Over by Bernard Waber. Boston: Houghton Mifflin, 1972 (Aages 5–6).

Ira not only learns courage as he goes to a sleep-over at his friend's house without his favorite teddy bear, but he also learns the value of being true to himself when he finally stops reacting to peer pressure and retrieves the toy.

The Man Who Walked Between the Towers by Mordicai Gerstein. Brookfield, CN: Roaring Brook, 2003 (Ages 6–7).

Based upon the true story of Philippe Petit who walked a tightrope strung between the two towers of the World Trade Center. Students learn courage and persistence, and consider a new perspective on these historic buildings.

Miss Rumphius by Barbara Cooney. New York: Puffin, 1982 (Ages 6–7).

We follow Alice from childhood to old age as she displays many remarkable qualities, such as courage, perseverance, compassion, and care for the environment.

The Rough-Face Girl by Rafe Martin. Illustrated by David Shannon. New York: G.P. Putnam's Sons, 1992 (Ages 5–6).

In this Native American Cinderella tale, the Rough-Face Girl demonstrates compassion, integrity, courage, and love of the environment.

Source: Contributed by Dr. Sheryl O'Sullivan, Professor of English, Azusa Pacific University, Azusa, California. Used with permission.

You can use the following techniques to help children learn through modeling:

- *Show.* For example, show children where the block corner is and how and where the blocks are stored.
- *Demonstrate.* Perform a task while students watch. For example, demonstrate the proper way to put the blocks away and how to store them. Extensions of the demonstration method are to have children practice the demonstration while you supervise and to ask a child to demonstrate to other children.
- *Model.* Modeling occurs when you practice the behavior you expect of the children. Also, you can call children's attention to the desired behavior when another child models it.
- *Supervise.* Supervision is a process of reviewing, insisting, maintaining standards, and following up. If children are not performing the desired behavior, you will need to review the behavior. You must be consistent in your expectations of desired behavior. Children will soon learn they do not have to put away their blocks if you allow them not to do it even once. Remember, you are responsible for setting up the environment that enables children's learning to take place.

You can also model and demonstrate social and group-living behaviors, including using simple courtesies (such as saying "please," "thank you," and "you're welcome") and practicing cooperation, sharing, and respect for others.

Step 10: Avoid Problems

It's easy to encourage children's misbehavior. Often teachers expect perfection and adult behavior from children. If you focus on building responsible behavior, there will be less

Fathers, Socioeconomic Status, and Children's Behaviors

The majority of our discussion in this chapter about guiding children's behavior has focused on what you can do in your classroom to guide children's behaviors. However, the behaviors children bring to classrooms and programs are the result of many different experiences and environments. For example, look at the figure below, which shows a few of the home/family environmental factors that influence children's behavior. For example, families' home environments, children's experiences in previous classrooms, and children's temperaments all help to determine how children behave.

Family socioeconomic status and parental background in particular exert powerful influences on children's behavior, their approaches to solving problems, and their particular life views regarding learning and social relationships. While a lot of attention is focused on mother–child interaction in the guiding of behavior, we must also consider how fathers influence their children's behavior.

Let's focus on fathers' SES and see how it influences their approach to guiding their children's behavior. Low-SES fathers report that they use more frequent verbal and corporal punishment when disciplining their children than do fathers from higher socioeconomic backgrounds.* Research is clear that verbal and physical punishments are good predictors of behavior problems. Across all SES levels, punitive parenting practices are associated with higher levels of disruptive behavior. So, punitive parenting practices exacerbate behaviors parents are trying to

eliminate or discourage. When fathers use punitive guidance practices with their children who are already disruptive, they may be providing them with a double whammy of negative behavior.

So, what can you do to help all low-SES parents, but particularly fathers, who need your help in learning how to positively guide children's behavior? Parents' sources of parenting information come mainly through discussions with other parents, and reading books on parenting.[†] You can use parent meetings and parent libraries to provide parents with resources they want and need in order to help them learn and use appropriate ways to deal with their children's misbehavior and help them develop new behaviors.

*A.D. Burbach, R.A. Fox, and B.C. Nicholson, "Challenging Behaviors in Young Children: The Father's Role," The Journal of Genetic Psychology, 2004, 165(2), 169–183.

[†]Christine Ateah, "Disciplinary Practices with Children: Parental Sources of Information, Attitudes, and Educational Needs," Issues in Comprehensive Pediatric Nursing, 2003, 26: 89–101.

Photo: David Mager / Pearson Learning Photo Studio

Complete an activity on the importance of parenting styles on child development at http://www.prenhall.com/morrison, Chapter 12—Journal: Diversity Tie-In.

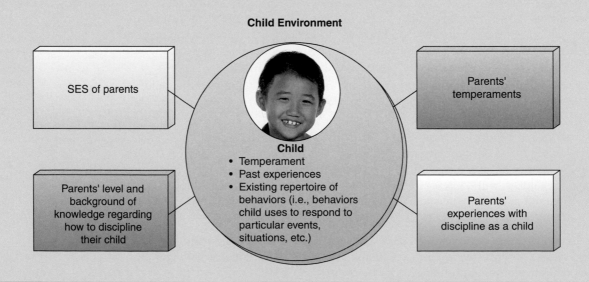

Child Environment

SES of parents

Parents' level and background of knowledge regarding how to discipline their child

Child
- Temperament
- Past experiences
- Existing repertoire of behaviors (i.e., behaviors child uses to respond to particular events, situations, etc.)

Parents' temperaments

Parents' experiences with discipline as a child

need to solve behavior problems. The Program in Action feature on pages 338–339 profiles the successes of a school employing the positive discipline philosophy.

Ignoring inappropriate behavior is probably one of the most overlooked strategies for guiding children's behavior. Some early childhood professionals feel guilty when they use this strategy. They believe that ignoring undesirable behaviors is not good teaching. Ignoring some inappropriate behavior can be an effective strategy, but it must be combined with positive reinforcement of desirable behavior. Thus, you ignore inappropriate behavior and at the same time reinforce appropriate behavior. A combination of positive reinforcement and ignoring can lead to desired behavior.

When children do something good or are on task, reward them. Use verbal and nonverbal reinforcement and privileges to help ensure that the appropriate behavior will continue. Review the affirmations listed in Figure 12.2. Catch children being good; that is, look for good behavior. This helps improve not only individual behavior, but group behavior as well.

> Read more about preventing challenging behavior in the classroom at http://www.prenhall.com/morrison, Chapter 12: Web Links.

Step 11: Develop a Partnership with Parents, Families, and Others

Involving parents and families is a wonderful way to gain invaluable insights about children's behaviors. Some things you can do to collaborate with parents on guiding children's behaviors are these:

- Share your philosophy of guiding behavior with parents.
- Share classroom rules and expectations with parents.
- Hold meetings for and with parents and share with them the information in this chapter and how to apply it to their learning about how to guide children's behavior in the home.
- Always be available in person or on the phone to discuss with parents questions or concerns they might have about their children's behavior.

Chapter 13 provides many helpful ideas to use in your collaboration with parents.

Scott Cunningham / Merrill

Social relationships play a powerful role in children's and teachers' everyday behaviors. Teachers must promote positive child–child and teacher–child relationships. What are some things you can do to promote positive social relationships in your classroom or program?

Step 12: Recognize and Value Basic Rights

Everyone involved in the process of education has basic rights that need to be recognized and honored. When this happens, guiding behavior is easier for everyone. Figure 12. 6 lists these basic rights. Consider now how you can and will honor them. When everyone's basic rights are respected, it is easier to guide and direct children's behavior. In addition, everyone "wins" in such a process.

Step 13: Teach Cooperative Living and Learning

You can do a lot to promote cooperative living in which children help each other direct their behavior. Recall from Chapter 3 our discussion of Vygotsky's theory of social relations. Children are born seeking social interactions, and social relations are necessary for children's learning and development. Peers help each other learn.

Children's natural social groups and play groups are ideal and natural settings in which to help children assist each other in learning new behaviors and being responsible for their own behavior. The classroom as a whole is an important social group. Classroom

The Grapevine (Texas) Elementary School staff had a vision. The vision emphasized the desire to encourage all learners to be responsible, intrinsically motivated, and self-directed in an environment of mutual respect. As we looked for a discipline management system that fit this philosophy, we recognized that we needed one that emphasized personal responsibility for behavior and cooperation instead of competition and that focused on developing a community of supportive members. We also discovered that we held several beliefs in common that should be the foundation of our discipline management plan:

1. All human beings have three basic needs—to feel connected (the ability to love and be loved), to feel capable (a sense of "I can" accomplish things), and to feel contributive (I count in the communities in which I belong).
2. Problem solving and solutions encourage responsible behavior. Punishment, by contrast, encourages rebellion and resentment.
3. Children can be creative decision makers and responsible citizens when given opportunities to direct the processes that affect the day-to-day environment in which they live.

4. Every inappropriate action does not necessitate a consequence, but rather can be used as a cornerstone of a problem-solving experience, ultimately leading to a true behavior change.

Our desire was, and is, to address the needs of the whole child as we educate our children to be responsible citizens.

ADOPTING THE PLAN

After much research, we decided to implement *Positive Discipline*, a discipline management system based on the concept of responsibilities rather than rules. Teachers established the following Grapevine Star Responsibilities:

I will be responsible for myself and my learning.
I will respect others and their property.
I will listen and follow directions promptly.
I will complete my class work and homework in a quality manner.

Furthermore, we decided that rewards—whether in the way of stickers, pencils, or award ceremonies—were not, on the whole, consistent with encouraging intrinsic motivation and the belief that all children should continuously monitor their own learning and behavior. Rather, the term *reward* should

FIGURE 12.6 Children's, Teachers', and Parents' Rights That Support Positive Behavior

Teachers' Rights	Children's Rights	Parents' Rights
• To be supported by administration and parents in appropriate efforts to help children guide their behavior • To have a partnership with parents so that they and their children can be successful in developing appropriate behavior • To be treated courteously and professionally by peers and others	• To be respected and treated courteously • To be treated fairly in culturally independent and gender-appropriate ways • To learn behaviors necessary for self-guidance • To have teachers who have high expectations for them • To learn and exercise independence • To achieve to their highest levels • To be praised and affirmed for appropriate behaviors and achievements • To learn and practice effective social skills • To learn and apply basic academic skills	• To share ideas and values of child rearing and discipline with teachers • To be involved in and informed about classroom and school discipline policies • To receive periodic reports and information about their children's behaviors • To be educated and informed about how to guide their children's behavior

be replaced with *celebration,* and these celebrations should be based on what children find personally significant.

Teachers also discussed the understanding that they would become facilitators of decision-making sessions instead of "general in command"; and they would encourage self-evaluation by students leading to solutions.

ENGAGING STUDENTS

Throughout the course of the year, students set goals each six-week period (usually one academic goal and one behavioral goal) and conferred with their teachers at the end of the six weeks to determine the extent of their achievement toward that goal. At the end of the year, students participated in a celebration of achievement. Each student chose the goal that held the most personal significance and received a certificate that detailed the goal. The principal read each chosen goal in the grade-level celebrations as the student walked across the stage and shook hands with the principal. Teachers, parents, and students all enjoyed this ceremony, which emphasized the worth of each individual and affirmed that learning was, and is, the ultimate goal of education and school (as opposed to a grade or series of marks on a report card).

Irene Boynton, a first-grade teacher, comments that Positive Discipline allows children to experience the rewards of feeling confident and healthy about making respectful, responsible choices because it is the "right" thing to do, not because they will receive something for their choice.

THE BENEFITS

Teachers at Grapevine Elementary, when asked to comment on Positive Discipline, say such things as "Is there any other way to teach?" and "We would never go back to playing referee again!" Students no longer ask "What am I going to get?" in response to a request to go the extra mile for another student or while working on a project. They are developing respect for themselves and for the rights and needs of others. The skills learned through Positive Discipline extend into academic areas, where we find that students are becoming more thoughtful, introspective, self-motivated, and effective problem solvers. We believe that we are fostering a safe, respectful community where children and adults thrive together in an atmosphere of mutual respect.

Visit Grapevine Elementary on the Web at http://www.gcisd-k12.org/schools/ges.

....

For more information on implementing additional components of Positive Discipline such as class meetings, "I" messages, and role-playing, refer to Positive Discipline in the Classroom *by Jane Nelsen, Lynn Lott, and Stephen Glenn. Contributed by Alicia King (original author: Nancy Robinson).*

 Reflect on the essentials of guiding children's behavior at http://www.prenhall.com/morrison, Chapter 12—Journal: Program in Action.

---

meetings in which teachers and children talk can serve many useful functions. They can talk about expected behaviors from day to day ("When we are done playing with toys, what do we do with them?"), review with children what they did in a particular center or situation, and help them anticipate what they will do in future situations ("Tomorrow morning when we visit the Senior Citizen Center . . . "). In all these situations, children are cooperatively engaged in thinking about, talking about, and learning how to engage in appropriate behavior.

In addition, you can initiate, support, and foster a cooperative, collaborative learning community in the classroom in which children are involved in developing and setting guidelines and devising classroom and, by extension, individual norms of behavior. Teachers "assist" children but do not do things for them, and they ask questions that make children think about their behavior—how it influences the class, themselves, and others. This process of cooperative living occurs daily. Discussions grow out of existing problems, and guidance is provided based on the needs of children and the classroom.

 Read how one teacher's methods of teaching conflict management influenced her students at Articles and Readings, Classroom Management, Module 9: Managing Problem Behaviors, Article 3: Turning Conflicts into Learning Experiences.

Step 14: Use and Teach Conflict Management

Quite often, conflicts result from children's interactions with others. Increasingly, teachers advocate teaching children ways to manage and resolve their own conflicts.

Teaching conflict resolution strategies is important for several reasons. First, it makes sense to give children the skills they need to handle and resolve their own conflicts.

COMPETENCY BUILDER

Tyrone entered the kindergarten classroom on the first day of the school year, trailing several feet behind his mom, who appeared to be unaware of his presence. She called out a greeting to another mom, and the two of them had an extended discussion about events in the neighborhood. Tyrone glanced around the room and headed purposefully toward the housekeeping center, where he grabbed a baby doll, threw it out of the doll bed, and then ran to the block box and grabbed a large block in each hand. At this point I deflected his trail of destruction and redirected his progress. "Good morning, welcome to my class. My name is Ms. Cheryl. What's your name?" The whirlwind stopped briefly to mumble a response that I could not understand and glared at me in open hostility. "Let's go talk to Mom," I suggested, touching his shoulder and directing him toward his mom.

BACKGROUND

My school is in an area that includes mostly low-socioeconomic households; ours is a Title I school, with 95 percent of our students on free or reduced-fee lunches. In any given year, one-half to two-thirds of our students entering kindergarten have had no preschool experience. Nevertheless, as an early childhood educator, it is my job to help these students develop behaviors that will ensure their success in education. That does not mean that I need only to teach them to write their names, recognize all their letters and numbers, sit quietly in their chairs, and raise their hands before they speak. These tasks are not ends in themselves but are important steps in encouraging children to love learning and to gain the self-regulation that supports it.

UNDERSTANDING BEHAVIOR

In our opening scenario, what important facts should we as educators recognize as signals that Tyrone has some behaviors that require adjustment to ensure his success in school? He seems unaware of the expected protocol for entering a classroom, that is, looking for an adult in charge to give him directions. His mother's apparent lack of interest in her child's behavior could be an indicator that Tyrone does not expect the adults around him to be involved with his activities. He may have been in an atmosphere that requires very little from him when it comes to following rules and, as indicated by his hostility, may see adult intervention as only restrictive rather than supportive and nurturing. Tyrone may even have an undiagnosed speech problem that prohibits adults and other children from understanding his needs. If adults in his world have failed to observe and interact with him, he is also probably lacking in basic language skills and vocabulary, which would limit his understanding. He appears to deal with his world in a very physical manner.

BEHAVIORS NECESSARY FOR SUCCESS IN SCHOOL

The following behaviors are necessary for children to succeed in school:

Behavior #1: *Recognition of authority*—Tyrone was not even aware that an adult was in charge of the classroom.

Behavior #2: *Trust in adults*—The process of building trust is lengthy, but Tyrone needs to learn to see adults as nurturing and supportive.

Behavior #3: *Use of verbal skills rather than physical reactions*—If Tyrone is lacking in language, his teacher can help provide language experiences, defining words, explaining everything in detail, showing and describing pictures, reading books aloud, helping with activities, and talk, talk, talking.

Behaviors #1 and #2 are especially complex; they stem from children's environments and experiences. However, I am

---

Second, teaching conflict resolution skills to children enables them to use these same skills as adults. Third, the peaceful resolution of interpersonal conflicts contributes, in the long run, to peaceful homes and communities. Children who are involved in efforts to resolve interpersonal behavior problems peacefully and intuitively learn that peace begins with them. Strategies used to teach and model conflict resolution include:

- *Model resolutions.* You can model resolutions for children: "Erica, please don't knock over Shantrell's building because she worked hard to build it"; "LaShawn, what is another way (instead of hitting) you can tell Marisa that she is sitting in your chair?"

- *Do something else.* Teach children to get involved in another activity. Children can learn that they do not always have to play with a toy someone else has. They can get involved in another activity with a different toy. They can do something else now and

committed to being one of the reasons a child succeeds and will dedicate great amounts of time and energy to changing behaviors that interfere with student learning. I follow certain steps to guide destructive behaviors into more successful ones.

STEP 1 — PLAN

Before that first day of school, I plan—what activities I will offer my students, what part of the day I will use for centers, how I can show my students the best ways to use materials, where I want them to keep their belongings, how I can explain my expectations about dealing with conflict, how I will deal with behavior that is inappropriate, and what I am going to say about procedures for our classroom.

STEP 2 — BE EXPLICIT

Many of my students are not accustomed to having an adult schedule their time for six hours, and many behavior problems stem from this new pressure to conform to an unfamiliar structure. Therefore, I want to be sure that all of my students fully understand what I expect. For example, I state exactly how I want them to move about the classroom, the cafeteria, the playground, and the school hallways. If they do not follow my instructions, I require them to practice. Many behaviors that inhibit success in school occur because students are not made aware of appropriate and inappropriate school procedures.

STEP 3 — MODEL BEHAVIOR

I model or have my students role-play expected behavior in interpersonal actions. Students who take other students' belongings, hit other students, or push and shove other students are taught to handle these issues through conflict-resolution methods. However, it takes numerous rounds of modeling and role-playing to make an impact on behavior that has been ingrained for five years at home and is still the norm when students return home.

STEP 4 — ROLE-PLAY

I spend some time each day having students role-play scenarios with incorrect behavior. We brainstorm about what the correct behavior would be. Hitting, pushing, name calling, destroying property are all common problems among our students. I ask my students how they feel if someone calls them a name (or exhibits any of the other negative behaviors).

STEP 5 — DEVELOP CLASSROOM RULES

I have five classroom rules:

1. We listen to each other.
2. We use our hands for helping, not hurting.
3. We use caring language.
4. We care about each other's feelings.
5. We are responsible for what we say and do.

STEP 6 — REINFORCE

Helping hard-to-manage children learn to guide their own behavior takes consistent reteaching and reinforcement. I correct every misbehavior I see, either using the "I don't like it when you . . . " statement or stating which rule has been broken. I use a very calm voice when I talk to my students and do not allow them to "tell" on each other. When a student comes to me with a tale of misbehavior, I ask, "Did you tell [*specific name*] how you feel?" Usually by the end of the first nine-week grading period, my students are using the behaviors and statements we have learned, and the tone of my classroom changes from a volatile one to a caring one. Spending some time at the beginning of the year changing behaviors and stating expectations gives my students the guidance they need to begin and to continue successful student careers.

Contributed by Cheryl Doyle, National Board Certified preschool teacher, Miami, Florida

play with the toy later. Chances are, however, that by getting involved in another activity they will forget about the toy for which they were ready to fight.

- *Talk it over.* Children can learn that talking about a problem often leads to a resolution and reveals that there are always two sides to an argument. Talking also helps children think about other ways to solve problems. Children should be involved in the solution of their interpersonal problems and classroom and activity problems.

- *Taking turns.* Taking turns is a good way for children to learn that they cannot always be first, have their own way, or do a prized activity. Taking turns brings equality and fairness to interpersonal relations.

- *Share.* Sharing is a good behavior to promote in any setting. Children have to be taught how to share and how to behave when others do not share. Children can be helped to select another toy rather than hitting or grabbing. Again, keep in mind that during the early years children are egocentric, and acts of sharing are likely to be motivated by expectations of a reward or approval such as being thought of as a "good" boy or girl.

- *Teach children to say "I'm sorry."* Saying "I'm sorry" is one way to heal and resolve conflicts. It can be a step toward good behavior. Children need to be reared in an environment in which they see and experience others apologizing for their inappropriate actions toward others.

The preceding Program in Action feature on pages 340–341 gives you guidelines for ensuring success for children who are hard to manage.

LOOKING TO THE FUTURE

As we have emphasized in this and other chapters, cognitive and social development and behavioral characteristics are interconnected. More early childhood teachers recognize that it does not make sense to teach children reading, writing, and arithmetic and not also teach them skills necessary for responsibly guiding their own behavior.

In our efforts to help prepare all children to live effectively and productively in a democracy, we are placing increasing emphasis on giving students experiences that will help promote efforts to run their classrooms as democracies. The idea of teaching this behavior through classrooms that are miniature democracies is not new. John Dewey was an advocate of this approach and championed democratic classrooms as a way of promoting democratic living. However, running a democratic classroom is easier said than done. It requires a confident professional who believes it is worth the effort.

Democratic learning environments are grounded in key foundational practices. These include:

- *Respect for children.* Throughout this text I have repeatedly emphasized the necessity for honoring and respecting children as human beings (refer to the list of children's basic rights in Figure 12.6 on page 338). When children are respected and honored then they are much more likely to engage in behavior that is respectful and honorable.

- *Time and opportunity to talk about behavior and develop strategies for guiding their behavior.* A good way to provide children time and opportunity to talk about behavior and classroom problems is through a class meeting (see Figure 12.4, page 334). An excellent resource for learning about and how to conduct class meetings is a NAEYC resource book, *Class Meetings: Young Children Solving Problems Together* by Emily Vance and Patricia Jimenez Weaver. Democratic learning environments require that students develop responsibility for their and others' behaviors and learning, that classrooms operate as communities, and that all children are respected and respectful of others.

- *The use of character education as a means of promoting responsible behavior.* Providing character education will continue to grow as a means of promoting fundamental behaviors that early childhood professionals and society believe are essential for living in a democratic society.

- *Teaching civility.* Civil behavior and ways to promote it are of growing interest at all levels of society. The specific teaching of **civil behavior**—how to treat others well and in turn be treated well—is seen as essential for living well in contemporary society. At a minimum, civil behavior includes manners, respect, and the ability to get along with people of all races, cultures, and socioeconomic backgrounds.

ACTIVITIES FOR PROFESSIONAL DEVELOPMENT

Ethical Dilemma

"Just Give Him a Good Whack"

Eduardo, age six, has just been assigned to Rachel's class. He acts out, hits other children, and screams when he doesn't get his own way. In a team meeting, Rachel asks for ideas on how to help guide Eduardo's behavior. One of Rachel's colleagues suggests that when he hits another child, she should "just give him a good whack on the bottom, and he'll soon get the message not to hit others."

How should Rachel handle disagreeing with a colleague over the best course of action to follow when dealing with a child's behavior problems? Should she suggest immediately that giving children "a good whack" is developmentally and culturally inappropriate, or should she talk after the meeting and share her views that she doesn't think physical punishment is a way to guide children's behavior, or should she report her colleague to the central administration or pursue another course of action?

Application Activities

1. Observe a primary classroom and identify aspects of the physical setting and atmosphere that influence classroom behavior. Can you suggest improvements?

2. In this chapter you learned fourteen steps for guiding children's behavior. Although they are all important, rank order the fourteen in importance to you. Your first choice will be 1, your second, 2, and so on.

3. List five behaviors you think are desirable in toddlers, five in preschoolers, and five in kindergartners. For each behavior, give two examples of how you would encourage and promote development of that behavior.

4. Interview five parents of young children to determine what they mean when they use the word *discipline*. What implications might these definitions have for you if you were their children's teacher?

 To take online practice tests on this chapter's material, go to the Companion Website at http://www.prenhall.com/morrison, select Chapter 12, then choose the Multiple Choice or the Essay module. For additional Web resources, choose Web Links.

13

PARENTS, FAMILIES, AND THE COMMUNITY
Building Partnerships for Student Success

Collaborating with Parents and Community

A. I am an advocate on behalf of children and families. I treat parents with dignity and respect. I involve parents, families, and community members in my program and help and encourage parents in their roles as their children's primary caregivers and teachers.

B. I know about, understand, and value the importance and complex characteristics of children's families and communities.[1]

C. I create respectful, reciprocal relationships that support and empower families.[2]

D. I involve families and communities in many aspects of children's development and learning.[3]

1. Why is collaboration between parents, families, and the community important?

2. What are the benefits of collaborating with parents, families, and the community?

3. How can you conduct an effective parent/family collaboration program?

One thing we can say with certainty about today's educational landscape is that parents, families, and communities are as much a part of the educational process as are the students, teachers, and staff. Efforts to involve families and communities in the process of educating the nation's youth are at an all-time high. One primary reason for these renewed efforts to involve parents is the overwhelming evidence that the effect of involving parents, families, and communities in the schools increases student achievement and promotes positive educational outcomes. Many research studies regarding parent involvement confirms the benefits of parent/community support.[4]

A positive and convincing relationship exists between family involvement and benefits for students, including improved academic achievement. This relationship holds across families of all economic, racial/ethnic, and educational backgrounds, as well as students of all ages. Students with involved parents, no matter their background, are more likely to earn higher grades and test scores, enroll in higher level programs, be promoted and earn credits, adapt well to school and attend regularly, have better social skills and behavior, and graduate and go on to higher education. Family involvement also has a protective effect; the more families can support their children's progress, the better their children do in school and the longer they stay in school.[5]

In fact, the public believes that nothing has a greater effect on students' level of achievement than parents (see Figure 13.1). This makes parental involvement in children's education even more critical.

NEW VIEWS OF PARENT/FAMILY AND COMMUNITY INVOLVEMENT

The current accountability and reform movements we discussed in Chapter 2 have convinced families that they should no longer be kept out of their children's schools. Families believe their children have a right to effective, high-quality teaching and care by

FIGURE 13.1

The Public's View of the Importance of Parents

Who is most important in determining how well or how poorly students perform in school? The response is—parents!

	National Totals (%)
Parents	43
Teachers	33
Students	20
Don't know	4

Source: Data from L. C. Rose and A. M. Gallup, "The Thirty-Seventh Annual Phi Delta Kappa/Gallup Poll of the Public's Attitudes Toward the Public Schools," *Phi Delta Kappan,* 2005, http://www.pdkintl.org/kappan/k0509pol.htm. Used with permission.

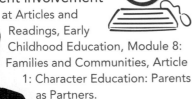

Read about the importance of parent involvement at Articles and Readings, Early Childhood Education, Module 8: Families and Communities, Article 1: Character Education: Parents as Partners.

high-quality teachers. Parents are more militant in their demands for high-quality education. Schools and other agencies have responded by seeking ways to involve families in this quest for quality. Educators and families realize that mutual cooperation is in everyone's best interest. As a result, approaches to parent, family, and community involvement have changed in these important ways:

- Schools and other agencies are expected to involve and collaborate with parents and families in significant ways. In addition to using traditional ways of involving parents in fund-raising and children's activities, schools now involve parents in decisions about hiring new teachers, school safety measures, and appropriate curriculum to help ensure that all children learn.

- Today, a major emphasis is on increasing student achievement. One of the best ways to do this is through involving parents in at-home learning activities with their children. Parent involvement is, now more than ever, a two-way street—from school to home and from home to school. The same reciprocal process applies to school–community collaboration.

- Parent and family involvement means that while teachers work with parents to help children learn, they also have to teach parents how to work with their children. Review again our discussion of family-centered teaching in Chapter 1.

- Parents, families, and the community are now viewed as the "owners" of schools. As one parent said to me, "I don't consider myself a visitor at school. I'm an owner!"

Teacher Paula McCullough shares how she helps parents take ownership of their children's education in order to increase student achievement. Her Professionalism in Practice feature on pages 348–349 will help you get children excited about learning.

CHANGING PARENTS AND FAMILIES: CHANGING INVOLVEMENT

The family of today is not the family of yesterday, nor will the family of today be the family of tomorrow. Today's parents are single, married, heterosexual, gay, lesbian, cousins, aunts, uncles, grandparents, brothers, and sisters. These changes in who and what parents are and what a family is have tremendous implications for parenting, child rearing, and education.

More young mothers are entering the workforce. Many children, 63 percent of whom are under age five, are spending thirty-six hours a week or more in the care of others.[6] Working parents are turning their young children over to others for care and spending less time with their children. Parents and other family members need more help with rearing children. As a result, opportunities have blossomed for child-serving agencies, such as child care centers and preschools, to assist and support parents in their child-rearing efforts. Over the next decade additional programs will provide more parents with child development and child-rearing information and training.

TEACHER PREP Observe how families of young children are changing and how teachers can involve these changing families at Video Classroom, Child Development, Module 3: Family, Culture, and Community, Video 3: Families.

Grandparents as Parents

Since the early 1990s, more grandparents are raising their grandchildren than ever before in American history. Nearly 6.1 million children, or 8 percent of all children under age eighteen, are living in homes maintained by grandparents.[7] Many of the children in homes headed by grandparents are "skipped-generation" children—neither parent is living with them, perhaps because of drug abuse, divorce, mental and physical illness, abandonment, teenage pregnancy, child abuse and neglect, incarceration, or even the death of the parents. Grandparent-parents in these skipped-generation households must provide for their grandchildren's basic needs and care, as well as make sure that they do well in school. Grandparents who are raising a new generation, often unexpectedly, need your support. Keep in mind that they are rearing their grandchildren in a world very different from the one in which they reared their children. You can help grandparents with this responsibility in a number of ways, including linking them with support groups such as Raising our Children's Children (ROCC) and the American Association of Retired Persons (AARP) Grandparent Information Center (http://www.aarp.org/life/grandparents).

Given the changes in families today, you can do a number of things as an early childhood professional to ensure that all parents and families are meaningfully involved. The following are some ideas for working with today's changing families:

PhotoDisc / Getty Images

- *Provide support services.* Support can extend from being a "listening ear" to organizing support groups and seminars on single parenting. You can help families link up with other agencies and groups, such as Big Brothers and Big Sisters and Families Without Partners. Through newsletters and fliers, professionals can offer families specific advice on how to help children become independent and how to meet the demands of living in single-parent families, stepfamilies, and other family configurations.

- *Provide child care.* As more families need child care, be an advocate for establishing care where none exists, extending existing services, and helping to arrange cooperative baby-sitting services. Providing child care for parent–teacher conferences and other school–parent/family activities is one way to meet parents' needs and make parent involvement programs successful.

- *Avoid criticism.* Be careful not to criticize parents for the jobs they are doing. They may not have extra time to spend with their children or know how to discipline them. Regardless of their circumstances, families need help, not criticism.

Grandparents acting as parents for their grandchildren are a growing reality in the United States today. What are some things you can do to ensure that grandparents will have the educational assistance and support they need so that their grandchildren will be successful in school?

Home and School: An Unbeatable Team!

Paula McCullough
USA Today All-USA Teacher Team

STEP 1 FORM PARTNERSHIPS WITH PARENTS

My philosophy of teaching is very simple: It is to teach the whole individual child, not a subject. Each child is unique, with different strengths and weaknesses, different likes and dislikes. To achieve my goal, I must form a partnership with the home. By working together, we can build a team whose mutual goal is the educational success of the child.

STEP 2 COMMUNICATE WITH FAMILIES

A strong relationship needs to exist between the school and home in order for the child to get the best education possible. This "unbeatable team" is established through communication. Communication needs to be varied, timely, and honest. Proper communication is the tool that allows me to motivate parents to find the necessary time to work with and support their children's educations. I use weekly newsletters, phone calls, notes home, weekly homework bags, parent conferences/meetings, and parent volunteers.

STEP 3 SEND NEWSLETTERS

I send out a weekly newsletter to inform my parents of "current events" in our classroom. Included in the newsletters are weekly progress reports, a list of spelling words, current areas of study, and special events/dates. I also include helpful tips on learning, such as how to help their child study spelling words, how to encourage reading for enjoyment and comprehension, or what games to play at home to practice reading/math skills.

STEP 4 ENCOURAGE FEEDBACK

To encourage a two-way communication between home and school, I include a place for comments in the newsletters. Individual notes are sent home and phone calls made when needed. Sometimes it is necessary to keep parents informed on a daily basis about their child's progress, behavior, and/or work habits. I send home a daily note that is signed by the parent and returned to school. I have found it helpful to write these notes on a carbonless copy message book so that I always have a copy (for those times when the student conveniently does not make it home with the note). Using different forms of communication keeps parents well informed of their child's progress, classroom policies/procedures, curriculum goals, and ideas on how best to help their child succeed at school.

STEP 5 PROVIDE HOMEWORK BAGS

Homework bags are sent home each week. Each bag contains a worksheet to practice the skills (math/reading) taught in class, a practice reader, a reading

---

Read how one school program involves grandparents at Articles and Readings, Educational Leadership, Module 13: The School and the Community, Article 3: It Takes 100 Grandparents.

TEACHER PREP

- *Adjust programs.* Adjust classroom and center activities to account for how particular children cope with their home situations. Children's needs for different kinds of activities depend on their experiences at home. For example, opportunities abound for role-playing, and such activities help bring into the open situations that children need to talk about. Use program opportunities to discuss families and the roles they play. Make it a point in the classroom to model, encourage, and teach effective interpersonal skills.

- *Be sensitive.* There are specific ways to sensitively approach today's changing family patterns. For example, avoid having children make presents for both parents when it is inappropriate to do so, and do not award prizes for bringing both parents to meetings. Be sensitive to the demands of school in relation to children's home lives.

- *Seek training.* Request in-service training to help you work with families. In-service programs can provide information about referral agencies, guidance techniques, ways to help families deal with their problems, and child abuse identification and prevention. Be alert to the signs of all kinds of child abuse, including mental, physical, and sexual abuse.

- *Increase parent contacts.* Encourage greater and different kinds of parent involvement through visiting homes; talking to families about children's needs; providing

activity, and a parent response form. The homework bags become increasingly more difficult as the student advances in abilities.

A variety of reading activities are included to keep students excited about learning. The reading activities are determined by the lesson and the practice reader enclosed in the homework bag. They include games (board games, teacher-made folder games, card games, etc.), art projects (with the materials included), writing projects (a suitcase with a variety of writing materials), and simple cooking recipes.

These homework bags encourage parent–child interaction as they work together on the same skills that are covered at school. The parents have firsthand experience in watching the academic growth of their child and discovering their child's weaknesses and strengths. The child gets to practice needed skills in a safe, warm environment with the added bonus of parental approval.

STEP 6 TEACH PARENTS

At the first of the year, I hold a meeting for my parents. I explain classroom procedures and how first graders learn to read and solve math problems. The parents are supplied with handouts on activities they can do at home to improve math and reading skills. I do not assume the parents are knowledgeable about how to help their child at home. I conduct a mini-lesson on the parents' role in teaching children to read. I model for them how they should guide their children when reading together by asking predicting questions, discussing cause/effect, using context clues, and so forth. At the end of the meeting, parents are given the opportunity to ask questions concerning their children's education. This gives me the opportunity to clarify any concepts or activities I had not clearly explained. Usually the questions asked need to be heard by the entire group. Parents realize that everyone has some of the same concerns: getting a reluctant child to read, homework hassles, improving weak math/reading skills, and challenging high achievers. Parents see that they are not alone in their child's educational journey.

STEP 7 RECRUIT PARENTS

Every year, I recruit parent volunteers to become involved in my class. These "helping hands" are used to encourage my students to develop skills and/or interests. Parents listen to my students read, play games with them, help individual students learn math facts or spelling words, make learning centers, and aid students in creating art projects. The use of parent volunteers helps to strengthen the relationship between school and home. It also makes parents more aware of the importance their role plays in the education of children.

By using a variety of activities, I get parents involved in their children's educations. If both members of the team—parents and teacher—meet their educational responsibilities, an unbeatable team is formed with the same goal in mind—*children excited about learning.*

Paula McCullough is a transitional first-grade teacher at Lakehoma Elementary, Mustang, Oklahoma.

Complete an activity on involving parents in their children's education at http://www.prenhall.com/morrison, Chapter 13—Projects: Professionalism in Practice.

information and opportunities to parents, grandparents, and other family members; gathering information from families (such as through interest inventories); and keeping in touch with parents. Make parent contacts positive.

PARENT/FAMILY INVOLVEMENT: WHAT IS IT?

Parent/family involvement is a process of helping parents and family members use their abilities to benefit themselves, their children, and the early childhood program. Families, children, and the program are all part of the process; consequently, all three parties should benefit from a well-planned program of involvement. Nonetheless, the focus in parent/family–child/interactions is the family, and you must work with and through families if you want to be successful.

As you think about your role in parent and family involvement, it would be helpful to review the six types of parent involvement, displayed in the accompanying Program in Action feature. These six types of parent/family involvement constitute a comprehensive approach to your work with parents. A worthy professional goal would be for you to try to have some of your parents involved in all six of these types of parental involvement through the program year.

Six Types of Parent/Family Involvement

As you think about your role in involving parents and families, it would be helpful to review the six types of involvement shown in the figure included here. A worthy professional goal would be to have some of your parents involved in all six of these types of parental involvement during the program year. Let's take a closer look at what you can do with each type, along with examples from actual practice.

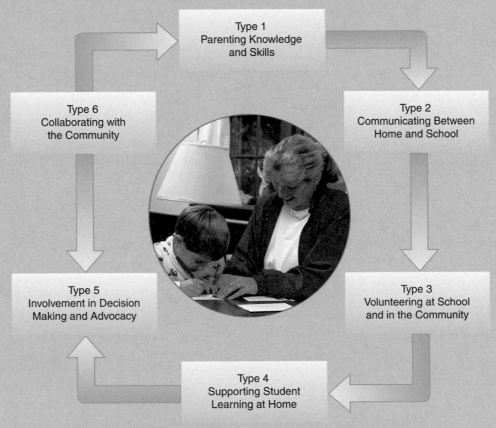

Type 1
Parenting Knowledge
and Skills

Type 6
Collaborating with
the Community

Type 2
Communicating Between
Home and School

Type 5
Involvement in Decision
Making and Advocacy

Type 3
Volunteering at School
and in the Community

Type 4
Supporting Student
Learning at Home

Source: Figure content reprinted by permission from J. L. Epstein, School, Family, and Community Partnerships: Your Handbook for Action, *2nd ed. Thousand Oaks, CA: Corwin Press. Also see http://www.partnershipschools.org.*

Photo: Scott Cunningham / Merrill

1. *Parenting*— Assist families with parenting and child-rearing skills, understanding child and adolescent development, and setting home conditions that support children as students at each age and grade level. Assist schools in understanding families.

   School #82 Early Childhood Center
   Buffalo, New York

   Several parents had approached School #82's math teacher, concerned that they were unable to help their children with math homework. The Early Childhood Center is trying to solve this problem with Adults-Only

   Free Math Tutoring, an evening of math instruction for parents who want to know what their children are learning. To try to meet parents' various needs, the building's math teacher designed a course that would cover the math from GED courses, as well as the math being taught in School #82's classes. The tutoring session, offered twice a month to accommodate parents' schedules, covered math skills taught from pre-kindergarten through fourth grade.

2. *Communicating*— Communicate with families about school programs and student progress through effective school-to-home and home-to-school communications.

Greendale School District
Greendale, Wisconsin

To help incoming kindergarteners and their families with "first day" anxiety, the Greendale School District and the Action Team for Partnerships (ATP) developed the Preschool Transition to Kindergarten program. The Kindergarten Adventure Program is an initial 90-minute program that allows incoming kindergarteners and their parents to meet the principal, teachers, and other students. The children also participate in activities such as finger plays, songs, story time, and a short recess. At the end of the event, preschoolers are partnered with a kindergartener to participate in free choice centers. Preschool students leave with a school folder and school supplies. Parent Information Night is the second phase of the transition program. Families have a picnic one evening in August and then receive information about kindergarten and volunteer opportunities, while children play games with high school volunteers. The district also holds a "Meet Your Teacher" hour before the first day of school, giving children a chance to meet their teachers, see their classrooms, and drop off their school supplies.

3. *Volunteering*— Improve recruitment, training, tasks, and schedules to involve families as volunteers and audiences at school or in other locations to support students and school programs.

Barnum School
Taunton, Massachusetts

To provide individual attention to pre-kindergarteners who have difficulty learning important readiness skills, the Barnum School developed the Barnum Buddy Program. The school recruited high school, parent, and community volunteers as "big buddies" to be paired with a "little buddy." These Barnum Buddies work together twice a week for 20 minutes at the school, reading books, playing learning games, and practicing skills that the teacher highlights for each student. Each child has a binder that includes a learning prescription, written by the classroom teacher, which indicates the specific skills the big buddy should focus on, along with notes on effective ways to work with the child. Each time the big buddy works with his or her little buddy, the child receives a paper to take home, indicating what skills have been worked on. The child's progress is then noted in the binder.

4. *Learning at home*— Involve families with their children in learning activities at home, including homework and other curriculum-related activities and decisions.

Bryant Woods Elementary School
Columbia, Maryland

This year the ATP at Bryant Woods Elementary School worked hard to improve its students' language arts skills by engaging families in home learning activities. While the ATP developed reading nights, the team realized that some of the ELL families living farthest from the school did not participate. Many have transportation and child care issues that prevent them from attending workshops. By holding an event in the community center at an apartment complex, the ATP worked around these issues, creating a small, comfortable setting to explore literacy development. The ATP invited area families to attend and share strategies to support literacy at home. Snacks and child care were provided. The literacy discussion brought out a rich dialogue, and ELL families spoke candidly. Teachers shared four areas of the language arts program with the parents: reading aloud, comprehension, vocabulary development, and journal writing. They talked about the importance and impact of each and demonstrated games and activities. Families received free books, games to make and play at home, journals, and informational materials. The ATP sent these materials home to families living in the neighborhood who could not attend the workshop.

5. *Decision making*— Include families as participants in school decisions, governance, and advocacy through PTA/PTO, school councils, committees, and other parent organizations.

Parents Plus
Milwaukee, Wisconsin

With an armload of free tickets to a popular ice-skating show, Parents Plus helped a small Milwaukee elementary school launch its ATP. Parents who completed a survey on school needs and volunteer potential received a free ticket and transportation for every family member to the touring ice show. In return, the school got almost a 100 percent response to its surveys, giving it a strong foundation for its parent involvement program. The tickets were donated to a Parents Plus staff member for use at the school. Parents Plus is Wisconsin's Parent Information and Resource Center (PIRC), funded through a grant from the U.S. Department of Education. Its mission is to support positive parenting skills and increase parent involvement in schools to improve student achievement. The Parents Plus representatives and school administrators wrote the survey questions so that they allowed parents to say how they felt about the school, what their needs were, and how willing they were to volunteer their time and talents for both the ATP and other school needs. Working on a team with school and community members empowers parents and "having a voice will make advocating an easier thing for parents to do," a Parents Plus representative said.

6. *Collaborating with the community*— Coordinate resources and services for families, students, and the school with businesses, agencies, and other groups, and provide services to the community.

Roger Wolcott Early Childhood Center
Windsor, Connecticut

The stars shone brightly at Roger Wolcott Early Childhood Center during a year-end fashion and variety

(continued)

show featuring the kindergarten students who attend the center's before- and after-school program. The youngsters from the after-school Tree House program modeled clothing and performed a song in sign language. Community members also shone in important ways behind the scenes. One of those was the owner of a new consignment shop who supplied the clothes for the models and provided refreshments for the event. A local Girl Scout troop also took a supporting role while working on a leadership badge. Its members volunteered to assist in designing and creating the backdrop of the stage. The school's outreach to the community and the resulting support from the community helped make this fashion extravaganza a great success. The parents were delighted to see their own children shine in the production. They were also asked to help the youngsters practice at home and accessorize their outfits. In addition to building community support and parent involvement, the fashion show attracted good publicity for the young school.

You can learn more about partnership program development in J. L. Epstein et al., *School, Family, and Community Partnerships: Your Handbook for Action,* 2nd ed. (Thousand Oaks, CA: Corwin Press, 2002) or online at www.partnershipschools.org.

Reprinted by permission of National Network of Partnership Schools at Johns Hopkins University (2002), http://www.csos.jhu.edu/p2000/nnps_model/ school/sixtypes.htm.

Journal about ways to implement these types of family involvement at http://www.prenhall.com/morrison, Chapter 13—Journal: Program in Action.

Education as a Family Affair

Education starts in the home, and what happens there profoundly affects development and learning. The greater the family's involvement in children's learning, the more likely it is that they will receive a high-quality education. Helping parents learn about child development, providing them with activities they can use to teach their children in the home, and supporting parents in their roles as their children's first teachers are powerful ways to help parents and children be successful.

Family-Centered Teaching

Family-centered teaching and learning focus on meeting the needs of children through the family unit. Family-centered teaching and learning make sense for a number of reasons. First, the family unit has the major responsibility for meeting children's needs. Children's development begins in the family system. The family is a powerful determiner of developmental processes, for better and for worse. What you want to do is maximize the best and diminish the worst. Helping parents and other family members meet their children's needs in appropriate ways means that everyone benefits. Enabling individuals in the family unit to become better parents and family members helps children and consequently promotes their success in school and life.

Second, family issues and problems must be addressed first to help children effectively. For instance, helping parents gain access to adequate and affordable health care increases the chances that the whole family, including children, will be healthy.

Third, you can do many things concurrently with children and their families that benefit both. Literacy is a good example. Adopting a family approach to literacy means that helping parents learn how to read so they can read aloud to their children helps ensure children's literacy development as well.

Even Start.   An example of family-centered education is the William F. Goodling Even Start Family Literacy Programs, a federally funded family literacy program that combines adult literacy and parenting training with early childhood education to break cycles of illiteracy that are often passed on from one generation to another.[8] **Even Start** is funded under Title I of the No Child Left Behind Act of 2001, operates through the public school system, and provides family-centered education. In particular, Even Start helps parents

TEACHERS, PRE-K–3, PROVIDE

- Family education
  - Literacy and math help
  - Nutrition education activities
  - Homework help
  - Technology education
- Basic counseling
  - Parenting help and skills
  - Assistance with problems of daily living
- Referrals to community agencies
  - Help with food, clothing, shelter

OUTCOMES/BENEFITS

- Increase knowledge, skills, and understanding of education process
- Help families and children address and solve problems
- Provide greater range of resources and more experts than school alone can provide
- Relieve families and children/youth of stress to make learning more possible
- Increase student achievement
- Promote school retention and prevent dropout

FIGURE 13.2 Family-Centered Teaching

Photo: Pearson Learning Photo Studio

become full partners in the education of their children, assists children in reaching their full potential, and provides literacy training for the parents. Even Start projects are designed to work cooperatively with existing community resources to provide a full range of services and to integrate early childhood education and adult education. Figure 13.2 will help you understand more about the outcomes of family-centered teaching.

Two-Generation and Intergenerational Family Programs

Two-generation programs involve parents and their children and are designed to help both generations and strengthen the family unit. Use the following guidelines to effectively involve all parents and families, including grandparents:

- *Support parents in their roles as first teachers of their children.* Support can include information, materials, and help with parenting questions.
- *Learn how families rear children and manage their families.* Political, social, and moral values of families all have implications for parent participation and ways to teach children.
- *Educate parents to be mentors, classroom aides, tutors, and homework helpers.* Also, communicate guidelines for helping students study for tests.
- *Support fathers in their roles as parents.* By supporting and encouraging fathers, you support the whole family.
- *Ask parents what goals they have for their children.* Use these goals to help you in your planning. Encourage parents to have realistically high expectations for their children.
- *Work with and through families.* Ask parents to help you in working with and involving other parents. Parents respond positively to other parents, so it makes sense to have parents helping families.
- *Get to know your children's parents and families in order to build relationships with them.* This allows for better communication. Home visits are a good way to do this.
- *Learn how to best communicate with parents based on their cultural communication preferences.* Take into account cultural features that can inhibit collaboration.

The Federal Government and Parent Involvement

Given the key role that parents play in student education, it should come as no surprise that federal and state governments are taking a leading role in ensuring that parents are involved in schools. The No Child Left Behind Act of 2001 (NCLB) has changed the way schools interact with parents. Prior to NCLB, parental involvement was largely determined by school district policies and administrator and teacher discretion. This is no longer the case: NCLB mandates a wide range of required procedures and activities relating to parental involvement.

The extent and range of parental involvement under NCLB is specific and comprehensive, at both the district and schoolhouse level. NCLB requires that at the school level, each school must:

Elizabeth Crews / Elizabeth Crews Photography

- Convene an annual meeting at a convenient time, to which all parents of participating children are invited and encouraged to attend; inform parents of their school's participation; and explain the requirements and the right of the parents to be involved.

- Involve parents in an organized, ongoing, and timely way in the planning, review, and improvement of programs, including the planning, review, and improvement of the school parental involvement policy and the joint development of the school-wide program plan.

Families continue to change and, as they do, you must adapt and adopt new ways of involving family members and providing for their needs. For example, growing numbers of fathers have sole responsibility for rearing their children. What can you do to ensure the involvement of single fathers in their programs?

- Provide parents with timely information about programs, a description and explanation of the curriculum, and the forms of academic assessment used to measure student progress and the proficiency levels students are expected to meet.

- Provide opportunities, if requested by parents, for regular meetings to formulate suggestions and to participate, as appropriate, in decisions relating to the education of their children and respond to any such suggestions as soon as practicably possible.

NCLB also requires that the district, parents, schools, and students enter into a compact of shared responsibility for ensuring high student achievement. The school compact describes the school's responsibility to provide high-quality curriculum and instruction in a supportive and effective learning environment.

ACTIVITIES FOR INVOLVING FAMILIES

Unlimited possibilities exist for family involvement, but a coordinated effort is required to build an effective, meaningful program that can bring about a change in education and benefit all concerned: families, children, professionals, and communities. The following are some activities you can implement to ensure you will be successful in your parent involvement activities. Using these activities will provide for significant family involvement. As the following Technology Tie-In feature notes, homework is one example of how early childhood professionals are encouraging parents to play a role in their children's academic success.

The following are examples of activities that allow for significant family involvement. The activities are organized according to the six types of parent/family involvement discussed earlier.

Homework assignments for all children are a growing reality in many of today's primary classrooms. Over the past decade homework has increased by 50 percent. First-grade teacher Karen Alverez at Aldama Elementary School in Los Angeles assigns her students forty-five minutes of homework every day, Monday through Thursday. Like Karen, teachers are assigning homework in response to higher standards and state tests that begin as early as kindergarten. Many teachers believe homework is one way of helping children learn the knowledge and skills mandated by school districts. Parents not only support homework, but they also expect their children to have homework.

Homework can be a challenge for parents and children. One of the issues parents and children have with homework is how to get the help they need with completing homework assignments. Keep in mind that quite often when you assign homework to children you are also assigning it to parents who are responsible for seeing that their children complete it! Over half of all parents are involved in their children's homework in one way or another.

The Internet is one source of help. B. J. Pinchbeck was nine years old when he founded B. J. Pinchbeck's Homework Helper, which lists more than 700 links to educational sites and is affiliated with the Discovery Channel. Other sources for homework help are

- Education Planet Inc.
- Jeeves for Kids
- Fact Monster Homework Center
- Yahooligans
- KidsClick!
- Bigchalk

Pick a grade from kindergarten through third and develop a homework assignment for your class. Use these Internet sites to complete it. Develop a set of guidelines for how children can use the Internet to help them with their homework.

 Locate additional resources for helping parents and children with homework at http://www.prenhall.com/morrison, Chapter 13—Journal: Technology Tie-In.

Type 1—Parenting Knowledge and Skills

- *Participating in workshops.* These workshops introduce families to the school's policies, procedures, and programs. Most families want to know what is going on in the school and would do a better job of parenting and educating if they knew how.

- *Attending adult education classes.* These classes provide members of the community with opportunities to learn about a range of subjects.

- *Attending training programs.* These programs give parents, family members, and others skills as classroom aides, club and activity sponsors, curriculum planners, and policy decision makers. When parents, family members, and community persons are viewed as experts, empowerment results.

- *Participation in classroom and center activities.* While not all families can be directly involved in classroom activities, encourage those who can. Those who are involved must have guidance, direction, and training. Involving parents and others as paid aides is also an excellent way to provide employment and training. Many programs, such as Head Start, actively support such a policy.

- *Resource libraries and materials centers.* Families benefit from books and other articles relating to parenting. Some programs furnish resource areas with comfortable chairs to encourage families to use these materials.

Type 2—Communicating Between Home and School

- *Support services such as car pools and baby-sitting.* This makes attendance and involvement possible.

- *Performances and plays.* These, especially ones in which children have a part, tend to bring families to school; however, the purpose of children's performances should not be solely to get families involved.

 Review strategies on increasing communication with families at http://www.prenhall.com/morrison, Chapter 13: Web Links.

- *Telephone hotlines.* When staffed by families, hotlines can help allay fears and provide information relating to child abuse, communicable diseases, and special events. Telephone networks are also used to help children and parents with homework and to monitor latchkey children.
- *Newsletters.* When planned with parents' help, newsletters are an excellent way to keep families informed about program events, activities, and curriculum information. Newsletters written in parents' native language help keep language-minority families informed.
- *Home learning materials and activities.* Putting out a monthly calendar of activities is one good way to keep families involved in their children's learning.
- *Involvement of families in writing individualized education programs (IEPs) for children with special needs.* Such involvement in writing an IEP is not only a legal requirement but also an excellent learning experience.

Type 3—Encouraging Volunteering at School and in the Community

- *Child care.* Families may not be able to attend programs and become involved if they do not have child care for their children. Child care makes their participation possible and more enjoyable.
- *Service exchanges.* When operated by early childhood programs and other agencies, exchanges help families in their needs for services. For example, one parent provided child care in her home in exchange for having her washing machine repaired. The possibilities for such exchanges are endless.
- *Welcoming committees.* A good way to involve families in any program is to have other families contact them when their children first join a program.

Type 4—Supporting Student Learning at Home

- *Offer books and other materials for home use.* Provide material for parents to read to their children.
- *Give suggestions to parents.* Provide parents with tips for how to help their children with homework.
- *Develop a website for parents.* A website informs them about the activities of your classroom. Give suggestions for how parents can extend and enrich classroom projects and activities at home.
- *Develop a "home learning kit."* This can consist of activities and materials (books, activity packets, etc.). Send these kits home with children.

Type 5—Involvement in Decision Making and Advocacy

- *Fairs and bazaars.* Schools should involve families in fund-raising.
- *Hiring and policy making.* Parents and community members can and should serve on committees that set policy and hire staff.
- *Curriculum development and review.* Parents' involvement in curriculum planning helps them learn about and understand what constitutes a quality program and what is involved in a developmentally appropriate curriculum. When families know about the curriculum, they are more supportive of it.

Type 6—Collaborating with the Community

- *Family nights, cultural dinners, carnivals, and potluck dinners.* Such events bring families and the community to the school in nonthreatening, social ways.
- *Parent support groups.* Parents need support in their roles. Support groups can provide parenting information, community agency information, and speakers.

Making Sure All Parents Are Involved

A goal of parent/family involvement is to involve all parents or legal guardians in their children's schooling and programs. This involvement is easier to do in some contexts than others. For example, in suburban, middle class, affluent schools, parental participation is facilitated as a result of parents' self-initiative in wanting to be involved in school and classroom activities. However, low-SES families, fathers, and minority groups may have a low rate of parental involvement. What can you do to help ensure that as many of your parents as possible are involved? With very little effort you can increase fathers' involvement in your program. For example, three things that you can do to increase father participation are:

1. Include the father's name on the school/class enrollment form.
2. Send written correspondence to fathers even if they live apart from their children.
3. Invite fathers to the centers to participate in educational activities with their children.*

You can ask parents how they want to be involved. In one study, researchers had parents "identify school activities they would like to do. Parents reported that they would like to: have lunch with their children, attend field trips, visit or observe the classroom, prepare materials for the teachers, help their children with homework, attend after-school activities, and write grants."† In similar research, parents told researchers they were interested in "helping with homework, joining the PTA, providing merchandise for the bake sale, and attending open house."‡

In addition to asking parents how they want to be involved, being available for and listening to parents are two additional critical factors of a successful parent involvement program. When researchers examined barriers to Latino parent involvement, "Parents wished that teachers would be available to speak about grades, be able to find interpreters during open house and at other times throughout the school day, and communicate with the parents when their child is in need of assistance."§

So, while we often think that we have to develop big initiatives to involve parents, the little things that we often overlook or take for granted may be the most effective for getting and keeping parents involved. Asking, inviting, listening, and being available can make all the difference!

*Stephen Green, "Reaching Out to Fathers: An Examination of Staff Efforts That Lead to Greater Father Involvement in Early Childhood" (2003). [Online.] Available at http://ecrp.uiuc.edu/v5n2/green.html.

†Tara Gbadamosi and Huey-Ling Lin, "Parent's Interests, Current Involvement and Level of Parental Involvement in School Activities," (2003).

‡Ibid.

§Fred A. Y. Ramirez, "Dismay and Disappointment: Parental Involvement of Latino Immigrant Parents," The Urban Review, Vol. 35, No. 2 (June 2003), p. 93.

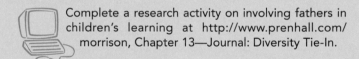

Complete a research activity on involving fathers in children's learning at http://www.prenhall.com/morrison, Chapter 13—Journal: Diversity Tie-In.

The Diversity Tie-In spotlights methods to increase participation in children's education.

Conducting Home Visits

Conducting home visits is becoming more commonplace for many teachers. In fact, California launched a $15 million initiative to pay teachers overtime for visiting students' homes.[9] Teachers who do home visiting are trained prior to going on the visits. Although not every state or district pays extra for home visits, more schools are building home visits into the school calendar, with a certain number of days being set aside for home visiting. Some districts and programs provide release time for visitation by hiring substitute teachers to enable classroom teachers to make home visits. A home visiting program can show that the teachers, principal, and school staff are willing to help "go more than halfway" to involve all parents in their children's education. Home visits help teachers demonstrate their interest in students' families and understand their students better by seeing them in their home environment.

These visits should not replace parent–teacher conferences or be used to discuss children's progress. When done early before any school programs can arise, they avoid putting parents on the defensive and signal that teachers are eager to work with all parents. Teachers who have made home visits say they build stronger relationships with parents and their children, and improve attendance and achievement. Although many "home" visits do occur in the home, they do not always have to. Sometimes parents are more comfortable meeting teachers away from the home in places such as community centers, churches, or the local YMCA or YWCA. These visits are still considered "home" visits.

Here are some guidelines for how you can be successful in your program of home visitation:

- Schedule the visits:
  - Some schools have scheduled home visits in the afternoon right after school. Others have found that early evening is more convenient for parents. Some schedule visits right before a new school year begins. A mix of times may be needed to reach all families.
  - Work with community groups (e.g., Boys and Girls Clubs, housing complexes, 4-H, YMCAs, and community centers) to schedule visits in neutral but convenient spaces.
- Make parents feel comfortable:
  - Send a letter home to parents explaining the desire to have teachers make informal visits to all students' homes. Include a form that parents can mail back to accept or decline the visit.
  - State clearly that the intent of your thirty-minute visit is to introduce yourself to family members and not to discuss the child's progress.
  - Suggest that families think about special things their children would want to share with the teacher.
  - Reduce parents' worries. One school included a note to parents that said "No preparation is required. In fact, our homes need to be vacuumed and all of us are on diets!" This touch of humor and casualness helps set a friendly and informal tone.
  - Make a phone call to parents who have not responded to explain the plan for home visits and reassure parents that it is to get acquainted and not to evaluate students.
  - Enlist community groups, religious organizations, and businesses to help publicize the home visits.[10]

Conducting Parent–Teacher Conferences

Significant parent involvement occurs through well-planned and well-conducted conferences between parents and early chilhood teachers, informally referred to as parent–teacher conferences. Such conferences are often the first contact many families have with school. Conferences are critical both from a public relations point of view and as a vehicle for helping families and professionals accomplish their goals. The following guidelines will help you as an early childhood professional prepare for and conduct successful conferences:

- *Plan ahead.* Be sure of the reason for the conference. What are your objectives? What do you want to accomplish? List the points you want to cover and think about what you are going to say.
- *Get to know the families.* This is not wasted time; the more effectively you establish rapport with families, the more you will accomplish in the long run.
- *Avoid an authoritative atmosphere.* Do not sit behind your desk while families sit in children's chairs. Treat families and others like the adults they are.
- *Communicate at parents' levels.* Do not condescend or patronize. Instead, use familiar words, phrases, and explanations families understand. Do not use jargon or complicated explanations, and speak in your natural style.

- *Accentuate the positive.* Make every effort to show and tell families that children are doing well. When you deal with problems, put them in the proper perspective: what a child is able to do, what the goals and purposes of the learning program are, what specific skill or concept you are trying to get the child to learn, and what problems the child is having in achieving the goal or purpose. Most importantly, explain what you plan to do to help the child achieve and what specific role families can have in meeting the achievement goals.

- *Give families a chance to talk.* You will not learn much about them if you do all the talking, nor are you likely to achieve your goals. Professionals are often accustomed to dominating a conversation, and many families will not be as verbal as you, so you will have to encourage families to talk.

- *Learn to listen.* An active listener holds eye contact, uses body language such as head nodding and hand gestures, does not interrupt, avoids arguing, paraphrases as a way of clarifying ideas, and keeps the conversation on track.

- *Follow up.* Ask families for a definite time for the next conference as you are concluding the current one. Having another conference is the best method of solidifying gains and extending support, but other acceptable means of follow-up are telephone calls, written reports, notes sent with children, and brief visits to the home. Although these types of contacts may appear casual, they should be planned for and conducted as seriously as any regular family–teacher conference.

- *Develop an action plan.* Never leave families with a sense of frustration, not knowing what you are doing or what they are to do. Every communication with families should end on a positive note, so that everyone knows what can be done and how to do it.

Making Contact by Telephone

Making a telephone call is an efficient way to contact families when it is impossible to arrange a face-to-face conference. Here are some tips you can use for your telephone contacts with parents:

- Since you cannot see someone on a telephone, it takes a little longer to build rapport and trust. The time you spend overcoming families' initial fears and apprehensions will pay dividends later.

- Constantly clarify what you are talking about and what you and the families have agreed to do, using such phrases as "What I heard you say then . . . " and "So far, we have agreed that. . . ."

- Do not act hurried. There is a limit to the amount of time you can spend on the phone, but you may be one of the few people who care about the parent and the child. Your telephone contact may be the major part of the family's support system.

Communicating with Parents over the Internet

The Internet provides another way for you to reach out to parents and keep them informed and involved. Most school districts have a web page that provides general information about the district and individual schools. Many teachers have their own classroom web page. Web pages are excellent ways to give parents and community members general information and let them virtually experience school and classroom events and accomplishments. Before you set up your class web page or begin communicating with parents via e-mail, here are some things to consider:

- Check with your school or program technology coordinator for guidelines and policies for web page development and communicating electronically with parents.

- Remember that not all parents are connected to the Internet. There is a great "digital divide" in the United States; low-income parents and minorities are less likely to have Internet access. You will have to consider how to provide families without Internet access the same information you provide to families who have Internet service.

Here are some guidelines to follow when you communicate with parents on the Internet:

- Observe all the rules of politeness and courtesy that you would in a face-to-face conversation.
- Observe all the rules of courteous Internet conversations. For example, don't use all capital letters (this is similar to SHOUTING).
- Remember that just like handwritten notes, electronic mail can be saved. In addition, electronic notes are much more easily transferred.
- Be straightforward and concise in your electronic conversations.
- Establish ground rules ahead of time about what you will and will not discuss electronically.

Involving Single-Parent Families

Explore websites devoted to encouraging family involvement in education at http://www.prenhall.com/morrison, Chapter 13: Web Links.

Many of the children you teach will be from single-parent families. Depending on where you teach, as many as 50 percent of your children could be from single-parent families. Here are some things you can do to ensure that single-parent families are involved:

- Many adults in one-parent families are employed during school hours and may not be available for conferences or other activities during that time. You must be willing to accommodate family schedules by arranging conferences at other times, perhaps early morning, noon, late afternoon, or early evening. Some employers, sensitive to these needs, give release time to participate in school functions, but others do not. In addition, professionals and principals need to think seriously about going to families, rather than having families always come to them.
- Remember that single parents have a limited amount of time to spend on involvement with their children's school and with their children at home. Therefore, when you talk with single-parent families, make sure that (1) the meeting starts on time, (2) you have a list of items to discuss, (3) you have sample materials available to illustrate all points, (4) you make specific suggestions relative to one-parent environments, and (5) the meeting ends on time. Because one-parent families are more likely to need child care assistance to attend meetings, child care should be planned for every parent meeting or activity.
- Suggest some ways that single parents can make their time with their children meaningful. If a child has trouble following directions, show families how to use home situations to help in this area. For example, children can learn to follow directions while helping with errands, meal preparation, or housework.
- Get to know families' lifestyles and living conditions. For instance, you can recommend that every child have a quiet place to study, but this may be an impossible demand for some households. You need to visit some of the homes in your community before you set meeting times, decide what family involvement activities to implement, and determine what you will ask of families during the year. All professionals, particularly early childhood professionals, need to keep in mind the condition of the home environment when they request that children bring certain items to school or carry out certain tasks at home. And when asking for parents' help, be sensitive to their talents and time constraints.

FIGURE 13.3

Involving Single and Working Parents

An increasing number of children live in single-parent and stepfamilies. Many also live with foster families and in other nontraditional family forms. In addition, in many two-parent families, both parents work full days, so children come home to an empty house. Thus, involving single and working parents presents many challenges to schools.

Communication

- Avoid making the assumption that students live with both biological parents.
- Avoid the traditional "Dear Parents" greeting in letters and other messages; instead use "Dear Parent", "Dear Family", "Friends", or some other form of greeting.
- Develop a system of keeping noncustodial parents informed of their children's school progress.
- Demonstrate sensitivity to the rights of noncustodial parents. Inform parents that schools may not withhold information from noncustodial parents who have the legal right to see their children's records.
- Develop a simple unobtrusive system to keep track of family changes:
  - At the beginning of the year ask for the names and addresses of individuals to be informed about each child and involved in school activities.
  - At midyear send a form to each child's parent or guardian to verify that the information is still accurate. Invite the parent or guardian to indicate any changes.
- Place flyers about school events on bulletin boards of major companies in the community that are family friendly to learning.

Involvement

- Hold parent–teacher conferences and other school events in the evenings.
- Welcome other children at such events, and provide organized activities or child care services.
- Provide teachers and counselors with in-service training that sensitizes them to special problems faced by children of single and working parents and by the parents themselves.
- Gather information on whether joint or separate parent conferences need to be scheduled with parents.
- Sponsor evening and weekend learning activities at which parents can participate and learn with their children.
- Work with local businesses to arrange released time from work so that parents can attend conferences, volunteer, or otherwise spend time at their child's school when it is in session.

Source: Reaching All Families: Creating Family-Friendly Schools, (Washington, DC: U.S. Department of Education, Office of Educational Research and Improvement, 1996).

- Help develop support groups for one-parent families within your school, such as discussion groups and classes on parenting for singles. And be sure to include the needs and abilities of one-parent families in your family involvement activities and programs. After all, single-parent families may represent the majority of families in your program.

Figure 13.3 provides some additional suggestions that can guide your involvement of single and working parents.

Involving Language-Minority Parents and Families

Forty-three percent of public school populations are considered to be members of a racial or ethnic minority group. The fact that the minority is now almost the majority is due to the growth in the proportion of students who are Hispanic. Hispanic students represent 19 percent of public school enrollment.[11]

Language-minority parents are individuals whose English proficiency is minimal and who lack a comprehensive knowledge of the norms and social systems in the United States. Language-minority families often face language and cultural barriers that greatly hamper their ability to become actively involved, although many have a great desire and willingness to participate in their children's education.

Because the culture of language-minority families often differs from the majority in a community, those who seek truly collaborative community, home, and school involvement must take into account the cultural features that can inhibit collaboration. Traditional styles of child rearing and family organization, attitudes toward schooling, organizations around which families center their lives, life goals and values, political influences, and methods of communication within the cultural group all have implications for parent participation.

Language-minority families often lack information about the U.S. educational system, including basic school philosophy, practice, and structure, which can result in misconceptions, fear, and a general reluctance to respond to invitations for involvement. Furthermore, this educational system may be quite different from schools with which these families are familiar. The Diversity Tie-In on the following page will help you invoke all minority parents.

SW Productions / Getty Images, Inc.–Photodisc

Your role as an early childhood professional includes learning how to effectively involve language-minority parents and families of many different cultures. How will you prepare yourself for this important role?

Community Involvement

A comprehensive program of involvement would not be complete without community involvement. More early childhood professionals realize that neither they alone nor the limited resources of their programs are sufficient to meet the needs of many children and families. Consequently, early education professionals are seeking ways to link families to community services and resources.

Community Resources. The community offers a vital and rich array of resources for helping you teach better and for helping you meet the needs of parents and their children. Schools and teachers cannot address the many issues facing children and youth without the partnership and collaboration of powerful sectors of society, including community agencies, businesses, and industry.

Following are suggested actions you can take to learn to use your community in your teaching:

- *Know your students and their needs.* Through observations, conferences with parents, and discussions with students, you can identify barriers to children's learning and discover what kind of help to seek.
- *Know your community.* Walk or drive around the community. Ask a parent to give you a tour to help familiarize you with agencies and individuals. Read the local newspaper, and attend community events and activities.
- *Ask for help and support from parents and the community.* Keep in mind that many parents will not be involved unless you personally ask them. The only encouragement many individuals and local businesses need is your invitation.

View a child's drawing depicting a recent school visit by a police officer at Student and Teacher Artifacts, Early Childhood Education, Module 7: Families and Community, Artifact 3: Trust a Policeman (Language Arts K–2).

TEACHER PREP

Because parents play such a powerful role in their children's educational development, early childhood programs must make every effort to involve the parents and families of *all* children. Unfortunately, many minority parents are not included at all or not to the extent to which they should be. The urgency of involving minority parents becomes more evident when we look at the population growth of minorities. For example, the Bureau of the Census estimates that by 2025, 25 percent of all school-age children in the United States will be Hispanic.

"Historically, we know that Hispanics don't feel welcome in schools, and that's been a barrier to recruiting Hispanic parents," said Mark Townsend, Colorado PTA president and a board member of the National PTA.*

To welcome and involve Hispanic parents, the National PTA launched its Hispanic outreach initiative in 2002 in California, Florida, and Texas, using billboards and other advertisements in Spanish, such as "Los buenos padres no nacen. Se hacen." ("Good parents are not born. They are developed.")

Across the country more emphasis will be placed on how to make Hispanic and other minority parents feel welcome and involved in their children's schools. According to Delia Pompa, chair of the National PTA Hispanic Outreach Advisory Board, "Whether or not your PTA serves a community that is heavily Hispanic, this initiative is just a first step in helping all PTAs reach out to parents of many languages and cultures. Through this Hispanic outreach initiative, we hope to learn and model best practices for reaching out to and including all parents in PTA."†

Programs that have successfully involved Hispanic parents recommend the following strategies:

- *Personal touch*—Use face-to-face communication in the Hispanic parents' primary language when first making contact. It may take several personal meetings before parents gain sufficient trust to actively participate.
  - Make home visits if possible, taking Spainish-speaking parents with you to interpret for you. Remember, parents trust parents!
  - Have parents invite other parents to school, where you can talk personally to a small group.

- Always greet parents whenever they come to school for any reason.
- *Nonjudgmental communication*—Avoid making Hispanic parents feel that they are to blame for or are doing something wrong. Support parents for their strengths rather than judging them for perceived failings.
  - Be an active listener—pay close attention to what parents are saying and how they are saying it.
  - Be willing to compromise.
- *Bilingual support*—Communicate with Hispanic parents in both Spanish and English.
  - Send all notes and flyers home in Spanish.
  - Spanish-speaking parents can help you compose notes and announcements.
  - Desginate a Hispanic parent as the contact for your classroom to keep other parents informed about upcoming meetings.
  - Establish a Spanish book corner where students and parents can check out bilingual or Spanish books to read together.
- *Staff development focused on Hispanic culture*—All staff must understand the key features of Hispanic culture—Latino history, traditions, values, and customs—and their impact on students' behavior and learning styles. For example, Hispanic children like peer-oriented learning, so mixed-age grouping and cooperative learning strategies work well. You should learn as much as possible about the children and their culture.
- *Community outreach*—Many Hispanic families can benefit from family literacy programs, vocational training, ESL programs, improved medical and dental services, and other community-based social services.†

---

* Medina, "Push on to Recruit Latinos for Parent-Teacher Groups, New York Times (Sept. 16, 2002) A. 14.

† Ibid.

† Linda Espinosa, "Hispanic Parent Involvement in Early Childhood Programs," ERIC Digest (1995), http://www.ericdigests.org/1996-1/hispanic.htm.

- *Develop a directory of community agencies.* Consult the business pages of local phone books, contact local chambers of commerce, and ask parents what agencies are helpful to them.
- *Compile a list of people who are willing to come to your classroom to speak to or work with your students.* You can start by asking parents to volunteer and to give suggestions and recommendations of others.

Only by helping families meet their needs and those of their children will you create opportunities for these children to reach their full potential. For this reason alone, family involvement programs and activities must be an essential part of every early childhood program.

School–Business Involvement

School–business involvement and partnerships are excellent means of strengthening programs and helping children and families. For their part, businesses are eager to develop the business–school connection in efforts to help schools better educate children.

The challenge to early childhood professionals is quite clear: merely seeking ways to involve parents in school activities is no longer a sufficient program of parent involvement. Today, the challenge is to make families the focus of our involvement activities so that their lives and their children's lives are made better. Anything less will not help families and children access and benefit from the opportunities of the twenty-first century.

National Organizations

National programs dedicated to family involvement are another rich resource for information and support. Some of these are listed here:

- Institute for Responsive Education (IRE), http://www.responsiveeducation.org
- Mega Skills Education Center, http://www.megaskillshsi.org
- National PTA, http://www.pta.org

Visit the websites of several national organizations that support school partnerships at http://www.prenhall.com/morrison, Chapter 13: Web Links.

Geri Enberg / Geri Enberg Photography

Community businesses and civic organizations offer many opportunities for collaborative partnerships that can lead to the achievement of common goals for making education better. Begin now to plan for ways that you will reach out to and involve the community in your classroom.

Another organization, the Family Involvement Partnership for Learning, promotes children's learning through the development of family–school–community partnerships. This organization began as a cooperative effort between the U.S. Department of Education and the National Coalition for Parent Involvement in Education (NCPIE). NCPIE has been meeting monthly since its founding in 1980 to advocate the involvement of families in their children's education and to promote relationships among home, school, and community that can enhance the education of all children and youth. NCPIE represents parents, schools, communities, religious groups, and businesses.[12]

Website Connections

Many websites are available to help parents become more involved in their children's education. For example, the Family Education Network (http://www.familyeducation.com) offers resources and features on a wide array of educational topics. You can find other sites by entering the following keywords into one of the Internet's many available search engines:

- Parent involvement,
- Community involvement,
- School partnerships,
- School/business relationships, or
- School/community collaboration.

THE CHALLENGE

The challenge to you and all early childhood professionals is quite clear: how to make families the focus of our involvement activities so that their lives and their children's lives are made better. Anything less will not help families and children access and benefit from the opportunities of the twenty-first century.

ACTIVITIES FOR PROFESSIONAL DEVELOPMENT

Ethical Dilemma

"I Really Don't Want to Get Involved"

Tyler Cove Elementary School has enrolled a number of new families who were displaced by a recent hurricane. Six-year-old Tamika, her mother, and three siblings arrived in town with only the clothes on their backs. Tamika has not had a change of clothing in several days. Although Carrie has no hurricane-displaced children in her third-grade class, she is very much concerned about their well-being. She mentions to Tamika's teacher that several community agencies are involved in hurricane relief and could provide Tamika and her family with clothing and other resources. Tamika's teacher is unresponsive. "I know, Carrie, but I don't have the time to mess around with this stuff. I've got all I can do to keep up with the things I have to do in the classroom. I don't want to make a lot of extra work for myself. Besides, I really don't want to get involved with these families; they just don't fit into our community."

What should Carrie do to help Tamika and her family? Should she report Tamika's teacher to the principal? Or should she offer to buy Tamika and her family clothing? Or should she call her friend at the Salvation Army for help? Or should she develop another strategy?

Application Activities

1. Develop a plan for family involvement in a grade in which you plan to teach.
   a. Write objectives for the program.
   b. Develop specific activities for involving families and for providing services to them.
   c. Explain how you would involve fathers, language-minority families, and families of children with disabilities.
2. Visit social services agencies in your area, and list the services they offer.
   a. Describe how you can work with these agencies to meet the needs of children and families.
   b. Invite agency directors to meet with your class to discuss how they and early childhood professionals can work cooperatively to help families and children.
   c. As families change, so, too, do the services they need. Conduct a family survey of a family to determine what services members believe they need most. Tell how you could help provide those services.

 To take online practice tests on this chapter's material, go to the Companion Website at http://www.prenhall.com/morrison, select Chapter 13, and then choose the Multiple Choice or the Essay module. For additional Web resources, choose Web Links.

appendix

NAEYC Code of Ethical Conduct and Statement of Commitment

PREAMBLE

NAEYC recognizes that those who work with young children face many daily decisions that have moral and ethical implications. The **NAEYC Code of Ethical Conduct** offers guidelines for responsible behavior and sets forth a common basis for resolving the principal ethical dilemmas encountered in early childhood care and education. The **Statement of Commitment** is not part of the Code but is a personal acknowledgement of an individual's willingness to embrace the distinctive values and moral obligations of the field of early childhood care and education. The primary focus of the Code is on daily practice with children and their families in programs for children from birth through 8 years of age, such as infant/toddler programs, preschool and prekindergarten programs, child care centers, hospital and child life settings, family child care homes, kindergartens, and primary classrooms. When the issues involve young children, then these provisions also apply to specialists who do not work directly with children, including program administrators, parent educators, early childhood adult educators, and officials with responsibility for program monitoring and licensing. (Note: See also the "Code of Ethical Conduct: Supplement for Early Childhood Adult Educators," online at http://www.naeyc.org/about/positions/asp/ethics04.)

Core Values

Standards of ethical behavior in early childhood care and education are based on commitment to the following core values that are deeply rooted in the history of the field of early childhood care and education. We have made a commitment to

- Appreciate childhood as a unique and valuable stage of the human life cycle
- Base our work on knowledge of how children develop and learn
- Appreciate and support the bond between the child and family
- Recognize that children are best understood and supported in the context of family, culture,[1] community, and society

- Respect the dignity, worth, and uniqueness of each individual (child, family member, and colleague)
- Respect diversity in children, families, and colleagues
- Recognize that children and adults achieve their full potential in the context of relationships that are based on trust and respect

Conceptual Framework

The Code sets forth a framework of professional responsibilities in four sections. Each section addresses an area of professional relationships: (1) with children, (2) with families, (3) among colleagues, and (4) with the community and society. Each section includes an introduction to the primary responsibilities of the early childhood practitioner in that context. The introduction is followed by a set of ideals (I) that reflect exemplary professional practice and by a set of principles (P) describing practices that are required, prohibited, or permitted.

The **ideals** reflect the aspirations of practitioners. The **principles** guide conduct and assist practitioners in resolving ethical dilemmas.[2] Both ideals and principles are intended to direct practitioners to those questions which, when responsibly answered, can provide the basis for conscientious decision making. While the Code provides specific direction for addressing some ethical dilemmas, many others will require the practitioner to combine the guidance of the Code with professional judgment.

The ideals and principles in this Code present a shared framework of professional responsibility that affirms our commitment to the core values of our field. The Code publicly acknowledges the responsibilities that we in the field have assumed, and in so doing supports ethical behavior in our work. Practitioners who face situations with ethical dimensions are urged to seek guidance in the applicable parts of this Code and in the spirit that informs the whole.

Often "the right answer"—the best ethical course of action to take—is not obvious. There may be no readily apparent, positive way to handle a situation. When one important value contradicts another, we face an ethical dilemma. When we face a dilemma, it is our professional responsibility to consult the Code and all relevant parties to find the most ethical resolution.

Source: From the National Association for the Education of Young Children, Washington, DC, 2005. Reprinted by permission. Revised April 2005. Endorsed by the Association for Childhood Education International.

[1]*Culture* includes ethnicity, racial identity, economic level, family structure, language, and religious and political beliefs, which profoundly influence each child's development and relationship to the world.

[2]There is not necessarily a corresponding principle for each ideal.

SECTION I: ETHICAL RESPONSIBILITIES TO CHILDREN

Childhood is a unique and valuable stage in the human life cycle. Our paramount responsibility is to provide care and education in settings that are safe, healthy, nurturing, and responsive for each child. We are committed to supporting children's development and learning; respecting individual differences; and helping children learn to live, play, and work cooperatively. We are also committed to promoting children's self-awareness, competence, self-worth, resiliency, and physical well-being.

Ideals

I-1.1—To be familiar with the knowledge base of early childhood care and education and to stay informed through continuing education and training.

I-1.2—To base program practices upon current knowledge and research in the field of early childhood education, child development, and related disciplines, as well as on particular knowledge of each child.

I-1.3—To recognize and respect the unique qualities, abilities, and potential of each child.

I-1.4—To appreciate the vulnerability of children and their dependence on adults.

I-1.5—To create and maintain safe and healthy settings that foster children's social, emotional, cognitive, and physical development and that respect their dignity and their contributions.

I-1.6—To use assessment instruments and strategies that are appropriate for the children to be assessed, that are used only for the purposes for which they were designed, and that have the potential to benefit children.

I-1.7—To use assessment information to understand and support children's development and learning, to support instruction, and to identify children who may need additional services.

I-1.8—To support the right of each child to play and learn in an inclusive environment that meets the needs of children with and without disabilities.

I-1.9—To advocate for and ensure that all children, including those with special needs, have access to the support services needed to be successful.

I-1.10—To ensure that each child's culture, language, ethnicity, and family structure are recognized and valued in the program.

I-1.11—To provide all children with experiences in a language that they know, as well as support children in maintaining the use of their home language and in learning English.

I-1.12—To work with families to provide a safe and smooth transition as children and families move from one program to the next.

Principles

P-1.1—Above all, we shall not harm children. We shall not participate in practices that are emotionally damaging, physically harmful, disrespectful, degrading, dangerous, exploitative, or intimidating to children. *This principle has precedence over all others in this Code*.

P-1.2—We shall care for and educate children in positive emotional and social environments that are cognitively stimulating and that support each child's culture, language, ethnicity, and family structure.

P-1.3—We shall not participate in practices that discriminate against children by denying benefits, giving special advantages, or excluding them from programs or activities on the basis of their sex, race, national origin, religious beliefs, medical condition, disability, or the marital status/family structure, sexual orientation, or religious beliefs or other affiliations of their families. (Aspects of this principle do not apply in programs that have a lawful mandate to provide services to a particular population of children.)

P-1.4—We shall involve all those with relevant knowledge (including families and staff) in decisions concerning a child, as appropriate, ensuring confidentiality of sensitive information.

P-1.5—We shall use appropriate assessment systems, which include multiple sources of information, to provide information on children's learning and development.

P-1.6—We shall strive to ensure that decisions such as those related to enrollment, retention, or assignment to special education services, will be based on multiple sources of information and will never be based on a single assessment, such as a test score or a single observation.

P-1.7—We shall strive to build individual relationships with each child; make individualized adaptations in teaching strategies, learning environments, and curricula; and consult with the family so that each child benefits from the program. If after such efforts have been exhausted, the current placement does not meet a child's needs, or the child is seriously jeopardizing the ability of other children to benefit from the program, we shall collaborate with the child's family and appropriate specialists to determine the additional services needed and/or the placement option(s) most likely to ensure the child's success. (Aspects of this principle may not apply in programs that have a lawful mandate to provide services to a particular population of children.)

P-1.8—We shall be familiar with the risk factors for and symptoms of child abuse and neglect, including physical, sexual, verbal, and emotional abuse and physical, emotional, educational, and medical neglect. We shall know and follow state laws and community procedures that protect children against abuse and neglect.

P-1.9—When we have reasonable cause to suspect child abuse or neglect, we shall report it to the appropriate community agency and follow up to ensure that appropriate action has been taken. When appropriate, parents or guardians will be informed that the referral will be or has been made.

P-1.10—When another person tells us of his or her suspicion that a child is being abused or neglected, we shall assist that person in taking appropriate action in order to protect the child.

P-1.11—When we become aware of a practice or situation that endangers the health, safety, or well-being of children, we have an ethical responsibility to protect children or inform parents and/or others who can.

SECTION II: ETHICAL RESPONSIBILITIES TO FAMILIES

Families[3] are of primary importance in children's development. Because the family and the early childhood practitioner have a common interest in the child's well-being, we acknowledge a primary responsibility to bring about communication, cooperation, and collaboration between the home and early childhood program in ways that enhance the child's development.

Ideals

I-2.1—To be familiar with the knowledge base related to working effectively with families and to stay informed through continuing education and training.

I-2.2—To develop relationships of mutual trust and create partnerships with the families we serve.

I-2.3—To welcome all family members and encourage them to participate in the program.

I-2.4—To listen to families, acknowledge and build upon their strengths and competencies, and learn from families as we support them in their task of nurturing children.

I-2.5—To respect the dignity and preferences of each family and to make an effort to learn about its structure, culture, language, customs, and beliefs.

I-2.6—To acknowledge families' child-rearing values and their right to make decisions for their children.

I-2.7—To share information about each child's education and development with families and to help them understand and appreciate the current knowledge base of the early childhood profession.

I-2.8—To help family members enhance their understanding of their children and support the continuing development of their skills as parents.

I-2.9—To participate in building support networks for families by providing them with opportunities to interact with program staff, other families, community resources, and professional services.

Principles

P-2.1—We shall not deny family members access to their child's classroom or program setting unless access is denied by court order or other legal restriction.

---

[3]The term *family* may include those adults, besides parents, with the responsibility of being involved in educating, nurturing, and advocating for the child.

P-2.2—We shall inform families of program philosophy, policies, curriculum, assessment system, and personnel qualifications, and explain why we teach as we do—which should be in accordance with our ethical responsibilities to children (see Section I).

P-2.3—We shall inform families of and, when appropriate, involve them in policy decisions.

P-2.4—We shall involve the family in significant decisions affecting their child.

P-2.5—We shall make every effort to communicate effectively with all families in a language that they understand. We shall use community resources for translation and interpretation when we do not have sufficient resources in our own programs.

P-2.6—As families share information with us about their children and families, we shall consider this information to plan and implement the program.

P-2.7—We shall inform families about the nature and purpose of the program's child assessments and how data about their child will be used.

P-2.8—We shall treat child assessment information confidentially and share this information only when there is a legitimate need for it.

P-2.9—We shall inform the family of injuries and incidents involving their child, of risks such as exposures to communicable diseases that might result in infection, and of occurrences that might result in emotional stress.

P-2.10—Families shall be fully informed of any proposed research projects involving their children and shall have the opportunity to give or withhold consent without penalty. We shall not permit or participate in research that could in any way hinder the education, development, or well-being of children.

P-2.11—We shall not engage in or support exploitation of families. We shall not use our relationship with a family for private advantage or personal gain, or enter into relationships with family members that might impair our effectiveness working with their children.

P-2.12—We shall develop written policies for the protection of confidentiality and the disclosure of children's records. These policy documents shall be made available to all program personnel and families. Disclosure of children's records beyond family members, program personnel, and consultants having an obligation of confidentiality shall require familial consent (except in cases of abuse or neglect).

P-2.13—We shall maintain confidentiality and shall respect the family's right to privacy, refraining from disclosure of confidential information and intrusion into family life. However, when we have reason to believe that a child's welfare is at risk, it is permissible to share confidential information with agencies, as well as with individuals who have legal responsibility for intervening in the child's interest.

P-2.14—In cases where family members are in conflict with one another, we shall work openly, sharing our observations of the child, to help all parties involved make informed decisions. We shall refrain from becoming an advocate for one party.

P-2.15—We shall be familiar with and appropriately refer families to community resources and professional support services. After a referral has been made, we shall follow up to ensure that services have been appropriately provided.

SECTION III: ETHICAL RESPONSIBILITIES TO COLLEAGUES

In a caring, cooperative workplace, human dignity is respected, professional satisfaction is promoted, and positive relationships are developed and sustained. Based upon our core values, our primary responsibility to colleagues is to establish and maintain settings and relationships that support productive work and meet professional needs. The same ideals that apply to children also apply as we interact with adults in the workplace.

A—Responsibilities to co-workers

Ideals

I-3A.1—To establish and maintain relationships of respect, trust, confidentiality, collaboration, and cooperation with co-workers.

I-3A.2—To share resources with co-workers, collaborating to ensure that the best possible early childhood care and education program is provided.

I-3A.3—To support co-workers in meeting their professional needs and in their professional development.

I-3A.4—To accord co-workers due recognition of professional achievement.

Principles

P-3A.1—We shall recognize the contributions of colleagues to our program and not participate in practices that diminish their reputations or impair their effectiveness in working with children and families.

P-3A.2—When we have concerns about the professional behavior of a co-worker, we shall first let that person know of our concern in a way that shows respect for personal dignity and for the diversity to be found among staff members, and then attempt to resolve the matter collegially and in a confidential manner.

P-3A.3—We shall exercise care in expressing views regarding the personal attributes or professional conduct of co-workers. Statements should be based on firsthand knowledge, not hearsay, and relevant to the interests of children and programs.

P-3A.4—We shall not participate in practices that discriminate against a co-worker because of sex, race, national origin, religious beliefs or other affiliations, age, marital status/family structure, disability, or sexual orientation.

B—Responsibilities to employers

Ideals

I-3B.1—To assist the program in providing the highest quality of service.

I-3B.2—To do nothing that diminishes the reputation of the program in which we work unless it is violating laws and regulations designed to protect children or is violating the provisions of this Code.

Principles

P-3B.1—We shall follow all program policies. When we do not agree with program policies, we shall attempt to effect change through constructive action within the organization.

P-3B.2—We shall speak or act on behalf of an organization only when authorized. We shall take care to acknowledge when we are speaking for the organization and when we are expressing a personal judgment.

P-3B.3—We shall not violate laws or regulations designed to protect children and shall take appropriate action consistent with this Code when aware of such violations.

P-3B.4—If we have concerns about a colleague's behavior, and children's well-being is not at risk, we may address the concern with that individual. If children are at risk or the situation does not improve after it has been brought to the colleague's attention, we shall report the colleague's unethical or incompetent behavior to an appropriate authority.

P-3B.5—When we have a concern about circumstances or conditions that impact the quality of care and education within the program, we shall inform the program's administration or, when necessary, other appropriate authorities.

C—Responsibilities to employees

Ideals

I-3C.1—To promote safe and healthy working conditions and policies that foster mutual respect, cooperation, collaboration, competence, well-being, confidentiality, and self-esteem in staff members.

I-3C.2—To create and maintain a climate of trust and candor that will enable staff to speak and act in the best interests of children, families, and the field of early childhood care and education.

I-3C.3—To strive to secure adequate and equitable compensation (salary and benefits) for those who work with or on behalf of young children.

I-3C.4—To encourage and support continual development of employees in becoming more skilled and knowledgeable practitioners.

Principles

P-3C.1—In decisions concerning children and programs, we shall draw upon the education, training, experience, and expertise of staff members.

P-3C.2—We shall provide staff members with safe and supportive working conditions that honor confidences and permit them to carry out their responsibilities through fair performance evaluation, written grievance procedures, constructive feedback, and opportunities for continuing professional development and advancement.

P-3C.3—We shall develop and maintain comprehensive written personnel policies that define program standards. These policies shall be given to new staff members and shall be available and easily accessible for review by all staff members.

P-3C.4—We shall inform employees whose performance does not meet program expectations of areas of concern and, when possible, assist in improving their performance.

P-3C.5—We shall conduct employee dismissals for just cause, in accordance with all applicable laws and regulations. We shall inform employees who are dismissed of the reasons for their termination. When a dismissal is for cause, justification must be based on evidence of inadequate or inappropriate behavior that is accurately documented, current, and available for the employee to review.

P-3C.6—In making evaluations and recommendations, we shall make judgments based on fact and relevant to the interests of children and programs.

P-3C.7—We shall make hiring, retention, termination, and promotion decisions based solely on a person's competence, record of accomplishment, ability to carry out the responsibilities of the position, and professional preparation specific to the developmental levels of children in his/her care.

P-3C.8—We shall not make hiring, retention, termination, and promotion decisions based on an individual's sex, race, national origin, religious beliefs or other affiliations, age, marital status/family structure, disability, or sexual orientation. We shall be familiar with and observe laws and regulations that pertain to employment discrimination. (Aspects of this principle do not apply to programs that have a lawful mandate to determine eligibility based on one or more of the criteria identified above.)

P-3C.9—We shall maintain confidentiality in dealing with issues related to an employee's job performance and shall respect an employee's right to privacy regarding personal issues.

SECTION IV: ETHICAL RESPONSIBILITIES TO COMMUNITY AND SOCIETY

Early childhood programs operate within the context of their immediate community made up of families and other institutions concerned with children's welfare. Our responsibilities to the community are to provide programs that meet the diverse needs of families, to cooperate with agencies and professions that share the responsibility for children, to assist families in gaining access to those agencies and allied professionals, and to assist in the development of community programs that are needed but not currently available.

As individuals, we acknowledge our responsibility to provide the best possible programs of care and education for children and to conduct ourselves with honesty and integrity. Because of our specialized expertise in early childhood development and education and because the larger society shares responsibility for the welfare and protection of young children, we acknowledge a collective obligation to advocate for the best interests of children within early childhood programs and in the larger community and to serve as a voice for young children everywhere.

The ideals and principles in this section are presented to distinguish between those that pertain to the work of the individual early childhood educator and those that more typically are engaged in collectively on behalf of the best interests of children—with the understanding that individual early childhood educators have a shared responsibility for addressing the ideals and principles that are identified as "collective."

Ideal (Individual)

1-4.1.—To provide the community with high-quality early childhood care and education programs and services.

Ideals (Collective)

I-4.2—To promote cooperation among professionals and agencies and interdisciplinary collaboration among professions concerned with addressing issues in the health, education, and well-being of young children, their families, and their early childhood educators.

I-4.3—To work through education, research, and advocacy toward an environmentally safe world in which all children receive health care, food, and shelter; are nurtured; and live free from violence in their home and their communities.

I-4.4—To work through education, research, and advocacy toward a society in which all young children have access to high-quality early care and education programs.

I-4.5—To work to ensure that appropriate assessment systems, which include multiple sources of information, are used for purposes that benefit children.

I-4.6—To promote knowledge and understanding of young children and their needs. To work toward greater societal acknowledgment of children's rights and greater social acceptance of responsibility for the well-being of all children.

I-4.7—To support policies and laws that promote the well-being of children and families, and to work to change those that impair their well-being. To participate in developing policies and laws that are needed, and to cooperate with other individuals and groups in these efforts.

I-4.8—To further the professional development of the field of early childhood care and education and to strengthen its commitment to realizing its core values as reflected in this Code.

Principles (Individual)

P-4.1—We shall communicate openly and truthfully about the nature and extent of services that we provide.

P-4.2—We shall apply for, accept, and work in positions for which we are personally well-suited and professionally qualified. We shall not offer services that we do not have the competence, qualifications, or resources to provide.

P-4.3—We shall carefully check references and shall not hire or recommend for employment any person whose competence, qualifications, or character makes him or her unsuited for the position.

P-4.4—We shall be objective and accurate in reporting the knowledge upon which we base our program practices.

P-4.5—We shall be knowledgeable about the appropriate use of assessment strategies and instruments and interpret results accurately to families.

P-4.6—We shall be familiar with laws and regulations that serve to protect the children in our programs and be vigilant in ensuring that these laws and regulations are followed.

P-4.7—When we become aware of a practice or situation that endangers the health, safety, or well-being of children, we have an ethical responsibility to protect children or inform parents and/or others who can.

P-4.8—We shall not participate in practices that are in violation of laws and regulations that protect the children in our programs.

P-4.9—When we have evidence that an early childhood program is violating laws or regulations protecting children, we shall report the violation to appropriate authorities who can be expected to remedy the situation.

P-4.10—When a program violates or requires its employees to violate this Code, it is permissible, after fair assessment of the evidence, to disclose the identity of that program.

Principles (Collective)

P-4.11—When policies are enacted for purposes that do not benefit children, we have a collective responsibility to work to change these practices.

P-4.12—When we have evidence that an agency that provides services intended to ensure children's well-being is failing to meet its obligations, we acknowledge a collective ethical responsibility to report the problem to appropriate authorities or to the public. We shall be vigilant in our follow-up until the situation is resolved.

P-4.13—When a child protection agency fails to provide adequate protection for abused or neglected children, we acknowledge a collective ethical responsibility to work toward the improvement of these services.

Glossary of Terms Related to Ethics

Code of Ethics. Defines the core values of the field and provides guidance for what professionals should do when they encounter conflicting obligations or responsibilities in their work.

Values. Qualities or principles that individuals believe to be desirable or worthwhile and that they prize for themselves, for others, and for the world in which they live.

Core Values. Commitments held by a profession that are consciously and knowingly embraced by its practitioners because they make a contribution to society. There is a difference between personal values and the core values of a profession.

Morality. Peoples' views of what is good, right and proper; their beliefs about their obligations; and their ideas about how they should behave.

Ethics. The study of right and wrong, or duty and obligation, that involves critical reflection on morality and the ability to make choices between values and the examination of the moral dimensions of relationships.

Professional Ethics. The moral commitments of a profession that involve moral reflection that extends and enhances the personal morality practitioners bring to their work, that concern actions of right and wrong in the workplace, and that help individuals resolve moral dilemmas they encounter in their work.

Ethical Responsibilities. Behaviors that one must or must not engage in. Ethical responsibilities are clear-cut and are spelled out in the Code of Ethical Conduct (for example, early childhood educators should never share confidential information about a child or family with a person who has no legitimate need for knowing).

Ethical Dilemma. A moral conflict that involves determining appropriate conduct when an individual faces conflicting professional values and responsibilities.

Sources for Glossary Terms and Definitions

Feeney, S., & N. Freeman. 1999. *Ethics and the early childhood educator: Using the NAEYC code.* Washington, DC: NAEYC.

Kidder, R. M. 1995. *How good people make tough choices: Resolving the dilemmas of ethical living.* New York: Fireside.

Kipnis, K. 1987. How to discuss professional ethics. *Young Children* 42 (4): 26–30.

STATEMENT OF COMMITMENT[4]

As an individual who works with young children, I commit myself to furthering the values of early childhood education as they are reflected in the ideals and principles of the NAEYC Code of Ethical Conduct. To the best of my ability I will

- Never harm children.
- Ensure that programs for young children are based on current knowledge and research of child development and early childhood education.
- Respect and support families in their task of nurturing children.
- Respect colleagues in early childhood care and education and support them in maintaining the NAEYC Code of Ethical Conduct.
- Serve as an advocate for children, their families, and their teachers in community and society.
- Stay informed of and maintain high standards of professional conduct.
- Engage in an ongoing process of self-reflection, realizing that personal characteristics, biases, and beliefs have an impact on children and families.
- Be open to new ideas and be willing to learn from the suggestions of others.
- Continue to learn, grow, and contribute as a professional.
- Honor the ideals and principles of the NAEYC Code of Ethical Conduct.

---

[4]This Statement of Commitment is not part of the Code but is a personal acknowledgment of the individual's willingness to embrace the distinctive values and moral obligations of the field of early childhood care and education. It is recognition of the moral obligations that lead to an individual becoming part of the profession.

endnotes

Chapter 1

1. National Association for the Education of Young Children, *NAEYC Standards for Early Childhood Professional Preparation: Initial Licensure Programs*, NAEYC Initial Licensure Standards (Washington, DC: NAEYC, July 2001).

2. Ibid.

3. Ibid.

4. Ibid.

5. The White House, "A Quality Teacher in Every Classroom: Improving Teacher Quality and Enhancing the Profession," *The New Provisions in the No Child Left Behind Act*, March 4, 2002, http://www.whitehouse.gov/infocus/education/teachers/index.html.

6. National Association for the Education of Young Children, *NAEYC Standards for Early Childhood Professional Preparation* (Washington, DC: NAEYC, 2001), 12.

7. Ibid., 20.

8. Ibid., 20–23.

9. L. Derman-Sparks and the A.B.C Task Force, *Anti-Bias Curriculum: Tools for Empowering Young Children* (Washington, DC: National Association for the Education of Young Children, 1998).

10. Ibid.

11. Ibid.

12. Ibid.

13. *NAEYC Standards for Early Childhood Professional Preparation*, 24.

14. Ibid., 24–25.

15. S. Feeney and K. Kipnis, *Code of Ethical Conduct and Statement of Commitment* (Washington, DC: National Association for the Education of Young Children, 1998). Used with permission.

16. S. Feeney and N. K. Freeman, *Ethics and the Early Childhood Educator: Using the NAEYC Code* (Washington, DC: National Association for the Education of Young Children, 2005).

17. Ibid.

18. Used with the permission of Mary Nelle Brunson, Assistant Chair, Department of Elementary Education, Stephen F. Austin State University, Nacogdoches, Texas.

19. National Council for Accreditation of Teacher Education, *NCATE Unit Standards: Glossary* (Washington, DC: NCATE, 2006), 53.

20. Nel Noddings, "Teaching Themes of Care," *Phi Delta Kappan*, 76(9), 1995, 675.

21. Council for Professional Recognition, *The 2004 National Survey of Child Development Associates, Executive Summary*, http://www.cdacouncil.org. Reprinted with permission.

22. Helen Raides et al., *Child Care Quality and Workforce Characteristics in Four Midwestern States* (Lincoln, NE: The Gallup Organization and Center for Children, Families, and the Law, University of Nebraska, October 31, 2003).

23. Carol Brunson Day, President and CEO, Council for Professional Recognition, personal communication, 2004.

Chapter 2

1. National Association for the Education of Young Children, *NAEYC Standards for Early Childhood Professional Preparation: Initial Licensure Programs*, NAEYC Initial Licensure Standards (Washington, DC: NAEYC, July 2001).

2. Ibid.

3. Jane Clifford, "If You Can Read This, Take Time to Say Thanks to a Teacher," *San Diego Union Tribune*, May 6, 2006, http://www.signonsandiego.com/uniontrib/20060506/news_1c06clifford.html.

4. Women's Educational Media, *Statistics on U.S. Families*, 2003, http://www.womedia.org/taf_statistics.htm.

5. Idaho Commission on Aging, *Grandparents as Parents*, 2000, http://www.idahoaging.com/programs/ps_caregiverGAP.htm.

6. *Texas Even Start Family Literacy Program*, Texas Youth Commission Prevention Summary, 2004, http://www.tyc.state.tx.us/prevention/evnstart.html.

7. Bureau of Labor Statistics, *Families with Own Children: Employment Status of Parents by Age of Youngest Child and Family Type, 2002–2003 Annual Averages*, April 2004, http://www.bls.gov/news.release/famee.t04.htm.

8. J. Barlow. *Personally Involved Father Figures Enhance Kids' Learning in School*, April 4, 2002, http://www.eurekalert.org/pub_releases/2002–04/uoia-pif040202.php.

9. U.S. Census Bureau, "Table FG1: Married Couple Family Groups, by Labor Force Status of Both Spouses, and Race and Hispanic Origin of the Reference Person," 2004, http://www.census.gov/population/socdemo/hh-fam/cps2004/tabFG1-all.csv.

10. Northern Illinois University, *Single Parent Families*, 2005, http://www.cedu.niu.edu/~shernoff/djs2/april_yackley.

11. Bureau of Labor Statistics, "Table 4: Families with Own Children: Employment Status of Parents by Age of Youngest Child and Family Type, 2004–05 Annual Averages," 2006 http://www.bls.gov/news.release/famee.t04.htm.

12. National Center for Health Statistics. "Table 1: Total Births and Percentage of Births with Selected Demographic Characteristics, by Race and Hispanic Origin of Mother: United States, Final 2003 and Preliminary" 2004 http://www.cdc.gov/nchs/data/hestat/prelimbirth04_tables.pdf.

13. Centers for Disease Control and Prevention, "Births: Preliminary Data for 2004," *National Vital Statistics Report*, 54(8), December 29, 2005, http://www.cdc.gov/nchs/data/nvsr/nvsr54/nvsr54_08.pdf.

14. Texas Department of State Health Services, *The Texas Guide to School Health Programs*, pp. 7–8, 2005, http://www.dshs.state.tx.us/schoolhealth.

15. American Lung Association, *Asthma & Children Fact Sheet*, 2005, http://www.lungusa.org/site/pp.asp?c=dvLUK9O0E&b=44352.

16. American Lung Association, *Home Control of Allergies and Asthma*, 2002, http://www.lungusa.org/site/pp.asp?c=dvLUK9O0E&b=22591.

17. Centers for Disease Control and Prevention, National Center for Environmental Health, *General Lead Information: Questions and Answers*, 2006, http://www.cdc.gov/nceh/lead/faq/about.htm.

18. Centers for Disease Control and Prevention, Agency for Toxic Substances and Disease Registry, *Lead Toxicity*, 1992, http://www.atsdr.cdc.gov/HEC/CSEM/lead/docs/lead.pdf.

19. American Heart Association, *Heart Disease and Stroke Statistics—2006 Update*, http://www.americanheart.org/downloadable/heart/1136308648540Statupdate2006.pdf.

20. American Heart Association, *Cardiovascular Statistics Updated for 2005: New Data on Risk Factors in America's Youth*, 2004, http://www.americanheart.org/presenter.jhtml?identifier=3027696.

21. American Obesity Association, *Obesity in Youth*, 2005, http://www.obesity.org/subs/fastfacts/obesity_youth.shtml.

22. S. Mustillo, A. Angold, A. Erkanli, G. Keeler, and E. J. Costello, "Obesity and Psychopathology: Developmental Trajectories," *Pediatrics*, 11, 2003, 851–859.

23. "Study: 8.8 Million Youth Obese," *USA Today*, 2003, http://www.usatoday.com/news/health/2003–01–01-obese-kids_x.htm.

24. Dayna Macy, "Rethinking Breakfast," *Yoga Journal*, 2003, http://www.yogajournal.com/health/853.cfm.

25. United States Department of Agriculture, Food and Nutrition Service, *National School Lunch Program: State Competitive Food Policies*, 2002, http://www.fns.usda.gov/cnd/Lunch/CompetitiveFoods/state_policies_2002.htm.

26. Ira Dreyfuss, "Schools Try for Healthier Food in Lunches," Associated Press, 2004, http://www.msnbc.msn.com/id/6160719.

27. Valerie Lee and David Burkam, Economic Policy Institute, *Inequality at the Starting Gate*, 2002, http://www.epi.org/content.cfm?id=617.

28. National Center for Children in Poverty, *Basic Facts About Low-Income Children: Birth to Age 18*, 2003, http://www.nccp.org/pub_lic06.html.

29. U.S. Department of Health and Human Services, *The 2006 HHS Poverty Guidelines*, January 2006, http://www.aspe.hhs.gov/poverty/06poverty.shtml.

30. U.S. Census Bureau, *Age and Sex of All People, Family Members and Unrelated Individuals Iterated by Income-to-Poverty Ratio and Race*, 2003, http://ferret.bls.census.gov/macro/032003/pov/new01_100.htm.

31. U.S. Census Bureau, *Annual Demographic Survey March Supplement*, 2004, http://ferret.bls.census.gov/macro/032004/pov/news45_100125_03.htm.

32. Teach-nology, *The Effects of Poverty on Teaching and Learning*, 2001, http://www.teach-nology.com/tutorials/teaching/poverty.

33. Ibid.

34. U.S. Department of Health and Human Services, *Oral Health in America: A Report of the Surgeon General* (Rockville, MD: DHHS, National Institute of Dental and Craniofacial Research, National Institutes of Health, 2000), http://www.surgeongeneral.gov/library/oralhealth.

35. National Institute of Child Health and Development, *The National Children's Study*, 2003, http://www.nichd.nih.gov/publications/pubs/TheNationalChildrensStudy.pdf.

36. Child Trends Research Brief, *Attending Kindergarten and Already Behind: A Statistical Portrait of Vulnerable Young Children*, 2003, http://www.childtrends.org/files/AttendingKindergartenRB.pdf#search='children%20lag%20behind'.

37. B. Hart and T. R. Risley, *The Social World of Children Learning to Talk* (Baltimore: Paul H. Brookes Publishing Co., 1999), p. 277.

38. National Association for the Education of Young Children, "Linguistic and Cultural Diversity—Building on America's Strengths," *Early Years Are Learning Years*, 2006; accessed March 19, 2007, at http://www.naeyc.org/resources/eyly/1996/03.htm.

39. Charles Dervarics, *Rural Children Lag in Early Childhood Educational Skills* (Washington, DC: Population Reference Bureau, January 2005); accessed March 19, 2007, at http://www.prb.org/PrintTemplate.cfm?Section=PRB&template=/ContentManagement/ContentDisplay.cfm&ContentID=12059.

40. Ronald Kotulak, *Inside the Brain: Revolutionary Discoveries of How the Mind Works* (Riverside, NJ: Andrews McMeel Publishing, 1997).

41. M. Lamb and J. Campos, *Development in Infancy: An Introduction*, 4th ed. (New York: Random House, 2002).

42. Purdue University Cooperative Extension Service, *Helping Children Cope with Stress*, 2003, http://www.ces.purdue.edu/terrorism/helpingchildren.html.

43. The White House, *Good Start, Grow Smart: The Bush Administration's Early Childhood Initiative*, 2002, http://www.whitehouse.gov/infocus/earlychildhood/earlychildhood.html.

44. U.S. Department of Education. *Student Achievement and School Accountability Programs*, 2006, http://www.ed.gov/programs/earlyreading/abstractsfinal2006.doc.

45. T. Smith, A. Kleiner, B. Parsad, and E. Farris, "Prekindergarten in U.S. Public Schools: 2000–2001," *Education Statistics Quarterly*, 5(1), Spring 2003, http://nces.ed.gov/pubs2003/2003607.pdf.

46. California Department of Education, *Preschool for All: A First-Class Learning Initiative*, 2006, http://www.cde.ca.gov/eo/in/se/yr05preschoolwp.asp?print=yes.

47. "State Should Make Plans for Universal Preschool," *The Modesto Bee*, 2005, http://www.modbee.com/opinion/story/10082353p–10909353c.html.

48. "Universal Preschool FAQs," 2007, http://www.universalpreschool.com/faq/#whatsup.

49. Dana Hull, "Universal Preschool Plan Fails; Backers Vow to Keep Working," *Mercury News*, 2006, http://www.mercurynews.com/mld/mercurynews/14759554.htm?template=contentModules/printstory.jsp.

50. State of Florida, Agency for Workforce Innovation, *School Readiness Programs*, 2005, http://www.floridajobs.org/earlylearning/sr_programs.html#CCEP.

Chapter 3

1. National Association for the Education of Young Children, *NAEYC Standards for Early Childhood Professional Preparation: Initial Licensure Programs*, NAEYC Initial Licensure Standards (Washington, DC: NAEYC, July 2001), 24.

2. Ibid.

3. Horace Mann, "Selected Quotes from the Production—What Experts, Historians and Witnesses Have to Say," *School: The Story of Public Education*, 2001, http://www.pbs.org/kcet/publicschool/pdf/quotes.pdf.

4. U.S. Department of Education, "Remarks by Secretary Spellings at No Child Left Behind Summit," April 27, 2006, http://www.ed.gov/news/pressreleases/2006/04/04272006.html.

5. Theresa Stephens Stapler, Central Elementary School, Carrollton, Georgia, personal communication, 2004.

6. John Amos Comenius, *The Great Didactic of John Amos Comenius*, Ed. and Trans. M. W. Keating (New York: Russell & Russell, 1967), 58.

7. Jean-Jacques Rousseau, *Emile, Or Education*, Trans. Barbara Foxley (New York: Dutton, Everyman's Library, 1933), 5.

8. Maria Montessori, *The Discovery of the Child*, Trans. M. J. Costelloe (Notre Dame, IN: Fides, 1967), 22.

9. Reginald D. Archambault, Ed., *John Dewey on Education: Selected Writings* (New York: Random House, 1964), 30.

10. W. Harms and I. DePencier, *100 Years of Learning at the University of Chicago Laboratory Schools* (Orlando Park, IL: Alpha Beta Press, 1996), http://www.ucls.uchicago.edu/about/history/education.shtml.

11. Jennifer Wolfe, *Learning from the Past—Historical Voices in Early Childhood Education* (Alberta: Piney Branch Press, 2002).

12. David M. Brodizinsky, Irving E. Sigel, and Roberta M. Golinkoff, "New Dimensions in Piagetian Theory and Research: An Integrative Perspective," in Irving E. Sigel, David M. Brodizinsky, and Roberta M. Golinkoff, Eds., *New Directions in Piagetian Theory and Practice* (Hillside, NJ: Erlbaum, 1981), 5.

13. P. G. Richmond, *An Introduction to Piaget* (New York: Basic Books, 1970), 68.

14. J. E. LeFebvre, "Make Believe Play," *Parenting the Preschooler*, http://www.uwex.edu/ces/flp/pp.

15. L. S. Vygotsky, *Mind in Society* (Cambridge, MA: Harvard University Press, 1978), 244.

16. Jonathon R. H. Tudge, "Processes and Consequences of Peer Collaboration: A Vygotskian Analysis," *Child Development*, 63, 1992, 1365.

17. Ibid.

18. Vygotsky, *Mind in Society*, 90.

19. Tudge, "Processes and Consequences," 1365.

Chapter 4

1. National Association for the Education of Young Children, *NAEYC Standards for Early Childhood Professional Preparation: Initial Licensure Programs*, NAEYC Initial Licensure Standards (Washington, DC: NAEYC, July 2001), 11.

2. National Association for the Education of Young Children, *Number of High-Quality Preschool & Child Care Programs Continues to Grow*, December 1, 2004, http://www.naeyc.org/about/releases/20041202.asp.

3. Public Education Network, *Open to the Public: The Public Speaks Out on No Child Left Behind A Summary of Nine Hearings*, September 2005–January 2006, http://www.publiceducation.org/2006_NCLB/main/2006_NCLB_National_Report.pdf.

4. U.S. Department of Education, *Questions and Answers on No Child Left Behind—Reading*, September 2003, http://www.ed.gov/nclb/methods/reading/reading.html.

5. B. Vossekuil, R. A. Fein, M. Reddy, R. Borum, and W. Modzeleski, *The Final Report and Findings of the Safe School Initiative: Implications for the Prevention of School Attacks in the United States* (Washington, DC: United States Secret Service and United States Department of Education, May 2002). http://www.secretservice.gov/ntac/ssi_final_report.pdf#search=%22school%20violence%20study%202002%20Department%20of%20Education%20Secret%20Service%22.

6. Bureau of Labor Statistics, "Table 5: Employment Status of the Population by Sex, Marital Status, and Presence and Age of Own Children Under 18, 2004–06 Annual Averages," 2006, http://www.bls.gov/news.release/famee.t05.htm.

7. National Institute of Child Health and Human Development, *The NICHD Study of Early Child Care and Youth Development: Study Summary; accessed* March 19, 2007, at http://secc.rti.org/summary.cfm.

8. High/Scope Education Research Foundation, *The High/Scope K–3 Curriculum: An Introduction* (Ypsilanti, MI: Author, 1989), 1.

9. Ibid.

10. Ibid.

11. Maria Montessori, *Dr. Montessori's Own Handbook* (New York: Schocken Books, 1965), 131.

12. "Students Prosper with Montessori Method," *Scientific American*, 29, September 2006, http://sciam.com/print_version.cfm?articleID=000D5CF0–96EF–151D–96EF83414B7F0000.

13. G. S. Morrison, *Contemporary Curriculum K–8* (Boston: Allyn & Bacon, 1993), 399.

14. S. F. Foster, "The Waldorf Schools: An Exploration of an Enduring Alternative School Movement" (Ph.D. dissertation, Florida State University, 1981), 18.

15. C. Bamford and E. Utne, "An Emerging Culture: Rudolf Steiner's Continuing Impact in the World," *Rudolf Steiner College Newsletter*, p. 3, http://www.steinercollege.org/newsletter.html.

16. Ibid.

17. Somerset School, http://waldorfworld.net/somerset.

18. U.S. Department of Health and Human Services Administration for Children & Families, *Head Start Program Fact Sheet: Fiscal Year 2006; accessed* March 19, 2007, at http://www.acf.hhs.gov/programs/hsb/research/2006.htm.

19. The White House, *Good Start, Grow Smart: The Bush Administration's Early Childhood Initiative—Strengthening Head Start*, April 2002; accessed March 19, 2007, http://www.whitehouse.gov/infocus/earlychildhood/sect5.html.

20. U.S. DHHS, Head Start Program Fact Sheet.

21. U.S. Department of Health and Human Services, *Head Start Program Performance Standards*, 45 CFR 1304 (Washington, DC: U.S. Government Printing Office, November 1984), 8–9.

Chapter 5

1. National Association for the Education of Young Children, *NAEYC Standards for Early Childhood Professional Preparation: Associate Degree Programs*, NAEYC Associate Standards (Washington, DC: NAEYC, July 2003), 11.

2. Ibid.

3. Anne Grosso de Leon, *After 20 Years of Educational Reform, Progress, but Plenty of Unfinished Business*, (New York: Carnegie Corporation of New York, Fall 2003); accessed August 21, 2006, at http://www.carnegie.org/results/03/index.html.

4. Ibid.

5. Ibid.

6. K. Paris, *Summary of Goals 2000: Educate America Act*, 1994; accessed August 21, 2006, at http://www.ncrel.org/sdrs/areas/issues/envrnmnt/stw/sw0goals.htm.

7. Ibid.

8. Education World, *National and State Standards; accessed* March 19, 2007, http://www.education-world.com/standards.

9. The White House, *Fact Sheet: No Child Left Behind—Strengthening America's Education System*, January 9, 2006, http://www.whitehouse.gov/news/releases/2006/01/print/20060109–3.html

10. Ibid.

11. C. Snow, M. S. Burns, and P. Griffin, Eds., *Preventing Reading Difficulties in Young Children* (Washington, DC: National Academies Press, 1998).

12. J. P. Shonkoff and D. Phillips, Eds., *From Neurons to Neighborhoods: The Science of Early Childhood Development* (Washington, DC: National Academies Press, 2000).

13. B. T. Bowman, S. Donovan, and M. S. Burns, Eds., *Eager to Learn: Educating Our Preschoolers* (Washington, DC: National Academies Press, 2000).

14. The White House, *Good Start, Grow Smart: The Bush Administration's Early Childcare Initiative*, 2002, http://www.whitehouse.gove/infocus/earlychildhood/earlychildhood.html.

15. The White House, *The No Child Left Behind Act: Challenging Students Through High Expectations*, October 2006, http://www.whitehouse.gov/news/releases/2006/10/20061005–2.html.

16. U.S. Department of Education, *Reading First: Over $4.3 Billion to Improve the Reading Skills of Young Children*, 2005, http://www.ed.gov/programs/readingfirst/nclb-reading-first.html.

17. U.S. Department of Education, *Early Reading First*, 2006, http://www.ed.gov/program/earlyreadingindex.html.

18. National Association for the Education of Young Children, *Early Learning Standards: Creating the Conditions for Success*, 2002, http://www.naeyc.org/about/positions/pdf/elstandardsstand.pdf.

19. Ibid.

20. K. Kauerz, "Straddling Early Learning and Early Elementary School" *Journal of the National Association for the Education of Young Children*, March 2005, http://www.journal.naeyc.org/btj/200503/01Kauerz.asp.

21. National Institute for Early Education Research, *The State of Preschool 2005*, amended November 2006, http://nieer.org/yearbook/pdf/yearbook.pdf.

22. The full version of these standards can be viewed online at http://www.ctb.com.

23. Commission on Behavioral and Social Sciences and Education, *Early Childhood Development and Learning; New Knowledge for Policy* (Washington DC: National Academies Press, 2001).

Chapter 6

1. National Association for the Education of Young Children, *NAEYC Standards for Early Childhood Professional Preparation: Initial Licensure Programs*, NAEYC Initial Licensure Standards (Washington, DC: NAEYC, July 2001).

2. Ibid.

3. NAEYC Academy for Early Childhood Program Accreditation, *Standard 4: NAEYC Accreditation Criteria for Assessment of Child Progress;* accessed March 19, 2007, at http://www.naeyc.org/academy/standards/standard4.

4. L. Shepard, S. L. Kagan, and E. Wurtz, *Principles and Recommendations for Early Childhood Assessments* (Washington, DC: National Education Goals Panel, December 14, 1998), 5–6.

5. Head Start National Reporting System. *What's New*, 2006, https://www.hsnrs.net/whatsnew.jsp.

Chapter 7

1. National Association for the Education of Young Children, *NAEYC Standards for Early Childhood Professional Preparation: Initial Licensure Programs*, NAEYC Initial Licensure Standards (Washington, DC: NAEYC, July 2001), 12.

2. U.S. Department of Health and Human Services Administration for Children & Families, "National Infant & Toddler Child Care Initiative Zero to Three," *Publications At-A-Glance Planning;* accessed February 27, 2007, at http://www.nccic.org/itcc/publications/planning.htm.

3. William J. Cromie, "Looking for the Nature of Human Nature," *Harvard University Gazette*, May 27, 2004, http://www.news.harvard.edu/gazette/2004/05.27/01-pinker.html.

4. P. Kuhl, *Early Language Acquisition: The Brain Comes Prepared* (St. Louis, MO: Parents as Teachers National Center, 1996).

5. Erik Erikson, *Childhood and Society*, 2nd ed. (New York: Norton, 1963; first pub., 1950), 249.

6. Ibid.

7. A. Thomas, S. Chess, and H. Birch, "The Origin of Personality," *Scientific American*, 1970, 102–109.

8. E. L. Newport, "Mother, I'd Rather Do It Myself: Some Effects and Non-Effects on Maternal Speech Style," in C. E. Snow and C. A. Ferguson, Eds., *Talking to Children* (Cambridge, England: Cambridge University Press, 1979), 112–129.

9. L. Acredelo and S. Goodwyn, *Baby Signs: How to Talk with Your Baby Before Your Baby Can Talk* (Chicago: Contemporary Books, 1996).

10. S. Bredekamp and C. Copple, Eds., *Developmentally Appropriate Practice in Early Childhood Programs* (Washington, DC: National Association for the Education of Young Children, 1997), 9.

11. American Academy of Pediatrics, "Campaign Launched to Avoid Sudden Death in Child Care Settings," January 29, 2003, http://www.aap.org/advocacy/archives/jansids.htm.

12. N. Engineer, C. Percaccio, and M. Kilgard, "Environment Shapes Auditory Processing," *New Horizons for Learning*, June 2004; accessed February 27, 2007, at http://www.newhorizons.org/neuro/engineer%20percaccio%20kilgard.htm.

13. U.S. Department of Health and Human Services Administration for Children and Families, *FY 2007 PRISM Protocol: Safe Environments*, 2007.

14. "Relationship as Curriculum," *Head Start Bulletin*, No. 73, 2002, http://www.headstartinfo.org/publications/hsbulletin73/hsb73_04.htm.

15. U.S. Department of Health and Human Services Administration for Children & Families, "A Commitment to Supporting the Mental Health of Our Youngest Children," October 23–24, 2000; accessed February 27, 2007, at http://www.acf.hhs.gov/programs/opre/ehs/mental_health/reports/imh_report/imh_rpt.pdf#search=%22A%20Committment%20to%20Supporting%20the%20Mental%20Health%20of%20Our%20Youngest%20Children%22

Chapter 8

1. National Association for the Education of Young Children, *NAEYC Standards for Early Childhood Professional Preparation: Initial Licensure Programs*, NAEYC Initial Licensure Standards (Washington, DC: NAEYC, July 2001), 16, 19.

2. Ibid.

3. U.S. Department of Health and Human Services Administration for Children and Families, *Number of Children in Early Care and*

Education Programs, National Childcare Information Center, April 19, 2006; accessed February 27, 2007, at http://www.nccic.org/poptopics/number-kidsece.html.

4. The White House, *Fact Sheet: America's Workforce: Ready for the 21st Century*, August 5, 2004; accessed February 27, 2007, at http://www.whitehouse.gov/news/releases/2004/08/20040805-6.html.

5. National Association of Child Care Resource and Referral Agencies, *What Do Parents Think About Child Care?*, 2006; accessed February 27, 2007, at http://www.naccrra.org/docs/policy/FocusGrpReport.pdf.

6. W. T. Dickens, I. Sawhill, and J. Tebbs, *Policy Brief #153: The Effects of Investing in Early Childhood Education on Economic Growth* (Washington, DC: The Brookings Institution, April 2006), http://www.brookings.edu/comm/policybriefs/pb153.pdf.

7. Ibid.

8. B. T. Bowman, M. S. Donovan, and M. S. Burns, Eds., *Eager to Learn: Educating Our Preschoolers*, Commission on Behavioral and Social Sciences and Education, National Research Council (Washington, DC: National Academies Press, 2000).

9. J. P. Shonkoff and D. A. Phillips, Eds., *From Neurons to Neighborhoods: The Science of Early Childhood Development* (Washington, DC: National Academies Press, 2000), 343.

10. Ibid., 338.

11. Ibid., 343.

12. National Governors Association, *A Governor's Guide to School Readiness: Building the Foundation for Bright Futures*, 2005.

13. C. Bruner, S. Floyd, and A. Copeman, "Seven Things Policy Makers Need to Know About School Readiness, Revised and Expanded Toolkit," *State Early Childhood Policy Technical Assistance Network*. (Des Moines, IA: Child and Family Policy Center, January 2005), 7.

14. D. S. Strickland and S. Riley-Ayers, *Early Literacy: Policy and Practice in the Preschool Years* (New Brunswick, NJ: National Institute for Early Education Research, April 2006).

15. Shonkoff and Phillips, *From Neurons to Neighborhoods*, 338

16. U.S. Department of Health and Human Services Administration for Children and Families, *Head Start Child Outcomes Framework Domain 6: Social and Emotional Development*, March 4, 2005; accessed February 27, 2007, at http://www.headstartinfo.org/leaders_guideeng/domain6.htm.

17. "Table POP5," *ChildStats.gov*, 2006; accessed February 27, 2007, at http://www.childstats.gov/americaschildren/tables/pop5.asp#a.

18. U.S. Census Bureau, "Detailed List of Languages Spoken at Home for the Population 5 Years and Over by State: 2000," 2000, http://www.census.gov/population/cen2000/phc-t20/tab05.pdf.

19. Ibid.

20. Ibid.

21. D. Phillips and N. A. Crowell, Eds., *Cultural Diversity and Early Education. Report of a Workshop National Research Council* (Washington, DC: National Academies Press, 1994).

22. M. Parten, "Social Participation Among Preschool Children," *Journal of Abnormal and Social Psychology*, 27, 1932, 243–269.

Chapter 9

1. National Association for the Education of Young Children, *NAEYC Standards for Early Childhood Professional Preparation: Initial Licensure Programs*, NAEYC Initial Licensure Standards (Washington, DC: NAEYC, July 2001), 12.

2. Ibid., 24.

3. Education Commission of the States, "How States Fund Full-Day Kindergarten," *State Notes Kindergarten*, updated August 2005, http://www.ecs.org/clearinghouse/63/10/6310.htm.

4. Ibid.

5. A. Matturro-Gault, "Off to the Write Start," *Scholastic*, June 1, 2005; accessed March 2, 2007, at http://www.scholastic.com/schoolage/kindergarten/atschool/writestart.htm.

6. National Association for the Education of Young Children, "Still Unacceptable Trends in Kindergarten Entry and Placement," *NAEYC Position Statement*, revision and updated, 2000, http://www.naeyc.org/about/positions/PsUnacc.asp.

7. Education Commission of the States, "Access to Kindergarten: Age Issues in State Statutes," *State Notes Kindergarten*, 2006, http://mb2.ecs.org/reports/Report.aspx?id=32.

8. K. Kauerz, "Straddling Early Learning and Early Elementary School" *Journal of the National Association for the Education of Young Children*, March 2005, http://www.journal.naeyc.org/btj/200503/01Kauerz.asp.

9. S. Martinez and T. Akey, *Full-Day Kindergarten 1997–98 Evaluation Report*, unpublished evaluation from Park Hill Public Schools, Kansas City, MO, March 1998, with follow-up study summary, May 1999.

10. International Reading Association & National Association for the Education of Young Children, "Learning to Read and Write: Developmentally Appropriate Practices for Young Children," *Young Children*, 53(4), July 1998, 39; accessed March 2, 2007, at http://www.naeyc.org/about/positions/pdf/psread98.pdf.

11. This digest was adapted from a position paper of the Association for Childhood Education International by Vito Perrone, "On Standardized Testing," which appeared in *Childhood Education*, Spring 1991, 132–142.

12. International Reading Association & National Association for the Education of Young Children, "Learning to Read and Write," 9.

13. J. T. Downer, K. M. La Paro, R. C. Pianta, and S. E. Rimm-Kaufman, "The Contribution of Classroom Setting and Quality of Instruction to Children's Behavior in Kindergarten Classrooms," *The Elementary School Journal*, 104(4), 2005.

14. *Pediatrics*, 117(5), May 2006, 1585–1598.

15. E. Y. Jung and M. M. Ostrosky, "Brief #12: Building Positive Teacher–Child Relationships," Center on the Social and Emotional Foundations for Early Learning, accessed March 2, 2007, at http://csefel.uiuc.edu/briefs/wwb12.html.

16. M. J. Adams, *Beginning to Read: Thinking and Learning About Print* (Urbana, IL: The Reading Research and Edu Center, 1990), 36–38.

17. Ibid., 8.

18. Entire section on shared reading adapted by permission from J. David Cooper, *Literacy: Helping Children Construct Meaning*, 5th ed. (Boston: Houghton Mifflin, 2003), 155–157.

19. L. M. Morrow, *Literacy Development in the Early Years: Helping Children Read and Write*, 5th ed. (Needham, MA: Allyn & Bacon, 2005). Copyright 2005. Reprinted/adapted by permission of Allyn & Bacon.

20. National Council of Teachers of Mathematics, *Curriculum Focal Points for Prekindergarten through Grade 8 Mathematics*, 2006, http://www.nctm.org/focalpoints.

21. National Council for Social Studies, "About NCSS," accessed March 2, 2007, at http://www.socialstudies.org/about/.

22. Georgia Department of Education, *Sequenced Lesson Plans*, 2003, http://www.glc.k12.ga.us/seqlps/sudspres.asp?SUID=255&SSUID=269&SSTitle=Kindergarten+Social+Studies.

23. K. L. Maxwell and S. K. Elder, "Children's Transition to Kindergarten," *Young Children*, 49(6), 56–63.

24. Clearing House on Early Education and Parenting, *Academic Redshirting*, March 2005; accessed March 2, 2007, at http://ceep.crc.uiuc.edu/poptopics/redshirting.html.

25. L. Starr, "Kindergarten Is for Kids," *Education World*, June 4, 2002, http://www.educationworld.com/a_issues/issues325.shtml.

26. D. Stipek, "At What Age Should Children Enter Kindergarten? A Question for Policy Makers and Parents," *Social Policy Report*, XVI(2), 2002, 11.

Chapter 10

1. National Association for the Education of Young Children, *NAEYC Standards for Early Childhood Professional Preparation: Initial Licensure Programs*, NAEYC Initial Licensure Standards (Washington, DC: NAEYC, July 2001), 12.

2. Ibid., 19.

3. American Obesity Association, *Obesity in Youth*, 2002; accessed March 5, 2007, at http://www.obesity.org/subs/fastfacts/obesity_youth.shtml.

4. Gary Ruskin, "The Fast Food Trap: How Commercialism Creates Overweight Children," *Mothering*, No. 121, November/December 2003; accessed March 5, 2007, at http://www.mothering.com/articles/growing_child/food/fast_food.html.

5. "Children and Computer Technology: Analysis and Recommendations," *The Future of Children*, 10(2), Fall 2000; accessed March 5, 2007, at http://www.futureofchildren.org/pubs-info2825/pubs-info_show.htm?doc_id=69787.

6. National Center for Educational Statistics, *Calories In, Calories Out: Food and Exercise in Public Elementary Schools*, 2005; accessed March 5, 2007, at http://nces.ed.gov/Pubs2006/nutrition.

7. "Lawmakers Call for Increased Activity to Combat Child Obesity," *Dallas Morning News*, February 8, 2007.

8. "Parents Launch 'Rescuing Recess' Drive," *CBS News*, May 16, 2006.

9. "Childhood Depression: Tips for Parents," *Mental Health America*, 2007; accessed March 5, 2007, at http://www.nmha.org/index.cfm?objectid=C7DF9240–1372–4D20-C81D80B5B7C5957B.

10. "Depression in Children," *Mental Health America*, 2007, accessed March 5, 2007, at http://www.nmha.org/index.cfm?objectid=CA866E0D–1372–4D20-C8872863D2EE2E90.

11. S. K. Bhatia and S. C. Bhatia, "Childhood and Adolescent Depression," *American Family Physician*, 75(1), January 2007, 74.

12. American Academy of Pediatrics, *Physical Fitness and Activity in Schools*, May 2005; accessed March 5, 2007, at http://aappolicy.aappublications.org/cgi/reprint/pediatrics;105/5/1156.pdf; 105/5/1156.

13. Institute of Medicine, *Schools Can Play a Role in Preventing Childhood Obesity*, September 2004; accessed March 5, 2007, at http://www.iom.edu/Object.File/Master/22/615/0.pdf.

14. Guidelines adapted by permission from David Cooper, *Helping Children Construct Meaning*, 5th ed. (Boston: Houghton Mifflin, 2003), 157–158.

15. National Council of Teachers of Mathematics, "Appendix: Table of Standards and Expectations—Algebra, accessed March 5, 2007, at http://standards.nctm.org/document/appendix/alg.htm.

16. Reprinted with permission from "Curriculum Focal Points for Prekindergarten Through Grade 8 Mathematics: A Quest for Coherence," National Council of Teachers of Mathematics (NCTM), 2006, p. 11.

17. National Council for Social Studies, "About NCSS," accessed March 5, 2007, at http://www.socialstudies.org/about/.

18. "Dancing to Music," *CanTeach*, accessed March 5, 2007, at http://www.canteach.ca/elementary/fadance1.html.

Chapter 11

1. National Association for the Education of Young Children, *NAEYC Standards for Early Childhood Professional Preparation: Initial Licensure Programs*, NAEYC Initial Licensure Standards (Washington, DC: NAEYC, July 2001), 11.

2. Ibid.

3. Ibid.

4. Public Law 105–17, 1997.

5. Ibid.

6. "Table 1–4. Students Ages 6 Through 11 Served Under IDEA, Part B, by Disability Category and State: Fall 2005," *IDEAdata.org*, accessed March 5, 2007, at https://www.ideadata.org/tables29th/ar_1–4.htm.

7. U.S. Department of Education, National Center for Education Statistics, *The Condition of Education 2005*, NCES 2005–094 (Washington, DC: U.S. Government Printing Office), 172.

8. A. Turnbull, H. Turnbull III, M. Shank, and D. Leal, *Exceptional Lives: Special Education in Today's Schools*, 2nd ed. (Upper Saddle River, NJ: Merrill/Prentice Hall, 1995), 64–71.

9. D. P. Hallahan and J. M. Kauffman, *Exceptional Learners: An Introduction to Special Education*, 10th ed. (Boston: Pearson/Allyn & Bacon, 2006), 31.

10. U.S. Department of Education, Office of Educational Research and Improvement, *Reaching All Families—Creating Family Friendly Schools*, 1996.

11. Autism Society of America, "What Is Autism?," accessed March 5, 2007, at http://www.autism-society.org/site/PageServer?pagename=about_whatis_home.

12. National Autism Association, http://www.nationalautismassociation.org/definitions.php.

13. Autism Society of America, "What Is Autism?"

14. "Facts About Autism," *Autism Speaks*, accessed March 5, 2007, at http://www.autismspeaks.org/whatisit/facts.php.

15. K. Painter, "Science Getting to the Roots of Autism," *USA Today*, January 12, 2004, accessed March 5, 2007, at http://www.usatoday.com/news/health/2004–01–12-autism-main_x.htm.

16. National Institute of Mental Health, *Autism Spectrum Disorders (Pervasive Developmental Disorders)*, 2004, accessed March 5, 2007, at http://www.nimh.nih.gov/publicat/autism.cfm.

17. D. Voltz et al., "A Framework for Inclusion in the Context of Standards-Based Reform," *Teaching Exceptional Children*, May/June 2005, 22.

18. Reprinted with permission from the *Diagnostic and Statistical Manual of Mental Disorders*, 4th ed., text revision. Copyright 2000

American Psychiatric Association; accessed March 5, 2007, at http://childdevelopmentinfo.com/disorders/add_symptoms.shtml.

19. American Academy of Pediatrics, "ADHD—Understanding Attention-Deficit/Hyperactivity Disorder," accessed March 5, 2007, at http://www.aap.org/healthtopics/adhd.cfm.

20. K. Jacob, Javits Gifted and Talented Students Education Act of 1988.

21. J. Gallagher, P. Weiss, K. Oglesby, and T. Thomas, *The Status of Gifted/Talented Education: United States Survey of Needs, Practices, and Policies* (Los Angeles: National/State Leadership Training Institute on the Gifted and Talented, 1983).

22. U.S. Department of Commerce, *Minority Business Development Agency, Minority Population Growth: 1995 to 2050*, 1999; accessed March 5, 2007, at http://www.mbda.gov/documents/mbdacolor.pdf.

23. Miami-Dade County Public Schools, *Miami-Dade County Public Schools Statistical Abstract 2002–2003*, July 2003; accessed March 5, 2007, at http://drs.dadeschools.net/Abstract/Abstract_2002–03.pdf.

24. Marie Cabo, Rita Dunn, and Kenneth Dunn, *Teaching Students to Read Through Their Individual Learning Styles* (Boston: Allyn & Bacon, 1991), 2.

25. V. Hildebrand, L. A. Phenice, M. M. Grey, and R. P. Hines, *Knowing and Serving Diverse Families* (Upper Saddle River, NJ: Merrill/Prentice Hall, 2000), 107.

Chapter 12

1. National Association for the Education of Young Children, *NAEYC Standards for Early Childhood Professional Preparation: Initial Licensure Programs*, NAEYC Initial Licensure Standards (Washington, DC: NAEYC, July 2001), 11.

2. Ibid.

3. S. B. Campbell, D. S. Shaw, and M. Gilliom, "Early Externalizing Behavior Problems: Toddlers and Preschoolers at Risk for Later Maladjustment," *Development and Psychopathology*, 12, 2000, 467–488.

4. L. S. Vygotsky, *Mind in Society* (Cambridge, MA: Harvard University Press, 1978), 86.

5. L. R. Roehler and D. J. Cantlon, *Scaffolding: A Powerful Tool in Social Constructivist Classrooms*, 1996, http://ed-web3.educ.msu.edu/literacy/papers/paperlr2.htm.

6. L. E. Berk and A. Winsler, *Scaffolding Children's Learning: Vygotsky and Early Childhood Education* (Washington, DC: National Association for the Education of Young Children, 1995), 45–46.

7. T. Gordon, *Teacher Effectiveness Training* (New York: Peter H. Hyden, 1974).

8. Ibid., 40.

Chapter 13

1. National Association for the Education of Young Children, *NAEYC Standards for Early Childhood Professional Preparation: Initial Licensure Programs*, NAEYC Initial Licensure Standards (Washington, DC: NAEYC, July 2001), 13.

2. Ibid.

3. Ibid.

4. A. T. Henderson and K. L. Mapp, *A New Wave of Evidence: The Impact of School, Family, and Community Connections on Student Achievement, Annual Synthesis 2002* (Austin, TX: Southwest Educational Development Laboratory, National Center for Family & Community Connections with Schools, 2002), accessed March 19, 2007, at http://www.sedl.org/connections/resources/evidence.pdf.

5. Maria Montessori, *Dr. Montessori's Own Handbook* (New York: Schocken, 1965), 133.

6. National Association of Child Care Resource and Referral Agencies, *Child Care in America*, accessed March 6, 2007, at http://www.naccrra.org/docs/Child_Care_In_America_Facts.pdf.

7. U.S. Census Bureau, "Facts for Features Grandparents Day 2006: Sept. 10," *U.S. Census Bureau News*, CB06-FF.13, July 10, 2006, accessed March 6, 2007, at http://www.census.gov/Press-Release/www/2006/cb06ff–13.pdf.

8. U.S. Department of Education, *Guidance for the William F. Goodling Even Start Literacy Programs*, September 29, 2003; accessed March 6, 2007, at http://www.ed.gov/policy/elsec/guid/evenstartguidance02.doc.

9. U.S. Department of Education, Office of Educational Research and Improvement, *Reaching All Families—Creating Family-Friendly Schools* (Washington, DC: U.S. Department of Education, 1996).

10. Ibid.

11. National Center for Education Statistics, "Racial/Ethnic Distribution of Public School Students," 2006; accessed March 6, 2007, at http://nces.ed.gov/programs/coe/2006/section1/indicator05.asp.

12. Family Involvement Partnership for Learning, *Community Update #23* (Washington, DC: FIPL, April 1995).

glossary

Accommodation The process involved in changing old methods and adjusting to new situations.

Active listening Involves interactions with a child to provide the child with proof that you understand what he or she is talking about.

Adult/child discourse A conversation between an adult/parent and a child.

Advocacy The act of engaging in strategies designed to improve the circumstances of children and families. Advocates move beyond their day-to-day professional responsibilities and work collaboratively to help others.

Anthroposophy The name Steiner gave to "the study of the wisdom of man"; the basic principle of Waldorf education.

Anti-bias curriculum An approach that seeks to provide children with an understanding of social and behavioral problems related to prejudice and seeks to provide them with the knowledge, attitude, and skills needed to combat prejudice.

Applied behavior analysis (ABA) Theory that behavior rewarded is more likely to be repeated than behavior ignored.

Assessment The process of collecting and recording information about children's development, learning, health, behavior, academic process, need for special services, and attainment in order to make a variety of educational decisions about children and programs.

Assimilation The taking in of sensory data through experiences and impressions and incorporating them into existing knowledge.

Asthma A chronic lung disorder that is marked by recurring episodes of airway obstruction manifested by labored breathing accompanied especially by wheezing and coughing and by a sense of constriction in the chest, and that is triggered by hyperreactivity to various stimuli (as allergens or rapid change in air temperature).

Atelier A special area or studio in a Reggio Emilia school for creating projects.

Atelierista A Reggio Emilia teacher trained in the visual arts who works with teachers and children.

Attachment An enduring emotional tie between a parent/caregiver and an infant that endures over time.

Attention deficit hyperactivity disorder (ADHD) A behavioral disorder in which children display cognitive delays as a result of difficulties with attention, impulse control, and hyperactivity.

Authentic assessment Assessment conducted through activities that require children to demonstrate what they know and are able to do; also referred to as *performance-based assessment.*

Autism A brain disorder that begins in early childhood and persists throughout life. Autism affects three crucial areas of development: communication, social interactions, and creative or imaginary play.

Autonomy An Erikson concept that occurs as toddlers mature physically and mentally and want to do things by themselves with no outside help.

Balanced approach A practice in which there is a balance between whole-language methods and phonics instruction that meets the specific needs of individual children.

Basic trust An Erikson concept that involves the trust, security, and basic optimism that an infant develops when nurtured and loved.

Behavior guidance A process by which teachers help all children learn to control and direct their behavior and become independent and self-reliant.

Benchmarks Statements that provide a description of student performance expected at specific grade levels, ages, or developmental levels. Benchmarks often are used in conjunction with standards.

Bias-free An environment, classroom setting, or program that is free of prejudicial behaviors.

Bonding A parent's initial emotional tie to an infant.

Bullying To treat abusively or affect by means of force or coercion.

Child care Comprehensive care and education of young children outside their homes.

Child development The study of how children change over time from birth to age eight.

Child Development Associate (CDA) An individual who has successfully completed the CDA assessment process and has been awarded the CDA credential. CDAs are able to meet the specific needs of children and work with parents and other adults to nurture children's physical, social, emotional, and intellectual growth in a child development framework.

Childhood depression A disorder affecting as many as one in thirty-three children that can negatively impact feelings, thoughts and behavior and can manifest itself with physical symptoms of illness.

Children with disabilities Children who need special education and related services because of mental retardation, hearing impairments, speech or language impairments, serious emotional disturbances, orthopedic impairments, autism, traumatic brain injury, other health impairments, or specific learning disabilities.

Chronosystem The environmental contexts and events that influence children over their lifetimes, such as living in a technological age.

Circular response Developmental reaction that typically begins to develop in early infancy in which infants' actions cause them to react or when another person prompts an infant to try to repeat the original action; similar to a stimulus–response or cause-and-effect relationship.

Civil behavior How to treat others well and in turn be treated well.

Cognitive theory Jean Piaget's proposition that children develop intelligence through direct experiences with the physical world. In this sense, learning is an internal (mental) process involving children's adapting new knowledge to what they already know.

Concrete operations The third stage of operational or logical thought, often referred to as the "hands-on" period of cognitive development because the ability to reason is based on tangible objects and real experiences.

Constructivist process The continuous mental organizing, structuring, and restructuring of experiences, in relation to schemes of thought, or mental images, that result in cognitive growth.

Content knowledge Refers to the discipline (math, science, social studies, art, music, etc.) knowledge teachers should possess.

Culture A group's way of life, including basic values, beliefs, religion, language, clothing, food, and practices.

Curriculum All of the experiences children have while in school.

Curriculum alignment The process of matching curriculum to the standards and to tests that measure student achievement.

Developmental screening A procedure designed to identify children who should receive more intensive assessment or diagnosis, for potential developmental delays.

Developmentally appropriate practice (DAP) Practice based on how children grow and develop and on individual and cultural differences.

Early childhood professional An educator who successfully teaches all children, promotes high personal standards, and continually expands his or her skills and knowledge.

Entitlement programs Programs and services children and families are entitled to because they meet the eligibility criteria for the services.

Ethical conduct Responsible behavior toward students and parents that allows you to be considered a professional.

Even Start Federally funded family literacy program that combines adult literacy and parenting training with early childhood education.

Exosystem Environments or settings in which children do not play an active role but which nonetheless influence their development.

Expanding horizons approach Also called the *expanding environments approach,* an approach to teaching social studies where the student is at the center of the expanding horizons and initial units, and at each grade level is exposed to a slowly widening environment.

Expressive language A preschooler's developing ability to talk fluently and articulately with teacher and peers, the ability to express oneself in the language of the school, and the ability to communicate needs and ideas.

Formal assessment Involves the use of standardized tests that have set procedures and instruction for administration and have been normed, meaning that it is possible to compare a child's score with the scores of a group of children who have already taken the same exam

Formal operations The fourth stage of operational intelligence. Children become capable of dealing with increasingly complex verbal and hypothetical problems and are less dependent on concrete objects.

Free and appropriate education (FAPE) The idea that children must receive a free education suited to their age, maturity level, condition of disability, achievements, and parental expectations.

Gifted and talented children As defined by federal law, children who demonstrate the potential for high performance in intellectual, creative, artistic, or leadership capacities.

Head Start A federal early childhood program serving children, ages three to five, who are socioeconomically challenged, and their families.

High/Scope educational model A constructivist educational model based on Piaget's cognitive development theory. High/Scope promotes the constructivist process of learning and broadens the child's emerging intellectual and social skills.

High-stakes testing An assessment test used to either admit children into programs or promote them from one grade to the next.

Holophrases One-word sentences toddlers use to communicate.

Home visitor program A program that involves visitation of children, parents, and other family members in their homes by trained personnel who provide information, training, and support.

"I" messages Messages that are designed to let children know that you have a problem with their behavior and that you want them to do something to change the behavior.

Impulse control The ability to stay on task, pay attention to a learning activity, work cooperatively with others, and not hit or interfere with the work of other children.

Independence The ability to work alone on a task, take care of oneself, and initiate projects without always being told what to do.

Individualized education program (IEP) A plan created to specify instruction for children with disabilities.

Individualized family service plan (IFSP) A plan created for infants and toddlers with disabilities and their families, specifying what services they will receive to help them reach their goals.

Infancy A child's first year of life.

Infant mental health Stage of emotional and social competence of young children.

Informal assessment The process of gathering information about students by means other than standardized tests.

Inquiry learning Involvement of children in activities and processes that lead to learning.

Integrated curriculum A curriculum in which one subject area is used to teach another.

Interpersonal skills The ability to get along and work with both peers and adults.

Interpretation A three-step process that includes examining the data/information that have been gathered, organizing and drawing conclusions from that data, and making decisions about teaching based on the conclusions.

Intersubjectivity Vygotskian concept based on the idea that individuals come to a task, problem, or conversation with their own subjective ways of making sense of it, and in the course of communication may arrive at some mutually agreed-on, or intersubjective, understanding.

Language experience approach A reading instruction method that links oral and written language. Based on the premise that what is thought can be said, what is said can be written, and what is written can be read.

Learned helplessness A condition that can develop when children perceive that they are not doing as well as they can or as well as their peers, lose confidence in their abilities and achievement, and then attribute their failures to a lack of ability. These children are passive and have learned to feel that they are helpless.

Learning Acquisition of knowledge, behaviors, skills, and attitudes.

Learning centers Areas of the classroom specifically set up to promote student-centered, hands-on, active learning. Learning centers are built and organized around student interests, themes, and academic subjects. Teachers plan for how children will use the centers, the materials the centers will contain, and the learning outcomes for each center.

Learning style The way a child is affected by his or her environment, emotions, sociological needs, physical characteristics, and psychological inclinations as he or she works to master new or difficult information or skills.

Least restrictive environment (LRE) Children with disabilities are educated with children who have no disabilities. Special classes, separate schooling, or other removal of children with disabilities from the regular educational environment occurs only when the nature or severity of the disability is such that education in regular classes with the use of supplementary aids and services cannot be achieved satisfactorily.

Literacy The ability to read, write, speak, and listen.

Locus of control The source or place of control; the goal of behavioral guidance is to help children learn that their locus of control is internal, that they are responsible for their behavior, and that the rewards for good behavior come from within themselves.

Macrosystem The broader culture in which children live (e.g., democracy, individual freedom, and religious freedom).

Mastery-oriented attributions Attributions that include trying hard (industriousness), paying attention, determination, and stick-to-itiveness.

Maturationist theory Theory that holds that language acquisition is innate in all children regardless of country or culture.

Mesosystem Links or interactions between microsystems.

Microsystem The environmental settings in which children spend a lot of their time (e.g., children in child care spend about thirty-three hours a week in the microsystem of child care).

Middle childhood Describes children in the Erikson's industry versus inferiority stage of social-emotional development. This occurs when children are six to nine years of age and is a time when they gain confidence in and ego satisfaction from completing demanding tasks.

Montessori method Preschool or grade school that provides programs that use the philosophy, procedures, and materials developed by Maria Montessori (see Chapter 3); for children ages one to eight years.

Multicultural awareness Appreciation for and understanding of people's cultures, socioeconomic status, and gender.

Multicultural infusion Permeating the curriculum with multicultural education to influence the way young children and teachers think about diversity issues.

Multiculturalism An approach to education based on the premise that all peoples in the United States should receive proportional attention in the curriculum.

Multidisciplinary assessment (MDA) A team approach using various methods to conduct a child's evaluation.

Multiple intelligences Howard Gardner's concept that people are "smart" in many ways; those intelligences include linguistic, musical, logical-mathematical, spatial, bodily-kinesthetic, interpersonal, intrapersonal, naturalistic, and existentialist.

Neural shearing The process of brain connections withering away when they are not used or used only a little.

No Child Left Behind Act A landmark act in education reform designed to improve student achievement and change the culture of America's schools.

Obesity Condition characterized by the excessive accumulation and storage of fat in the body.

Object permanence The concept that things out of sight continue to exist; this intellectual milestone typically begins to develop at four to eight months of age.

Observation The intentional, systematic act of looking at the behavior of a child or children in a particular setting, program, or situation; sometimes referred to as *kid-watching*.

Operation A reversible mental action.

Parent/family involvement Process of helping parents and family members use their abilities to benefit themselves, their children, and the early childhood program.

Pedagogical knowledge Refers to the knowledge about teaching and instructional practices teachers should possess.

Performance standards Specific examples of what students should know and do to demonstrate that they have mastered the knowledge and skills stated in the content standards.

Pervasive developmental disorders (PDDs) A category of neurological disorders characterized by severe and pervasive impairment in several areas of development.

Philosophy of education A set of beliefs about how children develop and learn and what and how they should be taught.

Phonics A method of teaching beginners to read and pronounce words by learning the phonetic value of letters, letter groups, and especially syllables.

Phonics instruction Teaching method that emphasizes teaching letter-sound correspondence so children can learn to combine sounds into words.

Portfolio A compilation of children's work samples, products, and teacher observations collected over time.

Poverty The state of one who lacks a usual or socially acceptable amount of money or material possessions.

Pre-first-grade A program designed to provide children who are developmentally behind their peers the time they need to grow and learn in a supportive environment.

Pre-kindergarten A class or program preceding kindergarten for children usually from three to four years old.

Private speech See *Self-discourse.*

Professional dispositions Values, commitments, and ethical decisions and practices that influence behavior toward students, families, colleagues, and members of the profession and community.

Professional knowledge Refers to the knowledge about the teaching profession teachers should possess.

Pruning See *Neural shearing.*

Psychosocial development Erik H. Erikson's theory that contends that cognitive and social development must occur simultaneously.

Readiness Being ready to learn; possessing the knowledge, skills, and abilities necessary for learning and for success in school.

Readiness screening A procedure designed to determine if children have the cognitive and behavioral skills necessary for kindergarten success.

Receptive language Skills that toddlers and preschoolers develop, such as listening to the teacher and following directions.

Reflective practice The active process of thinking before teaching, during teaching, and after teaching in order to make decisions about how to plan, assess, and teach.

Reggio Emilia approach An educational program named for a town in Italy where it originated. This early education method emphasizes the child's relationships with family, peers, teachers, and the wider community; small-group interaction; schedules set by the child's personal rhythms; and visual arts programs coordinated by a specially trained atelierista.

Responsive relationship The relationship between a caregiver and the child that involves the caregiver being responsive to the needs and interests of each child.

Scaffolding Assistance or support of some kind from a teacher, parent, caregiver, or peer to help children complete tasks they cannot complete independently.

Scientific method A process used as the basis of scientific inquiry that includes the recognition of a problem, the collection of data through observation and experiment, and the formulation and testing of hypotheses.

Screening procedures Procedures that give you and others a broad picture of what children know and are able to do, as well as their physical and emotional status.

Self-actualization Abraham Maslow's theory of motivation based on the satisfaction of needs; Maslow maintained that children cannot achieve self-actualization until certain basic needs, including food, shelter, safety, and love, are met.

Self-discourse An internal conversation between a person and himself or herself.

Self-regulation The ability of preschool children to control their emotions and behaviors, to delay gratification, and to build positive social relations with each other.

Sensory integration dysfunction (SID) A neurological disability in which the brain is unable to appropriately process information from the senses.

Shared reading A teaching method in which the teacher and children read together from text that is visible to all.

Sight word approach Also called *whole-word* or *look-say,* the approach involves presenting children with whole words so they develop a "sight vocabulary" that enables them to begin reading and writing.

Social constructivist approach A theory that says children construct or build their behavior as a result of learning from experience and from making decisions that lead to responsible behavior.

Socioeconomic status (SES) The social and economic background of an individual or individuals. It is a reflection of family income, maternal education level, and family occupation.

Standards Statements of what pre-K–12 students should know and be able to do.

Standards-based education (SBE) Curriculum, teaching, and testing based on local, state, and national standards.

Symbolic language Knowing the names of people, places, and things, words for concepts, and adjectives and prepositions.

Symbolic representation The understanding, which develops at about age two, that something else can stand for a mental image; for example, a word can represent real objects, something not present, and concepts.

Synaptogenesis The formation of connections, or synapses, among neurons; this process of brain development begins before birth and continues until age ten.

Telegraphic speech Two-word sentences, such as "go out" or "all gone," used by toddlers.

Temperament A child's general style of behavior.

Theory A statement of principles and ideas that attempts to explain events and how things happen.

Title I A federal program designed to improve the basic skills (reading and mathematics) of low-ability children from low-income families.

Toddlerhood The period of a child's life between one and three years of age.

Transition A passage from one learning setting, grade, program, or experience to another.

Universal kindergarten Kindergarten for all children.

Universal preschool Public preschool funded by tax dollars, and made available to all children ages two to five, regardless of need or family income.

Whole-language approach Philosophy of literacy development that advocates the use of real literature—reading, writing, listening, and speaking—to help children become motivated to read and write.

Zero to Three A national program promoting the healthy development of infants and toddlers.

Zone of proximal development (ZPD) That area of development into which a child can be led by a more competent partner. Also, the range of tasks that children cannot do independently but which they can learn with help.

index

Abecedarian Project, 204
Academic achievement. *See* Achievement
Academic goals, for preschoolers, 218
Academic materials, 103, 105
Academics, in primary grades, 273
Accardo, P. J., 174
Accommodation, 67, 314
Accountability, 130, 131, 165, 309
Achievement, 38, 130, 133, 273, 315. *See also* High-stakes testing
Achievement gaps, 32
Achievement needs, 76
Acredelo, Linda, 187
Active involvement, 192
Active learning, 97, 100–102, 106, 160, 208
Active listening, 325
Activity centers, 227
Adaptation, 66–67
Adaptive education, 296
Administration for Children and Families, 113, 196
Admission, into kindergarten, 239–240, 259
Adult/child discourse, 322–323
Adults, in Reggio Emilia approach, 108. *See also* Parents; Teachers
Advocacy, 11–13, 356
Aesthetic needs, 76
Affective needs, 76, 326
After-school child care, 96
AIDS, 299
Ainsworth, Mary, 178
Aldama Elementary School (Los Angeles, California), 356
Alimacani Elementary School (Jacksonville, Florida), 307
Alphabet knowledge, 245, 258
Alphabetic principle, 245
Alverez, Karen, 356
American Academy of Pediatrics, 48, 188
American Alliance for Theater and Education, 255
American Association of Elementary, Kindergarten, and Nursery School Educators, 64
American Council of Parent Cooperatives, 65
American Educational Research Association, 127
American Heart Association, 35
American Psychological Association, 127
Anecdotal record, 152
Anthroposophy, 110–111
Anti-bias curriculum, 6–8
Anti-Bias Curriculum: Tools for Empowering Young Children, 6, 8
Applied behavior analysis (ABA), 306
Appropriate assessment, 127–128
Appropriate education, 297

Arts, 82, 218–219, 255–256, 289
Artwork, inclusive, 314
Assessment, 146–147
 accountability and, 165
 appropriate, 106, 127–128
 authentic, 133, 149–150
 checklists, 158–160
 context of, 165, 166
 data-driven instruction, 274, 275
 definition of, 147
 diversity and, 168
 formal, 150–151
 Head Start National Reporting System (HSNRS), 166–167
 High/Scope, 99–100
 high-stakes testing, 167–168
 importance of, 147–149
 informal, 151–152
 lesson planning and, 136
 multidisciplinary, 297
 observation, 153–158, 159, 160–161
 parents and families, 164–165
 portfolios, 161–162
 professional development activities, 168–169
 purposes of, 148
 reliability, 149
 screening procedures, 164
 technology and, 163
Assimilation, 66–67
Assistive technology and services, 300, 310
Associate degree programs, 16, 17
Association for Childhood Education International (ACEI), 12, 64
Associative play, 219
Asthma, 34
Ateah, Christine, 336
Atelier, 109
Atelierista, 108, 109
Atlanta Children's Shelter, Inc. (ACS), 92–93
Atlanta Enterprise Center, 93
Attachment/attachment behaviors, 177–178
 avoidant attachment, 178
Attention deficit disorder (ADD), 308
Attention deficit hyperactivity disorder (ADHD), 307–308
Audiology, 300
Austin, Deborah, 222
Authentic assessment, 133, 149–150
Autism, 299, 305–306
Autonomy, 191
Autonomy versus shame and doubt, 77

Baby signing, 187
Baccalaureate programs, 16, 17
Baird, Gary W., 275

Bang, Molly, 269
Barnum School (Taunton, Massachusetts), 351
Basic needs, 73–75, 76
Basic trust, 191
Batelle Development Inventory, 151
Bathroom routines, in preschool, 228
Beardsley, Anna, 59
Beaty, Janice, 161
Before-school child care, 96
Behavior guidance, 321–322
 beliefs about, 325
 conflict management, 339–342
 cooperative living and learning, 337, 339
 democratic classrooms, 342
 developmentally appropriate practice, 325–326
 diversity and, 336
 empowerment, 329–331
 environment, 332–334
 expectations, 332, 333
 gifted and talented children, 328–329
 locus of control, 327–328, 330–331
 modeling, 334–335
 needs, 326–327
 parents and families, 337
 positive, 338–339
 problems, avoiding, 335, 337
 professional development activities, 343
 rights, 337, 338
 social constructivist approach to, 322–325
 technology and, 330–331
Behavior indicators, of kindergartners, 239
Belonging needs, 73, 76, 326
Belpre Elementary School (Belpre, Ohio), 260
Benchmarks, 130
Berenstain, Stan, 45
Berry, Joy Wilt, 43
Bias-free, 313
Bilbro-Berry, Laura, 80
Bilingual education, 298, 312, 313
Bilingualism, 210
Birch, Herbert, 179
Bloom, Benjamin, 278, 279
Blow, Susan, 64, 236
Blume, Judy, 45
Blumenschein, Sarah, 35
Bodily/kinesthetic intelligence, 79
Bodrova, Elena, 75
Boehm Test of Basic Concepts–Revised, 151
Bonding, 177
Book for Mothers, 59
Boynton, Irene, 339
Brain-compatible learning, 280–281
Brain development, 172–174
Brain research, 39–43
BRIGANCE screens and inventories, 151, 164

Bright Horizons Family Solutions, 96, 175, 188–189
Bronfenbrenner, Urie, 76, 78, 84
Brown, Jackye, 93
Brown, Marc, 43
Bryant Woods Elementary School (Columbia, Maryland), 351
Buddy system, 211
Bullying, 43, 45
Bultman, Scott, 61
Burbach, A. D., 336
Bureau of Indian Affairs (BIA), 58
Burkham, D. T., 38
Business–school involvement, 364
Byrd, Cathy, 135

Cadwallader, Lori D., 253
Cameras, 175, 247
   digital, 175, 247
   disposable, 175
   video, 175
Camp Can Do, 154
Capute, A. J., 174
Cardenas, Maria, 3
Caring, 14–15, 42
Carlisle Indian School, 58
Carnahan, Linda, 21
Carnegie Foundation, 65
Carolina Beach Elementary School (North Carolina), 135
Casa dei Bambini, 62
Center-based option, 115
Center child care, 96
Centers for Disease Control and Prevention (CDC), 34
Cephalocaudal development, 180
Chair for My Mother, A (Williams), 335
Challenging environments, 191–192
Character education, 218, 277–278, 342
Checklists, 23–24, 25, 151, 152
Chess, Stella, 179
Chicago Child–Parent Center Program, 204
Child care, 16, 88–89
   Atlanta Children's Shelter, Inc., 92–93
   importance of, 89, 91
   multicultural settings, 314
   NICHD Study of Early Child Care and Youth Development, 92–93, 98–99
   quality, 92, 97
Child Care and Development Block Grant, 124
Child Care Executive Partnership Act, 49
Child Care Executive Partnership Program, 49
Child Care Network, 96
Child care programs
   comparison of, 90–91
   Magnia Child Care, 94–95
   types of, 91–92, 96
Child-centered curriculum, 62, 88–89
Child-centered school, 62, 88–89

Child development
   content knowledge and, 4, 5–6
   definition, 55
   socioeconomic status and, 37–39
   Waldorf education and, 111
   See also Infants and toddlers; Kindergartners; Preschoolers
Child Development Associate (CDA), 4
   competency goals and functional areas, 18
   National Credentialing Program, 16, 18–19
   participants, 19, 20–21
Childhood depression, 271
Childhood development. *See* Kindergartners; Primary-age children
Childhood Education (journal), 64
Child Observation Record (COR), 100
Children First, 112
Children's Defense Fund, 12, 65
Children's House, 64
Children with disabilities, 294–295
   ADHD, 307–308
   autism, 305–306
   child care for, 96
   definition of, 296
   IDEA, 295, 297–305
   inclusion, 307
   Native American Head Start programs, 114
   professional development activities, 318–319
   teaching, 309, 311
   technology, 310
   terms related to, 296
   Waldorf education, 111
Children with special needs. *See* Children with disabilities
Choices, 330–331
Chronosystem, 78
Circular response, 181
City & Country School, 88–89
Civics, 255
Civility, 342
Clark, John T., 43
Clark, Nicole K., 43
Class Meetings: Young Children Solving Problems Together (NAEYC), 342
Classroom arrangement, 97, 99, 241–242. *See also* Environment
Classroom environment, 7. *See also* Environment
Classroom rules, 332, 333, 341
Cleanup time, 102
Coach Dads program, 33
Code of Ethical Conduct (NAEYC), 9–10, 367–372
Cognitive development
   infants and toddlers, 181–183
   kindergartners, 238–239
   preschoolers, 207, 208–209
   primary-age children, 271–272

   stages of, 67–71
   theory of, 63, 66
Cognitive play, 223
Collaboration, 10–11, 276
Colleagues, collaboration with, 11
Columbia Teachers College, 64
Combination option, 115
Comenius, John Amos, 56, 57, 64
Common School Arithmetic, 54
Common Sense Book of Baby and Child Care (Spock), 65
Communication, 55
   assessment and, 164–165
   Internet, 359–360
   parent/family involvement and, 348, 350–351, 355, 359–360, 361
Community
   assessment and, 148
   kindness and caring, 15
   multicultural education and, 317
   professional knowledge and, 10–11, 13
Community involvement, 344–345, 351–352, 356, 362–363
Community mentor, 311
Community resources, 362–363
Comprehension, 244, 245, 310
Computers, handheld, 163. *See also* Technology
Concepts
   integration of, 128
   preschoolers and, 221
Concrete operations, 68, 71, 271–272
Conferences, parent–teacher, 358–359
Conflict management, 339–342
Conflict resolution education, 276–277
Confronting Our Discomfort (Jacobson), 64
Constructivism, 63, 66–71. *See also* Behavior guidance; High/Scope
Constructivist process, 66
Consultant professional, 311
Content areas, 5
Content knowledge, 2, 3, 4–5
Content standards, 121. *See also* Standards
Continuous learning, 10
Cooney, Barbara, 335
Cooperative learning, 309, 337, 339
Cooperative living, 337, 339
Core values, 367, 372
Co-teaching, 280, 296
Creative arts, 289
Culp, K. M., 288
Cultural accommodation, 314
Cultural awareness, 314–315
Cultural differences, 270
Cultural diversity, 313. *See also* Diversity
Cultural identity, 6
Culturally fair education, 313
Cultural pluralism, 313
Cultural sensitivity, 314
Culture
   preschoolers and, 212
   primary grades, 270

readiness and, 214
See also Diversity
Culwell, Barbara, 280, 281
Curriculum
    alignment, 134, 135
    anti-bias, 6–8
    child-centered, 62, 88–89
    compacting, 328–329
    emergent, 222, 224
    gifted and talented students, 328–329
    Harger, Lu Ann, 154–155
    High/Scope, 100, 101
    infants and toddlers, 192–193, 194–196
    integrated, 63, 106, 259
    kindergarten, 243–256, 258–259, 260
    preschool, 217, 218–219
    primary grades, 283–289
    Reggio Emilia approach, 109
    standards and, 121, 133–134, 135
Curriculum Focal Points (NCTM), 285
Curtis, Jamie Lee, 269

Daily routines, 193, 196
Daily schedule, 99, 224–229
Dancing, 289
Danielson, Lou, 310
Data analysis, 274–275
Data collection, 274
Data-driven instruction, 273, 274–275
Data interpretation, 161
Deaf-blindness, 299
Deafness, 299
Decision making, 351, 356
Decoding, 245, 310
Delpit, L., 7
Democratic classrooms, 342
Demonstration, 335. *See also* Modeling
Denton, K., 315
Depression, childhood, 271
Derman-Sparks, L., 7
DesLauriers, Joann, 19, 22
Development. *See* Professional development
Developmental Indicators for the Assessment
    of Learning (DIAL-3), 151, 164
Developmentally and culturally appropriate
    practice (DCAP), 6, 7
Developmentally appropriate approaches, 5–8
Developmentally appropriate practice (DAP),
    6, 106, 325–326
Developmentally appropriate programs, for
    infants and toddlers, 187–189
Developmental screening, 258
Dewey, John
    democratic classrooms, 342
    preschool, 217, 219
    progressive education theory, 62–63,
        64, 83
Difficult children, 179
Dignity, 54–55
Disability, definition of, 296. *See also* Children
    with disabilities

"Disaster Planning at Day Care" (*Wall Street
    Journal*), 30
Disorganized attachment, 178
Dispositions, professional, 2, 3, 13–15
District standards, 136
Diversity, 294–295
    anti-bias curriculum, 6–8
    assessment and, 149, 168
    behavior guidance and, 336
    definition of, 313
    English language learners (ELLs), 40–41
    gifted and talented children, 308, 310–311
    Head Start, 114
    high-stakes testing, 168
    infants and toddlers, 189–190, 197, 200
    kindergartners, 260
    language experiences and language
        development, 41, 42
    multicultural awareness, 312–313
    multicultural infusion, 313–318
    multiculturalism and professionalism,
        10–11
    Native American education, 58–59
    parent/family involvement and, 357,
        361–362, 363
    preschoolers, 210–212
    primary-age children, 266, 270, 273, 276
    professional development activities,
        318–319
    readiness and, 214
    socioeconomic status, 37, 38
    standards and, 129
    Waldorf education and, 111
    See also Children with disabilities
Dr. Carlos J. Finley Elementary School
    (Miami, Florida), 276
Documentation, in Reggio Emilia
    approach, 109
Dodde, Josiah, 180
Doyle, Cheryl, 341
Dramatic play, 70
Drawing, 253
Dreamkeepers, The (Ladson-Billings), 7
Due process, 297
Duke, Nell, 266

*Eager to Learn: Educating Our
    Preschoolers*, 122
Early childhood development, in Native
    American Head Start programs, 114
Early childhood education, 28
    brain research, 39–43
    bullying, 43, 45
    families and, 29–34
    federal and state involvement in, 46–47
    new directions in, 48–50
    politics and, 45–46
    professional development activities,
        50–51
    socioeconomic status and child
        development, 37–39

technology and, 48
    violence, 43, 44
    wellness and healthy living, 34–37
Early childhood education history
    and theory, 53–57
    Bronfenbrenner, Urie, 76, 78, 84
    Comenius, John Amos, 57
    Dewey, John, 62–63, 83
    educational practices and, 81–84
    Erikson, Erik, 75–76, 77, 83
    Froebel, Friedrich Wilhelm, 60–61
    Gardner, Howard, 79–80, 84
    kindergarten, 236–237
    Locke, John, 57–58
    Luther, Martin, 57
    Maslow, Abraham, 72–75, 76, 83
    Montessori, Maria, 62, 83
    Owen, Robert, 60
    Pestalozzi, Johann Heinrich, 59–60
    Piaget, Jean, 63, 66–71, 83
    professional development activities,
        84–85
    Rousseau, Jean-Jacques, 58–59
    technology and, 82
    timeline, 64–66
    Vygotsky, Lev, 71–72, 73, 83
Early childhood professional organizations,
    12. *See also specific organizations*
Early childhood professionals, 3, 221–222,
    224. *See also* Professional development;
    Professional development goals
Early childhood programs, 86
    assessment and, 148
    child care, 88–93
    demand for, 87–88
    federal programs, 112–118
    High/Scope, 93–102
    infants and toddlers, 187–189
    Montessori method, 102–106
    professional development activities,
        118–119
    Reggio Emilia, 106–110, 112
    technology and, 107
    Waldorf education, 110–112
Early education and care settings, 296
Early elementary grades. *See* Primary grades
Early Head Start, 65, 112, 117–118
Early intervention, 296
Early learning standards, 125–126,
    132–133
Early literacy learning, 49
Early Reading First, 46, 124, 125
Eclectic Reader (McGuffey), 54, 64
Ecological theory, 76, 78
Economic Opportunity Act, 65
Economics, 255
Education Alternatives, Inc., 65
Education for All Handicapped
    Children Act, 65
Education of the Handicapped Act
    Amendments, 65

Educational practices
    early childhood education history
        and theory and, 81–84
    Montessori method, 106
    Reggio Emilia approach, 109
Educational reform, 131, 273–278, 279,
    280–281
Educational resources, inequality of, 266
Edwards, C., 91
eKidSkills, 330
eKidTools, 330
Elementary school, contemporary, 273–278,
    279, 280–281. *See also* Primary grades
Elffers, Joost, 269
Eliot, Abigail, 64
Ellis, D., 247
Emde, R. N., 196
Emergent curriculum, 222, 224
Emergent literacy skills, 310
Émile (Rousseau), 58, 64
Emotional development
    infants and toddlers, 175, 177–179
    kindergartners, 237–238
    preschoolers, 206
    primary-age children, 269–271
Emotional disturbance, 299
Employer-sponsored child care, 96
Empowerment, 329–331
English as a second language (ESL), 313,
    318–319
English language fluency, 211
English language learners (ELLs), 40–41
    definition of, 296
    high-stakes testing and, 168
    preschool, 215–211
    primary grades, 276
Enrichment classroom, 311
Entitlement programs, 112–113. *See also* Early
    Head Start; Head Start
Entrance age, for kindergartners, 239–240, 259
Environment
    behavior guidance and, 332–334
    classroom, 7
    infants and toddlers, 174–175, 190–192
    kindergarten, 241–243
    preschool, 209, 215–217
    primary grades, 278, 280–282, 283
    Reggio Emilia approach, 108–109
Environmental theory, 184
Epstein, J. L., 352
Equality, 266
Equilibrium, 67
Erikson, Erik, 65, 75–76, 77, 83, 175, 206
Escobar, Maria, 324, 325
Espinosa, Linda M., 210, 363
Ethical conduct, 9–10, 367–372
Ethical dilemma activities
    assessment, 168
    behavior guidance, 343
    diversity, 318
    early childhood education, 50

early childhood education history
    and theory, 84
early childhood programs, 118
infants and toddlers, 198
kindergarten, 261
parent/family involvement, 365
preschool, 232
primary grades, 289
professional development, 25
standards, 145
Ethical responsibilities, 369–372
Ethics, 372
Ethnicity. *See* Anti-bias curriculum; Diversity;
    Multiculturalism
Evaluation, 6
    contexts of, 16
    learning, 55
    NCLB, 124
    nondiscriminatory, 297
    See also Assessment
Even Start, 65, 352–353
Event sampling, 152
Exceptional student education, 296
Existentialist intelligence, 79
Exosystem, 78
Expanding horizons approach, 251, 254
Experiential background, 212
Experimentation, 182–183, 253

Face-to-face interaction, 309
Fairness, 149
Falkener Elementary School (Greensboro,
    North Carolina), 125
Families
    assessment and, 148, 164–165
    behavior guidance and, 336, 337
    collaboration with, 10–11
    early childhood education and, 29–34
    educational practices and, 81
    Harger, Lu Ann, 154
    Head Start and, 116
    language-minority, 361–362
    multicultural education and, 317
    Reggio Emilia approach and, 108
    single-parent, 360–361
Families Learning at School and Home
    (FLASH), 276
Families Without Partners, 347
Family and relative care, 96
Family-centered teaching, 352–353
Family child care, 94, 95, 96
Family Education network, 364
Family involvement. *See* Parent/family
    involvement
Family Involvement Partnership for
    Learning, 364
Family member roles, 30
Family responsibilities, 30
Family structure, 29–30
Family training, 300
Fathers, 31–33, 336. *See also* Parents

Federal control, 132–133
Federal programs, 112–118
Federal standards, 260. *See also* Standards
Federal support, 46–47
Feedback, 348
Feelings. *See* Emotional development
Feeney, S., 372
Fellman, Sandi, 43
Fine arts, 82
First words, 184
Fitness. *See* Healthy living
Fitzgerald, G., 331
Floor plans
    infants and toddlers, 190
    kindergarten, 241
    preschool, 216
    primary grades, 282, 283
Florida Comprehensive Assessment test, 136
Florida Department of Education, 46
Florida International University, 276
Florida Sunshine State Standards, 136
Follow Through, 65
Formal assessment, 150–151
Formal operations, 71, 384
Formative assessments, 275
Fox, R. A., 336
Frankenburg, William K., 180
Free and appropriate education (FAPE),
    297, 298, 300
Freeman, N., 372
Free play, 223
Free Waldorf School, 110
Freymann, Saxton, 269
Froebel, Friedrich Wilhelm, 54, 56, 60–61,
    62, 64, 236–237, 217
*From Neurons to Neighborhoods: The Science
    of Early Childhood Development,* 122
Froschl, Merle, 45
Full-day, full-year services, 48
Fuller, M. L., 7
Full inclusion, 296
Functional play, 223

Gallaudet, Thomas, 64
Games with rules, 223
Gardner, Howard, 78, 79–80, 84, 317
Garret, Joe, 168
Gbadamosi, Tara, 357
Genetics, 174–175
Genre-writing, 244
Geography, 254–255
Geometry, 250
Georgia Law Center, 93
Germino-Hausken, E., 315
Gerstein, Mordical, 335
Gifted and talented children, 308, 310–311,
    328–329
Gifts (Froebel), 60–61
Gimenez, Lourdes P., 276
Glenn, Stephen, 339
Goals. *See* Professional development goals

Goals 2000: Educate America Act, 66, 122
Gonzales, Maria, 224
Gonzalez, Graciela, 159
Gonzalez, José, 147
Good Start, Grow Smart, 124
Goodwyn, Susan, 187
Gordon, Thomas, 324
Grace Hill Neighborhood Health Centers,
    34–35
Grandparents, 347–349
Grapevine Elementary School (Texas),
    338–339
Grasping reflexes, 181
Great Didactic, The (Comenius), 57, 64
Green, Stephen, 357
Greendale School District (Greendale,
    Wisconsin), 351
Greenman, Jim, 189
Green River Community College, 20–21
Gronlund, Gaye, 130, 132–133
Grouping, mixed-age, 105
Group meeting/planning, in preschool, 225
Group processing, 309
Group time, in preschool, 228–229
Guidance, 56–57. *See also* Behavior
    guidance
Guided reading, 284

Hampton Place Baptist Church
    (Dallas, Texas), 314
Handheld computers, 163
Handicapped Children's Early Education
    Program, 65
Hands-on activities
    ELLs, 40
    kindergarten, 252
    preschoolers, 208
Hand washing, 228
Handwriting, 244
Hardman, Michael L., 306
Harger, Lu Ann, 154
Harris, Millie, 278, 280–281
Harris, William T., 64, 236
Hausman, Bonnie, 43
Head Start, 91, 112, 113
    Child Development Associate
        program, 19
    early childhood education and,
        39, 49
    eligibility for, 116
    health services, 116
    history, 65, 66
    Native American programs, 114
    nutrition, 116
    objectives, 113–115
    parent involvement and family
        partnerships, 116
    preschool and, 203, 210
    program options, 115–116
    Upper Des Moines Opportunity,
        Inc., 117

Head Start Bureau, 113
Head Start National Reporting System
    (HSNRS), 166–167
Head Start Outcomes Framework, 138, 139,
    140–143
Head Start Performance Standards, 138–139
Head Start Reauthorization, 65
Health
    infants and toddlers, 190–191
    kindergartners, 239
    preschoolers, 212, 219
    See also Mental health
Health impairments, 299. *See also* Children
    with disabilities
Health services, 114, 116, 300
Healthy living, 34–37, 219
Hearing impairment, 299
Height
    infants and toddlers, 172
    kindergartners, 237
    preschoolers, 205
    primary-age children, 267, 268
Helping Hands pledge, 14
Heredity, 174, 183
Hergenroeder, Ernie, 43
Hewitt, J. K., 196
High/Scope, 90, 93–94
    active learning, 100–102
    advantages, 102
    curriculum wheel, 100
    elements of, 97, 99–100
    Perry Preschool Project, 66, 204
    principles and goals, 94–95
High/Scope Educational Foundation, 65
High-stakes testing, 49, 136, 167–168,
    258–259
Hill, Patty Smith, 64, 236–237
Hinitz, Blythe, 45
History, in kindergarten, 255. *See also* Early
    childhood education history and theory
Holcombe, Amy, 125
Holland, Vickie, 135
Holophrasic speech, 184
Holvoet, Jennifer, 247
Holz, Diana Mamerto, 21
Home-based option, 115
Home learning, 351, 356
Homelessness, 92–93
Home visitor programs, 18
Home visits, 357–358
Homework bags, 348–349
Homework Helper, 356
Housewright, Linda, 138
Houston, Gloria, 80
Howard, Amir Diego, 168
How Are You Peeling? Foods with Moods
    (Freymann and Elffers), 269
How Gertrude Teaches Her Children
    (Pestalozzi), 59, 64
Huggins, Carrie, 163
Hyperactivity, 308

Ideals, 367–72
Identity, individual and cultural, 6
Illinois Early Learning Standards for Language
    Arts and Mathematics, 130, 131
Imagination, 111
"I" messages, 325
Imitation, 177
Impulse control, 212
Impulsivity, 308
Inattention, 307–308
Inclusion, 307
Inclusive artwork, 314
Inclusive classrooms, 159, 305, 306, 311
Inclusive services, continuum of, 305
Independence, 106, 212, 219
Independent study, 311, 329
Indian Health Service, 114
Individual accountability, 309
Individual identity, 6
Individualized education program (IEP),
    296, 298, 301, 302–304
Individualized family service plan (IFSP),
    296, 301, 304–305
Individualized instruction, 106
Individuals with Disabilities Education Act
    (IDEA), 295, 297–305, 310
Industry versus inferiority, 77
Infancy, 171
Infant mental health, 193, 196–197
Infant school, 60
Infants and toddlers, 170–172
    brain development, 172–174
    cognitive development, 181–183
    curriculum, 192–193, 194–196
    developmentally appropriate programs,
        187–189
    diversity and, 197
    environments for, 190–192
    IDEA and, 300
    language development, 183–187, 188–189
    mental health, 193, 196–197
    motor development, 180–181
    multiculturally appropriate practice,
        189–190
    nature, nurture, and development,
        174–175, 176
    portraits of, 198, 199–200
    professional development activities, 198
    social and emotional development, 175,
        177–179
    technology and, 175
Informal assessment, 151–152
Informal play, 223
Infusion, 313
Initiative versus guilt, 77
"In Kindergarten Playtime, a New Meaning
    for 'Play'" (*New York Times*), 30
Inquiry-based classrooms, 287
Inquiry learning, 287
Institute for Responsive Education
    (IRE), 364

Institute of Medicine, 274
Instruction, differentiating, 136. *See also* Teaching
Instructional materials
  anti-bias curriculum and, 7
  inequalities of, 266
  kindergarten, 256
  Montessori method and, 103–105
  multicultural education, 314, 315–316
  open-ended, 88
  preschool, 208
Integrated curriculum, 63, 106, 259
Integration, 296
Intellectual development, stages of, 67–71. *See also* Cognitive development
Intelligence, 40, 63, 316–317
Intentional preschool curriculum standards, 133
Interdependence, positive, 309
Intergenerational care, 96
Intergenerational family programs, 353
International Kindergarten Union (IKU), 64
International Year of the Family (IYF), 66
Internet communications, 359–360
Interpersonal intelligence, 79
Interpersonal skills, 212, 218, 309
Intersubjectivity, 72
Interviews, 152
Intrapersonal intelligence, 79
Intrapersonal skills, 218
Ira Sleeps Over (Waber), 335

Jacob K. Javits Gifted and Talented Students Education Act, 308
Jacobson, T., 7
Jefferson Place Transitional Program, 93
Johnston, Marianne, 45
Jones, Irene, 58, 59
Jones, T. G., 7
Jones, Tyron, 147

Kaiser Child Care Centers, 65
Kearn, Catherine M., 75
Kenayta Primary School, 58–59
Key experiences, 101
Kidder, R. M., 372
KidTools Support System (KTSS), 328, 330–331
Kindergarten, 234–235
  changing dynamics of, 240
  curriculum, 243–256, 258–259
  diversity and, 260
  entrance age, 239–240, 259
  environment, 241–243
  high-stakes testing, 258–259
  history and theory, 60, 64, 65, 236–237
  professional development activities, 261
  redshirting, 257
  standards in, 135
  technology and, 247

Kindergartners
  cognitive and language development, 238–239
  physical development, 237
  portraits of, 261, 262–263
  social and emotional development, 237–238
  support for, 256–257
Kindergarten Guide (Peabody and Mann), 236
Kindergarten readiness, 207–214
Kindergarten transition, 229
Kindness, 14–15
Kindness Promise, 14
King, Alicia, 339
King, Donna, 112
Kipnis, K., 372
Knowledge
  alphabet, 245, 258
  content, 2, 3, 4–5
  pedagogical, 2, 3, 5–8
  professional, 2, 3, 9–13
Knowledge Learning Company, 96
Kohlberg, Lawrence, 272
Koury, K., 331

Laboratory School, 64
Ladd, Mary, 16
Ladson-Billings, G., 7
Lamb, Susan Condie, 80
Landis, B., 59
Language arts
  kindergarten, 243–249, 258–259
  primary grades, 283–284
  standards, 131, 135
Language development, 41, 42
  infants and toddlers, 174, 183–187, 188–189, 192–193
  kindergartners, 238–239
  preschoolers, 207, 209–212, 218, 220, 221
Language experience approach (LEA), 246
Language experiences, 41, 42
Language impairment, 299
Language-minority parents and families, 361–362
La Petite Academy (Dublin, Ohio), 96, 161
Lead poisoning, 34–35
Learned helplessness, 269
Learning
  active, 97, 100–102, 106, 160, 208
  brain-compatible, 280–281
  definition of, 55
  evaluation of, 55
  Harger, Lu Ann, 155
  home, 351
  Reggio Emilia and, 107–110
  standards and, 130–134
Learning Care Group, Inc., 96
Learning centers, 225–228, 237
Learning Cheer, 14
Learning disabilities, 299

Learning materials. *See* Instructional materials
Learning styles, 316–317
Learning theories. *See* Early childhood education history and theory
Least restrictive environment (LRE), 296, 297
Lee, V. E., 38
Lekotek, 65
Leong, Deborah, 75
Lesson planning, 136–137
Lessow-Hurley, Judith, 40
Letter to the Mayors and Aldermen of All the Cities of Germany in Behalf of Christian Schools (Luther), 64
Lewis, Cindy, 163
Lifelong learning, 10
Limited English proficiency (LEP), 296
Limits, setting, 332
Lin, Huey-Ling, 357
Linguistic diversity. *See* Diversity
Listening, 32, 325
Listening experiences, 101
Literacy Decade, 66
Literacy development, 209
  assistive technology and, 310
  kindergartners, 243–249, 253
  preschoolers, 218, 220, 221
  primary-age children, 283–284
Literacy learning, 49
Literature
  kindergarten, 253
  multicultural, 316
  primary grades, 269
Locke, John, 56, 57–58
Locus of control, 327–328, 330–331
"Long Wait, The" (*Winston-Salem Journal*), 30
Lott, Lynn, 339
Lunch, in preschool, 228
Luther, Martin, 56, 57, 64

Macrosystem, 78
Madvig, Mary Jo, 117
Magnia Child Care, 94–95
Magnia, Albert, 94
Magnia, Martha, 95
Mainstreaming, 296
Make-believe play, 70
Malaguzzi, Loris, 106
Mandinach, E., 288
Mann, Horace, 53, 64
Mann, Mary, 236
Man Who Walked Between the Towers, The (Gerstein), 335
Martin, Rafe, 335
Maslow, Abraham, 72–75, 76, 82, 83
Master's degree programs, 16, 17
Mastery-oriented attributions, 268
Materials. *See* Instructional materials
Maternal education, 315
Mathematical/logical intelligence, 79

Mathematics
    academic materials for, 105
    kindergarten, 249–250
    preschool, 209
    primary grades, 284–286
    standards, 131, 135
Maturationist theory, 183–184
McArthur, Mindy, 147
McBride, Rachel, 163
McCain, Becky R., 45
McCullough, Paula, 346, 348–349
McGraw-Hill Publishing Company,
    137, 139, 144
McGuffey, William, 64
McLin, Eva, 64
McMillan, Margaret, 64
McMillan, Rachel, 64
Meaningful learning, 155
Measurement, 250, 285–286
Medical needs, children with, 96
Medical services, 300
Medlock, Lori, 307
Mega Skills Education Center, 364
Mellor, Kathy, 318–319
Mental constructs, 66–67. *See also* Schemes
Mental health
    infants and toddlers, 193, 196–197
    preschoolers, 212
    primary-age children, 271
Mental operations, 63
Mental retardation, 299
Merged classroom, 296
Merillat, Linda, 247
Mesosystem, 76, 78
Michigan Department of Education, 244
Microsystem, 76, 78
Middle childhood, 268. *See also*
    Primary-age children
Military schools, 280–281
Mini-Skool, 96
Minnieland Private Day School, 96
Minority students. *See* Diversity
Miss Rumphius (Cooney), 335
Mixed-age grouping, 105
Modeling, 334–335, 340, 341
Molt, Emil, 110
Monterosso, Anne, 260
Montessori, Maria, 54, 62, 64, 82, 83, 217
Montessori method, 62, 66, 82, 90,
    102–106
Moral development, of primary-age
    children, 272–273
Morality, 372
Morrow, L. M., 220
Motherese, 185, 186
Motivation, 328, 338–339
Motor development
    infants and toddlers, 180–181
    preschoolers, 205–206
    See also Physical development
Movement, in Waldorf education, 111

Multicultural awareness, 312–313
Multicultural infusion, 313–318
Multiculturalism, 6, 7, 10, 313. *See also*
    Diversity
Multicultural literature, 316
Multiculturally appropriate practice, 189–190
Multidisciplinary assessment (MDA), 297
Multiple disabilities, 299
Multiple intelligence theory, 78, 79–80, 317
Music, 82, 111, 218–219, 289
Music Educators National Conference, 255
Musical/rhythmic intelligence, 79
My Great Aunt Arizona (Houston), 80
MyPyramid for Kids, 35, 36

Nagourney, E., 48
National Academy of Sciences, 122
National Art Education Association, 255
National Association for Family Child Care
    (NAFCC), 94
National Association for the Education of
    Young Children (NAEYC), 4, 66
    appropriate assessment, 127
    assessment, 147
    Code of Ethical Conduct, 9–10, 367–372
    developmentally appropriate infant and
        toddler programs, 187–188
    early childhood programs, 87
    early learning standards, 125–126
    joining, 12
    Statement of Commitment, 367, 373
National Association of Early Childhood
    Specialists in State Departments of
    Education (NAECS/SDE), 4, 125, 127
National Association of Nursery Education
    (NANE), 64
National Center for Education Statistics
    (NCES), 129, 239, 312
National Center for Fathering, 32
National Center for Health Statistics, 172
National Center for Measurement in
    Education, 127
National Coalition for Parent Involvement in
    Education (NCPIE), 364
National Committee on Nursery Schools, 64
National Council for the Social Studies
    (NCSS), 316
National Council of Teachers of Mathematics
    (NCTM), 122, 123, 227, 249, 250,
    284–285
National Dance Association, 255
National Dissemination Center for Children
    with Disabilities (NICHCY), 299
National Education Standards and
    Improvement Council, 122
National Home Start Program, 65
National Institute for Early Education
    Research, 132
National Institute of Child Health and Human
    Development (NICHD), 92–93, 98–99
National PTA, 29, 363, 364

National PTA Hispanic Outreach Advisory
    Board, 363
National Reporting System Computer-Based
    Reporting System, 166
National Research Council, 122
National standards, 136–139, 140–143.
    See also Standards
Nation at Risk, A (U.S. Department of
    Education), 122
Native American education, 58–59
Native American Head Start
    programs, 114
Natural environment, 296
Naturalistic preschool curriculum
    standards, 133
Naturalist intelligence, 79
Nature versus nurture, 174–175, 176
Needs, 326–327
Needs hierarchy, 73–75, 76
Neill, A. S., 64
Nelson, Jane, 339
Neural shearing, 172. *See also* Pruning
New Horizon Child Care, 96
Newsletters, 348
Nicholson, B. C., 336
Nobel Learning Communities, 96
No Child Left Behind Act, 46, 66
    parent/family involvement, 352, 354
    primary grades and, 267, 274, 275, 283
    standards and, 122, 124–125
Noddings, Nel, 14–15
Nondiscriminatory evaluation, 297
Nonverbal affirmation and
    acknowledgment, 327
Nonverbal communication, in English
    language learning, 41
North Carolina State Standards, 135
"No Toy Is Better Than a Parent's Attention"
    (*Freelance Star*), 30
Numbers and operations, 250, 285
Nursery School of the Bureau of Educational
    Experiments, 64
Nursery schools, 64
Nurture. *See* Nature versus nurture
Nutrition, 34, 35–36, 116
Nutritional needs, 73, 76

Obesity, 35, 37, 265, 273–274
Object lessons (Pestalozzi), 59
Object permanence, 181–182
Observation, 146–147, 151
    conducting, 154–158, 160–161
    contexts of, 166
    guidelines, 152
    inclusive classrooms, 159
    purposes of, 152, 153–154
    technology and, 163
Occupational therapy, 300
Occupations (Froebel), 61
Office of Special Education and Rehabilitative
    Services, 299, 300, 301

Office of Vocational and Educational Services for Individuals with Disabilities, 304
Onlooker play, 219
Onset-rime, 245
Open-ended materials and methods, 88
Opening activities, in preschool, 225
Operation, 207
Operational thinking, 207
Orbis Pictus, 56, 57
Origins of Intelligence in Children, The (Piaget), 65
Orthographic awareness, 245
Orthopedic impairment, 299
Oshkosh Normal School, 64
O'Sullivan, Sheryl, 335
Other People's Children (Delpit), 7
Outdoor activities, in preschool, 28
Outdoor play, 223
Owen, Robert, 56, 60, 64

Parallel play, 219
Parent Cooperative Preschools International, 65
Parent Effectiveness Training (PET), 324
Parent/family involvement, 344–345
    activities for, 354–356
    changing, 346–349
    community involvement and, 362–363
    diversity and, 357
    family-centered teaching, 352–353
    federal government and, 354
    home visits, 357–358
    Internet communications, 359–360
    language-minority parents and families, 361–362
    national organizations, 364
    overview of, 349–354
    parent–teacher conferences, 358–359
    professional development activities, 365
    school–business involvement and, 364
    single-parent families, 360–361
    technology and, 356
    telephone contact, 359
    two-generation and intergenerational programs, 353
    views of, 345–346
    Website connections, 364
Parentese, 185, 186
Parenting, 350
Parenting knowledge and skills, 355
Parents
    anti-bias curriculum and, 8
    assessment and, 148, 164–165
    behavior guidance and, 336, 337, 338
    brain research and, 42
    collaboration with, 10–11
    educational practices and, 81
    fathers, 31–33
    Head Start and, 116
    IDEA and, 298
    IFSP and, 304

infants and toddlers, 177–178
language-minority, 361–362
Magnia Child Care, 95
multiculturalism and, 11
primary grades and, 275
Reggio Emilia approach and, 108
roles and responsibilities of, 30
single, 33, 360–361
teenage, 33–34
working, 31, 361
See also Families
Parents Plus (Milwaukee, Wisconsin), 351
Parent Teacher Association (PTA), 29
Parent–teacher conferences, 358–359
Parten, Mildred, 219
Peabody, Elizabeth, 64, 236
Peabody Picture Vocabulary Test–Revised (PPVT–R), 151
Pedagogical knowledge, 2, 3, 5–8
Pehrson, Christa, 15
Perfection, 328
Performance-based assessment. *See* Authentic assessment
Performance standards, 113, 121. *See also* Standards
Perry Preschool Project, 66, 204
Personal accomplishments, in multicultural education, 316
Personality development, 178–179
Personal responsibility, 309
Pervasive developmental disorders (PDDs), 305
Pestalozzi, Johann Heinrich, 56, 59–60, 64
Peterson, S. H., 195, 196
Philadelphia Centennial Exposition, 64
Philosophy of education, 19–22
Phonemes, 245
Phonemic awareness, 244, 245, 258, 310
Phonics, 245, 246
Phonics instruction, 246
Phonological awareness, 245
Phonological decoding, 310
Physical development
    kindergartners, 237
    preschoolers, 205–206, 221
    primary-age children, 267–268
Physical environment
    kindergartens, 241–242
    primary grades, 280–282, 283
    Reggio Emilia approach, 108–109
    See also Environment
Physical fitness. *See* Healthy living
Physical health, 212. *See also* Health
Physical needs, 76, 326
Physical therapy, 300
Piaget, Jean
    moral development, 272
    preschoolers, 219
    social constructivist approach, 322
    theory, 56, 63, 65, 66–71, 83
Pinchbeck, B. J., 356

Planning
    anti-bias curriculum, 8
    conflict management education, 341
    observation, 155–156, 160
    preschool, 225
Planning time, 101
Play, 8
    constructivism in, 63
    cooperative, 219
    make-believe, 70
    preschool, 217, 219–224, 228
    primary grades, 270–271
Politics, 45–46, 49, 267
Portfolios, 151, 152, 161–162
Positive behavior guidance, 338–339
Positive Discipline, 338–339
Positive interdependence, 309
Poverty, 37, 39
Practical life activities, 103
Praise, 74–75, 76, 327
Pratt, Caroline, 88
Pratt, Martha, 175, 176
Pre-kindergarten, 16
Preoperational stage, 68, 69–70
Preschool, 47, 202–203
    curriculum, 217, 218–219
    daily schedule, 224–229
    environment, 214–217
    play in, 217, 219–224
    popularity of, 203–205
    professional development activities, 233
    state standards, 214
Preschool curriculum standards, 133
Preschoolers
    cognitive development, 207, 208–209
    diversity and, 210–212
    kindergarten transition, 229
    language development, 207, 209–212, 220
    physical and motor development, 205–206
    portraits of, 230, 231–232
    professional development activities, 230, 233
    readiness, 207–214
    self-regulation, 206–207
    social and emotional development, 206
    technology and, 213
"Preschool Space Is at a Premium" (*Washington Post*), 30
Prestige needs, 76
Pretend play, 70, 223
Preventing Reading Difficulties in Young Children, 122
Primary-age children
    cognitive development, 271–272
    emotional development, 269–271
    moral development, 272–273
    physical development, 267–268
    portraits of, 289, 290–292
    social development, 268–269, 270–271

Primary grades, 264–267
  curriculum, 283–289
  diversity and, 266
  educational reform, 273–278, 279, 280–281
  environment, 278, 280–282, 283
  professional development activities, 289, 293
  technology and, 288
Principles, 367–372
Print awareness, 245, 258
Private speech, 322, 323–324
Problem ownership, 324–325
Problems, avoiding, 335, 337
Problem-solving, 209
Problem-solving chart, 251
Professional development, 2–3
  checklist, 23–24, 25
  pathways, 16–24
  primary grades and, 275
  technology and, 24–25, 26–27
Professional development activities, 25–27
  assessment, 168–169
  behavior guidance, 343
  children with disabilities, 318–319
  diversity, 318–319
  early childhood education, 50–51
  early childhood education history and theory, 84–85
  early childhood programs, 118–119
  infants and toddlers, 198
  kindergarten, 261
  parent/family involvement, 365
  preschool, 230, 233
  primary grades, 289, 293
  standards, 145
Professional development goals, 3–15
  content knowledge, 2, 3, 4–5
  pedagogical knowledge, 2, 3, 5–8
  professional dispositions, 2, 3, 13–15
  professional knowledge, 2, 3, 9–13
Professional dispositions, 2, 3, 13–15
Professional ethics, 372
Professionalism, 10–11
Professional knowledge, 2, 3, 9–13
Progressivism, 62
Proprietary child care, 96
Prosocial behaviors, 334–335
Prosocial education, 276–277
Protestant Reformation, 57
Proximodistal development, 180
Pruning, 172. See also Neural shearing
Psychological services, 300
Psychosocial development, 75–76, 77
Public Law 94–142, 65
Public Law 99–457, 65
Public schools, 46–47. See also Schools
"Push for Success Sends More Kids to Pre-K Tutoring" (Arizona Republic), 30

Quaid, Julie, 114
Questioning levels, hierarchy of, 278, 279

Race. See Anti-bias curriculum; Diversity; Multiculturalism
Railsback, J., 247
Raising Our Children's Children (ROCC), 347
Ramirez, Fred A. Y., 357
Ramsey, P., 7
Rating scale, 152
Readiness, 49, 207–214, 218
Readiness screening, 258
Reading
  academic materials for, 105
  balanced approach, 249
  kindergarten, 243–249
  primary grades, 283–284
Reading comprehension, 310
Reading experiences, in High/Scope curriculum, 101
Reading First, 124
Reading logs, 257
"Ready to Learn" plan, 65
Recall time, 102
Recess, 54, 270–271
Reconnecting Education and Dads to Kids (R.E.A.D. to Kids), 33
Redshirting, 257
Reflection, 176, 195, 196
Reflective practice, 11, 12
Reflexive responses, 181
Reform, of standards, 131
Reggio Emilia approach, 90, 106–110, 112
Reinforcement, 341
Relationship care, 193
Relationships, 107–108
  infants and toddlers, 177–178, 193, 194–196
  responsive, 193
Relaxation, 228
Reliability, of assessment, 149
Reports, national, 122
Representation, symbolic, 183, 184–185
Resistant attachment, 178
Resource room pullout, 311
Respect, 54–55, 194, 342
Respite care, 300
Responsibilities
  empowerment and, 330
  ethical, 369–72
  families, 30
  personal, 309
Responsive relationships, 193
Reverse mainstreaming, 296
Rewards, for behavior, 338–339
Rhythm, 111
Rideout, V. J., 44
Rights that support positive behavior, 337, 338
Risk-taking behavior, 328
Rivers Edge Elementary School (Richmond, Virginia), 270
Robinson, Nancy, 339

Rogers, Kerry, 307
Roger Wolcott Early Childhood Center (Windsor, Connecticut), 351–352
Role models, 35–37
Role-playing, 341
Rough-and-tumble play, 223
Rough-Face Girl, The (Martin), 335
Rousseau, Jean-Jacques, 54, 56, 58–59, 64
Routines, daily, 193, 196
Ruggles Street Nursery School, 64
Rules, classroom, 332, 333, 341
Running record, 152
Rural schools, 54
Rush, Marie, 307

Safety, for infants and toddlers, 190–191
Safety needs, 73, 76, 326
San Felipe Pueblo Elementary School, 59
Sarmalis, Ioannis, 21
Scaffolding, 72, 74–75, 208–209, 250–251, 322
Schedule, daily, 99, 224–229
Schemes, 66–67. See also Mental constructs
School #82 Early Childhood Center (Buffalo, New York), 350
School–business involvement, 364
School readiness, 49, 207–214, 218
Schools
  child-centered, 62, 88–89
  early education and, 46–47
  infant, 60
  military, 280–281
  nursery, 64
  rural,
  special, 311
School vouchers, 65
Schurz, Margarethe, 64, 236
Science
  kindergarten, 250–251, 252–253
  preschool, 209
  primary grades, 286–287
  standards, 135
Science as inquiry, 252
Screening instruments, 164
Screening procedures, 164
Secure attachment, 178
Security needs, 73, 76, 326
Self-actualization, 72–73, 76, 326–327
Self-directed learners, 338–339
Self-discourse, 322
Self-esteem, 221
Self-esteem needs, 73, 76, 326
Self-fulfillment needs, 76
Self-guided behavior, 323
Self-help skills, 218
Self-pacing, 105
Self-regulation, 206–207, 208, 321
Sensorimotor development, 181–183
Sensorimotor stage, 68–69
Sensory materials, 103–105
Shannon, David, 335

Shared reading, 246, 248
Sharing, 341–342
Sheffler, Vicki, 15
Showing, 335. *See also* Modeling
Sierra Vista Elementary School (Washo
 County, Nevada), 168
Sight vocabulary, 258
Sight words, 245–246
Signing, for infants, 187
Sims, Will, 161
Single parents, 33
Single-parent families, 360–361
Slow-to-warm-up children, 179
Small-group skills, 309
Smith, Darlene, 58–59
Snacks, in preschool, 228
Social affirmation and acknowledgment, 327
Social behaviors, 177
Social constructivist approach, 322–325. *See
 also* Behavior guidance; Constructivism
Social development, 107
 infants and toddlers, 175, 177–179, 192
 kindergartners, 237–238
 preschoolers, 206, 218, 221
 primary-age children, 268–269, 270–271
Social environment
 kindergartens, 242–243
 primary grades, 282
Social interactions, 8, 42, 309
Social studies
 kindergarten, 251, 254–255
 primary grades, 287, 289
 standards, 135
Social work services, 300
Sociocultural theory, 71–72
Sociodramatic play, 223
Socioeconomic status, 37–39, 266,
 315, 336
Software. *See* Technology
Solitary play, 219
Southern Early Childhood Association
 (SECA), 12
South Pointe Elementary School
 (Miami, Florida), 65
South San Antonio Independent School
 District, 46
Southwest Florida College, 16
Speaking experiences, in High/Scope
 curriculum, 101
Special class, 311
Special instruction, 300
Special needs. *See* Children with disabilities
Special projects, in preschool, 228
Special schools, 311
Specific learning disability, 299
Speech impairment, 299
Speech–language pathology, 300
Spelling, 244
Spellings, Margaret, 53
Spock, Benjamin, 65
Sprung, Barbara, 45

Sputnik, 65
Standards, 120–122
 appropriate assessment, 127–128
 diversity and, 129
 importance of, 128–130
 issues surrounding, 139, 144
 kindergarten, 260
 lesson planning and, 136–137
 NAEYC early learning standards,
 125–126
 national, 136–139, 140–143
 national reports, 122
 NCTM, 123
 No Child Left Behind Act, 124–125
 preschool, 214
 primary grades, 273
 professional development activities, 145
 reform, 131
 state, 136, 214, 260
 teaching and learning, 130–134
 technology and, 135
Stand for Children Campaign, 12, 65
Stapler, Theresa Stephens, 54
State control, 132–133
Statement of Commitment, 367, 373
State standards, 136, 214, 260. *See also*
 Standards
State support, 46–47
Steiner, Rudolf, 110–111
Storybooks, talking, 310
Stowers Elementary School (Fort Benning,
 Georgia), 280–281
Strange Situation, 178
Stride Rite Corporation, 65
Student achievement. *See* Achievement
Study of Early Child Care and Youth
 Development (SECC), 92–93, 98–99
Subject centers, 226–227
Success, praising, 74–75, 76. *See also*
 Achievement
Sudden infant death syndrome (SIDS), 188
Summative assessments, 275
Summerhill, 64
Sunshine House, 96
Supersize Generation, 35
Supervision, 335. *See also* Modeling
Support, children's efforts, 331
Symbolic play, 223
Symbolic representation, 183, 184–185
Synaptogenesis, 172

Tabors, P., 211
Taking turns, 341
Talking storybooks, 310
Taylor, Katherine Whiteside, 65
Teacher Effectiveness Training (TET),
 324–325
Teachers
 assessment and, 148
 behavior guidance and, 338
 educational practices and, 81

 IFSP and, 304–305
 infants and toddlers, 176
 Montessori, 102–103
 preschool play and, 224
 primary grades and, 278, 279, 280–281
 Reggio Emilia approach and, 108
 standards and, 130, 136, 138
Teaching
 children with disabilities, 309, 311
 English language learners, 210
 family-centered, 352–353
 gifted and talented children, 310–311
 standards and, 129, 130–134
Teaching Hispanic Children (Jones and
 Fuller), 64
Technology
 assessment and, 163
 assistive, 300, 310
 behavior guidance, 330–331
 early childhood education and, 48, 49
 early childhood education history and
 theory and, 82
 early childhood programs and, 107
 infants and toddlers, 175
 kindergarten and, 247
 parent/family involvement and, 356
 preschoolers and, 212, 213
 primary grades and, 265–267, 275, 288
 professional development and, 24–25,
 26–27
 standards and, 135
Technology centers, 227
Teenage parents, 33–34
Telegraphic speech, 185
Telephone contact, 359
Television, 43, 44
Temperament, 178–179
Testing, in primary grades, 273. *See also*
 High-stakes testing
Texas Even Start Family Literacy Program, 31
Theme-based learning centers, 226
Themes
 English language learning, 40
 multicultural education, 316
Theory, 55. *See also* Early childhood
 education history and theory
Thinking skills, 218
Thomas, Alexander, 179
Thomas, Pat, 45
Thurman, Nita, 54
Time
 kindergarten, 255–256
 Reggio Emilia approach, 108
Time sampling, 152
Timmons, Dayle, 307
Title I, 39, 352
Today I Feel Silly (Curtis), 269
Toddlerhood, 171. *See also* Infants
 and toddlers
Toileting, in preschool, 228
Toilet training, 180–181

Townsend, Mark, 363
Toy Loan, 65
Trachtenburg, Phyllis, 259
Traditional cameras, 175
Transitions, 229
Transportation and related costs, covered under IDEA, 300
Traumatic brain injury, 299
Trust, basic, 191
Trust versus mistrust, 77
Turcotte, Amy, 314
"Tutored at 2—Too Much, Too Soon?" (*San Diego Tribune*), 30
Two-generation family programs, 353
Typically developing children, 296

Unfolding, 58–59, 60
UNICEF, 37
United Nations Convention on the Rights of the Child, 65
U.S. Department of Agriculture Food and Nutrition Service, 36
U.S. Department of Education, 32, 65, 122, 239, 257, 364
U.S. Department of Health and Human Services, 113, 116, 196
Universal kindergarten, 239–240
Universal preschool, 47, 203
University of Chicago, 64
University of Oklahoma, 17
University of South Florida, 16
Unoccupied play, 219
Upper Des Moines Opportunity, Inc., 117
Urban Father–Child Partnership (UFP), 32–33

Values, 367, 372
Vandewater, A. E., 44
Van Scoter, J., 247
Verbal affirmation and acknowledgment, 327
Verbal/linguistic intelligence, 79
Violence, 43, 44, 265
Vision services, 300
Visual aids, for ELLs, 40
Visual impairment, 299
Visual/spatial intelligence, 79
Vocabulary development, 185, 211
Voices for America's Children, 12
Volunteering, 351, 355
Vouchers, 65
Vygotsky, Lev
    preschoolers, 219
    social constructivist approach, 322, 324
    theory, 71–72, 73, 74, 83

Waber, Bernard, 335
Waldorf education, 90–91, 110–112
Walking, in preschool, 228
Wartella, E. A., 44
Website connections, for parent/family involvement, 364
Weight
    infants and toddlers, 172
    kindergartners, 237
    preschoolers, 205
    primary-age children, 267, 268
Wellness, 34–37, 219
Weselak, Anna Marie, 29
West, Jerry, 239
What If All the Kids Are White? (Derman-Sparks and Ramsey), 7

When Sophie Gets Angry . . . Really, Really Angry (Bang), 269
White House Conference on Child Care, 65
Whole child education, 49
Whole-language approach, 246
William F. Goodling Even Start Family Literacy Programs, 352–353
Williams, George R., 33
Williams, Kerry C., 251
Williams, Vera, 335
Winebrenner, Susan, 328–329
Winston-Salem/Forsyth County School District, 40
Wittmer, D. S., 195, 196
Word recognition, 244
Words, first, 184
Working parents, 31, 361
Work sample, 152
Work time, 102
Wrap-around services, 49
Writing
    academic materials for, 105
    kindergarten, 244, 253
    primary grades, 269
    See also Literacy development

Year of the Elementary School (1986), 65
Yun, Vicki, 161

Zero reject, 297
Zero to Three, 39
Zill, Nicholas, 239
Zone of proximal development (ZPD), 71–72, 322, 323

PHOTO CREDITS FOR CHAPTER OPENERS